Tarascon Pocket Pharmacopoeia™

2002 Deluxe Lab-coat Pocket Edition

"Desire to take medicines ... distinguishes man from animals." *Sir William Osler*

CONTENTS

See Tarascon Publishing book ordering information on page 256.

- ***Tarascon Pocket Pharmacopoeia™ Classic edition***
- ***Tarascon Pocket Pharmacopoeia™ Deluxe edition***
- ***Tarascon Pocket Orthopaedica™***
- ***Tarascon Internal Medicine & Critical Care Pocketbook***
- ***Tarascon Adult Emergency Pocketbook***
- ***Tarascon Pediatric Emergency Pocketbook***
- ***How to be a Truly Excellent Junior Medical Student***

Tarascon Publishing®
Box 1159
Loma Linda, CA 92354

Website: www.tarascon.com
E-mail: info@tarascon.com
Phone: (800) 929-9926

"It's not how much you know, it's how fast you can find the answer."®

Important Caution Please Read This! The information in *Pocket Pharmacopoeia* is compiled from sources believed to be reliable, and exhaustive efforts have been put forth to make the book as accurate as possible. However the accuracy and completeness of this work cannot be guaranteed. Despite our best efforts this book may contain typographical errors and omissions. The *Pocket Pharmacopoeia* is intended as a quick and convenient reminder of information you have already learned elsewhere. The contents are to be used as a guide only, & health care professionals should use sound clinical judgment and individualize therapy to each specific patient care situation. This book is not meant to be a replacement for training, experience, continuing medical education, studying the latest drug prescribing literature, raw intelligence, good looks, or common sense. This book is sold without warranties of any kind, express or implied, and the publisher and editors disclaim any liability, loss, or damage caused by the contents. ***If you do not wish to be bound by the foregoing cautions and conditions, you may return your undamaged and unexpired book to our office for a full refund.***

The *Tarascon Pocket Pharmacopoeia* is edited by a panel of drug information experts with extensive peer review & input from practicing clinicians of multiple specialties. Our goal is to provide health professionals focused, core prescribing information in a convenient, organized, and concise fashion. We include FDA-approved dosing indications & those off-label uses that have a reasonable basis to support their use. Tarascon Publishing is independent from & has no affiliation with pharmaceutical companies. Although drug companies purchase & distribute our books as promotional items, the Tarascon editorial staff determines all book content.

If you obtained your *Pocket Pharmacopoeia* from a bookstore, please send us your address (info@tarascon.com). This allows you to be the first to know about new editions or updates! Got any ideas for improving future editions of the *Pocket Pharmacopoeia* without increasing its size? Write to us! We apologize in advance that time does not permit us to answer most inquiries. The cover woodcut is *The Apothecary* by Jost Amman, Frankfurt, 1574.

Tarascon Pocket Pharmacopoeia™ 2002 Deluxe Edition

ISBN 1-882742-22-2. A hospital is a big building with patients, but that's not important now.

D

HOW TO USE THE TARASCON POCKET PHARMACOPOEIA

The *Tarascon Pocket Pharmacopoeia* arranges drugs by clinical class with a comprehensive index in the back. Trade names are italicized and capitalized. Drug doses shown in mg/kg are generally intended for children, while fixed doses represent typical adult recommendations. Each drug entry is divided as follows:

WARNING – Black-box warnings, if any, with lower level warnings in the "notes" section.
ADULT – Selected adult FDA-approved indications & doses listed in typical frequency of use.
PEDS – Selected peds FDA-approved indications & doses listed in typical frequency of use.
UNAPPROVED ADULT – Selected adult non-FDA-approved (ie, "off-label") indications and doses listed in typical frequency of use.
UNAPPROVED PEDS – Selected pediatric non-FDA-approved (ie, "off-label") indications and doses listed in typical frequency of use.
FORMS – Formulations available from manufacturers (eg, tabs, caps, liquid, susp, cream, lotion, patches, etc), including specification of trade, generic, and over-the-counter forms. Scored pills are designated as such. Not all pharmacies stock all items, of course.
NOTES – Selected notes, additional warnings, major adverse drug interactions, dosage adjustment in renal/hepatic insufficiency, therapeutic levels, etc.

Each drug entry contains the following codes:

▶ **METABOLISM & EXCRETION**: **L** = primarily liver, **K** = primarily kidney, **LK** = both, but liver>kidney, **KL** = both, but kidney>liver, **LO** = liver & onions

♀ **SAFETY IN PREGNANCY**: **A** = Safety established using human studies, **B** = Presumed safety based on animal studies, **C** = Uncertain safety; no human studies and animal studies show an adverse effect, **D** = Unsafe - evidence of risk that may in certain clinical circumstances be justifiable, **X** = Highly unsafe - risk of use outweighs any possible benefit. For drugs which have not been assigned a category: **+**Generally accepted as safe, **?**Safety unknown or controversial, **-**Generally regarded as unsafe. **Ъ** Something in Russian.

SAFETY IN LACTATION: **+**Generally accepted as safe, **?**Safety unknown or controversial, **-**Generally regarded as unsafe. Many of our "**+**" listings are taken from the AAP website, and may differ from those recommended by manufacturers (www.aap.org/policy/00026.html).

© **DEA CONTROLLED SUBSTANCES**: **I** = High abuse potential, no accepted use (eg, heroin, marijuana), **II** = High abuse potential and severe dependence liability (eg, morphine, codeine, hydromorphone, cocaine, amphetamines, methylphenidate, secobarbital). Some states require triplicates. **III** = Moderate dependence liability (eg, *Tylenol #3, Vicodin*), **IV** = Limited dependence liability (benzodiazepines, propoxyphene, phentermine), **V** = Limited abuse potential (eg, *Lomotil*).

$ **RELATIVE COST**: Cost codes used are "per month" of maintenance therapy (eg, antihypertensives) or "per course" of short-term therapy (eg, antibiotics). Codes are calculated using average wholesale prices (at press time in US$) for the most common indication & route of each drug at a typical adult dosage. For maintenance therapy, costs are calculated based upon a 30 day supply or the quantity that might typically be used in a given month. For short-term therapy (≤10 days), costs are calculated on a single treatment course. When multiple forms are available (eg, generics), these codes reflect the least expensive generally available product. When drugs don't neatly fit into the classification scheme above, we have assigned codes based upon the relative cost of other similar drugs. <u>*These codes should be used as a rough guide only*</u>, as (1) they reflect cost, not charges, (2) pricing often varies substantially from location to location & time to time, and (3) HMOs, Medicaid, and buying groups often negotiate quite different pricing. Your mileage may vary. Check with your local pharmacy if you have any question.

Code	*Cost*
$	< $25
$$	$25 to $49
$$$	$50 to $99
$$$$	$100 to $199
$$$$$	≥ $200

CANADIAN TRADE NAMES: ***New this year!*** Unique common Canadian trade names not used in the USA are listed after a maple leaf symbol. Trade names used in both nations or only in the USA are displayed without such notation.

PAGE INDEX FOR TABLES

ABBREVIATIONS IN TEXT

AAP - American Academy of Pediatrics
ac – before meals
ADHD – attention deficit & hyperactivity disorder
AHA – American Heart Association
ANC – absolute neutrophil count
ASA – aspirin
bid - twice per day
BPH - benign prostatic hypertrophy
cap – capsule
CMV – cytomegalovirus
CrCl – creat clearance
d - day
D5W - 5% dextrose
IM - intramuscular
INR – international normalized ratio
DPI – dry powder inhaler
elem – elemental
ET - endotracheal
EPS – extrapyramidal symptoms
g - gram
gtts - drops
GERD - gastroesophageal reflux dz
GU – genitourinary
h - hour
HAART – highly active antiretroviral therapy
HCTZ - hydrochlorothiazide
HRT - hormone replacement therapy
HSV – herpes simplex virus
HTN – hypertension
IU - international units
IV - intravenous
JRA - juvenile rheumatoid arthritis
kg – kilogram
LFTs – liver fxn tests
mcg - microgram
MDI – metered dose inhaler
mEq - milliequivalent
mg - milligram
MI - myocardial infarction
min - minute
mL - milliliter
mo – months old
ng - nanogram
NS - normal saline
N/V – nausea and vomiting
OA – osteoarthritis
pc – after meals
PO - by mouth
PR - by rectum
prn - as needed
q – every
qd - once daily
qhs - at bedtime
qid - four times/day
qod – every other day
q pm – every evening
RA - rheumatoid arthritis
SC - subcutaneous
soln – solution
supp - suppository
susp - suspension
tab – tablet
TCAs – tricyclic antidepressants
TIA - transient ischemic attack
tid - 3 times/day
UC – ulcerative colitis
UTI – urinary tract infection
wk - week
yo - years old

CONVERSIONS

Temperature:	*Liquid:*	*Weight:*
F = (1.8) C + 32	1 fluid ounce = 30ml	1 kilogram = 2.2 lbs
C = (F - 32)/(1.8)	1 teaspoon = 5ml	1 ounce = 30 g
	1 tablespoon = 15ml	1 grain = 65 mg

Clinicians with a special interest in drug therapeutics are encouraged to subscribe to the *Prescriber's Letter*, an outstanding monthly newsletter detailing advances in drug therapy. Visit their website at www.prescribersletter.com or call 209-472-2240 for subscription information ($88 per year). (Not affiliated with Tarascon Publishing.)

Whose musical talent was lacking because of some quacking? The Sesame Street generation has disappointed us! Remember how Ernie couldn't play saxophone due to his rubber ducky in the rollicking, star-studded music video "Put Down the Ducky"? Go to the children's section of your local video store and rent "Sing Yourself Silly"; it's a classic. It took an Einstein to answer this one; the only correct answer was from a Dr. Paul Einstein (congratulations!) We will send a free copy of next year's edition to the first 25 who know whose first command went down the drain because of some grain.

OUTPATIENT PEDIATRIC DRUGS		*Age*	2m	4m	6m	9m	12m	15m	2y	3y	5y
		Kg	5	6½	8	9	10	11	13	15	19
		Lbs	11	15	17	20	22	24	28	33	42
med	**strength**	**freq**	**teaspoons of liquid per dose** (1 tsp= 5 ml)								
Tylenol (mg)		q4h	80	80	120	120	160	160	200	240	280
Tylenol (tsp)	160/t	q4h	½	½	¾	¾	1	1	1¼	1½	1¾
ibuprofen (mg)		q6h	-	-	75†	75†	100	100	125	150	175
ibuprofen (tsp)	100/t	q6h	-	-	¾†	¾†	1	1	1¼	1½	1¾
amoxicillin or	125/t	bid	1	1¼	1½	1¾	1¾	2	2¼	2¾	3½
Augmentin	200/t	bid	½	¾	1	1	1¼	1¼	1½	1¾	2¼
regular dose	250/t	bid	½	½	¾	¾	1	1	1¼	1¼	1¾
	400/t	bid	¼	½	½	½	¾	¾	¾	1	1
amoxicillin or	200/t	bid	--	1¼	1½	1¾	2	2¼	2½	3	4
Augmentin	250/t	bid	--	1¼	1½	1½	1¾	1¾	2¼	2½	3
high OM dose‡	400/t	bid	--	¾	¾	1	1	1¼	1½	1½	2
Augmentin ES‡	600/t	bid	--	½	½	¾	¾	¾	1	1¼	1½
azithromycin*§	100/t	qd	--	½†	½	½	½	½	¾	¾	1
"	200/t	qd	--	¼†	¼	¼	¼	¼	½	½	½
Bactrim/Septra	---	bid	½	¾	1	1	1	1¼	1½	1½	2
cefaclor*	125/t	bid	--	1†	1¼†	1½	1½	1¾	2	2½	3
"	250/t	bid	--	½†	¾†	¾	¾	1	1	1¼	1½
cefadroxil	125/t	bid	½	¾	1	1	1¼	1¼	1½	1¾	2
"	250/t	bid	¼	½	½	½	¾	¾	¾	1	1
cefdinir	125/t	qd	--	¾†	1	1	1	1¼	1½	1¾	2
cefixime	100/t	qd	--	½	¾	¾	¾	1	1	1¼	1½
cefprozil*	125/t	bid	--	¾†	1	1	1¼	1½	1½	2	2¼
"	250/t	bid	--	½†	½	½	¾	¾	¾	1	1¼
cefuroxime	125/t	bid	½	¾	¾	1	1	1	1¼	1½	2
cephalexin	125/t	qid	--	½†	¾†	¾†	1	1	1¼	1½	1¾
"	250/t	qid	--	¼†	¼†	½†	½	½	¾	¾	1
clarithromycin	125/t	bid	--	½†	½†	½	¾	¾	¾	1	1¼
"	250/t	bid	--	¼†	¼†	¼	½	½	½	½	¾
dicloxacillin	62½/t	qid	½	¾	1	1	1¼	1¼	1½	1¾	2
loracarbef*	100/t	bid	--	1†	1¼	1½	1½	1¾	2	2¼	3
nitrofurantoin	25/t	qid	¼	½	½	½	½	¾	¾	¾	1
Pediazole	---	tid	½	½	¾	¾	1	1	1	1¼	1½
penicillin	125/t	qid	½	½	¾	¾	1	1	1¼	1¼	1½
"	250/t	qid	--	¼	¼	½	½	½	¾	¾	1
Benadryl	12.5/t	q6h	½	½	¾	¾	1	1	1¼	1½	2
Dimetapp	---	q4h	-	-	¼†	¼†	½	¾	¾	1	1
prednisolone	15/t	qd	¼	½	½	¾	¾	¾	1	1	1¼
prednisone	5/t	qd	1	1¼	1½	1¾	2	2¼	2½	3	3¾
Robitussin	---	q4h	-	-	¼†	¼†	½	½	¾	¾	1
Rondec	---	q4h	-	-	-	-	¼†	¼†	½	½	1
Triaminic	---	q4h	-	¼	¼	¼	½	½	1	1	1
Tylenol w/ Codeine		q4h	-	-	-	-	-	-	-	1	1
Ventolin	2/t	tid	-	-	-	-	½	½	¾	¾	1
Zyrtec	5/t	qd	-	-	-	-	-	-	½	½	½

* Dose shown is for otitis media only; see dosing in text for alternative indications.

† Dosing at this age/weight not recommended by manufacturer.

‡ High dose (80-90 mg/kg/d) is for otitis media in children at high risk for penicillin-resistant S pneumoniae (age <2 yo, antibiotics within ≤3 months, day care).

§Give a double dose of azithromycin the first day.

PEDIATRIC VITAL SIGNS AND INTRAVENOUS DRUGS

Age		Pre-matr	New-born	2m	4m	6m	9m	12m	15m	2y	3y	5y
Weight	(Kg)	2	3½	5	6½	8	9	10	11	13	15	19
	(Lbs)	4½	7½	11	15	17	20	22	24	28	33	42
Maint fluids	(ml/h)	8	14	20	26	32	36	40	42	46	50	58
ET tube	(mm)	2½	3/3½	3½	3½	3½	4	4	4½	4½	4½	5
Defib	(Joules)	4	7	10	13	16	18	20	22	26	30	38
Systolic BP	(high)	70	80	90	100	110	110	120	120	120	120	120
	(low)	50	60	70	70	70	70	70	70	75	75	80
Pulse rate	(high)	145	145	180	180	180	160	160	160	150	150	135
	(low)	100	100	110	110	110	100	100	100	90	90	65
Resp rate	(high)	45	45	45	40	35	35	30	30	30	24	24
	(low)	35	35	35	30	25	25	20	20	20	16	14
adenosine	(mg)	0.2	0.3	0.5	0.6	0.8	0.9	1	1.1	1.3	1.5	1.9
atropine	(mg)	0.1	0.1	0.1	0.13	0.16	0.18	0.2	0.22	0.26	0.30	0.38
Benadryl	(mg)	-	-	5	6½	8	9	10	11	13	15	19
bicarbonate	(meq)	2	3½	5	6½	8	9	10	11	13	15	19
dextrose	(g)	2	3½	5	6½	8	9	10	11	13	15	19
epinephrine	(mg)	.02	.04	.05	.07	.08	.09	0.1	0.11	0.13	0.15	0.19
lidocaine	(mg)	2	3½	5	6½	8	9	10	11	13	15	19
morphine	(mg)	0.2	0.3	0.5	0.6	0.8	0.9	1	1.1	1.3	1.5	1.9
mannitol	(g)	2	3½	5	6½	8	9	10	11	13	15	19
diazepam	(mg)	0.6	1	1.5	2	2.5	2.7	3	3.3	3.9	4.5	5
lorazepam	(mg)	0.1	0.2	0.3	0.35	0.4	0.5	0.5	0.6	0.7	0.8	1.0
phenobarb	(mg)	30	60	75	100	125	125	150	175	200	225	275
ampicillin	(mg)	100	175	250	325	400	450	500	550	650	750	1000
ceftriaxone	(mg)	-	-	250	325	400	450	500	550	650	750	1000
cefotaxime	(mg)	100	175	250	325	400	450	500	550	650	750	1000
gentamicin	(mg)	6	7	10	13	16	18	20	22	26	30	38

THERAPEUTIC DRUG LEVELS

Drug	Level	Optimal Timing
amikacin peak	20-35 mcg/ml	1 hour after start of 30-60 min infusion
amikacin trough	<5 mcg/ml	Just prior to next dose
carbamazepine trough	4-12 mcg/ml	Just prior to next dose
cyclosporine trough	50-300 ng/ml	Just prior to next dose
digoxin	0.8-2.2 ng/ml	Just prior to next dose
ethosuximide trough	40-100 mcg/ml	Just prior to next dose
gentamicin peak	5-10 mcg/ml	1 hour after start of 30-60 min infusion
gentamicin trough	<2 mcg/ml	Just prior to next dose
lidocaine	1-5 mcg/ml	4-8 hours after start of infusion
lithium trough	0.6-1.2 meq/l	Just prior to first morning dose
NAPA	10-30 mcg/ml	Just prior to next procainamide dose
phenobarbital trough	15-40 mcg/ml	Just prior to next dose
phenytoin trough	10-20 mcg/ml	Just prior to next dose
primidone trough	5-12 mcg/ml	Just prior to next dose
procainamide	4-8 mcg/ml	Just prior to next dose
quinidine	1-4 mcg/ml	Just prior to next dose
theophylline	5-15 mcg/ml	8-12 hrs after once daily dose
tobramycin peak	5-10 mcg/ml	1 hour after start of 30-60 min infusion
tobramycin trough	<2 mcg/ml	Just prior to next dose
valproic acid trough	50-100 mcg/ml	Just prior to next dose
vancomycin trough	5-10 mcg/ml	Just prior to next dose

INHIBITORS, INDUCERS, AND SUBSTRATES OF CYTOCHROME P450 ISOZYMES

Bear in mind that inhibitors and inducers listed on the chart below do not necessarily cause clinically important drug interactions with the substrates listed below. This chart only predicts the *potential* for a drug interaction. Please refer to other resources for more definitive information when a drug interaction is suspected based on the information given in the chart. Many drugs are metabolized by subfamilies of hepatic cytochrome P450. A drug that inhibits the activity of a specific enzyme can block the metabolism of drugs that are substrates of that enzyme. If the body lacks other mechanisms for excreting these drugs, they can accumulate and cause toxicity. A drug that induces the activity of a specific enzyme can stimulate the metabolism of drugs that are substrates of that enzyme. This can lead to decreased levels of these drugs in the body and could reduce their efficacy.

CYP 1A2

Inhibitors: cimetidine, ciprofloxacin, clarithromycin, enoxacin, erythromycin, ♦fluvoxamine, isoniazid, mexiletine, norfloxacin, paroxetine, tacrine, zileuton.
Inducers: barbiturates, carbamazepine, charcoal-broiled foods, lansoprazole, omeprazole, phenytoin, rifampin, ritonavir, smoking.
Substrates: amitriptyline, caffeine, clomipramine, clozapine, cyclobenzaprinehaloperidol, imipramine, mirtazapine, olanzapine, propranolol, riluzole, ropinirole, R-warfarin, tacrine, theophylline, zileuton

CYP2C9

Inhibitors: amiodarone, cimetidne, cotrimoxazole, disulfiram, fluconazole, ♦fluvoxamine, imatinib, isoniazid, ketoconazole (weak), metronidazole, zafirlukast.
Inducers: barbiturates, carbamazepine, rifampin, rifapentine, St Johns wort.
Substrates: carvedilol, celecoxib, diclofenac, flurbiprofen, fluvastatin, glimepiride, ibuprofen, irbesartan, losartan, montelukast, naproxen, nateglinide, phenytoin, piroxicam, tolbutamide, torsemide, S-warfarin, zafirlukast

CYP 2C19

Inhibitors: felbamate, fluconazole, fluoxetine, fluvoxamine, modafinil, omeprazole, oxcarbazepine
Inducers: rifampin
Substrates: amitriptyline, citalopram, clomipramine, diazepam, esomeprazole, imipramine, lansoprazole, nelfinavir, omeprazole, pantoprazole, phenytoin, proguanil, R-warfarin

CYP2D6

Inhibitors: amiodarone, chloroquine, cimetidine, clomipramine, diphenhydramine, fluoxetine, fluphenazine, fluvoxamine, haloperidol, imatinib, paroxetine, perphenazine, pindolol, propafenone, propoxyphene, propranolol, quinacrine, ♦quinidine, ♦ritonavir, sertraline, terbinafine, thioridazine, venlafaxine.
Inducers: None.
Substrates: almotriptan, amitriptyline, carvedilolchlorpromazine, clomipramine, clozapine, codeine*, desipramine, dextromethorphan, dihydrocodeine*, donepezil, flecainide, fluoxetine, galantamine, haloperidol, hydrocodone*, imipramine, loratadine, maprotiline, methadone, methamphetamine metoprolol, mexiletine, mirtazapine, morphine, nortriptyline, oxycodone, paroxetine, perphenazine, propafenone, propoxyphene, propranolol, risperidone, ritonavir, thioridazine, timolol, tolterodine, tramadol*, trazodone, venlafaxine

CYP3A4

Inhibitors: amiodarone, amprenavir, clarithromycin, cyclosporine, danazol, delavirdine, diltiazem, efavirenz, erythromycin, ethinyl estradiol, fluconazole, fluvoxamine, grapefruit juice, imatinib, indinavir, itraconazole, ketoconazolenefazodone, nelfinavirquinine, ♦ritonavir, saquinavir, sertraline, Synercid, troleandomycin, verapamil, zafirlukast.
Inducers: barbiturates, carbamazepine, dexamethasone, efavirenz, ethosuximide, garlic supplements (suspected inducer), griseofulvin, modafinil, nafcillin, nevirapine, oxcarbazepine, phenytoin, primidone, rifabutin, ♣rifampin, rifapentine, St Johns wort.
Substrates: alfentanil, almotriptan, alprazolam, amlodipine, amprenavir, atorvastatin, bepridil, buspirone, carbamazepine, cerivastatin, cisapride, citalopram, clarithromycin, clomipramine, corticosteroids, cyclophosphamide, cyclosporine, dapsone, delavirdine, diazepam, diltiazem, disopyramide, dofetilide, donepezil, doxorubicin, efavirenz, erythromycin, ethinyl estradiol, etoposide, felodipine, fentanylfinasteride, galantamine, ifosfamide, imatinab, imipramine, indinavir, isradipine, itraconazole, ketoconazole, lansoprazole, lopinavir, loratadine, losartan, lovastatin, methadone, midazolam, mirtazapine, montelukast, nefazodone, nelfinavir, nicardipine, nifedipine, nimodipine, nisoldipine, paclitaxel, pimozide, quetiapine, quinidine, quinine, repaglinide, rifabutin, ritonavir, saquinavir, sertraline, sibutramine, sildenafil, simvastatin, sirolimus, sufentanil, tacrolimus, tamoxifen, testosterone, tolterodine, toremifene, triazolam, troleandomycin, verapamil, vinblastine, vincristine, R-warfarin, zaleplon, zileuton, ziprasidone, zolpidem, zonisamide

♦potent inhibitor ♣potent inducer * Metabolism by CYP2D6 required to convert to active analgesic metabolite; analgesia may be impaired by CYP2D6 inhibitors.

FORMULAS

Alveolar-arterial oxygen gradient = A-a = 148 - 1.2(PaCO2) - PaO2
[normal = 10-20 mmHg, breathing room air at sea level]

Calculated osmolality = 2Na + glucose/18 + BUN/2.8 + ethanol/4.6 + isopropanol/6 + methanol/3.2 + ethylene-glycol/6.2
[norm 280-295 meq/L. Na in meq/L; all others in mg/dL]

Pediatric IV maintenance fluids (see table on page 7)
4 ml/kg/hr **or** 100 ml/kg/day for first 10 kg, plus
2 ml/kg/hr **or** 50 ml/kg/day for second 10 kg, plus
1 ml/kg/hr **or** 20 ml/kg/day for all further kg

$$\text{mcg/kg/min} = \frac{16.7 \times \text{Drug Conc [mg/ml]} \times \text{Infusion Rate [ml/h]}}{\text{Weight [kg]}}$$

$$\text{Infusion rate [ml/h]} = \frac{\text{Desired mcg/kg/min} \times \text{Weight [kg]} \times 60}{\text{Drug concentration [mcg/ml]}}$$

Fractional excretion of sodium = $\left[\frac{\text{urine Na / plasma Na}}{\text{urine creat / plasma creat}}\right] \times 100\%$
[Pre-renal, etc <1%; ATN, etc >1%]

Anion gap = Na – (Cl + HCO3) [normal = 10-14 meq/L]

Creatinine clearance = $\frac{\text{(lean kg)(140 - age)(0.85 if female)}}{\text{(72)(stable creatinine)}}$
[normal >80]

Body surface area (BSA) = square root of: $\left[\frac{\text{height (cm)} \times \text{weight (kg)}}{3600}\right]$
[in m^2]

DRUGS THAT MAY PROLONG THE QT INTERVAL

amiodarone*‡	droperidol*	isradipine	**phenothiazines**§#	sumatriptan
arsenic trioxide*	erythromycin*‡	levofloxacin†	pimozide*‡	tamoxifen
bepridil*‡	flecainide*†	levomethadyl	procainamide*	tizanidine
beta agonists¶	fluoxetine*†	mefloquine	quetiapine§	tricyclic anti-
chloroquine	foscarnet	moexipril/HCTZ	quinidine*‡	depressants
cisapride*	fosphenytoin	moxifloxacin	quinine	venlafaxine
clarithromycin*	gatifloxacin	naratriptan	risperidone§	ziprasidone§
disopyramide*‡	haloperidol*§	nicardipine	sertraline*†	
dofetilide*	ibutilide*‡	octreotide	sotalol*‡	
dolasetron	indapamide*	pentamidine*‡	sparfloxacin	

Risk of drug-induced QT prolongation may be increased in women, elderly, ↓K, ↓Mg, bradycardia, starvation, & CNS injuries. Hepatorenal dysfunction & drug interactions can ↑ the concentration of QT interval-prolonging drugs. Coadministration of QT interval-prolonging drugs can have additive effects. (www.torsades.org) *Torsades reported in product labeling/case reports. †Association unclear. ‡↑Risk in women. § QT prolongation: thioridazine>ziprasidone>risperidone, quetiapine, haloperidol. ¶QT interval prolongation documented for salmeterol. #QT prolongation documented for chlorpromazine*, fluphenazine†, mesoridazine, thioridazine.*§

ANALGESICS: Antirheumatic Agents

auranofin (*Ridaura*) ▶K ♀C ▶- $$$$
WARNING - Gold toxicity may manifest as marrow suppression, proteinuria, hematuria.
ADULT - RA: Initial 3 mg PO bid or 6 mg PO qd. May increase to 3 mg PO tid after 6 months.
PEDS - RA: 0.1-0.15 mg/kg/day PO. Max dose 0.2 mg/kg/day. May be given qd or divided bid.
UNAPPROVED ADULT - Psoriatic arthritis: 3 mg PO bid or 6 mg PO qd.
FORMS - Trade: Caps 3 mg.
NOTES - Contraindicated in patients with a history of any of the following gold-induced disorders: anaphylactic reactions, necrotizing enterocolitis, pulmonary fibrosis, exfoliative dermatitis, bone marrow suppression. Proteinuria has developed in 3%-9% of patients. Diarrhea, rash, stomatitis, chrysiasis (gray-to-blue pigmentation of skin) may occur. Minimize exposure to sunlight or artificial UV light. Auranofin may increase phenytoin levels.

aurothioglucose (*Solganal*) ▶K ♀C ▶- $$$$$
WARNING - Evaluate patient at each injection for gold toxicity, including marrow suppression, proteinuria, hematuria.
ADULT - Early RA: weekly IM injections: 1st dose, 10 mg. 2nd & 3rd doses, 25 mg. 4th & subsequent doses, 50 mg. Continue the 50 mg dose weekly to a cumulative dose of 0.8-1g. If improvement is seen w/o toxicity, continue 25-50 mg q3-4 weeks.
PEDS - Early RA in 6-12 yo: 0.25 mg/kg IM 1st week. Increase by 0.25 mg/kg/dose IM q week to maintenance dose 1 mg/kg q week to total of 20 doses. If improvement is seen w/o toxicity, continue maintenance dose q2-4 weeks. Max dose 50 mg q week.
UNAPPROVED ADULT - Pemphigus: ≤25 mg IM q week.
UNAPPROVED PEDS - Pemphigus: Doses of 15-50 mg IM q wk have been used in 4-5 yo's.
NOTES - Administer only IM, preferably intragluteally, using an 18 gauge, 1.5-inch needle. Use 2-inch needle in obese patients. Patient should remain recumbent ~10 minutes & be observed for 15 minutes after each injection. Contraindicated in pregnancy, uncontrolled DM, severe debilitation, renal disease, hepatic dysfunction or hepatitis, marked HTN, uncontrolled CHF, SLE, blood dyscrasias, recent radiation & severe toxicity from previous exposure to gold or other heavy metals, urticaria, eczema & colitis. Arthralgia & dermatitis may occur.

azathioprine (*Imuran*) ▶LK ♀D ▶- $$$
WARNING - Chronic immunosuppression with azathioprine increases the risk of neoplasia.
ADULT - Severe RA: Initial dose 1 mg/kg (50-100 mg) PO qd or divided bid. Increase by 0.5 mg/kg/day at 6-8 weeks and thereafter at 4-week intervals, if no serious toxicity and if initial response is unsatisfactory. Max dose 2.5 mg/kg/day. In patients with clinical response, use the lowest effective dose for maintenance therapy.
PEDS - Not approved in children.
UNAPPROVED ADULT - Crohn's disease: 75-

100 mg PO qd. Myasthenia gravis: 2-3 mg/kg/day PO. Behcet's syndrome: 2.5 mg/kg/day PO.

UNAPPROVED PEDS - JRA:1-3 mg/kg/day PO.

FORMS - Generic/Trade: Tabs 50 mg, scored.

NOTES - May cause marrow suppression or GI hypersensitivity reaction characterized by severe nausea & vomiting. ACE inhibitors, allopurinol, & methotrexate may increase activity & toxicity. Azathioprine may decrease the activity of anticoagulants, cyclosporine, & neuromuscular blockers.

etanercept (*Enbrel*) ▶Serum ♀B ◗- $$$$$

WARNING - Serious infections, sepsis, and death have been reported with the use of etanercept. Patients who develop a new infection while undergoing treatment with etanercept should be monitored closely. The drug should be discontinued if a patient develops a serious infection or sepsis. Treatment with etanercept should not be started in patients with active infections (chronic or localized). Physicians should use caution when considering the use of etanercept in patients with a history of recurring infections or with underlying conditions (i.e., diabetes) which may predispose patients to infections. Rare cases of nervous system disorders including demyelinating disorders such as multiple sclerosis, myelitis, & optic neuritis have been reported.

ADULT - RA: 25 mg SC 2x/week.

PEDS - JRA 4-17 yo: 0.4 mg/kg SC 2x/week, to max single dose of 25 mg.

FORMS - Supplied in a carton containing four dose trays. Each dose tray contains one 25 mg single-use vial of etanercept, one syringe (1 mL Sterile Bacteriostatic Water for Injection, USP, containing 0.9% benzyl alcohol), one plunger, and two alcohol swabs.

NOTES - Appropriate SC injection sites are thigh, abdomen & upper arm. Rotate injection sites.

gold sodium thiomalate (*Aurolate*, ✱*Myochrysin*) ▶K ♀C ◗- $$$$$

WARNING - Evaluate patient at each injection for gold toxicity, including marrow suppression, proteinuria, hematuria.

ADULT - RA: weekly IM injections: 1st dose 10 mg. 2nd dose, 25 mg. 3rd & subsequent doses, 25-50 mg. Continue the 25-50 mg dose weekly to a cumulative dose of 0.8-1g. If improvement seen w/o toxicity, 25-50 mg every other week for 2-20 weeks. If stable, increase dosing intervals to q 3-4 weeks.

PEDS - JRA: test dose 10 mg IM, then 1 mg/kg, not to exceed 50 mg for a single injection. Continue this dose weekly to a cumulative dose of 0.8-1g. If improvement seen w/o toxicity, dose every other week for 2-20 weeks. If stable, increase dosing intervals to q 3-4 weeks.

NOTES - Administer only IM, preferably intragluteally. Have patient remain recumbent for approximately 10 minutes after injection. Contraindicated in pregnancy & in patients who have uncontrolled DM, severe debilitation, renal disease, hepatic dysfunction or hepatitis, marked HTN, uncontrolled CHF, SLE, blood dyscrasias, patients recently radiated & those with severe toxicity from previous exposure to gold or other heavy metals, urticaria, eczema & colitis. Arthralgia & dermatitis may occur.

hydroxychloroquine sulfate (*Plaquenil*) ▶K ♀C ◗? $$$

ADULT - RA: 400-600 mg PO qd to start, taken with food or milk. After clinical response, decrease to 200-400 mg PO qd. If no objective improvement within 6 months, discontinue. SLE: 400 mg PO qd-bid to start. Decrease to 200-400 PO qd for prolonged maintenance.

PEDS - Not approved in children.

UNAPPROVED PEDS - JRA or SLE: 3-5 mg/kg/day, up to a max of 400 mg/day PO qd or divided bid. Max dose 7 mg/kg/day. Take with food or milk.

FORMS - Generic/Trade: Tabs 200 mg, scored.

NOTES - May exacerbate psoriasis or porphyria. Irreversible retinal damage possible with long-term or high dosage. Baseline & periodic eye exams recommended. Monitor CBC periodically for marrow suppression. Anorexia, nausea & vomiting may occur. May increase digoxin and metoprolol levels.

infliximab (*Remicade*) ▶Serum ♀B ◗? $$$$$

WARNING - Serious, life-threatening infections, including sepsis & disseminated TB have been reported. Evaluate patients for latent TB, and treat if necessary, prior to initiation of infliximab. Hypersensitivity reactions may occur.

ADULT - RA: 3 mg/kg IV in combination with methotrexate at 0, 2 and 6 weeks. Give q8 weeks thereafer.

PEDS - Not approved in children.

NOTES - Headache, dyspnea, urticaria, nausea, infections, abdominal pain, & fever.

leflunomide (*Arava*) ▶LK ♀X ◗- $$$$$

WARNING - Exclude pregnancy before starting; women of childbearing potential must use reliable contraception.

ADULT - RA: initial: 100 mg PO qd x 3 days. Maintenance: 10-20 mg PO qd.

PEDS - Not approved in children.
FORMS - Trade: Tabs 10, 20, & 100 mg.
NOTES - Avoid in hepatic or renal insufficiency. Monitor LFTs. Avoid in men wishing to father children or with concurrent live vaccines. Rifampin increases and cholestyramine decreases leflunomide levels. Give charcoal or cholestyramine in case of overdose or drug toxicity. Cholestyramine: 8 g PO tid x 24 h. Repeat prn.

methotrexate (*Rheumatrex, Trexall*) ▶LK ♀X ▶- $$
WARNING - Deaths have occurred from hepatotoxicity, pulmonary disease, intestinal perforation and marrow suppression. Restrict use to patients with severe, recalcitrant, disabling rheumatic disease unresponsive to other therapy. Use with extreme caution in renal insufficiency. May see diarrhea. Folate deficiency states may increase toxicity. The American College of Rheumatology recommends supplementation with 1 mg/day of folic acid.
ADULT - Severe RA: 7.5 mg/week PO single dose or 2.5 mg PO q12h x 3 doses given as a course once weekly. May be increased gradually to a max weekly dose of 20 mg. After clinical response, reduce to lowest effective dose.
PEDS - Severe JRA: 10 mg/meters squared PO q week.
FORMS - Trade: Tabs 5, 7.5, 10 & 15 mg. Generic/Trade: Tabs 2.5 mg, scored.
NOTES - Contraindicated in pregnant & lactating women, alcoholism, liver disease, immunodeficiency, blood dyscrasias. Monitor CBC q month, liver & renal function q 1-3 months.

sulfasalazine (*Azulfidine, Azulfidine EN-tabs*, *✦Salazopyrin EN-Tabs, S.A.S.*) ▶L ♀B ▶- $
ADULT - RA: 500 mg PO qd-bid after meals to start. Increase to 1g PO bid. Ulcerative colitis: 500 mg -1g PO bid after meals to start. Increase to 1.5 -2g PO bid. After clinical response, decrease to 1g PO bid.
PEDS - Ulcerative colitis ≥2 yo: 40-60 mg/kg/day PO divided into 3-6 doses after meals. After clinical response, decrease to 30 mg/kg/day divided qid. JRA: ≥6 yo: 30-50 mg/kg/day (EN-Tabs) PO divided bid to max of 2g/day.
UNAPPROVED ADULT - Ankylosing spondylitis, collagenous colitis: 1-1.5g PO bid. Crohn's disease, psoriasis: 1.5-2g PO bid. Psoriatic arthritis: 1g PO bid.
FORMS - Generic/Trade: Tabs 500 mg, scored. Trade only: Enteric Coated, Delayed release (EN-Tabs) 500 mg.
NOTES - Avoid with hepatic or renal dysfunction, intestinal or urinary obstruction, & porphyria. Monitor CBCs & LFTs. Beware of hypersensitivity, marrow suppression, renal & liver damage, irreversible neuromuscular & CNS changes, fibrosing alveolitis, oligospermia & infertility. Decreases absorption of digoxin & folic acid. May turn body fluids, contact lenses, or skin orange-yellow. May decrease cyclosporine levels.

ANALGESICS: Muscle Relaxants

NOTE: May cause drowsiness/sedation, which may be enhanced by alcohol, sedatives, etc.

baclofen (*Lioresal*) ▶K ♀C ▶+ $$
ADULT - Spasticity related to MS or spinal cord disease/injury: 5 mg PO tid x 3 days, 10 mg PO tid x 3 days, 15 mg PO tid x 3 days, then 20 mg PO tid x 3 days. Max dose: 20 mg qid.
PEDS - Not approved in children.
UNAPPROVED ADULT - Trigeminal neuralgia: 30-80 mg/day PO divided tid-qid. Tardive dyskinesia: 40-60 mg/day PO divided tid-qid. Intractable hiccoughs: 15-30 mg PO divided tid.
UNAPPROVED PEDS - Spasticity: ≥ 2 yo: 10-15 mg/day PO divided q8h. Max doses 40 mg/day for 2-7 yo, 60 mg/day for ≥ 8 yo.
FORMS - Generic/Trade: Tabs 10 & 20 mg, trade scored.
NOTES - Hallucinations & seizures with abrupt withdrawal. Caution if impaired renal function. Efficacy not established for typical muscle relaxant indications: rheumatic disorders, stroke, cerebral palsy, Parkinson's disease.

carisoprodol (*Soma*) ▶LK ♀? ▶+ $
ADULT - Musculoskeletal pain: 350 mg PO tid-qid with meals and qhs.
PEDS - Not approved in children.
FORMS - Generic/Trade:Tabs 350 mg.
NOTES - Contraindicated in porphyria, caution in renal or hepatic insufficiency. Abuse potential. Use with caution if addiction-prone.

chlorzoxazone (*Paraflex, Parafon Forte DSC, Remular-S*) ▶LK ♀C ▶? $$
WARNING - If signs/symptoms of liver dysfunction are observed, discontinue use.
ADULT - Musculoskeletal pain: Start 500 mg PO tid-qid, increase prn to 750 mg tid-qid. After

clinical improvement, decrease to 250 mg PO tid-qid.
PEDS - Not approved in children.
UNAPPROVED PEDS - Musculoskeletal pain: 125-500 mg PO tid-qid or 20 mg/kg/day divided tid-qid depending on age & weight.
FORMS - Generic/Trade:Tabs & caplets 250 & 500 mg (Parafon Forte DSC 500 mg caplets scored).
NOTES - Use with caution in patients with history of drug allergies. Discontinue if allergic drug reactions occur or for signs/symptoms of liver dysfunction.

cyclobenzaprine (*Flexeril*) ▶LK ♀B ◗? $
ADULT - Musculoskeletal pain: 10 mg PO tid up to max dose of 60 mg/day. Not recommended in elderly or for use >2-3 weeks.
PEDS - Not approved in children.
FORMS - Generic/Trade: Tabs 10 mg.
NOTES - Contraindicated with recent or concomitant MAO inhibitor use, immediately post-MI, in patients with arrhythmias, conduction disturbances, CHF, & hyperthyroidism. Not effective for cerebral or spinal cord disease or in cerebral palsy. May have similar adverse effects & drug interactions as TCAs.

dantrolene (*Dantrium*) ▶LK ♀C ◗- $$$$
WARNING - Hepatotoxicity, monitor LFTs. Use the lowest possible effective dose.
ADULT - Chronic spasticity related to spinal cord injury, stroke, cerebral palsy, MS: 25 mg PO qd to start, increase to 25 mg bid-qid, then by 25 mg up to max of 100 mg bid-qid if necessary. Maintain each dosage level for 4-7 days to determine response. Use the lowest possible effective dose. Malignant hyperthermia: 1 mg/kg rapid IV push q6h continuing until symptoms subside or to a maximum cumulative dose of 10 mg/kg. Cumulative doses of up to 40 mg/kg have been used. Follow with 4-8 mg/kg/day PO divided tid-qid x 1-3 days to prevent recurrence.
PEDS - Chronic spasticity: 0.5 mg/kg PO bid to start; increase to 0.5 mg/kg tid-qid, then by increments of 0.5 mg/kg up to 3 mg/kg bid-qid. Max dose 100 mg PO qid. Malignant hyperthermia: use adult dose.
UNAPPROVED ADULT - Neuroleptic malignant syndrome, heat stroke: 1-3 mg/kg/day PO/IV divided qid.
FORMS - Trade: Caps 25, 50 & 100 mg.
NOTES - Photosensitization may occur. Warfarin may decrease protein binding & increase dantrolene's effect. The following website may be useful for malignant hyperthermia info: www.mhaus.org/ananesprotocol12.

diazepam (*Valium, Diastat*) ▶LK ♀D ◗- ©IV $$
ADULT - Skeletal muscle spasm, spasticity related to cerebral palsy, paraplegia, athetosis, stiff man syndrome: 2-10 mg PO/PR tid-qid. 5-10 mg IM/IV initially, then 5-10 mg q 3-4h prn.
PEDS - Skeletal muscle spasm: 0.1-0.8 mg/kg/day PO/PR divided tid-qid. 0.04-0.2 mg/kg/dose IV/IM q2-4h. Max dose 0.6 mg/kg within 8 hours.
FORMS - Generic/Trade: Tabs 2, 5 & 10 mg, trade scored. Generic: Oral soln 5 mg/5 ml & 5 mg/ml. Trade only: Rectal gel: 2.5 mg & 5 mg (pediatric), 10 mg (pediatric & adult), 15 mg & 20 mg (adult).
NOTES - Contraindicated in liver disease. Abuse potential. Long half-life may increases the risk of adverse effects in the elderly. Cimetidine, oral contraceptives, disulfiram, fluoxetine, isoniazid, ketoconazole, metoprolol, propoxyphene, propranolol, & valproic acid may increase diazepam concentrations. Diazepam may increase digoxin & phenytoin concentrations. Rifampin may increase the metabolism of diazepam.

metaxalone (*Skelaxin*) ▶LK ♀? ◗? $$$
ADULT - Musculoskeletal pain: 800 mg PO tid-qid.
PEDS - Not approved in children.
FORMS - Trade: Tabs 400 mg, scored.
NOTES - Contraindicated in serious renal or hepatic insufficiency or history of drug-induced hemolytic or other anemia. Beware of hypersensitivity reactions, leukopenia, hemolytic anemia, & jaundice.

methocarbamol (*Robaxin, Robaxin-750*) ▶LK ♀C ◗+ $$
ADULT - Musculoskeletal pain, acute relief: 1500 mg PO qid or 1000 mg IM/IV tid x 48-72h. Maintenance: 1000 mg PO qid, 750 mg PO q4h, or 1500 mg PO tid. Tetanus: specialized dosing.
PEDS - Tetanus: Specialized dosing.
FORMS - Generic/Trade: Tabs 500 & 750 mg. OTC in Canada.
NOTES - Max IV rate 3 ml/min to avoid syncope, hypotension, & bradycardia. Total parenteral dosage should not exceed 3g/day for >3 consecutive days, except in the treatment of tetanus. Urine may turn brown, black or green.

orphenadrine (*Norflex*) ▶LK ♀C ◗? $$
ADULT - Musculoskeletal pain: 100 mg PO bid. 60 mg IV/IM bid.
UNAPPROVED ADULT - Leg cramps: 100 mg

PO qhs.
FORMS - Generic/Trade: 100 mg sustained release. OTC in Canada.
NOTES - Contraindicated in glaucoma, pyloric or duodenal obstruction, BPH, & myasthenia gravis. Some products contain sulfites, which may cause allergic reactions. May increase anticholinergic effects of amantadine & decrease therapeutic effects of phenothiazines. Side effects include dry mouth, difficult urination, constipation, headache & GI upset.

quinine sulfate ▸L ♀X ◗? $
ADULT - Chloroquine resistant malaria. See Antimicrobial section (Antimalarial Agents).
PEDS - Not approved in children.
UNAPPROVED ADULT - Nocturnal leg cramps: 260-325 mg PO qhs.
FORMS - Rx: Generic: Caps 200, 260 & 325 mg. Tabs 260 mg.
NOTES - Hemolysis possible in G6PD deficiency. Cinchonism with overdose. Quinine may have quinidine-like activity & may exacerbate cardiac arrhythmias. Beware of hypersensitivity reactions, tinnitus & visual impairment. Do not use with mefloquine. Antacids may decrease quinine absorption; rifampin may increase its metabolism. Cimetidine may reduce quinine clearance & urinary alkalinizers may also increase levels. May increase warfarin, digoxin & neuromuscular blocker activity.

tizanidine (*Zanaflex*) ▸LK ♀C ◗? $$$$
ADULT - Muscle spasticity due to MS or spinal cord injury: 4-8 mg PO q6-8h prn, max dose 36 mg/day.
PEDS - Not approved in children.
FORMS - Trade: Tabs 4 mg, scored.
NOTES - Avoid with hepatic or renal insufficiency. Alcohol & oral contraceptives increase tizanidine levels. Concurrent antihypertensives may exacerbate hypotension. Dry mouth, somnolence, sedation, asthenia & dizziness most common side effects.

ANALGESICS: Non-Opioid Analgesic Combinations

NOTE: Refer to individual components for further information. Carisoprodol and butalbital may be habit-forming. May cause drowsiness and/or sedation, which may be enhanced by alcohol, sedatives, tranquilizers, etc. Avoid exceeding 4 g/day of acetaminophen in combo products. Caution people who drink >3 alcoholic drinks/day to limit acetaminophen use due to additive liver toxicity.

***Ascriptin* (ASA with Mg/Al hydroxide & Ca carbonate buffers)** ▸K ♀D ◗? $
WARNING - Multiple strengths; see FORMS.
ADULT - Pain: 1-2 tabs PO q4h.
PEDS - Not approved in children.
FORMS - OTC: Trade: Tabs 325 mg ASA/50 mg magnesium hydroxide/50 mg aluminum hydroxide/calcium carbonate (Asciptin). 325 mg ASA/75 mg magnesium hydroxide/75 mg aluminum hydroxide/calcium carbonate (Ascriptin A/D). 500 mg ASA/80 mg magnesium hydroxide/80 mg aluminum hydroxide/calcium carbonate (Ascriptin Maximum Strength).
NOTES - See NSAIDs - Salicylic Acid subclass warning.

***Esgic* (acetaminophen + butalbital + caffeine)** ▸LK ♀C ◗? $
ADULT - Tension or muscle contraction headache: 1-2 tabs or caps PO q4h.
PEDS - Not approved in children.
FORMS - Generic/Trade: Tabs/caps acetaminophen 325 mg/butalbital 50 mg/caffeine 40 mg.

***Fioricet* (acetaminophen + butalbital + caffeine)** ▸LK ♀C ◗? $
ADULT - Tension or muscle contraction headache: 1-2 tabs PO q4h.
PEDS - Not approved in children.
FORMS - Generic/Trade: Tabs 325 mg acetaminophen//50 mg butalbital/40 mg caffeine.

***Fiorinal* (ASA + butalbital + caffeine)** ▸KL ♀D ◗- ©III $
ADULT - Tension or muscle contraction headache: 1-2 tabs PO q4h.
PEDS - Not approved in children.
FORMS - Generic/Trade: Tabs 325 mg aspirin/50 mg butalbital/40 mg caffeine.
NOTES - See NSAIDs - Salicylic Acid subclass warning.

***Norgesic* (orphenadrine + ASA + caffeine)** ▸KL ♀D ◗? $$$
WARNING - Multiple strengths; see FORMS & write specific product on Rx.
ADULT - Pain: Norgesic, 1-2 tabs PO tid-qid. Pain: Norgesic Forte, 1 tab PO tid-qid.
PEDS - Not approved in children.
FORMS - Trade: Tabs Norgesic 25 mg orphenadrine/385 mg aspirin/30 mg caffeine. Norgesic Forte 50 mg orphenadrine/770 mg aspirin/60 mg caffeine.
NOTES - See NSAIDs - Salicylic Acid warning.

***Robaxisal* (methocarbamol + ASA)** ▸LK ♀D ◗? $

ADULT - Pain: 2 tabs PO qid.
PEDS - Not approved in children.
FORMS - Generic/Trade: Tabs 400 mg methocarbamol/325 mg ASA.
NOTES - See NSAIDs - Salicylic Acid subclass warning.

Soma Compound **(carisoprodol + ASA)** ▸LK ♀D ◗- $$
ADULT - Pain: 1-2 tabs PO qid.
PEDS - Not approved in children.
FORMS - Generic/Trade: Tabs 200 mg carisoprodol/325 mg ASA.
NOTES - Refer to individual components. See NSAIDs - Salicylic Acid subclass warning. Carisoprodol may be habit forming.

Ultracet **(tramadol + acetaminophen)** ▸KL ♀C ◗- ?
ADULT - Acute pain: 2 tabs PO q4-6h prn, max 8 tabs/day for no more than 5 days. If creatinine clearance < 30ml/min, increase the dosing interval to 12 hours. Consider a similar adjustment in elderly patients.
PEDS - Not approved in children.
FORMS - Trade: Tabs 37.5 mg tramadol/325 mg acetaminophen.
NOTES - Do not use with other acetaminophen-containing drugs due to potential for hepatotoxicity. Contraindicated in acute intoxication with alcohol, hypnotics, centrally acting analgesics, opioids or psychotropic drugs. Seizures may occur with concurrent antidepressants or in epileptics. Use with great caution with MAO inhibitors or in combination with SSRIs due to potential for serotonin syndrome; dose adjustment may be needed. Withdrawal symptoms may occur in patients dependent on opioids. The most frequent side effects are somnolence & constipation.

ANALGESICS: Nonsteroidal Anti-Inflammatories – COX-2 Inhibitors

NOTES: Less GI side effects than 1st generation NSAIDs & no effect on platelets, but other NSAID related side effects (renal dysfunction, fluid retention, CNS) are possible. Monitor INR with warfarin. Caution in aspirin-sensitive asthma.

celecoxib (*Celebrex*) ▸L ♀C (D in 3rd trimester) ◗? $$$
ADULT - OA: 200 mg PO qd or 100 mg PO bid. RA: 100 mg - 200 mg PO bid. Familial adenomatous polyposis (FAP), as an adjunct to usual care: 400 mg PO bid with food.
PEDS - Not approved in children.
FORMS - Trade: Caps 100 & 200 mg.
NOTES - Contraindicated in sulfonamide allergy. See rofecoxib for possible alternative in this situation. Fluconazole increases levels.

rofecoxib (*Vioxx*) ▸Plasma ♀C (D in 3rd trimester) ◗? $$$
ADULT - OA: 12.5-25 mg PO qd. Acute pain, primary dysmenorrhea: 50 mg PO qd.
PEDS - Not approved in children.
FORMS - Trade: Tabs 12.5, 25 & 50 mg. Suspension 12.5 mg/5 ml and 25 mg/5 ml.
NOTES - Rifampin decreases rofecoxib levels. Rofecoxib is not related to the sulfonamides and is not contraindicated in pts with such allergies. Use of 50 mg for >5 days pain management has not been studied.

ANALGESICS: Nonsteroidal Anti-Inflammatories – Salicylic Acid Derivatives

NOTES: Avoid in children/teenagers <17 yo with chickenpox or flu due to association with Reye's syndrome. May potentiate warfarin, heparin, valproic acid, methotrexate. Unlike ASA, derivatives may have less GI toxicity & negligible effects on platelet aggregation & renal prostaglandins.

aspirin (*Ecotrin, Empirin, Bayer, ASA,* ✤*Asaphen, Entrophen*) ▸K ♀D ◗? $
ADULT - Mild to moderate pain, fever: 325-650 mg PO/PR q4h prn. Acute rheumatic fever: 5-8 g/day, initially. RA/OA: 3.2-6g/day in divided doses.
PEDS - Mild to moderate pain, fever: 10-15 mg/kg/dose PO q4-6h not to exceed 60-80 mg/kg/day. JRA: 60-100 mg/kg/day PO divided q6-8h. Acute rheumatic fever: 100 mg/kg/day PO/PR x 2 weeks, then 75 mg/kg/day x 4-6 weeks. Kawasaki disease 80-100 mg/kg/day divided qid PO/PR until fever resolves, then 3-5 mg/kg/day PO qam x 7 weeks or longer if there is ECG evidence of coronary artery abnormalities.
FORMS - OTC: Tabs 81, 165, 325, 500, 650, controlled release tabs 650 (scored). Rx only: 800 mg controlled release tabs & 975 mg enteric coated. OTC: suppositories 120, 200, 300, & 600 mg.
NOTES - Consider discontinuation 1 week prior

to surgery because of the possibility of postoperative bleeding. Aspirin intolerance occurs in 4%-19% of asthmatics. Use caution in liver damage, renal insufficiency, peptic ulcer or bleeding tendencies.

choline magnesium trisalicylate (*Trilisate*) ▸K ♀C (D in 3rd trimester) ◗? $$$

ADULT - RA/OA: 1500 mg PO bid. Mild to moderate pain, fever: 1000-1500 mg PO bid.

PEDS - RA, mild to moderate pain: 50 mg/kg/day (up to 37kg) PO divided bid.

FORMS - Generic/Trade: Tabs 500, 750, & 1000 mg, scored. Liquid 500 mg/5 ml.

NOTES - Contraindicated in ASA allergy.

diflunisal (*Dolobid*) ▸K ♀C (D in 3rd trimester) ◗- $$$

ADULT - Mild to moderate pain: Initially: 500 mg-1g PO, then 250-500 mg PO q8-12h. RA/OA: 500 mg-1g PO divided bid. Max dose 1.5g/day.

PEDS - Not approved in children.

FORMS - Generic/Trade: Tabs 250 & 500 mg.

NOTES - Contraindicated in patients with ASA allergy.

salsalate (*Salflex, Disalcid*) ▸K ♀C (D in 3rd trimester) ◗? $$$

ADULT - RA/OA: 3000 mg/day PO divided q8-12h.

PEDS - Not approved in children.

FORMS - Generic/Trade: Tabs 500 & 750 mg, various scored. Trade only: Caps 500 mg.

NOTES - Contraindicated in patients with ASA allergy.

NSAIDSs – If one class fails, consider another. Salicylic acid derivatives: aspirin, diflunisal, salsalate, Trilisate. Propionic acids: flurbiprofen, ibuprofen, ketoprofen, naproxen, oxaprozin. Acetic acids: diclofenac, etodolac, indomethacin, ketorolac, nabumetone, sulindac, tolmetin. Fenamates: meclofenamate. Oxicams: meloxicam, piroxicam. COX-2 inhibitors: celecoxib, rofecoxib.

ANALGESICS: Nonsteroidal Anti-Inflammatories - Other

NOTE: Chronic use associated with renal insufficiency, gastritis, peptic ulcer disease, GI bleeds. Caution in liver disease. May cause fluid-retention or exacerbate CHF. May elevate BP or blunt effects of antihypertensives & loop diuretics. May increase levels of methotrexate, lithium, phenytoin, digoxin & cyclosporine. May potentiate warfarin. Caution in aspirin-sensitive asthma.

***Arthrotec* (diclofenac + misoprostol)** ▸LK ♀X ◗- $$$$

WARNING - Because of the abortifacient property of the misoprostol component, it is contraindicated in women who are pregnant. Caution in women with childbearing potential; effective contraception is essential.

ADULT - OA: one 50/200 PO tid. RA: one 50/200 PO tid-qid. If intolerant, may use 50/200 or 75/200 PO bid.

PEDS - Not approved in children.

FORMS - Trade: Tabs 50 mg/200 mcg & 75 mg/200 mcg diclofenac/misoprostol.

NOTES - Refer to individual components. Abdominal pain & diarrhea may occur. Check LFTs at baseline then periodically. See NSAIDs-Other subclass warning.

diclofenac (*Voltaren, Voltaren XR, Cataflam*) ▸L ♀B (D in 3rd trimester) ◗- $$$

WARNING - Multiple strengths; see FORMS & write specific product on Rx.

ADULT - OA: immediate or delayed release 50 mg PO bid-tid or 75 mg bid. Extended release 100 mg PO qd. RA: immediate or delayed release 50 mg PO tid-qid or 75 mg bid. Extended release 100 mg PO qd-bid. Ankylosing spondylitis: immediate or delayed release 25 mg PO qid & hs. Analgesia & primary dysmenorrhea: immediate or delayed release 50 mg PO tid.

PEDS - Not approved in children.

UNAPPROVED PEDS - JRA: 2-3 mg/kg/day PO.

FORMS - Generic/Trade: Tabs, immediate release (Cataflam) 50 mg. Tabs, delayed release (Voltaren) 25, 50, & 75 mg. Tabs, extended release (Voltaren XR) 100 mg.

NOTES - Check LFTs at baseline then periodically.

etodolac (*Lodine, Lodine XL*) ▸L ♀C (D in 3rd trimester) ◗- $$$

WARNING - Multiple strengths; see FORMS & write specific product on Rx.

ADULT - OA: 400 mg PO bid-tid. 300 mg PO bid-qid. 200 mg tid-qid. Extended release 400-1200 mg PO qd. Mild to moderate pain: 200-400 mg q6-8h. Max dose 1200 mg/day or if ≤ 60 kg, 20 mg/kg/day.

PEDS - Not approved in children.

UNAPPROVED ADULT - RA, ankylosing spondylitis: 300-400 mg PO bid. Tendinitis, bursitis & acute gout: 300-400 mg PO bid-qid then taper.

FORMS - Generic/Trade: Tabs, immediate release (Lodine) 400 mg. Trade only: Caps, immediate release (Lodine) 200 & 300 mg. Tabs, extended release (Lodine XL) 400,500,600 mg.

fenoprofen (*Nalfon Pulvules*) ▶L ♀C (D in 3rd trimester) ◗- $$

ADULT - Other drugs preferred due to nephrotoxicity risk.

PEDS - Not approved in children.

FORMS - Generic/Trade: Caps 200 & 300 mg. Generic only: Tabs 600 mg.

flurbiprofen (*Ansaid*, *Froben*) ▶L ♀B (D in 3rd trimester) ◗+ $$$

ADULT - RA/OA: 200-300 mg/day PO divided bid-qid. Max single dose 100 mg.

PEDS - Not approved in children.

UNAPPROVED ADULT - Ankylosing spondylitis: 150-300 mg/day PO divided bid-qid. Mild to moderate pain: 50 mg PO q6h. Primary dysmenorrhea: 50 mg PO qd at onset, d/c when pain subsides. Tendinitis, bursitis, acute gout, acute migraine: 100 mg PO at onset, then 50 mg PO qid, then taper.

UNAPPROVED PEDS - JRA: 4 mg/kg/day PO.

FORMS - Generic/Trade: Tabs immediate release 50 & 100 mg.

ibuprofen (*Motrin, Advil, Nuprin, Rufen*) ▶L ♀B (D in 3rd trimester) ◗+ $

ADULT - RA/OA: 200-800 mg PO tid-qid. Mild to moderate pain: 400 mg PO q4-6h. Primary dysmenorrhea: 400 mg PO q4h, prn. Fever: 200 mg PO q4-6h prn. Migraine pain: 200-400 mg PO not to exceed 400 mg in 24 hours (OTC dosing). Max dose 3.2g/day.

PEDS - JRA: 30-50 mg/kg/day PO divided q6h; max dose 2400 mg/24h. 20 mg/kg/day may be adequate for milder disease. Analgesic/antipyretic >6 mo: 5-10 mg/kg PO q6-8h, prn. Max dose 40 mg/kg/day.

FORMS - OTC: Caps, 200 mg. Tabs 100, 200 mg. Chewable tabs 50 & 100 mg. Caplets 200 mg. Liquid & suspension, 100 mg/5 ml, suspension 100 mg/2.5 ml. Infant drops, 50 mg/1.25 ml (calibrated dropper). Rx only: Tabs 400, 600 & 800 mg.

indomethacin (*Indocin, Indocin SR, Indocid, Indotec*) ▶L ♀B (D in 3rd trimester) ◗+ $

WARNING - Multiple strengths; see FORMS & write specific product on Rx.

ADULT - RA/OA, ankylosing spondylitis: 25 mg PO bid-tid to start. Increase incrementally to a total daily dose of 150-200 mg. Bursitis/tendinitis: 75-150 mg/day PO/PR divided tid-qid. Acute gout: 50 mg PO/PR tid until pain tolerable, rapidly taper dose to D/C. Sustained release: 75 mg PO qd-bid.

PEDS - Not approved in children.

UNAPPROVED ADULT - Primary dysmenorrhea: 25 mg PO tid-qid. Cluster headache: 75-150 mg SR PO qd. Polyhydramnios: 2.2-3.0 mg/kg/day PO.

UNAPPROVED PEDS - JRA: 1-3 mg/kg/day tid-qid to start. Increase prn to max dose of 4 mg/kg/d or 200 mg/d, whichever is less.

FORMS - Generic/Trade: Caps, immediate release 25 & 50 mg. Oral suspension 25 mg/5 ml. Suppositories 50 mg. Caps, sustained release 75 mg.

NOTES - Suppositories contraindicated with history of proctitis or recent rectal bleeding. May aggravate depression or other psychiatric disturbances.

ketoprofen (*Orudis, Actron, Oruvail, Orafen*) ▶L ♀B (D in 3rd trimester) ◗- $$$

ADULT - RA/OA: 75 mg PO tid or 50 mg PO qid. Extended release 200 mg PO qd. Mild to moderate pain, primary dysmenorrhea: 25-50 mg PO q6-8h prn.

PEDS - Not approved in children.

UNAPPROVED PEDS - JRA : 100-200 mg/meters squared/day PO. Max dose 320 mg/day.

FORMS - OTC: Tabs immediate release, 12.5 mg. Rx: Generic/Trade: Caps, immediate release 25, 50 & 75 mg. Caps, extended release 100, 150 & 200 mg.

ketorolac (*Toradol*) ▶L ♀C (D in 3rd trimester) ◗+ $

WARNING - Indicated for short-term (up to 5 days) therapy only. Ketorolac is a potent NSAID and can cause serious GI and renal adverse effects. It may also increase the risk of bleeding by inhibiting platelet function. Contraindicated in patients with active peptic ulcer disease, recent GI bleeding or perforation, a history of peptic ulcer disease or GI bleeding, and advanced renal impairment.

ADULT - Moderately severe, acute pain, single-dose treatment: 30-60 mg IM or 15-30 mg IV. Multiple-dose treatment: 15-30 mg IV/IM q6h. IV/IM doses are not to exceed 60 mg/day in patients ≥65 yo, <50 kg, & for patients with moderately elevated serum creatinine. Oral continuation therapy: 10 mg PO q4-6h prn, max dose 40 mg/day. Combined duration IV/IM and PO is not to exceed 5 days.

PEDS - Not approved in children.

UNAPPROVED PEDS - Pain: 0.5 mg/kg/dose IM/IV q6h not to exceed 30 mg q6h or 120 mg/day. > 50kg: 10 mg PO q6h prn not to ex-

ceed 40 mg/day.
FORMS - Generic/Trade: Tabs 10 mg.

meclofenamate ▶L ♀D ▶- $$$$$
ADULT - Mild to moderate pain: 50 mg PO q4-6h prn. Max dose 400 mg/day. Menorrhagia & primary dysmenorrhea: 100 mg PO tid for up to 6 days. RA/OA: 200-400 mg/day PO divided tid-qid.
PEDS - Not approved in children.
UNAPPROVED PEDS - JRA: 3-7.5 mg/kg/day PO; max dose 300 mg/day.
FORMS - Generic: Caps 50 & 100 mg.
NOTES - Reversible autoimmune hemolytic anemia with use for >12 months.

meloxicam (*Mobic*) ▶L ♀C (D in 3rd trimester) ▶? $$$
ADULT - OA: 7.5 mg tab PO qd.
PEDS - Not approved in children.
FORMS - Trade: Tabs 7.5 mg
NOTES - This is not a selective COX-2 inhibitor. The package inserts of the currently marketed COX-2 selective drugs, Vioxx and Celebrex, state their mechanism of action is due to inhibition of prostaglandin synthesis, primarily via inhibition of cyclooxygenase-2 (COX-2), and at therapeutic concentrations in humans, these two drugs do not inhibit the cyclooxygenase-1 (COX-1) isoenzyme. The FDA did not allow this wording in the Mobic prescribing information.

nabumetone (*Relafen*) ▶L ♀C (D in 3rd trimester) ▶- $$$
ADULT - RA/OA: Initial: two 500 mg tabs (1000mg) PO qd. May increase to 1500-2000 mg PO qd or divided bid. Dosages >2000 mg/day have not been studied.
PEDS - Not approved in children.
FORMS - Trade: Tabs 500 & 750 mg.

naproxen (*Naprosyn, Aleve, Anaprox, EC-Naprosyn, Naprelan*, ✤*Naxen*) ▶L ♀B (D in 3rd trimester) ▶+ $$$
WARNING - Multiple strengths; see FORMS & write specific product on Rx.
ADULT - RA/OA, ankylosing spondylitis, pain, dysmenorrhea, acute tendinitis & bursitis, fever: 250-500 mg PO bid. Delayed release: 375-500 mg PO bid (do not crush or chew). Controlled release: 750-1000 mg PO qd. Acute gout: 750 mg PO x 1, then 250 mg PO q8h until the attack subsides. Controlled release: 1000-1500 mg PO x 1, then 1000 mg PO qd until the attack subsides.
PEDS - JRA: 10-20 mg/kg/day PO divided bid. Max dose 1250 mg/24h. Pain >2 yo: 5-7 mg/kg/dose PO q8-12h.
UNAPPROVED ADULT - Acute migraine: 750 mg PO x 1, then 250-500 mg PO prn. Migraine prophylaxis, menstrual migraine: 500 mg PO bid.
FORMS - OTC: Generic/Trade: Tabs immediate release 200 mg. Rx: Generic/Trade: Tabs immediate release 250, 375 & 500 mg. Rx: Trade: Tabs (Naprelan), delayed release enteric coated, 375 & 500 mg. Tabs, controlled release 375 & 500 mg. Suspension 125 mg/5 ml.
NOTES - All dosing is based on naproxen content; 500 mg naproxen = 550 mg naproxen sodium.

oxaprozin (*Daypro*) ▶L ♀C (D in 3rd trimester) ▶- $$$
ADULT - RA/OA: 1200 mg PO qd. Max dose 1800 mg/day or 26 mg/kg/day, whichever is lower.
PEDS - Not approved in children.
FORMS - Generic/Trade: Caplets 600 mg, trade scored.

piroxicam (*Feldene, Fexicam*) ▶L ♀B (D in 3rd trimester) ▶+ $$$
ADULT - RA/OA: 20 mg PO qd or divided bid.
PEDS - Not approved in children.
UNAPPROVED ADULT - Primary dysmenorrhea: 20-40 mg PO qd x 3 days.
FORMS - Generic/Trade: Caps 10 & 20 mg.

sulindac (*Clinoril*) ▶L ♀B (D in 3rd trimester) ▶- $$$
ADULT - RA/OA, ankylosing spondylitis: 150 mg PO bid. Bursitis, tendinitis, acute gout: 200 mg PO bid, decrease after response. Max dose: 400 mg/day.
PEDS - Not approved in children.
UNAPPROVED PEDS - JRA: 4 mg/kg/day PO divided bid.
FORMS - Generic/Trade: Tabs 150 & 200 mg.
NOTES - Sulindac-associated pancreatitis & a potentially fatal hypersensitivity syndrome have occurred.

tolmetin (*Tolectin*) ▶L ♀C (D in 3rd trimester) ▶+ $$$
ADULT - RA/OA: 400 mg PO tid to start. Range 600-1800 mg/day PO divided tid.
PEDS - JRA ≥ 2 yo: 20 mg/kg/day PO divided tid-qid to start; range 15-30 mg/kg/day divided tid-qid; max dose 2g/24h.
UNAPPROVED PEDS - Pain ≥ 2 yo: 5-7 mg/kg/dose PO q6-8h. Max dose 2g/24h.
FORMS - Generic/Trade: Tabs 200 (trade scored) & 600 mg. Caps 400 mg.
NOTES - Rare anaphylaxis.

OPIOIDS*	Approximate equianalgesic		Recommended starting dose			
			Adults >50kg		Children/Adults 8 to 50 kg	
	IV / SC / IM	*PO*	*IV / SC / IM*	*PO*	*IV / SC / IM*	*PO*
Opioid Agonists						
morphine	10 mg q3-4h	†30 mg q3-4h †60 mg q3-4h	10 mg q3-4h	30 mg q3-4h	0.1 mg/kg q3-4h	0.3 mg/kg q3-4h
codeine	75 mg q3-4h	130 mg q3-4h	60 mg q2h	60 mg q3-4h	n/r	1 mg/kg q3-4h
fentanyl	0.1 mg q1h	n/a	0.1 mg q1h	n/a	n/r	n/a
hydromor-phone	1.5 mg q3-4h	7.5 mg q3-4h	1.5 mg q3-4h	6 mg q3-4h	0.015 mg/kg q3-4h	0.06 mg/kg q3-4h
hydrocodone	n/a	30 mg q3-4h	n/a	10 mg q3-4h	n/a	0.2 mg/kg q3-4h
levorphanol	2 mg q6-8h	4 mg q6-8h	2 mg q6-8h	4 mg q6-8h	0.02 mg/kg q6-8h	0.04 mg/kg q6-8h
meperidine§	100 mg q3h	300 mg q2-3h	100 mg q3h	n/r	0.75 mg/kg q2-3h	n/r
oxycodone	n/a	30 mg q3-4h	n/a	10 mg q3-4h	n/a	0.2 mg/kg q3-4h
oxymorphone	1 mg q3-4h	n/a	1 mg q3-4h	n/a	n/r	n/r
Opioid Agonist-Antagonist and Partial Agonist						
buprenor-phine	0.3-0.4 mg q6-8h	n/a	0.4 mg q6-8h	n/a	0.004 mg/kg q6-8h	n/a
butorphanol	2 mg q3-4h	n/a	2 mg q3-4h	n/a	n/r	n/a
nalbuphine	10 mg q3-4h	n/a	10 mg q3-4h	n/a	0.1 mg/kg q3-4h	n/a
pentazocine	60 mg q3-4h	150 mg q3-4h	n/r	50 mg q4-6h	n/r	n/r

*Approximate dosing, adapted from 1992 AHCPR guidelines, www.ahcpr.gov. Individualize all dosing, especially in the elderly, children, and patients with chronic pain, opioid tolerance, or hepatic/renal insufficiency. Many recommend initially using lower than equivalent doses when switching between different opioids. Not available = "n/a". Not recommended = "n/r". Do not exceed 4g/day of acetaminophen or aspirin when using opioid combination formulations. Methadone is excluded due to poor consensus on equivalence. The contributions of Robert Arnold, MD and David Weissman, MD to this table are kindly acknowledged.

†30 mg with around the clock dosing, and 60 mg with a single dose or short-term dosing (ie, the opioid-naïve).

§Doses should be limited to <600 mg/24 hrs and total duration of use <48 hrs; not for chronic pain.

ANALGESICS: Opioid Agonist-Antagonists

NOTE: May cause drowsiness and/or sedation, which may be enhanced by alcohol, sedatives, etc. Partial agonist-antagonists may result in withdrawal effects in the opioid-dependent.

buprenorphine (*Buprenex*) ▶L ♀C ▶? ©V $

ADULT - Moderate to severe pain: 0.3-0.6 mg IM or slow IV, q6-8h prn. Max single dose 0.6 mg.

PEDS - Moderate to severe pain: 2-12 yo: 2-6 mcg/kg/dose IM or slow IV q4-6h. Max single dose 6 mcg/kg.

NOTES - May cause bradycardia, hypotension & respiratory depression. Concurrent use with diazepam has resulted in respiratory & cardiovascular collapse.

butorphanol (*Stadol, Stadol NS*) ▶LK ♀C ▶+ ©IV $$$

WARNING - Approved as a nasal spray in 1991 and has been promoted as a safe treatment for migraine headaches. There have been numerous reports of dependence-addiction & major psychological disturbances. These problems have been documented by the FDA. Stadol NS should be used for patients with infrequent but severe migraine attacks for whom all other common ablative treatments have failed. Experts recommended a restriction to no more than two bottles (30 sprays) per month in patients who are appropriate candidates for this medication.

ADULT - Pain, including post-operative pain: 0.5-2 mg IV q3-4h prn. 1-4 mg IM q3-4h prn. Obstetric pain during labor: 1-2 mg IV/IM at full term in early labor, repeat after 4h. Last resort for migraine pain: 1 mg nasal spray (1 spray in one nostril)..If no pain relief in 60-90 min, may give a 2nd spray in the other nostril. Additional doses q3-4h prn.

PEDS - Not approved in children.

FORMS - Nasal spray 1 mg/spray, 2.5 ml bottle (14-15 doses/bottle).

NOTES - May increases cardiac workload.

nalbuphine (*Nubain*) ▶LK ♀? ◗? $

ADULT - Moderate to severe pain: 10-20 mg SC/IM/IV q3-6h prn. Max dose 160 mg/day.

PEDS - Not approved in children.

pentazocine (*Talwin, Talwin NX*) ▶LK ♀C ◗? ©IV $

WARNING - The oral form (Talwin NX) may cause fatal reactions if injected.

ADULT - Moderate to severe pain: Talwin: 30 mg IM/IV q3-4h prn, max dose 360 mg/day. Talwin NX: 1 tab PO q3-4h, max 12 tabs/day.

PEDS - Not approved in children.

FORMS - Generic/Trade: Tabs 50 mg with 0.5 mg naloxone, trade scored.

NOTES - Rotate injection sites. Can cause hallucinations, disorientation, and seizures. Concomitant sibutramine may precipitate serotonin syndrome.

ANALGESICS: Opioid Agonists

NOTE: May cause drowsiness and/or sedation, which may be enhanced by alcohol, sedatives, tranquilizers, etc. Patients with chronic pain may require more frequent & higher dosing. Opioids commonly create constipation. All opioids are pregnancy class D if used for prolonged periods or in high doses at term.

codeine ▶LK ♀C ◗+ ©II $

WARNING - Do not use IV in children due to large histamine release/& cardiovascular effects.

ADULT - Mild to moderate pain: 15-60 mg PO/IM/IV/SC q4-6h. Antitussive: 10-20 mg PO q4-6h prn.

PEDS - Mild to moderate pain in ≥1yo: 0.5-1 mg/kg PO/SC/IM q4-6h, max dose 60 mg/dose. Antitussive: 2-5 yo: 2.5-5 mg PO q4-6h prn, max dose: 30 mg/day. 6-12 yo: 5-10 mg PO q4-6h prn, max dose 60 mg/day.

FORMS - Generic: Tabs 15, 30, & 60 mg. Oral soln: 15 mg/5 ml.

fentanyl (*Duragesic Patches, Actiq, Fentanyl Oralet*) ▶L ♀C ◗? ©II $$$$$

WARNING - Duragesic Patches and Actiq are contraindicated in the management of acute or postoperative pain due to potentially life-threatening respiratory depression in opioid non-tolerant patients. Fentanyl Oralet can only be used as an anesthetic premedication or for inducing sedation prior to a diagnostic/therapeutic procedure in a monitored anesthesia care setting. Instruct patients and their caregivers that even used patches/lozenges on a stick can be fatal to a child or pet. Dispose via toilet.

ADULT - (Duragesic Patches): Chronic pain: 25-100 mcg/hr patch q72 hours. Titrate dose to the needs of the patient. Some patients require q48 hr dosing. May wear more than one patch to achieve the correct analgesic effect. (Actiq): Breakthrough cancer pain: 200-1600 mcg sucked over 15 min, max dose 4 lozenges on a stick/day. Premedication for anesthesia (Oralet): 5-15 mcg/kg, 20-40 minutes prior to procedure, sucked over 15 min up to 400 mcg as a max single dose (See FORMS).

PEDS - Transdermal (Duragesic): not approved in children. Actiq: not approved < 16yo. Oralet: anesthetic premedication in a hospital setting: specialized doses for children weighing between 10-40 kg. See Full Prescribing Info.

FORMS - Trade: Transdermal patches 25, 50, 75, & 100 mcg/h (Duragesic). Transmucosal forms: lozenges on a stick, raspberry flavored 200, 400, 600, 800, 1,200, & 1,600 mcg (Actiq lozenges on a stick). 100, 200, 300, 400 mcg (Fentanyl Oralet lozenges).

FENTANYL TRANSDERMAL DOSE (based on ongoing morphine requirement)

morphine (IV/IM)	*morphine (PO)*	*Transdermal fentanyl*
8-22 mg/day	45-134 mg/day	25 mcg/hr
23-37 mg/day	135-224 mg/day	50 mcg/hr
38-52 mg/day	225-314 mg/day	75 mcg/hr
53-67 mg/day	315-404 mg/day	100 mcg/hr

NOTES - Do not use patches for acute pain. Oral transmucosal fentanyl doses of 5mcg/kg provide effects similar to 0.75-1.25 mcg/kg of fentanyl IM. Lozenges & lozenges on a stick should be sucked, not chewed. Flush lozenge remnants (without stick) down the toilet. For transdermal systems: apply patch to non-hairy skin. Clip (not shave) hair if have to apply to hairy area. Fever or external heat sources may increase fentanyl released from patch. Dispose of a used patch by folding with the adhesive side of the patch adhering to itself, then flush it down the toilet immediately upon removal. Do not cut the patch in half. Keep all forms of fentanyl out of the reach of children or pets. For Duragesic patches and Actiq lozenges on a stick: Titrate dose as high as necessary to relieve cancer pain or other types of non-malignant pain where chronic opioids are necessary.

hydromorphone (*Dilaudid, Dilaudid-5*) ▶L ♀C ▶? ©II $$$$$

ADULT - Moderate to severe pain: 2-4 mg PO q4-6h; 0.5-2 mg SC/IM or slow IV q4-6h prn initial dose (opioid naïve). 3 mg PR q6-8h.

PEDS - Not approved in children.

UNAPPROVED PEDS - Pain =< 12 yo: 0.03-0.08 mg/kg PO q4-6h prn. 0.015 mg/kg/dose IV q4-6h prn. Pain >12 yo: use adult dose.

FORMS - Generic/Trade: Tabs 2, 4, & 8 mg (8 mg trade scored). Liquid 5 mg/5 ml (Dilaudid). Suppositories 3 mg. Trade only: Tabs 1,3 mg.

NOTES - May be given by slow IV injection over 2-5 minutes. SC/IM/IV doses after initial dose should be individualized. Titrate dose as high as necessary to relieve cancer pain or other types of non-malignant pain where chronic opioids are necessary. 1.5 mg IV = 7.5 mg PO.

levorphanol (*Levo-Dromoran*) ▶L ♀C ▶? ©II $$$$$

ADULT - Moderate to severe pain: 2 mg PO/SC q6-8h. Increase to 4 mg, if necessary. May be given by slow IV injection.

PEDS - Not approved in children.

FORMS - Trade: Tabs 2 mg, scored.

meperidine (*Demerol*) ▶LK ♀C but + ▶- ©II $

ADULT - Moderate to severe pain: 50-150 mg IM/SC/PO q3-4h prn. OB analgesia: when pains become regular, 50-100 mg IM/SC q1-3h. May also be given slow IV diluted to 10 mg/ml, or by continuous IV infusion diluted to 1 mg/ml.

PEDS - Moderate to severe pain: 1-1.8 mg/kg IM/SC/PO or slow IV (see adult dosing) up to adult dose, q3-4h prn.

FORMS - Generic/Trade:Tabs 50 (trade scored) & 100 mg. Syrup 50 mg/5 ml (trade banana flavored).

NOTES - Avoid in renal insufficiency, MAO inhibitor therapy, or in elderly due to risk of metabolite accumulation, and increased risk of CNS disturbance and seizures. Poor oral absorption/efficacy. 75 mg meperidine IV,IM,SC = 300 mg meperidine PO. Due to the risk of seizures at high doses, meperidine is not a good choice for treatment of chronic pain. Not recommended in children.

methadone (*Dolophine, Methadose*) ▶L ♀C ▶? ©II $$$

ADULT - Severe pain: 2.5-10 mg IM/SC/PO q3-4h prn. Detoxification treatment: 15-40 mg PO qd to start. Decrease by 20% q1-2 days, not to exceed 3 weeks. Maintenance: 20-120 mg PO qd in an approved narcotic addiction treatment program.

PEDS - Not approved in children.

UNAPPROVED PEDS - Pain =<12 yo: 0.8 mg/kg/24h divided q4-6h PO/SC/IM/IV prn. Max 10 mg/dose.

FORMS - Generic/Trade: Tabs 5, 10, various scored. Oral concentrate: 10 mg/ml. Dispersable tabs 40 mg. Generic only: Oral soln 5 & 10 mg/5 ml.

NOTES - Rifampin may decrease methadone levels and precipitate withdrawal. The HIV drugs nevirapine & possibly efavirenz may decrease methadone levels; monitor for opioid withdrawal sx and increase methadone if necessary. Titrate dose as high as necessary to relieve cancer pain or other types of non-malignant pain where chronic opioids are necessary.

morphine sulfate (*MS Contin, Kadian, Roxanol, Oramorph SR, MSIR*, *✤Statex*) ▶LK ♀C ▶+ ©II $$$$

WARNING - Multiple strengths; see FORMS & write specific product on Rx.

ADULT - Moderate to severe pain: 10-30 mg PO q4h (immediate release tabs, caps, or oral soln). Controlled release (MS Contin, Oramorph SR): 30 mg PO q8-12h. (Kadian): 20 mg PO q12-24h. 10 mg q4h IM/SC. 2.5-15 mg/70kg IV over 4-5 min. 10-20 mg PR q4h.

PEDS - Moderate to severe pain: 0.1-0.2 mg/kg up to 15 mg IM/SC/IV q2-4h.

UNAPPROVED PEDS - Moderate to severe pain: 0.2-0.5 mg/kg/dose PO (immediate release) q4-6h. 0.3-0.6 mg/kg/dose PO q12h (controlled release).

FORMS - Generic/Trade: Tabs, immediate release: 15 & 30 mg. Trade: Caps 15 & 30 mg. Generic/Trade: Oral soln (Roxanol) 10 mg/5 ml, 10 mg/2.5 ml, 20 mg/5 ml, 20 mg/ml (concentrate) & 100 mg/5 ml (concentrate). Rectal suppositories 5, 10, 20 & 30 mg. Controlled release tabs (MS Contin, Oramorph SR) 15, 30, 60, 100; 200 mg MS Contin only. Controlled release caps (Kadian) 20, 30, 50, 60 & 100 mg. Do not break, chew, or crush MS Contin or Oramorph SR. Kadian caps may be opened & sprinkled in applesauce for easier administration, however the pellets should not be crushed or chewed.

NOTES - Titrate dose as high as necessary to relieve cancer pain or other types of non-malignant pain where chronic opioids are necessary. The active metabolite may accumulate in hepatic/renal insufficiency leading to increased analgesic & sedative effects.

oxycodone (*Roxicodone, OxyContin, Percolone, OxyIR, OxyFAST*, ✤*Endocodone, Supeudol*) ▸L ♀C ◗- ©II $$$$

WARNING - Do not Rx Oxycontin tabs on a prn basis; 80 & 160 mg tabs for use in opioid tolerant patients only. Multiple strengths; see FORMS & write specific product on Rx. Do not break, chew, or crush controlled release preparations.

ADULT - Moderate to severe pain: 5 mg PO q6h prn. Controlled release tabs: 10-40 mg PO q12h. (No supporting data for shorter dosing intervals for controlled release tabs.)

PEDS - Not approved in children.

UNAPPROVED PEDS - Pain ≤12yo: 0.03 mg/kg/dose q4-6h PO prn to max of 10 mg/dose.

FORMS - Generic/Trade: Immediate release: Tabs (scored) & caps 5 mg. Oral soln 5 mg/5 ml. Oral concentrate 20 mg/ml. Trade: Controlled release tabs (OxyContin): 10, 20, 40 mg, & 80 mg & 160 mg.

NOTES - Titrate dose as high as necessary to relieve cancer pain or other types of non-malignant pain where chronic opioids are necessary. Distribution of Oxycontin 160 mg tabs temporarily suspended as of May 2001.

oxymorphone (*Numorphan*) ▸L ♀C ◗? ©II $

ADULT - Moderate to severe pain: 1-1.5 mg IM/SC q4-6h prn. 0.5 mg IV initial dose in healthy patients then q4-6h prn, increase dose until pain adequately controlled. 5 mg PR q4-6h prn.

PEDS - Not approved in children.

FORMS - Trade only: Suppositories 5 mg.

propoxyphene (*Darvon-N, Darvon Pulvules*) ▸L ♀C ◗+ ©IV $

ADULT - Mild to moderate pain: 65 mg (Darvon) to 100 mg (Darvon-N) PO q4h prn. Max dose 6 caps/day.

PEDS - Not approved in children.

FORMS - Generic/Trade: Caps 65 mg. Trade only: 100 mg (Darvon-N).

NOTES - Caution in renal & hepatic dysfunction. Norpropoxyphene, a toxic metabolite can accumulate in renal insufficiency & cause QRS prologation. May increase the effects of warfarin & carbamazepine.

ANALGESICS: Opioid Analgesic Combinations

NOTE: Refer to individual components for further information. May cause drowsiness and/or sedation, which may be enhanced by alcohol, sedatives, etc. Opioids, carisoprodol, and butalbital may be habit-forming. Avoid exceeding 4 g/day of acetaminophen in combination products. Caution people who drink >3 alcoholic drinks/day to limit acetaminophen use due to additive liver toxicity. Opioids commonly create constipation.

***Anexsia* (hydrocodone + acetaminophen)** ▸LK ♀B ◗- ©III $

WARNING - Multiple strengths; see FORMS & write specific product on Rx.

ADULT - Moderate pain: 1 tab PO q4-6h prn.

PEDS - Not approved in children.

FORMS - Generic/Trade: Tabs 5/500, 7.5/650, 10/660 mg hydrocodone/mg acetaminophen, scored.

***Capital with Codeine suspension* (acetaminophen + codeine)** ▸LK ♀C ◗? ©V $

ADULT - Moderate pain: 15 ml PO q4h prn.

PEDS - Moderate pain 3-6 yo: 5 ml PO q4-6h prn. 7-12 yo: 10 ml PO q4-6h prn. >12yo use adult dose.

FORMS - Generic = oral soln. Trade = suspension. Both codeine 12 mg/acetaminophen 120 mg/5 ml (trade, fruit punch flavor).

***Darvocet* (propoxyphene + acetaminophen)** ▸L ♀C ◗? ©IV $

WARNING - Multiple strengths; see Forms below & write specific product on Rx.

ADULT - Moderate pain: 1 tab (100/650) or 2 tabs (50/325) PO q4h prn.

PEDS - Not approved in children.

FORMS - Generic/Trade: Tabs 50/325 (Darvocet N-50) & 100/650 (Darvocet N-100), mg

propoxyphene/mg acetaminophen.
NOTES - Norpropoxyphene, a toxic metabolite can accumulate in renal insufficiency & cause QRS prologation.

Darvon Compound-65 Pulvules **(propoxyphene + ASA + caffeine)** ▶LK ♀D ▶- ©IV $
ADULT - Moderate pain: 1 cap PO q4h prn.
PEDS - Not approved in children.
FORMS - Generic/Trade: Caps, 65 mg propoxyphene/389 mg ASA/32.4 mg caffeine.
NOTES - Norpropoxyphene, a toxic metabolite can accumulate in renal insufficiency & cause QRS prologation.

Empirin with Codeine **(ASA + codeine, ✤*Frosst 292*)** ▶LK ♀D ▶- ©III $
WARNING - Multiple strengths; see FORMS & write specific product on Rx.
ADULT - Moderate pain: 1-2 tabs PO q4h prn.
PEDS - Not approved in children.
FORMS - Generic/Trade: Tabs 325/30(Empirin with codeine #3) & 325/60 (Empirin with codeine #4), mg ASA/mg codeine.

Fioricet with Codeine **(acetaminophen + butalbital + caffeine + codeine)** ▶LK ♀C ▶- ©III $$$
ADULT - Moderate pain: 1-2 caps PO q4h prn, max dose 6 caps/day.
PEDS - Not approved in children.
FORMS - Generic/Trade: Caps, 325 mg acetam/50 mg butal/40 mg caffeine/30 mg codeine.

Fiorinal with Codeine **(ASA + butalbital + caffeine + codeine)** ▶LK ♀D ▶- ©III $$$
ADULT - Moderate pain: 1-2 caps PO q4h prn, max dose 6 caps/day.
PEDS - Not approved in children.
FORMS - Trade: Caps, 325 mg ASA/50 mg butalbital /40 mg caffeine/30 mg codeine.

Lorcet **(hydrocodone + acetaminophen)** ▶LK ♀B ▶- ©III $
WARNING - Multiple strengths; see FORMS & write specific product on Rx.
ADULT - Moderate pain: 1-2 tabs (5/500) PO q4-6h prn, max dose 8 tabs/day. 1 tab PO q4-6h prn (7.5/650 & 10/650).
PEDS - Not approved in children.
FORMS - Generic/Trade: Caps, 5/500. (Lorcet HD) Tabs, 7.5/650 (Lorcet Plus). Trade: Lorcet -10/650, mg hydrocodone/mg acetam, scored.

Lortab **(hydrocodone + acetaminophen)** ▶LK ♀B ▶- ©III $
WARNING - Multiple strengths; see FORMS & write specific product on Rx.
ADULT - Moderate pain: 1-2 tabs 2.5/500 & 5/500 PO q4-6h prn, max dose 8 tabs/day. 1 tab 7.5/500 & 10/500 PO q4-6h prn, max dose 5 tabs/day. Elixir 15ml PO q4-6h prn, max 6 doses/day.
PEDS - Not approved in children.
FORMS - Trade: Tabs Lortab 2.5/500. Generic/Trade: Lortab 5/500 (scored), Lortab 7.5/500 (trade scored) & Lortab 10/500 mg hydrocodone/mg acetaminophen. Elixir: 7.5/500 mg hydrocodone/mg acetaminophen/15 ml.

Maxidone **(hydrocodone + acetaminophen)** ▶LK ♀B ▶- ©III $$
ADULT - Moderate pain: 1 tab PO q4-6h prn, max dose 5 tabs/day.
PEDS - Not approved in children.
FORMS - Trade: Tabs 10/750 mg hydroc/aceta.

Norco **(hydrocodone + acetaminophen)** ▶L ♀C ▶? ©III $$
ADULT - Moderate to severe pain: 1-2 tabs PO q4-6h prn (5/325). 1 tab (7.5/325 & 10/325) PO q4-6h prn up to 6 tabs/day.
PEDS - Not approved in children.
FORMS - Trade: Tabs: 5/325, 7.5/325 & 10/325 mg hydrocodone/mg acetaminophen, scored.

Percocet **(oxycodone + acetaminophen)** ▶L ♀C ▶- ©II $
WARNING - Multiple strengths; see FORMS & write specific product on Rx.
ADULT - Moderate-severe pain: 1-2 tabs PO q6h prn (2.5/325 & 5/325). 1 tab PO q6 prn (7.5/500 & 10/650).
PEDS - Not approved in children.
FORMS - Trade: Tabs Percocet 2.5/325, Percocet 7.5/500, Percocet 10/650. Generic/Trade: Tabs Percocet 5/325 mg oxycod/mg acetamin.

Percodan **(oxycodone + ASA)** ▶LK ♀D ▶- ©II $
WARNING - Multiple strengths; see FORMS below & write specific product on Rx.
ADULT - Moderate to severe pain: 1 tab (5/325) PO q6h prn, 1-2 tabs (2.5/325) q6h prn.
PEDS - Not approved in children.
UNAPPROVED PEDS - Moderate to severe pain in 6-12 yo: ¼ Demi tab PO q6h prn; >12 yo ½ Demi tab PO q6h prn.
FORMS - Generic/Trade: Tabs Perodan 5/325 (trade scored). Trade only: 2.5/325(Percodan Demi) scored, mg oxycodone/mg ASA.

Roxicet **(oxycodone + acetaminophen)** ▶L ♀C ▶- ©II $
WARNING - Multiple strengths; see FORMS & write specific product on Rx.
ADULT - Moderate to severe pain: 1 tab PO q6h prn. Oral soln: 5 ml PO q6h prn.
PEDS - Not approved in children.
FORMS - Generic/Trade: Tablet Roxicet 5/325,

scored. Caplet Roxicet 5/500, scored. Generic: Caps 5/500. Trade only: Roxicet oral soln 5/325 per 5 ml, mg oxycodone/mg acetamin.

Soma Compound with Codeine **(carisoprodol + ASA + codeine)** ▸L ♀C ◗- ©III $$$

ADULT - Moderate to severe musculoskeletal pain: 1-2 tabs PO qid prn.

PEDS - Not approved in children.

FORMS - Trade: Tabs 200 mg carisoprodol/325 mg ASA/16 mg codeine.

NOTES - Refer to individual components.

Talacen **(pentazocine + acetaminophen)** ▸L ♀C ◗? ©IV $$$

ADULT - Moderate pain: 1 tab PO q4h prn.

PEDS - Not approved in children.

FORMS - Trade: Tabs 25 mg pentazocine/650 mg acetaminophen, scored.

NOTES - Serious skin reactions, including erythema multiforme & Stevens-Johnson syndrome have been reported.

Tylenol with Codeine **(codeine + acetaminophen)** ▸LK ♀C ◗? ©III (Tabs), V(elixir) $

WARNING - Multiple strengths; see FORMS & write specific product on Rx.

ADULT - Moderate pain: 1-2 tabs PO q4h prn.

PEDS - Moderate pain 3-6 yo: 5 ml PO q4-6h prn. 7-12 yo 10 ml PO q4-6h prn.

FORMS - Generic/Trade: Tabs Tylenol #2 (15/300), Tylenol #3 (30/300), Tylenol #4 (60/300). Tylenol with Codeine Elixir 12/120 per 5 ml, mg codeine/mg acetaminophen.

Tylox **(oxycodone + acetaminophen)** ▸L ♀C ◗- ©II $

ADULT - Moderate-severe pain: 1 cap PO q6h prn.

PEDS - Not approved in children.

FORMS - Generic/Trade: Caps, 5 mg oxycodone/500 mg acetaminophen.

Vicodin **(hydrocodone + acetaminophen)** ▸LK ♀B ◗? ©III $

WARNING - Multiple strengths; see FORMS & write specific product on Rx.

ADULT - Moderate pain: 5/500 (max dose 8 tabs/day) & 7.5/750 (max dose of 5 tabs/day): 1-2 tabs PO q4-6h prn. 10/660: 1 tab PO q4-6h prn (max of 6 tabs/day).

PEDS - Not approved in children.

FORMS - Generic/Trade: Tabs Vicodin (5/500), Vicodin ES (7.5/750), Vicodin HP (10/660), scored, mg hydrocodone/mg acetaminophen.

Vicoprofen **(hydrocodone + ibuprofen)** ▸LK ♀- ◗? ©III $$

ADULT - Moderate pain: 1 tab PO q4h prn, max dose 6 tabs/day.

PEDS - Not approved in children.

FORMS - Trade: Tabs 7.5 mg hydrocodone/200 mg ibuprofen.

NOTES - See NSAIDs-Other subclass warning.

Wygesic **(propoxyphene + acetaminophen)** ▸L ♀C ◗? ©IV $

ADULT - Moderate pain: 1 tab PO q4h prn.

PEDS - Not approved in children.

FORMS - Generic/Trade: Tabs 65 mg propoxyphene/650 mg acetaminophen.

NOTES - Norpropoxyphene, a toxic metabolite can accumulate in renal insufficiency & cause QRS prologation.

Zydone **(hydrocodone + acetaminophen)** ▸LK ♀B ◗? ©III $$

WARNING - Multiple strengths; see FORMS & write specific product on Rx.

ADULT - Moderate pain: 1-2 tabs (5/400) PO q4-6h prn, max dose 8 tabs/day. 1 tab (7.5/400, 10/400) q4-6h prn, max 6 tabs/day.

PEDS - Not approved in children.

FORMS - Trade: All Brands are named Zydone - Tabs (5/400), (7.5/400) & (10/400) mg hydrocodone/mg acetaminophen.

ANALGESICS: Opioid Antagonists

NOTE: May result in withdrawal in the opioid dependent, including life-threatening withdrawal if administered to neonates born to opioid-dependent mothers. Rare pulmonary edema, cardiovascular instability, hypotension, HTN, v-tach & v-fib have been reported with opioid reversal.

nalmefene (*Revex*) ▸L ♀B ◗? $$$

ADULT - Opioid overdosage: 0.5 mg/70 kg IV. If needed, this may be followed by a second dose of 1 mg/70 kg, 2-5 minutes later. Max cumulative dose 1.5 mg/70kg. If suspicion of opioid dependency, initially administer a challenge dose of 0.1 mg/70 kg. Post-operative opioid reversal: 0.25 mcg/kg IV followed by 0.25 mcg/kg incremental doses at 2-5 minute intervals, stopping as soon as the desired degree of opioid reversal is obtained. Max cumulative dose 1 mcg/kg.

PEDS - Not approved in children.

FORMS - Trade: Injection 100 mcg/ml nalmefene for postoperative reversal (blue label). 1 mg/ml for opioid overdose (green label).

NOTES - Recurrence of respiratory depression is possible, even after an apparently adequate initial response to nalmefene treatment.

naloxone (*Narcan*) ▶LK ♀B ▶? $

ADULT - Management of opioid overdose: 0.4-2 mg IV. May repeat IV at 2-3 minute intervals up to 10 mg. Use IM/SC/ET if IV not available. Intravenous infusion: 2 mg in 500 ml D5W or NS (0.004 mg/ml); titrate according to response. Partial post-operative opioid reversal: 0.1-0.2 mg IV at 2-3 minute intervals; repeat IM doses may be required at 1-2 hr intervals.

PEDS - Management of opioid overdose: 0.01 mg/kg IV. Give a subsequent dose of 0.1 mg/kg prn. Use IM/SC/ET if IV not available. Partial post-operative opioid reversal: 0.005-0.01 mg IV at 2-3 minute intervals.

NOTES - Watch patients for re-emergence of narcotic effects.

ANALGESICS: Other Analgesics

acetaminophen (*Tylenol, Panadol, Tempra,* ✱*Atasol*) ▶LK ♀B ▶+ $

ADULT - Analgesic/antipyretic: 325-1000 mg PO q4-6h prn; 650 mg PR q4-6h prn. Max 4g/day. OA: extended release: 2 caplets PO q8h around the clock. Max dose 6 caplets/ day.

PEDS - Analgesic/antipyretic: 10-15 mg/kg q4-6h PO/PR prn. Max 5 doses/day.

UNAPPROVED ADULT - OA: 1,000 mg PO qid.

FORMS - OTC: Tabs 160, 325, 500, 650 mg. Chewable Tabs 80 mg. Gelcaps 500 mg. Caps 325 & 500 mg. Sprinkle Caps 80 & 160 mg. Extended release caplets 650 mg. Liquid 80 mg/2.5 ml, 80, 120, 160 mg/5 ml, 500 mg/15 ml. Drops 80 mg/0.8 ml & 80 mg/1.66 ml, & 100 mg/ml. Suppositories 80, 120, 125, 300, 325, & 650 mg.

NOTES - Hepatotoxicity with chronic use, especially in alcoholics. Do not use chronically with ≥3 drinks/day. Rectal administration may produce lower/less reliable plasma levels.

lidocaine (*Lidoderm*) ▶LK ♀B ▶? $$$$

WARNING - Contraindicated in allergy to amide-type anesthetics.

ADULT - Postherpetic neuralgia: apply up to 3 patches once for up to 12h within a 24h period.

PEDS - Not approved for use in children.

FORMS - Trade: Patch 5%, box of 30.

NOTES - Apply only to intact skin to cover the most painful area. Patches may be cut into smaller sizes w/scissors prior to removal of the release liner. Store and dispose out of the reach of children & pets to avoid possible toxicity from ingestion.

tramadol (*Ultram*) ▶KL ♀C ▶- $$$$

ADULT - Moderate to moderately severe pain: 50-100 mg PO q4-6h prn; max dose 400 mg/day. If >75 yo, <300 mg/day PO in divided doses. If creatinine clearance <30 ml/min, increase the dosing interval to 12 hours. If cirrhosis, decrease dose to 50 mg PO q12h.

PEDS - Not approved in children < 16 yo.

FORMS - Trade: Tabs immed release 50 mg.

NOTES - Contraindicated in acute intoxication with alcohol, hypnotics, centrally acting analgesics, opioids or psychotropic drugs. Seizures may occur with concurrent antidepressants or in epileptics. Use with great caution with MAO inhibitors or in combination with SSRIs due to potential for serotonin syndrome; dose adjustment may be needed. Withdrawal symptoms may occur in patients dependent on opioids. Carbamazepine decreases tramadol levels. The most frequent side effects are nausea & constipation.

***Women's Tylenol Menstrual Relief* (acetaminophen + pamabrom)** ▶LK ♀B ▶+ $

ADULT - Menstrual cramps: 2 caplets PO q4-6h.

PEDS - >12 yo: use adult dose.

FORMS - OTC: Caplets 500 mg acetaminophen/25 mg pamabrom (diuretic).

NOTES - Hepatotoxicity with chronic use, especially in alcoholics.

ANESTHESIA: Anesthetics & Sedatives

alfentanil (*Alfenta*) ▶L ♀C ▶? ©II $

ADULT - IV general anesthesia adjunct; specialized dosing.

PEDS - Not approved in children.

dexmedetomidine (*Precedex*) ▶L ♀C ▶? $$$$

ADULT - ICU sedation <24h: Load 1 mcg/kg over 10 min followed by infusion 0.2-0.7 mcg/kg/h titrated to desired sedation endpoint.

PEDS - Not recommended <18 yo.

NOTES - Alpha 2 adrenergic agonist with sedative properties. Beware of bradycardia and hypotension.

etomidate (*Amidate*) ▶L ♀C ▶? $

ADULT - Anesthesia induction: 0.3 mg/kg IV.

PEDS - Age ≥10 yo: Adult dosing. Age <10 yo: Not approved.

UNAPPROVED PEDS - Anesthesia induction: 0.3 mg/kg IV.

NOTES - Adrenocortical suppression, but rarely of clinical significance.

fentanyl (*Sublimaze, Oralet, Actiq*) ▶L ♀C ▶? ©II $

ADULT - Anesthetic premedication: 5-15 mcg/kg up to 400 mcg lozenge (Oralet) 20-40 min pre-procedure. IV adjunct to general anesthesia: specialized dosing.

PEDS - Anesthetic premedication: 5-15 mcg/kg up to 400 mcg lozenge (Oralet) 20-40 min pre-procedure. IV adjunct to general anesthesia & procedural sedation, specialized dosing.

UNAPPROVED ADULT - Procedural sedation: 50 mcg IV, may repeat q3 min, adjust to desired effect.

UNAPPROVED PEDS - Procedural sedation: 1 mcg/kg/dose IV, may repeat q3 min, adjust to desired effect.

FORMS - Trade: Oralet lozenges 100,200,300, 400 mcg; Actiq lozenges 200,400,600,800, 1200,1600 mcg.

ketamine (*Ketalar*) ▶L ♀? ▶? ©III $

WARNING - Emergence delirium limits value in adults; such reactions are rare in children.

ADULT - Dissociative sedation: 1-2 mg/kg IV over 1-2 min or 4-5 mg/kg IM.

PEDS - Dissociative sedation: 1-2 mg/kg IV over 1-2 min or 4-5 mg/kg IM.

NOTES - Raises BP and intracranial pressure; avoid if coronary artery disease, HTN, head or eye injury. Concurrent atropine minimizes hypersalivation; can be combined in same syringe with ketamine for IM use.

methohexital (*Brevital*, *✤Brietal*) ▶L ♀B ▶? ©IV $

ADULT - Anesthesia induction: 1-1.5 mg/kg IV.

PEDS - Safety in children not established.

UNAPPROVED PEDS - Sedation for diagnostic imaging: 25 mg/kg PR

NOTES - Duration 5 minutes.

midazolam (*Versed*) ▶LK ♀D ▶- ©IV $

WARNING - Beware of respiratory depression/apnea. Administer with appropriate monitoring.

ADULT - Sedation/anxiolysis: 0.07-0.08 mg/kg IM (5 mg in average adult); or 1 mg IV slowly q2-3 min up to 5 mg. Anesthesia induction: 0.3-0.35 mg/kg IV over 20-30 seconds.

PEDS - Sedation/anxiolysis: 0.25-1.0 mg/kg to maximum of 20 mg PO, or 0.1-0.15 mg/kg IM. IV route (6 mo to 5 yo): Initial dose 0.05-0.1 mg/kg IV, then titrated to max 0.6 mg/kg. IV route (6-12 yo): Initial dose 0.025-0.05 mg/kg IV, then titrated to max 0.4 mg/kg.

UNAPPROVED PEDS - Sedation/anxiolysis: Intranasal 0.2-0.4 mg/kg. Rectal: 0.25-0.5 mg/kg PR. Higher oral dosing: 0.5-0.75 mg/kg PO, max 20 mg/kg.

FORMS - Oral liquid 2 mg/ml

NOTES - Use lower doses in the elderly, chronically ill, and those receiving concurrent CNS depressants.

propofol (*Diprivan*) ▶L ♀B ▶- $$$

WARNING - Beware of respiratory depression/apnea. Administer with appropriate monitoring.

ADULT - Anesthesia (<55 yo): 40 mg IV q10 sec until induction onset (typical 2-2.5 mg/kg). Follow with maintenance infusion generally 100-200 mcg/kg/min. Lower doses in elderly or for sedation. ICU ventilator sedation: infusion 5-50 mcg/kg/min.

PEDS - Anesthesia (≥3 yo): 2.5-3.5 mg/kg IV over 20-30 seconds, followed with infusion 125-300 mcg/kg/min. Not recomm. if <3 yo.

NOTES - Avoid with egg or soy allergies.

remifentanil (*Ultiva*) ▶L ♀C ▶? ©II $$

ADULT - IV general anesthesia adjunct; specialized dosing.

PEDS - IV general anesthesia adjunct; specialized dosing.

sufentanil (*Sufenta*) ▶L ♀C ▶? ©II $$

ADULT - IV anesthesia adjunct: specialized dosing.

PEDS - IV anesthesia adjunct: specialized dosing.

thiopental (*Pentothal*) ▶L ♀C ▶? ©III $

ADULT - Anesthesia induction: 3-5 mg/kg IV.

PEDS - Anesthesia induction: 3-5 mg/kg IV.

UNAPPROVED PEDS - Sedation for diagnostic imaging: 25 mg/kg PR

NOTES - Duration 5 min. Hypotension, histamine release, extravasation tissue necrosis.

ANESTHESIA: Local Anesthetics

bupivacaine (*Marcaine, Sensorcaine*) ▶LK ♀C ▶? $

WARNING - Not for OB anesthesia or children.

ADULT - Local anesth, nerve block: 0.25% inj.

PEDS - Not recommended in children <12 yo.
FORMS - 0.25%. With epinephrine: 0.25%
NOTES - Onset 5 mins, duration 2-4h (longer with epi). Amide group. Max dose 1.5 mg/kg or 3.0 mg/kg with epinephrine.

etidocaine (*Duranest*) ▶LK ♀B ▶? $
ADULT - Nerve block, peridural, caudal: 1%. Dental block: 1.5%.
PEDS - Nerve block, peridural, caudal: 1% soln. Dental block: 1.5%.
FORMS - 1% soln. With epinephrine: 1%, 1.5%.
NOTES - Onset 3-5 mins, duration 5-10h (longer with epinephrine). Amide group.

lidocaine (*Xylocaine*) ▶LK ♀B ▶? $
ADULT - Local anesthesia: 0.5-1% injection.
PEDS - Local anesthesia: 0.5-1% injection.
FORMS - 0.5,1,1.5,2%. With epi: 0.5,1,1.5,2%.
NOTES - Onset <2 mins, duration 30-60 mins (longer with epi). Amide group. Potentially toxic dose 3-5 mg/kg without epinephrine, and 5-7 mg/kg with epinephrine.

mepivacaine (*Carbocaine*, ✱*Polocaine*) ▶LK ♀C ▶? $
ADULT - Nerve block: 1%-2% injection.
PEDS - Nerve block: 1%-2% injection.
FORMS - 1,1.5,2,3%.
NOTES - Onset 3-5 mins, duration 45-90 mins. Amide group.

ANESTHESIA: Neuromuscular Blockers

NOTE: Should be administered only by those skilled in airway management and resp support.

atracurium (*Tracrium*) ▶Plasma ♀C ▶? $
ADULT - Paralysis: 0.4-0.5 mg/kg IV.
PEDS - Paralysis ≥ 2yo: 0.4-0.5 mg/kg IV.
NOTES - Duration 15-30 minutes.

cisatracurium (*Nimbex*) ▶Plasma ♀B ▶? $$
ADULT - Paralysis: 0.15-0.2 mg/kg IV.
PEDS - Paralysis: 0.1 mg/kg IV over 5-10 sec.
NOTES - Duration 30-60 minutes.

doxacurium (*Nuromax*) ▶K ♀C ▶? $
ADULT - Paralysis: 0.05 mg/kg IV.
PEDS - Paralysis: 0.03 mg/kg IV.
NOTES - Duration ~100 minutes.

mivacurium (*Mivacron*) ▶Plasma ♀C ▶? $
ADULT - Paralysis: 0.15 mg/kg IV over 5-15 seconds.
PEDS - Paralysis in children aged 2-12 years: 0.2 mg/kg IV over 5-15 seconds.
NOTES - Duration 20 minutes.

pancuronium (*Pavulon*) ▶LK ♀C ▶? $
ADULT - Paralysis: 0.04 to 0.1 mg/kg IV.
PEDS - Paralysis (beyond neonatal age): 0.04 to 0.1 mg/kg IV.
NOTES - Duration 45 minutes.

rocuronium (*Zemuron*) ▶L ♀B ▶? $$
ADULT - Paralysis: 0.6 mg/kg IV. Rapid sequence intubation: 0.6 to 1.2 mg/kg IV. Continuous infusion: 10 to 12 mcg/kg/min; first verify spontaneous recovery from bolus dose.
PEDS - Paralysis (age >3 mo): 0.6 mg/kg IV. Continuous infusion: 12 mcg/kg/min; first verify spontaneous recovery from bolus dose.
NOTES - Duration 30 minutes.

succinylcholine (*Anectine, Quelicin*) ▶Plasma ♀C ▶? $
ADULT - Paralysis: 0.6-1.1 mg/kg IV.
PEDS - Paralysis (≥5 yo): 1 mg/kg IV. Paralysis (<5 yo): 2 mg/kg IV after pretreatment with atropine 0.02 mg/kg to prevent bradycardia.
NOTES - Avoid in hyperkalemia, myopathies, eye injuries, rhabdomyolysis, subacute burn. If immediate cardiac arrest & ET tube is correctly placed & no tension pneumo evident, strongly consider empiric treatment for hyperkalemia.

vecuronium (*Norcuron*) ▶LK ♀C ▶? $
ADULT - Paralysis: 0.08-0.1 mg/kg IV bolus. Continuous infusion: 0.8 to 1.2 mcg/kg/min; 1st verify spontaneous recovery from bolus dose.
PEDS - Paralysis (age ≥10 yrs): 0.08-0.1 mg/kg IV bolus. Continuous infusion: 0.8 to 1.2 mcg/kg/min; first verify spontaneous recovery from bolus dose. Age 1-10 years: may require a slightly higher initial dose and may also require supplementation slightly more often than older patients. Age 7 weeks to 1 year: moderately more sensitive on a mg/kg dose compared to adults and take 1.5 x longer to recover. Age <7 weeks: Safety has not been established.
NOTES - Duration 15-30 minutes.

ANTIMICROBIALS: Aminoglycosides

NOTES: See also dermatology & ophthalmology.

amikacin (*Amikin*) ▶K ♀D ▶? $$$$
WARNING - Nephrotoxicity, ototoxicity.
ADULT - Gram negative infections: 15 mg/kg/day up to 1500 mg/day IM/IV divided q8-12h. Peak 20-35 mcg/ml, trough <5 mcg/ml.

PEDS - Gram neg infections: 15 mg/kg/day up to 1500 mg/day IM/IV divided q8-12h. Neonates: 10 mg/kg load, then 7.5 mg/kg IM/IV q12h.
UNAPPROVED ADULT - Once daily dosing: 15 mg/kg IV q24h. Second-line for tuberculosis: 7.5-10 mg/kg IM/IV qd.
UNAPPROVED PEDS - Severe Infections: 15-22.5 mg/kg/day IV divided q8h. Some experts recommend 30 mg/kg/day. Once daily dosing: 15 mg/kg IV q24h. Some consider once-daily aminoglycosides investigational in children.
NOTES - May enhance effects of neuromuscular blockers. Avoid other ototoxic/nephrotoxic drugs. Individualize dose in renal dysfunction, burn patients. Base dose on average of actual and ideal body weight in obesity.

gentamicin (*Garamycin*, ✱*Cidomycin*) ▸K ♀D ◗? $$
WARNING - Nephrotoxicity, ototoxicity.
ADULT - Gram negative infections: 3-5 mg/kg/day IM/IV divided q8h. Peak 5-10 mcg/ml, trough <2 mcg/ml. See table for prophylaxis of bacterial endocarditis.
PEDS - Gram negative infections: 2-2.5 mg/kg IM/IV q8h. Infants ≥1 week old, >2 kg: 2.5 mg/kg IM/IV q8h. Infants <1 week old, >2 kg: 2.5 mg/kg IM/IV q12h. Cystic fibrosis: 9 mg/kg/day IV in divided doses with target peak of 8-12 mcg/ml.
UNAPPROVED ADULT - Once daily dosing: 5-7 mg/kg IV q24h.
UNAPPROVED PEDS - Once daily dosing: 5-7 mg/kg IV q24h. Age <1 week and full-term: 4 mg/kg IV q24h. Some consider qd aminoglycosides investigational in children.
NOTES - May enhance effects of neuromuscular blockers. Avoid other ototoxic/nephrotoxic drugs. Individualize dose in renal dysfunction, burn patients. Base dose on average of actual and ideal body weight in obesity.

spectinomycin (*Trobicin*) ▸K ♀B ◗? $$
ADULT - Discontinued in June 2001. CDC-recommended alternatives for gonorrhea in patients who cannot take cephalosporins/quinolones: Rapid cephalosporin desensitization (with expert consultation) for cephalosporin-allergic pregnant women. Due to high rates of resistance, quinolones are not recommended for use in Hawaii or for infections acquired in Asia or the Pacific. Azithromycin 2 g PO single dose is a potential alternative. Observe patients for GI intolerance for ≥30 minutes after the azithromycin dose.
PEDS - Discontinued in June 2001.

streptomycin ▸K ♀D ◗+ $$$$
WARNING - Nephrotoxicity, ototoxicity. Monitor audiometry, renal function, and electrolytes.
ADULT - Combined therapy for tuberculosis: 15 mg/kg up to 1 g IM qd or 25-30 mg/kg up to 1.5 g IM 2-3 times weekly.
PEDS - Combined therapy for tuberculosis: 20-40 mg/kg up to 1 g IM qd or 25-30 mg/kg up to 1.5 g IM 2-3 times weekly.
UNAPPROVED ADULT - Same IM dosing can be given IV.
FORMS - Generic: 1 g vials for parenteral use.
NOTES - May enhance effects of neuromuscular blockers. Avoid other ototoxic/nephrotoxic drugs. Individualize dose in renal dysfunction.

tobramycin (*Nebcin, TOBI*) ▸K ♀D ◗? $$$$
WARNING - Nephrotoxicity, ototoxicity.
ADULT - Gram negative infections: 3-5 mg/kg/day IM/IV divided q8h. Peak 5-10 mcg/ml, trough <2 mcg/ml. Parenteral for cystic fibrosis: 10 mg/kg/day IV divided q6h with target peak of 8-12 mcg/ml. Nebulization for cystic fibrosis (TOBI): 300 mg neb bid 28 days on, then 28 days off.
PEDS - Gram negative infections: 2-2.5 mg/kg IV q8h or 1.5-1.9 mg/kg IV q6h. Premature/full-term neonates ≤1 week old: Up to 4 mg/kg/day divided q12h. Parenteral for cystic fibrosis: 10 mg/kg/day IV divided q6h with target peak of 8-12 mcg/ml. Nebulization for cystic fibrosis (TOBI) ≥6 yo: 300 mg neb bid 28 days on, then 28 days off.
UNAPPROVED ADULT - Once daily dosing: 5-7 mg/kg IV q24h.
UNAPPROVED PEDS - Once daily dosing: 5-7 mg/kg IV q24h. Some consider once-daily aminoglycosides investigational in children.
FORMS - TOBI 300 mg ampules for nebulizer.
NOTES - May enhance neuromuscular blockers. Avoid other ototoxic/nephrotoxic drugs. Individualize dose in renal dysfunction, burn patients. Base dose on average of actual & ideal body weight in obesity. Routine monitoring of levels not required with nebulized TOBI.

ANTIMICROBIALS: Antifungal Agents

amphotericin B deoxycholate (*Fungizone*) ▸Tissues ♀B for IV, C for PO ◗? $$$
WARNING - IV route not for noninvasive fungal infections (oral thrush, vaginal or esophageal

candidiasis) in normal neutrophil counts.

ADULT - Fungizone IV - Life-threatening systemic fungal infections: Test dose 1 mg slow IV. Wait 2-4 h, and if tolerated start 0.25 mg/kg IV qd. Advance to 0.5-1.5 mg/kg/day depending on fungal type. Maximum dose 1.5 mg/kg/day. Infuse over 2-6 h. Hydrate with 500 ml NS before and after infusion to decrease risk of nephrotoxicity. Fungizone oral susp. Oral candidiasis: 1 ml PO swish & swallow qid given between meals for ≥2 weeks.

PEDS - Fungizone oral susp - Oral candidiasis: 1 ml PO swish & swallow qid given between meals for ≥2 weeks.

UNAPPROVED ADULT - Alternative dosing regimen: Give 1 mg test dose as part of first infusion (separate IV bag not needed); if tolerated continue infusion, giving target dose of 0.5 to 1.5 mg/kg on first day. Candidal cystitis: Bladder irrigation with 50 mcg/ml soln periodically or continuously x 5-10 days.

UNAPPROVED PEDS - Fungizone IV. Systemic life-threatening fungal infections: Test dose 0.1 mg/kg slow IV. Wait 2-4 h, and if tolerated start 0.25 mg/kg IV qd. Advance to 0.5-1.5 mg/kg/day depending on fungal type. Maximum dose 1.5 mg/kg/day. Infuse over 2-6 h. Alternative dosing regimen: Give 1 mg test dose as part of first infusion (separate IV bag not needed); if tolerated continue infusion, giving target dose of 0.5 to 1.5 mg/kg on first day.

FORMS - Trade: Oral susp 100 mg/ml.

NOTES - Fungizone IV: Acute infusion reactions, anaphylaxis, nephrotoxicity, hypokalemia, hypomagnesemia, acidosis, anemia. Monitor renal and hepatic function, CBC, serum electrolytes. Lipid formulations better tolerated, preferred in renal dysfunction. Fungizone oral susp poorly absorbed.

amphotericin B lipid formulations (*Abelcet, Amphotec, AmBisome*) ▶? ♀B ◗? $$$$$

ADULT - Abelcet: Invasive fungal infections in patients refractory/intolerant to amphotericin deoxycholate: 5 mg/kg/day IV at 2.5 mg/kg/h. Shake infusion bag every 2 h. AmBisome: Infuse IV over 2 h. Empiric therapy of fungal infections in febrile neutropenia: 3 mg/kg/day IV. Aspergillus, candidal, cryptococcal infections in patients refractory/intolerant to amphotericin deoxycholate: 3-5 mg/kg/day IV. Cryptococcal meningitis in HIV infection: 6 mg/kg/day. Amphotec: Aspergillosis in patients refractory/ intolerant to amphotericin deoxycholate: Test dose of 10 ml over 15-30 minutes, observe 30 minutes, then 3-4 mg/kg/day IV at 1 mg/kg/h.

PEDS - Abelcet. Invasive fungal infections in patients refractory/intolerant to amphotericin deoxycholate: 5 mg/kg/day IV at 2.5 mg/kg/h. Shake infusion bag every 2 h. AmBisome. Infuse IV over 2 h. Empiric therapy of fungal infections in febrile neutropenia: 3 mg/kg/day IV. Aspergillus, candidal, cryptococcal infections in patients refractory/intolerant to amphotericin deoxycholate: 3-5 mg/kg/day. Cryptococcal meningitis in HIV infection: 6 mg/kg/day. Amphotec. Aspergillosis in patients refractory/ intolerant to amphotericin deoxycholate: Test dose of 10 ml over 15-30 minutes, observe 30 minutes, then 3-4 mg/kg/day IV at 1 mg/kg/h.

NOTES - Acute infusion reactions, anaphylaxis, nephrotoxicity, hypokalemia, hypomagnesemia, acidosis. Lipid formulations better tolerated than amphotericin deoxycholate, preferred in renal dysfunction. Monitor renal and hepatic function, CBC, electrolytes.

caspofungin (*Cancidas*) ▶KL ♀C ◗? $$$$$

ADULT - Invasive aspergillosis in patients refractory/intolerant to other antifungals: 70 mg loading dose on day 1, then 50 mg qd. Infuse IV over 1 h. Consider 70 mg qd in patients not responding to 50 mg qd.

PEDS - Not approved in children.

NOTES - Administration with cyclosporine increases caspofungin levels & hepatic transaminases; risk of concomitant use unclear. Caspofungin decreases tacrolimus levels. Consider increasing caspofungin dose to 70 mg/day in patients with a poor response who are taking CYP 450 inducers (efavirenz, nelfinavir, nevirapine, phyenytoin, rifampin, dexamethasone, carbamazepine). Do not dilute caspofungin in dextrose. Dosage adjustment in moderate liver dysfunction (Child-Pugh score 7-9): 70 mg loading dose on day 1, then 35 mg qd.

clotrimazole (*Mycelex*, ✤*Canesten*) ▶L ♀C ◗? $$$

ADULT - Oral candidiasis: 1 troche dissolved slowly in mouth 5x/day x 14 days. Prevention of oropharyngeal candidiasis in immunocompromised patients: 1 troche dissolved slowly in mouth tid until end of chemotherapy/high-dose corticosteroids.

PEDS - Treatment of oropharyngeal candidiasis, ≥3 yo: 1 troche dissolved slowly in mouth 5x/day x 14 days.

FORMS - Trade: Oral troches 10 mg.

NOTES - Abnormal LFTs, usually mild.

fluconazole (*Diflucan*) ▶K ♀C ◗- $$$$

ADULT - Oropharyngeal/esophageal candidiasis: 200 mg IV/PO first day, then 100 mg IV/PO qd for ≥14 days for oropharyngeal, ≥3 weeks & 2 weeks past symptom resolution for esophageal. Consider chronic suppressive therapy for HIV-infected patients. Vaginal candidiasis: 150 mg PO single dose. Systemic candidiasis: 400 mg IV/PO qd. Candidal UTI, peritonitis: 50-200 mg IV/PO qd. Cryptococcal meningitis: 400 mg IV/PO qd until 10-12 weeks after cerebrospinal fluid is culture negative. Suppression of cryptococcal meningitis relapse in AIDS: 200 mg IV/PO qd. Prevention of candidiasis after bone marrow transplant: 400 mg IV/PO qd starting several days before neutropenia and continuing until ANC >1000 cells/mm3 x 7 days.

PEDS - Oropharyngeal/esophageal candidiasis: 6 mg/kg IV/PO first day, then 3 mg/kg IV/PO qd for ≥14 days for oropharyngeal, ≥3 weeks & 2 weeks past symptom resolution for esophageal. Consider chronic suppressive therapy for HIV-infected patients. Systemic candidiasis: 6-12 mg/kg IV/PO qd. Cryptococcal meningitis: 12 mg/kg IV/PO on first day, then 6 mg/kg IV/PO qd until 10-12 weeks after cerebrospinal fluid is culture negative. Suppression of cryptococcal meningitis relapse in AIDS: 6 mg/kg IV/PO qd.

UNAPPROVED ADULT - Onychomycosis, fingernail: 150-300 mg PO q week x 3-6 mo. Onychomycosis, toenail: 150-300 mg PO q week x 6-12 mo. Prevention of recurrent oropharyngeal/vaginal/esophageal candidiasis in HIV infection: 100-200 mg PO qd.

UNAPPROVED PEDS - Prevention of recurrent oropharyngeal/esophageal candidiasis in HIV infection: 3-6 mg/kg PO qd.

FORMS - Trade: Tabs 50,100,150,200 mg; susp 10 & 40 mg/ml.

NOTES - Hepatotoxicity. Many drug interactions, including increased levels of cyclosporine, phenytoin, theophylline, and increased INR with warfarin. Do not use with cisapride. Dosing in renal dysfunction: Reduce maintenance dose by 50% for CrCl 11-50 ml/min. Hemodialysis: Give recommended dose after each dialysis. Oral susp stable for 2 weeks after mixing.

flucytosine (*Ancobon*) ▶K ♀C ▶- $$$$$

WARNING - Extreme caution in renal or bone marrow impairment. Monitor hematologic, hepatic, renal function in all patients.

ADULT - Candidal/cryptococcal infections: 50-150 mg/kg/day PO divided qid.

PEDS - Not approved in children.

UNAPPROVED PEDS - Candidal/cryptococcal infections: 50-150 mg/kg/day PO divided qid.

FORMS - Trade: Caps 250, 500 mg.

NOTES - Flucytosine is given with other antifungal agents. Myelosuppression. Reduce nausea by taking caps a few at a time over 15 minutes. Monitor flucytosine levels. Peak 70-80 mg/L, trough 30-40 mg/L. Reduce dose in renal dysfunction.

griseofulvin microsize (*Fulvicin-U/F, Grifulvin-V*) ▶Skin ♀C ▶? $$

ADULT - Tinea: 500 mg PO qd x 4-6 weeks for capitis, 2-4 weeks for corporis, 4-8 weeks for pedis, 4 months for fingernails, 6 months for toenails. Can use 1000 mg/day for pedis and unguium.

PEDS - Tinea: 11 mg/kg PO qd x 4-6 weeks for capitis, 2-4 weeks for corporis, 4-8 weeks for pedis, 4 months for fingernails, 6 months for toenails.

UNAPPROVED PEDS - Tinea capitis: AAP recommends 15-20 mg/kg (max 1 g) PO qd x 4-6 weeks and 2 weeks past symptom resolution. Some infections may require 20-25 mg/kg/day or ultramicrosize griseofulvin at 5-10 mg/kg (max 750 mg) PO qd.

FORMS - Generic/Trade: Tabs 500 mg. Trade: Tabs 250, caps 250, susp 125 mg/5 ml.

NOTES - Do not use in liver failure, porphyria. Photosensitivity, lupus-like syndrome/ exacerbation of lupus. Decreased INR with warfarin, decreased efficacy of oral contraceptives. Ultramicrosize formulations available with different strengths and dosing.

itraconazole (*Sporanox*) ▶L ♀C ▶- $$$$$

WARNING - Contraindicated with cisapride, dofetilide, lovastatin, PO midazolam, pimozide, quinidine, simvastatin, triazolam. Negative inotrope; not for onychomycosis therapy if ventricular dysfunction, CHF, or hx of CHF. Consider stopping the drug if CHF signs/sx develop during use for other indications. Use for other indications in CHF only if benefit exceeds risk.

ADULT - Caps - Take caps with full meal. Onychomycosis, toenails: 200 mg PO qd x 12 weeks. Onychomycosis "pulse dosing", fingernails: 200 mg PO bid for 1st wk of month x 2 months. Confirm diagnosis with nail specimen lab testing before prescribing. Aspergillosis in patients intolerant/refractory to amphotericin, blastomycosis, histoplasmosis: 200 mg IV bid x 4 doses, each IV dose over 1h, then 200 mg qd. Can also give 200 mg PO bid or qd. Treat for at least 3 months. For life-threatening infections, load with 200 mg IV bid x 4 doses or 200 mg PO tid x 3 days. Empiric therapy of suspected fungal infection in febrile neutropenia: 200 mg IV bid x 4 doses, then 200 mg IV qd for ≤14 days. Continue oral sol'n 200 mg (20 ml) PO bid until significant neutropenia resolved. Oral sol'n - Swish & swallow in 10 ml increments on empty stomach. Oropharyngeal candidiasis: 200 mg PO swish & swallow qd x 1-2 weeks. Oropharyngeal candidiasis unresponsive to fluconazole: 100 mg PO swish & swallow bid. Esophageal candidiasis: 100-200 mg PO swish & swallow qd x at least 3 weeks & 2 weeks past symptom resolution.

PEDS - Not approved in children.

UNAPPROVED ADULT - Caps - Onychomycosis "pulse dosing", toenails: 200 mg PO bid for 1st wk of month x 3-4 months. Confirm diagnosis with nail specimen lab testing before prescribing. Prevention of recurrent oropharyngeal, vaginal, or esophageal candidiasis in HIV infection: 200 mg oral solution PO qd.

UNAPPROVED PEDS - Caps for systemic fungal infections, 3-16 yo: 100 mg PO qd. Oral solution for prevention of recurrent esophageal candidiasis in HIV infection: 5 mg/kg PO qd.

FORMS - Trade: Cap 100 mg, oral soln 10 mg/ml.

NOTES - Hepatotoxicity; monitor LFTs in patients with liver dysfunction or hx of drug-induced hepatotoxicity. Decreased absorption of itraconazole with antacids, H2 blockers, proton pump inhibitors, or achlorhydria; increased absorption of tabs taken with cola beverages. Carbamazepine, grapefruit juice (avoid), isoniazid, phenobarbital, phenytoin, rifabutin & rifampin reduce itraconazole levels. Itraconazole inhibits cytochrome P450 3A4 metabolism of many drugs. Caps and oral sol'n not interchangeable. Women should not get pregnant during and for 2 months after taking itraconazole for onychomycosis. Do not use IV itraconazole if CrCl <30 ml/min.

ketoconazole (*Nizoral*) ▶L ♀C ▶- $$$$

WARNING - Hepatotoxicity: inform patients of risk & monitor. Do not use with cisapride, midazolam, pimozide, triazolam.

ADULT - Systemic fungal infections: 200-400 mg PO qd.

PEDS - Systemic fungal infections, ≥2 yo: 3.3-6.6 mg/kg PO qd.

UNAPPROVED ADULT - Tinea versicolor: 400 mg PO single dose or 200 mg PO qd x 7 days. Prevention of recurrent oropharyngeal, vaginal, or esophageal candidiasis in HIV infection: 200 mg PO qd.

UNAPPROVED PEDS - Prevention of recurrent mucocutaneous candidiasis in HIV infection: 5-10 mg/kg/day PO qd or bid; max 400 mg bid.

FORMS - Generic/Trade: Tabs 200 mg.

NOTES - First-dose anaphylaxis rare. Antacids, H2 blockers, proton pump inhibitors, achlorhydria decrease absorption. Isoniazid & rifampin reduce ketoconazole levels. Ketoconazole inhibits cytochrome P450 3A4 metabolism of many drugs. High doses decrease serum testosterone, ACTH-induced corticosteroid levels.

nystatin (*Mycostatin*, ✤*Nilstat, Nyaderm*) ▶Not absorbed ♀B ▶? $

ADULT - Thrush: 4-6 ml PO swish & swallow qid or suck on 1-2 troches 4-5 x daily.

PEDS - Thrush, infants: 2 ml/dose PO with 1 ml in each cheek qid. Premature and low weight infants: 0.5 ml PO in each cheek qid. Thrush, older children: 4-6 ml PO swish & swallow qid or suck on 1-2 troches 4-5 x daily.

FORMS - Generic/Trade: Susp 100,000 units/ml. Trade: Troches 200,000 units.

terbinafine (*Lamisil*) ▶LK ♀B ▶- $$$$$

ADULT - Onychomycosis: 250 mg PO qd x 6 weeks for fingernails, x 12 weeks for toenails.Confirm diagnosis with nail specimen lab testing before prescribing.

PEDS - Not approved in children.

UNAPPROVED ADULT - Onychomycosis "pulse dosing": 500 mg PO qd for 1st week of month x 2 months for fingernails, 4 months for toenails. Confirm diagnosis with nail specimen lab testing before prescribing.

UNAPPROVED PEDS - Onychomycosis: 67.5 mg PO qd for <20 kg, 125 mg PO qd for 20-40 kg, 250 mg PO qd for >40 kg x 6 weeks for fingernails, x 12 weeks for toenails. Confirm diagnosis with nail specimen lab testing before prescribing.

FORMS - Trade: Tabs 250 mg.

NOTES - Hepatotoxicity; monitor AST & ALT at baseline. Neutropenia. Do not use in liver disease or CrCl <50 ml/min.

ANTIMICROBIALS: Antimalarials

NOTES: For help treating malaria or getting antimalarials, call the CDC "malaria hotline" (770) 488-7788 Monday-Friday 8 am to 4:30 pm EST. After hours / weekend (404) 639-2888. Informa-

tion is also available at:
http://www.cdc.gov/travel/diseases.htm#malaria.

chloroquine phosphate (*Aralen*) ▶KL ♀C but + ▶+ $

WARNING - Review product labeling for precautions and adverse effects before prescribing.

ADULT - Doses given as chloroquine phosphate. Malaria prophylaxis, chloroquine-sensitive areas: 500 mg PO q wk from 1-2 weeks before exposure to 4 weeks after. Malaria: On day 1, give 1 g PO x 1, then 500 mg PO 6 h later. Give 500 mg PO qd on days 2 & 3. Extraintestinal amebiasis: 1 g PO qd x 2 days, then 500 mg PO qd x 2-3 weeks.

PEDS - Doses given as chloroquine phosphate. Malaria prophylaxis for chloroquine-sensitive areas: 8.3 mg/kg (up to 500 mg) PO q wk from 1-2 weeks before exposure to 4 weeks after. Malaria: On day 1, give 16.7 mg/kg PO x 1, then 8.3 mg/kg 6 h later. Give 8.3 mg/kg PO qd on days 2 & 3. Do not exceed adult dose. Chloroquine phosphate 8.3 mg/kg = 5 mg/kg base.

FORMS - Trade/Generic: Tabs 250, 500 mg (500 mg phosphate equivalent to 300 mg base).

NOTES - Dose-related retinopathy with long-term/high-dose therapy; eye exams required. Discontinue if muscle weakness develops. May exacerbate psoriasis. As little as 1 g can cause fatal overdose in a child. Chloroquine resistance common in most malaria areas; use only for malaria acquired in area without resistance. Fatalities have been reported with chloroquine treatment of malaria acquired in areas where chloroquine resistance is common. Maternal use of antimalarial prophylaxis doesn't harm breast-fed infant or protect infant from malaria.

doxycycline (*Vibramycin, Vibra-Tabs, Doryx,* ✤*Doxycin*) ▶LK ♀D ▶? $

ADULT - Malaria prophylaxis: 100 mg PO qd starting 1-2 days before exposure until 4 weeks after. Usual dose for other indications: 100 mg PO bid on first day, then 100 mg/day PO divided qd or bid. Severe infections: 100 mg PO bid. Chlamydia, nongonococcal urethritis: 100 mg PO bid x 7 days. Acne vulgaris: Up to 100 mg PO bid. Syphilis if penicillin-allergic: 100 mg PO bid x 14 days if primary, secondary, early latent, x 4 weeks if late latent or tertiary. Not for neurosyphilis. Periostat for periodontitis: 20 mg PO bid 1 h before breakfast and dinner. Intravenous: 200 mg on first day in 1-2 infusions, then 100-200 mg/day in 1-2 infusions. See http://jama.ama-assn.org/issues/v281n18/pdf/jst80027.pdf for anthrax bioterrorism dosing.

PEDS - Avoid in children <8 yo due to teeth staining. Malaria prophylaxis: 2 mg/kg/day up to 100 mg PO qd starting 1-2 days before exposure until 4 weeks after. Usual dose for other indications, children ≤45 kg: 4.4 mg/kg/day PO divided bid on first day, then 2.2-4.4 mg/kg/day PO divided qd or bid. Use adult dose for children >45 kg. Most PO and IV doses are equivalent. See http://jama.ama-assn.org/issues/v281n18/pdf/jst80027.pdf for anthrax bioterrorism dosing.

UNAPPROVED ADULT - See table for treatment of pelvic inflammatory disease. Lyme disease: 100 mg PO bid x 14-28 days. Prevention of Lyme disease in highly endemic area, with deer tick attachment ≥48h: 200 mg PO single dose with food within 72 h of tick bite. Ehrlichiosis: 100 mg IV/PO bid x 7-14 days. Malaria treatment: 100 mg PO bid x 7 days with quinine.

UNAPPROVED PEDS - Avoid in children <8 yo due to teeth staining. Lyme disease: 1-2 mg/kg up to 100 mg PO bid x 14-28 days. Malaria treatment: 2 mg/kg/day x 7 days with quinine.

FORMS - Generic/Trade: Tabs 100 mg, caps 50,100 mg. Trade: Susp 25 mg/5 ml, syrup 50 mg/5 ml (contains sulfites). Periostat: Caps 20 mg.

NOTES - Photosensitivity, pseudotumor cerebri, increased BUN, pain with IV infusion. May decrease efficacy of oral contraceptives. Increased INR with warfarin. Do not give antacids or calcium supplements within 2 h of doxycycline. Barbiturates, carbamazepine, and phenytoin may decrease doxycycline levels. Preferred over tetracycline in renal dysfunction. Maternal use of antimalarial prophylaxis doesn't harm breast-fed infant or protect infant from malaria. Take with fluids to decrease esophageal irritation. Doxycycline can be given with food/milk.

***Fansidar* (sulfadoxine + pyrimethamine)** ▶KL ♀C ▶- $

WARNING - Can cause life-threatening Stevens-Johnson syndrome and toxic epidermal necrolysis. Stop treatment at first sign of rash, bacterial/fungal infection, or change in CBC.

ADULT - Treatment of chloroquine-resistant P falciparum malaria: 2-3 tabs PO single dose.

PEDS - CDC regimen for self-treatment: 5-10 kg: ½ tab, 11-20 kg: 1 tab, 21-30 kg: 1½ tab, 31-45 kg: 2 tabs, >45 kg: 3 tabs.

FORMS - Trade: Tabs sulfadoxine 500 mg +

pyrimethamine 25 mg.
NOTES - Do not use in sulfonamide allergy. Hemolytic anemia in G6PD deficiency. Fansider resistance is common in many malarious regions.

***Malarone* (atovaquone + proguanil)** ▶Fecal excretion; LK ♀C ▶? $$$$

ADULT - Prevention of malaria: 1adult tab PO qd from 1-2 days before exposure until 7 days after. Treatment of malaria: 4 adult tabs PO qd x 3 days. Take with food or a milky drink at the same time each day. Repeat dose if vomiting occurs within 1 hour after dose.
PEDS - Safety & efficacy not established in children <11 kg. Prevention of malaria: Give PO qd from 1-2 days before exposure until 7 days after: 1 ped tab for 11-20 kg; 2 ped tabs for 21-30 kg; 3 ped tabs for 31-40 kg; 1adult tab for >40 kg. Treatment of malaria: Give PO qd x 3 days: 1adult tab for 11-20 kg; 2 adult tabs for 21-30 kg; 3 adult tabs for 31-40 kg; 4 adult tabs for >40 kg. Take with food or milky drink at same time each day. Repeat dose if vomiting occurs within 1 h after dose.
FORMS - Trade: Adult tabs atovaquone 250 mg + proguanil 100 mg; pediatric tabs 62.5 mg + 25 mg.
NOTES - Vomiting common with malaria treatment doses of Malarone; atovaquone absorption decreased in patients with diarrhea/vomiting. Monitor paresitemia and consider antiemetic in Malarone-treated patients who are vomiting. Plasma levels of atovaquone may be decreased by tetracycline, metoclopramide (use another anti-emetic if possible), and rifampin (avoid).

mefloquine (*Lariam*) ▶L ♀C ▶? $$

ADULT - Malaria prophylaxis, chloroquine-resistant areas: 250 mg PO q week from 1 week before exposure to 4 weeks after. Malaria treatment: 1250 mg PO single dose. Take on full stomach with at least 8 oz water.
PEDS - Not approved in children.
UNAPPROVED PEDS - Malaria prophylaxis, chloroquine-resistant areas: CDC recommends these PO doses q week starting 1 week before exposure to 4 weeks after: 15-19 kg, ¼ tab; 20-30 kg, ½ tab; 31-45 kg, ¾ tab; >45 kg, 1 tab. Malaria treatment, <45 kg: 15 mg/kg PO, then 10 mg/kg PO given 8-12 h after first dose. Take on full stomach with at least 8 oz water.
FORMS - Trade: Tabs 250 mg.
NOTES - Cardiac conduction disturbances including QT prolongation; do not use with halofantrine, quinine, quinidine. Psychiatric disturbances. May cause dizziness - warn patients about driving & hazardous tasks. May decrease valproate levels. Increased risk of seizures when used with chloroquine. Maternal use of antimalarial prophylaxis doesn't harm breast-fed infant or protect infant from malaria.

primaquine phosphate ▶L ♀- ▶- $

WARNING - Review product labeling for precautions and adverse effects before prescribing.
ADULT - Prevention of relapse after leaving malarious region or after treatment for P vivax or P ovale: 26.3 mg PO qd x 14 days.
PEDS - Not approved in children.
UNAPPROVED ADULT - Pneumocystis in patients intolerant to trimethoprim/sulfamethoxazole: 30 mg primaquine base (2 tabs) PO qd plus clindamycin 600-900 mg IV q8h or 300-450 mg PO q8h x 21 days.
UNAPPROVED PEDS – Relapse prevention after leaving malarious region or after treatment for P vivax or P ovale: 0.5 mg/kg PO qd x 14 d.
FORMS - Generic: Tabs 26.3 mg (equiv to 15 mg base).
NOTES - Hemolytic anemia with G6PD deficiency, methemoglobinemia with NADH methemoglobin reductase deficiency. Stop if dark urine or anemia. Avoid in patients with rheumatoid arthritis or SLE, recent quinacrine use, or use of other bone marrow suppressants.

quinidine gluconate ▶LK ♀C ▶+ $$$$

ADULT - Life-threatening malaria: Load with 10 mg/kg of quinidine gluconate (max 600 mg) IV over 1-2h, then 0.02 mg/kg/min. Treat x 72 h, until parasitemia <1%, or PO meds tolerated.
PEDS - Safety and efficacy not established in children.
UNAPPROVED PEDS - Life-threatening malaria: Load with 10 mg/kg IV over 1-2h, then 0.02 mg/kg/min. Treat x 72 h, until parasitemia <1%, or PO meds tolerated. Dose given as quinidine gluconate.
NOTES - QRS widening, QT interval prolongation, hypotension, hypoglycemia. Monitor EKG and BP. Drug interactions with amiodarone and other anti-arrhythmics, digoxin, phenytoin, phenobarbital, rifampin, verapamil. Rapid shipment of quinidine gluconate can be arranged by calling Eli Lilly at (800) 821-0538.

quinine sulfate ▶L ♀X ▶+? $

ADULT - Malaria: 600-650 mg PO tid x 3-7 days. Also give doxycycline or Fansidar.
UNAPPROVED PEDS - Malaria: 25-30 mg/kg/day up to 2 g/day PO divided q8h x 3-7 days. Also give doxycycline or Fansidar.

FORMS - Generic: Tabs 260 mg, caps 200,325 mg.
NOTES - Thrombocytopenia, cinchonism, hemolytic anemia with G6PD deficiency, cardiac conduction disturbances, hearing impairment with high levels. Many drug interactions.

ANTIMICROBIALS: Antimycobacterial Agents

NOTES: Two or more drugs are needed for the treatment of active mycobacterial infections. Guidelines for management of mycobacterial infections at http://www.thoracic.org/statements/.

clofazimine (*Lamprene*) ▶Fecal excretion ♀C ▶? $
UNAPPROVED ADULT - Mycobacterium avium complex treatment: 100 mg PO qd.
FORMS - Trade: Caps 50 mg.
NOTES - Abdominal pain common; rare reports of splenic infarction, bowel obstruction, and GI bleeding. Pink to brownish-black skin pigmentation that may persist for months to years after drug is discontined. Discoloration of urine, body secretions.

dapsone, *Avlosulfon* ▶LK ♀C ▶+? $
ADULT - Leprosy: 100 mg PO qd with rifampin +/- clofazimine or ethionamide.
PEDS - Leprosy: 1 mg/kg/day (up to 100 mg) PO qd with other antimycobacterial agents.
UNAPPROVED ADULT - Pneumocystis prophylaxis: 100 mg PO qd. Pneumocystis treatment: 100 mg PO qd with trimethoprim 5 mg/kg PO tid x 21 days.
UNAPPROVED PEDS - Pneumocystis prophylaxis age ≥1 mo: 2 mg/kg up to 100 mg PO qd.
FORMS - Generic: Tabs 25,100 mg.
NOTES - Blood dyscrasias, severe allergic skin reactions, sulfone syndrome, hemolysis in G6PD deficiency, hepatotoxicity, neuropathy, photosensitivity, leprosy reactional states. Didanosine, rifampin may decrease dapsone levels, but dapsone dosage adjustment not needed in leprosy. Monitor CBC q wk x 4, then monthly x 6, then twice yearly. Monitor LFTs.

ethambutol (*Myambutol*, *Etibi*) ▶LK ♀B ▶+ $$$$$
ADULT - Tuberculosis: 15-25 mg/kg up to 2500 mg PO qd.
PEDS - Tuberculosis: 15-25 mg/kg up to 2500 mg PO qd.
UNAPPROVED ADULT - Mycobacterium avium complex treatment: 15-25 mg/kg up to 2500 mg PO qd.
UNAPPROVED PEDS - Prevention of recurrent mycobacterium avium complex disease in HIV infection: 15 mg/kg up to 900 mg PO qd with clarithromycin/azithromycin +/- rifabutin.
FORMS - Trade: Tabs 100,400 mg.
NOTES - Optic neuritis; test color vision and visual acuity monthly if >15 mg/kg/day. Give 2h before/after aluminum-containing antacids, sucralfate, buffered didanosine. Reduce dose/ monitor levels in renal impairment.

isoniazid (*INH*, *Isotamine*) ▶LK ♀C but + ▶+ $
WARNING - Hepatotoxicity. Obtain baseline LFTs. Monitor LFTs periodically in high-risk patients (HIV, signs/hx of liver disease, abnormal LFTs at baseline, pregnancy/postpartum, alcoholism/regular alcohol use). Consider LFTs if >35 yo on individual basis, especially if treated with other medications for chronic medical conditions. Tell all patients to stop INH and call immediately for symptoms of hepatotoxicity.
ADULT - Tuberculosis treatment: 5 mg/kg up to 300 mg PO qd or 15 mg/kg up to 900 mg twice weekly. TB prevention: 300 mg PO qd.
PEDS - Tuberculosis treatment: 10-20 mg/kg up to 300 mg PO qd. Tuberculosis prevention: 10 mg/kg up to 300 mg PO qd.
UNAPPROVED ADULT - American Thoracic Society regimen for latent tuberculosis: 5 mg/kg/day up to 300 mg PO qd for 9 months (6 months acceptable for HIV-negative patients, but less effective than 9 months).
UNAPPROVED PEDS - American Thoracic Society regimen for latent tuberculosis: 10-20 mg/kg up to 300 mg PO qd for 9 months.
FORMS - Generic: Tabs 100,300 mg, syrup 50 mg/5 ml.
NOTES - Peripheral neuropathy (high risk if alcoholism, diabetes, uremia, malnutrition, HIV); treat high-risk patients with pyridoxine 10-25 mg PO qd. Pyridoxine also recommended if pregnancy, seizure disorder, or breast-fed infant of mother who is taking INH. Many drug interactions.

pyrazinamide, *Tebrazid* ▶LK ♀C ▶? $$$
ADULT - Tuberculosis: 15-30 mg/kg up to 2000 mg PO qd.
PEDS - Tuberculosis: 15-30 mg/kg up to 2000 mg PO qd.
UNAPPROVED ADULT - American Thoracic Society regimen for latent tuberculosis: 15-20 mg/kg up to 2 g PO qd for 2 months, WITH ri-

fampin 10 mg/kg up to 600 mg PO qd.
FORMS - Generic: Tabs 500 mg.
NOTES - Hepatotoxicity, hyperuricemia. Obtain LFTs at baseline. Monitor periodically in high-risk patients (HIV infection, alcoholism, pregnancy, signs/history of liver disease, abnormal LFTs at baseline). Avoid in renal dysfunction.

rifabutin (*Mycobutin*) ▶L ♀B ▶? $$$$$
ADULT - Prevention of disseminated mycobacterium avium complex disease in AIDS: 300 mg PO qd or 150 mg PO bid.
PEDS - Not approved in children.
UNAPPROVED ADULT - Tuberculosis or mycobacterium avium complex treatment in AIDS: 300 mg PO qd. Dosage adjustments of rifabutin when given with anti-HIV drugs: 150 mg PO qod or 3 times/week with ritonavir or lopinavir/ritonavir (Kaletra); 150 mg PO qd with amprenavir, indinavir, or nelfinavir; 450-600 mg PO qd with efavirenz.
UNAPPROVED PEDS - Mycobacterium avium complex prophylaxis: ≥6 yo, 300 mg PO qd. <6 yo, 5 mg/kg (up to 300 mg) PO qd.
FORMS - Trade: Caps 150 mg.
NOTES - Uveitis, hepatotoxicity, thrombocytopenia. Obtain CBC and LFTs at baseline. Monitor periodically in high-risk patients (HIV infection, alcoholism, pregnancy, signs/ history of liver disease, abnormal LFTs at baseline). Do not use rifabutin alone in patients with active TB. Rifabutin may induce liver metabolism of other drugs including oral contraceptives, protease inhibitors, and fluconazole. Fluconazole, clarithromycin, and protease inhibitors increase rifabutin levels (dosage adjustments above). Do not use with delavirdine or saquinavir. Increase indinavir dose to 1000 mg PO q8h. Urine, body secretion, soft contact lenses may turn orange-brown.

***Rifamate* (isoniazid + rifampin)** ▶LK ♀C ▶+ $$$$
WARNING - Hepatotoxicity.
ADULT - Tuberculosis: 2 caps PO qd on empty stomach.
PEDS - Not approved in children.
FORMS - Trade: Caps isoniazid 150 mg + rifampin 300 mg.
NOTES - See components. Monitor LFTs at baseline and periodically during therapy.

rifampin (*Rimactane, Rifadin*, ✱*Rofact*) ▶L ♀C ▶+ $$$
ADULT - Tuberculosis: 10 mg/kg up to 600 mg PO/IV qd. Neisseria meningitidis carriers: 600 mg PO bid x 2 days. Take on empty stomach.
PEDS - Tuberculosis: 10-20 mg/kg up to 600 mg PO/IV qd. Neisseria meningitidis carriers: ≥1 mo, 10 mg/kg up to 600 mg PO bid x 2 days. <1 mo, 5 mg/kg PO bid x 2 days. Take on empty stomach.
UNAPPROVED ADULT - Prophylaxis of H influenza type b infection: 20 mg/kg up to 600 mg PO qd x 4 days. Leprosy: 600 mg PO q month with dapsone. American Thoracic Society regimen for latent tuberculosis: 10 mg/kg up to 600 mg PO qd x 4 months.Take on empty stomach.

UNAPPROVED PEDS - Prophylaxis of H influenza type b infection: ≥1 mo, 20 mg/kg up to 600 mg PO qd x 4 days. <1 mo, 10 mg/kg PO qd x 4 days. Prophylaxis of invasive meningococcal disease: ≥1 mo, 10 mg/kg up to 600 mg PO bid x 2 days. <1 mo, 5 mg/kg PO bid x 2 days. American Thoracic Society regimen for latent tuberculosis: 10-20 mg/kg up to 600 mg PO qd x 4 months. Take on empty stomach.
FORMS - Generic/Trade: Caps 150,300 mg. Pharmacists can make oral suspension.
NOTES - Hepatotoxicity, thrombocytopenia, exacerbation of porphyria. When treating tuberculosis, obtain CBC and LFTs at baseline. Monitor periodically in high-risk patients (HIV infection, alcoholism, pregnancy, signs/history of liver disease, abnormal LFTs at baseline). Induces hepatic metabolism of many drugs including oral contraceptives. Do not use with amprenavir, delavirdine, indinavir, nelfinavir, saquinavir, lopinavir/ritonavir (Kaletra). Adjust dose with hepatic impairment. Colors urine, body secretions, soft contact lenses red-orange. Adult regimen for latent tuberculosis can be given for 2 months with pyrazinamide (see entry for pyrazinamide).

rifapentine (*Priftin*) ▶Esterases, fecal ♀C ▶? $$$
ADULT - Tuberculosis: 600 mg PO twice weekly x 2 months, then once weekly x 4 months (twice weekly if HIV).
PEDS - Not approved in children <12 yo.
FORMS - Trade: Tabs 150 mg.
NOTES - Obtain CBC and LFTs at baseline. Monitor LFTs periodically in high-risk patients (HIV infection, alcoholism, pregnancy, signs/ history of liver disease, abnormal LFTs at baseline). Urine, body secretions, contact lenses, and dentures may turn red-orange. May induce liver metabolism of other drugs including oral contraceptives. Avoid with protease inhibitors. Do not use in porphyria.

***Rifater* (isoniazid + rifampin + pyrazinamide)** ▶LK ♀C ▶? $$$$$

WARNING - Hepatotoxicity.
ADULT - Tuberculosis, initial 2 mo of treatment: 6 tabs PO qd if ≥55 kg, 5 tabs qd if 45-54 kg, 4 tabs qd if ≤ 44 kg. Take on empty stomach. Can finish treatment with Rifamate.
PEDS - Ratio of formulation may not be appropriate for children <15 yo.
FORMS - Trade: Tab Isoniazid 50 mg + rifampin 120 mg + pyrazinamide 300 mg.
NOTES - See components. Monitor LFTs at baseline and during therapy.

ANTIMICROBIALS: Antiparasitics

albendazole (*Albenza*) ▶L ♀C ▶? $$$
ADULT - Hydatid disease, neurocysticercosis: ≥60 kg - 400 mg PO bid. <60 kg - 15 mg/kg/day (up to 800 mg/day) PO divided bid. Treatment duration varies. Take with food.
PEDS - Hydatid disease, neurocysticercosis: ≥60 kg - 400 mg PO bid. <60 kg: 15 mg/kg/day (up to 800 mg/day) PO divided bid. Treatment duration varies. Take with food.
UNAPPROVED ADULT - Hookworm, whipworm, pinworm, roundworm: 400 mg PO single dose. Repeat in 2 weeks for pinworm. Cutaneous larva migrans: 200 mg PO bid x 3 days. Strongyloidiasis: 400 mg PO qd x 3 days. Systemic microsporidia: 400 mg PO bid.
UNAPPROVED PEDS - Roundworm, hookworm, pinworm, whipworm: 400 mg PO single dose. Repeat in 2 weeks for pinworm. Cutaneous larva migrans: 200 mg PO bid x 3 days.
FORMS - Trade: Tabs 200 mg.
NOTES - Monitor LFTs, WBC. Consider corticosteroids & anticonvulsants in neurocysticercosis. Get negative pregnancy test before treatment & warn against getting pregnant until a month after treatment. Treat close contacts for pinworms.

atovaquone (*Mepron*) ▶Fecal ♀C ▶? $$$$$
ADULT - Pneumocystis in patients intolerant to trimethoprim/sulfamethoxazole: Treatment - 750 mg PO bid x 21 days. Prevention - 1500 mg PO qd. Take with meals.
PEDS - Pneumocystis in patients intolerant to trimethoprim/sulfamethoxazole, 13-16 yo: Treatment, 750 mg PO bid x 21 days. Prevention, 1500 mg PO qd. Take with meals. Efficacy & safety not established for <13 yo.
UNAPPROVED PEDS - Prevention of recurrent pneumocystis in HIV infection: 1-3 mo, 30 mg/kg PO qd. 4-24 mo, 45 mg/kg PO qd. >24 mo, 30 mg/kg PO qd. Take with a meal.
FORMS - Trade: Susp 750 mg/5 ml, foil pouch 750 mg/5 ml, 1500 mg/10 ml.
NOTES - Efficacy of atovaquone may be decreased by rifampin (consider using alternative), rifabutin, and rifapentine.

iodoquinol (*Yodoxin, diiodohydroxyquin,* ✤*Diodoquin*) ▶Not absorbed ♀? ▶? $$
ADULT - Intestinal amebiasis: 650 mg PO tid after meals x 20 days.
PEDS - Intestinal amebiasis: 40 mg/kg/day PO divided tid x 20 days. Do not exceed adult dose.
FORMS - Generic/Trade: Tabs 650 mg. Trade: Tabs 210 mg, powder 25 g.
NOTES - Optic neuritis/atrophy, peripheral neuropathy with prolonged high doses. Interference with some thyroid function tests for up to 6 months after treatment.

ivermectin (*Stromectol*) ▶L ♀C ▶? $
ADULT - Strongyloidiasis: 200 mcg/kg PO single dose. Onchocerciasis: 150 mcg/kg PO q3-12 months. Take with water.
PEDS - For children ≥15 kg. Strongyloidiasis: 200 mcg/kg PO single dose. Onchocerciasis: 150 mcg/kg PO single dose q 3-12 months. Take with water.
UNAPPROVED ADULT - Scabies: 200 mcg/kg PO single dose. Cutaneous larva migrans: 150 -200 mcg/kg PO single dose. Take with water.
UNAPPROVED PEDS - Scabies: 200 mcg/kg PO single dose. Cutaneous larva migrans: 150-200 mcg/kg PO single dose. Take with water. Safety and efficacy not established in children <15 kg.
FORMS - Trade: Tab 3 mg.
NOTES - Mazzotti & ophthalmic reactions with treatment for onchocerciasis. May need repeat/monthly treatment for strongyloidiasis in immunocompromised/HIV-infected patients.

mebendazole (*Vermox*) ▶L ♀C ▶? $
ADULT - Pinworm: 100 mg PO single dose; consider repeat dose in 2 weeks. Roundworm, whipworm, hookworm: 100 mg PO bid x 3 days.
PEDS - Pinworm: 100 mg PO single dose; consider repeat dose in 2 weeks. Roundworm, whipworm, hookworm: 100 mg PO bid x 3 d.
FORMS - Trade/Generic: Chew tab 100 mg.
NOTES - Treat close contacts for pinworms. Retreat if not cured in 3 weeks.

metronidazole (*Flagyl*, ✤*Trikacide*) ▶KL ♀B(- in 1st trimester) ◗?- $

ADULT - Acute amebic dysentery: 750 mg PO tid x 5-10 days. Amebic liver abscess: 500-750 mg PO tid x 5-10 days. Trichomoniasis: Treat patient & sex partners with 2g PO single dose, 250 mg PO tid x 7 days, or 375 mg PO bid x 7 days. Flagyl ER for bacterial vaginosis: 750 mg PO qd x 7 days on empty stomach. H pylori: See table in GI section. Anaerobic bacterial infections: Load 1 g or 15 mg/kg IV, then 500 mg or 7.5 mg/kg IV/PO q6h, each IV dose over 1h (not to exceed 4 g/day). Prophylaxis, colorectal surgery: 15 mg/kg IV completed 1 h preop, then 7.5 mg/kg IV q6h x 2 doses.

PEDS - Amebiasis: 35-50 mg/kg/day PO (max of 750 mg/dose) divided tid x 10 days.

UNAPPROVED ADULT - Giardia: 250 mg PO tid x 5-7 days. Bacterial vaginosis: 500 mg PO bid x 7 days. Bacterial vaginosis in pregnancy (not 1st trimester): 250 mg PO tid x 7 days. Trichomoniasis (CDC alternative to single dose): 500 mg PO bid x 7 days. Pelvic inflammatory disease: see STD table. Clostridium difficile diarrhea: 250 mg PO qid or 500 mg PO tid x 10 days.

UNAPPROVED PEDS - Giardia: 15 mg/kg/day PO divided tid x 5-7 days. Clostridium difficile diarrhea: 30-50 mg/kg/day PO (not to exceed adult dose) divided tid or qid x 7-10 days. Trichomoniasis: 5 mg/kg PO tid (max 2 g/day) x 7 days. Anaerobic bacterial infections: 30 mg/kg/day IV/PO divided q6h, each IV dose over 1 h (not to exceed 4 g/day).

FORMS - Generic/Trade: Tabs 250,500 mg. Trade: Caps 375 mg, Flagyl ER tabs 750 mg.

NOTES - Peripheral neuropathy with long-term use, seizures. Disulfiram-like reaction with alcohol; avoid alcohol during & for 3 days after treatment. Do not give within 2 weeks of disulfiram. Interactions with barbiturates, lithium, phenytoin. Increased INR with warfarin. Decrease dose in liver dysfunction. Darkens urine. Follow treatment for amebic dysentery or liver abscess with a course of a luminal agent (iodoquinol, paromomycin).

paromomycin (*Humatin*) ▶Not absorbed ♀C ◗- $$$$

ADULT - Intestinal amebiasis: 25-35 mg/kg/day PO divided tid with/after meals x 5-10 days.

PEDS - Intestinal amebiasis: 25-35 mg/kg/day PO divided tid with/after meals x 5-10 days.

UNAPPROVED ADULT - Cryptosporidiosis in HIV infection: 1 g PO bid or 500-750 mg PO tid or qid.

FORMS - Trade: Caps 250 mg.

NOTES - Nephrotoxicity possible with systemic absorption in inflammatory bowel disease. Not effective for extra-intestinal amebiasis.

pentamidine (*Pentam, NebuPent*, ✤*Pentacarina*) ▶K ♀C ◗- $$$$$

ADULT - Pneumocystis treatment: 4 mg/kg IM/IV qd x 14-21 days. NebuPent for pneumocystis prevention: 300 mg nebulized q 4 weeks.

PEDS - Pneumocystis treatment: 4 mg/kg IM/IV qd x 14 days. NebuPent not approved in children.

UNAPPROVED PEDS - NebuPent, ≥5 yo: 300 mg nebulized q 4 weeks.

FORMS - Trade: Aerosol 300 mg.

NOTES - Fatalities due to severe hypotension, hypoglycemia, cardiac arrhythmias with IM/IV. Have patient lie down, check BP, and keep resuscitation equipment handy during IM/IV injection. Hyperglycemia, neutropenia, nephrotoxicity, pancreatitis, and hypocalcemia. Monitor BUN, serum creatinine, blood glucose, CBC, LFTs, serum calcium, and ECG. Bronchospasm with inhalation. Reduce IM/IV dose in renal dysfunction.

praziquantel (*Biltricide*) ▶LK ♀B ◗- $$$

ADULT - Schistosomiasis: 20 mg/kg PO q4-6h x 3 doses. Liver flukes: 25 mg/kg PO q4-6h x 3 doses.

PEDS - Schistosomiasis: 20 mg/kg PO q4-6h x 3 doses. Liver flukes: 25 mg/kg PO q4-6h x 3 doses.

UNAPPROVED ADULT - Neurocysticercosis: 50 mg/kg/day PO divided tid x 15 days. Fish, dog, beef, pork intestinal tapeworms: 10 mg/kg PO single dose.

UNAPPROVED PEDS - Neurocysticercosis: 50-100 mg/kg/day PO divided tid x 15 days. Fish, dog, beef, pork intestinal tapeworms: 10 mg/kg PO single dose.

FORMS - Trade: Tabs 600 mg.

NOTES - Contraindicated in ocular cysticercosis. May cause drowsiness. Phenytoin, carbamazepine, and dexamethasone may lower praziquantel levels enough to cause treatment failure. Take with liquids during a meal. Do not chew tabs.

pyrantel (*Pin-X, Pinworm*, ✤*Combantrin*) ▶Not absorbed ♀- ◗? $

ADULT - Pinworm, roundworm: 11 mg/kg up to 1 g PO single dose. Repeat in 2 weeks for pinworm.

PEDS - Pinworm, roundworm: 11 mg/kg up to 1 g PO single dose. Repeat in 2 weeks for pinworm.

UNAPPROVED ADULT - Hookworm: 11 mg/kg up to 1 g PO qd x 3 days.
UNAPPROVED PEDS - Hookworm: 11 mg/kg up to 1 g PO qd x 3 days.
FORMS - OTC: Caps 62.5 mg, liquid 50 mg/ml.
NOTES - Purging not necessary. Treat close contacts for pinworms.

pyrimethamine (*Daraprim*) ▶L ♀C ▶- $$
ADULT - Toxoplasmosis, immunocompetent patients: 50-75 mg PO qd x 1-3 weeks, then reduce dose by 50% for 4-5 more weeks. Give with leucovorin (10-15 mg qd) and sulfadiazine. Reduce initial dose in seizure disorders.
PEDS - Toxoplasmosis: 1 mg/kg/day PO divided bid x 2-4 days, then reduce by 50% x 1 month. Give with sulfadiazine & leucovorin. Reduce initial dose in seizure disorders.
UNAPPROVED ADULT - CNS toxoplasmosis in AIDS: 200 mg PO x 1, then 75-100 mg qd. Secondary prevention after CNS toxoplasmosis in AIDS: 25-75 mg PO qd. Give with leucovorin (10-15 mg qd) and sulfadiazine or clindamycin. Reduce initial dose in seizure disorders.
UNAPPROVED PEDS - AAP regimen for toxoplasmosis: 2 mg/kg/day PO x 3 days, then 1 mg/kg/day (max 25 mg/day) PO (duration of treatment varies). Give with leucovorin (10-25 mg PO with each dose of pyrimethamine) & sulfadiazine. Secondary prevention after CNS toxoplasmosis in HIV infection: 1 mg/kg or 15 mg/m2 (max 25 mg/day) PO qd with leucovorin 5 mg PO every 3 days and sulfadiazine. Reduce initial dose in seizure disorders.
FORMS - Trade: Tabs 25 mg.
NOTES - Hemolytic anemia in G6PD deficiency, dose-related folate deficiency, hypersensitivity. Monitor CBC.

thiabendazole (*Mintezol*) ▶LK ♀C ▶? $
ADULT - Helminths: 22 mg/kg/dose up to 1500 mg PO bid. Treat x 2 days for strongyloidiasis, cutaneous larva migrans. Take after meals.
PEDS - Helminths: 22 mg/kg/dose up to 1500 mg PO bid. Treat x 2 days for strongyloidiasis, cutaneous larva migrans. Limited use in children <13.5 kg. Take after meals.
FORMS - Trade: Chew tab 500 mg, susp 500 mg/5 ml.
NOTES - May cause drowsiness.

trimetrexate (*Neutrexin*) ▶LK ♀D ▶- $$$$$
WARNING - Must use with leucovorin to prevent toxicity (bone marrow suppression, oral & GI mucosal ulcers, renal & hepatic dysfunction). Must give leucovorin for 72h after last dose of trimetrexate.
ADULT - Pneumocystis pneumonia in AIDS/ immunocompromised patients who cannot take / do not respond to trimethoprim/sulfamethoxazole: 45 mg/m2 IV infused over 1h qd x 21 days. Must also give leucovorin 20 mg/m2 IV/ PO q6h x 24 days. Round PO leucovorin doses up to next higher 25 mg increment. Refer to package insert for dosage adjustments for hematologic, renal, hepatic, mucosal toxicity.
PEDS - Safety and efficacy not established in children. Adult dose has been used in compassionate use.
NOTES - Stop zidovudine while using trimetrexate. Monitor ANC, platelets, renal & hepatic function ≥ twice/wk. Many drug interactions.

ANTIMICROBIALS: Antiviral Agents - Anti-CMV

cidofovir (*Vistide*) ▶K ♀C ▶- $$$$$
WARNING - Nephrotoxicity. Granulocytopenia - monitor neutrophil counts.
ADULT - CMV retinitis in AIDS: Induction 5 mg/kg IV q week x 2 wks, maintenance 5 mg/kg every other week. Give probenecid 2 g PO 3h before and 1 g 2h and 8h after infusion. Give normal saline with each infusion.
PEDS - Not approved in children.
NOTES - Fanconi-like syndrome. Stop nephrotoxic drugs at least 1 week before cidofovir. Get serum creatinine, urine protein before each dose. Do not use if serum creatinine >1.5 mg/dl, CrCl ≤55 ml/min, or urine protein ≥100 mg/dl (≥2+). Decrease to 3 mg/kg if serum creatinine increases by 0.3-0.4 mg/dl from baseline. Stop if ≥0.5 mg/dl increase in serum creatinine or ≥3+ proteinuria. Hold zidovudine/decrease dose by 50% on days cidofovir is given. Tell women not to get pregnant during & for 1 month after cidofovir. Tell men to use barrier contraceptive during & for 3 months after cidofovir. Ocular hypotony - monitor intraocular pressure.

foscarnet (*Foscavir*) ▶K ♀C ▶? $$$$$
WARNING - Nephrotoxicity; seizures due to mineral/electrolyte imbalance.
ADULT - Hydrate before each infusion. CMV retinitis in AIDS: Induction 60 mg/kg IV (over 1 h) q8h or 90 mg/kg IV (over 1.5-2 h) q12h x 2-3 weeks. Maintenance 90-120 mg/kg IV qd over 2h. Acyclovir-resistant HSV infections in im-

munocompromised patients: 40 mg/kg IV (over 1 h) q8-12h x 2-3 weeks or until healed.

PEDS - Not approved in children. Deposits into teeth & bone of young animals.

UNAPPROVED PEDS - Hydrate before each infusion. CMV retinitis in AIDS: Induction 60 mg/kg IV (over 1 h) q8h or 90 mg/kg IV (over 1.5-2 h) q12h x 2-3 weeks. Maintenance 90-120 mg/kg IV qd over 2h. Acyclovir-resistant HSV infections in immunocompromised patients: 40 mg/kg IV (over 1 h) q8h x 2-3 weeks or until healed.

NOTES - Granulocytopenia, anemia, vein irritation, penile ulcers. Decreased ionized serum calcium, especially with IV pentamidine. Must use IV pump to avoid rapid administration. Monitor renal function, serum calcium, magnesium, phosphate, potassium. Reduce dose in renal impairment. Stop foscarnet if CrCl decreases to <0.4 ml/min/kg.

ganciclovir (*DHPG, Cytovene*) ▸K ♀C ◗- $$$$$

WARNING - Neutropenia, anemia, thrombocytopenia. Do not use if ANC <500/mm3 or platelets <25,000/mm3.

ADULT - CMV retinitis. Induction: 5 mg/kg IV q12h x 14-21 days. Maintenance: 6 mg/kg IV qd x 5 days/week; 5 mg/kg IV qd; 1000 mg PO tid; or 500 mg PO 6 times/day (q3h while awake) with food. Prevention of CMV disease in advanced AIDS: 1000 mg PO tid with food. Prevention of CMV disease after organ transplant: 5 mg/kg IV q12h x 7-14 days, then 6 mg/kg IV qd x 5 days/week or 1000 mg PO tid with food. Give IV infusion over 1 h.

PEDS - Safety and efficacy not established in children; potential carcinogenic or reproductive adverse effects.

UNAPPROVED PEDS - CMV retinitis in immunocompromised patient: Induction 5 mg/kg IV q12h x 14-21 days. Maintenance 5 mg/kg IV qd or 6 mg/kg IV qd x 5 days/week.

FORMS - Trade: Caps 250, 500 mg.

NOTES - Phlebitis/pain at infusion site, neutropenia which may be exacerbated by zidovudine, increased seizure risk if used with imipenem-cilastatin. Monitor CBC, creatinine. Reduce dose if CrCl <70 ml/min. Adequate hydration required. Potential teratogen. Women should not get pregnant during treatment. Men should use barrier contraceptive during & for ≥3 months after ganciclovir. Potential carcinogen. Consider following guidelines for handling/ disposal of cytotoxic agents.

valganciclovir (*Valcyte*) ▸K ♀C ◗- $$$$$

WARNING - Neutropenia, anemia, thrombocytopenia. Do not use if ANC <500/mm3, platelets <25,000/mm3, hemoglobin <8 g/dL. Monitor CBC frequently, esp if history of drug-induced neutropenia (eg ganciclovir, zidovudine), baseline ANC <1000/mm3, myelosuppressive drugs, radiation, or after conversion from ganciclovir to valganciclovir. Cytopenia may occur at any time, may worsen with continued use, & usually resolves within 3-7 days after discontinuation.

ADULT - CMV retinitis in AIDS patients. Induction: 900 mg PO bid x 21 days. Maintenance: 900 mg PO qd. Give with food. Valganciclovir tabs and ganciclovir caps not interchangeable on mg per mg basis.

PEDS - Safety and efficacy not established in children; potential carcinogenic or reproductive adverse effects.

FORMS - Trade: Tabs 450 mg.

NOTES - Prodrug of ganciclovir; contraindicated in ganciclovir allergy. Potential teratogen. Women should not get pregnant during treatment. Men should use barrier contraceptive during & for ≥3 months after treatment. CNS toxicity; warn patients about risks of hazardous tasks. Potential drug interactions with didanosine, mycophenolate, probenecid. May increase serum creatinine; monitor renal function & adjust dose prn. Reduce induction and maintenance doses if CrCl <60 ml/min. Use ganciclovir instead of valganciclovir in hemodialysis patients. Potential carcinogen. Avoid direct contact with broken/crushed tabs; do not intentionally break/crush tabs. Consider following guidelines for handling/ disposal of cytotoxic agents.

ANTIMICROBIALS: Antiviral Agents - Anti-Herpetic

acyclovir (*Zovirax*, ✤*Avirax*) ▸K ♀B ◗+ $$

ADULT - Genital herpes: 200 mg PO q4h (5x/day) x 10 days for first episode, x 5 days for recurrent episodes. Herpes prophylaxis: 400 mg PO bid. Zoster: 800 mg PO q4h (5x/day) x 7-10 days. Varicella: 800 mg PO qid x 5 days. IV: 5-10 mg/kg IV q8h, each dose over 1 h. Treat as soon as possible after symptom onset.

PEDS - Safety and efficacy of PO acyclovir not

established in children <2 yo. Varicella: 20 mg/kg PO qid x 5 days. Use adult dose if >40 kg. AAP does not recommend routine treatment of varicella with acyclovir. Consider use in otherwise healthy children >12 yo, those with chronic cutaneous or pulmonary disease, corticosteroid use, or chronic salicylate use. IV: 250-500 mg/m2 q8h, each dose over 1h. Treat as soon as possible after symptom onset.

UNAPPROVED ADULT - Genital herpes: 400 mg PO tid x 7-10 days for first episode, x 5 days for recurrent episodes. Orolabial herpes (controversial indication): 400 mg PO 5x/day. Treat as soon as possible after symptom onset.

UNAPPROVED PEDS - Primary gingivostomatitis: 15 mg/kg PO 5x/day x 7 days. First-episode genital herpes: 80 mg/kg/day PO divided tid (max 1.2 g/day) x 7-10 days. Use adult dose for adolescents. Treat as soon as possible after symptom onset.

FORMS - Generic/Trade: Caps 200 mg, tabs 400,800 mg. Trade: Susp 200 mg/5 ml.

NOTES - Need adequate hydration with IV administration. Severe drowsiness with acyclovir plus zidovudine. Reduce dose in renal dysfunction.

famciclovir (*Famvir*) ▶K ♀B ▶? $$$

ADULT - Recurrent genital herpes: 125 mg PO bid x 5 days. Herpes prophylaxis: 250 mg PO bid. Recurrent orolabial/genital herpes in HIV patients: 500 mg PO bid x 7 days. Zoster: 500 mg PO tid x 7 days. Treat as soon as possible after symptom onset.

PEDS - Not approved in children.

UNAPPROVED ADULT - First-episode genital herpes: 250 mg PO tid x 7-10 days. Varicella in young adults: 500 mg PO tid x 5 days. Orolabial herpes (controversial indication): 250 mg PO tid. Treat as soon as possible after symptom onset.

UNAPPROVED PEDS - Varicella in adolescents: 500 mg PO tid x 5 days.

FORMS - Trade: Tabs 125,250,500 mg.

NOTES - Reduce dose for CrCl <60 ml/min.

valacyclovir (*Valtrex*) ▶K ♀B ▶? $$$

ADULT - First-episode genital herpes: 1 g PO bid x 10 days. Recurrent genital herpes: 500 mg PO bid x 3 days. Herpes prophylaxis: 500-1000 mg PO qd. Zoster: 1 g PO tid x 7 days.

PEDS - Not approved in children.

UNAPPROVED ADULT - Orolabial herpes in immunocompromised patients, including HIV-infection: 1 g PO tid x 7 days. Chickenpox in young adults: 1 g PO tid x 5 days. Treat as soon as possible after symptom onset.

UNAPPROVED PEDS - Chickenpox in adolescents: 1 g PO tid x 5 days. Treat as soon as possible after symptom onset.

FORMS - Trade: Tabs 500,1000 mg.

NOTES - Thrombotic thrombocytopenic purpura/hemolytic uremic syndrome at dose of 8 g/day. Reduce dose for CrCl <50 ml/min. Metabolized to acyclovir.

ANTIMICROBIALS: Antiviral Agents - Anti-HIV – Non-Nucleoside Reverse Transcriptase Inhibitors

NOTE: Many serious drug interactions - always check before prescribing! Consider monitoring LFTs in patients receiving highly active antiretroviral therapy (HAART).

delavirdine (*Rescriptor,* DLV) ▶L ♀C ▶- $$$$$

WARNING - Not for monotherapy.

ADULT - Combination therapy for HIV infection: 400 mg PO tid.

PEDS - Combination therapy for HIV infection, ≥16 yo: 400 mg PO tid. Safety and efficacy not established in younger children.

UNAPPROVED PEDS - Combination therapy for HIV, adolescents <16 yo: 400 mg PO tid.

FORMS - Trade: Tabs 100,200 mg.

NOTES - Rash common in the first month of therapy. Many drug interactions. Inhibits hepatic cytochrome P450 3A4 & 2C9. Monitor LFTs when used with saquinavir. Do not use with rifampin, rifabutin, St John's wort, H2 blockers, proton pump inhibitors. Take at least 1 h before/after buffered didanosine or antacids. Reduce indinavir dose when taken with delavirdine. Can dissolve tabs in water. For achlorhydria, take with acidic drink (cranberry/ orange juice).

efavirenz (*Sustiva,* EFV) ▶L ♀C ▶- $$$$$

WARNING - Not for monotherapy.

ADULT - Combination therapy for HIV infection: 600 mg PO qhs. Avoid with high-fat meal.

PEDS - Combo therapy for HIV infection, ≥3 yo: 10-15 kg: 200 mg PO qhs. 15-20 kg: 250 mg qhs. 20-24.9 kg: 300 mg qhs. 25-32.4 kg: 350 mg qhs. 32.5-39.9 kg: 400 mg qhs. ≥40 kg: 600 mg qhs. Do not give with high-fat meal.

FORMS - Trade: Caps 50,100,200 mg.

NOTES - Psychiatric/CNS reactions (warn about driving & hazardous tasks), rash (stop if severe), increased cholesterol (monitor). May avoid morning "hangover" by giving first dose at 6-8 pm instead of qhs & starting drug over weekend. False-positive cannabinoid screening test. Monitor LFTs if given with ritonavir or to patients with hepatitis B or C. Inducer of cytochrome P450 3A4. Many drug interactions. Do not give with cisapride, midazolam, triazolam, ergot derivatives, St John's wort. Decreases levels of saquinavir - do not use with saquinavir as sole protease inhibitor. Decreases levels of amprenavir, clarithromycin (consider alternative), methadone, rifabutin. Get negative pregnancy test before use in women of child-bearing potential and recommend birth control while on efavirenz.

nevirapine (*Viramune,* NVP) ▶LK ♀C ▶- $$$$$

WARNING - Life-threatening skin reactions, hypersensitivity, hepatotoxicity. Monitor clinical and lab status intensively during first 12 weeks of therapy (consider LFTs at baseline, before and 2 weeks after dose increase, and at least once monthly) and frequently thereafter. Stop nevirapine and never rechallenge if clinical hepatitis, severe rash, or rash with constitutional sx. Not for monotherapy.

ADULT - Combination therapy for HIV infection: 200 mg PO qd x 14 days, then 200 mg PO bid. Dose titration reduces risk of rash. If rash develops at initial dose, do not increase dose until it resolves. If nevirapine is stopped for >7 days, restart with initial dose. Do not use prednisone during dose titration to prevent rash.

PEDS - Combination therapy for HIV infection, 2 mo - 8 yo: 4 mg/kg PO qd x 14 days, then 7 mg/kg PO bid. ≥8 yo: 4 mg/kg PO qd x 14 days, then 4 mg/kg PO bid. Total daily dose not to exceed 400 mg. Dose titration reduces risk of rash. If rash develops at initial dose, do not increase dose until it resolves. If nevirapine is stopped for more than 7 days, restart with initial dose. Do not use prednisone during dose titration to prevent rash.

UNAPPROVED ADULT - Prevention of maternal-fetal HIV transmission, maternal dosing: 200 mg PO single dose at onset of labor.

UNAPPROVED PEDS - Prevention of maternal-fetal HIV transmission, neonatal dosing: 2 mg/kg PO single dose within 3 days of birth.

FORMS - Trade: Tabs 200 mg, susp 50 mg/5 ml.

NOTES - Induces hepatic cytochrome P450 3A. Increase indinavir dose. Monitor for opiate withdrawal in patients receiving methadone and increase methadone dose if needed. Do not give with ketoconazole, hormonal contraceptives, saquinavir, St John's wort.

ANTIMICROBIALS: Antiviral Agents - Anti-HIV – Nucleoside Reverse Transcriptase Inhibitors

NOTE: Consider monitoring LFTs in patients receiving highly active anti-retroviral therapy .

abacavir (*Ziagen,* ABC) ▶L ♀C ▶- $$$$$

WARNING - Potentially fatal hypersensitivity reactions (look for fever, rash, GI symptoms, fatigue, cough, dyspnea, pharyngitis, or other respiratory symptoms). Stop abacavir permanently if symptoms of acute illness can't be clearly differentiated from hypersensitivity reaction. Never restart after a hypersensitivity reaction. More severe symptoms, including life-threatening hypotension and death, will recur within hours. Reactions have occurred after restarting abacavir in patients who did not have a previously recognized hypersensitivity reaction. When considering reintroduction of abacavir, find out why the drug was stopped. Do not restart if hypersensitivity is suspected. Otherwise, restart only with caution and ready access to medical care. Abacavir may cause lactic acidosis with hepatic steatosis.

ADULT - Combination therapy for HIV infection: 300 mg PO bid.

PEDS - Combination therapy for HIV, 3 mo - 16 yo: 8 mg/kg up to 300 mg PO bid.

FORMS - Trade: Tabs 300 mg, oral soln 20 mg/ml.

***Combivir* (lamivudine + zidovudine)** ▶LK ♀C ▶- $$$$$

WARNING - Lactic acidosis with hepatic steatosis. Zidovudine: bone marrow suppression, myopathy.

ADULT - Combination therapy for HIV infection: 1 tab PO bid.

PEDS - Combination therapy for HIV infection, ≥12 yo: 1 tab PO bid.

FORMS - Trade: Tabs lamivudine 150 mg + zidovudine 300 mg.

NOTES - See components. Monitor CBC. Not for patients <50 kg, those with CrCl ≤50 mL/min, or those requiring dosage adjustment.

didanosine (*Videx, Videx EC,* ddl) ▶LK ♀B ◗- $$$$$

WARNING - Potentially fatal pancreatitis; avoid use with other drugs that can cause pancreatitis. Lactic acidosis with hepatic steatosis; fatalities reported in pregnant women receiving didanosine + stavudine.

ADULT - Combination therapy for HIV infection: Buffered tabs: 200 mg PO bid for ≥60 kg, 125 mg PO bid for <60 kg. Use at least 2 (but not >4) tabs per dose to get adequate buffering. Use qd only when less frequent dosing required (may be less effective): 400 mg PO qd for ≥60 kg, 250 mg PO qd for <60 kg. Buffered powder: 250 mg PO bid for ≥60 kg, 167 mg PO bid for <60 kg. Videx EC: 400 mg PO qd for ≥60 kg, 250 mg PO qd for <60 kg. Take all formulations on empty stomach.

PEDS - Combination therapy for HIV infection: 120 mg/m2 PO bid. Give on empty stomach. Give at least 2 buffered tabs (but not >4) per dose to get adequate buffering. Videx EC not approved for children.

UNAPPROVED PEDS - Combination therapy for HIV infection: Infants <3 mo: 50 mg/m2 PO q12h. Usual dose in combo with other antiretrovirals: 90 mg/m2 PO q12h. Dosage range: 90-150 mg/m2 PO q12h (may need higher dose in patients with CNS disease.) Give on empty stomach.

FORMS - Trade: chew/dispersible buffered tabs 25,50,100,150,200 mg, packets of buffered powder for oral soln 100,167,250 mg, pediatric powder for oral soln 10 mg/ml (buffered with antacid). Delayed-release caps (Videx EC) 125,200,250,400 mg.

NOTES - Peripheral neuropathy, retinal changes, optic neuritis, retinal depigmentation in children, hyperuricemia. Diarrhea with buffered powder for oral sol'n. Consider dose reduction if hepatic dysfunction or CrCl <60 ml/min. Tabs contain phenylalanine & 8.6 mEq magnesium/tab. 1380 mg Na/packet of buffered powder. Use caution with other drugs that can cause neuropathy. Do not use with allopurinol. Give some medications at least 1 h (amprenavir, delavirdine, indinavir), 2 h (ciprofloxacin, levofloxacin, ofloxacin, itraconazole, ketoconazole, ritonavir, dapsone, tetracyclines), or 4 h (moxifloxacin, gatifloxacin) before buffered didanosine. Videx EC is not buffered. Pediatric oral sol'n stable in refrigerator for 30 days.

lamivudine (*Epivir, Epivir-HBV,* 3TC, ✤*Heptovir*) ▶K ♀C ◗- $$$$$

WARNING - Lactic acidosis with hepatic steatosis. Lower dose of lamivudine in Epivir-HBV can cause HIV resistance - test for HIV before prescribing Epivir-HBV.

ADULT - Epivir (with zidovudine) for HIV infection: 150 mg PO bid, 2 mg/kg PO bid for adults <50 kg. Epivir-HBV for chronic hepatitis B: 100 mg PO qd.

PEDS - Epivir (with zidovudine) for HIV infection: 3 mo-12 yo, 4 mg/kg up to 150 mg PO bid. 12-16 yo, 150 mg PO bid. Epivir-HBV for chronic hepatitis B not approved in children.

UNAPPROVED ADULT - Use in combination with stavudine.

UNAPPROVED PEDS - Epivir in combination therapy for HIV infection: Infants <30 days, 2 mg/kg PO bid. Children, 4 mg/kg PO bid. Adolescents <50 kg, 2 mg/kg PO bid. Adolescents ≥50 kg, 150 mg PO bid. Epivir-HBV for chronic hepatitis B: 2-12 yo, 3 mg/kg PO qd. 13-17 yo, 100 mg PO qd.

FORMS - Trade: Epivir, 3TC: Tabs 150 mg, oral soln 10 mg/ml. Epivir-HBV, Heptovir. Tabs 100 mg, oral soln 5 mg/ml.

NOTES - In non-HIV infected patients treated for chronic hepatitis B, lamivudine resistance reported and linked to poor treatment response. Hepatitis B resistance also reported in patients with both HIV & hepatitis B infection treated with antiretroviral regimens containing lamivudine. Epivir: Pancreatitis in children. Dosage adjustment in renal dysfunction, adults & >16 yo: 150 mg PO qd for CrCl 30-49 ml/min; 150 mg PO load, then 100 mg PO qd for CrCl 15-29 ml/min; 150 mg PO load, then 50 mg PO qd for CrCl 5-14 ml/min; 50 mg PO load, then 25 mg PO qd for CrCl <5 ml/min. Epivir-HBV: Exacerbation of hepatitis B after discontinuation. Dosing in adults with renal dysfunction: 100 mg PO load, then 50 mg PO qd for CrCl 30-49 ml/min; 100 mg PO load, then 25 mg PO qd for CrCl 15-29 ml/min; 35 mg PO load, then 15 mg PO qd for CrCl 5-14 ml/min; 35 mg PO load, then 10 mg PO qd for CrCl <5 ml/min.

stavudine (*Zerit,* d4T) ▶LK ♀C ◗- $$$$$

WARNING - Lactic acidosis with hepatic steatosis; fatalities reported in pregnant women receiving didanosine + stavudine. Potentially fatal pancreatitis and hepatotoxicity with didanosine + stavudine +/- hydroxyurea.

ADULT - Combination therapy for HIV infection: 40 mg PO q12h, 30 mg PO q12h if <60 kg. Hold for peripheral neuropathy. If symptoms resolve completely, can restart at 20 mg PO

q12h, 15 mg PO q12h if <60 kg.
PEDS - Combination therapy for HIV infection: <30 kg: 1 mg/kg PO bid. 30-59.9 kg: 30 mg bid. ≥60 kg: 40 mg bid.
FORMS - Trade: Caps 15,20,30,40 mg; oral soln 1 mg/ml.
NOTES - Peripheral neuropathy. Do not use with zidovudine. Dosing for adults with renal dysfunction: 20 mg PO q12h for CrCl 26-50 ml/min, 20 mg PO q24h for CrCl 10-25 ml/min. For <60 kg: 15 mg PO q12h for CrCl 26-50 ml/min, 15 mg PO q24h for CrCl 10-25 ml/min. Oral soln stable in refrigerator for 30 days.

***Trizivir* (abacavir + lamivudine + zidovudine)** ▶LK ♀C ▶- $$$$$
WARNING - Lactic acidosis with hepatic steatosis. Abacavir: Life-threatening hypersensitivity reactions (see abacavir entry for details). Never restart after a reaction. Zidovudine: Bone marrow suppression, myopathy.
ADULT - HIV infection: 1 tab PO bid.
PEDS - HIV infection in adolescents ≥40 kg: 1 tab PO bid.
FORMS - Trade: Tabs abacavir 300 mg + lamivudine 150 mg + zidovudine 300 mg.
NOTES - See components. Monitor CBC. Not for patients <40 kg, those with CrCl ≤50 mL/min or those who require dosage adjustment.

zalcitabine (*Hivid,* ddC) ▶K ♀C ▶- $$$$$
WARNING - Peripheral neuropathy, pancreatitis, lactic acidosis with hepatic steatosis, hepatotoxicity.
ADULT - Combination therapy for HIV infection: 0.75 mg PO q8h on an empty stomach.
PEDS - Combination therapy for HIV infection, ≥13 yo: 0.75 mg PO q8h on an empty stomach. Safety and efficacy not established in younger children.
UNAPPROVED PEDS - HIV infection, <13 yo: 0.005-0.01 mg/kg PO q8h. Take on an empty stomach.
FORMS - Trade: Tabs 0.375, 0.75 mg.
NOTES - Monitor amylase, triglycerides if high risk of pancreatitis. Do not give with didanosine, IV pentamidine. Do not give at the same time as magnesium/aluminum antacids. If neuropathy develops, hold zalcitabine. If symptoms resolve, restart at 0.375 mg PO q8h. Dosing in adults with renal dysfunction: 0.75 mg PO q12h for CrCl 10-40 ml/min, 0.75 mg PO q24h for CrCl <10 ml/min.

zidovudine (*Retrovir,* AZT, *azidothymidine,* ZDV) ▶LK ♀C ▶- $$$$$
WARNING - Bone marrow suppression, myopathy, lactic acidosis with hepatic steatosis.
ADULT - Combination therapy for HIV infection: 600 mg/day PO divided bid or tid. IV dosing: 1 mg/kg IV over 1 h 5-6 x/day. Prevention of maternal-fetal HIV transmission, maternal dosing (>14 weeks of pregnancy): 200 mg PO tid or 300 mg PO bid until start of labor. During labor, 2 mg/kg IV over 1 h, then 1 mg/kg/h until delivery.
PEDS - Combination therapy for HIV infection: 3 mo-12 yo - 180 mg/m2 q6h not to exceed 200 mg q6h. Adolescents - 200 mg PO tid or 300 mg PO bid. Prevention of maternal-fetal HIV transmission, infant dosing: 2 mg/kg PO q6h from within 12 h of birth until 6 weeks old. Can also give infants 1.5 mg/kg IV over 30 min q6h.
FORMS - Trade: Cap 100 mg, tab 300 mg, syrup 50 mg/5 ml.
NOTES - Do not use with stavudine. Monitor CBC. Consider holding & reducing dose for hemoglobin <7.5 g/dl or decrease >25% from baseline, or granulocyte count <750/mm3 or decrease >50% from baseline. Peritoneal dialysis or hemodialysis: 100 mg PO q6-8h or 1 mg/kg IV q6-8h.

ANTIMICROBIALS: Antiviral Agents - Anti-HIV - Protease Inhibitors

NOTES: Many serious drug interactions - always check before prescribing! Potential cardiac dysrhythmias with cisapride. Consider monitoring LFTs in patients receiving highly active antiretroviral therapy. Protease inhibitors can cause spontaneous bleeding in hemophiliacs, hyperglycemia, hyperlipidemia, and fat redistribution.

amprenavir (*Agenerase,* APV) ▶L ♀C ▶- $$$$$
WARNING - Oral solution contraindicated in children <4 yo, pregnancy, hepatic/renal failure, therapy with metronidazole/disulfiram due to potential propylene glycol toxicity. Use oral solution only if amprenavir caps or other protease inhibitor can't be used.
ADULT - Combination therapy for HIV infection: 1200 mg PO bid.
PEDS - Combination therapy for HIV infection, caps: 13-16yo, 1200 mg PO bid. 4-12 yo or 13-16yo <50kg, 20 mg/kg PO bid or 15 mg/kg PO tid. Maximum daily dose of 2400 mg. Combination therapy for HIV infection, oral soln: 4-12 yo

or 13-16 yo <50 kg, 22.5 mg/kg PO bid or 17 mg/kg PO tid. Maximum daily dose of 2800 mg.

FORMS - Trade: Caps 50,150 mg, oral soln 15 mg/ml.

NOTES - Life-threatening skin reactions, cross-sensitivity with sulfonamides possible. Contains vitamin E; tell patients not to take more. Inhibits cytochrome P450 3A4. Do not give with bepridil, cisapride, ergot alkaloids, lovastatin, midazolam, rifampin, St John's wort, simvastatin, triazolam. Monitor levels of some antiarrhythmics, tricyclic antidepressants. Monitor INR with warfarin. Reduce rifabutin dose by at least 50% and monitor for neutropenia with weekly and prn CBC. Ritonavir and delavirdine increase amprenavir levels; efavirenz and saquinavir decrease amprenavir levels. May reduce efficacy of hormonal contraceptives. Take at least 1 hour before/after buffered didanosine/antacids. Do not take with high-fat meal. Oral sol'n and caps not interchangeable on mg per mg basis.

indinavir (*Crixivan,* IDV) ▶LK ♀C ▶- $$$$$

ADULT - Combination therapy for HIV infection: 800 mg PO q8h between meals with water (at least 48 oz/day to prevent kidney stones).

PEDS - Not approved in children.

UNAPPROVED ADULT - Combination therapy for HIV infection: 800 mg PO bid with ritonavir 200 mg PO bid.

UNAPPROVED PEDS - Combination therapy for HIV infection, adolescents: 800 mg PO q8h between meals with water (at least 48 oz/day to prevent kidney stones). Children: 350-500 mg/m2/dose (max of 800 mg/dose) PO q8h.

FORMS - Trade: Caps 200,333,400 mg.

NOTES - Nephrolithiasis, hemolytic anemia, possible hepatitis. Inhibitor of cytochrome P450 3A4. Do not give with cisapride, ergot alkaloids, midazolam, pimozide, rifampin, St John's wort, triazolam. Many other drug interactions. Indinavir levels decreased by amprenavir and carbamazepine (consider alternative anticonvulsant). Indinavir may increase risk of myopathy from atorvastatin, lovastatin, simvastatin. Give indinavir and buffered didanosine 1 h apart on empty stomach. Reduce rifabutin dose by 50% and increase indinavir dose to 1000 mg PO q8h when taken together. Reduce indinavir dose to 600 mg PO q8h when given with ketoconazole, itraconazole 200 mg bid, or delavirdine 400 mg tid. Increase indinavir dose to 1000 mg PO q8h when given with efavirenz, nevirapine. For mild to moderate hepatic cirrhosis, give 600 mg PO q8h.

***Kaletra* (lopinavir + ritonavir)** ▶L ♀D ▶- $$$$$

ADULT - Combination therapy for HIV infection: 3 caps or 5 ml PO bid. Consider 4 caps or 6.5 ml PO bid if using efavirenz/nevirapine and reduced susceptibility to lopinavir is suspected. Take with food.

PEDS - Combination therapy for HIV infection, 6 mo - 12 yo: lopinavir 12 mg/kg PO bid for 7-14.9 kg, 10 mg/kg PO bid for 15-40 kg. Do not exceed adult dose. Use adult dose for >12 yo or >40 kg. If using efavirenz/ nevirapine and reduced susceptibility to lopinavir is suspected, consider increasing to 13 mg/kg PO bid for 7-14.9 kg, 11 mg/kg PO bid for 15-45 kg. Do not exceed adult dose. Use adult dose for >12 yo or >45 kg. Take with food.

FORMS - Trade: Caps 133.3 mg lopinavir + 33.3 mg ritonavir. Oral soln 80 mg lopinavir + 20 mg ritonavir/ml.

NOTES - Pancreatitis. Ritonavir (inhibitor of cytochrome P450 3A4 & 2D6) included to inhibit metabolism and boost levels of lopinavir. Do not give Kaletra with drugs that are metabolized by these enzymes if they cause dangerous effects at high levels (cisapride, flecainide, ergot alkaloids, midazolam, pimozide, propafenone, triazolam). Do not give with lovastatin, simvastatin, St John's wort, rifampin. Many other drug interactions including decreased efficacy of oral contraceptives. May reduce methadone levels & require higher methadone dose. Give buffered didanosine 1 h before or 2 h after Kaletra. Do not exceed single 25 mg dose of sildenafil in 48 h. Reduce rifabutin dose to 150 mg PO qod or 3 times/week. Monitor INR with warfarin. Oral sol'n contains alcohol. Use caps/oral sol'n within 2 months if patient stores at room temperature.

nelfinavir (*Viracept,* NFV) ▶L ♀B ▶- $$$$$

ADULT - Combination therapy for HIV infection: 750 mg PO tid or 1250 mg PO bid with meals.

PEDS - Combination therapy for HIV infection, ≥2 yo: 20-30 mg/kg/dose (up to 750 mg) PO tid with meals.

FORMS - Trade: Tab 250 mg, powder 50 mg/g.

NOTES - Diarrhea common. Inhibitor of cytochrome P450 3A4. Many drug interactions. Do not give with amiodarone, cisapride, ergot alkaloids, lovastatin, midazolam, pimozide, quinidine, rifampin, simvastatin, St John's wort, triazolam. Decreases efficacy of oral contraceptives. May reduce methadone levels & require higher methadone dose. Reduce rifabutin dose by 50% when used with nelfinavir (use nelfinavir 1250 mg bid). Give nelfinavir 2 h before/1 h after buffered didanosine. Oral powder stable for 6 h after mixing. Oral powder contains phenylalanine.

ritonavir (*Norvir*, RTV) ▶L ♀B ▶- $$$$$

WARNING - Do not give with most antiarrhythmics, most benzodiazepines, bepridil, bupropion, cisapride, clozapine, ergot alkaloids, meperidine, pimozide, piroxicam, propoxyphene, St John's wort.

ADULT - Combination therapy for HIV infection: Begin 300 mg PO bid with meals, and increase by increments of 100 mg bid every 2-3 days to 600 mg bid. Best tolerated regimen with saquinavir appears to be ritonavir 400 mg PO bid with saquinavir (Fortovase preferred) 400 mg PO bid.

PEDS - Combination therapy for HIV infection: 250 mg/m2 PO q12h, increasing by 50 mg/m2/dose every 2-3 days to 400 mg/m2 PO q12h. Maximum dose is 600 mg PO bid. Give with meals.

UNAPPROVED ADULT - Combination therapy for HIV infection: 200 mg PO bid with indinavir 800 mg PO bid.

FORMS - Trade: Cap 100 mg, oral soln 80 mg/ml.

NOTES - Nausea & vomiting, alterations in AST, ALT, GGT, CPK, uric acid, pancreatitis. Inhibitor of hepatic cytochrome P450 3A & 2D6. Many drug interactions including decreased efficacy of oral contraceptives. May reduce methadone levels & require higher methadone dose. Avoid using with lovastatin or simvastatin. Do not exceed single 25 mg dose of sildenafil in 48 h. Give ritonavir 2.5h before/after buffered didanosine. Reduce rifabutin dose to 150 mg PO qod or 3 times/week. Contains alcohol. Do not refrigerate oral soln. Refrigerate caps if possible, but stable for 30 days at <77 degrees F.

saquinavir (*Fortovase, Invirase*, SQV, *FTV*) ▶L ♀B ▶? $$$$$

ADULT - Combination therapy for HIV infection. Fortovase: 1200 mg PO tid with/after meals. Invirase: 600 mg PO tid within 2 h after meals.

PEDS - Combination therapy for HIV, ≥16 yo. Fortovase: 1200 mg PO tid with/after meals. Invirase: 600 mg PO tid within 2 h after meals. Safety & efficacy not established in younger children.

UNAPPROVED ADULT - Combination therapy for HIV infection: Preferred regimen with ritonavir is 400 mg (Fortovase preferred) PO bid with ritonavir 400 mg PO bid.

UNAPPROVED PEDS - Fortovase, combination therapy for HIV infection: 33 mg/kg PO q8h. Use adult dose in adolescents.

FORMS - Trade: Fortovase (soft gel), Invirase (hard gel) caps 200 mg.

NOTES - Fortovase preferred over Invirase. Do not give with cisapride, ergot derivatives, garlic supplements, midazolam, pimozide, St John's wort, triazolam. Delavirdine increases saquinavir levels. Monitor LFTs if given with delavirdine. Rifampin, nevirapine, and efavirenz significantly lower levels of saquinavir; avoid combo therapy. Rifabutin lowers saquinavir levels; avoid combo unless ritonavir also used. Do not exceed single 25 mg dose of sildenafil in 48 h. Use Fortovase caps within 3 months when stored at room temperature.

ANTIMICROBIALS: Antiviral Agents - Anti-Influenza

NOTES: Whenever possible, immunization is the preferred method of prophylaxis. Consider chemoprophylaxis in high-risk patients vaccinated after influenza activity has begun, care-givers for high-risk patients, patients with immunodeficiency (including HIV infection), and those who request it. Provide chemoprophylaxis to all residents during institutional outbreaks of influenza, continuing for ≥2 weeks or until 1 week after end of outbreak.

amantadine (*Symmetrel*) ▶K ♀C ▶? $

ADULT - Influenza A: 100 mg PO bid. ≥65 yo: 100 mg PO qd.

PEDS - Safety and efficacy not established in infants <1 yo. Influenza A, treatment or prophylaxis, ≥10 yo: 100 mg PO bid.1-9 yo and any child <40 kg: 5 mg/kg/day up to 150 mg/day PO divided bid.

FORMS - Generic: Cap 100 mg. Trade: Tab 100 mg. Generic/Trade: Syrup 50 mg/5 ml.

NOTES - CNS toxicity, suicide attempts, neuroleptic malignant syndrome with dosage reduction/withdrawal, orthostatic hypotension. CNS toxicity increased by concomitant antihistamines or anticholinergics. For influenza prophylaxis, start as soon as possible and continue for ≥10 days after known exposure. For treatment, start within 48 h of symptom onset, continue for 3-5 days or until 24-48 h after signs/sx resolve. Do not stop abruptly in Parkinson's disease. Dosage reduction in adults with renal dysfunction: 200 mg PO 1st day, then 100 mg PO qd for CrCl 30-50 ml/min. 200 mg PO 1st day, then 100 mg PO qod for CrCl 15-29 ml/min. 200 mg PO q week for CrCl <15 ml/min or hemodialysis.

oseltamivir (*Tamiflu*) ▶LK ♀C ▶? $$$

ADULT - Influenza A/B, treatment: 75 mg PO bid x 5 days starting within 2 days of symptom onset. Prophylaxis: 75 mg PO qd. Start within 2 days of exposure and continue for ≥ 7 days.

PEDS - Influenza A/B treatment ≥1 yo: 30 mg PO bid for ≤15 kg, 45 mg PO bid for 16-23 kg, 60 mg PO bid for 24-40 kg, 75 mg PO bid for >40 kg or ≥13 yo. Treat for 5 days starting within 2 days of symptom onset. Prophylaxis ≥13 yo: 75 mg PO qd. Start within 2 days of exposure and continue for ≥ 7 days.

FORMS - Trade: Caps 75 mg, susp 12 mg/ml.

NOTES - Patients with suspected influenza may have primary/ concomitant bacterial pneumonia. Antibiotics may be indicated. Dosage adjustment for CrCl 10-30 ml/min: 75 mg PO qd x 5 days for treatment, 75 mg PO qod for prophylaxis. Susp stable for 10 days at room temperature.

rimantadine (*Flumadine*) ▶LK ♀C ▶- $$

ADULT - Prophylaxis/treatment of influenza A: 100 mg PO bid. Start treatment within 48 h of symptom onset and continue x 7 days. Consider dosage reduction to 100 mg/day if side effects in patients >65 yo.

PEDS - Prophylaxis of influenza A, ≥10 yo: 100 mg PO bid. 1-9 yo or any child <40 kg: 5 mg/kg/day up to 150 mg/day PO divided qd or bid.

FORMS - Trade: Tabs 100 mg, syrup 50 mg/5 ml.

NOTES - CDC recommends treatment for 3-5 days or until 24-48 h after signs/sx resolve. Reduce dose to 100 mg qd if severe hepatic dysfunction, CrCl ≤10 ml/min, elderly nursing home patients.

zanamivir (*Relenza*) ▶K ♀C ▶? $$

ADULT - Influenza A/B, treatment: 2 puffs bid x 5 days. Take 2 doses on day 1 at least 2 h apart. Start within 2 days of symptom onset.

PEDS - Influenza A/B, treatment, ≥7 yo: 2 puffs bid x 5 days. Take 2 doses on day 1 at least 2 h apart. Start within 2 days of symptom onset. Not approved in children <7 yo.

UNAPPROVED ADULT - Influenza A/B, prophylaxis: 2 puffs qd.

FORMS - Trade: Rotadisk inhaler 5 mg/puff (20 puffs).

NOTES - May cause bronchospasm & worsening pulmonary function in patients with asthma or chronic obstructive pulmonary disease; not generally recommended for patients with underlying airways disease. Discontinue zanamivir in any patient who develops bronchospasm/decline in respiratory function. Patients with suspected influenza may have primary/ concomitant bacterial pneumonia. Antibiotics may be indicated. Instruct patient how to use inhaler.

ANTIMICROBIALS: Antiviral Agents - Other

interferon alfa-2b (*Intron A*) ▶K? ♀C ▶? $$$$$

ADULT - Chronic hepatitis B: 5 million units/day or 10 million units 3 times/week SC/IM x 16 weeks. Chronic hepatitis C: 3 million units SC/IM 3 times/week x 16 weeks. Continue for 18-24 mo if ALT normalized. Other indications: condylomata acuminata, AIDS-related Kaposi's sarcoma.

PEDS - Not approved in children.

FORMS - Trade: Powder/sol'n for injection 3,5, 10 million units/vial. Sol'n for injection 18,25 million units/multidose vial. Multidose injection pens 3,5,10 million units/dose (6 doses/pen).

NOTES - Depression, suicidal behavior, thyroid abnormalities, hepatotoxicity, flu-like sx, pulmonary & cardiovascular reactions, retinal damage, neutropenia, thrombocytopenia. Increases theophylline levels. Monitor CBC, TSH, LFTs, electrolytes. For severe adverse effects, reduce dose/hold until resolved. In chronic hepatitis B, reduce dose by 50% for granulocytes <750/mm3 or platelets <50,000/ mm3. Hold for granulocytes <500/mm3 or platelets <30,000/mm3. Give SC for platelets <50,000/mm3.

interferon alfacon-1 (*Infergen*) ▶Plasma ♀C ▶? $$$$$

ADULT - Chronic hepatitis C: 9 mcg SC 3 times/week for 24 weeks. Increase to 15 mcg SC 3 times/week x 24 weeks for relapse/no response to 9 mcg dose. Reduce to 7.5 mcg SC 3 times/week for intolerable adverse effects with 9 mcg dose.

PEDS - Not approved in children.
FORMS - Trade: Vials injectable soln 9,15 mcg.
NOTES - Depression, suicidal behavior, thyroid abnormalities, cardiovascular reactions, retinal damage, flu-like symptoms, thrombocytopenia, neutropenia, exacerbation of autoimmune disorders. Refrigerate injectable soln.

palivizumab (*Synagis*) ▶L ♀C ▶? $$$$$
ADULT - None
PEDS - Prevention of respiratory syncytial virus pulmonary disease in high-risk patients: 15 mg/kg IM q month during RSV season with first injection before season starts (November to April in northern hemisphere). Consider for children <2 yo treated for chronic lung disease in last 6 mo; infants born <28 wk gestation who are now <12 mo; infants born 29-32 wk gestation who are now <6 mo.
NOTES - Preservative-free - use within 6 h of reconstitution. Not more than 1 ml per injection site.

peginterferon alfa-2b (*PEG-Intron*) ▶K? ♀C ▶- $$$$$
WARNING - May cause or aggravate serious neuropsychiatric, autoimmune, ischemic, & infectious diseases. Frequent clinical & lab monitoring recommended. Discontinue if signs/sx of these conditions are persistently severe or worsen.
ADULT - Chronic hepatitis C in patients without previous alpha interferon treatment. Give SC once weekly for 1 year. Pickdose and vial strength based on weight. Monotherapy: 1 mcg/kg/week. ≤45 kg: 40 mcg (0.4 ml, 50 mcg/0.5 ml vial). 46-56 kg: 50 mcg (0.5 ml, 50 mcg/0.5 ml vial). 57-72 kg: 64 mcg (0.4 ml, 80 mcg/0.5 ml vial). 73-88 kg: 80 mcg (0.5 ml, 80 mcg/0.5 ml vial). 89-106 kg: 96 mcg (0.4 ml, 120 mcg/0.5 ml vial). 107-136 kg: 120 mcg (0.5 ml, 120 mcg/0.5 ml vial). 137-160 kg: 150 mcg (0.5 ml, 150 mcg/0.5 ml vial). Combo therapy with oral ribavirin (see Rebetol entry): 1.5 mcg/kg/week. <40 kg: 50 mcg (0.5 ml, 50 mcg/0.5 ml vial). 40-50 kg: 64 mcg (0.4 ml, 80 mcg/0.5 ml vial). 51-60 kg: 80 mcg (0.5 ml, 80 mcg/0.5 ml vial). 61-75 kg: 96 mcg (0.4 ml, 120 mcg/0.5 ml vial). 76-85 kg: 120 mcg (0.5 ml, 120 mcg/0.5 ml vial). >95 kg: 150 mcg (0.5 ml, 150 mcg/0.5 ml vial). Give at bedtime or with antipyretic to minimize flu-like sx. Consider stopping treatment if HCV RNA is not below limit of detection after 24 weeks of therapy.
PEDS - Not approved in children.
FORMS - Trade: 50,80,120,150 mcg/0.5 ml single-use vials with diluent, 2 syringes, and alcohol swabs.
NOTES - Monitor for depression, suicidal behavior, other severe neuropsychiatric effects. Thrombocytopenia, neutropenia, thyroid dysfunction, hyperglycemia, cardiovascular events, ulcerative & hemorrhagic colitis, pancreatitis, hypersensitivity reactions, flu-like sx, pulmonary & retinal damage. Use cautiously if CrCl <50 ml/min. Monitor CBC, blood chemistry. Baseline EKG in patients with cardiac disease. Baseline eye exam in patients with diabetes/ HTN. Maintain hydration, esp. early in therapy. For severe adverse effects, reduce dose by 50% or hold until resolved. Discontinue if reaction recurs or persists. Reduce dose if neutrophils <750/mm3 or platelets <80,000/mm3. Stop if neutrophils <500/mm3 or platelets <50,000/mm3. Peginterferon should be used immediately after reconstitution, but can be refrigerated for up to 24 h.

***Rebetron* (interferon alfa-2b + ribavirin)** ▶K ♀X ▶- $$$$$
WARNING - Teratogenic. Contraindicated in pregnant women or their male partners. Female patients and female partners of male patients must avoid pregnancy by using 2 forms of birth control during and for 6 months after discontinuation of ribavirin. Obtain pregnancy test at baseline and monthly.
ADULT - Chronic hepatitis C: Interferon alfa-2b 3 million units SC 3 times/week and ribavirin (Rebetol) 600 mg PO bid if >75 kg; 400 mg q am and 600 q pm if ≤75 kg. Get CBC at baseline, weeks 2 & 4, then as needed. Reduce ribavirin to 200 mg q am and 400 mg q pm if hemoglobin <10 g/dl. Stop if hemoglobin <8.5 g/dl. In stable cardiovascular disease, reduce to 600 mg/day if hemoglobin drops ≥2 g/dl over 4 weeks. Stop if hemoglobin <12 g/dl 4 weeks after dosage reduction. Experts recommend 48 weeks of treatment for genotype 1 if HCV RNA negative at 24 weeks. Stop treatment if HCV RNA positive at 24 weeks. Treat other genotypes for 24 weeks.
PEDS - Not approved in children.
FORMS - Trade: Each kit contains 2-week supply of interferon alfa-2b, ribavirin caps 200 mg.
NOTES - Interferon alfa-2b: Depression, suicidal behavior, thyroid abnormalities, flu-like symptoms, pulmonary reactions, retinal damage, hypersensitivity reactions, exacerbation of autoimmune disorders/psoriasis. Give SC for platelets <50,000/mm3. Ribavirin: Hemolytic anemia. Do not use ribavirin in significant/ unstable heart disease.

ribavirin - inhaled (*Virazole*) ▶Lung ♀X ▶- $$$$$

WARNING - Beware of sudden pulmonary deterioration with ribavirin. Drug precipitation may cause ventilator dysfunction.

ADULT - None.

PEDS - Severe respiratory syncytial virus infection: Aerosol 12-18 hours/day x 3-7 days.

NOTES - Minimize exposure to health care workers, especially pregnant women.

ribavirin - oral (*Rebetol*) ▶Cellular, K ♀X ▶- $$$$$

WARNING - Teratogenic. Contraindicated in pregnant women or their male partners. Female patients and female partners of male patients must avoid pregnancy by using 2 forms of birth control during and for 6 months after discontinuation of ribavirin. Obtain pregnancy test at baseline and monthly. Hemolytic anemia that may worsen cardiac disease. Do not use in significant/ unstable heart disease. Baseline ECG for patients with pre-existing cardiac abnormalities.

ADULT - Chronic hepatitis C. In combo with interferon alfa-2b: 600 mg PO bid if >75 kg; 400 mg q am and 600 mg q pm if ≤75 kg. Get CBC at baseline, weeks 2 & 4, and prn. Reduce ribavirin to 200 mg q am and 400 mg q pm if hemoglobin <10 g/dl. Stop if hemoglobin <8.5 g/dl. In stable cardiovascular disease, reduce to 600 mg/day if hemoglobin drops ≥2 g/dl over 4 weeks. Stop if hemoglobin <12 g/dl 4 weeks after dosage reduction. In combo with peginterferon alfa 2b: 400 mg PO bid. Get CBC at baseline, weeks 2 & 4, and prn. Reduce dose by 200 mg/day if hemoglobin <10 g/dl. Stop if hemoglobin <8.5 g/dl. In stable cardiovascular disease, reduce by 200 mg/day if hemoglobin drops ≥2 g/dl over 4 weeks. Stop if hemoglobin <12 g/dl after lower dose.

PEDS - Not approved in children.

FORMS - Trade: Caps 200 mg.

NOTES - Not for use with peginterferon if CrCl <50 ml/min.

OVERVIEW OF BACTERIAL PATHOGENS (selected)

Gram Positive Aerobic Cocci: *Staph epidermidis* (coagulase negative), *Staph aureus* (coagulase positive), Streptococci: *S pneumoniae* (pneumococcus), *S pyogenes* (Group A), *S agalactiae* (Group B), enterococcus

Gram Positive Aerobic / Facultatively Anaerobic Bacilli: *Bacillus, Corynebacterium diphtheriae, Erysipelothrix rhusiopathiae, Listeria monocytogenes, Nocardia*

Gram Negative Aerobic Diplococci: *Moraxella catarrhalis, Neisseria gonorrhoeae, Neisseria meningitidis*

Gram Negative Aerobic Coccobacilli: *Haemophilus ducreyi, Haemophilus influenzae*

Gram Negative Aerobic Bacilli: *Acinetobacter, Bartonella* species, *Bordetella pertussis, Brucella, Burkholderia cepacia, Campylobacter, Francisella tularensis, Helicobacter pylori, Legionella pneumophila, Pseudomonas aeruginosa, Stenotrophomonas maltophilia, Vibrio cholerae, Yersinia*

Gram Negative Facultatively Anaerobic Bacilli: *Aeromonas hydrophila, Eikenella corrodens, Pasteurella multocida,* Enterobacteriaceae: *E coli, Citrobacter, Salmonella, Shigella, Klebsiella, Enterobacter, Hafnia, Serratia, Proteus, Providencia*

Anaerobes: *Actinomyces, Bacteroides fragilis, Clostridium botulinum, Clostridium difficile, Clostridium perfringens, Clostridium tetani, Fusobacterium, Lactobacillus, Peptostreptococcus*

Defective Cell Wall Bacteria: *Chlamydia pneumoniae, Chlamydia psittaci, Chlamydia trachomatis, Coxiella burnetii, Myocoplasma pneumoniae, Rickettsia prowazekii, Rickettsia rickettsii, Rickettsia typhi, Ureaplasma urealyticum*

Spirochetes: *Borrelia burgdorferi, Leptospira, Treponema pallidum*

Mycobacteria: *M avium complex, M kansasii, M leprae, M tuberculosis*

ANTIMICROBIALS: Carbapenems

imipenem-cilastatin (*Primaxin*) ▶K ♀C ▶? $$$$$

ADULT - Pneumonia, sepsis, endocarditis, polymicrobic, intra-abdominal, gynecologic, bone & joint, skin infections. Normal renal function, ≥70 kg - Mild infection: 250-500 mg IV q6h. Moderate infection: 500 mg IV q6-8h or 1 g IV q8h. Severe infection: 500 mg IV q6h to 1 g IV q6-8h. Complicated UTI: 500 mg IV q6h. See product labeling for doses in adults <70 kg. Can give up to 1.5 g/day IM for mild/moderate infections.

PEDS - Pneumonia, sepsis, endocarditis, polymicrobic, intra-abdominal, bone & joint, skin infections. age >3 mo: 15-25 mg/kg IV q6h. 1-3 mo: 25 mg/kg IV q6h. 1-4 weeks old: 25 mg/kg IV q8h. <1 week old: 25 mg/kg IV q12h. Not for children with CNS infections, or <30 kg with renal dysfunction.

UNAPPROVED ADULT - Malignant otitis externa, empiric therapy for neutropenic fever: 500 mg IV q6h.

NOTES - Possible cross-sensitivity with other beta-lactams, pseudomembranous colitis, superinfection, seizures (especially if given with ganciclovir, elderly with renal dysfunction, or cerebrovascular or seizure disorder). See product labeling for dose if CrCl <70 ml/min. Not for CrCl <5 ml/min unless dialysis started within 48 h.

meropenem (*Merrem IV*) ▶K ♀B ◗? $$$$$

ADULT - Intra-abdominal infections: 1 g IV q8h.

PEDS - Meningitis: age ≥3 mo, 40 mg/kg/dose IV q8h. >50 kg, 2 g IV q8h. Intra-abdominal infection: age ≥3 mo, 20 mg/kg/dose IV q8h. >50 kg, 1 g IV q8h.

UNAPPROVED ADULT - Meningitis: 40 mg/kg (up to max of 2 g) IV q 8h. Hospital-acquired pneumonia, complicated UTI, malignant otitis externa: 1 g IV q8h.

NOTES - Possible cross-sensitivity with other beta-lactams; pseudomembranous colitis; superinfection; seizures; thrombocytopenia in renal dysfunction. May reduce valproic acid levels to subtherapeutic range. For adults with renal dysfunction: 1 g IV q12h for CrCl 26-50 ml/min, 500 mg IV q12h for CrCl 10-25 ml/min, 500 mg IV q24h for CrCl <10 ml/min.

ANTIMICROBIALS: Cephalosporins - 1st Generation

cefadroxil (*Duricef*) ▶K ♀B ◗+ $$$

ADULT - Simple UTI: 1-2 g/day PO divided qd-bid. Other UTIs: 1 g PO bid. Skin infections: 1 g/day PO divided qd-bid. Group A streptococcal pharyngitis (second-line to penicillin): 1 g/day PO divided qd-bid x 10 days. See table for prophylaxis of bacterial endocarditis.

PEDS - UTIs, skin infections: 30 mg/kg/day PO divided bid. Group A streptococcal pharyngitis/tonsillitis (second-line to penicillin), impetigo: 30 mg/kg/day PO divided qd-bid. Treat streptococcal pharyngitis for 10 days.

FORMS - Generic/Trade: Tabs 1000 mg, caps 500 mg. Trade: Susp 125,250, & 500 mg/5 ml.

NOTES - Cross-sensitivity with penicillins possible, pseudomembranous colitis. Renal dysfunction in adults: 1 g load, then 500 mg PO q12h for CrCl 25-50 ml/min, 500 mg PO q24h for CrCl 10-25 ml/min, 500 mg PO q36h for CrCl <10 ml/min.

cefazolin (*Ancef, Kefzol*) ▶K ♀B ◗+ $$$

ADULT - Pneumonia, sepsis, endocarditis, skin, bone & joint, genital infections. Mild infections due to gram-positive cocci: 250-500 mg IM/IV q8h. Moderate/severe infections: 0.5-1 g IM/IV q6-8h. Life-threatening infections: 1-1.5 g IV q6h. Simple UTI: 1 g IM/IV q12h. Pneumococcal pneumonia: 500 mg IM/IV q12h. Surgical prophylaxis: 1 g IM/IV 30-60 min preop, additional 0.5-1 g during surgery >2h, and 0.5-1 g q6-8h x 24h postop. See table for prophylaxis of bacterial endocarditis.

PEDS - Pneumonia, sepsis, endocarditis, skin, bone & joint infections. Mild/moderate infections, age ≥1 mo: 25-50 mg/kg/day IM/IV divided q6-8h. Severe infections, age ≥1 mo: 100 mg/kg/day IV divided q6-8h. See table for prophylaxis of bacterial endocarditis.

NOTES - Cross-sensitivity with penicillins possible, pseudomembranous colitis. Renal dysfunction in adults: Usual 1st dose, then usual dose q8h for CrCl 35-54 ml/min, 50% of usual dose q12h for CrCl 11-34 ml/min, 50% of usual dose q18-24h for CrCl <10 ml/min. Renal dysfunction in children: Usual 1st dose, then 60% of usual dose q12h for CrCl 40-70 ml/min, 25% of usual dose q12h for 20-40 ml/min, 10% of usual dose q24h for CrCl 5-20 ml/min.

cephalexin (*Keflex, Keftab*) ▶K ♀B ◗? $

ADULT - Pneumonia, bone, GU infections. Usual dose: 250-500 mg PO qid. Maximum dose: 4g/day. Group A streptococcal pharyngitis (second-line to penicillin), skin infections, simple UTI: 500 mg PO bid. Treat streptococcal pharyngitis for 10 days. See table for prophylaxis of bacterial endocarditis.

PEDS - Pneumonia, GU, bone, skin infections, group A streptococcal pharyngitis (second-line to penicillin). Usual dose: 25-50 mg/kg/day PO in divided doses. Max dose: 100 mg/kg/day. Can give bid for streptococcal pharyngitis in children >1 yo, skin infections. Group A strep-

tococcal pharyngitis, skin infections, simple UTI in patients >15 yo: 500 mg PO bid. Treat streptococcal pharyngitis for 10 days. Not for otitis media and sinusitis.
FORMS - Generic/Trade: Caps 250,500 mg, tabs 250,500 mg, susp 125 & 250 mg/5 ml. Keftab: 500 mg.
NOTES - Cross-sensitivity with penicillins possible, pseudomembranous colitis.

ANTIMICROBIALS: Cephalosporins - 2nd Generation

cefaclor (*Ceclor*) ▶K ♀B ◗? $$$
ADULT - Otitis media, pneumonia, group A streptococcal pharyngitis (second-line to penicillin), UTI, skin infections: 250-500 mg PO tid. Ceclor CD: Acute exacerbation of chronic bronchitis, secondary bacterial infection of acute bronchitis: 500 mg PO bid with food. Group A streptococcal pharyngitis, skin infections: 375 mg PO bid with food. Treat streptococcal pharyngitis for 10 days.
PEDS - Pneumonia, group A streptococcal pharyngitis (second-line to penicillin), UTI, skin infections: 20-40 mg/kg/day up to 1 g/day PO divided bid for pharyngitis, tid for other infections. Treat streptococcal pharyngitis x 10d. Otitis media: 40 mg/kg/day PO divided bid.
FORMS - Generic/Trade: Caps 250,500 mg, susp 125,187,250,375 mg/5 ml. Trade: Extended release (Ceclor CD) 375,500 mg.
NOTES - Serum sickness-like reactions with repeated use, cross-sensitivity with penicillins possible, pseudomembranous colitis. Do not give Ceclor CD within 1 h of antacids. CDC recommends 10 days of therapy for otitis media if <2 yo and 5-7 days if ≥2 yo. Poor activity against penicillin-nonsusceptible pneumococci.

cefotetan (*Cefotan*) ▶K/Bile ♀B ◗? $$$$$
ADULT - Usual dose: 1-2 g IM/IV q12h. UTI: 0.5-2 g IM/IV q12h or 1-2 g IM/IV q24h. Pneumonia, gynecologic, intra-abdominal, bone & joint infections: 1-3 g IM/IV q12h. Skin infections: 1-2 g IM/IV q12h or 2 g IV q24h. Surgical prophylaxis: 1-2 g IV 30-60 min preop. Give after cord clamp for C-section.
PEDS - Not approved in children.
UNAPPROVED PEDS - Usual dose: 40-80 mg/kg/day IV divided q12h.
NOTES - Cross-sensitivity with penicillins possible, pseudomembranous colitis, hemolytic anemia, clotting impairment rarely. Disulfiram-like reaction with alcohol. Dosing reduction in adults with renal dysfunction: Usual dose q24h for CrCl 10-30 ml/min, usual dose q48h for CrCl <10 ml/min.

cefoxitin (*Mefoxin*) ▶K ♀B ◗+ $$$$$
ADULT - Pneumonia, UTI, sepsis, intra-abdominal, gynecologic, skin, bone & joint infections: Uncomplicated, 1 g IV q6-8h. Moderate to severe, 1 g IV q4h or 2 g IV q6-8h. Infections requiring high doses, 2 g IV q4h or 3 g IV q6h. Uncontaminated gastrointestinal surgery, vaginal/abdominal hysterectomy: 2 g IV 30-60 min preop, then 2 g IV q6h x 24h. C-section: 2 g IV after cord clamped or 2 g IV q4h x 3 doses with 1st dose given after cord clamped.
PEDS - Pneumonia, UTI, sepsis, intra-abdominal, skin, bone & joint infections, age ≥3 mo: 80-160 mg/kg/day IV divided into 4-6 doses, not to exceed 12 g/day. Surgical prophylaxis: 30-40 mg/kg IV 30-60 min preop and for not more than 24h postop.
NOTES - Eosinophilia & increased AST with high doses in children, cross-sensitivity with penicillins possible, pseudo-membranous colitis. Dosing reduction in adults with renal dysfunction: Load with 1-2 g IV; then 1-2 g IV q8-12h for CrCl 30-50 ml/min, 1-2 g IV q12-24h for CrCl 10-29 ml/min, 0.5-1 g IV q12-24h for CrCl 5-9 ml/min, 0.5 g IV q24-48h for CrCl <5 ml/min. Give 1-2 g loading dose after each hemodialysis.

cefprozil (*Cefzil*) ▶K ♀B ◗+ $$$
ADULT - Group A streptococcal pharyngitis (second-line to penicillin): 500 mg PO qd x 10 days. Sinusitis: 250-500 mg PO bid. Acute exacerbation of chronic/secondary infection of acute bronchitis: 500 mg PO bid. Skin infections: 250-500 mg PO bid or 500 mg PO qd.
PEDS - Otitis media: 15 mg/kg/dose PO bid. Group A streptococcal pharyngitis (second-line to penicillin): 7.5 mg/kg/dose PO bid x 10 days. Sinusitis: 7.5-15 mg/kg/dose PO bid. Skin infections: 20 mg/kg PO qd. Use adult dose for ≥13 yo.
FORMS - Trade: Tabs 250,500 mg, susp 125 & 250 mg/5 ml.
NOTES - Cross-sensitivity with penicillins possible, pseudomembranous colitis. CDC recommends 10 days of therapy for otitis media if <2 yo and 5-7 days if ≥2 yo. Oral susp contains phenylalanine. Give 50% of usual dose at usual interval for CrCl <30 ml/min.

CEPHALOSPORINS – GENERAL ANTIMICROBIAL SPECTRUM

1st generation: gram positive (including Staph aureus); basic gram negative coverage
2nd generation: diminished Staph aureus, improved gram negative coverage compared to 1st generation; some with anaerobic coverage
3rd generation: further diminished Staph aureus, further improved gram negative coverage compared to 1st & 2nd generation; some with Pseudomonal coverage & diminished streptococcal coverage
4th generation: same as 3rd generation plus coverage against Pseudomonas & Staph aureus

cefuroxime (*Zinacef, Ceftin*, ✱*Kefurox*) ▸K ♀B ◗? $$$

ADULT - IM/IV cefuroxime. Uncomplicated pneumonia, simple UTI, skin infections, disseminated gonorrhea: 750 mg IM/IV q8h. Bone & joint, or severe/complicated infections: 1.5 g IV q8h. Sepsis: 1.5 g IV q6h to 3 g IV q8h. Gonorrhea: 1.5 g IM single dose split into 2 injections, given with probenecid 1 g PO. Surgical prophylaxis: 1.5 g IV 30-60 min preop, then 750 mg IM/IV q8h for prolonged procedures. Open heart surgery: 1.5 g IV q12h x 4 with 1st dose at induction of anesthesia. Cefuroxime axetil tabs. Group A streptococcal pharyngitis (second-line to penicillin), acute sinusitis: 250 mg PO bid x 10 days. Acute exacerbation of chronic/secondary infection of acute bronchitis, skin infections: 250-500 mg PO bid. Early Lyme disease: 500 mg PO bid x 20 days. Simple UTI: 125-250 mg PO bid. Gonorrhea: 1 g PO single dose.

PEDS - IM/IV cefuroxime. Most infections: 50-100 mg/kg/day IM/IV divided q6-8h. Bone & joint infections: 150 mg/kg/day IM/IV divided q8h not to exceed maximum adult dose. Cefuroxime axetil tabs. Group A streptococcal pharyngitis (second-line to penicillin): 125 mg PO bid x 10 days. Otitis media, sinusitis: 250 mg PO bid x 10 days. Cefuroxime axetil oral susp. Group A streptococcal pharyngitis: 20 mg/kg/day (up to 500 mg/day) PO divided bid x 10 days. Otitis media, sinusitis, impetigo: 30 mg/kg/day (up to 1 g/day) PO divided bid x 10 days. Use adult dose for ≥13 yo.

UNAPPROVED PEDS - Early lyme disease: 30 mg/kg/day PO divided bid (max 500 mg/dose).

FORMS - Trade: Tabs 125,250,500 mg, susp 125 & 250 mg/5 ml.

NOTES - Cross-sensitivity with penicillins possible, pseudomembranous colitis. CDC recommends 10 days of therapy for otitis media if <2 yo and 5-7 days if ≥2 yo. Dosage adjustment for renal dysfunction in adults: 750 mg IM/IV q12h for CrCl 10-20 ml/min, 750 mg IM/IV q24h for CrCl <10 ml/min. Give supplemental dose after hemodialysis. Tabs & susp not bioequivalent on mg/mg basis. Do not crush tabs.

loracarbef (*Lorabid*) ▸K ♀B ◗? $$$

ADULT - Acute exacerbation of chronic bronchitis, pneumonia, sinusitis, uncomplicated pyelonephritis: 400 mg PO bid. Secondary infection of acute bronchitis: 200-400 mg PO bid. Group A streptococcal pharyngitis (second-line to penicillin): 200 mg PO bid x 10 days. Skin infections: 200 mg PO bid. Simple UTI: 200 mg PO qd. Take on empty stomach.

PEDS - Otitis media, sinusitis: 30 mg/kg/day PO divided bid. Use susp for otitis media. Group A streptococcal pharyngitis (second-line to penicillin), impetigo: 15 mg/kg/day up to 500 mg/day PO divided bid. Treat pharyngitis for 10 days. Use adult dose for ≥13 yo. Take on empty stomach.

FORMS - Trade: Caps 200,400 mg, susp 100 & 200 mg/5 ml.

NOTES - Cross-sensitivity with penicillins possible, pseudomembranous colitis. CDC recommends 10 days of therapy for otitis media if <2 yo and 5-7 days if ≥2 yo. Poor activity against penicillin-nonsusceptible pneumococci. Dosing in renal dysfunction: 50% of recommended dose at usual interval or full recommended dose at twice the usual interval for CrCl 10-49 ml/min, give recommended dose q3-5 days for CrCl <10 ml/min. Give supplemental dose following hemodialysis.

ANTIMICROBIALS: Cephalosporins – 3rd Generation

cefdinir (*Omnicef*) ▸K ♀B ◗? $$$

ADULT - Community-acquired pneumonia, skin infections: 300 mg PO bid x 10 days. Sinusitis: 600 mg PO qd or 300 mg PO bid x 10 days. Group A streptococcal pharyngitis (second-line to penicillin), acute exacerbation of chronic bronchitis,: 600 mg PO qd x 10 days or 300 mg PO bid x 5-10 days.

PEDS - Group A streptococcal pharyngitis (second-line to penicillin), otitis media: 14 mg/kg/

day PO divided bid x 5-10 days or qd x 10 d. Sinusitis: 14 mg/kg/day PO divided qd-bid x 10 days. Skin infections: 14 mg/kg/day PO divided bid x 10 days. Use adult dose for ≥13 yo.

FORMS - Trade: Cap 300 mg, susp 125 mg/5 ml.

NOTES - Cross-sensitivity with penicillins possible, pseudomembranous colitis. CDC recommends 10 days of therapy for otitis media if <2 yo and 5-7 days if ≥2 yo. Take 2 h before/after antacids/iron supplements. Dosage reduction for renal dysfunction: 300 mg PO qd for adults with CrCl <30 ml/min. 7 mg/kg/day PO qd up to 300 mg/day for children with CrCl <30 ml/min. Hemodialysis: 300 mg or 7 mg/kg PO after hemodialysis, then 300 mg or 7 mg/kg PO qod.

cefixime (*Suprax*) ▶K/Bile ♀B ◗? $$$

ADULT - Simple UTI, group A streptococcal pharyngitis (second-line to penicillin), acute bacterial bronchitis, acute exacerbation of chronic bronchitis: 400 mg PO qd or 200 mg PO bid. Gonorrhea: 400 mg PO single dose.

PEDS - Otitis media: 8 mg/kg/day susp PO divided qd-bid. Group A streptococcal pharyngitis (second-line to penicillin): 8 mg/kg/day PO divided qd-bid x 10 days. Use adult dose for >50 kg or ≥13 yo.

UNAPPROVED PEDS - Febrile UTI (3-24 mo): 16 mg/kg PO on first day, then 8 mg/kg PO qd to complete 14 days. Gonorrhea: 8 mg/kg (max 400 mg) PO single dose for <45 kg, 400 mg PO single dose for ≥45 kg.

FORMS - Trade: Tabs 200,400 mg, susp 100 mg/5 ml.

NOTES - Cross-sensitivity with penicillins possible, pseudomembranous colitis. CDC recommends 10 days of therapy for otitis media if <2 yo and 5-7 days if ≥2 yo. Less effective than amoxicillin for pneumococcal otitis media. Poor activity against penicillin-nonsusceptible pneumococci and S aureus. Susp stable at room temp or refrigerated x 14 days. Dosing in renal dysfunction: 75% of usual dose at usual interval for CrCl 21-60 ml/min or hemodialysis. 50% of usual dose at usual interval for CrCl <20 ml/min or continuous peritoneal dialysis.

cefoperazone (*Cefobid*) ▶Bile/K ♀B ◗? $$$$$

ADULT - Peritonitis, sepsis, respiratory, intra-abdominal, skin infections, endometritis, pelvic inflammatory disease & other gynecologic infections: Usual dose 2-4 g/day IV divided q12h. Infections with less sensitive organisms/severe infections: 6-12 g/day IV divided q6-12h. Use q6h for Pseudomonas infections. 1-2 g doses can be given IM.

PEDS - Not approved in children.

UNAPPROVED PEDS - Mild to moderate infections, age ≥1 mo: 100-150 mg/kg/day IM/IV divided q8-12h.

NOTES - Cross-sensitivity with penicillins possible, pseudomembranous colitis, possible clotting impairment. Disulfiram-like reaction with alcohol. Not for meningitis.

cefotaxime (*Claforan*) ▶KL ♀B ◗+ $$$$$

ADULT - Pneumonia, sepsis, GU & gynecologic, skin, intra-abdominal, bone & joint infections: Uncomplicated, 1 g IM/IV q12h. Moderate/severe, 1-2 g IM/IV q8h. Infections usually requiring high doses, 2 g IV q6-8h. Life-threatening, 2 g IV q4h. Meningitis: 2g IV q4-6h. Gonorrhea: 0.5-1 g IM single dose.

PEDS - Neonates, ≤1 week old: 50 mg/kg/dose IV q12h. 1-4 weeks old: 50 mg/kg/dose IV q8h. Pneumonia, sepsis, GU, skin, intra-abdominal, bone/joint, CNS infections, 1 mo-12 yo: 50-180 mg/kg/day IM/IV divided q4-6h. AAP recommends 225-300 mg/kg/day IV divided q6-8h for S pneumoniae meningitis.

NOTES - Cross-sensitivity with penicillins possible, pseudomembranous colitis, arrhythmias with bolus injection through central venous catheter. Decrease dose by 50% for CrCl <20 ml/min.

cefpodoxime (*Vantin*) ▶K ♀B ◗? $$$

ADULT - Community-acquired pneumonia, acute exacerbation of chronic bronchitis: 200 mg PO bid. Group A streptococcal pharyngitis (second-line to penicillin): 100 mg PO bid x 5-10 days. Skin infections: 400 mg PO bid. Simple UTI: 100 mg PO bid. Gonorrhea: 200 mg PO single dose. Give tabs with food.

PEDS - Otitis media: 10 mg/kg/day PO divided bid/qd. Group A streptococcal pharyngitis (second-line to penicillin): 10 mg/kg/day divided bid x 5-10 days. Use adult dose for >13 yo.

FORMS - Trade: Tabs 100,200 mg, susp 50 & 100 mg/5 ml.

NOTES - Cross-sensitivity with penicillins possible, pseudomembranous colitis. CDC recommends 10 days of therapy for otitis media if <2 yo and 5-7 days if ≥ 2 yo. Do not give antacids within 2 h before/after cefpodoxime. Dosing in renal dysfunction: Increase dosing interval to q24h for CrCl <30 ml/min. Give 3 times/week after dialysis for hemodialysis patients. Susp stable for 14 days refrigerated.

ceftazidime (*Ceptaz, Fortaz, Tazidime, Tazicef*) ▶K ♀B ◗+ $$$$$

ADULT - Simple UTI: 250 mg IM/IV q12h. Complicated UTI: 500 mg IM/IV q8-12h. Uncomplicated pneumonia, mild skin infections: 500 mg - 1g IM/IV q8h. Serious gynecologic, intra-abdominal, bone & joint, life-threatening infections, meningitis, empiric therapy of neutropenic fever: 2 g IV q8h. Pseudomonas lung infections in cystic fibrosis: 30-50 mg/kg IV q8h to max of 6 g/day.

PEDS - Use sodium formulations in children (Fortaz, Tazidime, Tazicef). UTIs, pneumonia, skin, intra-abdominal, bone & joint infections, 1 mo - 12 yo: 100-150 mg/kg/day IV divided q8h to max of 6 g/day. Meningitis, 1 mo - 12 yo: 150 mg/kg/day IV divided q8h to max of 6 g/day. Infants up to 4 weeks old: 30 mg/kg IV q12h. Use adult dose & formulations if ≥12 yo.

UNAPPROVED ADULT - P aeruginosa osteomyelitis of the foot from nail puncture: 2 g IV q8h.

UNAPPROVED PEDS - AAP dosing for infants >2 kg: 50 mg/kg IV q8-12h for <1 week old, q8h for ≥1 week old.

NOTES - Cross-sensitivity with penicillins possible, pseudomembranous colitis. Elevated levels in renal impairment can cause CNS toxicity. Dosing in adults with renal dysfunction: 1 g IV q12h for CrCl 31-50 ml/min; 1 g q24h for CrCl 16-30 ml/min; load with 1 g, then 500 mg q24h for CrCl 6-15 ml/min; load with 1 g, then 500 mg q48h for CrCl <5 ml/min. Load with 1 g IV in hemodialysis patients, then 1 g IV after each hemodialysis session. Continuous ambulatory peritoneal dialysis: 1 g IV load, then 500 mg q24h.

ceftibuten (*Cedax*) ▶K ♀B ▶? $$$

ADULT - Acute exacerbation of chronic bronchitis, otitis media not due to S pneumoniae, group A streptococcal pharyngitis (second-line to penicillin): 400 mg PO qd x 10 days.

PEDS - Otitis media not due to S pneumoniae, group A streptococcal pharyngitis (second-line to penicillin), age >6 mo: 9 mg/kg up to 400 mg PO qd. Give susp on empty stomach.

FORMS - Trade: Cap 400 mg, susp 90 & 180 mg/5 ml.

NOTES - Cross-sensitivity with penicillins possible, pseudomembranous colitis. CDC recommends 10 days of therapy for otitis media if <2 yo and 5-7 days if ≥2 yo. Poor activity against S aureus and S pneumoniae. Dosing in adults with renal dysfunction: 200 mg PO qd for CrCl 30-49 ml/min, 100 mg PO qd for CrCl 5-29 ml/min. Dosing in children with renal dysfunction: 4.5 mg/kg PO qd for CrCl 30-49 ml/min, 2.25 mg/kg PO qd for CrCl 5-29 ml/min. Hemodialysis: adults 400 mg PO and children 9 mg/kg PO after each dialysis session. Susp stable for 14 days refrigerated.

ceftizoxime (*Cefizox*) ▶K ♀B ▶? $$$$$

ADULT - Simple UTI: 500 mg IM/IV q12h. Pneumonia, sepsis, intra-abdominal, skin, bone & joint infections: 1-2 g IM/IV q8-12h. Pelvic inflammatory disease: 2 g IV q8h. Life-threatening infections: 3-4 g IV q8h. Gonorrhea: 1 g IM single dose. Split 2 g IM dose into 2 injections.

PEDS - Pneumonia, sepsis, intra-abdominal, skin, bone & joint infections, age ≥6 mo: 50 mg/kg/dose IV q6-8h. Up to 200 mg/kg/day for serious infections, not to exceed max adult dose.

NOTES - Cross-sensitivity with penicillins possible; pseudomembranous colitis; transient rise in eosinophils, ALT, AST, CPK in children. Not for meningitis. Dosing in adults with renal dysfunction: For less severe infection load with 500 mg - 1 g IM/IV, then 500 mg q8h for CrCl 50-79 ml/min, 250-500 mg q12h for CrCl 5-49 ml/min, 500 mg q48h or 250 mg q24h for hemodialysis. For life-threatening infection, give loading dose, then 750 mg - 1.5 g IV q8h for CrCl 50-79 ml/min, 500 mg - 1 g q12h for CrCl 5-49 ml/min, 500 mg - 1 g q48h or 500 mg q24h for hemodialysis. For hemodialysis patients, give dose at end of dialysis.

ceftriaxone (*Rocephin*) ▶K/Bile ♀B ▶+ $$$$$

ADULT - Pneumonia, UTI, pelvic inflammatory disease (hospitalized), sepsis, meningitis, skin, bone & joint, intra-abdominal infections: Usual dose 1-2 g IM/IV q24h (max 4 g/day divided q12h). Gonorrhea: single dose 125 mg IM (250 mg if ambulatory treatment of PID).

PEDS - Meningitis: 100 mg/kg/day (max 4 g/day) IV divided q12-24h. Skin, pneumonia, other serious infections: 50-75 mg/kg/day (max 2 g/day) IM/IV divided q12-24h. Otitis media: 50 mg/kg (max 1 g) IM single dose.

UNAPPROVED ADULT - Lyme disease carditis, arthritis, meningitis: 2 g IV qd. Chancroid: 250 mg IM single dose. Disseminated gonorrhea: 1 g IM/IV q24h.

UNAPPROVED PEDS - Refractory otitis media (no response after 3 days of antibiotics): 50 mg/kg IM q24h x 3 doses. Lyme disease carditis, arthritis, meningitis: 75-100 mg/kg IM/IV qd (max 2 g/day). Prophylaxis, invasive meningococcal disease: Single IM dose of 125 mg for ≤12 yo, 250 mg for >12 yo. Gonorrhea: 125 mg IM single dose. Gonococcal bacteremia: If <45 kg give 50 mg/kg (up to 1 g) IM/IV qd x 7 days, if ≥45 kg give 50 mg/kg (up to 2 g) IM/IV qd x

10-14 days. Gonococcal ophthalmia neonatorum/ gonorrhea prophylaxis in newborn: 25-50 mg/kg up to 125 mg IM/IV single dose at birth. Disseminated gonorrhea, infants: 25-50 mg/kg/day IM/IV qd x 7 days. Typhoid fever: 50-75 mg/kg IM/IV qd x 14 days.

NOTES - Possible cross-sensitivity with penicillins, pseudomembranous colitis, prolonged prothrombin time due to vitamin K deficiency, biliary sludging/symptoms of gallbladder disease. Do not give to neonates with hyperbilirubinemia. Dilute in 1% lidocaine for IM use. Do not exceed 2 g/day in patients with both hepatic & renal dysfunction.

SEXUALLY TRANSMITTED DISEASES & VAGINITIS*

Bacterial vaginosis: 1) metronidazole 5 g of 0.75% gel intravaginally bid or qhs for 5 days. 2) clindamycin 5 g of 2% cream intravaginally qhs for 7 days. 3) metronidazole 500 mg PO bid for 7 days or extended-release 750 mg PO qd for 7 days. In pregnancy (2nd or 3rd trimesters): metronidazole 250 mg PO tid for 7 days.

Candidal vaginitis: 1) intravaginal clotrimazole, miconazole, terconazole, nystatin, tioconazole, or butoconazole. 2) fluconazole 150 mg PO single dose.

Chancroid: 1) azithromycin 1 g PO single dose. 2) ceftriaxone 250 mg IM single dose.

Chlamydia: 1) azithromycin 1 g PO single dose. 2) doxycycline 100 mg PO bid for 7days. 3) ofloxacin 300 mg PO bid for 7 days. 4) erythromycin base 500 mg PO qid for 7 days.

Chlamydia (in pregnancy): 1) erythromycin base 500 mg PO qid for 7 days or 250 mg PO qid for 14 days. 2) amoxicillin 500 mg PO tid for 7 days. 3) azithromycin 1 g PO single dose.

Epididymitis: 1) ceftriaxone 250 mg IM single dose + doxycycline 100 mg PO bid x 10 days. 2) ofloxacin 300 mg PO bid x 10 days if enteric organisms suspected or cephalosporin/doxycycline allergic.

Gonorrhea: 1) ceftriaxone 125 mg IM single dose. 2) cefixime 400 mg PO single dose. 3) ciprofloxacin 500 mg PO single dose. 4) ofloxacin 400 mg PO single dose. Treat chlamydia empirically. Rapid cephalosporin desensitization (with expert consultation) advised for cephalosporin-allergic pregnant women. Due to high resistance rates, quinolones not recommended for use in Hawaii or for infections acquired in Asia or the Pacific. Azithromycin 2 g PO single dose is a potential alternative. Observe patients for >=30 minutes after the dose for GI side effects.

Gonorrhea, disseminated: Initially treat with ceftriaxone 1 g IM/IV q24h until 24-48 h after improvement. Alternatives if β-lactam allergic: 1) ciprofloxacin 500 mg IV q12h. 2) ofloxacin 400 mg IV q12h. Complete 1 week of treatment with 1) cefixime 400 mg PO bid. 2) ciprofloxacin 500 mg PO bid. 3) ofloxacin 400 mg PO bid.

Gonorrhea, meningitis: ceftriaxone 1-2 g IV q12h for 10-14 days.

Gonorrhea, endocarditis: ceftriaxone 1-2 g IV q12h for at least 4 weeks.

Granuloma inguinale: 1) trimethoprim-sulfamethoxazole 1 double-strength tab PO bid for at least 3 weeks. 2) doxycycline 100 mg PO bid for at least 3 weeks.

Herpes simplex (genital, first episode): 1) acyclovir 400 mg PO tid for 7-10 days. 2) famciclovir 250 PO tid for 7-10 days. 3) valacyclovir 1 g PO bid for 7-10 days.

Herpes simplex (genital, recurrent): 1) acyclovir 400 mg PO tid for 5 days. 2) famciclovir 125 mg PO bid for 5 days. 3) valacyclovir 500 mg PO bid for 5 days.

Herpes simplex (suppressive therapy): 1) acyclovir 400mg PO bid. 2) famciclovir 250 mg PO bid. 3) valacyclovir 250 mg PO bid (250 mg tab not available; split 500 mg tab) or 500-1000 mg PO qd.

Lymphogranuloma venereum: 1) doxycycline 100 mg PO bid for 21 days. 2) erythromycin base 500 mg PO qid for 21 days.

Pelvic inflammatory disease (PID), inpatient regimens: 1) cefotetan 2 g IV q12h/ cefoxitin 2 g IV q6h + doxycycline 100 mg IV/PO q12h. 2) clindamycin 900 mg IV q8h + gentamicin 2 mg/kg IM/IV loading dose, then 1.5 mg/kg IM/IV q8h (See gentamicin entry for alternative qd dosing). Can switch to PO therapy within 24 h of improvement.

Pelvic inflammatory disease (PID), outpatient treatment: 1) ceftriaxone 250 mg IM + doxycycline 100 mg PO bid for 14 days. 2) ofloxacin 400 mg PO bid + metronidazole 500 mg PO bid for 14 days.

Proctitis, proctocolitis, enteritis: ceftriaxone 125 mg IM single dose + doxycycline 100 mg PO bid x7d.

Sexual assault prophylaxis: ceftriaxone 125 mg IM single dose + metronidazole 2 g PO single dose + azithromycin 1 g PO single dose/doxycycline 100 mg PO bid for 7 days.

Syphilis (primary and secondary): 1) benzathine penicillin 2.4 million units IM single dose. 2) doxycycline 100 mg PO bid for 2 weeks if penicillin allergic.

SEXUALLY TRANSMITTED DISEASES & VAGINITIS, cont'd*

Syphilis (early latent, i.e. duration <1 y): 1) benzathine penicillin 2.4 million units IM single dose. 2) doxycycline 100 mg PO bid for 2 weeks if penicillin allergic.
Syphilis (late latent or unknown duration): 1) benzathine penicillin 2.4 million units IM q week for 3 doses. 2) doxycycline 100 mg PO bid for 4 weeks if penicillin allergic.
Syphilis (tertiary): 1) benzathine penicillin 2.4 million units IM q week for 3 doses. 2) doxycycline 100 mg PO bid for 4 weeks if penicillin allergic.
Syphilis (neuro): 1) penicillin G 3-4 million units IV q4h for 10-14 days. 2) procaine penicillin 2.4 million units IM qd + probenecid 500 mg PO qid, both for 10-14 days.
Syphilis in pregnancy: Treat only with penicillin regimen for stage of syphilis as noted above. Use penicillin desensitization protocol if penicillin-allergic.
Trichomonal vaginitis: metronidazole 2 g PO single dose or 500 mg bid for 7days. Can use 2 g single dose in pregnant women.
Urethritis, Cervicitis: Test for chlamydia and gonorrhea. Treat based on test results or treat for both if testing not available or if patient unlikely to return for follow-up.
Urethritis (persistent/recurrent): 1) metronidazole 2 g PO single dose + erythromycin base 500 mg PO qid for 7 days.

* *MMWR 1998; 47* or http://www.ama-assn.org/special/std/treatmnt/guide/stdgd98/stdgd98.htm
http:www.cdc.gov/std/specshortage.htm
Treat sexual partners for all except herpes, candida, and bacterial vaginosis.

ANTIMICROBIALS: Cephalosporins - 4th Generation

cefepime (*Maxipime*) ▶K ♀B ▶? $$$$$
ADULT - Mild, moderate UTI: 0.5-1 g IM/IV q12h. Severe UTI, complicated intra-abdominal, skin infections: 2 g IV q12h. Pneumonia: 1-2 g IV q12h. Empiric therapy of febrile neutropenia: 2 g IV q8h.
PEDS - UTI, skin infections, pneumonia, ≤40 kg: 50 mg/kg IV q12h. Empiric therapy for febrile neutropenia, ≤40 kg: 50 mg/kg IV q8h. Do not exceed adult dose.
UNAPPROVED ADULT - P aeruginosa osteomyelitis of the foot from nail puncture: 2 g IV q12h.
NOTES - Cross-sensitivity with penicillins possible, pseudomembranous colitis. Elevated levels in renal impairment can cause CNS toxicity. Refer to product labeling for dosing if CrCl <60 ml/min.

ANTIMICROBIALS: Macrolides

azithromycin (*Zithromax*) ▶L ♀B ▶? $$
ADULT - Community-acquired pneumonia: 500 mg IV over 1 h qd x at least 2 days, then 500 mg PO qd x 7-10 days total. Pelvic inflammatory disease: 500 mg IV qd x 1-2 days, then 250 mg PO qd x 7 days total. Oral for acute exacerbation of chronic bronchitis, community-acquired pneumonia, group A streptococcal pharyngitis (second-line to penicillin), skin infections: 500 mg PO on 1st day, then 250 mg PO qd x 5 days total. Chlamydia, chancroid: 1 g PO single dose. Gonorrhea: 2 g PO single dose. Observe patient for ≥30 minutes for poor GI tolerability. Mycobacterium avium complex prevention: 1200 mg PO q week.
PEDS - Oral for otitis media, community-acquired pneumonia: 10 mg/kg up to 500 mg PO on 1st day, then 5 mg/kg up to 250 mg qd to complete 5 days. Group A streptococcal pharyngitis (2nd line to penicillin): 12 mg/kg up to 500 mg PO qd x 5 days. Take susp on empty stomach.
UNAPPROVED ADULT - See table for prophylaxis of bacterial endocarditis. Nongonococcal urethritis: 1 g PO single dose. Campylobacter gastroenteritis: 500 mg PO qd x 3 days. Traveler's diarrhea: 500 mg PO on 1st day, then 250 mg PO qd x 5 days total; or 1 g PO single dose. Mycobacterium avium complex treatment in AIDS: 500 mg PO qd. Two or more drugs are needed for the treatment of active mycobacterial infections. Legionaires' disease: 1000 mg IV/PO on 1st day, then 500 mg IV/PO qd.
UNAPPROVED PEDS - Mycobacterium avium complex prevention: 20 mg/kg PO q week not

to exceed adult dose. Mycobacterium avium complex treatment: 5 mg/kg PO qd. Two or more drugs are needed for the treatment of active mycobacterial infections. Chlamydia trachomatis: 20 mg/kg (max of 1 g) PO single dose for <45 kg, 1 g PO single dose for ≥45 kg. Pertussis: 10 mg/kg/day PO x 5 days. See table for bacterial endocarditis prophylaxis.

FORMS - Trade: Tab 250,600 mg, packet 1000 mg, susp 100 & 200 mg/5 ml. Z-Pak: #6, 250 mg tabs.

NOTES - Severe allergic/skin reactions rarely, IV site reactions, hearing loss with prolonged use. Does not inhibit cytochrome P450 enzymes. Do not take at the same time as Al/Mg antacids. Contraindicated with pimozide.

clarithromycin (*Biaxin, Biaxin XL*) ▶KL ♀C ▶? $$$

ADULT - Group A streptococcal pharyngitis (second-line to penicillin): 250 mg PO bid x 10 days. Acute sinusitis: 500 mg PO bid x 14 days. Acute exacerbation of chronic bronchitis (S pneumoniae/M catarrhalis), pneumonia, skin infections: 250 mg PO bid x 7-14 days. Acute exacerbation of chronic bronchitis (H influenzae): 500 mg PO bid x 7-14 days. H pylori: See table in GI section. Mycobacterium avium complex prevention/ treatment: 500 mg PO bid. Two or more drugs are needed for the treatment of active mycobacterial infections. Biaxin XL: Acute sinusitis: 1000 mg PO qd x 14 days. Acute exacerbation of chronic bronchitis, community-acquired pneumonia: 1000 mg PO qd x 7 days. Take Biaxin XL with food.

PEDS - Group A streptococcal pharyngitis (2nd line to penicillin), pneumonia, sinusitis, otitis media, skin infections: 7.5 mg/kg PO bid x 10 days. Mycobacterium avium complex prevention/treatment: 7.5 mg/kg PO bid up to 500 mg bid. Two or more drugs are needed for the treatment of active mycobacterial infections.

UNAPPROVED ADULT - See table for prophylaxis of bacterial endocarditis. Pertussis: 500 mg PO bid x 7 days.

UNAPPROVED PEDS - See endocarditis prophylaxis table. Pertussis: 7.5 mg/kg PO bid x 5-7 days. Prophylaxis of pertussis in household contacts: 7.5 mg/kg PO bid x 14 days.

FORMS - Trade: Tab 250,500 mg, susp 125 & 250 mg/5 ml; Extended release (Biaxin XL) 500 mg. Biaxin XL-Pak: #14, 500 mg tabs.

NOTES - Rare arrhythmias in patients with prolonged QT. Cytochrome P450 3A4 & 1A2 inhibitor. Contraindicated w/ cisapride, pimozide. Many drug interactions including increased levels of carbamazepine, cyclosporine, digoxin, disopyramide, lovastatin, simvastatin, tacrolimus, & theophylline. Ergot toxicity with ergotamine/dihydroergotamine. Monitor INR with warfarin. CDC recommends 10 days of therapy for otitis media if <2 yo and 5-7 days if ≥2 yo. Dosage reduction for renal insufficiency patients taking ritonavir: Decrease by 50% for CrCl 30-60 ml/min, decrease by 75% for CrCl <30 ml/min. Do not refrigerate susp.

dirithromycin (*Dynabac*) ▶L ♀C ▶? $$$

ADULT - 500 mg PO qd x 5-7 days for acute exacerbation of chronic bronchitis and skin infections, x 7 days for secondary infection of acute bronchitis, x 10 days for group A streptococcal pharyngitis (second-line to penicillin), and x 14 days for community-acquired pneumonia. Take with food or within 1 h of eating.

PEDS - Not approved in children <12 yo.

FORMS - Trade: Tab 250 mg.

NOTES - Serum levels are inadequate for treatment of bacteremia.

erythromycin base (*Eryc, E-mycin*) ▶L ♀B ▶+ $

ADULT - Respiratory, skin infections: 250-500 mg PO qid or 333 mg PO tid. Mycoplasma pneumonia, pertussis: 500 mg PO q6h. S aureus skin infections: 250 mg PO q6h or 500 mg PO q12h. Secondary prevention of rheumatic fever: 250 mg PO bid. Nongonococcal urethritis, chlamydia in pregnancy: 500 mg PO qid x 7 days or 250 mg PO qid x 14 days if high dose not tolerated. Erythrasma: 250 mg PO tid x 21 days. Legionnaires' disease: 2 g/day PO in divided doses x 14-21 days.

PEDS - Usual dose: 30-50 mg/kg/day PO divided qid x 10 days. Can double dose for severe infections. Pertussis: 40-50 mg/kg/day PO divided qid x 14 days. Chlamydia, newborn - <45 kg: 50 mg/kg/day PO divided qid x 10-14 days.

UNAPPROVED ADULT - Chancroid: 500 mg PO qid x 7 days.

FORMS - Generic/Trade: Tab 250, 333, 500 mg, delayed-release cap 250.

NOTES - Rare arrhythmias in patients with prolonged QT. May aggravate myasthenia gravis. Cytochrome P450 3A4 & 1A2 inhibitor. Many drug interactions including increased levels of carbamazepine, cyclosporine, digoxin, disopyramide, tacrolimus, theophylline, some benzodiazepines and statins. Monitor INR with warfarin. Increased vinblastine toxicity. Contraindicated with cisapride, pimozide, sparfloxacin.

erythromycin estolate ▶L ♀B ▶+ $

WARNING - Hepatotoxicity, primarily in adults.

ADULT - Usual dose: 250 mg PO qid. Secondary prevention of rheumatic fever: 250 mg PO bid. Chlamydia (except during pregnancy): 500 mg PO qid x 7 days or 250 mg PO qid x 14 days for patients who can't tolerate higher dose. Legionnaires' disease: 2 g/day in divided doses x 14-21 days.

PEDS - Usual dose: 30-50 mg/kg/day PO divided bid-qid. Can double for severe infections. Group A streptococcal pharyngitis: 20-40 mg/kg/day PO divided bid to qid x 10d. Secondary prevention of rheumatic fever: 250 mg PO bid. Pertussis: 40-50 mg/kg/day PO divided qid x 14 days.

FORMS - Generic/Trade: Caps 250 mg, susp 125 & 250 mg/5 ml.

NOTES - Contraindicated in liver disease. Rare arrhythmias in patients with prolonged QT. May aggravate myasthenia gravis. Cytochrome 450 3A4 & 1A2 inhibitor. Many drug interactions including increased levels of carbamazepine, cyclosporine, digoxin, disopyramide, tacrolimus, theophylline, some benzodiazepines and statins. Monitor INR with warfarin. Increased vinblastine toxicity. Contraindicated with cisapride, pimozide, sparfloxacin.

erythromycin ethyl succinate (*EES*) ▶L ♀B ▶+ $

ADULT - Usual dose: 400 mg PO qid. Nongonococcal urethritis, chlamydia in pregnancy: 800 mg PO qid x 7 days or 400 mg PO qid x 14 days if high dose not tolerated. Secondary prevention of rheumatic fever: 400 mg PO bid. Legionnaires' disease: 3.2 g/day PO in divided doses x 14-21 days.

PEDS - Usual dose: 30-50 mg/kg/day PO divided qid. Maximum dose: 100 mg/kg/day. Group A streptococcal pharyngitis: 40 mg/kg/day PO divided bid to qid x 10 days. Secondary prevention of rheumatic fever: 400 mg PO bid. Pertussis: 40-50 mg/kg/day up to 2 g/day PO divided qid x 14 days.

FORMS - Generic/Trade: Tab 400 tab, susp 200 & 400 mg/5 ml. Trade: Chew tab 200 tab.

NOTES - Rare arrhythmias in patients with prolonged QT. May aggravate myasthenia gravis. Cytochrome P450 3A4 & 1A2 inhibitor. Many drug interactions including increased levels of carbamazepine, cyclosporine, digoxin, disopyramide, tacrolimus, theophylline, some benzodiazepines and statins. Monitor INR with warfarin. Increased vinblastine toxicity. Contraindicated with cisapride, pimozide, sparfloxacin.

erythromycin lactobionate, ✤***Erythrocin*** ▶L ♀B ▶+ $$$$$

ADULT - For severe infections/PO not possible: 15-20 mg/kg/day (max 4g) IV divided q6h. Legionnaires' disease: 4 g/day IV divided q6h.

PEDS - For severe infections/PO not possible: 15-20 mg/kg/day (max 4g) IV divided q6h.

UNAPPROVED PEDS - 20-50 mg/kg/day IV divided q6h.

NOTES - Dilute and give slowly to minimize venous irritation. Reversible hearing loss with high doses, allergic reactions, arrhythmias in patients with prolonged QT, exacerbation of myasthenia gravis. Cytochrome P450 3A4 & 1A2 inhibitor. Many drug interactions including increased levels of carbamazepine, cyclosporine, digoxin, disopyramide, tacrolimus, theophylline, some benzodiazepines and statins. Monitor INR with warfarin. Increased vinblastine toxicity. Contraindicated with cisapride, pimozide, sparfloxacin.

***Pediazole* (erythromycin ethyl succinate + sulfisoxazole)** ▶KL ♀C ▶- $

ADULT - None

PEDS - Otitis media, age >2 mo: 50 mg/kg/day (based on EES dose) PO divided tid-qid.

FORMS - Generic/Trade: Susp, erythromycin ethyl succinate 200 mg + sulfisox 600 mg/5 ml.

NOTES - Sulfisoxazole: Stevens-Johnson syndrome, toxic epidermal necrolysis, hepatotoxicity, blood dyscrasia, hemolysis in G6PD deficiency. Increased INR with warfarin. Erythromycin: Rare arrhythmias in patients with prolonged QT. May aggravate myasthenia gravis. Cytochrome P450 3A4 & 1A2 inhibitor. Many drug interactions including increased levels of carbamazepine, cyclosporine, digoxin, disopyramide, tacrolimus, theophylline, some benzodiazepines and statins. Monitor INR with warfarin. Increased vinblastine toxicity. Contraindicated with cisapride, pimozide, sparfloxacin. CDC recommends 10 days of therapy for otitis media if <2 yo and 5-7 days if ≥2 yo.

ANTIMICROBIALS: Penicillins - 1st generation - Natural

benzathine penicillin (*Bicillin L-A*) ▶K ♀B ▶? $

ADULT - Group A streptococcal pharyngitis: 1.2 million units IM single dose. Prevention of rheumatic fever: 1.2 million units IM q month or 600,000 units IM q 2 weeks. Primary, secondary, early latent syphilis: 2.4 million units IM single dose. Tertiary, late latent syphilis: 2.4 million units IM q week x 3 doses.

PEDS - Group A streptococcal pharyngitis: <27 kg, 300,000-600,000 units IM single dose. ≥ 27 kg, 900,000 units IM single dose. Prevention of rheumatic fever: 1.2 million units IM q month or 600,000 units IM q 2 weeks. Primary, secondary, early latent syphilis: 50,000 units/kg (up to 2.4 million units) IM single dose. Late latent syphilis: 50,000 units/kg (up to 2.4 million units) IM x 3 weekly doses.

UNAPPROVED ADULT - Prophylaxis of diphtheria/treatment of carriers: 1.2 million units IM single dose.

UNAPPROVED PEDS - Prophylaxis of diphtheria/treatment of carriers: 1.2 million units IM single dose for ≥30 kg or ≥6 yo. 600,000 units IM single dose for <30 kg or <6 yo.

NOTES - Anaphylaxis rarely, cross-sensitivity with cephalosporins possible. Do not give IV. Doses last 2-4 wks. Not for neurosyphilis.

benzylpenicilloyl polylysine (*Pre-Pen*) ▸K ♀? ◗? $

ADULT - Skin testing for penicillin allergy: 1 drop in needle scratch, then 0.01-0.02 ml intradermally if no reaction.

PEDS - Not approved in children.

NOTES - Systemic allergic reactions; do not test if known to be highly sensitive to penicillin.

***Bicillin CR* (procaine and benzathine penicillin)** ▸K ♀B ◗? $

ADULT - Scarlet fever, erysipelas, upper-respiratory, skin and soft-tissue infections due to Group A strep: 2.4 million units IM single dose. Pneumococcal infections other than meningitis: 1.2 million units IM q2-3 days until temperature normal for 48 h.

PEDS - Scarlet fever, erysipelas, upper-respiratory, skin & soft-tissue infections due to Group A strep: 2.4 million units IM for >27 kg, 900,000-1.2 million units IM for 13.6-27 kg, 600,000 units IM for <13.6 kg. Pneumococcal infections other than meningitis: 600,000 units IM q2-3 days until temperature normal for 48 h.

FORMS - Trade: for IM use in mixes of 1.2/1.2 million, 300/300, 600/600, 300/900 thousand units procaine/benzathine penicillin.

NOTES - Contraindicated if hypersensitive to procaine. Anaphylaxis rarely, cross-sensitivity with cephalosporins possible. Do not give IV.

penicillin G ▸K ♀B ◗? $$$

ADULT - Penicillin-sensitive pneumococcal pneumonia: 8-12 million units/day IV divided q4-6h. Penicillin-sensitive pneumococcal meningitis: 24 million units/day IV divided q2-4h. Enterococcal endocarditis: 18-30 million units/day by IV continuous infusion or divided q4h for ≥4-6 weeks with gentamicin or streptomycin. Penicillin-sensitive viridans streptococci/S bovis endocarditis: 12-18 million units/day by IV continuous infusion or divided q4h x 4 weeks alone or 2 weeks with gentamicin. Neurosyphilis: 3-4 million units IV q4h x10-14 d. See http://jama.ama-assn.org/issues/v281n18/pdf/jst80027.pdf for anthrax bioterrorism dosing.

PEDS - Mild to moderate infections: 25,000-50,000 units/kg/day IV divided q6h. Severe infections: 250,000-400,000 units/kg/day IV divided q4-6h. Neonates <1 week, >2 kg: 25,000 units/kg IV q8h. Neonates ≥1 week, >2 kg: 25,000 units/kg IV q6h. Group B streptococcal meningitis: ≤7 days old, 250,000-450,000 units/kg/d IV divided q8h. >7 days old, 450,000 units/kg/d IV divided q6h. Congenital syphilis: 50,000 units/kg/dose IV q12h during first 7 days of life, then q8h thereafter x 10d total.

UNAPPROVED ADULT - Prevention of perinatal group B streptococcal disease: Give to mother 5 million units IV at onset of labor/after membrane rupture, then 2.5 million units IV q4h until delivery. Diphtheria: 100,000-150,000 units/kg/day IV divided q6h x 14 days.

UNAPPROVED PEDS - Diphtheria: 100,000-150,000 units/kg/day IV divided q6h x 14 days.

NOTES - Anaphylaxis rarely, cross-sensitivity with cephalosporins possible. 2 mEq sodium/million units of penicillin G sodium. 1.7 mEq potassium & 0.3 mEq sodium/million units of penicillin G potassium. Decrease dose by 50% if CrCl <10 ml/min.

penicillin V (*Pen-Vee K, Veetids*, ✤*Ledercillin VK*) ▸K ♀B ◗? $

ADULT - Usual dose: 250-500 mg PO qid. AHA dosing for group A streptococcal pharyngitis: 500 mg PO bid or tid x 10 days. Secondary prevention of rheumatic fever: 250 mg PO bid. Vincent's infection: 250 mg PO q6-8h.

PEDS - Usual dose: 25-50 mg/kg/day PO divided tid or qid. Use adult dose for ≥12 yo. AHA dosing for group A streptococcal pharyngitis: 250 mg PO bid or tid x 10 days. Secondary prevention of rheumatic fever: 250 mg PO bid.

UNAPPROVED PEDS - Prevention of pneumococcal infections in functional/anatomic asplenia: 125 mg PO bid for <5 yo, 250 mg PO bid for ≥5 yo.

FORMS - Generic/Trade: Tabs 250,500 mg, oral

soln 125 & 250 mg/5 ml.
NOTES - Anaphylaxis rarely, cross-sensitivity with cephalosporins possible. Oral soln stable in refrigerator for 14 days.

procaine penicillin (*Wycillin*) ▶K ♀B ◗? $
ADULT - Pneumococcal & streptococcal infections, Vincent's infection, erysipeloid: 0.6-1.0 million units IM qd. Neurosyphilis: 2.4 million units IM qd plus probenecid 500 mg PO q6h, both for 10-14 days.
PEDS - Pneumococcal & streptococcal infections, Vincent's infection, erysipeloid, <27 kg: 300,000 units IM qd. AAP dose for mild-to-moderate infections, >1 mo: 25,000-50,000 units/kg/day IM divided qd-bid. Congenital syphilis: 50,000 units/kg IM qd x 10 days.
NOTES - Peak 4h, lasts 24h. Contraindicated if procaine allergy; skin test if allergy suspected. Anaphylaxis rarely, cross-sensitivity with cephalosporins possible, transient CNS reactions with high doses.

ANTIMICROBIALS: Penicillins - 2nd generation - Penicillinase-Resistant

cloxacillin, ✤*Orbenin* ▶KL ♀B ◗? $
ADULT - Staph infections: 250-500 mg PO qid on empty stomach.
PEDS - Staph infections: 50-100 mg/kg/day PO divided q6h on empty stomach. Use adult dose for ≥20 kg.
FORMS - Generic: Caps 250,500 mg, oral soln 125 mg/5 ml.
NOTES - Anaphylaxis rarely, cross-sensitivity with cephalosporins possible. Oral soln stable in refrigerator for 14 days.

dicloxacillin (*Dynapen*) ▶KL ♀B ◗? $
ADULT - Mild to moderate upper respiratory, skin & soft-tissue infections: 125 mg PO qid. Pneumonia, disseminated infections: 250-500 mg PO qid. Take on empty stomach.
PEDS - Mild to moderate upper respiratory, skin & soft-tissue infections, age >1 mo: 12.5 mg/kg/day PO divided qid. Pneumonia, disseminated infections, age >1 mo: 25 mg/kg/day PO divided qid. Follow-up therapy after IV antibiotics for staph osteomyelitis: 50-100 mg/kg/day PO divided qid. Use adult dose for ≥40 kg. Give on empty stomach.
FORMS - Generic/Trade: Caps 250,500 mg. Trade: Susp 62.5 mg/5 ml.
NOTES - Anaphylaxis rarely, cross-sensitivity with cephalosporins possible. Oral susp stable at room temperature for 7d, in refrigerator 14d.

nafcillin (*Nallpen*) ▶L ♀B ◗? $$$$
ADULT - Staph infections, usual dose: 500 mg IM q4-6h or 500-2000 mg IV q4h. Osteomyelitis: 1-2 g IV q4h. Methicillin-susceptible staph endocarditis: 2 g IV q4h x 4-6 weeks or longer.
PEDS - Not approved for IV use. Staph infections, usual dose: Neonates, 10 mg/kg IM q12h. <40 kg, 25 mg/kg IM q12h.
UNAPPROVED PEDS - Mild to moderate infections: 50-100 mg/kg/day IM/IV divided q6h. Severe infections: 100-200 mg/kg/day IM/IV divided q4-6h. Neonates <1 week, >2 kg: 25 mg/kg IM/IV q8h. Neonates ≥1 week, >2 kg: 25-35 mg/kg IM/IV q6h.
NOTES - Anaphylaxis rarely, cross-sensitivity with cephalosporins possible. Reversible neutropenia with prolonged use. Decreased INR with warfarin. Decreased cyclosporine levels.

oxacillin (*Bactocill*) ▶KL ♀B ◗? $
ADULT - Staph infections: 500-1000 mg PO q4-6h or 250 mg-2g IM/IV q4-6h. Osteomyelitis: 1.5-2 g IV q4h. Oral best taken on an empty stomach.
PEDS - Staph infections: 50-100 mg/kg/day PO divided qid. Oral best taken on an empty stomach. Mild to moderate infections: 100-150 mg/kg/day IM/IV divided q6h. Severe infections: 150-200 mg/kg/day IM/IV divided q4-6h. Use adult dose for ≥40 kg. AAP regimens for newborns >2 kg: <1 week, 25-50 mg/kg IM/IV q8h. ≥1 week, 25-50 mg/kg IM/IV q6h.
FORMS - Generic: Caps 250,500 mg, oral soln 250 mg/5 ml.
NOTES - Anaphylaxis rarely, cross-sensitivity with cephalosporins possible. Hepatic dysfunction possible with doses >12 g/day; monitor LFTs. Oral soln stable for 3 days at room temperature, 14 days refrigerated.

PENICILLINS - GENERAL ANTIMICROBIAL SPECTRUM

1st generation: Most streptococci; oral anaerobic coverage
2nd generation: Most streptococci; Staph aureus
3rd generation: Most streptococci; basic gram negative coverage
4th generation: Pseudomonas

PROPHYLAXIS FOR BACTERIAL ENDOCARDITIS*

For dental, oral, respiratory tract, or esophageal procedures	
Standard regimen	amoxicillin[1] 2 g PO 1h before procedure
Unable to take oral meds	ampicillin[1] 2 g IM/IV within 30 minutes before procedure
Allergic to penicillin	clindamycin[2] 600 mg PO; or cephalexin[1] or cefadroxil[1] 2 g PO; or azithromycin[3] or clarithromycin[3] 500 mg PO 1h before procedure
Allergic to penicillin and unable to take oral meds	clindamycin[2] 600 mg IV; or cefazolin[4] 1 g IM/IV within 30 minutes before procedure
For genitourinary and gastrointestinal (excluding esophageal) procedures	
High-risk patients	ampicillin[1] 2 g IM/IV plus gentamicin 1.5 mg/kg (max 120 mg) within 30 min of starting procedure; 6h later ampicillin[4] 1 g IM/IV or amoxicillin[4] 1 g PO.
High-risk patients allergic to ampicillin	vancomycin[2] 1 g IV over 1-2h plus gentamicin 1.5 mg/kg IV/IM (max 120 mg) complete within 30 minutes of starting procedure
Moderate-risk patients	amoxicillin[1] 2 g PO or ampicillin[1] 2 g IM/IV within 30 minutes of starting procedure
Moderate-risk patients allergic to ampicillin	vancomycin[2] 1 g IV over 1-2h complete within 30 minutes of starting procedure

**JAMA 1997; 277:1794* or http://www.americanheart.org/Scientific/statements/1997/079701.html
Footnotes for pediatric doses: 1 = 50 mg/kg; 2 = 20 mg/kg; 3 = 15 mg/kg; 4 = 25 mg/kg. Total pediatric dose should not exceed adult dose.

ANTIMICROBIALS: Penicillins – 3rd Generation - Aminopenicillins

amoxicillin (*Amoxil, Polymox, Trimox*) ▶K ♀B ▶+ $

ADULT - ENT, skin, GU infections: 250-500 mg PO tid or 500-875 mg PO bid. Pneumonia: 500 mg PO tid or 875 mg PO bid. H pylori: See table in GI section. See table for prophylaxis of bacterial endocarditis.

PEDS - ENT, skin, GU infections: 20-40 mg/kg/day PO divided tid or 25-45 mg/kg/day PO divided bid. Pneumonia: 40 mg/kg/day PO divided tid or 45 mg/kg/day PO divided bid. Infants <3 mo: 30 mg/kg/day PO divided q12h. See table for bacterial endocarditis prophylaxis.

UNAPPROVED ADULT - Early Lyme disease: 500 mg PO tid x 3 weeks. Chlamydia in pregnancy: 500 mg PO tid x 7 days. See http://jama.ama-assn.org/issues/v281n18/pdf/jst80027.pdf for anthrax bioterrorism dosing.

UNAPPROVED PEDS - Otitis media in children at high risk for penicillin-resistant S pneumoniae (age <2 yo, antibiotics within ≤3 months, day care): 80-90 mg/kg/day PO divided bid-tid. Prevention of recurrent otitis media: 20 mg/kg PO qd (prophylactic use may contribute to PRSP). Lyme disease: 25-50 mg/kg/day (up to 1-2 g/day) PO divided tid x 21 days. See http://jama.ama-assn.org/issues/v281n18/pdf/jst80027.pdf for anthrax bioterrorism dosing.

FORMS - Generic/Trade: Caps 250,500 mg, tabs 500,875 mg, chews 125,250 mg, susp 125, 250 mg/5 ml. Trade: chews 200,400 mg, susp 200 & 400mg/5 ml, infant drops 50 mg/ml.

NOTES - Anaphylaxis rarely; cross-sensitivity with cephalosporins possible; rash in patients with mononucleosis. CDC recommends 10 days of therapy for otitis media if <2 yo and 5-7 days if ≥2 yo. Dosing in adults with renal dysfunction: Do not use 875 mg tab for CrCl < 30 ml/min. Use 250-500 mg PO bid for CrCl 10-30 ml/min, 250-500 mg PO qd for CrCl <10 ml/min or hemodialysis. Give additional dose both during & at end of dialysis. Oral susp & infant drops stable for 14 days at room temperature or in the refrigerator.

amoxicillin-clavulanate (*Augmentin, Augmentin ES, ✱Clavulin*) ▶K ♀B ▶? $$$

ADULT - Pneumonia, otitis media, sinusitis, skin infections, UTIs: Usual dose - 500 mg PO bid or 250 mg PO tid. More severe infections: 875 mg PO bid or 500 mg PO tid.

PEDS - 200,400 chewables & 200,400/5 ml susp for bid administration: Pneumonia, otitis media, sinusitis: 45 mg/kg/day PO divided bid. Less severe infections such as skin, UTIs: 25 mg/kg/day PO divided bid. 125,250 chewables

& 125,250/5 ml susp for tid administration: Pneumonia, otitis media, sinusitis: 40 mg/kg/day PO divided tid. Less severe infections such as skin, UTIs: 20 mg/kg/day PO divided tid. Age <3 months: Use 125 mg/5 ml susp and give 30 mg/kg PO q12 hr. Use adult dose for ≥40 kg. Augmentin ES-600 susp for ≥3 mo and <40 kg. Recurrent/ persistent otitis media with risk factors (antibiotics for otitis media in past 3 months and either age ≤2 yo or daycare): 90 mg/kg/day PO divided bid with food x 10 days.

UNAPPROVED ADULT - Acute sinusitis in areas with >30% drug-resistent S pneumoniae and/or antibiotic use in past month OR clinical failure after 3 days of antibiotics: 875 mg bid or 500 mg tid with extra amox to provide dose of 3 to 3.5 g/day. Do not increase Augmentin beyond standard dose. Prevention of infection after dog/cat bite: 875 mg PO bid or 500 mg PO tid x 3-5 days. Treatment of infected dog/cat bite: 875 mg PO bid or 500 mg PO tid, duration of treatment based on response.

UNAPPROVED PEDS - Group A streptococcal pharyngitis, repeated culture-positive episodes: 45 mg/kg/day PO divided bid x 10 days.

FORMS - Trade: (amoxicillin + clavulanate) Tabs 250+125, 500+125, 875+125 mg, chewables 125+31.25, 200+28.5, 250+62.5, 400+57 mg, susp 125+31.25, 200+28.5, 250+62.5, & 400+57 mg/5 ml. Augmentin ES-600 susp 600+42.9 mg/5 ml.

NOTES - Anaphylaxis rarely; cross-sensitivity with cephalosporins possible; rash in patients with mononucleosis; diarrhea common (less diarrhea with bid dosing). CDC recommends 10 days of therapy for otitis media if <2 yo and 5-7 days if ≥2 yo. Clavulanate content varies: do not substitute two 250 mg tabs for 500 mg tab, 250 mg chewable for 250 mg tab, or other suspensions for ES-600. 200,400 mg chewables, 200,400 mg/5 ml and ES-600 susp contain phenylalanine. 250 mg tab contains too much clavulanate for children <40kg. Suspensions stable in refrigerator for 10 days.

ampicillin (*Principen*, ✤*Ampicin*) ▶K ♀B ▶? $$$

ADULT - Pneumonia, soft tissue infections: 250-500 mg IM/IV/PO q6h. Gastrointestinal infections, UTIs: 500 mg IM/IV/PO q6h. Sepsis, meningitis: 150-200 mg/kg/day IV divided q3-4h. Enterococcal endocarditis: 12 g/day IV continuous infusion or divided q4h for 4-6 wks or longer with gentamicin or streptomycin. See table for prophylaxis of bacterial endocarditis. Take oral ampicillin on an empty stomach.

PEDS - Pneumonia, soft tissue infections: 25-50 mg/kg/day IM/IV/PO divided qid. Gastrointestinal infections, UTIs: 50-100 mg/kg/day IM/IV/PO divided qid. Use adult doses for ≥40 kg. Give oral ampicillin on an empty stomach. Sepsis, CNS infections: 100-200 mg/kg/day IV divided q3-4h. Group B streptococcal meningitis: ≤1 week old, 200-300 mg/kg/day IV divided q8h. ≥1 week old, 300 mg/kg/day IV divided q4-6h. Give with gentamicin initially. See table for prophylaxis of bacterial endocarditis.

UNAPPROVED ADULT - Prevention of neonatal group B streptococcal disease: Give to mother 2 g IV during labor, then 1-2 g IV q4-6h until delivery.

UNAPPROVED PEDS - AAP regimens. Mild to moderate infections: 100-150 mg/kg/day IM/IV divided q6h or 50-100 mg/kg/day PO divided qid. Severe infections: 200-400 mg/kg/day IM/IV divided in 4 doses. Infants >2 kg: 25-50 mg/kg IV q8h if <1 week old and q6h if ≥ 1 week old.

FORMS - Generic/Trade: Caps 250,500 mg, susp 125 & 250 mg/5 ml.

NOTES - Anaphylaxis rarely; cross-sensitivity with cephalosporins possible; rash in patients with mononucleosis or taking allopurinol; pseudomembranous colitis. 3.1 mEq sodium/g IV ampicillin. Susp stable for 7 days at room temperature, 14 days in the refrigerator. Reduce dosing interval to q12-24h for CrCl <10 ml/min. Give dose after hemodialysis.

ampicillin-sulbactam (*Unasyn*) ▶K ♀B ▶? $$$$$

ADULT - Skin, intra-abdominal, gynecologic infections: 1.5-3 g IM/IV q6h.

PEDS - Skin infections, ≥1 yo: <40 kg, 300 mg/kg/day IV divided q6h. ≥40 kg: adult dose.

UNAPPROVED PEDS - AAP regimens. Mild to moderate infections: 100-150 mg/kg/day of ampicillin IM/IV divided in 4 doses. Severe infections: 200-400 mg/kg/day of ampicillin IM/IV divided in 4 doses.

NOTES - Anaphylaxis rarely; cross-sensitivity with cephalosporins possible; rash in patients with mononucleosis or taking allopurinol; pseudomembranous colitis. 5 mEq sodium/1.5 g Unasyn. Dosing in renal impairment: Give usual dose q6-8h for adults with CrCl ≥30 ml/min, q12h for CrCl 15-29 ml/min, q24 h for CrCl 5-14 ml/min.

ANTIMICROBIALS: Penicillins - 4th generation - Extended Spectrum

mezlocillin (*Mezlin*) ▶KL ♀B ◗? $$$$$

ADULT - Pneumonia, sepsis, intra-abdominal, skin, gynecologic infections: 3 g IV q4h or 4 g IV q6h. Simple UTI: 1.5-2 g IM/IV q6h. Complicated UTI: 3 g IV q6h. Life-threatening infections: Up to 4 g IV q4h.

PEDS - Serious infections. Infants ≤7 days: 75 mg/kg IM/IV q12h. Infants >7 days, >2 kg: 75 mg/kg IM/IV q6h. Infants >1 mo, children <12 yo: 50 mg/kg IM/IV q4h.

UNAPPROVED ADULT - Empiric therapy of neutropenic fever: 3 g IV q4h or 4 g IV q6h with an aminoglycoside.

NOTES - Anaphylaxis rarely; cross-sensitivity with cephalosporins possible; hypokalemia; bleeding & coagulation abnormalities possible especially with renal impairment. May prolong neuromuscular blockade with non-depolarizing muscle relaxants. Not more than 2 g/IM injection site. 1.9 mEq sodium/g mezlocillin. Adult dosing with renal dysfunction: Simple UTI: 1.5 g IV q8h for CrCl ≤30 ml/min. Complicated UTI: 1.5 g IV q6h for CrCl 10-30 ml/min, 1.5 g IV q8h for CrCl <10 ml/min. Serious systemic infections: 3 g IV q8h for CrCl 10-30 ml/min, 2 g IV q8h for CrCl <10 ml/min. Life-threatening infections: 3 g IV q6h for CrCl 10-30 ml/min, 2 g IV q6h for CrCl <10 ml/min. Serious systemic infections, hemodialysis: 3-4 g IV q12h, then 3-4 g after dialysis. Serious systemic infections, peritoneal dialysis: 3 g IV q12h.

piperacillin (*Pipracil*) ▶K/Bile ♀B ◗? $$$$$

ADULT - Simple UTI, community-acquired pneumonia: 6-8 g/day IM/IV divided q6-12h. Complicated UTI: 8-16 g/day IV divided q6-8h. Serious infections: 12-18 g/day IV divided q4-6h. Max dose: 24 g/day.

PEDS - Safety and efficacy not established in children <12 yo. Use adult dose for ≥12 yo.

UNAPPROVED ADULT - Empiric therapy of neutropenic fever: 3 g IV q4h or 4 g IV q6h with an aminoglycoside.

UNAPPROVED PEDS - Mild to moderate infections: 100-150 mg/kg/day IV divided q6h. Severe infections: 200-300 mg/kg/day IV divided q4-6h.

NOTES - Anaphylaxis rarely; cross-sensitivity with cephalosporins possible; hypokalemia; bleeding & coagulation abnormalities possible especially with renal impairment. May prolong neuromuscular blockade with non-depolarizing muscle relaxants. 1.85 mEq sodium/g piperacillin. Adult dosing with renal dysfunction: Serious infections: 4 g IV q8h for CrCl 20-40 ml/min, 4 g IV q12h for CrCl <20 ml/min. Complicated UTI: 3 g IV q8h for CrCl 20-40 ml/min, 3 g IV q12h for CrCl <20 ml/min. Simple UTI: 3 g IV q12h for CrCl <20 ml/min.

piperacillin-tazobactam (*Tazocin, Zosyn*) ▶K ♀B ◗? $$$$$

ADULT - Appendicitis, peritonitis, skin infections, postpartum endometritis, pelvic inflammatory disease, moderate community-acquired pneumonia: 3.375 g IV q6h. Nosocomial pneumonia: 3.375 g IV q4h (with aminoglycoside initially and if P. aeruginosa is cultured).

PEDS - Not approved in children <12 yo.

UNAPPROVED ADULT - Serious infections: 4.5 g IV q6h.

UNAPPROVED PEDS - 240 mg/kg/day of piperacillin IV divided q8h.

NOTES - Anaphylaxis rarely; cross-sensitivity with cephalosporins possible; hypokalemia; bleeding & coagulation abnormalities possible especially with renal impairment. 2.35 mEq sodium per 1 g piperacillin in Zosyn/Tazocin. Dosing in renal impairment: 2.25 g IV q6h for CrCl 20-40 ml/min, 2.25 g IV q8h for CrCl <20 ml/min. Hemodialysis: Maximum dose of 2.25 g IV q8h plus 0.75 g after each dialysis.

ticarcillin (*Ticar*) ▶K ♀B ◗+ $$$$$

ADULT - Sepsis, pneumonia, skin & soft tissue, intra-abdominal, female GU infections: 3 g IV q4h or 4 g IV q6h. Simple UTI: 1 g IM/IV q6h. Complicated UTI: 3 g IV q6h.

PEDS - Sepsis, pneumonia, skin & soft tissue, intra-abdominal infections, <40 kg: 200-300 mg/kg/day IV divided q4-6h. Simple UTI, <40 kg: 50-100 mg/kg/day IM/IV divided q6-8h. Complicated UTI, <40 kg: 150-200 mg/kg/day IV divided q4-6h. Use adult dose for ≥40 kg. Severe infections, neonates ≥2 kg: <1 week, 75 mg/kg IV q8h. >1 week, 100 mg/kg IV q8h or 75 mg/kg IV q6h.

NOTES - Anaphylaxis rarely; cross-sensitivity with cephalosporins possible; hypokalemia; bleeding & coagulation abnormalities possible especially with renal impairment. Not more than 2 g/IM injection site. Up to 6.5 mEq sodium/g ticarcillin. Adult dosing with renal dysfunction: 3 g IV load, then 2 g IV q4h for CrCl 30-60 ml/min, 2 g IV q8h for CrCl 10-30 ml/min, 2 g IV q12h or 1 g IM q6h for CrCl <10 ml/min. Liver dysfunction and CrCl <10 ml/min: 2 g IV q24h or 1 g IM q12h. Peritoneal dialysis: 3 g IV q12h. Hemodialysis: 2 g IV q12h and 3 g IV after each dialysis session.

ticarcillin-clavulanate (*Timentin*) ▶K ♀B ▶? $$$$$

ADULT - Systemic infections or UTIs: 3.1 g IV q4-6h. Gynecologic infections: Moderate, 200 mg/kg/day IV divided q6h. Severe, 300 mg/kg/day IV divided q4h. Adults <60 kg: 200-300 mg/kg/day (based on ticarcillin content) IV divided q4-6h. Use q4h dosing interval for Pseudomonas infections.

PEDS - Mild to moderate infections: ≥60 kg, 3.1 g IV q6h. Age ≥3 mo and <60 kg, 200 mg/kg/day (based on ticarcillin content) IV divided q6h. Severe infections: ≥60 kg, 3.1 g IV q4h. Age ≥3 mo and <60 kg, 300 mg/kg/day (based on ticarcillin content) IV divided q4h.

NOTES - Timentin 3.1 g = 3 g ticarcillin + 0.1 g clavulanate. Anaphylaxis rarely; cross-sensitivity with cephalosporins possible; hypokalemia; bleeding & coagulation abnormalities possible especially in patients with renal impairment. 4.75 mEq sodium/g Timentin. IV dosing in adults with renal dysfunction: Load with 3.1 g, then 2 g q4h for CrCl 30-60 ml/min, 2 g q8h for CrCl 10-30 ml/min, 2 g q12h for CrCl <10 ml/min, 2 g q24h for CrCl <10 ml/min and liver dysfunction. Peritoneal dialysis: 3.1 g q12h. Hemodialysis: 3.1 g load, then 2 g q12h and 3.1 g after each dialysis.

ANTIMICROBIALS: Quinolones - 1st Generation

NOTES: Important quinolone drug interactions with warfarin, antacids, iron, zinc, magnesium, sucralfate, cimetidine, caffeine, cyclosporine, hydantoins, theophylline, etc.

nalidixic acid (*NegGram*) ▶KL ♀C ▶? $$$$$

ADULT - UTI: 1 g PO qid for 1-2 weeks, may reduce to 2 g/day thereafter.

PEDS - UTI, age ≥3 mo: 55 mg/kg/day PO divided qid, may reduce to 33 mg/kg/d thereafter.

FORMS - Trade: Tabs 0.25,0.5,1 g, susp 250 mg/5 ml.

NOTES - CNS toxicity; photosensitivity; hemolytic anemia in G6PD deficiency. Contraindicated if seizure history. Arthropathy in animal studies - use cautiously in prepubertal children. Monitor CBC and LFTs if used for >2 weeks.

ANTIMICROBIALS: Quinolones - 2nd Generation

NOTES: Avoid in children unless absolutely necessary due to potential cartilage toxicity. Important quinolone drug interactions with antacids, iron, zinc, magnesium, sucralfate, cimetidine, caffeine, cyclosporine, phenytoin, anticoagulants, theophylline, etc.

ciprofloxacin (*Cipro*) ▶LK ♀C ▶? $$$

ADULT - UTI: 250-500 mg PO bid or 200-400 mg IV q12h. Simple UTI: 100 mg PO bid x 3 days. Pneumonia, skin, bone/joint infections: 400 mg IV q8-12h or 500-750 mg PO bid. Treat bone/joint infections x 4-6 weeks. Acute sinusitis: 500 mg PO bid x 10 days. Chronic bacterial prostatitis: 500 mg PO bid x 28 days. Infectious diarrhea: 500 mg PO bid x 5-7 days. Typhoid fever: 500 mg PO bid x 10 days. Gonorrhea: 250 mg PO single dose (not for use in Hawaii or for infections acquired in Asia or the Pacific). Nosocomial pneumonia: 400 mg IV q8h. Complicated intra-abdominal infection (with metronidazole): 400 mg IV q12 h, then 500 mg PO bid. Empiric therapy of febrile neutropenia: 400 mg IV q8h with piperacillin. Inhalation anthrax, post-exposure: 400 mg IV or 500 mg PO q12h.

PEDS - Safety and efficacy not established in children; arthropathy in juvenile animals. Still limited data, but several case series of pediatric patients treated with ciprofloxacin show no evidence of arthropathy. Inhalation anthrax, post-exposure: 10 mg/kg/dose up to 400 mg IV or 15 mg/kg/dose up to 500 mg PO q12h.

UNAPPROVED ADULT - Acute uncomplicated pyelonephritis: 500 mg PO bid x 7 days. CDC regimen, gonorrhea: 500 mg PO single dose (not for use in Hawaii or for infections acquired in Asia or the Pacific). Chancroid: 500 mg PO bid x 3 days. Prophylaxis, high-risk GU surgery: 500 mg PO or 400 mg IV. Prophylaxis, invasive meningococcal disease: 500 mg PO single dose. Traveler's diarrhea (treatment preferred over prophylaxis): Treatment - 500 mg PO bid x 3 days or 750 mg PO single dose. Prophylaxis - 500 mg PO qd for up to 3 weeks. Malignant otitis externa: 400 mg IV or 750 mg PO q12h. Legionnaires' disease: 400 mg IV q8h or 750 mg PO q12h.

UNAPPROVED PEDS - Acute pulmonary exacerbation of cystic fibrosis: 10 mg/kg/dose IV q8h x 7 days, then 20 mg/kg/dose PO q12h to complete 10-21 days of treatment.

FORMS - Trade: Tabs 100,250,500,750 mg, susp 250 & 500 mg/5 ml.

NOTES - Tendon rupture, phototoxicity, CNS toxicity, crystalluria if alkaline urine, hypersensitivity reactions. Ciprofloxacin inhibits cytochrome P450 1A2, an enzyme that metabolizes caffeine, clozapine, tacrine, theophylline, and warfarin. Give antacids, iron, sucralfate, calcium, zinc, buffered didanosine 6 h before or 2 h after ciprofloxacin. Watch for hypoglycemia with glyburide. Do not give oral susp in feeding tube. Consider monitoring serum levels if changing renal function or renal & hepatic impairment. Therapeutic peak concentration 1-2 h after dose: 2-4 mcg/ml. Dosing in adults with renal dysfunction: 250-500 mg PO q12h for CrCl 30-50 ml/min; 250-500 mg PO q18h or 200-400 mg IV q18-24h for CrCl 5-29 ml/min; 250-500 mg PO q24h given after dialysis for hemodialysis/peritoneal dialysis.

enoxacin (*Penetrex*) ▶LK ♀C ▶? $$

ADULT - Gonorrhea: 400 mg PO single dose (not for use in Hawaii or for infections acquired in Asia or the Pacific). Simple UTI: 200 mg PO bid x 7 days. Complicated UTI: 400 mg PO bid x 14 days. Take on empty stomach.

PEDS - Safety and efficacy not established in children; arthropathy in juvenile animals.

FORMS - Trade: Tabs 200,400 mg.

NOTES - Tendon rupture, CNS toxicity, hypersensitivity reactions, phototoxicity. Enoxacin inhibits cytochrome P450 1A2, an enzyme that metabolizes caffeine, clozapine, tacrine, theophylline, and warfarin. May increase digoxin levels. Give ranitidine, antacids, iron, sucralfate 8 h before or 2 h after enoxacin. Give 50% of usual dose q12h for CrCl ≤30 ml/min.

lomefloxacin (*Maxaquin*) ▶LK ♀C ▶? $$$

ADULT - Acute exacerbation of chronic bronchitis not due to S pneumoniae, simple UTI due to K pneumoniae, P mirabilis, S saprophyticus: 400 mg PO qd x 10 days. Simple E coli UTI: 400 mg PO qd x 3 days. Complicated UTI: 400 mg PO qd x 14 days. Take in the evening to decrease risk of phototoxicity.

PEDS - Safety and efficacy not established in children; arthropathy in juvenile animals.

FORMS - Trade: Tabs 400 mg.

NOTES - Arthropathy in immature animals, tendon rupture in humans, CNS toxicity, hypersensitivity reactions, high risk of phototoxicity. Avoid sunlight during and for several days after treatment. Give Al/Mg antacids, sucralfate 4 h before or 2 h after lomefloxacin. Dosing in renal dysfunction: 400 mg PO load, then 200 mg PO qd for CrCl 11-39 ml/min or hemodialysis.

norfloxacin (*Noroxin*) ▶LK ♀C ▶? $$

ADULT - Simple UTI due to E coli, K pneumoniae, P mirabilis: 400 mg PO bid x 3 days. UTI due to other organisms: 400 mg PO bid x 7-10 days. Complicated UTI: 400 mg PO bid x 10-21 days. Gonorrhea: 800 mg PO single dose (not recommended for use in Hawaii or for infections acquired in Asia or the Pacific). Acute/chronic prostatitis: 400 mg PO bid x 28 days. Take on an empty stomach.

PEDS - Safety and efficacy not established in children; arthropathy in juvenile animals.

UNAPPROVED ADULT - Traveler's diarrhea treatment (preferred over prophylaxis): 400 mg PO bid x 3 days. Travelers diarrhea prophylaxis: 400 mg PO qd for up to 3 weeks. Gastroenteritis: 400 mg PO bid x 5 days for campylobacter, x 3-7 days for salmonella, x 3 doses for shigella. Take on an empty stomach.

FORMS - Trade: Tabs 400 mg.

NOTES - Tendon rupture, CNS toxicity, hypersensitivity reactions, phototoxicity, crystalluria with high doses. Maintain adequate hydration. Norfloxacin inhibits cytochrome P450 1A2, an enzyme that metabolizes caffeine, clozapine, tacrine, theophylline, and warfarin. Increased INR with warfarin. Do not take with dairy products. Give antacids, iron, sucralfate, multivitamins 2 h before/after norfloxacin. Dosing for CrCl <30 ml/min: 400 mg PO qd.

ofloxacin (*Floxin*) ▶LK ♀C ▶? $$$

ADULT - IV & PO doses are the same. Acute exacerbation of chronic bronchitis, community-acquired pneumonia, skin infections: 400 mg bid x 10 days. Gonorrhea: 400 mg PO single dose (not for use in Hawaii or Asia-Pacific infections). Chlamydia: 300 mg bid x 7 days. Pelvic inflammatory disease: See table. Simple UTI due to E coli, K pneumoniae: 200 mg bid x 3 days. Simple UTI due to other organisms: 200 mg bid x 7 days. Complicated UTI: 200 mg bid x 10 days. Chronic bacterial prostatitis: 300 mg PO bid x 6 weeks.

PEDS - Safety and efficacy not established in children; arthropathy in juvenile animals.

UNAPPROVED ADULT - Epididymitis: 300 mg PO bid x 10 days. Shigella gastroenteritis: 300 mg PO bid x 3 days. See http://jama.ama-assn.org/issues/v281n18/pdf/jst80027.pdf for anthrax bioterrorism dosing.

FORMS - Trade: Tabs 200,300,400 mg.

NOTES - Tendon rupture, CNS toxicity, hypersensitivity reactions, phototoxicity. Give antacids, iron, sucralfate, multivitamins containing zinc, buffered didanosine 2h before/after ofloxacin. May decrease metabolism of theophylline, increase INR with warfarin. Monitor glucose with antidiabetic agents. Dosing in renal dysfunction: Usual dose given q24h for CrCl 20-50 ml/min, 50% of usual dose q24h for CrCl <20 ml/min.

QUINOLONES- GENERAL ANTIMICROBIAL SPECTRUM

1st generation: gram negative (excluding Pseudomonas), urinary tract only
2nd generation: gram negative (including Pseudomonas); Staph aureus but not pneumococcus; some atypicals
3rd generation: gram negative (including Pseudomonas); gram positive (including Staph aureus and pneumococcus); expanded atypical coverage
4th generation: same as 3rd generation plus broad anaerobic coverage

ANTIMICROBIALS: Quinolones – 3rd Generation

NOTES: Avoid in children unless absolutely necessary due to potential cartilage toxicity. Important quinolone drug interactions with antacids, iron, zinc, magnesium, sucralfate, cimetidine, caffeine, cyclosporine, phenytoin, anticoagulants, theophylline, etc.

levofloxacin (*Levaquin*) ▶KL ♀C ▶? $$$

ADULT - IV & PO doses are the same. Acute exacerbation of chronic bronchitis: 500 mg qd x 7 days. Community-acquired pneumonia, including penicillin-resistant S pneumoniae: 500 mg qd x 7-14 days. Acute sinusitis: 500 mg qd x 10-14 days. Skin infections: 500 mg qd x 7-10 daysdays if uncomplicated, 750 mg qd x 7-14 days if complicated. Simple UTI: 250 mg PO qd x 3 days. Complicated UTI, acute pyelonephritis: 250 mg PO qd x 10 days.

PEDS - Safety and efficacy not established in children; arthropathy in juvenile animals.

UNAPPROVED ADULT - Acute uncomplicated pyelonephritis: 500 mg PO qd x 7 days. Legionnaires' disease: 1 g IV/PO on 1st day, then 500 mg IV/PO qd. See http://jama.ama-assn.org/issues/v281n18/pdf/jst80027.pdf for anthrax bioterrorism dosing.

FORMS - Trade: Tabs 250,500,750 mg.

NOTES - Tendon rupture, CNS toxicity, hypersensitivity reactions, phototoxicity. Give Mg/Al antacids, iron, sucralfate, multivitamins containing zinc, buffered didanosine 2 h before/after PO levofloxacin. Increased INR with warfarin. Monitor glucose with antidiabetic agents. Dosing in renal dysfunction: For most indications and CrCl <50 ml/min, load with 500 mg, then 250 mg qd for CrCl 20-49 ml/min, 250 mg qod CrCl 10-19 ml/min, hemodialysis, peritoneal dialysis. For complicated UTI/pyelonephritis and CrCl 10-19 ml/min, give 250 mg qod.

sparfloxacin (*Zagam*) ▶KL ♀C ▶? $$$

ADULT - Acute exacerbation of chronic bronchitis, community-acquired pneumonia,: 400 mg PO 1st day, then 200 mg qd x 10 days total.

PEDS - Safety and efficacy not established in children; arthropathy in juvenile animals.

FORMS - Trade: Tabs 200 mg.

NOTES - Can prolong QT interval; contraindicated with prolonged QT interval, drugs that prolong QT interval; avoid in proarrhythmic conditions. High risk of phototoxicity; avoid bright sunlight until 5 days after treatment is stopped. Tendon rupture, CNS toxicity, hypersensitivity reactions. Give antacids, iron, sucralfate, multivitamins containing zinc 4 h after sparfloxacin. Dosing in renal dysfunction: 400 mg PO 1st day, then 200 mg PO qod x 9 days total for CrCl <50 ml/min.

ANTIMICROBIALS: Quinolones - 4th Generation

NOTES: Avoid in children unless absolutely necessary due to potential cartilage toxicity. Important quinolone drug interactions with antacids, iron, zinc, magnesium, sucralfate, cimetidine, caffeine, cyclosporine, phenytoin, anticoagulants, theophylline, etc.

gatifloxacin (*Tequin*) ▶K ♀C ▶- $$$

ADULT - IV & PO doses are the same. Community-acquired pneumonia: 400 mg qd x 7-14 days. Acute exacerbation of chronic bronchitis, complicated UTI, acute pyelonephritis: 400 mg qd x 7-10 days. Acute sinusitis: 400 mg qd x 10 days. Simple UTI: 400 mg single dose or 200 mg qd x 3 days. Gonorrhea: 400 mg single dose (not for use in Hawaii or for patients who became infected in Asia or the Pacific).

PEDS - Safety and efficacy not established in children; arthropathy in juvenile animals.

UNAPPROVED ADULT - IV & PO doses are the same. Acute uncomplicated pyelonephritis: 400 mg qd x 7 days.

FORMS - Trade: Tabs 200,400 mg.

NOTES - Tendon rupture, CNS toxicity, hypersensitivity reactions. Potential for QT interval prolongation unknown. Avoid using in proarrhythmic conditions or with drugs that prolong QT interval. Monitor blood glucose in diabetics receiving insulin/oral hypoglycemics. Give PO gatifloxacin 4 h before Al/Mg antacids, iron, multivitamins with zinc, buffered didanosine. May increase digoxin levels. Dosing for renal dysfunction in adults: 400 mg loading dose on day 1. On day 2, reduce dose to 200 mg PO qd for CrCl <40 ml/min, hemodialysis, continuous peritoneal dialysis.

moxifloxacin (*Avelox*) ▶LK ♀C ▶- $$$

ADULT - Acute sinusitis, community-acquired pneumonia: 400 mg PO qd x 10 days. Acute exacerbation of chronic bronchitis: 400 mg PO qd x 5 days. Uncomplicated skin infections due to S aureus or S pyogenes: 400 mg PO qd x 7 days.

PEDS - Safety and efficacy not established in children; arthropathy in juvenile animals.

UNAPPROVED ADULT - UTI: 400 mg PO qd x 3 days.

FORMS - Trade: Tabs 400 mg.

NOTES - Prolonged QT interval, tendon rupture, CNS toxicity, hypersensitivity reactions. Avoid using in proarrhythmic conditions or with drugs that prolong QT interval, including Class 1A and Class III antiarrhythmics. Give at least 4 h before or 8 h after Mg/Al antacids, iron, multivitamins with zinc, sucralfate, buffered didanosine. Monitor INR with warfarin. Avoid in moderate or severe hepatic insufficiency.

trovafloxacin (*Trovan, alatrofloxacin*) ▶LK ♀C ▶- $$$$$

WARNING - Hepatotoxicity. Only for treatment of serious/life-threatening infections. Therapy must begin in hospital or long-term care facility. Do not use for more than 14 days.

ADULT - IV & PO doses equivalent. Community-acquired pneumonia: 200 mg IV/PO qd x 7-14 days. Nosocomial pneumonia: 300 mg IV qd, then 200 mg PO qd for 10-14 days total. Complicated intra-abdominal infections, gynecologic/pelvic infections: 300 mg IV qd, then 200 mg PO qd x 7-14 days total. Complicated skin infections, diabetic foot: 200 mg IV/PO, then 200 mg PO qd x 10-14 days.

PEDS - Safety and efficacy not established in children; arthropathy in juvenile animals.

FORMS - Trade: Tabs 100, 200 mg.

NOTES - Pancreatitis, tendon rupture, CNS toxicity, hypersensitivity reactions, phototoxicity. Wait 2 h to give IV morphine after PO trovafloxacin taken on empty stomach and 4 h after PO trovafloxacin taken with a meal. Give Al/Mg antacids, iron, sucralfate, buffered didanosine, Bicitra 2 h before/after PO trovafloxacin.

ANTIMICROBIALS: Sulfonamides

***Bactrim, Cotrim, Septra, Sulfatrim* (trimethoprim + sulfamethoxazole, TMP/SMX, cotrimoxazole)** ▶K ♀C ▶+ $

ADULT - UTI, shigellosis, acute exacerbation of chronic bronchitis: 1 tab PO bid, double strength (DS, 160 TMP/800 SMX). Travelers' diarrhea: 1 DS tab PO bid x 5 days. Pneumocystis treatment: 15-20 mg/kg/day (based on TMP) IV divided q6-8h or PO divided q6h x 21 days total. Pneumocystis prophylaxis: 1 DS tab PO qd.

PEDS - UTI, shigellosis, otitis media: 5 ml susp per 10 kg (up to 20 ml) per dose PO bid. Pneumocystis treatment: 15-20 mg/kg/day (based on TMP) IV divided q6-8h or 5 ml susp per 8 kg per 8 kg per dose PO q6h. Pneumocystis prophylaxis: 150 mg/m2/day (based on TMP) PO divided bid on 3 consecutive days each week. Do not use in infants <2 mo; may cause kernicterus.

UNAPPROVED ADULT - Bacterial prostatitis: 1 DS tab PO bid x 10-14 days for acute, x 1-3 months for chronic. Sinusitis: 1 DS tab PO bid x 10 days. Burkholderia cepacia pulmonary infection in cystic fibrosis: 5 mg/kg (based on TMP) IV q6h. Pneumocystis prophylaxis: 1 SS tab PO qd. Nocardiosis: 1 DS tab PO bid for 6 mo, indefinitely if AIDS.

UNAPPROVED PEDS - Head lice unresponsive to usual therapy: 10 mg/kg/day (based on

TMP) PO divided bid x 10 days in combo with standard doses of permethrin 1%.

FORMS - Generic/Trade: Tabs 80 mg TMP/400 mg SMX (single strength), 160 mg TMP/800 mg SMX (double strength; DS), susp 40 mg TMP/200 mg SMX per 5 ml. 20 ml susp = 2 SS tabs = 1 DS tab.

NOTES - Not effective for streptococcal pharyngitis. No activity against penicillin-nonsusceptible pneumococci. Blood dyscrasias; Stevens-Johnson syndrome; toxic epidermal necrolysis; hepatitis; hemolysis in G6PD deficiency. Bone marrow depression with high IV dosing. Significantly increased INR with warfarin; avoid concomitant use if possible. Increases levels of methotrexate, phenytoin. Avoid sulfonamides in woman with breastfeeding infant who is ill, stressed, premature, or has hyperbilirubinemia or glucose-6-phosphate dehydrogenase deficiency. CDC recommends 10 days of therapy for otitis media if <2 yo and 5-7 days if ≥2 yo. Dosing in renal dysfunction: Use 50% of usual dose for CrCl 15-30 ml/min. Don't use for CrCl <15 ml/min.

***Pediazole* (erythromycin ethyl succinate + sulfisoxazole)** ▶KL ♀C ◗- $

ADULT - None

PEDS - Otitis media,age >2 mo: 50 mg/kg/day (based on EES dose) PO divided tid-qid.

FORMS - Generic/Trade: Susp, erythromycin ethyl succinate 200 mg, sulfisox 600 mg/5 ml.

NOTES - Sulfisoxazole: Stevens-Johnson syndrome; toxic epidermal necrolysis; hepatotoxicity; blood dyscrasias; hemolysis in G6PD deficiency. Significantly increased INR with warfarin; avoid concomitant use if possible. Erythromycin: Rare arrhythmias in patients with prolonged QT. May aggravate myasthenia gravis. Cytochrome P450 3A4 & 1A2 inhibitor. Many drug interactions including increased levels of carbamazepine, cyclosporine, digoxin, disopyramide, tacrolimus, theophylline, some benzodiazepines and statins. Monitor INR with warfarin. Increased vinblastine toxicity. Contraindicated with cisapride, pimozide, sparfloxacin. CDC recommends 10 days of therapy for otitis media if <2 yo and 5-7 days if ≥2 yo.

sulfadiazine, ✤*Coptin* ▶K ♀C ◗+ $$$$$

ADULT - Usual dose: 2-4 g PO initially, then 2-4 g/day divided into 3-6 doses. Secondary prevention of rheumatic fever: 1 g PO qd. Toxoplasmosis treatment: 1-1.5 g PO qid with pyrimethamine and leucovorin.

PEDS - Not for infants <2 mo, except as adjunct to pyrimethamine for congenital toxoplasmosis. Usual dose: Give 75 mg/kg PO initially, then 150 mg/kg/day up to 6 g/day divided into 4-6 doses. Secondary prevention of rheumatic fever, <27 kg: 500 mg PO qd. Use adult dose for >27 kg.

UNAPPROVED ADULT - Secondary prevention after CNS toxoplasmosis in AIDS: 0.5-1 g PO qid with pyrimethamine and leucovorin.

UNAPPROVED PEDS - Not for infants <2 mo, except as adjunct to pyrimethamine for congenital toxoplasmosis. AAP regimen for toxoplasmosis: 100-200 mg/kg/day PO with pyrimethamine and leucovorin (duration varies). Secondary prevention after CNS toxoplasmosis in HIV-infection: 85-120 mg/kg/day PO divided in 2-4 doses with pyrimethamine and leucovorin.

FORMS - Generic: Tab 500 mg.

NOTES - Not effective for streptococcal pharyngitis. Blood dyscrasias; Stevens-Johnson syndrome; toxic epidermal necrolysis; hepatitis; photosensitivity; hemolytic anemia in G6PD deficiency. Maintain fluid intake to prevent crystalluria/stone formation. Reduce dose in renal insufficiency. May increase INR with warfarin. May increase levels of methotrexate, phenytoin. Avoid sulfonamides in woman with breastfeeding infant who is ill, stressed, premature, or has hyperbilirubinemia or glucose-6-phosphate dehydrogenase deficiency.

sulfamethoxazole (*Gantanol*) ▶K ♀C ◗- $

ADULT - Mild to moderate infections: 2 g load, then 1 g PO bid. Severe infections: 2 g load, then 1 g PO tid.

PEDS - Usual dose: 50-60 mg/kg PO load, then 25-30 mg/kg/dose PO bid. Not to exceed 75 mg/kg/day. Not for infants <2 mo, except as adjunct to pyrimethamine for congenital toxoplasmosis.

FORMS - Trade: Tabs 500 mg.

NOTES - Not effective for streptococcal pharyngitis. Blood dyscrasias; Stevens-Johnson syndrome; toxic epidermal necrolysis; hepatitis; photosensitivity; hemolytic anemia in G6PD deficiency. Maintain fluid intake to prevent crystalluria/stone formation. Significantly increased INR with warfarin; avoid concomitant use if possible. May increase levels of methotrexate, phenytoin. Avoid sulfonamides in woman with breastfeeding infant who is ill, stressed, premature, or has hyperbilirubinemia or glucose-6-phosphate dehydrogenase deficiency. Reduce dose in renal failure.

sulfisoxazole (*Gantrisin Pediatric*) ▶KL ♀C ◗+ $

PEDS - Usual dose: 75 mg/kg PO load, then 150 mg/kg/day PO divided q4-6h (max 6 g/day). Not for infants <2 mo, except as adjunct to pyrimethamine for congenital toxoplasmosis.
UNAPPROVED PEDS - Prophylaxis for recurrent otitis media: 50 mg/kg PO qhs.
FORMS - Trade: susp 500 mg/5ml. Generic: Tabs 500 mg.
NOTES - Blood dyscrasias, Stevens-Johnson syndrome; toxic epidermal necrolysis; hepatitis; photosensitivity; hemolytic anemia in G6PD deficiency. May increase levels of methotrexate, phenytoin. Significantly increased INR with warfarin; avoid concomitant use if possible. Reduce dose in renal failure. Maintain fluid intake to prevent crystalluria/stone formation. Avoid sulfonamides in woman with breastfeeding infant who is ill, stressed, premature, or has hyperbilirubinemia or glucose-6-phosphate dehydrogenase deficiency.

ANTIMICROBIALS: Tetracyclines

doxycycline (*Vibramycin, Doryx*, ✤*Doxycin*) ▶LK ♀D ◗? $
ADULT - Usual dose: 100 mg PO bid on first day, then 100 mg/day PO divided qd or bid. Severe infections: 100 mg PO bid. Chlamydia, nongonococcal urethritis: 100 mg PO bid x 7 days. Acne vulgaris: Up to 100 mg PO bid. Periostat for periodontitis: 20 mg PO bid 1 h before breakfast and dinner. Primary, secondary, early latent syphilis if penicillin-allergic: 100 mg PO bid x 14 days. Late latent or tertiary syphilis if penicillin allergic: 100 mg PO bid x 4 weeks. Not for neurosyphilis. Malaria prophylaxis: 100 mg PO qd starting 1-2d before exposure until 4 wks after. Intravenous: 200 mg on first day in 1-2 infusions, then 100-200 mg/day in 1-2 infusions. See http://jama.ama-assn.org/issues/v281n18/pdf/jst80027.pdf for anthrax bioterrorism dosing.
PEDS - Avoid in children <8 yo due to teeth staining. Usual dose, children ≤45 kg: 4.4 mg/kg/day PO divided bid on first day, then 2.2-4.4 mg/kg/day PO divided qd or bid. Use adult dose for children >45 kg. Malaria prophylaxis: 2 mg/kg/day up to 100 mg PO qd starting 1-2 days before exposure until 4 weeks after. Most PO and IV doses are equivalent. See http://jama.ama-assn.org/issues/v281n18/pdf/jst80027.pdf for anthrax bioterrorism dosing.
UNAPPROVED ADULT - See table for treatment of pelvic inflammatory disease. Lyme disease: 100 mg PO bid x 14-28 days. Prevention of Lyme disease in highly endemic area, with deer tick attachment ≥48h: 200 mg PO single dose with food within 72 h of tick bite. Ehrlichiosis: 100 mg IV/PO bid x 7-14 days. Malaria treatment: 100 mg PO bid x 7 days with quinine.
UNAPPROVED PEDS - Avoid in children <8 yo due to teeth staining. Lyme disease: 1-2 mg/kg PO up to 100 mg bid x 14-28 days. Malaria treatment: 2 mg/kg/day PO x 7d with quinine.
FORMS - Generic/Trade: Tabs 100 mg, caps 50,100 mg. Trade: Susp 25 mg/5 ml, syrup 50 mg/5 ml (contains sulfites), Periostat: Caps 20 mg.
NOTES - Photosensitivity, pseudotumor cerebri, increased BUN, pain with IV infusion. May decrease efficacy of oral contraceptives. Increased INR with warfarin. Do not give antacids or calcium supplements within 2 h of doxycycline. Barbiturates, carbamazepine, and phenytoin may decrease doxycycline levels. Preferred over tetracycline in renal dysfunction. Take with fluids to decrease esophageal irritation. Doxycycline can be given with food/milk.

minocycline (*Minocin, Dynacin*) ▶LK ♀D ◗? $$
ADULT - Usual dose: 200 mg IV/PO 1st dose, then 100 mg q12h. IV and PO doses are the same. Not more than 400 mg/day IV.
PEDS - Avoid in children <8 yo due to teeth staining. Usual dose: 4 mg/kg PO 1st dose, then 2 mg/kg bid. IV and PO doses are the same.
UNAPPROVED ADULT - Acne vulgaris: 50 mg PO bid. Nocardiosis: 200 mg PO bid x 6 months.
FORMS - Generic/Trade: Caps 50,75,100 mg. Trade: Susp 50 mg/5 ml.
NOTES - Dizziness, photosensitivity, pseudotumor cerebri, hepatotoxicity, lupus. May decrease efficacy of oral contraceptives. Increased INR with warfarin. Do not give antacids or calcium supplements within 2h of minocycline. May cause drowsiness. Take with fluids (not milk) to decrease esophageal irritation. Use with caution in renal dysfunction; doxycycline preferred.

tetracycline (*Sumycin*, ✤*Tetracyn*) ▶LK ♀D ◗? $

ADULT - Usual dose: 250-500 mg PO qid on empty stomach. H pylori: See table in GI section. Primary, secondary, early latent syphilis if penicillin-allergic: 500 mg PO qid x 14 days. Late latent syphilis if penicillin allergic: 500 mg PO qid x 28 days.

PEDS - Avoid in children <8 yo due to teeth staining. Usual dose: 25-50 mg/kg/day PO divided bid-qid on empty stomach.

FORMS - Generic/Trade: Caps 250,500 mg. Trade: Tabs 250, 500 mg, susp 125 mg/5 ml.

NOTES - Photosensitivity; pseudotumor cerebri; increased BUN/hepatotoxicity in patients with renal dysfunction. May decrease efficacy of oral contraceptives. Increased INR with warfarin. Do not give antacids or calcium supplements within 2 h of tetracycline. Use with caution in renal dysfunction; doxycycline preferred. Take with fluids (not milk) to decrease esophageal irritation.

ANTIMICROBIALS: Other Antimicrobials

aztreonam (*Azactam*) ▶K ♀B ▶+ $$$$$

ADULT - UTI: 500 mg-1 g IM/IV q8-12h. Pneumonia, sepsis, skin, intra-abdominal, gynecologic infections: Moderate, 1-2 g IM/IV q8-12h. Severe or P aeruginosa infections, 2 g IV q6-8h. Use IV route for doses >1 g.

PEDS - Serious gram-negative infections, usual dose: 30 mg/kg/dose IV q6-8h.

UNAPPROVED PEDS - P aeruginosa pulmonary infection in cystic fibrosis: 50 mg/kg/dose IV q6-8h.

NOTES - Dosing in adults with renal dysfunction: 1-2 g IV load, then 50% of usual dose for CrCl 10-30 ml/min. 0.5-2 g IV load, then 25% of usual dose for CrCl <10 ml/min. For life-threatening infections, also give 12.5% of initial dose after each hemodialysis.

chloramphenicol (*Chloromycetin*) ▶LK ♀C ▶- $$$$$

WARNING - Serious & fatal blood dyscrasias. Dose-dependent bone marrow suppression common.

ADULT - Typhoid fever, rickettsial infections: 50 mg/kg/day IV divided q6h. Up to 75-100 mg/kg/day IV for serious infections untreatable with other agents.

PEDS - Severe infections including meningitis: 50-100 mg/kg/day IV divided q6h.

NOTES - Monitor CBC every 2 days. Monitor serum levels. Therapeutic peak: 10-20 mcg/ml. Trough: 5-10 mcg/ml. Use cautiously in acute intermittent porphyria/G6PD deficiency. Gray baby syndrome in preemies and newborns. Barbiturates, rifampin decrease chloramphenicol levels. Chloramphenicol increases barbiturate, phenytoin levels and may increase INR with warfarin. Dosing in adults with hepatic dysfunction: 1 g IV load, then 500 mg q6h.

clindamycin (*Cleocin*, ✤*Dalacin C*) ▶L ♀B ▶? $$

WARNING - Pseudomembranous colitis.

ADULT - Serious anaerobic, streptococcal, staph infections: 600-900 mg IV q8h or 150-450 mg PO qid. See table for prophylaxis of bacterial endocarditis.

PEDS - Serious anaerobic, streptococcal, staph infections: 20-40 mg/kg/day IV divided q6-8h or 8-20 mg/kg/day (as Caps) PO divided tid-qid or 8-25 mg/kg/day (as palmitate oral soln) PO divided tid-qid. Do not give <37.5 mg of oral soln PO tid for ≤10 kg. Infants <1 mo: 15-20 mg/kg/day IV divided tid-qid. See table for prophylaxis of bacterial endocarditis.

UNAPPROVED ADULT - Bacterial vaginosis: 300 mg PO bid x 7 days. Oral/dental infection: 300 mg PO qid. Prevention of perinatal group B streptococcal disease: 900 mg IV to mother q8h until delivery. CNS toxoplasmosis, AIDS (with leucovorin, pyrimethamine): treatment 600 mg PO/IV q6h; secondary prevention 300-450 mg PO q6-8h. Group A streptococcal pharyngitis, repeated culture-positive episodes: 600 mg/day PO in 2-4 divided doses x 10 days.

UNAPPROVED PEDS - Group A streptococcal pharyngitis, repeated culture-positive episodes: 20-30 mg/kg/day PO divided q8h x 10 days.

FORMS - Generic/Trade: Cap 150 mg. Trade: Cap 75,300 mg, oral soln 75 mg/5 ml.

NOTES - Not for meningitis. Do not give orally at the same time as kaolin-pectin antidiarrheals. Not more than 600 mg/IM injection site.

fosfomycin (*Monurol*) ▶K ♀B ▶? $$

ADULT - Simple UTI in women: One 3 g packet PO single dose. Dissolve granules in 1/2 cup of water.

PEDS - Not approved in children <12 yo.

FORMS - Trade: 3 g packet of granules.

NOTES - Metoclopramide decreases urinary excretion of fosfomycin. No benefit with multiple dosing. Single dose less effective than ciprofloxacin or TMP/SMX; equivalent to nitrofurantoin.

furazolidone (*Furoxone*) ▶K ♀C ▶? $$

PEDS - Contraindicated in infants <1 month old. Bacterial/protozoal diarrhea and enteritis: 1 mo-1 yo, 8-17 mg PO qid. 1-4 yo, 17-25 mg PO qid. ≥5 yo, 25-50 mg PO qid.

FORMS - Trade: Susp 50 mg/15 ml.

NOTES - Orthostatic hypotension, hypoglycemia, hemolysis in G6PD deficiency. Inhibits MAO; may interact with MAOIs, anorexiants, levodopa, meperidine, sympathomimetics, tricyclic antidepressants, high tyramine foods. Disulfiram-like reaction; avoid alcohol within 4 days of treatment. May turn urine brown.

linezolid (*Zyvox*) ▶Esterase, fecal excretion ♀C ▶? $$$$$

ADULT - IV & PO doses are the same. Vancomycin-resistant E. faecium infections: 600 mg IV/PO q12h x 14-28 days. Pneumonia, complicated skin infections: 600 mg IV/PO q12h x 10-14 days. Uncomplicated skin infections: 400 mg PO q12h x 10-14 days. Infuse over 30-120 minutes.

PEDS - Safety and efficacy not established in children.

UNAPPROVED PEDS - Limited data suggest a dose of 10 mg/kg IV q 8-12h.

FORMS - Trade: Tabs 600 mg, susp 100 mg/5 ml. 400 mg tab FDA-approved, but not marketed.

NOTES - Myelosuppression. Monitor CBC weekly, esp if >2 weeks of therapy, pre-existing myelosuppression, other myelosuppressive drugs, or chronic infection treated with other antibiotics. Consider discontinuation if myelosuppression occurs or worsens. Inhibits MAO; may interact with adrenergic and serotonergic drugs, high tyramine foods. Limit tyramine to <100 mg/meal. Reduce initial dose of dopamine/epinephrine. Oral susp contains phenylalanine & 8.5 mg sodium/5 ml. Store susp at room temperature; stable for 21 days. Gently turn bottle over 3-5 times before giving a dose; do not shake.

methenamine hippurate (*Hiprex, Urex*) ▶KL ♀C ▶? ?

ADULT - Long-term suppression of UTI: 1 g PO bid.

PEDS - Long-term suppression of UTI: 0.5-1 g PO bid for 6-12 yo, 1 g PO bid for >12 yo.

FORMS - Trade: Tabs 1g.

NOTES - Not for UTI treatment. Contraindicated if renal or severe hepatic impairment, severe dehydration. Acidify urine if Proteus, Pseudomonas infections. Give 1-2 g vitamin C PO q4h if urine pH >5. Avoid sulfonamides, alkalinizing foods/medications.

methenamine mandelate (*Mandelamine*) ▶KL ♀C ▶? $$

ADULT - Long-term suppression of UTI: 1 g PO qid after meals and qhs.

PEDS - Long-term suppression of UTI: 18.4 mg/kg PO qid for <6 yo, 500 mg PO qid for 6-12 yo. Give after meals and qhs.

FORMS - Generic/Trade: Tabs 0.5,1 g. Generic: Susp 0.5 g/5 ml.

NOTES - Not for UTI treatment. Contraindicated with renal or severe hepatic impairment, severe dehydration. Acidify urine for Proteus, Pseudomonas infections. If urine pH >5, give 1-2 g vitamin C PO q4h. Avoid alkalinizing foods/medications, avoid sulfonamides.

metronidazole (*Flagyl, Trikacide*) ▶KL ♀B(-in 1st trimester) ▶?- $

ADULT - Trichomoniasis: Treat patient & sex partners with 2 g PO single dose, 250 mg PO tid x 7 days, or 375 mg PO bid x 7 days. Flagyl ER for bacterial vaginosis: 750 mg PO qd x 7 days on empty stomach. H pylori: See table in GI section. Anaerobic bacterial infections: Load 1 g or 15 mg/kg IV, then 500 mg or 7.5 mg/kg IV/PO q6h, each IV dose over 1h (not to exceed 4 g/day). Prophylaxis, colorectal surgery: 15 mg/kg IV completed 1 h preop, then 7.5 mg/kg IV q6h x 2 doses. Acute amebic dysentery: 750 mg PO tid x 5-10 days. Amebic liver abscess: 500-750 mg PO tid x 5-10 days.

PEDS - Amebiasis: 35-50 mg/kg/day PO (max of 750 mg/dose) divided tid x 10 days.

UNAPPROVED ADULT - Bacterial vaginosis: 500 mg PO bid x 7 days. Bacterial vaginosis in pregnancy (not 1st trimester): 250 mg PO tid x 7 days. Trichomoniasis (CDC alternative to single dose): 500 mg PO bid x 7 days. Pelvic inflammatory disease: see STD table. Clostridium difficile diarrhea: 250 mg PO qid or 500 mg PO tid x 10 days. Giardia: 250 mg PO tid x 5-7 days.

UNAPPROVED PEDS - Clostridium difficile diarrhea: 30-50 mg/kg/day PO divided tid or qid x 7-10 days (not to exceed adult dose). Trichomoniasis: 5 mg/kg PO tid (max 2 g/day) x 7 days. Giardia: 15 mg/kg/day PO divided tid x 5-7 days. Anaerobic bacterial infections: 30 mg/kg/day IV/PO divided q6h, each IV dose over 1h (not to exceed 4 g/day).

FORMS - Generic/Trade: Tabs 250,500 mg. Trade: Caps 375 mg. Flagyl ER tabs 750 mg.

NOTES - Peripheral neuropathy with long-term use, seizures. Disulfiram-like reaction with alcohol; avoid alcohol during & for 3 days after treatment. Do not give within 2 weeks of disulfiram. Interactions with barbiturates, lithium, phenytoin. Increased INR with warfarin. Decrease dose in liver dysfunction. Darkens urine. Follow therapy for amebic dysentery or liver abscess with a course of a luminal agent (iodoquinol, paromomycin).

nitrofurantoin (*Furadantin, Macrodantin, Macrobid*) ▶KL ♀B ◗+? $$

WARNING - Pulmonary fibrosis with prolonged use.

ADULT - Acute uncomplicated cystitis: 50-100 mg PO qid with food/milk x 7 days or x 3 days after sterile urine. Long-term suppressive therapy: 50-100 mg PO qhs. Sustained release Macrobid: 100 mg PO bid with food/milk x 7 days.

PEDS - UTI: 5-7 mg/kg/day PO divided qid x 7 days or x 3 days after sterile urine. Long-term suppressive therapy: Doses as low as 1 mg/kg/day PO divided qd-bid. Give with food/milk. Macrobid, >12 yo: 100 mg PO bid with food/milk x 7 days.

FORMS - Macrodantin: Caps 25,50,100 mg. Generic: Caps 50,100 mg. Furadantin: Susp 25 mg/5 ml. Macrobid: Caps 100 mg.

NOTES - Contraindicated if CrCl <60 ml/min, pregnancy ≥38 weeks, infant <1 mo. Hemolytic anemia in G6PD deficiency (including susceptible infants exposed through breastmilk), hepatotoxicity, peripheral neuropathy. May turn urine brown. Do not use for complicated UTI or pyelonephritis.

rifampin (*Rimactane, Rifadin, Rofact*) ▶L ♀C ◗+ $$$

ADULT - Tuberculosis: 10 mg/kg up to 600 mg PO/IV qd. Neisseria meningitidis carriers: 600 mg PO bid x 2 days. Take on empty stomach.

PEDS - Tuberculosis: 10-20 mg/kg up to 600 mg PO/IV qd. Neisseria meningitidis carriers: age ≥1 mo, 10 mg/kg up to 600 mg PO bid x 2 days. Age <1 mo, 5 mg/kg PO bid x 2 days. Take on empty stomach.

UNAPPROVED ADULT - Prophylaxis of H influenza type b infection: 20 mg/kg up to 600 mg PO qd x 4 days. Leprosy: 600 mg PO q month with dapsone. American Thoracic Society regimen for latent tuberculosis: 10 mg/kg/day up to 600 mg PO qd for 4 months. Take on empty stomach.

UNAPPROVED PEDS - Prophylaxis of H influenza type b infection: age ≥1 mo, 20 mg/kg up to 600 mg PO qd x 4 days. Age <1 mo, 10 mg/kg PO qd x 4 days. Prophylaxis of invasive meningococcal disease: age ≥1 mo, 10 mg/kg up to 600 mg PO bid x 2 days. Age <1 mo, 5 mg/kg PO bid x 2 days. American Thoracic Society regimen for latent tuberculosis: 10-20 mg/kg/day up to 600 mg PO qd for 4 months. Take on empty stomach.

FORMS - Generic/Trade: Caps 150,300 mg. Pharmacists can make oral suspension.

NOTES - Hepatotoxicity, thrombocytopenia, exacerbation of porphyria. When treating tuberculosis, obtain CBC and LFTs at baseline. Monitor periodically in high-risk patients (HIV infection, alcoholism, pregnancy, signs/ history of liver disease, abnormal LFTs at baseline). Induces hepatic metabolism of many drugs including oral contraceptives. Do not use with amprenavir, delavirdine, indinavir, nelfinavir, saquinavir,lopinavir/ritonavir (Kaletra). Adjust dose with hepatic impairment. Colors urine, body secretions, contact lenses red-orange. Adult regimen for latent tuberculosis can be given for 2 months with pyrazinamide (see entry for pyrazinamide).

***Synercid* (quinupristin + dalfopristin)** ▶Bile ♀B ◗? $$$$$

ADULT - Vancomycin-resistant E faecium infections (Not active against E. faecalis): 7.5 mg/kg IV q8h, each dose over 1 h. Complicated staphylococcal/ streptococcal skin infections: 7.5 mg/kg IV q12h, each dose over 1 h.

PEDS - Safety and efficacy not established in children.

UNAPPROVED PEDS - Vancomycin-resistant E faecium infections (Not active against E. faecalis): 7.5 mg/kg IV q8h, each dose over 1 h. Complicated staphylococcal/streptococcal skin infections: 7.5 mg/kg IV q12h, each dose over 1 h.

NOTES - Venous irritation - flush with D5W (not normal saline/heparin) after peripheral infusion, arthralgias/myalgias, hyperbilirubinemia. Cytochrome P450 3A4 inhibitor. Increases levels of cyclosporine, midazolam, nifedipine, others.

trimethoprim (*Primsol*, *✤Proloprim*) ▶K ♀C ◗- $

ADULT - Uncomplicated UTI: 100 mg PO bid or 200 mg PO qd.

PEDS - Safety not established in infants <2 mo; Otitis media, age ≥ 6 mo (not for M catarrhalis): 10 mg/kg/day PO divided bid x 10 days.

UNAPPROVED ADULT - Prophylaxis of recurrent UTI: 100 mg PO qhs.

FORMS - Generic/Trade: Tabs 100,200 mg. Primsol: Oral soln 50 mg/5 ml.

NOTES - Contraindicated in megaloblastic anemia due to folate deficiency. Blood dyscrasias. Trimethoprim alone not first-line for otitis media. Inhibits metabolism of phenytoin and procainamide. Dosing in adults with renal dysfunction: 50 mg PO q12h for CrCl 15-30 ml/min. Do not use if CrCl <15 ml/min.

vancomycin (*Vancocin*) ▶K ♀C ▶? $$$$$

ADULT - Severe staph infections, endocarditis: 1g IV q12h, each dose over 1h or 30 mg/kg/day IV divided q12h. Clostridium difficile diarrhea: 500-2000 mg/day PO divided tid-qid x 7-10 days. IV administration ineffective for this indication. See table for prophylaxis of bacterial endocarditis.

PEDS - Severe staph infections, endocarditis: 10 mg/kg IV q6h. Infants <1 week old: 15 mg/kg IV load, then 10 mg/kg q12h. Infants 1 week - 1 mo: 15 mg/kg IV load, then 10 mg/kg q8h. Clostridium difficile diarrhea: 40 mg/kg/day up to 2000 mg/day PO divided tid-qid x 7-10 days. IV administration ineffective for this indication.

UNAPPROVED PEDS - AAP dosing for infants: 10-15 mg/kg IV q8-12h for infants <1 week. 10-15 mg/kg IV q6-8h for infants ≥1 week. Bacterial meningitis: 60 mg/kg/day IV divided q6h.

FORMS - Generic/Trade: oral soln 1 g/20 ml bottle. Trade: Caps 125,250 mg; oral soln 500 mg/6 ml.

NOTES - "Red Neck" (or "Red Man") syndrome with rapid IV administration, vein irritation with IV extravasation, reversible neutropenia, ototoxicity or nephrotoxicity rarely. Enhanced effects of neuromuscular blockers. Use caution with other ototoxic/nephrotoxic drugs. Peak 30-40 mcg/ml 1.5-2.5 h after 1-h infusion, trough 5-10 mcg/ml. Individualize dose if renal dysfunction. Oral vancomycin poorly absorbed; do not use for extraluminal infections.

CARDIOVASCULAR: ACE Inhibitors

	Hypertension		Congestive Heart Failure		
ACE INHIBITOR DOSING	*Initial*	*Max*	*Initial*	*Target*	*Max*
benazepril (*Lotensin*)	10 mg qd*	80/d	-	-	-
captopril (*Capoten*)	25 mg bid/tid	450/d	6.25-12.5 mg tid	50 mg tid	150 mg tid
enalapril (*Vasotec*)	5 mg qd/bid*	40/d	2.5 mg bid	10 mg bid	20 mg bid
fosinopril (*Monopril*)	10 mg qd	80/d	5-10 mg qd	20 mg qd	40 mg qd
lisinopril (*Zestril/Prinivil*)	10 mg qd	80/d	5 mg qd	20 mg qd	40 mg qd
moexipril (*Univasc*)	7.5 mg qd*	30/d	-	-	-
perindopril (Aceon)	4 mg qd	16/d	-	-	-
quinapril (*Accupril*)	10 mg qd*	80/d	2.5-5 mg bid	20 mg bid	20 mg bid
ramipril (*Altace*)	2.5 mg qd*	20/d	1.25-2.5 mg bid	5 mg bid	10 mg bid
trandolapril (*Mavik*)	1-2 mg qd	8/d	0.5-1 mg qd	4 mg qd	4 mg qd

**May require bid dosing for 24-hour BP control.*

NOTES: See also antihypertensive combinations. To minimize the risk of hypotension in diuretic treated patients, hold diuretic dose (if possible) for 2-3 days before starting an ACE inhibitor and use a low ACE inhibitor dose. If diuretics cannot be held, then reduce the dose (if possible). Use with caution in volume depleted or hyponatremic patients. Hyperkalemia possible, especially if used concomitantly with other drugs that increase K+ and in patients with CHF or renal impairment. ACE inhibitor use during the second and third trimester of pregnancy may cause injury or death to the developing fetus.

benazepril (*Lotensin*) ▶LK ♀C (1st trimester) D (2nd & 3rd) ▶? $$

ADULT - HTN: Start 10 mg PO qd, usual maintenance dose 20-40 mg PO qd or divided bid, max 80 mg/day, but added effect not apparent >40 mg/day. Elderly, renal impairment, or concomitant diuretic therapy: Start 5 mg PO qd.

PEDS - Not approved in children.

UNAPPROVED ADULT - Renal protective dosing: 10 mg PO qd.

FORMS - Trade: Tabs, non-scored 5,10,20,40 mg.

NOTES - BID dosing may be required for 24-hour BP control.

captopril (*Capoten*) ▶LK ♀C (1st trimester) D (2nd & 3rd) ▶+ $$$

ADULT - HTN: Start 25 mg PO bid-tid, usual maintenance dose 25-150 mg PO bid-tid, max 450 mg/day (max 150 mg/day typical). Elderly, renal impairment, or concomitant diuretic therapy: Start 6.25-12.5 mg PO bid-tid. CHF: Start 6.25-12.5 mg PO tid, usual 50-100 mg PO tid, max 450 mg/day (max 150 mg/day typical).

PEDS - Not approved in children.

UNAPPROVED ADULT - Hypertensive urgency: 12.5-25 mg PO, repeated once or twice if necessary at intervals of ≥30-60 minutes. Renal protecive dosing: 25 mg PO tid or 50 mg bid.

UNAPPROVED PEDS - HTN: Neonates: initial dose 0.1-0.4 mg/kg/day PO divided q6-8h. Infants: initial dose 0.15-0.3 mg/kg/dose, titrate to effective dose, max dose 6 mg/kg/day divided qd-qid. Children: initial dose 0.5-1 mg/kg/day PO divided tid. Titrate to effective dose, maximum dose 6 mg/kg/day.

FORMS - Generic/Trade: Tabs, scored 12.5,25, 50,100 mg.

NOTES - A captopril solution or suspension (1 mg/mL) can be made by dissolving Tabs in distilled water or flavored syrup. The solution is stable for 7days at room temperature.

enalapril (*Vasotec*) ▶LK ♀C (1st trimester) D (2nd & 3rd) ◗+ $$

ADULT - HTN: Start 5 mg PO qd, usual maintenance dose 10-40 mg PO qd or divided bid, max 40 mg/day. If oral therapy not possible, can use 1.25 mg IV q6h over 5 minutes, and increase up to 5 mg IV q6h if needed. Renal impairment or concomitant diuretic therapy: Start 2.5 mg PO qd. CHF: Start 2.5 mg PO bid, usual 10-20 mg PO bid, max 40 mg/day.

PEDS - Not approved in children.

UNAPPROVED ADULT - Hypertensive crisis: 1.25-5 mg IV q6h. Renal protective dosing: 10-20 mg PO qd.

UNAPPROVED PEDS - HTN: Start 0.1 mg/kg/day PO qd or divided bid, titrate to effective dose, maximum dose 0.5 mg/kg/day; 0.005-0.01 mg/kg/dose IV q8-24 hours.

FORMS - Generic/Trade: Tabs, scored 2.5,5, non-scored 10, 20 mg.

NOTES - BID dosing may be required for 24-hour BP control. An enalapril oral suspension (0.2 mg/ml) can be made by dissolving one 2.5 mg tab in 12.5 ml sterile water, use immediately.

fosinopril (*Monopril*) ▶LK ♀C (1st trimester) D (2nd & 3rd) ◗? $$

ADULT - HTN: Start 10 mg PO qd, usual maintenance dose 20-40 mg PO qd or divided bid, max 80 mg/day, but added effect not apparent above 40 mg/day. CHF: Start 10 mg PO qd, usual 20-40 mg PO qd, max 40 mg/day.

PEDS - Not approved in children.

FORMS - Trade: Tabs, scored 10, non-scored 20, 40 mg.

NOTES - Elimination 50% renal, 50% hepatic. Accumulation of drug negligible with impaired renal function.

lisinopril (*Prinivil, Zestril*) ▶K ♀C (1st trimester) D (2nd & 3rd) ◗? $$

ADULT - HTN: Start 10 mg PO qd, usual maintenance dose 20-40 mg PO qd, max 80 mg/day, but added effect not apparent above 40 mg/day. Renal impairment or concomitant diuretic therapy: Start 2.5-5 mg PO qd. CHF, acute MI: start 2.5-5 mg PO qd, usual 5-20 mg PO qd, max 40 mg/day.

PEDS - Not approved in children.

FORMS - Trade: Tabs, non-scored 2.5,10,20, 40, scored 5 mg.

moexipril (*Univasc*) ▶LK ♀C (1st trimester) D (2nd & 3rd) ◗? $

ADULT - HTN: Start 7.5 mg PO qd, usual maintenance dose 7.5-30 mg PO qd or divided bid, max 30 mg/day. Renal impairment or concomitant diuretic therapy: Start 3.75 mg PO qd.

PEDS - Not approved in children.

FORMS - Trade: Tabs, scored 7.5,15 mg.

NOTES - BID dosing may be required for 24-hour BP control.

perindopril (*Aceon*, ✤*Coversyl*) ▶K ♀C (1st trimester) D (2nd & 3rd) ◗? $$

ADULT - HTN: Start 4 mg PO qd, usual maintenance dose 4-8 mg PO qd or divided bid, max 16 mg/day.

PEDS - Not approved in children.

FORMS - Trade: Tabs, scored 2,4,8 mg.

NOTES - BID dosing does not provide clinically significant BP lowering compared to once daily dosing.

quinapril (*Accupril*) ▶LK ♀C (1st trimester) D (2nd & 3rd) ◗? $$

ADULT - HTN: Start 10 mg PO qd, usual maintenance dose 20-80 mg PO qd or divided bid, max 80 mg/day, but added effect not apparent above 40 mg/day. Renal impairment or concomitant diuretic therapy: Start 2.5-5 mg PO qd. CHF: Start 5 mg PO bid, usual maintenance dose 20-40 mg/day divided bid.

PEDS - Not approved in children.

FORMS - Trade: Tabs, scored 5, non-scored 10,20,40 mg.

NOTES - BID dosing may be required for 24-hour BP control.

ramipril (*Altace*) ▶LK ♀C (1st trimester) D (2nd & 3rd) ◗? $$

ADULT - HTN: Start 2.5 mg PO qd, usual maintenance dose 2.5-20 mg PO qd or divided bid,

max 20 mg/day. CHF: Start 2.5 mg PO bid, usual maintenance dose 5 mg PO bid. Reduce cardiovascular morbidity and mortality: Start 2.5 mg PO qd for 1 week, then 5 mg qd for 3 weeks, increase as tolerated to maintenance dose 10 mg qd.
PEDS - Not approved in children.
FORMS - Trade: Caps, 1.25,2.5,5,10 mg.
NOTES - BID dosing may be required for 24-hour BP control. cap contents can be sprinkled on applesauce and eaten or mixed with 120 mL of water or apple juice and swallowed. Mixtures are stable for 24 hr at room temperature or 48 hr refrigerated.

trandolapril (*Mavik*) ▶LK ♀C (1st trimester) D (2nd & 3rd) ▶? $$
ADULT - HTN: Start 1 mg PO qd in non-black patients or 2 mg PO qd in black patients, usual maintenance dose 2-4 mg PO qd or divided bid, max 8 mg/day, but added effect not apparent above 4 mg/day. Renal impairment or concomitant diuretic therapy: Start 0.5 mg PO qd. CHF/post MI: Start 0.5-1 mg PO qd, titrate to target dose 4 mg PO qd.
PEDS - Not approved in children.
FORMS - Trade: Tabs, scored 1, non-scored 2,4 mg.

CARDIOVASCULAR: Angiotensin Receptor Blockers (ARBs)

NOTES: See also antihypertensive combinations. To minimize the risk of hypotension in diuretic treated patients, hold diuretic dose (if possible) for 2-3 days before starting an ARB and use a low ARB dose. If diuretics can not be held, reduce the dose (if possible). Use with caution in volume depleted or hyponatremic patients. ARB use during the second and third trimester of pregnancy may cause injury or death to the developing fetus. Use with caution, if at all, in patients with a history of ACE inhibitor induced angioedema.

candesartan (*Atacand*) ▶K ♀C (1st trimester) D (2nd & 3rd) ▶? $$
ADULT - HTN: Start 16 mg PO qd, max 32 mg/day. Volume depleted patients: Start 8 mg PO qd.
PEDS - Not approved in children.
FORMS - Trade: Tabs, non-scored 4,8,16,32 mg.

eprosartan (*Teveten*) ▶Fecal excretion ♀C (1st trimester) D (2nd & 3rd) ▶? $$
ADULT - HTN: Start 600 mg PO qd, maximum 800 mg/day given qd or divided bid.
PEDS - Not approved in children.
FORMS - Trade: tab, scored 400, non-scored 600 mg.

irbesartan (*Avapro*) ▶L ♀C (1st trimester) D (2nd & 3rd) ▶? $$
ADULT - HTN: Start 150 mg PO qd, max 300 mg/day. Volume depleted patients: Start 75 mg PO qd.
PEDS - Not approved in children.
FORMS - Trade: Tabs, non-scored 75,150,300 mg.

losartan (*Cozaar*) ▶L ♀C (1st trimester) D (2nd & 3rd) ▶? $$
ADULT - HTN: Start 50 mg PO qd, max 100 mg/day given qd or divided bid. Volume depleted patients or history of hepatic impairment: Start with 25 mg PO qd.
PEDS - Not approved in children.
UNAPPROVED ADULT - Renal protective dosing: 50-100 mg PO qd.
FORMS - Trade: Tabs, non-scored 25,50,100 mg.

telmisartan (*Micardis*) ▶L ♀C (1st trimester) D (2nd & 3rd) ▶? $$
ADULT - HTN: Start 40 mg PO qd, max 80 mg/day.
PEDS - Not approved in children.
FORMS - Trade: Tabs, non-scored 40,80 mg.
NOTES - Swallow Tabs whole, do not break or crush. Caution in hepatic insufficiency.

valsartan (*Diovan*) ▶L ♀C (1st trimester) D (2nd & 3rd) ▶? $$
ADULT - HTN: Start 80 mg PO qd, max 320 mg/d.
PEDS - Not approved in children.
FORMS - Trade: Caps 80,160 mg.

CARDIOVASCULAR: Antiadrenergic Agents

clonidine (*Catapres*) ▶KL ♀C ▶? $
ADULT - HTN: Start 0.1 mg PO bid, usual maintenance dose 0.2-1.2 mg/day divided bid-tid, max 2.4 mg/day. Transdermal (Catapres-TTS): Start 0.1 mg/24 hour patch q week, titrate to desired effect, max effective dose 0.6 mg/24

hour (two, 0.3 mg/24 hour patches).
PEDS - HTN: Start 5-7 mcg/kg/day PO divided q6-12 hr, titrate at 5-7 day intervals to 5-25 mcg/kg/day divided q6h; max 0.9 mg/day. Transdermal therapy not recommended in children.
UNAPPROVED ADULT - HTN urgency: Initially, 0.1-0.2 mg PO, followed by 0.1 mg q1h as needed up to a total dose of 0.5-0.7 mg.
FORMS - Generic/Trade: Tabs, non-scored 0.1,0.2,0.3 mg. Trade only: Patch, 0.1,0.2,0.3 mg/24 hours.
NOTES - Sedation. Can get rebound HTN with abrupt discontinuation of tabs, especially at doses ≥ 0.8 mg/d. Taper therapy over 4-7 days to avoid rebound HTN. Dispose of used patches carefully, keep away from children.

doxazosin (*Cardura*) ▶L ♀C ◗? $$
WARNING - Not first line agent for hypertension. Increased risk of CHF in patients who used doxazosin compared to diuretic in treating HTN.
ADULT - HTN: Start 1 mg PO qhs, max 16 mg/day. BPH: see urology section.
PEDS - Not approved in children.
FORMS - Generic/Trade: Tabs, scored 1,2,4,8 mg.
NOTES - Dizziness, drowsiness, lightheadedness, syncope. Bedtime dosing may avoid side effects. Initial 1 mg dose is used to decrease postural hypotension that may occur after the first few doses. If therapy is interrupted for several days, restart at the 1 mg dose. Monitor BP after first dose, after each dose adjustment, and periodically thereafter.

guanabenz (*Wytensin*) ▶LK ♀C ◗- $$
WARNING - Start 2-4 mg PO bid, max 32 mg/day. Sedation, rebound HTN with abrupt discontinuation especially with high doses.
ADULT - HTN: Start 2-4 mg PO bid, max 32 mg/day.
PEDS - Children >12 years of age: initial dose 0.5-2 mg/day divided bid, usual maintenance dose 4-24 mg/day divided bid.
FORMS - Generic/Trade: Tabs, non-scored 4, scored 8 mg.
NOTES - Sedation. Can get rebound HTN with abrupt discontinuation, especially at higher doses (32 mg/day). Taper therapy over 4-7 days to avoid rebound HTN.

guanadrel (*Hylorel*) ▶K ♀B ◗? $$$
ADULT - HTN: Start 5 mg PO bid, usual maintenance dose 20-75 mg divided bid-qid.
PEDS - Not approved in children.
FORMS - Trade: Tabs, scored, 10,25 mg.
NOTES - Orthostatic hypotension may occur during dose titration. Monitor BP standing and supine. Decrease dosing frequency with renal impairment - start 5 mg PO qd; CrCl 30-60 ml/min, q24 hours; CrCl < 30 ml/min, q48 hours.

guanethidine (*Ismelin*) ▶L ♀C ◗- $$
WARNING - Orthostatic hypotension can occur; monitor BP standing and supine. Patient should be educated on symptoms of low BP and to avoid sudden or prolonged standing or exercise while using guanethidine.
ADULT - HTN: Start 10 mg PO qd, increase dose slowly (i.e. 5-7 days), usual maintenance dose 25-50 mg qd.
PEDS - Not approved in children.
UNAPPROVED PEDS - HTN: Start 0.2 mg/kg/day qd, increase every 7-10 days as needed by 0.2 mg/kg/day increments, max dose 3 mg/kg/day. Do not exceed max adult dose 50 mg qd.
FORMS - Trade: Tabs, scored, 10,25 mg.

guanfacine (*Tenex*) ▶K ♀B ◗? $
ADULT - HTN: Start 1 mg PO qhs, increase to 2-3 mg qhs if needed after 3-4 weeks, max 3 mg/day.
PEDS - HTN: ≥12 years of age, same as adult.
FORMS - Generic/Trade: Tabs, non-scored 1,2 mg.
NOTES - Sedation. Most of the drug's therapeutic effect is seen at 1 mg/day. Rebound HTN with abrupt discontinuation, but generally BP returns to pretreatment measurements slowly without ill effects.

methyldopa (*Aldomet*) ▶LK ♀B ◗+ $
ADULT - HTN: Start 250 mg PO bid-tid, usual maintenance dose 500-3000 mg/day divided bid-qid, max 3000 mg/day. Hypertensive crisis: 250-500 mg IV q6h, maximum 1gm IV q6h.
PEDS - HTN: 10 mg/kg/day PO divided bid-qid, titrate dose to a max dose 65 mg/kg/day.
FORMS - Generic/Trade: Tabs, non-scored 125,250,500 mg.
NOTES - Drug of choice for pregnancy-induced HTN, except near term or during labor. Otherwise, reserved as a 2nd or 3rd line agent for HTN. IV form has a slow onset of effect and other agents preferred for rapid reduction of BP. Hemolytic anemia possible.

prazosin (*Minipress*) ▶L ♀C ◗? $$
WARNING - Not first line agent for hypertension. Increased risk of CHF in patients who used doxazosin compared to diuretic in treating HTN.
ADULT - HTN: Start 1 mg PO bid-tid, usual

maintenance dose 20 mg/day divided bid-tid, max 40 mg/day, but doses > 20 mg/day usually do not increase efficacy.
PEDS - Not approved in children.
UNAPPROVED PEDS - HTN: Start 0.005 mg/kg PO single dose; increase slowly as needed up to maintenance dose 0.025-0.150 mg/kg/day divided q6 hours; max dose 0.4 mg/kg/day.
FORMS - Generic/Trade: Caps 1,2,5 mg.
NOTES - To avoid syncope, start with 1 mg qhs, and increase dose gradually.

reserpine (*Serpasil*) ▶LK ♀C ◗- $
ADULT - HTN: Start 0.05-0.1 mg PO qd or 0.1 mg PO qod, max dose 0.25 mg/day.
PEDS - Not approved in children.
FORMS - Generic: Tabs, scored, 0.1,0.25 mg.
NOTES - Drowsiness, fatigue, lethargy. May cause depression at higher doses, avoid use in patients with depression.

terazosin (*Hytrin*) ▶LK ♀C ◗? $$
WARNING - Not first line agent for hypertension. Increased risk of CHF in patients who used doxazosin compared to diuretic in treating HTN.
ADULT - HTN: Start 1 mg PO qhs, usual effective dose 1-5 mg PO qd or divided bid, max 20 mg/day. BPH: see urology section.
PEDS - Not approved in children.
FORMS - Generic (Tabs)/Trade (Caps): 1,2,5,10 mg.
NOTES - Dizziness, drowsiness, lightheadedness, syncope. Bedtime dosing may avoid side effects. Initial 1 mg dose is used to decrease postural hypotension that may occur after the first few doses. If therapy is interrupted for several days, restart at the 1 mg dose. Monitor BP after first dose, after each dose adjustment, and periodically thereafter.

CARDIOVASCULAR: Anti-Dysrhythmics / Cardiac Arrest

adenosine (*Adenocard*) ▶Plasma ♀C ◗? $$$
ADULT - PSVT conversion (not A-fib): 6 mg rapid IV & flush, preferably through a central line. If no response after 1-2 mins then 12 mg. A third dose of 12 mg may be given prn.
PEDS - PSVT conversion: initial dose 50-100 mcg/kg, give subsequent doses q2 min prn by increasing 50-100 mcg/kg each time, up to a max single dose of 300 mcg/kg.
UNAPPROVED PEDS - PSVT converson: Initial dose 0.1-0.2 mg/kg IV bolus; increase dose by 0.05 mg/kg increments every 2 minutes to max dose 0.25 mg/kg or 12 mg.
NOTES - Half-life is <10 seconds. Need higher dose if on theophylline or caffeine, lower dose if on dipyridamole or carbamazepine. Do not confuse with adenosine PHOSPHATE used for the symptomatic relief of varicose vein complications.

amiodarone (*Cordarone, Pacerone*) ▶L ♀D ◗- $$$$
ADULT - Life-threatening ventricular arrhythmia: Load 150 mg IV over 10 min, then 1 mg/min x 6 hrs, then 0.5 mg/min x 18h. Mix in D5W. Oral loading dose 800-1600 mg PO qd for 1-3 weeks, reduce dose to 400-800 mg qd for 1 month when arrhythmia is controlled or adverse effects are prominent, then reduce to lowest effective dose, usually 200-400 mg qd.
PEDS - Not approved in children.
UNAPPROVED ADULT - Refractory atrial fibrillation: loading dose 600-800 mg PO qd for 7-10 days, then 200-400 mg qd. Cardiac arrest/VF: 300 mg IV push, repeat dose 150 mg IV prn. Stable monomorphic ventricular tachycardia: 150 mg IV over 10 min, repeat q10-15 min prn.
UNAPPROVED PEDS - Ventricular arrhythmia: Loading dose 10-15 mg/kg/day PO for 4-14 days and/or until arrhythmia is controlled or adverse effects are prominent, then reduce dose to 5 mg/kg/d for several weeks. Reduce to lowest effective dose. IV therapy limited data; 5 mg/kg IV over 30 minutes; followed by 5 mcg/kg/min infusion; increase infusion as needed up to max 10 mcg/kg/min. Give loading dose in 1 mg/kg aliquots with each aliquot given over 5-10 min. Do not exceed 30 mg/min.
FORMS - Generic/Trade: Tabs, scored 200 mg.
NOTES - Photosensitivity with oral therapy. Pulmonary toxicity. Hypo or hyperthyroidism possible. Long elimination half-life, approximately 25-50 days. May increase digoxin levels by 70% and INRs with warfarin therapy by 100%. A dosage reduction in warfarin of 33-50% is recommended. Give bid if intolerable GI effects occur with qd dosing. IV therapy may cause hypotension in adults and gasping respirations, hypotension, bradycardia, and cardiovascular collapse in neonates. Adverse effects on male reproductive tract development in relation to plasticizers from IV tubing may occur in children. Administration in infants and toddlers

using IV bolus doses may be considered instead of IV tubing. Contraindicated with marked sinus bradycardia and second or third degree heart block in the absence of a functioning pacemaker.

atropine ▶K ♀C ▶- $

ADULT - Bradyarrhythmia/CPR: 0.5-1.0 mg IV q3-5 mins, max 0.04 mg/kg (2 mg).

PEDS - CPR: 0.02 mg/kg/dose IV q5 mins for 2-3 doses prn (max single dose 0.5 mg); minimum single dose, 0.1 mg; max cumulative dose 1 mg.

UNAPPROVED ADULT - ET administration prior to IV access: 2-2.5 x the recommended IV dose in 10 ml of NS or distilled water.

bicarbonate sodium ▶K ♀C ▶? $

ADULT - Cardiac arrest: 1 mEq/kg/dose IV initially, followed by repeat doses up to 0.5 mg/kg at 10 minute intervals during continued arrest. Severe acidosis: 2-5 mEq/kg dose IV administered as a 4-8 hour infusion. Repeat dosing based on lab values.

PEDS - Cardiac arrest: Neonates or infants < 2 years of age, 1 mEq/kg dose IV slow injection initially, followed by repeat doses up to 1 mEq/kg at 10 minute intervals during continued arrest. To avoid intracranial hemorrhage due to hypertonicity, use a 1:1 dilution of 8.4% (1 mEq/mL) sodium bicarbonate and dextrose 5% or use the 4.2% (0.5 mEq/mL) product.

NOTES - Full correction of bicarbonate deficit should not be attempted during the first 24h. May paradoxically exacerbate intracellular acidosis.

bretylium (*Bretylol*, ✤*Bretylate*) ▶K ♀C ▶? $$

ADULT - Ventricular arrhythmia: Initial 5 mg/kg IV bolus over 1 minute, then 10 mg/kg if needed at 5-30 minute intervals up to a total 30-35 mg/kg. Infusion 500 mg in 50 ml D5W (10 mg/mL) at 1-3 mg/min (6-18 mL/h).

PEDS - Not approved in children.

UNAPPROVED PEDS - Ventricular fibrillation: Initial dose 5 mg/kg IV, followed by 10 mg/kg IV if ventricular fibrillation persists.

NOTES - Hyperthermia; considered 2nd line agent due to delayed onset of antiarrhythmic action, hypotension (occurs commonly), and increased ventricular irritability.

digoxin (*Lanoxin, Lanoxicaps, Digitek*) ▶KL ♀C ▶+ $

ADULT - Atrial fibrillation/CHF: 0.125-0.25 mg PO qd. Rapid A-fib: Load 0.5 mg IV, then 0.25 mg IV q6h x 2 doses, maintenance 0.125-0.375 mg IV/PO qd.

PEDS - Arrhythmia: Oral loading dose with Tabs or elixir: premature neonate, 20-30 mcg/kg; full-term neonate, 25-35 mcg/kg; 1-24 months, 35-60 mcg/kg; 2-5 years, 30-40 mcg/kg; 5-10 years, 20-35 mcg/kg; > 10 years, 10-15 mcg/kg. Use 25-35% of oral loading dose for maintenance dose. Caution - pediatric doses are in mcg, elixir product is labeled in mg/ml.

FORMS - Generic/Trade: Tabs, scored (Lanoxin, Digitek) 0.125,0.25, 0.5 mg; elixir 0.05 mg/mL. Trade only: Caps (Lanoxicaps), 0.05,0.1, 0.2 mg.

NOTES - Adjust dose based on response and therapeutic serum levels (range from 0.8-2.2 ng/mL). Higher levels may be needed for atrial fibrillation. Toxicity exacerbated by hypokalemia. 100 mcg Lanoxicaps = 125 mcg Tabs or elixir. Avoid administering digoxin IM due to severe local irritation. Elimination prolonged with renal impairment, monitor serum levels carefully. Many drug and herb interactions.

digoxin-immune Fab (*Digibind*) ▶K ♀C ▶? $$$$$

ADULT - Digoxin toxicity: 2-20 vials IV, one formula is: Number vials = (serum dig level in ng/mL) x (kg) / 100.

PEDS - Same as adult.

NOTES - Do not draw serum digoxin concentrations after administering digoxin-immune Fab; levels will be falsely elevated for several days. One vial binds approximately 0.5 mg digoxin.

disopyramide (*Norpace, Norpace CR*, ✤*Rythmodan-LA*) ▶KL ♀C ▶+ $$$$

WARNING - Proarrhythmic. Increased mortality in patients with non-life threatening ventricular arrhythmias and structural heart disease (i.e. MI, LV dysfunction).

ADULT - Rarely indicated, consult cardiologist. Ventricular arrhythmia: 400-800 mg PO daily in divided doses (immediate-release, q6h or extended-release, q12h).

PEDS - Ventricular arrhythmia: Divide dose q6h. <1 yr, 10-30 mg/kg/day; 1-4 yrs, 10-20 mg/kg/day; 4-12 yrs, 10-15 mg/kg/day; 12-18 yrs, 6-15 mg/kg/day.

FORMS - Generic/Trade: caps, immediate-release, 100,150 mg; extended-release, 100,150 mg.

NOTES - Anticholinergic side effects (dry mouth, constipation, blurred vision, urinary hesitancy) commonly occur. Reduce dose in patients with CrCl < 40 mL/min.

dofetilide (*Tikosyn*) ▶KL ♀C ▶- $$$$

WARNING - Consult cardiologist before using. Tikosyn is available only to hospitals and prescribers who have received appropriate dosing and treatment initiation education. Contraindicated if CrCl is < 20 ml/min or QTc interval >440 msec, or > 500 msec in patients with ventricular conduction abnormalities. Tikosyn must be initiated or re-initiated in a setting with continuous ECG monitoring and with personnel trained to manage serious ventricular arrhythmias. Monitor in this setting for ≥3 days. Do not discharge if ≤12 h since electrical or pharmacological conversion to normal sinus rhythm.

ADULT - A-fib/flutter: Specialized dosing based on creatinine clearance and QTc interval.

PEDS - Not approved in children.

FORMS - Trade: Caps, 0.125,0.25,0.5 mg.

NOTES - Use in patients with heart rates < 50 bpm has not been studied. Monitor K+ and Mg+ (low levels increase risk of arrhythmias). Monitor renal function and QTc interval q3h during therapy initiation. Tikosyn effects may be increased by known cytochrome P450 3A4 inhibitors and other agents. Contraindicated when used with SMZ-TMP, verapamil, cimetidine, and ketoconazole.

epinephrine (*EpiPen, EpiPen Jr*) ▶Plasma ♀C ◗- $

ADULT - Cardiac arrest: 1 mg (1:10,000 solution) IV, repeat every 3-5 minutes if needed; infusion 1 mg in 250 mL D5W (4 mcg/mL) at 1-4 mcg/min (15-60 mL/h). Anaphylaxis: 0.1-0.5 mg SC/IM (1:1,000 solution), may repeat SC dose every 10-15 minutes for anaphylactic shock.

PEDS - Cardiac arrest: 0.01 mg/kg IV/IO or 0.1 mg/kg ET, repeat 0.1-0.2 mg/kg IV/IO/ET every 3-5 minutes if needed. Neonates: 0.01-0.03 mg/kg IV/ET, repeat every 3-5 minutes if needed; IV infusion start 0.1 mcg/kg/min, increase in increments of 0.1 mcg/kg/min if needed, max 1 mcg/kg/min. Anaphylaxis: 0.01 mg/kg SC, may repeat SC dose at 20 min to 4h intervals depending on severity of condition.

UNAPPROVED ADULT - Symptomatic bradycardia unresponsive to atropine: 2-10 mcg/min IV infusion. ET administration prior to IV access: 2-2.5 x the recommended IV dose in 10 ml of NS or distilled water.

FORMS - Adults: EpiPen Auto-injector delivers 0.3 mg (1:1,000 soln) IM dose. Children: EpiPen Jr. Autoinjector delivers 0.15 mg (1:2,000 solution) IM dose.

NOTES - Use the 1:10,000 injectable solution for IV use in cardiac arrest (10 mL = 1 mg). For pediatric patients, use 1:10,000 for initial IV dose, then 1:1,000 for subsequent dosing or ET doses. Use the 1:1,000 injectable solution for SC/IM use in anaphylaxis (0.1 mL = 0.1 mg).

flecainide (*Tambocor*) ▶K ♀C ◗- $$$$

WARNING - Proarrhythmic. Increased mortality in patients with non-life threatening ventricular arrhythmias, structural heart disease (i.e. MI, LV dysfunction), and chronic atrial fibrillation.

ADULT - Rarely indicated, consult cardiologist. PSVT, PAF: Start 50 mg PO q12h, max dose 300 mg/day. Sustained VT: Start 100 mg PO q12h, max dose 400 mg/day.

PEDS - Not approved in children. Consult pediatric cardiologist.

FORMS - Trade: Tabs, non-scored 50, scored 100,150 mg.

NOTES - Decrease dose by 25-50% with CrCl < 20 mL/min.

ibutilide (*Corvert*) ▶K ♀C ◗? $$$$$

WARNING - Proarrhythmic.

ADULT - Recent onset A-fib/flutter: 1 mg (10 mL) IV over 10 mins, may repeat if no response after 10 additional minutes. Patients < 60 kg: 0.01 mg/kg up to 1 mg IV over 10 min, may repeat if no response after 10 additional minutes. Useful in combination with DC cardioversion if DC cardioversion alone is unsuccessful.

PEDS - Not approved in children.

NOTES - Keep on cardiac monitor ≥4 hours. Use with caution when QT interval is >500 ms or in patients already using class Ia or III antiarrhythmics. Stop infusion when arrhythmia is terminated.

isoproterenol (*Isuprel*) ▶LK ♀C ◗? $$

ADULT - Refractory bradycardia or third degree AV block: 0.02-0.06 mg (1-3 mL of a 1:50,000 dilution) IV bolus or IV infusion (2 mg in 250 ml D5W = 8 mcg/mL) at 5 mcg/min; 5 mcg/min = 37 mL/h. General dose range 2-20 mcg/min.

PEDS - Refractory bradycardia or third degree AV block: Start IV infusion 0.05 mcg/kg/min, increase every 5-10 min by 0.1 mcg/kg/min until desired effect or onset of toxicity, max 2 mcg/kg/min. 10 kg: 0.1 mcg/kg/min = 8 mL/h.

lidocaine (*Xylocaine, Xylocard*) ▶LK ♀B ◗? $

ADULT - Ventricular arrhythmia: Load 1 mg/kg IV, then 0.5 mg/kg IV q8-10min as needed to max 3 mg/kg. IV infusion: 4 gm in 500 mL D5W (8 mg/ml) at 1-4 mg/min.

PEDS - Ventricular arrhythmia: Loading dose 1 mg/kg IV/IO slowly; may repeat for 2 doses 10-15 minutes apart; max 3-5 mg/kg in one hour. ET tube: Use 2-2.5 times IV dose. IV infusion:

4 gm in 500 mL D5W (8 mg/ml) at 20-50 mcg/kg/min. 10 kg: 40 mcg/kg/min = 3 mL/h.

UNAPPROVED ADULT - ET administration prior to IV access: 2-2.5 x the recommended IV dose in 10 ml of NS or distilled water.

NOTES - Reduce infusion in CHF, liver disease, elderly. Not for routine use after acute MI.

mexiletine (*Mexitil*) ▶L ♀C ▶- $$$

WARNING - Proarrhythmic. Increased mortality in patients with non-life threatening ventricular arrhythmias and structural heart disease (i.e. MI, LV dysfunction).

ADULT - Rarely indicated, consult cardiologist. Ventricular arrhythmia: Start 200 mg PO q8h with food or antacid, max dose 400 mg/day. Patients responding to q8h dosing may be converted to q12h dosing with careful monitoring, max dose 450 mg q12h.

PEDS - Not approved in children.

FORMS - Generic/Trade: Caps, 150,200,250 mg.

NOTES - Patients may require decreased dose with severe liver disease.

moricizine (*Ethmozine*) ▶L ♀B ▶? $$$$

WARNING - Proarrhythmic. Increased mortality in patients with non-life threatening ventricular arrhythmias and structural heart disease (i.e. MI, LV dysfunction).

ADULT - Rarely indicated, consult cardiologist. Ventricular arrhythmia: Start 200 mg PO q8h, max dose 900 mg/day. Patients responding to q8h dosing may be converted to q12h dosing with careful monitoring.

PEDS - Not approved in children.

FORMS - Trade: Tabs, non-scored 200,250,300 mg.

procainamide (*Procanbid, Pronestyl*) ▶LK ♀C ▶- $$$

WARNING - Proarrhythmic. Increased mortality in patients with non-life threatening ventricular arrhythmias and structural heart disease (i.e. MI, LV dysfunction). Positive ANA titer, lupus erythematosus-like syndrome.

ADULT - Ventricular arrhythmia: 50 mg/kg/day PO; 250-625 mg PO q3h (immediate-release products), 500-1250 mg PO q6h (SR products), 500-1000 mg PO q12h (Procanbid product). IV dosing: Load 100 mg IV q10 min or 20 mg/min (150 mL/h) until: 1) QRS widens >50%, 2) dysrhythmia suppressed, 3) hypotension, or 4) total of 17 mg/kg or 1000 mg. Infusion 2g in 250 ml D5W (8 mg/mL) at 2-6 mg/min (15-45 mL/h). If rhythm unresponsive, guide therapy by serum procainamide/NAPA levels.

PEDS - Not approved in children.

UNAPPROVED PEDS - Arrhythmia: 15-50 mg/kg/day PO immediate-release products divided q 3-6 h; 2-6 mg/kg IV over 5 min, max loading dose 100 mg, repeat loading dose every 5-10 min as needed up to max 15 mg/kg; 20-80 mcg/kg/min IV infusion, max dose 2 g/day. Consult peds cardiologist or intensivist.

FORMS - Generic/Trade: tabs, immediate-release, non-scored and caps (Pronestyl) 250,375,500 mg. Generic only: tabs, sustained-release, non-scored (generic procainamide SR, q6h dosing), 250,500,750 mg. Trade only: tabs, extended-release, non-scored (Procanbid, q12h dosing) 500,1000 mg.

NOTES - Do not break or crush SR or XR products. Swallow Tabs whole.

propafenone (*Rythmol*) ▶L ♀C ▶? $$$$

WARNING - Proarrhythmic. Increased mortality in patients with non-life threatening ventricular arrhythmias and structural heart disease (i.e. MI, LV dsyfunction).

ADULT - Rarely indicated, consult cardiologist. PSVT, PAF, sustained VT: Initial 150 mg PO q8h, increase to 225 mg q8h in 3-4 days if needed, max 300 mg q8h.

PEDS - Not approved in children.

FORMS - Trade: Tabs, scored 150,225,300 mg.

quinidine gluconate (*Quinaglute, Quinalan, Quinate*) ▶LK ♀C ▶- $$

WARNING - Proarrhythmic. Increased mortality in patients with non-life threatening ventricular arrhythmias and structural heart disease (i.e. MI, LV dysfunction).

ADULT - Prevention of atrial fibrillation/flutter and ventricular premature complexes: 324-648 mg PO q8-12h. Consider inpatient rhythm and QT monitoring during institution of therapy, especially with LV dysfunction.

PEDS - Not approved in children.

UNAPPROVED PEDS - Arrhythmia: Test dose 2 mg/kg IV (max 200 mg), then 2-10 mg/kg IV q3-4h prn.

FORMS - Generic/Trade: Tabs, extended-release, non-scored (Quinaglute) 324, scored (Quinalan) 324 mg.

NOTES - Extended-release Tabs may be broken in half & swallowed. Do not chew or crush.

quinidine sulfate (*Quinidex, Quinora*) ▶LK ♀C ▶- $

WARNING - Proarrhythmic. Increased mortality in patients with non-life threatening ventricular arrhythmias and structural heart disease (i.e. MI, LV dysfunction).

ADULT - Conversion of atrial fibrillation: immediate-release, 300-400 mg PO q6h. Atrial fibrillation/flutter: immediate-release, 200-400

lation/flutter: immediate-release, 200-400 mg PO 6-8h; extended-release, 300-600 mg PO q8-12h. Consider inpatient rhythm and QT monitoring during institution of therapy, especially in patients with LV dysfunction.

PEDS - Not approved in children.

UNAPPROVED PEDS - Arrhythmia: Test dose 2 mg/kg PO (max 200 mg), then 15-60 mg/kg/day divided q6h.

FORMS - Generic/Trade: Tabs, non-scored immediate-release 200,300 mg (Quinora). Generic/Trade: Tabs, extended-release 300 mg (Quinidex Extentabs).

NOTES - Due not chew or crush extended-release Tabs.

sotalol (*Betapace, Betapace AF*, ✤*Rylosol, Sotacar*) ▸K ♀B ◗- $$$$

WARNING - Patients should be in a facility for ≥3 days with ECG monitoring, cardiac resuscitation available, and creatinine clearance calculated when initiating or re-initiating Betapace AF. Do not substitute Betapace for Betapace AF.

ADULT - Ventricular arrhythmia (Betapace), A-fib/A-flutter (Betapace AF): Start 80 mg PO bid, usual maintenance dose 160-320 mg/day divided bid, max 640 mg/day.

PEDS - Not approved in children.

FORMS - Generic/Trade: Tabs, scored 80,120, 160,240 mg. Trade only: 80,120,160 mg (Betapace AF).

NOTES - Proarrhythmic. Caution, higher incidence of torsades de pointes with doses >320 mg/day, use in women, or CHF. Adjust dose if CrCl < 60 mL/min.

tocainide (*Tonocard*) ▸L ♀C ◗? $$$

WARNING - Blood dyscrasis, pulmonary fibrosis. Proarrhythmic. Increased mortality in patients with non-life threatening ventricular arrhythmias and structural heart disease (i.e. MI, LV dysfunction).

ADULT - Rarely indicated, consult cardiologist. Ventricular arrhythmia: Start 400 mg PO q8h, max dose 2400 mg/day. Patients responding to q8h dosing may be converted to q12h dosing with careful monitoring.

PEDS - Not approved in children.

FORMS - Trade: Tabs, scored 400,600 mg.

vasopressin (*Pitressin, ADH*, ✤*Pressyn*) ▸LK ♀C ◗? $

UNAPPROVED ADULT - Ventricular fibrillation: 40 units IV once.

CARDIOVASCULAR: Anti-Hyperlipidemic Agents - Bile Acid Sequestrants

cholestyramine (*Questran, Questran Light, Prevalite, LoCHOLEST, LoCHOLEST Light*) ▸Fecal excretion ♀C ◗+ $$$

ADULT - Elevated LDL cholesterol: Start 4 g PO qd-bid before meals, usual maintenance 12-24 g/day in divided doses bid-qid before meals, max 24 g/day.

PEDS - Not approved in children.

UNAPPROVED ADULT - Cholestasis-associated pruritis: 4-8 g bid-tid.

UNAPPROVED PEDS - Elevated LDL cholesterol: Start 240 mg/kg/day PO divided tid before meals, usual maintenance 8-16 g/day divided tid.

FORMS - Generic/Trade: Powder for oral suspension, 4 g cholestyramine resin / 9 g powder (Questran, LoCHOLEST), 4 g cholestyramine resin / 5 g powder (Questran Light), 4 g cholestyramine resin / 5.5 g powder (Prevalite, LoCHOLEST Light).

NOTES - BID dosing recommended, but may divide up to 6x/day. Mix powder with 60-180 mL of water, milk, fruit juice, or drink. Avoid carbonated liquids for mixing. GI problems common, mainly constipation. Administer other drugs at least 1 hour before or 4-6 h after cholestyramine to avoid decreased absorption of the other agent. May cause elevation of HDL cholesterol and no change or elevated triglycerides.

colesevelam (*Welchol*) ▸Not absorbed ♀B ◗+ $$$$

ADULT - Elevated LDL cholesterol: 3 tabs bid with meals or 6 tabs once daily with a meal, max dose 7 tabs/day. Same dose when used in combination with other agents (i.e. statin drug).

PEDS - Not approved in children.

FORMS - Trade: Tabs, non-scored, 625 mg.

NOTES - Take with a full glass of water or other non-carbonated liquid. GI problems common, mainly constipation. May cause elevation of HDL cholesterol and triglycerides.

colestipol (*Colestid, Colestid Flavored*) ▸Fecal excretion ♀B ◗+ $$$

ADULT - Elevated LDL cholesterol: Tabs: Start 2 g PO qd-bid, max 16 g/day. Granules: Start 5 g PO qd-bid, increase by 5 g increments as tolerated at 1-2 month intervals, max 30 g/day.

PEDS - Not approved in children.

UNAPPROVED PEDS - 125-250 mg/kg/day PO in divided doses bid-qid, dosing range 10-20 g/day.
FORMS - Trade: Tab 1 g. Granules for oral suspension, 5 g / 7.5 g powder.
NOTES - Mix granules in at least 90 mL of water, milk, fruit juice, or drink. Avoid carbonated liquids for mixing. Swallow Tabs whole with a full glass of liquid to avoid tab disintegration in the esophagus. GI problems common, mainly constipation. Administer other drugs at least 1 hour before or 4-6 h after colestipol to avoid decreased absorption of the other agent. May cause elevation of HDL cholesterol and no change or elevated triglycerides .

LIPID RESPONSE* (%change)	Cholesterol	LDL	HDL	Triglycerides	LFT MONITORING FOR STATINS**
atorvastatin 10 mg	-29%	-39%	+6%	-19%	B, 12 wk, semiannually
fluvastatin 40 mg	-19%	-25%	+4%	-14%	B, 12 wk
lovastatin 20 mg	-17%	-24%	+7%	-10%	B, 6 & 12 wk, semiannually
pravastatin 20 mg	-24%	-32%	+2%	-11%	B, 12 wk
simvastatin 20 mg	-28%	-38%	+8%	-15%	B, 6 mo, 12 mo ***

*Doses are recommended starting doses. Data taken from prescribing information. **Schedule for LFT monitoring when starting therapy and after each dosage increase. Stop statin therapy if LFTs are > 3 times upper limit of normal. ***For first year only or after last dose increase. Get LFTs 3,6,12 months after increasing to 80 mg. B = baseline, LDL = low-density lipoprotein, LFT = liver function tests, HDL = high-density lipoprotein, N/A = not available.

CARDIOVASCULAR: Anti-Hyperlipidemic Agents – HMG-CoA Reductase Inhibitors ("Statins")

NOTES: Hepatotoxicity - monitor LFTs periodically (see table). Myopathy a concern especially when combined with fibric acid agents (gemfibrozil, fenofibrate) and niacin. Weigh potential risk of combination therapy against potential benefit.

atorvastatin (*Lipitor*) ▶L ♀X ▶- $$$
ADULT - Hypercholesterolemia: Start 10 mg PO qd with or without food, increase at no less than 4-week intervals to a max of 80 mg/day.
PEDS - Homozygous familial hypercholesterolemia in children ≥9 years of age: Start 10 mg PO qd, max 80 mg/day.
FORMS - Trade: Tabs, non-scored 10,20,40,80 mg.
NOTES - Metabolism may be decreased by known inhibitors of cytochrome P450 3A4 enzyme system (erythromycin, clarithromycin, cyclosporine, ketoconazole, itraconazole, HIV protease inhibitors, nefazodone, grapefruit and grapefruit juice), increasing risk of myopathy. Increased risk of myopathy and rhabdomyolysis when used with a fibric acid agent.

cerivastatin (*Baycol*) ▶LK ♀X ▶- $$
WARNING - Combined use with gemfibrozil (Lopid) is contraindicated due to increased risk of rhabdomyolysis.
ADULT - Withdrawn from the market, 8/01.
PEDS - Not approved in children.
FORMS - Trade: Tabs, non-scored 0.2,0.3,0.4 ,0.8 mg.
NOTES - Metabolism may be decreased by known inhibitors of cytochrome P450 3A4 enzyme system (erythromycin, clarithromycin, cyclosporine, ketoconazole, itraconazole, HIV protease inhibitors, nefazodone, grapefruit and grapefruit juice), increasing risk of myopathy.

fluvastatin (*Lescol, Lescol XL*) ▶L ♀X ▶- $$
ADULT - Hypercholesterolemia: Start 20 mg PO qhs for LDL-C reduction to a goal of <25%, 40-80 mg qhs for goal of ≥25%, max 80 mg/day, give 80 mg/day qd (Lescol XL) or 40 mg bid.
PEDS - Not approved in children.
FORMS - Trade: Caps, 20,40 mg; tab, extended-release, non-scored 80 mg.
NOTES - Not metabolized substantially by the cytochrome P450 isoenzyme 3A4, so less potential for drug interactions. Increased risk of myopathy and rhabdomyolysis when used with a fibric acid agent.

lovastatin (*Mevacor*) ▶L ♀X ▶- $$$
ADULT - Hypercholesterolemia: Start 20 mg PO with the evening meal, increase at no less than 4 week intervals to a max of 80 mg/day. Daily doses may be divided bid.
PEDS - Not approved in children.
FORMS - Trade:Tabs, non-scored 10,20,40 mg.

NOTES - Metabolism significantly decreased by known inhibitors of cytochrome P450 3A4 enzyme system (erythromycin, clarithromycin, cyclosporine, ketoconazole, itraconazole, HIV protease inhibitors, nefazodone, grapefruit and grapefruit juice), increasing risk of myopathy. Increased risk of myopathy and rhabdomyolysis when used with a fibric acid agent.

pravastatin (*Pravachol*) ▶L ♀X ◗- $$$

ADULT - Hypercholesterolemia: Start 10-40 mg PO qd, increase at ≥4 week intervals to a max of 40 mg/day. Renal or hepatic impairment: Start 10 mg PO qd.

PEDS - Not approved in children.

FORMS - Trade:Tabs, non-scored 10,20,40 mg.

NOTES - Not metabolized substantially by the cytochrome P450 isoenzyme 3A4, less potential for drug interactions. Increased risk of myopathy and rhabdomyolysis when used with a fibric acid agent.

simvastatin (*Zocor*) ▶L ♀X ◗- $$$$

ADULT - Hypercholesterolemia: Start 20 mg PO qpm, 40 mg qpm for LDL-C reduction >45%, increase prn at ≥4 week intervals to max 80 mg/day.

PEDS - Not approved in children.

FORMS - Trade: Tabs, non-scored 5,10,20,40, 80 mg.

NOTES - Metabolism significantly decreased by known inhibitors of cytochrome P450 3A4 enzyme system (erythromycin, clarithromycin, cyclosporine, ketoconazole, itraconazole, HIV protease inhibitors, nefazodone, grapefruit and grapefruit juice), increasing risk of myopathy. Increased risk of myopathy and rhabdomyolysis when used with a fibric acid agent.

LDL CHOLESTEROL GOALS[1]

Risk Category	*LDL Goal (mg/dL)*	*Lifestyle Changes at LDL (mg/dL)*[2]	*Also Consider Meds at LDL (mg/dL)*
CHD or equivalent risk[3] (10-year risk >20%)	<100	≥100	≥130 (100-129: Rx optional)
2+ risk factors[4] (10-year risk ≤20%)	<130	≥130	10-yr risk 10-20%: ≥130 10-yr risk <10%: ≥160
0 to 1 risk factor (10-year risk <10%)	<160	≥160	≥190 (160-189: Rx optional)

1. CHD=coronary heart disease. LDL=low density lipoprotein. Adapted from NCEP: *JAMA* 2001; 285:2486. All 10-year risks based upon Framingham stratification. **2**. Dietary modification, weight reduction, exercise. **3**. Equivalent risk defined as diabetes, other atherosclerotic disease (peripheral artery disease, abdominal aortic aneurysm, symptomatic carotid artery disease), or multiple risk factors such that 10 year risk >20%. **4**. Risk factors: Cigarette smoking, HTN (BP≥140/90 mmHg or on antihypertensive meds), low HDL (<40 mg/dL), family hx of CHD (1° relative: ♂ <55 yo, ♀ <65 yo), age (♂ ≥45 yo, ♀ ≥55 yo).

CARDIOVASCULAR: Anti-Hyperlipidemic Agents - Other

clofibrate (*Atromid-S*) ▶LK ♀C ◗- $$$$

ADULT - Hypertriglyceridemia: 1000 mg PO bid.

PEDS - Not approved in children.

FORMS - Generic/Trade: Caps, 500 mg.

NOTES - May increase the effect of warfarin. Increased risk of myopathy and rhabdomyolysis when used with a statin.

fenofibrate (*Tricor*) ▶LK ♀C ◗- $$$

ADULT - Hypertriglyceridemia: Start 67 mg (1 cap) PO qd with a meal. Increase at ≥4 week intervals; usual maintenance dose is 134-200 mg PO qd with a meal. Max dose 200 mg qd.

PEDS - Not approved in children.

FORMS - Trade: cap, 67,134,200 mg.

NOTES - Monitor LFTs, dose related hepatotoxicity. Increased risk of myopathy and rhabdomyolysis when used with a statin.

gemfibrozil (*Lopid*, ✤*Lipidil Micro*) ▶LK ♀C ◗? $$

ADULT - Hypertriglyceridemia: 600 mg PO bid before meals. Some patients may respond to increased doses up to 1.5 g/day.

PEDS - Not approved in children.

FORMS - Generic/Trade: Tabs, scored 600 mg.

NOTES - Increased risk of myopathy and rhabdomyolysis when used with a statin.

niacin (*nicotinic acid, vitamin B3, Niacor, Nicolar, Niaspan*) ▶K ♀C ◗? $

ADULT - Hyperlipidemia: Start 50-100 mg PO bid-tid with meals, increase slowly, usual main-

tenance range 1.5-3 g/day, max 6 g/day. Extended-release (Niaspan): Start 500 mg qhs with a low-fat snack for 4 weeks, increase as needed every 4 weeks to max 2000 mg.
PEDS - Not approved in children.
FORMS - Generic (OTC): Tabs, scored 25,50, 100,150,500 mg. Trade: Tabs, immediate-release, scored (Niacor), 500 mg; ext'd-release, non-scored (Niaspan), 500,750,1000 mg.
NOTES - Extended-release formulations not listed here may have greater hepatotoxicity. Do not break, chew, or crush extended-release niacin, swallow whole. Aspirin or ibuprofen, 30 minutes before niacin doses may decrease flushing reaction. Titrate niacin slowly to avoid flushing events. Niacin may worsen glucose control, peptic ulcer disease, gout, headaches, and menopausal flushing. Significantly lowers LDL-cholesterol and triglycerides, raises HDL-cholesterol. Increased risk of myopathy and rhabdomyolysis when used with a fibric acid agent or a statin.

omega-3 fatty acid (fish oil) (*Promega, Cardio-Omega 3, Sea-Omega, Marine Lipid Concentrate, SuperEPA 1200*) ▶L ♀? ◗? $$
PEDS - Note approved in children.
UNAPPROVED ADULT - Hypertriglyceridemia: 3-5 gm EPA+DHA content daily. Secondary prevention of CHD: 750-1000 mg EPA+DHA content daily.
FORMS - Trade/Generic: cap, shown as EPA+DHA mg content, 240 (Promega Pearls), 300 (Cardi-Omega 3, Max EPA), 400 (Promega), 500 (Sea-Omega), 600 (Marine Lipid Concentrate, SuperEPA 1200), 875 mg (SuperEPA 2000).
NOTES - Dose dependent GI upset, increase LDL-cholesterol, excessive bleeding, hyperglycemia. Marine Lipid Concentrate, Super EPA 1200 mg cap contains EPA 360 mg + DHA 240 mg, daily dose = 5-8 Caps. Treatment doses lowers triglycerides by 30-50%. Safe to use with other cholesterol lowering drugs. Caps contain vitamin E. Vitamin E content increases with cap strength.

CARDIOVASCULAR: Antihypertensive Combinations

ACE Inhibitor/Diuretic: *Accuretic, Capozide, Lotensin HCT, Prinizide, Uniretic, Vaseretic, Zestoretic.* ACE Inhibitor/Calcium Channel Blocker: *Lexxel, Lotrel, Tarka.* ARB/Diuretic: *Atacand HCT, Avalide, Diovan HCT, Hyzaar, Micardis HCT.* Beta-blocker/Diuretic: *Corzide, Inderide, Inderide LA, Lopressor HCT, Tenoretic, Timolide, Ziac.* Diuretic combinations: *Aldactazide, Dyazide, Maxzide, Maxzide-25, Moduretic, Moduret.* Diuretic/miscellaneous antihypertensive: *Aldoclor-250, Aldoril-15, Aldoril-25, Aldoril D30, Aldoril D50, Apresazide, Combipres, Diutensin-R, Enduronyl, Enduronyl Forte, Minizide, Rauzide, Renese-R, Salutensin, Salutensin-Demi, Ser-Ap-Es.*

NOTES: Dosage should first be adjusted by using each drug separately. See component drugs for metabolism, pregnancy, and lactation.

***Accuretic* (quinapril + HCTZ)** $$
ADULT - HTN: Establish dose using component drugs first. Dosing interval: qd.
PEDS - Not approved in children.
FORMS - Trade: Tabs, 10/12.5, 20/12.5, 20/25.

***Aldactazide* (spironolactone + HCTZ)** $$
ADULT - HTN: Establish dose using component drugs first. Dosing interval: qd-bid.
PEDS - Not approved in children.
FORMS - Generic/Trade: Tabs, non-scored 25/25, scored 50/50 mg.

***Aldoclor-250* (methyldopa + chlorothiazide, ✤*Supres*)** $$
ADULT - HTN: Establish dose using component drugs first. Dosing interval: bid.
PEDS - Not approved in children.
FORMS - Trade: Tabs, non-scored, 250/250 mg.

***Aldoril* (methyldopa + HCTZ)** $
ADULT - HTN: Establish dose using component drugs first. Dosing interval: bid.
PEDS - Not approved in children.
FORMS - Generic/Trade: Tabs, non-scored, 250/15 (Aldoril-15), 250/25 mg (Aldoril-25). Trade: Tabs, non-scored, 500/30 (Aldoril D30), 500/50 mg (Aldoril D50).

***Apresazide* (hydralazine + HCTZ)** $$
ADULT - HTN: Establish dose using component drugs first. Dosing interval: bid.
PEDS - Not approved in children.
FORMS - Generic/Trade: Caps 25/25, 50/50, 100/50.

***Atacand HCT* (candesartan + HCTZ)** $$
ADULT - HTN: Establish dose using component drugs first. Dosing interval: qd.

PEDS - Not approved in children.
FORMS - Trade: tab, non-scored 16/12.5, 32/12.5 mg.

***Avalide* (irbesartan + HCTZ)** $$
ADULT - HTN: Establish dose using component drugs first. Dosing interval: qd.
PEDS - Not approved in children.
FORMS - Trade: Tabs, non-scored 150/12.5, 300/12.5 mg.

***Capozide* (captopril + HCTZ)** $$
ADULT - HTN: Establish dose using component drugs first. Dosing interval: bid-tid.
PEDS - Not approved in children.
FORMS - Generic/Trade: Tabs, scored 25/15, 25/25, 50/15, 50/25 mg.

***Combipres* (clonidine + chlorthalidone)** $$
ADULT - HTN: Establish dose using component drugs first. Dosing interval: bid.
PEDS - Not approved in children.
FORMS - Generic/Trade: Tabs, non-scored 0.1/15, 0.2/15, 0.3/15 mg.

***Corzide* (nadolol + bendroflumethiazide)** $$
ADULT - HTN: Establish dose using component drugs first. Dosing interval: qd.
PEDS - Not approved in children.
FORMS - Trade: Tabs, scored 40/5, 80/5 mg.

***Diovan HCT* (valsartan + HCTZ)** $$
ADULT - HTN: Establish dose using component drugs first. Dosing interval: qd.
PEDS - Not approved in children.
FORMS - Trade: Tabs, non-scored 80/12.5, 160/12.5 mg.

***Diutensen-R* (reserpine + methyclothiazide)** $$$$
ADULT - HTN: Establish dose using component drugs first. Dosing interval: qd.
PEDS - Not approved in children.
FORMS - Trade: Tabs, non-scored, 0.1/2.5 mg.

***Dyazide* (triamterene + HCTZ)** $
ADULT - HTN: Establish dose using component drugs first. Dosing interval: qd.
PEDS - Not approved in children.
FORMS - Generic/Trade: Caps, (Dyazide) 37.5/25, (generic only) 50/25 mg.
NOTES - Dyazide 37.5/25 cap same combination as Maxzide-25 tab.

***Enduronyl* (deserpidine, methyclothiazide)** $$
ADULT - HTN: Establish dose using component drugs first. Dosing interval: qd.
PEDS - Not approved in children.
FORMS - Trade: Tabs, non-scored, 0.25/5 (Enduronyl), 0.5/5 mg (Enduronyl Forte).

***Hyzaar* (losartan + HCTZ)** $$
ADULT - HTN: Establish dose using component drugs first. Dosing interval: qd.
PEDS - Not approved in children.
FORMS - Trade: Tabs, non-scored 50/12.5, 100/25 mg.

***Inderide* (propranolol + HCTZ)** $
ADULT - HTN: Establish dose using component drugs first. Dosing interval: bid.
PEDS - Not approved in children.
FORMS - Generic/Trade: Tabs, scored 40/25, 80/25 mg.

***Inderide LA* (propranolol + HCTZ)** $$
ADULT - HTN: Establish dose using component drugs first. Dosing interval: qd.
PEDS - Not approved in children.
FORMS - Generic/Trade:Caps, extended-release 80/50, 120/50, 160/50 mg.
NOTES - Do not crush or chew cap contents. Swallow whole.

***Lexxel* (enalapril + felodipine)** $$
ADULT - HTN: Establish dose using component drugs first. Dosing interval: qd.
PEDS - Not approved in children.
FORMS - Trade:Tabs, non-scored 5/2.5,5/5 mg.
NOTES - Do not crush or chew, swallow whole.

***Lopressor HCT* (metoprolol + HCTZ)** $$$
ADULT - HTN: Establish dose using component drugs first. Dosing interval: qd-bid.
PEDS - Not approved in children.
FORMS - Trade: Tabs, scored 50/25, 100/25, 100/50 mg.

***Lotensin HCT* (benazepril + HCTZ)** $$
ADULT - HTN: Establish dose using component drugs first. Dosing interval: qd.
PEDS - Not approved in children.
FORMS - Trade: Tabs, scored 5/6.25, 10/12.5, 20/12.5, 20/25 mg.

***Lotrel* (amlodipine + benazepril)** $$$
ADULT - HTN: Establish dose using component drugs first. Dosing interval: qd.
PEDS - Not approved in children.
FORMS - Trade: cap, 2.5/10, 5/10, 5 /20 mg.

***Maxzide* (triamterene + HCTZ)** $
ADULT - HTN: Establish dose using component drugs first. Dosing interval: qd.
PEDS - Not approved in children.
FORMS - Generic/Trade: Tabs, scored (Maxzide-25) 37.5/25 (Maxzide) 75/50 mg.

***Maxzide-25* (triamterene + HCTZ)** $
ADULT - HTN: Establish dose using component drugs first. Dosing interval: qd.
PEDS - Not approved in children.
FORMS - Generic/Trade: Tabs, scored (Maxzide-25) 37.5/25 (Maxzide) 75/50 mg.

***Micardis HCT* (telmisartan + HCTZ)** $$

ADULT - HTN: Establish dose using component drugs first. Dosing interval: qd.
PEDS - Not approved in children.
FORMS - Trade: Tabs, non-scored 40/12.5, 80/12.5 mg.
NOTES - Swallow tabs whole, do not break or crush. Caution in hepatic insufficiency.

***Minizide* (prazosin + polythiazide)** $$
ADULT - HTN: Establish dose using component drugs first. Dosing interval: bid-tid.
PEDS - Not approved in children.
FORMS - Trade: cap, 1/0.5, 2/0.5, 5/0.5 mg.

***Moduretic* (amiloride + HCTZ, ✤*Moduret*)** $
ADULT - HTN: Establish dose using component drugs first. Dosing interval: qd.
PEDS - Not approved in children.
FORMS - Generic/Trade: Tabs, scored 5/50 mg.

***Prinzide* (lisinopril + HCTZ)** $$
ADULT - HTN: Establish dose using component drugs first. Dosing interval: qd.
PEDS - Not approved in children.
FORMS - Trade: Tabs, non-scored 10/12.5, 20/12.5, 20/25 mg.

***Rauzide* (rauwolfia + bendroflumethiazide)** $$
ADULT - HTN: Establish dose using component drugs first. Dosing interval: qd.
PEDS - Not approved in children.
FORMS - Trade: Tabs, non-scored, 50/4 mg.

***Renese-R* (reserpine + polythiazide)** $$
ADULT - HTN: Establish dose using component drugs first. Dosing interval: qd.
PEDS - Not approved in children.
FORMS - Trade: Tabs, scored, 0.25/2 mg.

***Salutensin* (reserpine + hydroflumethiazide)** $$
ADULT - HTN: Establish dose using component drugs first. Dosing interval: qd.
PEDS - Not approved in children.
FORMS - Trade: Tabs, non-scored, 0.125/25 (Salutensin-Demi), 0.125/50 mg (Salutensin)

***Ser-Ap-Es* (hydralazine + HCTZ + reserpine)** $
ADULT - HTN: Establish dose using component drugs first. Dosing interval: qd-bid.
PEDS - Not approved in children.
FORMS - Generic: Tabs, non-scored, 25/15/0.1 mg.

***Tarka* (trandolapril + verapamil)** $$
ADULT - HTN: Establish dose using component drugs first. Dosing interval: qd.
PEDS - Not approved in children.
FORMS - Trade: Tabs, non-scored 2/180, 1/240, 2/240, 4/240 mg.
NOTES - Contains extended release verapamil. Do not chew or crush; swallow whole.

***Tenoretic* (atenolol + chlorthalidone)** $$
ADULT - HTN: Establish dose using component drugs first. Dosing interval: qd.
PEDS - Not approved in children.
FORMS - Generic/Trade: Tabs, scored 50/25, non-scored 100/25 mg.

***Timolide* (timolol + HCTZ)** $$
ADULT - HTN: Establish dose using component drugs first. Dosing interval: qd-bid.
PEDS - Not approved in children.
FORMS - Trade: Tabs, non-scored 10/25 mg.

***Uniretic* (moexipril + HCTZ)** $
ADULT - HTN: Establish dose using component drugs first. Dosing interval: qd-bid.
PEDS - Not approved in children.
FORMS - Trade: Tabs, scored 7.5/12.5, 15/25 mg.

***Vaseretic* (enalapril + HCTZ)** $$
ADULT - HTN: Establish dose using component drugs first. Dosing interval: qd-bid.
PEDS - Not approved in children.
FORMS - Generic/Trade: Tabs, non-scored 5/12.5, 10/25 mg.

***Zestoretic* (lisinopril + HCTZ)** $$
ADULT - HTN: Establish dose using component drugs first. Dosing interval: qd.
PEDS - Not approved in children.
FORMS - Trade: Tabs, non-scored 10/12.5, 20/12.5, 20/25 mg.

***Ziac* (bisoprolol + HCTZ)** $$
ADULT - HTN: Establish dose using component drugs first. Dosing interval: qd.
PEDS - Not approved in children.
FORMS - Generic/Trade: Tabs, non-scored 2.5/6.25, 5/6.25, 10/6.25 mg.

CARDIOVASCULAR: Antihypertensives - Miscellaneous

diazoxide (*Hyperstat*) ▶L ♀C ▶- $$$$
ADULT - Severe HTN: 1-3 mg/kg (up to 150 mg) IV q5-15 min until BP is controlled.
PEDS - Severe HTN: same as adult.
UNAPPROVED ADULT - Preeclampsia/eclampsia: 30 mg IV every few minutes until control of BP is achieved.
NOTES - Severe hyperglycemia possible. Monitor for edema and CHF exacerbation during administration; diuretic therapy may be

needed. See endocrine section for diazoxide use in managing hypoglycemia.

epoprostenol (*Flolan*) ▶Plasma ♀B ◗? $$$$$

ADULT - Pulmonary HTN: Acute dose ranging, 2 ng/kg/min increments via IV infusion until the patient develops symptomatic intolerance (mean maximal dose without symptoms 8.6 ng/kg/min), start continuous chronic IV infusion at 4 ng/kg/min less than the patient's maximum-tolerated infusion (MTI) rate for acute dose ranging. If the MTI rate is < 5 ng/kg/min, start chronic IV infusion at one-half the MTI.

PEDS - Not approved in children.

NOTES - Administer by continuous IV infusion via a central venous catheter. Temporary peripheral IV infusions may be used until central access is established.

fenoldopam (*Corlopam*) ▶LK ♀B ◗? $$$$$

ADULT - Severe HTN: 10 mg in 250 ml D5W (40 mcg/mL), start at 0.1 mcg/kg/min (for 70 kg adult = 11 mL/h), titrate q15 min, usual effective dose 0.1 to 1.6 mcg/kg/min.

PEDS - Not approved in children.

hydralazine (*Apresoline*) ▶LK ♀C ◗+ $

ADULT - HTN: Start 10 mg PO bid-qid for 2-4 days, increase to 25 mg bid-qid, then 50 mg bid-qid if necessary, max 400 mg/day. Hypertensive emergency: 10-50 mg IM or 10-20 mg IV. Use lower doses initially & repeat prn to control BP. Preeclampsia/eclampsia: 5-10 mg IV initially, followed by 5-10 mg IV every 20-30 min as needed to control BP.

PEDS - Not approved in children.

UNAPPROVED ADULT - CHF: Start 10-25 mg PO tid, target dose 75 mg tid, max 100 mg tid. Use in combination with isosorbide dinitrate.

UNAPPROVED PEDS - HTN: Start 0.75-1 mg/kg/day PO divided bid-qid, increase slowly over 3-4 weeks up to 7.5 mg/kg/day; initial IV dose 1.7-3.5 mg/kg/day divided in 4-6 doses. HTN urgency: 0.1-0.2 mg/kg IM/IV q4-6 h as needed. Max single dose, 25 mg PO and 20 mg IV.

FORMS - Generic/Trade: Tabs, non-scored 10,25,50,100 mg.

NOTES - Headache, nausea, dizziness, tachycardia, peripheral edema, lupus-like syndrome.

mecamylamine (*Inversine*) ▶K ♀C ◗- $$$$$

ADULT - Severe HTN: Start 2.5 mg PO bid, increase as needed by 2.5 mg increments no sooner than every 2 days, usual maintenance dose 25 mg/day divided tid.

PEDS - Not approved in children.

FORMS - Trade: Tabs, scored, 2.5 mg.

NOTES - Orthostatic hypotension, especially during dosage titration. Monitor BP standing and supine. Rebound, severe hypertension with sudden drug withdrawal. Discontinue slowly and use other antihypertensives.

metyrosine (*Demser*) ▶K ♀C ◗? $$$$

ADULT - Pheochromocytoma: Start 250 mg PO qid, increase by 250-500 mg/day as needed, max dose 4 g/day.

PEDS - Pheochromocytoma >12 yo: Same as adult.

FORMS - Trade: Caps, 250 mg.

minoxidil (*Loniten*) ▶K ♀C ◗- $$

ADULT - Refractory HTN: Start 2.5-5 mg PO qd, increase at no less than 3 day intervals, usual dose 10-40 mg qd, max 100 mg/day.

PEDS - Not approved in children < 12 yo.

UNAPPROVED PEDS - HTN: Start 0.2 mg/kg PO qd, increase every 3 days as needed up to 0.25-1 mg/kg/day qd or divided bid; max 50 mg/day.

FORMS - Generic/Trade: Tabs, scored, 2.5,10 mg.

NOTES - Edema, weight gain, hypertrichosis, may exacerbate CHF. Usually used in combination with a diuretic and a beta-blocker to counteract side effects .

nitroprusside sodium (*Nipride, Nitropress*) ▶RBC's ♀C ◗- $

WARNING - Reconstituted solution must be further diluted before use. Cyanide toxicity may occur, especially with high infusion rates (10 mcg/kg/min), hepatic/renal impairment, and prolonged infusions (> 10 min). Protect from light.

ADULT - Hypertensive emergency: 50 mg in 250 ml D5W (200 mcg/mL), start at 0.3 mcg/kg/min (for 70 kg adult = 6 mL/h) via IV infusion, titrate slowly, usual range 0.3-10 mcg/kg/min, max 10 mcg/kg/min.

PEDS - Severe HTN: Same as adult.

NOTES - Discontinue if inadequate response after 10 minutes. Check thiocyanate levels. Protect IV infusion minibag from light.

phenoxybenzamine (*Dibenzyline*) ▶KL ♀C ◗? $$$$$

ADULT - Pheochromocytoma: Start 10 mg PO bid, increase slowly qod as needed, usual dose 20-40 mg bid-tid, max 120 mg/day.

PEDS - Not approved in children.

UNAPPROVED PEDS - Pheochromocytoma: 0.2 mg/kg/day PO qd, initial dose ≤10 mg, increase slowly qod as needed, usual dose 0.4-1.2 mg/kg/day.

FORMS - Brand: Caps, 10 mg.

NOTES - Patients should be observed after

each dosage increase for symptomatic hypotension and other adverse effects. Do not use for essential HTN.

phentolamine (*Regitine, Rogitine*) ▶Plasma ♀C ◗? $$

ADULT - Diagnosis of pheochromocytoma: 5 mg IV/IM. Rapid IV administration is preferred. An immediate, marked decrease in BP should occur, typically, 60 mm Hg SBP and 25 mm Hg DBP decrease in 2 minutes. HTN during pheochromocytoma surgery: 5 mg IV/IM 1-2h pre-op, 5 mg IV during surgery prn.

PEDS - Diagnosis of pheochromocytoma: 0.05-0.1 mg/kg IV/IM, up to 5 mg per dose. Rapid IV administration is preferred. An immediate, marked decrease in BP should occur, typically, 60 mm Hg SBP and 25 mm Hg DBP decrease in 2 minutes. HTN during pheochromocytoma surgery: 0.05-0.1 mg/kg IV/IM 1-2h pre-op, repeat q2-4h prn.

UNAPPROVED ADULT - IV extravasation of catecholamines: 5-10 mg in 10 mL NS, inject 1-5 mL (in divided doses) around extravasation site. Hypertensive crisis: 5-15 mg IV.

UNAPPROVED PEDS - IV extravasation of catecholamines: neonates, 2.5-5 mg in 10 mL NS, inject 1 mL (in divided doses) around extravasation site; children, same as adult.

NOTES - Weakness, flushing, hypotension; priapism with intracavernous injection. Use within 12h of extravasation. Distributed to hospital pharmacies, at no charge, only for use in life-threatening situations. Call (888) 669-6682 for ordering.

tolazoline (*Priscoline*) ▶L ♀C ◗? $$

PEDS - Persistent pulmonary HTN in newborns: Test dose 1-2 mg/kg IV over 10 minutes via a scalp vein, then IV infusion 0.5-2 mg/kg/h.

UNAPPROVED ADULT - Peripheral vasospastic disorders: 10-50 mg qid IV/IM/SC, initiate therapy with smaller doses and titrate up as needed.

NOTES - Response to therapy should be seen within 30 minutes of loading dose. Limited experience with IV infusions lasting longer than 36-48 hours.

trimethaphan (*Arfonad*) ▶? ♀- ◗? ?

ADULT - Hypertensive emergency associated with surgery: Begin IV infusion at 3-4 mg/min and titrate drip rate to lower BP. 500 mg in 500 ml D5W only (1 mg/ml).

PEDS - Hypertensive emergency associated with surgery: Begin IV infusion at 50 mcg/kg/min and titrate drip rate to lower BP. Usual dose range 50-150 mcg/kg/min.

NOTES - Significant interpatient variability in BP response. Monitor BP frequently during use.

CARDIOVASCULAR: Antiplatelet Drugs

abciximab (*ReoPro*) ▶Plasma ♀C ◗? $$$$$

ADULT - Platelet aggregation inhibition, prevention of acute cardiac ischemic events associated with PTCA: 0.25 mg/kg IV bolus over 1 min via separate infusion line 10-60 min before procedure, then 0.125 mcg/kg/min up to 10 mcg/min infusion for 12h. Unstable angina not responding to standard therapy: 0.25 mg/kg IV bolus over 1 min via separate infusion line, followed by 10 mcg/min IV infusion for 18-24h, concluding 1h after PTCA.

PEDS - Not approved in children.

NOTES - Thrombocytopenia possible. Discontinue abciximab, heparin, and aspirin if uncontrollable bleeding occurs.

***Aggrenox* (dipyridamole + aspirin)** ▶LK ♀D ◗? $$$

ADULT - Platelet aggregation inhibition/prevention of TIAs and strokes: 1 cap bid.

PEDS - Not approved in children.

FORMS - Trade: Caps, 200/25 mg.

NOTES - The dipyridamole component is extended-release. Do not crush or chew Caps. May need supplemental aspirin for prevention of MI.

aspirin (*Ecotrin, Empirin, Halfprin, Bayer, ASA*, ✤*Entrophen*) ▶K ♀D ◗? $

ADULT - Platelet aggregation inhibition: 81-325 mg PO qd.

PEDS - See analgesic section for pain/antipyretic doses.

FORMS - Generic/Trade (OTC): tabs, 325,500 mg; chewable 81 mg; enteric-coated 81,165 mg (Halfprin), 81,325,500 mg (Ecotrin), 650,975 mg. Trade only: tabs, controlled-release 650,800 mg (ZORprin, Rx). Generic only (OTC): suppository 120,200,300,600 mg.

NOTES - Crush or chew tabs (including enteric-coated products) in first dose with acute MI. Higher doses of aspirin (1.3 g/day) have not been shown to be superior to low doses in preventing TIAs and strokes.

clopidogrel (*Plavix*) ▶LK ♀B ◗? $$$

WARNING - May cause life-threatening thrombotic thrombocytopenia purpura (TTP), usually during the first two weeks of therapy.

ADULT - Platelet aggregation inhibition/reduction of atherosclerotic events: 75 mg PO qd with or without food.

PEDS - Not approved in children.

UNAPPROVED ADULT - Acute coronary syndrome: 300 mg loading dose, then 75 mg PO qd in combination with aspirin 81-325 mg PO qd x 3-12 months. Prevention of coronary stent occlusion: 150-300 mg loading dose, then 75 mg PO qd in combination with aspirin 325 mg PO qd for 2-4 weeks.

FORMS - Trade: Tab, non-scored 75 mg.

NOTES - Prolongs bleeding time. Discontinue use 7 days before surgery. Loading dose 150-300 mg PO on day 1 may be used for prevention of cardiac stent occlusion. Contraindicated with active pathologic bleeding (peptic ulcer or intracranial bleed).

dipyridamole (*Persantine*) ▶L ♀B ▶? $$

ADULT - Prevention of thromboembolic complications of cardiac valve replacement: 75-100 mg PO qid. Use in combination with warfarin.

PEDS - Not approved in children < 12 yo.

UNAPPROVED ADULT - Platelet aggregation inhibition: 150-400 mg/day PO divided tid-qid.

FORMS - Generic/Trade: Tabs, non-scored 25,50,75 mg.

NOTES - Not effective for angina.

eptifibatide (*Integrilin*) ▶K ♀B ▶? $$$$$

ADULT - Acute coronary syndromes (unstable angina and non-Q wave MI): Load 180 mcg/kg IV bolus, then IV infusion 2 mcg/kg/min for up to 72 hr. Discontinue infusion prior ot CABG. If percutaneous cardiovascular intervention (PCI; mainly PTCA) occurs during the infusion, decrease the infusion to 0.5 mcg/kg/min at the time of the procedure. PCI in patients not presenting with acute coronary syndrome: Load 135 mcg/kg IV bolus just before procedure, then IV infusion 0.5 mcg/kg/min for 20-24 hr after the procedure.

PEDS - Not approved in children.

UNAPPROVED ADULT - Alternative dosing for PCI in patients not presenting with acute coronary syndrome: Load 180 mcg/kg IV bolus, then IV infusion 2 mcg/kg/min for 20-24 hr after the procedure. Nonurgent coronary stenting: Two 180 mcg/kg IV boluses 10 minutes apart followed by 2 mcg/kg/min IV infusion for 18-24 hr.

NOTES - Thrombocytopenia possible. Concomitant aspirin, heparin use recommended, unless contraindicated.

ticlopidine (*Ticlid*) ▶L ♀B ▶? $$$$

WARNING - May cause life-threatening neutropenia, agranulocytosis, and thrombotic thrombocytopenia purpura (TTP). TTP usually occurs during the first two weeks of treatment.

ADULT - Due to adverse effects, other drugs preferred. Platelet aggregation inhibition/reduction of thrombotic stroke: 250 mg PO bid with food.

PEDS - Not approved in children.

UNAPPROVED ADULT - Due to adverse effects, other drugs preferred. Prevention of graft occlusion with CABG: 250 mg PO bid. Prevention of cardiac stent occlusion: 250 mg PO bid in combo with aspirin 325 mg PO qd for 4 weeks.

FORMS - Generic/Trade: Tab, non-scored 250 mg.

NOTES - Check CBC every 2 weeks during the first 3 months of therapy. Neutrophil counts usually return to normal within 1-3 weeks following discontinuation. Loading dose 500 mg PO on day 1 may be used for prevention of cardiac stent occlusion.

tirofiban (*Aggrastat*) ▶K ♀B ▶? $$$$$

ADULT - Acute coronary syndromes (unstable angina and non-Q wave MI): Start 0.4 mcg/kg/min IV infusion for 30 mins, then decrease to 0.1 mcg/kg/min for 48-108 hr or until 12-24 hr after coronary intervention.

PEDS - Not approved in children.

NOTES - Thrombocytopenia possible. Concomitant aspirin, heparin use recommended, unless contraindicated. Dose heparin to keep PTT twice normal. Decrease rate of infusion by 50% in patients with CrCl < 30 mL/min. Dilute concentrate solution before using.

CARDIOVASCULAR: Beta Blockers

NOTES: See also antihypertensive combinations. Discontinue therapy by tapering over 2 weeks. Avoid using nonselective beta-blockers and use agents with beta1 selectivity cautiously in asthma / obstructive lung disease. Beta 1 selectivity diminishes at high doses.

acebutolol (*Sectral*, ✤*Monitan*) ▶LK ♀B ▶- $$

ADULT - HTN: Start 400 mg PO qd or 200 mg PO bid, usual maintenance 400-800 mg/day,

max 1200 mg/day. Twice daily dosing appears to be more effective than qd dosing.
PEDS - Not approved in children < 12.
UNAPPROVED ADULT - Angina: Start 200 mg PO bid, increase as needed up to 800 mg/day.
FORMS - Generic/Trade: Caps, 200,400 mg.
NOTES - Has mild intrinsic sympathomimetic activity (partial beta agonist activity). Beta1 receptor selective.

atenolol (*Tenormin*) ▶K ♀D ▶- $
ADULT - Acute MI: 5 mg IV over 5 min, repeat in 10 min, follow with 50 mg PO 10 min after IV dosing in patients tolerating the total IV dose, increase as tolerated to 100 mg/day given qd or divided bid. HTN: Start 25-50 mg PO qd or divided bid, maximum 100 mg/day. Renal impairment, elderly: Start 25 mg PO qd, increase as needed. Angina: Start 50 mg PO qd or divided bid, increase as needed to max of 200 mg/day.
PEDS - Not approved in children.
UNAPPROVED PEDS - HTN: 1-1.2 mg/kg/dose PO qd, max 2 mg/kg/day.
FORMS - Generic/Trade: Tabs, non-scored 25,100; scored, 50 mg.
NOTES - Doses >100 mg/day usually do not provide further BP lowering. Beta1 receptor selective.

betaxolol (*Kerlone*) ▶LK ♀C ▶? $
ADULT - HTN: Start 5-10 mg PO qd, max 20 mg/day. Renal impairment, elderly: Start 5 mg PO qd, increase as needed.
PEDS - Not approved in children.
FORMS - Generic/Trade: Tabs, scored 10, non-scored 20 mg.
NOTES - Beta1 receptor selective.

bisoprolol (*Zebeta*) ▶LK ♀C ▶? $$
ADULT - HTN: Start 2.5-5 mg PO qd, max 20 mg/day. Renal impairment: Start 2.5 mg PO qd, increase as needed.
PEDS - Not approved in children.
UNAPPROVED ADULT - Compensated heart failure: Start 1.25 mg PO qd, double dose every 2 weeks as tolerated up to max 20 mg/day.
FORMS - Generic/Trade: Tabs, scored 5, non-scored 10 mg.
NOTES - Monitor closely for CHF exacerbation and hypotension when titrating dose. Avoid use in patients with decompensated CHF (i.e. NYHA class IV heart failure). Stabilize dose of digoxin, diuretics, and ACEI before starting bisoprolol. Beta1 receptor selective.

carteolol (*Cartrol*) ▶K ♀C ▶? $$
ADULT - HTN: Start 2.5 mg PO qd, usual maintenance dose 2.5-5 mg qd, max 10 mg qd. Doses > 10 mg daily generally do not produce additional BP lowering.
PEDS - Not approved in children.
FORMS - Trade: Tabs, non-scored, 2.5,5 mg.
NOTES - Decrease dosing frequency with renal impairment - CrCl 20-60 ml/min, q48 hours; CrCl < 20 ml/min, q72 hours. Avoid in asthma and obstructive lung disease. Has mild intrinsic sympathomimetic activity (partial beta agonist activity).

carvedilol (*Coreg*) ▶L ♀C ▶? $$$
ADULT - Compensated heart failure: Start 3.125 mg PO bid with food, double dose q2 weeks as tolerated up to max of 25 mg bid (if <85 kg) or 50 mg bid (if >85 kg). HTN: Start 6.25 mg PO bid, maximum 50 mg/day. Not first line agent for HTN.
PEDS - Not approved in children.
FORMS - Trade: Tabs, non-scored 3.125, scored, 6.25,12.5,25 mg.
NOTES - Monitor closely for CHF exacerbation and hypotension when titrating dose. Avoid use in patients with decompensated CHF (i.e. NYHA class IV heart failure). Stabilize dose of digoxin, diuretics, and ACEI before starting carvedilol. Avoid use in severe hepatic impairment. Alpha1, beta1, and beta2 receptor blocker. Contraindicated in asthma.

esmolol (*Brevibloc*) ▶K ♀C ▶? $$
ADULT - SVT/HTN emergency: Mix infusion 5 g in 500 mL (10 mg/mL), load with 500 mcg/kg IV over 1 minute (70 kg: 35 mg or 3.5 mL) then IV infusion 50 mcg/kg/min for 4 min (70 kg: 100 mcg/kg/min = 40 mL/h). If optimal response is not attained, repeat IV load and increase IV infusion to 100 mcg/kg/min for 4 min. If necessary, additional boluses (500 mcg/kg/min over 1 min) may be given followed by IV infusion with increased dose by 50 mcg/kg/min for 4 min. Max IV infusion rate 200 mcg/kg/min.
PEDS - Not approved in children.
UNAPPROVED PEDS - Same schedule as adult except loading dose 100-500 mcg/kg IV over 1 min and IV infusion 25-100 mcg/kg/min. IV infusions may be increased by 25-50 mcg/kg/min every 5-10 min. Titrate dose based on patient response.
NOTES - Hypotension. Beta1 receptor selective. Half-life = 9 minutes.

labetalol (*Trandate, Normodyne*) ▶LK ♀C ▶+ $$
ADULT - HTN: Start 100 mg PO bid, usual maintenance dose 200-600 mg bid, max 2400 mg/day. HTN emergency: Start 20 mg slow IV

injection, then 40-80 mg IV q10min as needed up to 300 mg total cumulative dose or start 0.5-2 mg/min IV infusion, adjust rate as needed up to total cumulative dose 300 mg.

PEDS - Not approved in children.

UNAPPROVED PEDS - HTN: 4 mg/kg/day PO divided bid, increase as needed up to 40 mg/kg/day. IV: Start 0.3-1 mg/kg/dose (max 20 mg) slow IV injection q10 min or 0.4-1 mg/kg/h IV infusion up to 3 mg/kg/hr.

FORMS - Generic/Trade: Tabs, scored 100,200 (Trandate, Normodyne), 300 (Trandate), non-scored 300 mg (Normodyne).

NOTES - Hypotension. Contraindicated in asthma. Alpha1, beta1, and beta2 receptor blocker.

metoprolol (*Lopressor, Toprol XL*, ♣*Betaloc*) ▶L ♀C ◗? $$

ADULT - Acute MI: 5 mg IV q5-15 min up to 15 mg. If tolerated, start 50 mg PO q6h for 48h, then 100 mg PO bid. If usual IV dose is not tolerated, start 25-50 mg PO q6h. If early IV therapy is contraindicated, patient should be titrated to 100 mg PO bid as soon as possible. HTN: Start 25-50 mg PO bid or 50-100 mg PO qd (extended-release), increase as needed up to 450 mg/day (immediate-release) or 400 mg/day (extended-release). Compensated heart failure: Start 12.5-25 mg (extended-release) PO qd, double dose every 2 weeks as tolerated up to max 200 mg/day. Angina: Start 50 mg PO bid or 100 mg PO qd (extended-release), increase as needed up to 400 mg/day.

PEDS - Not approved in children.

UNAPPROVED ADULT - CHF: Start 6.25-12.5 mg (immediate release) PO bid, double dose q2 weeks as tolerated up to max 200 mg/day. Atrial tachyarrhythmia: 2.5-5 mg IV q2-5 min as needed to control rapid ventricular response, max 15 mg over 10-15 min.

FORMS - Generic/Trade: tabs, scored 50,100 mg. Trade only: tabs, extended-relese, scored (Toprol XL) 25,50,100,200 mg.

NOTES - Monitor closely for CHF exacerbation and hypotension when titrating dose. Avoid use in patients with decompensated CHF (i.e. NYHA class IV heart failure or pulmonary edema). Stabilize dose of digoxin, diuretics, and ACEI before starting metoprolol. Beta1 receptor selective. Extended-release Tabs may be broken in half, but do not chew or crush.

nadolol (*Corgard*) ▶K ♀C ◗- $$

ADULT - HTN: Start 20-40 mg PO qd, usual maintenance dose 40-80 mg/day, max 320 mg/day. Renal impairment: Start 20 mg PO qd, adjust dosage interval based on severity of renal impairment - CrCl 31-50 mL/min, q24-36h; CrCl 10-30 mL/min, q24-48h; CrCl < 10 mL/min, q40-60h. Angina: Start 40 mg PO qd, usual maintenance dose 40-80 mg/day, max 240 mg/day.

PEDS - Not approved in children.

UNAPPROVED ADULT - Rebleeding esophageal varices: 40-160 mg/day PO. Titrate dose to reduce heart rate to 25% below baseline. Ventricular arrhythmia: 10-640 mg/day PO.

FORMS - Generic/Trade: Tabs, scored 20,40,80,120,160 mg.

NOTES - Beta1 and beta2 receptor blocker.

penbutolol (*Levatol*) ▶LK ♀C ◗? $$$

ADULT - HTN: Start 20 mg PO qd, usual maintenance dose 20-40 mg, max 80 mg/day.

PEDS - Not approved in children.

FORMS - Trade: Tabs, scored 20 mg.

NOTES - Has mild intrinsic sympathomimetic activity (partial beta agonist activity). Beta1 and beta2 receptor blocker.

pindolol (*Visken*) ▶K ♀B ◗? $$$

ADULT - HTN: Start 5 mg PO bid, usual maintenance dose 10-30 mg/day, max 60 mg/day.

PEDS - Not approved in children.

UNAPPROVED ADULT - Angina: 15-40 mg/day PO in divided doses tid-qid.

FORMS - Generic/Trade: Tabs, scored 5,10 mg.

NOTES - Has mild intrinsic sympathomimetic activity (partial beta agonist activity). Beta1 and beta2 receptor blocker. Contraindicated with thioridazine.

propranolol (*Inderal, Inderal LA*) ▶L ♀C ◗+ $

ADULT - HTN: Start 20-40 mg PO bid, usual maintenance dose 160-480 mg/day, max 640 mg/day; extended-release (Inderal LA): start 60-80 mg PO qd, usual maintenance dose 120-160 mg/day, max 640 mg/day. Angina: Start 10-20 mg PO tid/qid, usual maintenance 160-240 mg/day, max 320 mg/day; extended-release (Inderal LA): start 80 mg PO qd, same usual dosage range and max for HTN. Migraine prophylaxis: Start 40 mg PO bid or 80 mg PO qd (extended-release), max 240 mg/day. Cardiac arrhythmia: 10-30 mg PO tid/qid. MI: 180-240 mg/day PO in divided doses bid-qid. Pheochromocytoma surgery: 60 mg PO in divided doses bid-tid beginning 3 days before surgery, use in combination with an alpha blocking agent. IV: reserved for life-threatening arrhythmia, 1-3 mg IV, repeat dose in 2 min if needed, additional doses should not be given in < 4h. Not for use in hypertensive emergency.

PEDS - HTN: Start 1 mg/kg/day PO divided bid, usual maintenance dose 2-4 mg/kg/day PO divided bid, max 16 mg/kg/day.

UNAPPROVED ADULT - Rebleeding esophageal varices: 20-180 mg PO bid. Titrate dose to reduce heart rate to 25% below baseline.

UNAPPROVED PEDS - Arrhythmia: 0.01-0.1 mg/kg/dose (max 1 mg/dose) by slow IV push. Manufacturer does not recommend IV propranolol in children.

FORMS - Generic/Trade: Tabs, scored 10,20,40,60,80 (Generic only), 90 mg. Solution 20,40 mg/5 ml. Concentrate, 80 mg/mL. Caps, extended-release 60,80,120,160 mg.

NOTES - Do not substitute extended-release product for immediate-release product on mg-for-mg basis. Dosage titration may be necessary with extended-release product when converting from immediate-release Tabs. Extended-release Caps may be opened, and the contents sprinkled on food for administration. cap contents should be swallowed whole without crushing or chewing. Beta1 and beta2 receptor blocker. Contraindicated with thioridazine.

timolol (*Blocadren*) ▶LK ♀C ◗? $$

ADULT - HTN: Start 10 mg PO bid, usual maintenance 20-40 mg/day, max 60 mg/day. MI: 10 mg PO bid, started 1-4 weeks post-MI. Migraine headaches: Start 10 mg PO bid, use 20 mg/day qd or divided bid for prophylaxis, increase as needed up to max 60 mg/day. Stop therapy if satisfactory response not obtained after 6-8 weeks of max dose.

PEDS - Not approved in children.

UNAPPROVED ADULT - Angina: 15-45 mg/day PO divided tid-qid.

FORMS - Generic/Trade: Tabs, non-scored 5, scored 10,20 mg.

NOTES - Beta1 and beta2 receptor blocker.

CARDIOVASCULAR: Calcium Channel Blockers (CCBs) - Dihydropyridines

NOTES: See also antihypertensive combinations. Peripheral edema, especially with higher doses. Extended / controlled / sustained-release tabs should be swallowed whole; do not chew or crush. Avoid concomitant grapefruit / grapefruit juice, which may enhance effect.

amlodipine (*Norvasc*) ▶L ♀C ◗? $$

ADULT - HTN: Start 2.5 to 5 mg PO qd, max 10 qd. Angina: Start 5 mg PO qd, usual maintenance dose 10 mg PO qd.

PEDS - Not approved in children.

UNAPPROVED ADULT - HTN: max 20 mg/day qd or divided bid.

FORMS - Trade: Tabs, non-scored 2.5,5,10 mg.

NOTES - HTN control improved with 5-10 mg PO qd in patients with CHF (already on ACEI, digoxin, and diuretics) without worsening morbidity or mortality.

bepridil (*Vascor*) ▶L ♀C ◗- $$$$

WARNING - Rarely used because of proarrhythmic effects.

ADULT - Chronic stable angina: Start 200 mg PO qd, increase after 10 days as needed to 300 mg qd, max dose 400 mg qd.

PEDS - Not approved in children.

FORMS - Trade: Tabs, scored 200, non-scored 300, 400 mg.

NOTES - Rare agranulocytosis may occur.

felodipine (*Plendil*, ✤*Renedil*) ▶L ♀C ◗? $$

ADULT - HTN: Start 2.5-5 mg PO qd, usual maintenance dose 5-10 mg/day, max 10 mg/day.

PEDS - Not approved in children.

UNAPPROVED ADULT - HTN: max 20 mg/day qd or divided bid.

FORMS - Trade: Tabs, extended-release, non-scored 2.5,5,10 mg.

NOTES - Extended-release tab. HTN control improved with 5-10 mg PO qd in patients with CHF (already on ACEI, digoxin, and diuretics) without worsening CHF.

isradipine (*DynaCirc, DynaCirc CR*) ▶L ♀C ◗? $$$

ADULT - HTN: Start 2.5 mg PO bid, usual maintenance 5-10 mg/day, max 20 mg/day divided bid (max 10 mg/day in elderly). Controlled-release (DynaCirc CR): Start 5 mg PO qd, usual maintenance dose 5-10 mg/day, max 20 mg/day.

PEDS - Not approved in children.

FORMS - Trade: Caps 2.5,5 mg; tab, controlled-release 5,10 mg.

nicardipine (*Cardene, Cardene SR*) ▶L ♀C ◗? $$

ADULT - HTN: sustained-release (Cardene SR), Start 30 mg PO bid, usual maintenance dose 30-60 mg PO bid, max 120 mg/day; immediate-release, Start 20 mg PO tid, usual maintenance dose 20-40 mg PO tid, max 120 mg/day. Hypertensive emergency/short-term manage-

ment of acute HTN: Begin IV infusion at 5 mg/h, titrate infusion rate by 2.5 mg/h q15min as needed, max 15 mg/h. Angina: immediate-release, Start 20 mg PO tid, usual maintenance dose 20-40 mg tid.
PEDS - Not approved in children.
UNAPPROVED PEDS - HTN: 1-5 mcg/kg/min IV infusion.
FORMS - Generic/Trade: caps, immediate-release 20,30 mg. Trade only: caps, sustained-release 30,45,60 mg.
NOTES - Hypotension, especially with immediate-release Caps and IV. Decrease dose if hepatically impaired. Use sustained-release Caps for HTN only, not for angina.

nifedipine (*Procardia, Adalat, Procardia XL, Adalat CC*) ▶L ♀C ▶+ $$
ADULT - HTN: extended-release, Start 30-60 mg PO qd, max 120 mg/day. Angina: extended-release, Start 30-60 mg PO qd, max 120 mg/day; immediate-release, Start 10 mg PO tid, usual maintenance dose 10-20 mg tid, max 120 mg/day.
PEDS - Not approved in children.
UNAPPROVED PEDS - HTN: 0.25-0.5 mg/kg/dose PO q4-6 h as needed, max 10 mg/dose or 3 mg/kg/day.
FORMS - Generic/Trade: Caps, 10,20 mg. Tabs, extended-release 30,60,90 mg.
NOTES - Avoid sublingual administration of immediate-release cap, may cause excessive hypotension, stroke. Do not use immediate-release Caps for treating HTN or hypertensive emergencies. Extended-release Tabs can be substituted for immediate-release Caps at the same dose in patients whose angina is controlled.

nisoldipine (*Sular*) ▶L ♀C ▶? $$
ADULT - HTN: Start 20 mg PO qd, usual maintenance 20-40 mg/day, max 60 mg/day. Impaired hepatic function, elderly: Start 10 mg PO qd, titrate as needed.
PEDS - Not approved in children.
FORMS - Trade: Tabs, extended-release 10,20, 30,40 mg.

CARDIOVASCULAR: Calcium Channel Blockers (CCBs) - Other

NOTE: See also antihypertensive combinations.

diltiazem (*Cardizem, Diltia XT, Tiazac, Dilacor, Tiamate*) ▶L ♀C ▶+ $$
ADULT - Rapid atrial fibrillation: 20 mg (0.25 mg/kg) IV bolus over 2 min. If needed and patient tolerated IV bolus with no hypotension, rebolus 15 min later with 25 mg (0.35 mg/kg). IV infusion: Start 10 mg/h, increase by 5 mg/h (usual range 5-15 mg/h). HTN: Once daily, extended-release (Cardizem CD, Dilacor XR, Tiazac): Start 120-240 mg PO qd, usual maintenance range 240-360 mg/day, max 540 mg/day. Twice daily, sustained-release (Cardizem SR): Start 60-120 mg PO bid, max 360 mg/day. Angina: immediate-release, Start 30 mg PO qid, max 360 mg/day divided tid-qid. Extended-release, 120-180 mg PO qd, max 540 mg/day.
PEDS - Not approved in children. Diltiazem injection should be avoided in neonates due to potential toxicity from benzyl alcohol in the injectable product .
FORMS - Generic/Trade: tabs, immediate-release, non-scored (Cardizem) 30, scored 60,90,120 mg; caps, sustained-release (Cardizem SR q12h) 60,90,120 mg, extended-release (Cardizem CD qd) 120,180,240,300, 360 mg. Trade only: tabs, extended-release (Tiamate qd) 120 mg, (Tiazac qd) 120,180, 240,300,360,420 mg, (Dilacor XR, Diltia XT qd) 120,180,240 mg.
NOTES - Contents of extended-release Caps may be sprinkled over food (apple sauce) and administered. Do not chew or crush cap contents.

verapamil (*Isoptin, Calan, Covera-HS, Verelan PM, ✤Chronovera*) ▶L ♀C ▶+ $$
ADULT - SVT: 5-10 mg (0.075-0.15 mg/kg) IV over 2 min. A second dose of 10 mg IV may be given 15-30 min later if needed. PSVT/rate control with atrial fibrillation: 240-480 mg/day PO divided tid-qid. Angina: Start 40-80 mg PO tid-qid, max 480 mg/day; sustained-release (Isoptin SR, Calan SR, Verelan), start 120-240 mg PO qd, max 480 mg/day (use bid dosing for doses > 240 mg/day with Isoptin SR and Calan SR); extended-release (Covera-HS), start 180 mg PO qhs, max 480 mg/day. HTN: Same as angina, except (Verelan PM) start 100-200 mg PO qhs, max 400 mg/day; (Covera-HS) start 180 mg PO qhs, max 480 mg/day; immediate-release tabs should be avoided in treating HTN.
PEDS - SVT: (1-15 yo) 2-5 mg (0.1-0.3 mg/kg) IV, max dose 5 mg. Repeat dose once in 30 min if needed, max second dose 10 mg. Im-

mediate-release and sustained-release Tabs not approved in children.
FORMS - Generic/Trade: tabs, immediate-release, scored 40,80,120 mg; sustained-release, non-scored (Calan SR, Isoptin SR) 120, scored 180,240 mg; caps, sustained-release (Verelan) 120,180,240,360 mg. Trade only: tabs, extended-release (Covera HS) 180,240 mg; caps, extended-release (Verelan PM) 100,200,300 mg.
NOTES - Avoid concomitant grapefruit and grapefruit juice, which may significantly enhance effect. Scored, sustained-release Tabs (Calan SR, Isoptin SR) may be broken and each piece swallowed whole, do not chew or crush. Other extended-release Tabs (Covera HS) should be swallowed whole. Contents of sustained-release Caps may be sprinkled on food (apple sauce) and administered. Do not chew or crush cap contents.

CARDIOVASCULAR: Diuretics - Carbonic Anhydrase Inhibitors

acetazolamide (*Diamox*) ▸LK ♀C ◗+ $$
ADULT - Edema: Rarely used, start 250-375 mg IV/PO qam given intermittently (qod or 2 consecutive days followed by none for 1-2 days) to avoid loss of diuretic effect. Acute mountain sickness: 0.5-1 gm PO divided bid-tid or sustained-release 500 mg PO qd-bid beginning 24-48hr before ascent and for 48 hr at high altitude.
PEDS - Diuretic: 5 mg/kg PO/IV qam.
FORMS - Generic/Trade: Tabs, 125,250 mg; Trade only: cap, sustained-release 500 mg.
NOTES - A suspension (250 mg/5 mL) can be made by crushing and mixing tabs in flavored syrup. The suspension is stable for 7 days at room temperature. One tab may be softened in 2 teaspoons of hot water, then add to 2 teaspoons of honey or syrup, and swallowed at once. Tabs and compounded suspension may have a bitter taste. Avoid use in patients with sulfa allergy. Prompt descent is necessary if severe forms of high altitude sickness (i.e. pulmonary or cerebral edema) occur.

CARDIOVASCULAR: Diuretics - Loop

NOTES: Give second dose of bid schedule in mid afternoon to avoid nocturia. Possible hypersensitivity in patients allergic to sulfonamide containing drugs.

bumetanide (*Bumex*, ✤*Burinex*) ▸K ♀C ◗? $
ADULT - Edema: 0.5-2 mg PO qd, repeat doses at 4-5 hr intervals as needed until desired response is attained, max 10 mg/day; 0.5-1 mg IV/IM, repeat doses at 2-3 hr intervals as needed until desired response is attained, max 10 mg/day. Dosing for 3-4 consecutive days followed by no drug for 1-2 days is acceptable. BID dosing may enhance diuretic effect. IV injections should be over 1-2 min. An IV infusion may be used, change bag every 24 hours.
PEDS - Not approved in children.
UNAPPROVED PEDS - Edema: 0.015-0.1 mg/kg/dose PO/IV/IM qd or qod.
FORMS - Generic/Trade: Tabs, scored 0.5,1,2 mg.
NOTES - 1 mg bumetanide is roughly equivalent to 40 mg furosemide. IV administration is preferred when GI absorption is impaired.

ethacrynic acid (*Edecrin*) ▸K ♀B ◗? $$
ADULT - Edema: 0.5-1 mg/kg IV, max 50 mg IV; 25 mg PO qd on day one, followed by 50 mg PO bid on day two, followed by 100 mg PO in the morning and 50-100 mg PO in the evening depending on the response to the morning dose, max 400 mg/day.
PEDS - Not approved in children.
UNAPPROVED ADULT - HTN: 25 mg PO qd, max 100 mg/day divided bid-tid.
UNAPPROVED PEDS - Edema: 1 mg/kg IV; 25 mg PO qd, increase slowly by 25 mg increments as needed. Ethacrynic acid should not be administered to infants.
FORMS - Trade: Tabs, scored 25,50 mg.
NOTES - Rarely used. Ototoxicity possible. Does not contain a sulfonamide group; may be useful in sulfa-allergic patients. Do not administer SC or IM due to local irritation. IV ethacrynic acid should be reconstituted to a concentration of 50 mg/mL and given slowly by IV infusion over 20-30 min.

furosemide (*Lasix*) ▸K ♀C ◗? $
ADULT - Edema: Start 20-80 mg IV/IM/PO, increase dose by 20-40 mg every 6-8h until desired response is achieved, max 600 mg/day. Give maintenance dose qd or divided bid. IV

infusion: 0.05 mg/kg/h, titrate rate to desired response. HTN: Start 20-40 mg bid, adjust dose as needed based on BP response. Thiazide diuretics generally preferred for HTN.
PEDS - Edema: 0.5-2 mg/kg/dose IV/IM/PO q6-12h, max 6 mg/kg/dose. IV infusion: 0.05 mg/kg/h, titrate rate to achieve desired response.
FORMS - Generic/Trade: Tabs, non-scored 20, scored 40,80 mg. Oral solution 10 mg/mL, 40 mg/5 ml.
NOTES - Loop diuretics are agent of choice for edema with decreased renal function (CrCl < 30 mL/min or Scr > 2.5 mg/dl).

torsemide (*Demadex*) ▶LK ♀B ◗? $
ADULT - Edema: Start 5-20 mg IV/PO qd, double dose as needed to desired response, max 200 mg as a single dose. HTN: Start 5 mg PO qd, increase as needed every 4-6 weeks, max 100 mg PO qd or divided bid. Thiazide diuretics generally preferred for HTN.
PEDS - Not approved in children.
FORMS - Trade: Tabs, scored 5,10,20,100 mg.
NOTES - Loop diuretics are agent of choice for edema with decreased renal function (CrCl < 30 mL/min or Scr > 2.5 mg/dl).

CARDIOVASCULAR: Diuretics - Potassium Sparing

NOTES: See also antihypertensive combinations. Beware of hyperkalemia. Use cautiously with other agents that may cause hyperkalemia (ie. ACE inhibitors)

amiloride (*Midamor*) ▶LK ♀B ◗? $$
ADULT - Diuretic-induced hypokalemia: Start 5 mg PO qd, increase as needed based on serum potassium, max 20 mg/day. Edema/HTN: Start 5 mg PO qd in combination with another diuretic, usually a thiazide diuretic for HTN, increase as needed based on serum potassium, max 20 mg/day. Other diuretics may need to be added when treating edema.
PEDS - Not approved in children.
UNAPPROVED ADULT - Hyperaldosteronism: 10-40 mg PO qd. Do not use combination product (Moduretic) for treatment of hyperaldosteronism.
UNAPPROVED PEDS - Edema: 0.625 mg/kg qd for children weighing 6-20 kg.
FORMS - Generic/Trade: Tabs, non-scored 5 mg.
NOTES - Spironolactone is generally preferred for treating primary hyperaldosteronism. Thiazide diuretics may worsen hypokalemia in patients with hyperaldosteronism.

spironolactone (*Aldactone*) ▶LK ♀D ◗+ $
ADULT - Edema (cirrhosis, nephrotic syndrome): Start 100 mg PO qd or divided bid, maintain for 5 days, increase as needed to achieve diuretic response, usual dose range 25-200 mg/day. Other diuretics may be needed. HTN: 50-100 mg PO qd or divided bid, generally used in combination with a thiazide diuretic to maintain serum potassium, increase dose as needed based on serum potassium and BP.
PEDS - Edema: 3.3 mg/kg PO qd or divided bid.
UNAPPROVED ADULT - CHF: 25-50 mg PO qd.
UNAPPROVED PEDS - Edema/HTN: 1-3.3 mg/kg/day, qd or divided bid.
FORMS - Generic/Trade: Tabs, non-scored 25; scored 50,100 mg.
NOTES - Gynecomastia, impotence in males. Dosing more frequently than BID not necessary.

triamterene (*Dyrenium*) ▶LK ♀B ◗- $$$
ADULT - Edema (cirrhosis, nephrotic syndrome, CHF): Start 100 mg PO bid, max 300 mg/day. Most patients can be maintained on 100 mg PO qd or qod after edema is controlled. Other diuretics may be needed.
PEDS - Not approved in children.
UNAPPROVED PEDS - Edema: 4 mg/kg/day divided bid after meals, increase to 6 mg/kg/day if needed, max 300 mg/day.
FORMS - Trade: Caps, 50,100 mg.
NOTES - Combo product with HCTZ (eg, Dyazide, Maxzide) available for HTN.

CARDIOVASCULAR: Diuretics - Thiazide Type

NOTES: See also antihypertensive combinations. Possible hypersensitivity in patients allergic to sulfonamide containing drugs.

bendroflumethiazide (*Naturetin*) ▶L ♀D ◗? $$
ADULT - HTN/Edema: Start 5 mg PO qam, usual maintenance dose 5-20 mg/day qd or divided bid.

PEDS - Not approved in children.
FORMS - Trade: Tabs, scored, 5,10 mg.
NOTES - May dose qod or 3-5 days/week as maintenance therapy to control edema.

chlorothiazide (*Diuril*) ▶L ♀D ▶+ $

ADULT - HTN: Start 125-250 mg PO qd or divided bid, max 1000 mg/day divided bid. Edema: 500-2000 mg PO/IV qd or divided bid. Dosing on alternate days or for 3-4 consecutive days followed by no drug for 1-2 days is acceptable.
PEDS - Edema: Infants: Start 10-20 mg/kg/day PO qd or divided bid, up to 30 mg/kg/day divided bid. Children 6 mo-2 yo: 10-20 mg/kg/day PO qd or divided bid, max 375 mg/day. Children 2-12 yo: start 10-20 mg/kg/day PO qd or divided bid, up to 1g/day. IV formulation not recommended for infants or children.
FORMS - Generic/Trade: Tabs, scored 250,500 mg. Trade only: suspension, 250 mg/5 ml.
NOTES - Do not administer SC or IM.

chlorthalidone (*Hygroton, Thalitone*) ▶L ♀D ▶+ $

ADULT - HTN: (Hygroton) Start 12.5-25 mg PO qd, usual maintenance dose 12.5-50 mg/day, max 50 mg/day. (Thalitone) Start 15 mg PO qd, usual maintenance 30-45 mg/day, max 50 mg/day. Edema: (Hygroton) Start 50-100 mg PO qd after breakfast or 100 mg qod or 100 mg 3 times/week, usual maintenance dose 150-200 mg/day, max 200 mg/day. (Thalitone) Start 30-60 mg PO qd or 60 mg qod, usual maintenance dose 90-120 mg PO qd or qod.
PEDS - Not approved in children.
UNAPPROVED PEDS - Edema: 2 mg/kg PO 3 times weekly.
FORMS - Trade only: Tabs, non-scored (Thalitone) 15 mg. Generic/Trade: Tabs, non-scored (Thalitone, Hygroton) 25,50, scored (Hygroton) 100 mg.
NOTES - Thalitone has greater bioavailability than Hygroton product, do not interchange. Doses greater than 50 mg/day for HTN are usually associated with hypokalemia with little added BP control.

hydrochlorothiazide (*HCTZ, Oretic, HydroDIURIL, Esidrix, Microzide*) ▶L ♀D ▶+ $

ADULT - HTN: Start 12.5-25 mg PO qd, usual maintenance dose 12.5-50 mg/day, max 50 mg/day. Edema: 25-100 mg PO qd or in divided doses or 50-100 mg PO qod or 3-5 days/week, max 200 mg/day.
PEDS - Edema: 1-2 mg/kg/day PO qd or divided bid, max 37.5 mg/day in infants up to 2 yo, max 100 mg/day in children 2-12 yo.
FORMS - Generic/Trade: Tabs, scored 25,50,100 mg; cap, 12.5 mg; solution, 50 mg/5 ml, concentrate, 100 mg/mL.
NOTES - Doses as low as 6.25 mg qd may be effective in combination with other antihypertensives. Doses greater than 50 mg/day for HTN may cause hypokalemia with little added BP control.

hydroflumethiazide (*Diucardin*) ▶L ♀D ▶? $$

ADULT - HTN: Start 50 mg PO bid, usual maintenance dose 50-100 mg/day divided bid, max 200 mg/day. Edema: Start 50 mg PO qd or bid, usual maintenance dose 25-200 mg/day. Divide daily doses ≥ 100 mg bid.
PEDS - Not approved in children.
FORMS - Trade: Tabs, scored, 50 mg.
NOTES - May dose qod or 3-5 days/week as maintenance therapy to control edema.

indapamide (*Lozol*, ✤*Lozide*) ▶L ♀D ▶? $

ADULT - HTN: Start 1.25-2.5 mg PO qd, max 5 mg/day. Edema/CHF: 2.5-5 mg PO qam.
PEDS - Not approved in children.
FORMS - Generic/Trade: Tabs, non-scored 1.25, 2.5 mg.

methyclothiazide (*Enduron, Aquatensen*) ▶L ♀D ▶? $

ADULT - HTN: Start 2.5 mg PO qd, usual maintenance dose 2.5-5 mg/day. Edema: Start 2.5 mg PO qd, usual maintenance dose 2.5-10 mg/day.
PEDS - Not approved in children.
FORMS - Generic/Trade: Tabs, scored, 5 mg.
NOTES - May dose qod or 3-5 days/week as maintenance therapy to control edema.

metolazone (*Zaroxolyn, Mykrox*) ▶L ♀D ▶? $

ADULT - Edema (CHF, renal disease): 5-10 mg PO qd, max 10 mg/day in CHF, 20 mg/day in renal disease (Zaroxolyn). Reduce to lowest effective dose as edema resolves. May be given qod as edema resolves. HTN: Start 0.5 mg PO qd, max 1 mg/day (Mykrox), 2.5-5 mg PO qd, max 10 mg/day (Zaroxolyn).
PEDS - Not approved in children.
UNAPPROVED PEDS - Edema: 0.2-0.4 mg/kg/day qd or divided bid.
FORMS - Trade: Tabs, non-scored (Mykrox) 0.5, (Zaroxolyn) 2.5,5,10 mg.
NOTES - Mykrox has greater bioavailability than Zaroxolyn, do not interchange. Generally used for CHF, not HTN. When used with furosemide or other loop diuretics, administer metolazone 30 min before loop diuretic.

polythiazide (*Renese*) ▶L ♀D ▶? $

ADULT - HTN: Start 2 mg PO qd, usual maintenance dose 2-4 mg qd. Edema: 1-4 mg PO qd.

PEDS - Not approved in children.

FORMS - Trade: Tabs, scored, 1,2,4 mg.

NOTES - May dose qod or 3-5 days/week as maintenance therapy to control edema.

trichlormethiazide (*Naqua*) ▶L ♀D ▶? $

ADULT - HTN/Edema: Start 2 mg PO qd, usual maintenance dose 2-4 mg qd.

PEDS - Not approved in children.

FORMS - Generic/Trade: Tabs, non-scored, 4 mg.

NOTES - May dose qod or 3-5 days/week as maintenance therapy to control edema.

CARDIOVASCULAR: Nitrates

NOTE: Sildenafil (*Viagra*) use contraindicated with nitrates.

amyl nitrite ▶Lung ♀X ▶- $

ADULT - Angina: 0.3 ml inhaled as needed.

PEDS - Not approved in children.

NOTES - May cause headache and flushing. Flammable. Avoid use in areas with open flames. To avoid syncope, use only when lying down.

isosorbide dinitrate (*Isordil, Sorbitrate, Dilatrate-SR*) ▶L ♀C ▶? $

ADULT - Acute angina: 2.5-10 mg SL or chewed immediately, repeat as needed every 5-10 minutes up to 3 doses in 30 min. SL and chew Tabs may be used prior to events likely to provoke angina. Angina prophylaxis: Start 5-20 mg PO tid (7 am, noon, & 5 pm), max 40 mg tid. Sustained-release (Isordil Tembids, Dilatrate SR): Start 40 mg PO bid, max 80 mg PO bid (8 am & 2 pm).

PEDS - Not approved in children.

UNAPPROVED ADULT - CHF: 10-40 mg PO tid (7 am, noon, & 5 pm), max 80 mg tid. Use in combination with hydralazine.

FORMS - Generic/Trade: Tabs, scored 5,10,20, 30,40, chewable, scored 5,10, sustained-release, scored 40, sublingual Tabs, non-scored 2.5,5,10 mg. Trade only: cap, sustained-release (Dilatrate-SR, Isordil Tembids) 40 mg.

NOTES - Headache possible. Use SL or chew Tabs for an acute angina attack. Extended-release tab may be broken, but do not chew or crush, swallow whole. Allow for a nitrate-free period of 10-14 h each day to avoid nitrate tolerance.

isosorbide mononitrate (*ISMO, Monoket, Imdur*) ▶L ♀C ▶? $$

ADULT - Angina: 20 mg PO bid (8 am and 3 pm). Extended-release (Imdur): Start 30-60 mg PO qd, max 240 mg/day.

PEDS - Not approved in children.

FORMS - Generic/Trade: Tabs, non-scored (ISMO, bid dosing) 20, scored (Monoket, bid dosing) 10,20, extended-release, scored (Imdur, qd dosing) 30,60, non-scored 120 mg.

NOTES - Headache. Extended-release tab may be broken, but do not chew or crush, swallow whole. Do not use for acute angina.

nitroglycerin intravenous infusion (*Tridil, NitroBid IV*) ▶L ♀C ▶? $

ADULT - Perioperative HTN, acute MI/CHF, acute angina: mix 50 mg in 250 mL D5W (200 mcg/mL), start at 10-20 mcg/min IV (3-6 mL/h), then titrate upward by 10-20 mcg/min every 3-5 min until desired effect is achieved.

PEDS - Not approved in children.

UNAPPROVED ADULT - Hypertensive emergency: Start 10-20 mcg/min IV infusion, titrate up to 100 mcg/min. Antihypertensive effect is usually evident in 2-5 min. Effect may persist for only 3-5 min after infusion is stopped.

UNAPPROVED PEDS - IV infusion: start 0.25-0.5 mcg/kg/min, increase by 0.5-1 mcg/kg/min q3-5 min as needed, max 5 mcg/kg/min.

NOTES - Nitroglycerin migrates into polyvinyl chloride (PVC) tubing. Use lower initial doses (5 mcg/min) with non-PVC tubing. Use with caution in inferior/right ventricular myocardial infarction. Nitroglycerin-induced venodilation can cause severe hypotension.

nitroglycerin ointment (*Nitrol, Nitro-bid*) ▶L ♀C ▶? $

ADULT - Angina prophylaxis: Start 0.5 inch q8h applied to non-hairy skin area, maintenance 1-2 inches q8h, maximum 4 inches q4-6h.

PEDS - Not approved in children.

FORMS - Generic/Trade: Ointment, 2%.

NOTES - 1 inch ointment is approximately 15 mg nitroglycerin. Allow for a nitrate-free period of 10-14 h each day to avoid nitrate tolerance. Generally change to oral tabs or transdermal patch for long-term therapy. Do not use topical therapy (ointment, transdermal system) for acute angina.

nitroglycerin spray (*Nitrolingual*) ▶L ♀C ▶?

$$
ADULT - Acute angina: 1-2 sprays under the tongue at the onset of attack, repeat as needed, max 3 sprays in 15 min.
PEDS - Not approved in children.
FORMS - Trade: Solution, 0.4 mg/spray (200 sprays/canister).
NOTES - May be preferred over SL Tabs in patients with dry mouth. Patient can see how much medicine is left in bottle.

nitroglycerin sublingual (*Nitrostat, Nitro-Quick*) ▶L ♀C ▶? $
ADULT - Acute angina: 0.4 mg under tongue or between the cheek and gum, repeat dose every 5 min as needed up to 3 doses in 15 min. A dose may be given 5-10 min before activities that might provoke angina.
PEDS - Not approved in children.
FORMS - Generic/Trade: Sublingual tabs, non-scored 0.3,0.4,0.6 mg; in bottles of 100 or package of 4 bottles with 25 tabs each.
NOTES - Headache. May produce a burning/tingling sensation when administered, although this should not be used to assess potency. Store in original glass bottle to maintain potency/stability. Traditionally, unused Tabs should be discarded 6 months after the original bottle is opened; however the Nitrostat product is stable for 24 months after the bottle is opened or until the expiration date on the bottle, whichever is earlier. If used rarely, prescribe package with 4 bottles with 25 Tabs each.

nitroglycerin sustained release (*Nitrong, Nitroglyn*) ▶L ♀C ▶? $
ADULT - Angina prophylaxis: Start 2.5 or 2.6 mg PO bid-tid, then titrate upward as needed.
PEDS - Not approved in children.
FORMS - Trade only: tabs, scored, extended-release (Nitrong) 2.6,6.5,9 mg. Generic/Trade: cap, extended-release (Nitroglyn) 2.5,6.5,9,13 mg.
NOTES - Headache. Extended-release tab may be broken, but do not chew or crush, swallow whole. cap should be swallowed whole. Do not use extended-release Tabs or Caps for acute angina attack. Allow for a nitrate-free period of 10-14 h each day to avoid nitrate tolerance.

nitroglycerin transdermal (*Deponit, Minitran, Nitrodisc, Nitro-Dur, Transderm-Nitro*, ✤*Trinipatch*) ▶L ♀C ▶? $$
ADULT - Angina prophylaxis: Start with lowest dose and apply 1 patch for 12-14 h each day to non-hairy skin.
PEDS - Not approved in children.
FORMS - Trade: Transdermal system, doses in mg/h: Nitro-Dur 0.1,0.2,0.3,0.4,0.6,0.8; Minitran 0.1,0.2,0.4,0.6; Nitrodisc 0.2,0.3,0.4; Deponit 0.2,0.4; Transderm-Nitro 0.1,0.2,0.4,0.6,0.8. Generic only: Transdermal system, doses in mg/h: 0.2,0.4,0.6.
NOTES - Do not use topical therapy (ointment, transdermal system) for acute angina attack. Allow for a nitrate-free period of 10-14 h each day to avoid nitrate tolerance.

nitroglycerin transmucosal (*Nitroguard*) ▶L ♀C ▶? $$$
ADULT - Acute angina and prophylaxis: 1-3 mg PO, between lip and gum or between cheek and gum, q 3-5 h while awake.
PEDS - Not approved in children.
FORMS - Trade: Tabs, controlled-release, 1,2,3 mg.
NOTES - May cause headache and flushing. Allow for a nitrate-free period of 10-14 h each day to avoid nitrate tolerance.

CARDIOVASCULAR: Pressors / Inotropes

dobutamine (*Dobutrex*) ▶Plasma ♀D ▶- $
ADULT - Inotropic support in cardiac decompensation (CHF, surgical procedures): 250 mg in 250 ml D5W (1 mg/mL) at 2-20 mcg/kg/min. 70 kg: 5 mcg/kg/min = 21 mL/h.
PEDS - Not approved in children.
UNAPPROVED PEDS - Same as adult. Use lowest effective dose.
NOTES - For short-term use, up to 72 hours.

dopamine (*Intropin*) ▶Plasma ♀C ▶- $
ADULT - Pressor: 400 mg in 250 ml D5W (1600 mcg/ mL), start 5 mcg/kg/min, increase as needed by 5-10 mcg/kg/min increments at 10 min intervals, max 50 mcg/kg/min. 70 kg: 5 mcg/kg/min = 13 mL/h.
PEDS - Not approved in children.
UNAPPROVED ADULT - Symptomatic bradycardia unresponsive to atropine: 5-20 mcg/kg/min IV infusion.
UNAPPROVED PEDS - Respiratory distress syndrome: 5 mcg/kg/min IV infusion; max rate 20-50 mcg/kg/min.
NOTES - Doses in mcg/kg/min: 2-4 = (traditional renal dose; recent evidence suggests ineffective) dopaminergic receptors; 5-10 = (cardiac dose) dopaminergic and beta1 receptors; >10

= dopaminergic, beta1, and alpha1 receptors.

ephedrine ▶K ♀C ▶? $

ADULT - Pressor: 10-25 mg IV slow injection, with repeat doses every 5-10 min as needed, max 150 mg/day. Orthostatic hypotension: 25 mg PO qd-qid. Bronchospasm: 25-50 mg PO q3-4h prn.

PEDS - Not approved in children.

UNAPPROVED PEDS - Pressor: 3 mg/kg/day SC or IV in 4-6 divided doses.

FORMS - Generic: Caps, 25,50 mg.

epinephrine ▶Plasma ♀C ▶- $

ADULT - Cardiac arrest: 0.5-1 mg (1:10,000 solution) IV, repeat every 3-5 minutes if needed; infusion 1 mg in 250 mL D5W (4 mcg/mL) at 1-4 mcg/min (15-60 mL/h). Anaphylaxis: 0.1-0.5 mg SC/IM (1:1,000 solution), may repeat SC dose every 10-15 minutes for anaphylactic shock.

PEDS - Cardiac arrest: 0.01 mg/kg IV/IO or 0.1 mg/kg ET, repeat 0.1-0.2 mg/kg IV/IO/ET every 3-5 minutes if needed. Neonates: 0.01-0.03 mg/kg IV/ET, repeat every 3-5 minutes if needed; IV infusion start 0.1 mcg/kg/min, increase in increments of 0.1 mcg/kg/min if needed, max 1 mcg/kg/min. Anaphylaxis: 0.01 mg/kg (0.01 ml/kg of 1:1000 injection) SC, may repeat SC dose at 20 minute to 4 hour intervals depending on severity of condition.

UNAPPROVED ADULT - Symptomatic bradycardia unresponsive to atropine: 2-10 mcg/min IV infusion. ET administration prior to IV access: 2-2.5 x the recommended IV dose in 10 ml of NS or distilled water.

NOTES - Use the 1:10,000 injectable solution for IV use in cardiac arrest (10 mL = 1 mg). Use the 1:1000 injectable solution for SC/IM use in anaphylaxis (0.1 mL = 0.1 mg).

inamrinone (*Inocor*) ▶K ♀C ▶? $$$$$

ADULT - CHF (NYHA class III,IV): 0.75 mg/kg bolus IV over 2-3 min, then infusion 100 mg in 100 mL NS (1 mg/mL) at 5-10 mcg/kg/min. 70 kg: 5 mcg/kg/min = 21 mL/h. An additional IV bolus of 0.75 mg/kg may be given 30 min after initiating therapy if needed. Total daily dose should not exceed 10 mg/kg.

PEDS - Not approved in children.

UNAPPROVED ADULT - CPR: 0.75 mg/kg bolus IV over 2-3 min, followed by 5-15 mcg/kg/min.

UNAPPROVED PEDS - Inotropic support: 0.75 mg/kg IV bolus over 2-3 minutes, followed by 3-5 mcg/kg/min (neonates) or 5-10 mcg/kg/min (children) maintenance infusion.

NOTES - Thrombocytopenia possible. Children may require higher bolus doses, 3-4.5 mg/kg. Name changed from "amrinone" to avoid medication errors.

mephentermine (*Wyamine*) ▶Plasma ♀C ▶- $$$$

ADULT - Hypotension during anesthesia: 0.5 mg/kg/dose, usually 15-30 mg IM, max 80 mg/dose. Spinal anesthesia: 30-45 mg IV, repeat 30 mg dose prn to maintain BP. Spinal anesthesia in cesarean section: 15 mg IV, repeat dose prn to maintain BP.

PEDS - Not approved in children.

UNAPPROVED PEDS - Hypotension during anesthesia: 0.4 mg/kg/dose IM.

metaraminol (*Aramine*) ▶Plasma ♀C ▶- $

ADULT - Acute hypotension during spinal anesthesia: 500-1500 mcg IV bolus followed by 100 mg in 250 ml D5W (400 mcg/mL) IV infusion, start 5 mcg/kg/min (70 kg = 53 mL/h). Prevention of hypotension: 2-10 mg IM/SC.

PEDS - Not approved in children.

UNAPPROVED PEDS - Acute hypotensive during spinal anesthesia: 0.1 mg/kg SC/IM, wait at least 10 min before repeat dose. Severe hypotension/shock: 0.01 mg/kg IV and, if needed, continue with IV infusion 0.4 mg/kg diluted and administered at a rate to maintain BP.

methoxamine (*Vasoxyl*) ▶Plasma ♀C ▶- $$$$$

ADULT - Acute hypotension during spinal anesthesia: 3-5 mg IV slow injection, may supplement with 10-15 mg IM for a prolonged effect. IM doses used with initial IV bolus range from 5-20 mg. Termination of SVT: 10 mg IV over 3-5 min.

PEDS - Not approved in children.

UNAPPROVED ADULT - Severe, acute hypotension during spinal anesthesia: Slow IV infusion, 35-40 mg in 250 mL D5W.

UNAPPROVED PEDS - Acute hypotensive during spinal anesthesia: 0.25 mg/kg IM or 0.08 mg/kg slow IV injection.

midodrine (*ProAmatine*, ✽*Amatine*) ▶LK ♀C ▶? $$$$$

ADULT - Orthostatic hypotension: Start 10 mg PO tid while awake, increase dose as needed to max 40 mg/day. Renal impairment: Start 2.5 mg tid while awake, increase dose as needed.

PEDS - Not approved in children.

FORMS - Trade: Tabs, scored 2.5,5 mg.

NOTES - The last daily dose should be no later than 6 pm to avoid supine HTN during sleep.

milrinone (*Primacor*) ▶K ♀C ▶? $$$$$

ADULT - CHF (NYHA class III,IV): Load 50 mcg/kg IV over 10 min, then begin IV infusion of 0.375-0.75 mcg/kg/min. Renal impairment: reduce IV infusion rate (mcg/kg/min) as follows, CrCl 50-41 mL/min, 0.43; CrCl 40-31 mL/min, 0.38; CrCl 30-21 mL/min, 0.33; CrCl 20-11 mL/min, 0.28; CrCl 10-6 mL/min, 0.23; CrCl ≤5 mL/min, 0.2.

PEDS - Not approved in children.

UNAPPROVED PEDS - Inotropic support: Limited data, 50 mcg/kg IV bolus over 10 minutes, followed by 0.5-1 mcg/kg/min IV infusion, titrate to effect within dosing range.

norepinephrine (*Levophed*) ▶Plasma ♀C ▶? $

ADULT - Acute hypotension: 4 mg in 500 mL D5W (8 mcg/mL), start IV infusion 8-12 mcg/min, ideally through central line, adjust rate to maintain BP, average maintenance dose 2-4 mcg/min. 3 mcg/min = 20 mL/h.

PEDS - Not approved in children.

UNAPPROVED PEDS - Acute hypotension: Start 0.05-0.1mcg/kg/min IV infusion, titrate to desired effect, max dose 2 mcg/kg/min.

NOTES - Avoid extravasation, do not administer IV push or IM.

phenylephrine (*Neo-Synephrine*) ▶Plasma ♀C ▶- $$$

ADULT - Mild to moderate hypotension: 0.1-0.2 mg slow IV injection, do not exceed 0.5 mg in initial dose, repeat dose as needed no less than every 10-15 min; 1-10 mg SC/IM, initial dose should not exceed 5 mg. Infusion for severe hypotension: 20 mg in 250 ml D5W (80 mcg/mL), start 100-180 mcg/min (75-135 mL/h), usual dose once BP is stabilized 40-60 mcg/min.

PEDS - Not approved in children.

UNAPPROVED PEDS - Mild to moderate hypotension: 5-20 mcg/kg IV bolus every 10-15 minutes as needed; 0.1-0.5 mcg/kg/min IV infusion, titrate to desired effect.

NOTES - Avoid SC or IM administration during shock, use IV route to ensure drug absorption.

CARDIAC PARAMETERS AND FORMULAS	Normal
Cardiac output (CO) = heart rate x stroke volume	4-8 l/min
Cardiac index (CI) = CO/BSA	2.8-4.2 l/min/m2
MAP (mean arterial press) = [(SBP - DBP)/3] + DBP	80-100 mmHg
SVR (systemic vasc resis) = (MAP - CVP)x(80)/CO	800-1200 dyne/sec/cm5
PVR (pulm vasc resis) = (PAM - PCWP)x(80)/CO	45-120 dyne/sec/cm5
QT_C = QT / square root of RR	0.38-0.42
Right atrial pressure (central venous pressure)	0-8 mmHg
Pulmonary artery systolic pressure (PAS)	20-30 mmHg
Pulmonary artery diastolic pressure (PAD)	10-15 mmHg
Pulmonary capillary wedge pressure (PCWP)	8-12 mmHg (post-MI ~16 mmHg)

CARDIOVASCULAR: Thrombolytics

alteplase (*t-PA, Activase*) ▶L ♀C ▶? $$$$$

ADULT - Acute MI: (patients > 67 kg) 15 mg IV bolus, then 50 mg IV over 30 min, then 35 mg IV over the next 60 min; (patients ≤67 kg) 15 mg IV bolus, then 0.75 mg/kg (not to exceed 50 mg) IV over 30 min, then 0.5 mg/kg (not to exceed 35 mg) IV over the next 60 min. Concurrent heparin infusion. Acute ischemic stroke: 0.9 mg/kg up to 90 mg infused over 60 min, with 10% of dose as initial IV bolus over 1 minute; start within 3 h of symptom onset. Acute pulmonary embolism: 100 mg IV over 2h, then restart heparin when PTT ≤ twice normal.

PEDS - Not approved in children.

NOTES - Must be reconstituted. Solution must be used within 8h after reconstitution.

anistreplase (*APSAC, Eminase*) ▶L ♀C ▶? $$$$$

ADULT - Acute MI: 30 units IV over 2-5 mins.

PEDS - Not approved in children.

NOTES - Must be reconstituted. Solution must be used within 30 min after reconstitution. Do not shake vial.

reteplase (*Retavase*) ▶L ♀C ▶? $$$$$

ADULT - Acute MI: 10 units IV over 2 minutes; repeat dose in 30 min.

PEDS - Not approved in children.

NOTES - Must be reconstituted with sterile water for injection to 1 mg/ml concentration. Solution must be used within 4 h after reconstitution.

streptokinase (*Streptase, Kabikinase*) ▶L ♀C ▶? $$$$$

ADULT - Acute MI: 1.5 million units IV over 60 min. Pulmonary embolism: 250,000 units IV loading dose over 30 min, followed by 100,000 units/h IV infusion for 24 h (maintain infusion for 72 h if concurrent DVT suspected). DVT: 250,000 units IV loading dose over 30 min, followed by 100,000 units/h IV infusion for 24 hours. Occluded arteriovenous catheter: 250,000 units instilled into the catheter, remove solution containing 250,000 units of drug from catheter after 2 h using a 5-mL syringe.

PEDS - Not approved in children.

NOTES - Must be reconstituted. Solution must be used within 8 h of reconstitution. Do not shake vial. Do not repeat use in less than one year.

tenecteplase (*TNKase*) ▶L ♀C ▶? $$$$$

ADULT - Acute MI: Single IV bolus dose over 5 seconds based on body weight; < 60 kg, 30 mg; 60-69 kg, 35 mg; 70-79 kg, 40 mg; 80-89 kg, 45 mg; ≥ 90kg, 50 mg.

PEDS - Not approved in children.

NOTES - Must be reconstituted. Solution must be used within 8h after reconstitution.

urokinase (*Abbokinase, Abbokinase Open-Cath*) ▶L ♀B ▶? $$$$$

ADULT - Pulmonary embolism: 4400 units/kg IV loading dose over 10 min, followed by IV infusion 4400 units/kg/h for 12 hours. Occluded IV catheter: 5000 units instilled into the catheter with a tuberculin syringe, remove solution containing 5000 units of drug from catheter after 5 min using a 5-mL syringe. Aspiration attempts may be repeated q5min. If unsuccessful, cap catheter and allow 5000 unit solution to remain in catheter for 30-60 min before again attempting to aspirate solution and residual clot.

PEDS - Not approved in children.

UNAPPROVED ADULT - Acute MI: 2-3 million units IV infusion over 45-90 min. Give one-half the total dose as a rapid initial IV injection over 5 min.

UNAPPROVED PEDS - Arterial or venous thrombosis: 4400 units/kg IV loading dose over 10 minutes, followed by 4400 units/kg/hr for 12-72 hours. Occluded IV catheter: same as adult.

NOTES - Currently this product is not available from the manufacturer, availability unknown. Must be reconstituted. Do not shake vial.

THROMBOLYTIC THERAPY FOR ACUTE MI *Indications*:* Chest pain ≤12 hours; and either ST elevation ≥1 mm in 2 contiguous leads or left BBB obscuring ST-segment analysis. *Absolute contraindications*: Prior hemorrhagic stroke or any stroke within 6-12 months; brain neoplasm, suspected aortic dissection. *Relative contraindications* (weigh benefits against higher risk): Ready availability of high-volume interventional cath lab; major surgery or trauma in prior 14-21 days; bleeding diathesis or current warfarin with INR >2; prolonged CPR (>10 min); age ≥75 years, pregnancy; uncorrected GI bleeding within 3 months; severe uncontrolled HTN (>180/110) before or during treatment; venous/arterial puncture to noncompressible site (eg, internal jugular or subclavian); brain aneurysm or AVM; coma. Menses are NOT a contraindication. Streptokinase contraindicated if given in prior year.

**Circulation* 1999; 100:1016

CARDIOVASCULAR: Volume Expanders

albumin (*Albuminar, Buminate, Albumarc, ♣Plasbumin*) ▶L ♀C ▶? $$$$

ADULT - Shock, burns: 500 mL of 5% solution (50 mg/mL) infused as rapidly as tolerated. Repeat infusion in 30 min if response is inadequate. 25% solution may be used with or without dilution if necessary. Undiluted 25% solution should be infused at 1 ml/min to avoid too rapid plasma volume expansion.

PEDS - Shock, burns: 10-20 mL/kg IV infusion at 5-10 mL/min using 50 mL of 5% solution.

UNAPPROVED PEDS - Shock/hypovolemia: 1 g/kg/dose IV rapid infusion. Hypoproteinemia: 1 g/kg/dose IV infusion over 30-120 min.

NOTES - Fever, chills. Monitor for plasma volume overload (dyspnea, fluid in lungs, abnormal increase in BP or CVP). Less likely to cause hypotension than plasma protein fraction, more purified. In treating burns, large volumes of crystalloid solutions (0.9% sodium chloride) are used to maintain plasma volume with albumin. Use 5% solution in pediatric hypovolemic patients. Use 25% solution in pediatric patients with volume restrictions.

dextran (*Rheomacrodex, Gentran, Macrodex*) ▶K ♀C ▶? $$$$

ADULT - Shock/hypovolemia: Dextran 40, Dextran 70 and 75, up to 20 mL/kg during the first 24 hours, up to 10 mL/kg/day thereafter, do not continue for longer than 5 days. The first 500

mL may be infused rapidly with CVP monitoring. DVT/PE prophylaxis during surgery: Dextran 40, 50-100 g IV infusion the day of surgery, continue for 2-3 days post-op with 50 g/day. 50 g/day may be given every 2nd or 3rd day thereafter up to 14 days.
PEDS - Total dose should not exceed 20 mL/kg.
UNAPPROVED ADULT - DVT/PE prophylaxis during surgery: Dextran 70 and 75 solutions have been used. Other uses: to improve circulation with sickle cell crisis, prevention of nephrotoxicity with radiographic contrast media, toxemia of late pregnancy.
NOTES - Monitor for plasma volume overload (dyspnea, fluid in lungs, abnormal increase in BP or CVP) and anaphylactoid reactions. May impair platelet function. Less effective that other agents for DVT/PE prevention.

hetastarch (*Hespan, Hextend*) ▸K ♀C ▸? $$
ADULT - Shock/hypovolemia: 500-1000 mL IV infusion, total daily dose usually should not exceed 20 mL/kg (1500 mL). Renal impairment: CrCl < 10 mL/min, usual initial dose followed by 20-25% of usual dose.
PEDS - Not approved in children.
UNAPPROVED PEDS - Shock/hypovolemia: 10 ml/kg/dose; do not exceed 20 ml/kg/day.
NOTES - Monitor for plasma volume overload (dyspnea, fluid in lungs, abnormal increase in BP or CVP). Little or no antigenic properties compared to dextran.

plasma protein fraction (*Plasmanate, Protenate, Plasmatein*) ▸L ♀C ▸? $$$$
ADULT - Shock/hypovolemia: Adjust initial rate according to clinical response and BP, but rate should not exceed 10 mL/min. As plasma volume normalizes, infusion rate should not exceed 5-8 mL/min. Usual dose 250-500 mL. Hypoproteinemia: 1000-1500 mL/day IV infusion.
PEDS - Shock/hypovolemia: Initial dose 6.6-33 mL/kg infused at a rate of 5-10 mL/min.
NOTES - Fever, chills, hypotension with rapid infusion. Monitor for plasma volume overload (dyspnea, fluid in lungs, abnormal increase in BP or CVP). Less pure than albumin products.

CARDIOVASCULAR: Other

alprostadil (*Prostin VR Pediatric, prostaglandin E1*) ▸Lung ♀- ▸- ?
PEDS - Temporary maintenance of patent ductus arteriosus in neonates: Start 0.1 mcg/kg/min IV infusion. Reduce dose to minimal amount that maintains therapeutic response. Max dose 0.4 mcg/kg/min.

cilostazol (*Pletal*) ▸L ♀C ▸? $$$
WARNING - Contraindicated in congestive heart failure of any severity.
ADULT - Intermittent claudication: 100 mg PO bid on empty stomach. 50 mg PO bid with cytochrome P450 3A4 inhibitors (like ketoconazole, itraconazole, erythromycin, diltiazem) or cytochrome P450 2C19 inhibitors (like omeprazole). Claudication may not improve for 2-12 weeks.
PEDS - Not approved in children.
FORMS - Trade: Tabs 50, 100 mg.
NOTES - Avoid grapefruit juice.

indomethacin (*Indocin IV*, *✤Indocid*) ▸KL ♀- ▸- ?
PEDS - Closure of patent ductus arteriosus in neonates: Initial dose 0.2 mg/kg IV, if additional doses necessary, dose and frequency (q12h or q24h) based on neonate's age and urine output.
NOTES - Administer prepared IV solution over 5-10 seconds.

isoxsuprine (*Vasodilan*) ▸KL ♀C ▸? $
ADULT - Adjunctive therapy for cerebral vascular insufficiency and PVD: 10-20 mg PO tid-qid.
PEDS - Not approved in children.
FORMS - Generic/Trade: Tabs, 10,20 mg.
NOTES - Drug has questionable therapeutic effect.

nesiritide (*Natrecor*) ▸K, plasma ♀C ▸? $$$$$
ADULT - Decompenstated CHF: 2 mcg/kg IV bolus over 60 seconds, then 0.01 mcg/kg/min IV infusion for up to 48 hours. Do not initiate at higher doses. Limited experience with increased doses: 0.005 mcg/kg/min increments, preceded by 1 mcg/kg bolus, no more frequently than q3h up to max infusion dose 0.03 mcg/kg/min. 1.5 mg vial in 250mL D5W (6 mcg/mL). 70 kg: 2 mcg/kg bolus = 23.3 ml, 0.01 mcg/kg/min infusion = 7 mL/h.
PEDS - Not approved in children.
NOTES - Contraindicated as primary therapy for cardiogenic shock and when SBP <90 mmHg. Discontinue if dose-related symptomatic hypotension occurs and support BP prn. May restart infusion with dose reduced by 30% (no bolus dose) once BP stabilized. Do not shake reconstituted vial, and dilute vial prior to ad-

ministration. Incompatible with heparin and many other injectable drugs; administer agents using separate IV lines.

papaverine ▶LK ♀C ◗? $

ADULT - Cerebral and peripheral ischemia: Start 150 mg PO bid, increase to max 300 mg bid prn. Start 30 mg IV/IM, dose range 30-120 mg q3h prn. Give IV doses over 1-2 min.

PEDS - Not approved in children.

FORMS - Generic: cap, ext'd-release, 150 mg.

pentoxifylline (*Trental*) ▶L ♀C ◗? $$

ADULT - Intermittent claudication: 400 mg PO tid with meals. For CNS/GI adverse effects, decrease dose to 400 mg PO BID. Claudication may not improve for 2-8 weeks.

PEDS - Not approved in children.

FORMS - Generic/Trade: Tabs 400 mg.

NOTES - Contraindicated with recent cerebral/retinal bleed. Increases theophylline levels. Increases INR with warfarin.

CONTRAST MEDIA: MRI Contrast

gadodiamide (*Omniscan*) ▶K ♀C ◗? $$$$

ADULT - Non-iodinated, non-ionic IV contrast for MRI.

PEDS - Non-iodinated, non-ionic IV contrast.

gadopentetate (*Magnevist*) ▶K ♀C ◗? $$$

ADULT - Non-iodinated IV contrast for MRI.

PEDS - >2 yo: Non-iodinated IV contrast for MRI.

CONTRAST MEDIA: Radiography Contrast

NOTE: Beware of allergic or anaphylactoid reactions. Avoid IV contrast in renal insufficiency or dehydration. Hold metformin (Glucophage) prior to or at the time of iodinated contrast dye use and for 48 h after procedure. Restart after procedure only if renal function is normal.

barium sulfate ▶Not absorbed ♀? ◗+ $

ADULT - Non-iodinated GI (eg, oral, rectal) contrast.

PEDS - Non-iodinated GI (eg, oral, rectal) contrast.

NOTES - Contraindicated if gastric or intestinal perforation. Use with caution in GI obstruction. May cause abdominal distention, cramping, and constipation with oral use.

diatrizoate (*Hypaque, Renografin, Gastrografin, MD-Gastroview, Cystografin*) ▶K ♀C ◗? $

ADULT - Iodinated, ionic, high osmolality IV or GI contrast.

PEDS - Iodinated, ionic, high osmolality IV or GI contrast.

NOTES - High osmolality contrast may cause tissue damage if infiltrated/extravasated. IV: Hypaque, Renografin. GI: Gastrografin, MD-Gastroview.

iohexol (*Omnipaque*) ▶K ♀B ◗? $$$

ADULT - Iodinated, non-ionic, low osmolality IV and oral/body cavity contrast.

PEDS - Iodinated, non-ionic, low osmolality IV and oral/body cavity contrast.

iopamidol (*Isovue*) ▶K ♀? ◗? $$

ADULT - Iodinated, non-ionic, low osmolality IV contrast.

PEDS - Iodinated, non-ionic, low osmolality IV contrast.

iothalamate (*Conray*) ▶K ♀B ◗- $

ADULT - Iodinated, ionic, high osmolality IV contrast.

PEDS - Iodinated, ionic, high osmolality IV contrast.

NOTES - High osmolality contrast may cause tissue damage if infiltrated/extravasated.

ioversol (*Optiray*) ▶K ♀B ◗? $$

ADULT - Iodinated, non-ionic, low osmolality IV contrast.

PEDS - Iodinated, non-ionic, low osmolality IV contrast.

ioxaglate (*Hexabrix*) ▶K ♀B ◗- $$$

ADULT - Iodinated, ionic, low osmolality IV contrast.

PEDS - Iodinated, ionic, low osmolality IV contrast.

DERMATOLOGY: Acne Preparations

NOTES: For topical agents, wash area prior to application. Wash hands before & after application; avoid eye area.

adapalene (*Differin*) ▶Bile ♀C ◗? $$

ADULT - Acne: apply qhs.

PEDS - Not approved in children.

UNAPPROVED PEDS - Acne: apply qhs.
FORMS - Trade only: gel 0.1%, 15,45 g.
NOTES - During early weeks of therapy, acne exacerbation may occur. May cause erythema, scaling, dryness, pruritus, and burning in up to 40% of patients. Therapeutic results take 8-12 weeks.

azelaic acid (*Azelex*) ▶K ♀B ◗? $$$
ADULT - Acne: apply bid.
PEDS - Not approved in children.
UNAPPROVED PEDS - Acne: apply qhs.
FORMS - Trade only: cream 20%, 30g.
NOTES - Improvement occurs within 4 weeks. Monitor for hypopigmentation esp in patients with dark complexions. Avoid use of occlusive dressings.

***BenzaClin* (clindamycin + benzoyl peroxide)** ▶K ♀B ◗? $$$
ADULT - Acne: apply bid.
PEDS - Not approved in children.
UNAPPROVED PEDS - Acne: apply qhs.
FORMS - Trade only: gel clindamycin 1% + benzoyl peroxide 5%; 19.7 g.
NOTES - Must be refrigerated, expires 2 months after mixing.

***Benzamycin* (erythromycin + benzoyl peroxide)** ▶LK ♀B ◗? $$$
ADULT - Acne: apply bid.
PEDS - Not approved in children.
UNAPPROVED PEDS - Acne: apply qhs.
FORMS - Trade only: gel erythromycin 3% + benzoyl peroxide 5%; 23.3, 46.6 g.

benzoyl peroxide (*Benzac, Clearasil, Desquam, ✤Acetoxyl, Solugel*) ▶LK ♀C ◗? $
ADULT - Acne: Cleansers: wash qd-bid. Creams/gels/lotion: apply qd initially, gradually increase to bid-tid if needed.
PEDS - Not approved in children.
UNAPPROVED PEDS - Acne: Cleansers: wash qd-bid. Creams/gels/lotion: apply qd initially, gradually increase to bid-tid if needed.
FORMS - OTC and Rx generic: liquid 2.5,5,10%, bar 5,10%, mask 5%, lotion 5,5.5,10%, cream 5,10%, cleanser 10%, gel 2.5,4,5, 6,10,20%.
NOTES - If excessive drying or peeling occurs, reduce frequency of application. Use with PABA-containing sunscreens may cause transient skin discoloration. May discolor fabric.

clindamycin (*Cleocin T*, ✤*Dalacin T*) ▶L ♀B ◗- $
ADULT - Acne: apply bid.
PEDS - Not approved in children.
UNAPPROVED ADULT - Rosacea: apply lotion bid.
UNAPPROVED PEDS - Acne: apply bid.
FORMS - Generic/Trade: gel 10 mg/ml 7.5, 30g, lotion 10 mg/ml 60 ml, soln 10 mg/ml 30,60 ml.
NOTES - Concomitant use with erythromycin may decrease effectiveness. Most common adverse effects dryness, erythema, burning, peeling, oiliness and itching. Pseudomembranous colitis has been reported with topical use.

doxycycline (*Vibramycin, Doryx*) ▶LK ♀D ◗+ $$
ADULT - Acne vulgaris: 100 mg PO bid.
PEDS - Avoid in children <8 yo due to teeth staining.
UNAPPROVED PEDS - Acne vulgaris: children > 8 y: 2.2 mg/kg PO given as a single daily dose or divided bid; maximum 100 mg PO bid.
FORMS - Generic only: tabs 50 mg, caps 20, 50 mg. Generic/Trade: Tabs 100 mg, caps 50,100 mg. Trade only: susp 25 mg/5 ml, syrup 50 mg/5 ml (contains sulfites).
NOTES - Photosensitivity, pseudotumor cerebri, increased BUN. Decreased efficacy of oral contraceptives. Increased INR with warfarin. Do not give antacids or calcium supplements within 2 h of doxycycline. Barbiturates, carbamazepine, and phenytoin may decrease doxycycline levels.

erythromycin (*Eryderm, Erycette, Erygel, A/T/S*) ▶L ♀B ◗? $$
ADULT - Acne: apply bid.
PEDS - Not approved in children.
UNAPPROVED PEDS - Acne: apply bid.
FORMS - Generic: solution 1.5% 60 ml, 2% 60,120 ml, pads 2%, gel 2% 30,60 g, ointment 2% 25 g.
NOTES - May be more irritating when used with other acne products. Concomitant use with clindamycin may decrease effectiveness.

isotretinoin (*Accutane*) ▶LK ♀X ◗- $$$$$
WARNING - Contraindicated in pregnant women or in women who may become pregnant. If used in a woman of childbearing age, patient must have severe, disfiguring acne, be reliable, comply with mandatory contraceptive measures, receive written and oral instructions about hazards of taking during pregnancy, have a negative serum pregnancy test within 2 weeks of starting, and begin therapy on second or third day of menstrual period. Must use 2 forms of effective contraception from 1 month prior until 1 month after discontinuation of therapy. May cause depression; monitor for symptoms. Consider informed consent.
ADULT - Severe, recalcitrant cystic acne: 0.5-2 mg/kg/day PO divided bid for 15-20 weeks.

Typical target dose is 1 mg/kg/day. May repeat second course of therapy after > 2 months off therapy.
PEDS - Not approved in children.
UNAPPROVED ADULT - Prevention of second primary tumors in patients treated for squamous-cell carcinoma of the head and neck: 50-100 mg/m2/day PO. Also been used in keratinization disorders.
UNAPPROVED PEDS - Severe, recalcitrant cystic acne: 0.5-2 mg/kg/day PO divided bid for 15-20 weeks. Typical target dose is 1 mg/kg/day. Maintenance therapy for neuroblastoma: 100-250 mg/m2/day PO in 2 divided doses.
FORMS - Trade only: caps 10,20,40 mg.
NOTES - May cause headache, cheilitis, drying of mucous membranes including eyes, nose, mouth, hair loss, abdominal pain, pyuria, joint and muscle pain/stiffness, conjunctivitis, elevated ESR, and changes in serum lipids and LFTs. Pseudotumor cerebri has occurred during therapy. May cause corneal opacities, decreased night vision, and inflammatory bowel disease. Avoid concomitant vitamin A, tetracycline and minocycline. May decrease carbamazepine concentrations. Avoid exposure to sunlight.

sodium sulfacetamide (*Klaron*) ▶K♀C ◗? $$
ADULT - Acne: apply bid.
PEDS - Not approved in children.
FORMS - Trade only: lotion 10% 59 ml.
NOTES - Cross-sensitivity with sulfa or sulfite allergy.

***Sulfacet-R* (sodium sulfacetamide + sulfur)** ▶K ♀C ◗? $$
ADULT - Acne, rosacea, seborrheic dermatitis: apply qd-tid.
PEDS - Not approved in children.
FORMS - Trade and generic: lotion (sodium sulfacetamide 10% & sulfur 5%) 25 g.
NOTES - Avoid with sulfa allergy, renal failure.

tazarotene (*Tazorac*) ▶L ♀X ◗? $$$
ADULT - Acne: apply 0.1% gel qhs. Psoriasis: apply qhs.
PEDS - Not approved in children.
UNAPPROVED PEDS - Acne: apply 0.1% gel qhs. Psoriasis: apply qhs.
FORMS - Trade only: gel 0.05% 30,100g, 0.1% 30, 100g.
NOTES - Desquamation, burning, dry skin, erythema, pruritus may occur in up to 30% of patients. May cause photosensitivity.

tretinoin (*Retin-A, Renova, Retisol-A,* ✤*Stievaa*) ▶LK ♀C ◗? $$
ADULT - Acne (Retin A): apply qhs. Wrinkles, hyperpigmentation, tactile roughness (Renova): apply qhs.
PEDS - Not approved in children.
UNAPPROVED ADULT - Used in skin cancer and lamellar ichthyosis, mollusca contagiosa, verrucae plantaris, verrucae planae juvenilis, hyperpigmented lesions in black individuals, ichthyosis vulgaris, and pityriasis rubra pilaris.
FORMS - Generic/Trade: cream 0.025% 20,45 g, 0.05% 20,45 g, 0.1% 20,45 g, gel 0.025% 15,45 g, liquid 0.05% 28 ml. Trade only: Renova cream 0.05% 40,60 g.
NOTES - May induce erythema, peeling. Minimize sun exposure. Concomitant use with sulfur, resorcinol, benzoyl peroxide, or salicylic acid may result in skin irritation.

DERMATOLOGY: Antibacterials

bacitracin ▶Not absorbed ♀C ◗? $
ADULT - Minor cuts, wounds, burns or skin abrasions: apply qd-tid.
PEDS - Not approved in children.
UNAPPROVED PEDS - Minor cuts, wounds, burns or skin abrasions: apply qd-tid.
FORMS - OTC Generic/Trade: ointment 500 units/g 1,15,30g.

gentamicin (*Garamycin*) ▶K ♀D ◗? $
ADULT - Skin infections: apply tid-qid.
PEDS - Skin infections > 1 yo: apply tid-qid.
FORMS - Generic/Trade: ointment 0.1% 15,30 g, cream 0.1% 15,30 g.

mafenide (*Sulfamylon*) ▶LK ♀C ◗? $$$
ADULT - Adjunctive treatment of burns: apply qd-bid.
PEDS - Adjunctive treatment of burns: apply qd-bid.
FORMS - Trade only: cream 37, 114, 411 g, 5% topical solution 50 g packets.
NOTES - Can cause metabolic acidosis. Contains sulfites.

metronidazole (*Noritate, MetroGel, MetroLotion*) ▶KL ♀B(- in 1st trimester) ◗- $$$
ADULT - Rosacea: apply bid.
PEDS - Not approved in children.
UNAPPROVED ADULT - A 1% solution prepared from the oral Tabs has been used in the treatment of infected decubitus ulcers.
FORMS - Trade only: gel (MetroGel) 0.75% 29

g, cream (Noritate) 1% 30 g, lotion (MetroLotion) 0.75% 59 ml.

NOTES - Results usually noted within 3 weeks, with continuing improvement through 9 weeks. Avoid using vaginal prep on face due to irritation because of formulation differences.

mupirocin (*Bactroban*) ▶Not absorbed ♀B ▶? $$

ADULT - Impetigo: apply tid x 3-5 days. Infected wounds: apply tid x 10 days. Nasal MRSA eradication: 0.5 g in each nostril bid x 5 days.

PEDS - Impetigo (mupirocin cream/ointment); apply tid. Infected wounds: apply tid x 10 days. Nasal form not approved in children <12 yo.

FORMS - Trade only: cream/ointment 2% 15,30 g, nasal ointment 2% 1 g single-use tubes (for MRSA eradication).

***Neosporin cream* (neomycin + polymyxin)** ▶K ♀C ▶? $

ADULT - Minor cuts, wounds, burns or skin abrasions: apply qd-tid.

PEDS - Not approved in children.

UNAPPROVED PEDS - Minor cuts, wounds, burns or skin abrasions: apply qd-tid.

FORMS - OTC trade only: neomycin 3.5 mg/g + polymyxin 10,000 units/g 15 g and unit dose 0.94 g.

***Neosporin ointment* (bacitracin + neomycin + polymyxin)** ▶K ♀C ▶? $

ADULT - Minor cuts, wounds, burns or skin abrasions: apply qd-tid.

PEDS - Not approved in children.

UNAPPROVED PEDS - Minor cuts, wounds, burns or skin abrasions: apply qd-tid.

FORMS - OTC Generic/Trade: bacitracin 400 units/g + neomycin 3.5 mg/g + polymyxin 5,000 units/g 2.4,9.6,14.2,15,30 g & unit dose 0.94 g.

NOTES - Also known as triple antibiotic ointment.

***Polysporin* (bacitracin + polymyxin)** ▶K ♀C ▶? $

ADULT - Minor cuts, wounds, burns or skin abrasions: apply qd-tid.

PEDS - Not approved in children.

UNAPPROVED PEDS - Minor cuts, wounds, burns or skin abrasions: apply qd-tid.

FORMS - OTC trade only: ointment 15,30 g and unit dose 0.9 g, powder 10 g, aerosol 90 g.

silver sulfadiazine (*Silvadene*, ✤*Dermazin, Flamazine*) ▶LK ♀B ▶- $

ADULT - Burns: apply qd-bid.

PEDS - Not approved in children.

UNAPPROVED PEDS - Burns: apply qd-bid.

FORMS - Generic/Trade: cream 1% 20,50,85, 400,1000g.

NOTES - Avoid in sulfa allergy. Leukopenia, primarily decreased neutrophil count in up to 20% of patients. Significant absorption may occur and serum sulfa concentrations approach therapeutic levels. Avoid in G6PD deficiency. Use caution in pregnancy nearing term, premature infants, infants ≤2 months and in patients with renal or hepatic dysfunction.

DERMATOLOGY: Antifungals

amphotericin B (*Fungizone*) ▶K ♀B ▶? $$$$

ADULT - Cutaneous and mucocutaneous Candida infections: apply bid-qid.

PEDS - Not approved in children.

UNAPPROVED PEDS - Candidiasis of diaper area: apply bid-qid.

FORMS - Trade only: cream 3% 20 g, lotion 3% 30 ml, ointment 3% 20 g.

NOTES - May discolor fabrics. Cream may discolor skin. Lotion and ointment may discolor nails, but not skin.

butenafine (*Mentax*) ▶L ♀B ▶? $$$

ADULT - Treatment of tinea pedis: apply qd for 4 weeks or bid x 7 days. Tinea coporis, tinea versicolor, or tinea cruris: apply qd for 2 weeks.

PEDS - Not approved in children.

FORMS - Trade only: cream 1% 15,30 g.

NOTES - Most common adverse effects include contact dermatitis, burning, and worsening of condition. If no improvement in 4 weeks, reevaluate diagnosis.

ciclopirox (*Loprox, Penlac*) ▶K ♀B ▶? $$

ADULT - Tinea pedis, cruris, corporis, and versicolor, candidiasis (cream, lotion): apply bid. Onchomycosis of fingernails/toenails (nail solution): apply daily to affected nails; apply over previous coat; remove with alcohol every 7 days.

PEDS - Not approved in children.

FORMS - Trade only: cream (Loprox) 1% 15,30,90 g, lotion (Loprox) 1% 30,60 ml, nail solution (Penlac) 8%.

NOTES - Clinical improvement of tinea usually occurs within first week. Patients with tinea versicolor usually exhibit clinical and mycological clearing after 2 weeks. If no improvement in 4 weeks, reevaluate diagnosis. For nail solution, infected portion of each nail should be removed by health care professional as frequently as monthly. Oral antifungal therapy is more effective for onychomycosis than Penlac.

clotrimazole (*Lotrimin, Mycelex,* ✱*Canesten*) ▸L ♀B ◗? $

ADULT - Treatment of tinea pedis, cruris, corporis, and versicolor, and cutaneous candidiasis: apply bid.

PEDS - Treatment of tinea pedis, cruris, corporis, versicolor, cutaneous candidiasis: apply bid.

FORMS - OTC & Rx generic/Trade: cream 1% 15, 30, 45, 90 g, solution 1% 10,30 ml. Trade only: lotion 1% 30 ml.

NOTES - If no improvement in 4 weeks, reevaluate diagnosis.

econazole (*Spectazole,* ✱*Ecostatin*) ▸Not absorbed ♀C ◗? $$

ADULT - Treatment of tinea pedis, cruris, corporis, and versicolor: apply qd. Cutaneous candidiasis: apply bid.

PEDS - Not approved in children.

FORMS - Trade only: cream 1% 15,30,85g.

NOTES - Treat candidal infections, tinea cruris and tinea corporis for 2 weeks and tinea pedis for 1 month to reduce risk of recurrence.

haloprogin (*Halotex*) ▸KL ♀B ◗? $$$

ADULT - Treatment of tinea pedis, cruris, corporis, manuum, and versicolor: apply bid.

PEDS - Not approved in children.

FORMS - Trade only: cream 1% 15,30 g, solution 1% 10,30 ml.

NOTES - Treat for 2-3 weeks. Intertriginous areas may require 4 weeks of therapy.

ketoconazole (*Nizoral*) ▸L ♀C ◗? $

ADULT - Shampoo (2%): Tinea versicolor: apply to affected area, leave on for 5 min, rinse. Cream: cutaneous candidiasis, tinea coporis, cruris, and versicolor: apply qd. Seborrheic dermatitis: apply cream (2%) bid. Dandruff: apply shampoo (1%) twice a week.

PEDS - Not approved in children < 12 years.

UNAPPROVED ADULT - Seborrheic dermatitis: apply cream (2%) qd.

UNAPPROVED PEDS - Shampoo (2%): Tinea versicolor: apply to affected area, leave on for 5 min, rinse. Cream: cutaneous candidiasis, tinea coporis, cruris, and versicolor: apply qd. Seborrheic dermatitis: apply cream (2%) bid. Dandruff: apply shampoo (1%) twice a week.

FORMS - Trade only: shampoo 1% (OTC), 2%, 120 ml, cream 2% 15,30,60 g.

NOTES - Treat candidial infections, tinea cruris, corporis and versicolor for 2 weeks. Treat seborrheic dermatitis for 4 weeks. Treat tinea pedis for 6 weeks.

miconazole (*Monistat-Derm, Micatin*) ▸L ♀+ ◗? $

ADULT - Tinea pedis, cruris, corporis, and versicolor, cutaneous candidiasis: apply bid.

PEDS - Not approved in children.

UNAPPROVED PEDS - Tinea pedis, cruris, corporis, and versicolor, cutaneous candidiasis: apply bid.

FORMS - OTC generic: ointment 2% 29 g, spray 2% 105 ml, solution 2% 7.39, 30 ml. Generic/Trade: cream 2% 15,30,90 g, powder 2% 90 g, spray powder 2% 90,100 g, spray liquid 2% 105,113 ml.

NOTES - Symptomatic relief generally occurs in 2-3 days. Treat candida, tinea cruris, tinea corporis for 2 weeks, tinea pedis for 1 month to reduce risk of recurrence.

naftifine (*Naftin*) ▸LK ♀B ◗? $$

ADULT - Tinea pedis, cruris, and corporis: apply qd (cream) or bid (gel).

PEDS - Not approved in children.

FORMS - Trade only: cream 1% 15,30,60 g, gel 1% 20,40, 60 g.

NOTES - If no improvement in 4 weeks, reevaluate diagnosis.

nystatin (*Mycostatin*) ▸Not absorbed ♀C ◗? $

ADULT - Cutaneous or mucocutaneous Candida infections: apply bid-tid.

PEDS - Cutaneous or mucocutaneous Candida infections: apply bid-tid.

FORMS - Generic/Trade: cream 100,000 units/g 15,30,240 g, ointment 100,000 units/g 15,30 g, powder 100,000 units/g 15 g.

NOTES - For fungal infections of the feet, dust feet and footwear with powder.

oxiconazole (*Oxistat, Oxizole*) ▸? ♀B ◗? $$

ADULT - Tinea pedis, cruris, and corporis: apply qd-bid. Tinea versicolor (cream only): apply qd.

PEDS - Cream: Tinea pedis, cruris, and corporis: apply qd-bid. Tinea versicolor: apply qd.

FORMS - Trade only: cream 1% 15,30,60 g, lotion 1% 30 ml.

terbinafine (*Lamisil, Lamisil AT*) ▸L ♀B ◗? $$$

ADULT - Tinea pedis: apply bid. Tinea cruris and corporis: apply qd-bid. Tinea versicolor (solution): apply bid.

PEDS - Not approved in children.

UNAPPROVED ADULT - Cutaneous candidiasis.

UNAPPROVED PEDS - Tinea pedis: apply bid. Tinea cruris and corporis: apply qd-bid. Tinea versicolor (solution): apply bid.

FORMS - Trade only: cream 1% 15,30 g, gel

1% 5,15,30 g OTC: Trade only (Lamisil AT): cream 1% 12,24 g, spray pump solution 1% 30 ml.
NOTES - In many patients, improvement noted within 7 days, but therapy should continue for a minimum of 1 week, maximum of 4 weeks. Topical therapy not effective for nail fungus.

tolnaftate (*Tinactin*) ▶? ♀? ▶? $
ADULT - Tinea pedis, cruris, corporis, and versicolor: apply bid. Prevention of tinea pedis (powder and aerosol): apply prn.
PEDS - > 2 yo: Tinea pedis, cruris, corporis, and versicolor: apply bid. Prevention of tinea pedis (powder and aerosol): apply prn.
FORMS - OTC Generic/Trade: cream 1% 15,30 g, solution 1% 10,15 ml, powder 1% 45,90 g, spray powder 1% 100,105,150 g, spray liquid 1% 60,120 ml. Trade only: gel 1% 15 g.

DERMATOLOGY: Antiparasitics (topical)

NOTE: See also acne preparations

***A-200* (pyrethrins + piperonyl butoxide, ✤*R&C*)** ▶L ♀C ▶? $
ADULT - Lice: Apply shampoo, wash after 10 min. Reapply in 5-7 days.
PEDS - Lice: Apply shampoo, wash after 10 min. Reapply in 5-7 days.
FORMS - OTC Generic/Trade: shampoo (0.33% pyrethrins, 4% piperonyl butoxide) 60,120,240 ml.
NOTES - Use caution if allergic to ragweed. Avoid contact with mucous membranes.

crotamiton (*Eurax*) ▶? ♀C ▶? $$
ADULT - Scabies: massage cream/lotion into entire body from chin down, repeat 24 h later, bathe 48 h later. Pruritus: massage into affected areas prn.
PEDS - Not approved in children.
UNAPPROVED PEDS - Scabies: massage cream/lotion into entire body from chin down, repeat 24h later, bathe 48h later. Pruritus: massage into affected areas prn.
FORMS - Trade only: cream 10% 60 g, lotion 10% 60,480 ml.
NOTES - Patients with scabies should change bed linen and clothing in am after second application and bathe 48h after last application.

lindane ▶L ♀B ▶? $
ADULT - Head/crab lice: Lotion: apply 30-60 ml to affected area, wash off after 12h. Shampoo: apply 30-60 ml, wash off after 4 min. Scabies (lotion): apply 30-60 ml to total body from neck down, wash off after 8-12h.
PEDS - Lindane penetrates human skin and has potential for CNS toxicity. Studies indicate potential toxic effects of topical lindane are greater in young. Maximum dose for children < 6 yo is 30 ml.
FORMS - Generic/Trade: lotion 1% 30,60,480 ml, shampoo 1% 30,60,480 ml.
NOTES - Lindane not indicated as primary treatment for any parasitic disease. Do not use in infants. For patients with lice, reapply if living lice noted after 7 days. After shampooing, comb with fine tooth comb to remove nits. Can cause seizures in epileptics or if overused/misused in children.

malathion (*Ovide*) ▶? ♀B ▶? $$
ADULT - Head lice: apply to dry hair, let dry naturally, wash off in 8-12 hrs.
PEDS - Head lice in children > 6 yo: apply to dry hair, let dry naturally, wash off in 8-12 hrs.
FORMS - Trade only: lotion 0.5% 59 ml.
NOTES - Do not use hair dryer; flammable. Avoid contact with eyes. Use a fine tooth comb to remove nits and dead lice. Application may be repeated in 7-9 days.

permethrin (*Elimite, Acticin, Nix*, ✤*Kwellada-P*) ▶L ♀B ▶? $$
ADULT - Scabies (cream): massage cream into entire body (avoid mouth, eyes, nose), wash off after 8-14h. 30 g is typical adult dose. Head lice (liquid): apply to clean, towel-dried hair, saturate hair and scalp, wash off after 10 min.
PEDS - Scabies (cream) > 2 mo: massage cream into entire body (avoid mouth, eyes, nose), wash off after 8-14h. Head lice (liquid) in children > 2 yo: saturate hair and scalp, wash off after 10 min.
FORMS - Trade only: cream (Elimite, Acticin) 5% 60 g. OTC Trade/generic: liquid creme rinse (Nix) 1% 60 ml.
NOTES - If necessary, may repeat application in 7 days.

***RID* (pyrethrins + piperonyl butoxide)** ▶L ♀C ▶? $
ADULT - Lice: Apply shampoo/mousse, wash after 10 min. Reapply in 5-10 days.
PEDS - Lice: Apply shampoo/mousse, wash after 10 min. Reapply in 5-10 days.
FORMS - OTC Generic/Trade: shampoo 60, 120,240 ml. Trade only: mousse 5.5 oz..
NOTES - Use caution if allergic to ragweed. Avoid contact with mucus membranes.

DERMATOLOGY: Antipsoriatics

acitretin (*Soriatane*) ▶L ♀X ▶- $$$$$

WARNING - Contraindicated in pregnancy and avoid pregnancy for 3 years following medication discontinuation. Females of child bearing age must avoid alcohol while on medication and for 2 months following therapy since alcohol prolongs elimination of a teratogenic metabolite. Use in reliable females of reproductive potential only if they have severe, unresponsive psoriasis, have received written and oral warnings of the teratogenic potential, are using 2 reliable forms of contraception, and have had a negative serum pregnancy test within 1 week prior to starting therapy. It is unknown whether residual acitretin in seminal fluid poses a risk to the fetus while a male patient is taking the drug or after it is discontinued.

ADULT - Severe psoriasis: initiate at 25-50 mg PO qd.

PEDS - Not approved in children.

UNAPPROVED ADULT - Lichen planus: 30 mg/day PO for 4 weeks, then titrate to 10-50 mg/day for 12 weeks total. Sjogren-Larsson syndrome: 0.47 mg/kg/day PO. Also used in Darier's disease, palmoplantar pustulosis, nonbullous and bullous ichthyosiform erythroderma, lichen sclerosus et atrophicus of the vulva and plamoplantar lichen nitidus.

UNAPPROVED PEDS - Has been used in children with lamellar ichthyosis. Pediatric use is not recommended. Adverse effects on bone growth are suspected.

FORMS - Trade only: cap 10,25 mg.

NOTES - Transient worsening of psoriasis may occur, and full benefit may take 2-3 mo. Elevated LFTs may occur in 1/3 of patients; monitor LFTs at 1-2 week intervals until stable and then periodically thereafter. Monitor serum lipid concentrations every 1-2 weeks until response to drug is established. May decrease tolerance to contact lenses due to dry eyes. Avoid prolonged exposure to sunlight. May cause hair loss. May cause depression. Many adverse drug reactions.

anthralin (*Anthra-Derm, Drithocreme*, ♣*Anthrascalp*) ▶? ♀C ▶- $$

ADULT - Quiescent/chronic psoriasis: apply qd.

PEDS - Not approved in children.

UNAPPROVED PEDS - Quiescent/chronic psoriasis: apply qd.

FORMS - Trade only: ointment 0.1% 42.5 g, 0.25% 42.5 g, 0.4% 60 g, 0.5% 42.5 g, 1% 42.5 g, cream 0.1% 50 g, 0.2% 50 g, 0.25% 50 g, 0.5% 50 g. Generic/Trade: cream 1% 50 g.

NOTES - Short contact periods (i.e. 15-20 minutes) followed by removal with an appropriate solvent (soap or petrolatum) may be preferred. May stain fabric, skin or hair.

calcipotriene (*Dovonex*) ▶L ♀C ▶? $$$

ADULT - Moderate plaque psoriasis: apply bid.

PEDS - Not approved in children.

UNAPPROVED PEDS - Moderate plaque psoriasis: apply bid.

FORMS - Trade only: ointment 0.005% 30,60,100 g, cream 0.005% 30,60,100 g, scalp solution 0.005% 60 ml.

NOTES - Avoid contact with face. Burning, itching, and skin irritation may occur in 10-15%.

tazarotene (*Tazorac*) ▶Bile ♀X ▶? $$$

ADULT - Acne: apply qhs. Psoriasis: apply qhs.

PEDS - Not approved in children.

UNAPPROVED PEDS - Acne: apply qhs. Psoriasis: apply qhs.

FORMS - Trade only: gel 0.05% 30,100 g, 0.1% 30, 100 g.

NOTES - Desquamation, burning, dry skin, erythema, pruritus may occur in up to 30% of patients. May cause photosensitivity.

DERMATOLOGY: Antivirals (topical)

acyclovir (*Zovirax*) ▶K ♀C ▶? $$$

ADULT - Initial episodes of herpes genitalis: apply q3h (6 times/d) x 7 days. Non-life threatening mucocutaneous herpes simplex in immunocompromised patients: apply q3h (6 times/d) x 7 days.

PEDS - Not approved in children.

UNAPPROVED PEDS - Initial episodes of herpes genitalis: apply q3h (6 times/d) x 7 days. Non-life threatening mucocutaneous herpes simplex in immunocompromised patients: apply q3h (6 times/d) x 7 days.

FORMS - Trade only: ointment 5% 3,15 g.

NOTES - Use finger cot or rubber glove to apply ointment to avoid dissemination. Burning/stinging may occur in up to 28% of patients.

Oral form more effective than topical for herpes genitalis.

docosanol (*Abreva*) ▶Not absorbed ♀B ▶? $

ADULT - Oral-facial herpes simplex: apply 5x/day until healed.

PEDS - Not approved in children.

FORMS - OTC: Trade only: cream 10% 2 g.

imiquimod (*Aldara*) ▶Not absorbed ♀B ▶? $$$$

ADULT - External genital and perianal warts: apply 3 times/week at bedtime. Wash off after 6-10 hours.

PEDS - Not approved in children.

UNAPPROVED ADULT - Giant molluscum contagiosum: apply 3 times weekly for 6-10 hours.

FORMS - Trade only: cream 5% 250 mg single use packets.

NOTES - May be used for up to 16 weeks. May weaken condoms and diaphragms. Avoid sexual contact while cream is on. Most common adverse effects include erythema, itching, erosion, burning, excoriation, edema and pain.

penciclovir (*Denavir*) ▶Not absorbed ♀B ▶? $$$

ADULT - Recurrent herpes labialis: apply q2h while awake x 4 days.

PEDS - Not approved in children.

UNAPPROVED PEDS - Recurrent herpes labialis: apply q2h while awake x 4 days.

FORMS - Trade only: cream 1% 2 g tubes.

NOTES - Start therapy as soon as possible during prodrome. For moderate to severe cases of herpes labialis, systemic treatment with famciclovir or acyclovir may be preferred.

podofilox (*Condylox*, ✤*Condyline*) ▶? ♀C ▶? $$$

ADULT - External genital warts (gel and solution) and perianal warts (gel only): apply bid for 3 consecutive days of a week and repeat for up to 4 weeks.

PEDS - Not approved in children.

FORMS - Trade only: gel 0.5% 3.5 g, solution 0.5% 3.5 ml.

podophyllin (*Podocon-25, Podofin, Podofilm*) ▶? ♀- ▶- $$

ADULT - Genital wart removal: Initial application: apply to wart and leave on for 30-40 min to determine patient's sensitivity. Thereafter, use minimum contact time necessary (1-4h depending on result). Remove dried podophyllin with alcohol or soap and water.

PEDS - Not approved in children.

FORMS - Not to be dispensed to patients. For hospital/clinic use; not intended for outpatient prescribing. Trade only: liquid 25% 15 ml.

NOTES - Not to be dispensed to patients. Do not treat large areas or numerous warts all at once. Contraindicated in diabetics, pregnancy, patients using steroids or with poor circulation, and on bleeding warts.

DERMATOLOGY: Corticosteroid / Antimicrobial Combinations

***Cortisporin* (neomycin + polymyxin + hydrocortisone)** ▶LK ♀C ▶? $

ADULT - Corticosteroid-responsive dermatoses with secondary infection: apply bid-qid.

PEDS - Not approved in children.

UNAPPROVED PEDS - Corticosteroid-responsive dermatoses with secondary infection: apply bid-qid.

FORMS - Generic/Trade: cream 7.5 g, ointment 15 g.

NOTES - Due to concerns about nephrotoxicity and ototoxicity associated with neomycin, do not use over wide areas or for prolonged periods of time.

***Lotrisone* (clotrimazole + betamethasone, ✤*Lotriderm*)** ▶L ♀C ▶? $$$

ADULT - Tinea pedis, cruris, and corporis: apply bid.

PEDS - Not approved in children.

FORMS - Trade only: cream (clotrimazole 1% + betamethasone 0.05%) 15,45 g.

NOTES - Treat tinea cruris and corporis for 2 weeks and tinea pedis for 4 weeks. Should not be used for diaper dermatitis due to risk of adrenal suppression.

***Mycolog II* (nystatin + trimacinolone)** ▶L ♀C ▶? $

ADULT - Cutaneous candidiasis: apply bid.

PEDS - Not approved in children.

UNAPPROVED PEDS - Sometimes used for diaper dermatitis, but this is not recommended due to risk of adrenal suppression.

FORMS - Generic/Trade: cream 15,30,60,120 g, ointment 15,30,60,120 g.

NOTES - Avoid occlusive dressings.

DERMATOLOGY: Hemorrhoid Care

dibucaine (*Nupercainal*) ▶L ♀? ▶? $

ADULT - Hemorrhoids or other anorectal disor-

ders: apply tid-qid prn.
PEDS - Not approved in children.
UNAPPROVED PEDS - Hemorrhoids or other anorectal disorders; children > 2yo or > 35 pounds: apply tid-qid prn.
FORMS - OTC Generic/Trade: ointm't 1% 30g.
NOTES - Do not use if <2 yo or <35 pounds.

hydrocortisone (*Anusol HC*) ▸L ♀? ◗? $
ADULT - External anal itching: apply cream tid-qid prn or supp bid.
PEDS - Not approved in children.
FORMS - Generic/Trade: cream 1% (Anusol HC-1), 2.5% 30 g (Anusol HC), suppository 25 mg (Anusol HC).

pramoxine (*Anusol Hemorrhoidal Ointment, Fleet Pain Relief, ProctoFoam NS*) ▸Not absorbed ♀+ ◗+ $
ADULT - Hemorrhoids: apply ointment, pads, or foam up to 5 times/day prn.
PEDS - Not approved in children.
FORMS - OTC Trade only: ointment (Anusol Hemorrhoidal Ointment), pads (Fleet Pain Relief), aerosol foam (ProctoFoam NS).

starch (*Anusol Suppositories*) ▸Not absorbed ♀+ ◗+ $
ADULT - Hemorrhoids: 1 suppository PR up to 6 times/day prn or after each bowel movement.
PEDS - Not approved in children.
FORMS - OTC Trade only: suppositories (51% topical starch; soy bean oil, tocopheryl acetate).

witch hazel (*Tucks*) ▸? ♀+ ◗+ $
ADULT - Hemorrhoids: Apply to anus/perineum up to 6 times/day prn.
PEDS - Not approved in children.
FORMS - OTC Generic/Trade: pads,gel.

DERMATOLOGY: Topical Corticosteroids

NOTES: After long-term use, do not discontinue abruptly; switch to a less potent agent or alternate use of corticosteroids and emollient products. Monitor for hyperglycemia / adrenal suppression if used for long period of time or over a large area of the body, especially in children. Chronic administration may interfere with pediatric growth & development.

alclometasone dipropionate (*Aclovate*) ▸L ♀C ◗? $$
ADULT - Inflammatory and pruritic manifestations of corticosteroid-responsive dermatoses: apply sparingly 2-3 times/day.
PEDS - Inflammatory and pruritic manifestations of corticosteroid-responsive dermatoses in children ≥1 yo: apply sparingly 2-3 times/day. Safety and efficacy for >3 weeks have not been established.
FORMS - Trade only: ointment 0.05% 15,45,60 g, cream 0.05% 15,45,60 g.

amcinonide (*Cyclocort*) ▸L ♀C ◗? $$
ADULT - Inflammatory and pruritic manifestations of corticosteroid-responsive dermatoses: apply sparingly 2-3 times/day.
PEDS - Inflammatory and pruritic manifestations of corticosteroid-responsive dermatoses: apply sparingly 2-3 times/day.
FORMS - Trade only: ointment 0.1% 15,30,60 g, cream 0.1% 15,30,60 g, lotion 0.1% 20,60 ml.

augmented betamethasone dipropionate (*Diprolene*) ▸L ♀C ◗? $$
ADULT - Inflammatory and pruritic manifestations of corticosteroid-responsive dermatoses: apply sparingly 1-2 times/day.
PEDS - Not approved in children.
FORMS - Trade only: ointment 0.05% 15,45 g, cream 0.05% 15,45 g, gel 0.05% 15,45g, lotion 0.05% 30,60 ml.
NOTES - Do not use occlusive dressings. Do not use for longer than 2 consecutive weeks and do not exceed a total dose of 45-50 g/week or 50 ml/week of the lotion.

betamethasone dipropionate (*Diprosone, Maxivate, Topisone*) ▸L ♀C ◗? $
ADULT - Inflammatory and pruritic manifestations of corticosteroid-responsive dermatoses: apply sparingly 1-2 times/day.
PEDS - Inflammatory and pruritic manifestations of corticosteroid-responsive dermatoses: apply sparingly 1-2 times/day.
FORMS - Generic/Trade: ointment 0.05% 15,45 g, cream 0.05% 15,45 g, lotion 0.05% 20,60 ml. Trade only: aerosol 0.1% 85 g.
NOTES - Do not use occlusive dressings.

betamethasone valerate (*Luxiq*) ▸L ♀C ◗? $
ADULT - Inflammatory and pruritic manifestations of corticosteroid-responsive dermatoses: apply sparingly 1-2 times/day. Dermatoses of scalp: apply small amount of foam to scalp bid.
PEDS - Inflammatory and pruritic manifestations of corticosteroid-responsive dermatoses: apply sparingly 1-2 times/day.
FORMS - Generic: ointm't 0.1% 15,45 g, cream 0.01% 15 g, cream 0.1% 15,45,110 g, lotion 0.1% 20,60 ml, foam (Luxiq) 0.12%100 g.

clobetasol (*Temovate, Dermovate, Cor-*

max) ▶L ♀C ▶? $$

ADULT - Inflammatory and pruritic manifestations of corticosteroid-responsive dermatoses: apply sparingly 2 times/day.

PEDS - Not approved in children.

FORMS - Generic/Trade: oint 0.05% 15,30,45,60 g, cream 0.05% 15,30,45,60 g, scalp application 0.05% 25,50 ml, gel 0.05% 15,30,60 g.

NOTES - Adrenal suppression at doses as low as 2 g/day. Do not use occlusive dressings. Do not use for longer than 2 consecutive weeks and do not exceed a total dose of 50 g/week.

clocortolone pivalate (*Cloderm*) ▶L♀C▶? $$

ADULT - Inflammatory and pruritic manifestations of corticosteroid-responsive dermatoses: apply sparingly 3 times/day.

PEDS - Inflammatory and pruritic manifestations of corticosteroid-responsive dermatoses: apply sparingly 3 times/day.

FORMS - Trade only: cream 0.1% 15,45 g.

desonide (*DesOwen, Desocort, Tridesilon*) ▶L ♀C ▶? $

ADULT - Inflammatory and pruritic manifestations of corticosteroid-responsive dermatoses: apply sparingly 2-3 times/day.

PEDS - Inflammatory and pruritic manifestations of corticosteroid-responsive dermatoses: apply sparingly 2-3 times/day.

FORMS - Generic/Trade: cream 0.05% 15,60 g, ointment 0.05% 15,60 g. Trade only: lotion 0.05% 60,120 ml.

NOTES - Do not use with occlusive dressings.

desoximetasone (*Topicort, Topicort LP*) ▶L ♀C ▶? $$

ADULT - Inflammatory and pruritic manifestations of corticosteroid-responsive dermatoses: apply sparingly 2 times/day.

PEDS - Safety and efficacy have not been established for Topicort 0.25% ointment. For inflammatory and pruritic manifestations of corticosteroid-responsive dermatoses (cream and gel): apply sparingly 2 times/day.

FORMS - Generic/Trade: cream 0.05% 15,60 g, cream 0.25%15,60,120 g, gel 0.05% 15,60 g. Trade only: ointment 0.25% 15,60 g.

diflorasone diacetate (*Psorcon, Maxiflor*) ▶L ♀C ▶? $$

ADULT - Inflammatory and pruritic manifestations of corticosteroid-responsive dermatoses: apply sparingly 2 times/day.

PEDS - Not approved in children.

FORMS - Generic/Trade: ointment 0.05% 15,30,60 g, cream 0.05% 15,30,60 g.

NOTES - Doses of 30 g/day of diflorasone 0.05% cream for 1 week resulted in adrenal suppression in some psoriasis patients.

fluocinolone acetonide (*Synalar, Fluoderm*) ▶L ♀C ▶? $

ADULT - Inflammatory and pruritic manifestations of corticosteroid-responsive dermatoses: apply sparingly 2-4 times/day.

PEDS - Inflammatory and pruritic manifestations of corticosteroid-responsive dermatoses: apply sparingly 2-4 times/day.

FORMS - Generic/Trade: ointment 0.025% 15,30,60 g, cream 0.01% 15,30,60 g, cream 0.025% 15,30,60 g, shampoo 0.01% 180 ml, solution 0.01% 20,60 ml, shampoo 0.01% 180 ml, oil 0.01% 120 ml.

fluocinonide (*Lidex, Lidex-E, Lyderm*, ✤*Topactin*) ▶L ♀C ▶? $

ADULT - Inflammatory and pruritic manifestations of corticosteroid-responsive dermatoses: apply sparingly 2-4 times/day.

PEDS - Inflammatory and pruritic manifestations of corticosteroid-responsive dermatoses: apply sparingly 2-4 times/day.

FORMS - Generic/Trade: cream 0.05% 15,30,60,120 g, ointment 0.05% 15,30,60 g, solution 0.05% 20,60 ml, gel 0.05% 15,30,60,120 g.

flurandrenolide (*Cordran, Cordran SP*) ▶L ♀C ▶? $

ADULT - Inflammatory and pruritic manifestations of corticosteroid-responsive dermatoses: apply sparingly 2-3 times/day.

PEDS - Inflammatory and pruritic manifestations of corticosteroid-responsive dermatoses: apply sparingly 2-3 times/day.

FORMS - Trade only: ointment 0.025% 30,60 g, ointment 0.05% 15,30,60 g, cream 0.025% 30, 60 g, cream 0.05% 15,30,60 g, tape 4mcg/cm2. Generic/Trade: lotion 0.05% 15,60 ml.

fluticasone propionate (*Cutivate*) ▶L ♀C ▶? $$

ADULT - Eczema: apply sparingly 1-2 times/day. Other inflammatory and pruritic manifestations of corticosteroid-responsive dermatoses: apply sparingly 2 times/day.

PEDS - Children > 3 mo old: Eczema: apply sparingly 1-2 times/day. Other inflammatory and pruritic manifestations of corticosteroid-responsive dermatoses: apply sparingly 2 times/day.

FORMS - Trade only: cream 0.05% 15,30,60 g, ointment 0.005% 15,60 g.

NOTES - Do not use with an occlusive dressing.

halcinonide (*Halog*) ▶L ♀C ▶? $$

ADULT - Inflammatory and pruritic manifestations of corticosteroid-responsive dermatoses: apply sparingly 2-3 times/day.

PEDS - Inflammatory and pruritic manifestations of corticosteroid-responsive dermatoses: apply sparingly 2-3 times/day.
FORMS - Trade only: ointment 0.1% 15,30,60 g cream 0.1% 15,30,60 g, soln 0.1% 20,60 ml.

halobetasol propionate (*Ultravate*) ▶L ♀C ▶? $$
ADULT - Inflammatory and pruritic manifestations of corticosteroid-responsive dermatoses: apply sparingly 1-2 times/day.
PEDS - Not approved in children.
FORMS - Trade only: ointment 0.05% 15,45 g, cream 0.05% 15,45 g.
NOTES - Do not use occlusive dressings. Do not use for >2 consecutive weeks and do not exceed a total dose of 50 g/week.

hydrocortisone (*Cortizone, Hycort, Tegrin-HC, Dermolate, Synacort*, ✱*Cortoderm*) ▶L ♀C ▶? $
ADULT - Inflammatory and pruritic manifestations of corticosteroid-responsive dermatoses: apply sparingly 2-4 times/day.
PEDS - Inflammatory and pruritic manifestations of corticosteroid-responsive dermatoses: apply sparingly 2-4 times/day.
FORMS - Products available OTC & Rx depending on labeling. 2.5% preparation available Rx only. Generic: ointment 0.5% 30 g, ointment 1% 15, 20,30,60,120 g, ointment 2.5% 20,30 g, cream 0.5% 15,30,60 g, cream 1% 20,30,60, 90,120 g, cream 2.5% 15,20,30,60,120 g, lotion 0.25% 120 ml, lotion 0.5% 30,60,120 ml, lotion 1% 60,120 ml, lotion 2% 30 ml, lotion 2.5% 60 ml.

CORTICOSTEROIDS – TOPICAL*

Group / Agent	*Trade Name*	*Concentration*	*Formulation*	*Frequency*
Group I (Most Potent)				
augmented betamethasone dipropionate	*Diprolene*	0.05%	L, O, G	qd-bid
clobetasol propionate	*Temovate, Cormax*	0.05%	C, O, G, S	qd-bid
diflorasone diacetate	*Psorcon*	0.05%	O	qd-tid
halobetasol propionate	*Ultravate*	0.05%	C, O	qd-bid
Group II				
amcinonide	*Cyclocort*	0.1%	O	bid-tid
augmented betamethasone dipropionate	*Diprolene AF*	0.05%	C	qd-bid
betamethasone dipropionate	*Diprosone*	0.05%	O	qd-bid
"	*Maxivate*	0.05%	C, O	qd-bid
desoximetasone	*Topicort*	0.25%	C, O	bid
"	*Topicort*	0.05%	G	bid
diflorasone diacetate	*Maxiflor*	0.05%	O	qd-tid
fluocinonide	*Lidex*	0.05%	C, O, G, S	bid-qid
halcinonide	*Halog*	0.1%	C, O, S	bid-tid
mometasone furoate	*Elocon*	0.1%	O	qd
Group III				
amcinonide	*Cyclocort*	0.1%	C,L	bid-tid
betamethasone dipropionate	*Diprosone*	0.05%	C	qd-bid
betamethasone valerate	*Betatrex, Valisone*	0.1%	O	qd-bid
diflorasone diacetate	*Maxiflor*	0.05%	C	bid-qid
fluticasone propionate	*Cutivate*	0.005%	O	bid
triamcinolone acetonide	*Aristocort A*	0.1%	C, O	bid-tid
Group IV				
desoximetasone	*Topicort LP*	0.05%	C	bid
fluocinolone acetonide	*Synalar*	0.025%	O	bid-qid
flurandrenolide	*Cordran*	0.05%	O	bid-qid
hydrocortisone valerate	*Westcort*	0.2%	O	bid-tid
mometasone furoate	*Elocon*	0.1%	C, L	qd
triamcinolone acetonide	*Aristocort, Kenalog*	0.1%	O	bid-tid

Group V				
betamethasone dipropionate	*Diprosone, Maxivate*	0.05%	L	qd-bid
betamethasone valerate	*Valisone, Betatrex*	0.1%	C, L	qd-bid
clocortolone pivalate	*Cloderm*	0.1%	C	tid
desonide	*DesOwen,Tridesilon*	0.05%	O	bid-tid
flucinolone acetonide	*Synalar*	0.025%	C	bid-qid
flurandrenolide	*Cordran*	0.05%	C, L	bid-tid
"	*Cordran*	0.025%	O	bid-tid
fluticasone propionate	*Cutivate*	0.05%	C	qd-bid
hydrocortisone butyrate	*Locoid*	0.1%	C, O, S	bid-tid
hydrocortisone valerate	*Westcort*	0.2%	C	bid-tid
prednicarbate	*Dermatop*	0.1%	C	bid
triamcinolone acetonide	*Aristocort, Kenalog*	0.1%	C	bid-tid
"	*Kenalog*	0.025%	O, L	bid-tid
Group VI				
alclometasone dipropionate	*Aclovate*	0.05%	C, O	bid-tid
desonide	*DesOwen*	0.05%	C, L	bid-tid
"	*Tridesilon*	0.05%	C	bid-qid
fluocinolone acetonide	*Synalar*	0.01%	C, S	bid-qid
triamcinolone acetonide	*Aristocort, Kenalog*	0.025%	C	bid-tid
Group VII (Least Potent)				
hydrocortisone	*Hytone, others*	0.5,1, 2.5%	C, O, L	qd-qid

***C-cream, G-gel, L-lotion, O-ointment, S-solution**. Adapted from Habif, *Clinical Dermatology*, 3rd ed, and data from Ferndale Laboratories, Ferndale, Michigan. Potency based on vasoconstrictive assays, which may not correlate with efficacy.

hydrocortisone acetate (*Cortaid, Corticaine, Micort-HC Lipocream*) ▸L ♀C ◗? $

ADULT - Inflammatory and pruritic manifestations of corticosteroid-responsive dermatoses: apply sparingly 2-4 times/day.

PEDS - Inflammatory and pruritic manifestations of corticosteroid-responsive dermatoses: apply sparingly 2-4 times/day.

FORMS - OTC Generic/Trade: ointment 0.5% 15,30 g, ointment 1% 30g, cream 0.05% 15,30 g. Rx only generic/trade: cream 1% 15,20,30, 120 g, 2.5% 30 g (Micort-HC Lipocream).

hydrocortisone butyrate (*Locoid*) ▸L ♀C ◗? $$

ADULT - Inflammatory and pruritic manifestations of corticosteroid-responsive dermatoses: apply sparingly 2-3 times/day. Seborrheic dermatitis (solution only): apply 2-3 times/day.

PEDS - Inflammatory and pruritic manifestations of corticosteroid-responsive dermatoses: apply sparingly 2-3 times/day. Seborrheic dermatitis (solution only): apply 2-3 times/day.

FORMS - Trade only: ointment 0.1% 15,45 g, cream 0.1% 15,45 g, solution 0.1% 30,60 ml.

hydrocortisone probutate (*Pandel*) ▸L ♀C ◗? $

ADULT - Inflammatory and pruritic manifestations of corticosteroid-responsive dermatoses: apply sparingly 1-2 times/day.

PEDS - Not approved in children.

FORMS - Trade only: cream 0.1% 15,45 g, 1% 15,45 g.

hydrocortisone valerate (*Westcort*) ▸L ♀C ◗? $$

ADULT - Inflammatory and pruritic manifestations of corticosteroid-responsive dermatoses: apply sparingly 2-3 times/day.

PEDS - Safety and efficacy of Westcort ointment have not been established in children. Inflammatory and pruritic manifestations of corticosteroid-responsive dermatoses (cream only): apply sparingly 2-3 times/day.

FORMS - Generic/Trade: ointment 0.2% 15,45, 60 g, cream 0.2% 15,45,60 g.

mometasone furoate (*Elocon*, ✤*Elocom*) ▸L ♀C ◗? $

ADULT - Inflammatory and pruritic manifestations of corticosteroid-responsive dermatoses: apply sparingly once daily.

PEDS - Inflammatory and pruritic manifestations of corticosteroid-responsive dermatoses ≥2 yo: apply sparingly once daily. Safety and efficacy for >3 weeks have not been established.

FORMS - Trade only: ointment 0.1% 15,45 g,

cream 0.1% 15,45 g, lotion 0.1% 30,60 ml.
NOTES - Do not use an occlusive dressing.

prednicarbate (*Dermatop*) ▸L ♀C ◗? $$
ADULT - Inflammatory and pruritic manifestations of corticosteroid-responsive dermatoses: apply sparingly 2 times/day.
PEDS - Inflammatory and pruritic manifestations of corticosteroid-responsive dermatoses in children ≥1 yo: apply sparingly 2 times/day. Safety and efficacy for >3 weeks have not been established.
FORMS - Trade only: cream 0.1% 15,60 g.

triamcinolone acetonide (*Kenalog, Aristocort*) ▸L ♀C ◗? $
ADULT - Inflammatory and pruritic manifestations of corticosteroid-responsive dermatoses: apply sparingly 3-4 times/day.
PEDS - Inflammatory and pruritic manifestations of corticosteroid-responsive dermatoses: apply sparingly 3-4 times/day.
FORMS - Generic/Trade: ointment 0.025% 15, 28,57,80,113 g, ointment 0.1% 15,28,57,60,80, 113 g, ointment 0.5% 15,20,28,57,113 g, cream 0.025% 15,20, 30,60,80,90,120 g, cream 0.5% 15,20,30,60,120 g, cream 0.1% 15,60,80 g, lotion 0.025% 60 ml, lotion 0.1% 15,60 ml. Trade only: aerosol 23,63 g.

DERMATOLOGY: Other Dermatologic Agents

alitretinoin (*Panretin*) ▸Not absorbed ♀D ◗- $$$$$
WARNING - May cause fetal harm if significant absorption were to occur. Women of child-bearing age should be advised to avoid becoming pregnant during treatment.
ADULT - Cutaneous lesions of AIDS-related Kaposi's sarcoma: apply bid-qid.
PEDS - Not approved in children.
FORMS - Trade only: gel 60 g.

aminolevulinic acid (*Levulan Kerastick*) ▸Not absorbed ♀C ◗? $$$
ADULT - Non-hyperkeratotic actinic keratoses: apply solution to lesions on scalp or face; expose to special light source 14-18 h later.
PEDS - Not approved in children.
FORMS - Trade only: 20% solution single use ampules.
NOTES - Solution should be applied by health-care personnel. Advise patients to avoid sunlight during 14-18 h period before blue light illumination.

becaplermin (*Regranex*) ▸Minimal absorption ♀C ◗? $$$$$
ADULT - Diabetic neuropathic ulcers: apply qd and cover with saline-moistened gauze for 12 hours. Rinse after 12 h and cover with saline gauze without medication.
PEDS - Not approved in children.
FORMS - Trade only: gel 0.01% 2,7.5,15 g.
NOTES - Length of gel to be applied calculated by size of wound (length x width x 0.6 = amount of gel in inches). If ulcer does not decrease by 30% in size by 10 weeks, or complete healing has not occurred by 20 weeks, continued therapy should be reassessed.

calamine ▸? ♀? ◗? $
ADULT - Itching due to poison ivy/oak/sumac, insect bites, or minor irritation: apply up to tid-qid prn.
PEDS - Itching due to poison ivy/oak/sumac, insect bites, or minor irritation (> 2 yo): apply up to tid-qid prn.
FORMS - OTC Generic: lotion 120, 240, 480 ml.

capsaicin (*Zostrix, Zostrix-HP*) ▸? ♀? ◗? $
ADULT - Pain due to rheumatoid arthritis, osteoarthritis, and neuralgias such as zoster or diabetic neuropathies: apply to affected area up to tid-qid.
PEDS - Children > 2yo: Pain due to rheumatoid arthritis, osteoarthritis, and neuralgias such as zoster or diabetic neuropathies: apply to affected area up to tid-qid.
UNAPPROVED ADULT - Psoriasis and intractable pruritus, postmastectomy/ postamputation neuromas (phantom limb pain), vulvar vestibulitis, apocrine chromhidrosis and reflex sympathetic dystrophy.
FORMS - OTC Generic/Trade: cream 0.025%45,60 g, 0.075% 30,60 g, lotion 0.025% 59 ml, 0.075% 59 ml, gel 0.025% 15,30 g, 0.05% 43 g, roll-on 0.075% 60 ml.
NOTES - Burning occurs in ≥30% patients but diminishes with continued use. Pain more commonly occurs when applied < 3-4 times/day. Wash hands immediately after application.

coal tar (*Polytar, Tegrin*) ▸? ♀? ◗? $
ADULT - Dandruff, seborrheic dermatitis: apply shampoo at least twice a week. Psoriasis: apply to affected areas qd to qid or use shampoo on affected areas.
PEDS - Children >2 yo: Dandruff, seborrheic dermatitis: apply shampoo at least twice a

week. Psoriasis: apply to affected areas qd to qid or use shampoo on affected areas.
FORMS - OTC Generic/Trade: shampoo, conditioner, cream, ointment, gel, lotion, soap, oil.
NOTES - May cause photosensitivity for up to 24 h after application.

diclofenac (*Solaraze*) ▶LK ♀B ▶? ?
ADULT - Actinic keratosis: apply bid x 2-3 months.
PEDS - Not approved in children.
FORMS - Trade only: 3% gel: 25,50 g.
NOTES - Complete healing of lesions may not be evident for up to 30 days after discontinuation of therapy.

doxepin (*Zonalon*) ▶L ♀B ▶- $
ADULT - Pruritus associated with atopic dermatitis, lichen simplex chronicus, eczematous dermatitis: apply qid for up to 8 days.
PEDS - Not approved in children.
FORMS - Trade only: cream 5% 30,45 g.
NOTES - Risk of systemic toxicity increased if applied to > 10% of body.

eflornithine (*Vaniqa*) ▶K ♀C ▶? $$
ADULT - Reduction of facial hair: apply to face bid at least 8 h apart.
PEDS - Not approved in children.
FORMS - Trade only: cream 13.9% 30 g.
NOTES - Takes ≥4-8 weeks to see an effect.

***EMLA* (lidocaine + prilocaine)** ▶LK ♀B ▶? $$
ADULT - Topical anesthesia for minor dermal procedures (eg, IV cannulation, venipuncture) apply 2.5 g over 20-25 cm2 area or 1 disc at least 1 hour prior to procedure, for major dermal procedures (ie, skin grafting harvesting) apply 2 g per 10 cm2 area ≥ 2h prior to procedure.
PEDS - Prior to circumcision in infants > 37 weeks gestation: apply a max dose 1g over max of 10 cm2. Topical anesthesia: Children age 1-3 mo or <5 kg: apply a max 1 g over max of 10 cm2; age 4-12 mo and > 5kg: apply max 2 g over a max of 20 cm2; age 1-6 yo and > 10kg: apply max 10g over max of 100 cm2; age 7-12 yo and > 20kg: apply max 20g over max of 200 cm2.
FORMS - Trade only: cream (2.5% lidocaine + 2.5% prilocaine) 5,30 g, disc 1 g.
NOTES - Cover cream with an occlusive dressing. Do not use in children <12 mo if child is receiving treatment with methemoglobin-inducing agents. Patients with glucose-6-phosphate deficiencies are more susceptible to methemoglobinemia. Dermal analgesia increases for up to 3 h under occlusive dressings, and persists for 1-2 h after removal.

finasteride (*Propecia*) ▶L ♀X ▶- $$
ADULT - Androgenetic alopecia in men: 1 mg PO qd.
PEDS - Not approved in children.
UNAPPROVED ADULT - Androgenetic alopecia in postmenopausal women (no evidence of efficacy): 1 mg PO qd.
FORMS - Trade only: tab 1 mg.
NOTES - May require ≥3 months before benefit seen. Monitor PSA before therapy; finasteride will decrease PSA by 50% in patients with BPH, even wth prostate cancer. Contraindicated in pregnancy or possible pregnancy. Women should not handle crushed or broken tabs if they are or could be pregnant.

fluorouracil (*5FU, Efudex, Fluoroplex*) ▶L ♀X ▶- $$$$$
ADULT - Actinic or solar keratoses: apply bid to lesions x 2-6 wks. Superficial basal cell carcinomas: apply 5% cream/solution bid.
PEDS - Not approved in children.
UNAPPROVED ADULT - Condylomata acuminata: a 1% solution in 70% ethanol and the 5% cream has been used.
FORMS - Trade only: cream 5% 25 g (Efudex), 1% 30 g (Fluoroplex), solution 1% 30 ml (Fluoroplex), 2% 10 ml (Efudex), 5% 10 ml (Efudex).
NOTES - May cause severe irritation & photosensitivity.

hydroquinone (*Eldopaque, Eldoquin, Esoterica, Lustra, Melanex, Solaquin*) ▶? ♀C ▶? $$$
ADULT - Temporary bleaching of hyperpigmented skin conditions (ie, chloasma, melasma, freckles, senile lentigines, ultraviolet-induced discoloration from oral contraceptives, pregnancy, or hormone replacement therapy): apply bid to affected area.
PEDS - Not approved in children.
FORMS - OTC Generic/Trade: cream 1.5,2,4%, lotion 2%, solution 3%, gel 4%.
NOTES - Responses may take 3 weeks - 6 months. Use a sunscreen on treated, exposed areas.

lactic acid (*Lac-Hydrin*) ▶? ♀? ▶? $$
ADULT - Ichthyosis vulgaris and xerosis (dry, scaly skin): apply bid to affected area.
PEDS - Ichthyosis vulgaris and xerosis (dry, scaly skin) in children > 2 yo: apply bid to affected area.
FORMS - Trade only: cream 12% 140,385 g, lotion 12% 150,360 ml.
NOTES - Frequently causes irritation.

lidocaine (*Xylocaine, Lidoderm, Numby*

Stuff) ▶LK ♀B ▶? $$
ADULT - Topical anesthesia: apply to affected area prn. Dose varies with anesthetic procedure, degree of anesthesia required and individual patient response. Post-herpetic neuralgia (patch): apply up to 3 patches for up to 12h within a 24h period.
PEDS - Topical anesthesia: apply to affected area prn. Dose varies with anesthetic procedure, degree of anesthesia required and individual patient response. Max 3 mg/kg/dose, do not repeat dose within 2 hours.
FORMS - For membranes of mouth and pharynx: spray 10%, ointment 5%, liquid 5%, solution 2,4%, dental patch. For urethral use: jelly 2%. Patch (Lidoderm) 5%.

masoprocol (*Actinex*) ▶LK ♀B ▶? ?
ADULT - Actinic (solar) keratoses: apply bid to affected areas.
PEDS - Not approved in children.
FORMS - Trade only: cream 10% 30 g.
NOTES - Most common adverse effects include erythema, flaking (46%), itching (32%), dryness (27%), edema (14%), burning (12%), and soreness (5%).

minoxidil (*Rogaine, Rogaine Forte, Rogaine Extra Strength, Minoxidil for Men*, ✤*Minox*) ▶K ♀C ▶- $$
ADULT - Androgenetic alopecia in men or women: 1 ml to dry scalp bid.
PEDS - Not approved in children.
UNAPPROVED ADULT - Alopecia areata.
UNAPPROVED PEDS - Alopecia: Apply to dry scalp bid.
FORMS - OTC Trade only: solution 2%, 60 ml, 5%, 60 ml, 5% (Rogaine Extra Strength) 60 ml.
NOTES - Alcohol content may cause burning and stinging. Evidence of hair growth usually takes ≥4 months. If treatment is stopped, new hair will be shed in a few months.

oatmeal (*Aveeno*) ▶Not absorbed ♀? ▶? $
ADULT - Pruritus from poison ivy/oak, varicella: apply lotion qid prn. Also available in packets to be added to bath.
PEDS - Pruritus from poison ivy/oak, varicella: apply lotion qid prn. Also available in bath packets for tub.
FORMS - OTC Generic/Trade: lotion, packets.

selenium sulfide (*Selsun, Exsel, Versel*) ▶? ♀C ▶? $
ADULT - Dandruff, seborrheic dermatitis: Massage 5-10 ml of shampoo into wet scalp, allow to remain 2-3 minutes, rinse. Apply twice a week for 2 weeks. For maintenance, less frequent administration needed. Tinea versicolor: Apply 2.5% shampoo/lotion to affected area, allow to remain on skin 10 min, rinse. Repeat qd x 7days.
PEDS - Dandruff, seborrheic dermatitis: Massage 5-10 ml of shampoo into wet scalp, allow to remain 2-3 minutes, rinse. Apply twice a week for 2 weeks. For maintenance, less frequent administration needed. Tinea versicolor: Apply 2.5% lotion/shampoo to affected area, allow to remain on skin 10 min, rinse. Repeat qd x 7days.
FORMS - OTC Generic/Trade: lotion/shampoo 1% 120,210,240, 330 ml, 2.5% 120 ml. Rx generic/trade: lotion/shampoo 2.5% 120 ml.

***Solag* (mequinol + tretinoin)** ▶Not absorbed ♀X ▶? ?
ADULT - Solar lentigines: apply bid separated by at least 8 hrs.
PEDS - Not approved in children.
FORMS - Trade only: soln 30 ml (mequinol 2% + tretinoin 0.01%).
NOTES - Use in non-Caucasians has not been evaluated. Avoid in patients taking photosensitizers. Minimize exposure to sunlight.

tacrolimus (*Protopic*) ▶Minimal absorption ♀C ▶? $$$$
ADULT - Atopic dermatitis: apply bid.
PEDS - Children < 2yo: not approved. Children 2-15 yo: Atopic dermatitis: apply 0.03% oint bid.
FORMS - Trade only: ointment 0.03% 30,60 g, 0.1% 30,60 g.
NOTES - Do not use with an occlusive dressing. Continue treatement for 1 week after clearing of symptoms.

ENDOCRINE & METABOLIC: Androgens / Anabolic Steroids

NOTES: See OB/GYN for other hormones.

fluoxymesterone (*Halotestin*) ▶L ♀X ▶? ©III $$
ADULT - Inoperable breast cancer in women: 5-10 mg PO bid- qid x 1-3 months. Hypogonadism: 5-20 mg PO qd.
PEDS - Delayed puberty in males: 2.5-10 mg PO qd x 4-6 months.
FORMS - Trade: Tabs 2, 5 mg. Generic/Trade: Tabs 10 mg.
NOTES - Transdermal or injectable therapy preferred to oral for hypogonadism. Use cautiously

in children and monitor bone maturation q6 months. Prolonged use of high doses of androgens has been associated with the development of hepatic adenomas, hepatocellular carcinoma, and peliosis hepatitis.

methyltestosterone (*Android, Methitest, Testred, Virilon*, *♣Metandren*) ▶L ♀X ◗? ©III $$$

ADULT - Inoperable breast cancer in women: 50-200 mg/day PO in divided doses. Hypogonadism: 10-50 mg PO qd.

PEDS - Delayed puberty in males: 10 mg PO qd x 4-6 months.

FORMS - Trade: Tabs 10 mg, Caps 10 mg. Generic/Trade: Tabs 25 mg.

NOTES - Transdermal or injectable therapy preferred to oral for hypogonadism. Use cautiously in children and monitor bone maturation q6 months. Prolonged use of high doses of androgens has been associated with the development of hepatic adenomas, hepatocellular carcinoma, and peliosis hepatitis.

nandrolone decanoate (*Deca-Durabolin, Hybolin Decanoate*) ▶L ♀X ◗- ©III $$

WARNING - Peliosis hepatitis, liver cell tumors, and lipid changes have occurred secondary to androgenic anabolic steroid use.

ADULT - Anemia of renal disease: women 50-100 mg IM q wk, men 100-200 mg IM q wk.

PEDS - Anemia of renal disease age 2- 13 yo: 25- 50 mg IM q3-4 weeks.

FORMS - Generic/Trade: injection 100 mg/ml, 200 mg/ml. Trade only: injection 50 mg/ml.

NOTES - Use cautiously in children and monitor bone maturation q6 months.

testosterone (*Androderm, Androgel, Testoderm, Testoderm TTS, Depo-Testosterone, Depotest, Testro-L.A., Virilon IM, Delatestryl, Everone, Testro AQ*) ▶L ♀X ◗? ©III $$$

ADULT - Hypogonadism: injectable enanthate or cypionate- 50-400 mg IM q2-4 weeks. Androderm- 5 mg patch qhs to clean, dry area of skin on back, abdomen, upper arms, or thighs. Non-virilized patients start with 2.5 mg patch qhs. Testoderm TTS (5 mg): 1 patch to arm/ back/ upper buttock qd. Testoderm (4 or 6 mg) or Testoderm with adhesive (6 mg)- start with 6 mg/day. Apply to clean, dry, scrotal skin only. Decrease to 4 mg/day if scrotal area cannot accommodate a 6 mg/day system. Androgel 1% (5 g): apply 1 foil packet of gel to clean, dry, intact skin of the shoulders, upper arms, or abdomen. May increase dose to 7.5-10 g after 2 weeks. Adjust doses based on serum testosterone concentrations.

PEDS - Not approved in children.

FORMS - Trade only: patch 5 mg (Testoderm TTS). patch 4,6 mg (Testoderm). patch 2.5,5 mg (Androderm). gel 1%-2.5, 5 g (Androgel). injection 200 mg/ml (enanthate). Generic/ Trade: injection 100, 200 mg/ml (cypionate).

NOTES - Do not apply Testoderm TTS, Androgel, or Androderm to scrotum. Prolonged use of high doses of androgens has been associated with the development of hepatic adenomas, hepatocellular carcinoma, and peliosis hepatitis. May cause prostatic hyperplasia or prostate cancer. Monitor hemoglobin, LFTs, lipids, PSA.

ENDOCRINE & METABOLIC: Bisphosphonates

alendronate (*Fosamax*) ▶K ♀C ◗- $$$

ADULT - Postmenopausal osteoporosis prevention (5 mg PO qd or 35 mg PO weekly) & treatment (10 mg qd or 70 mg PO weekly). Glucocorticoid-induced osteoporosis treatment: 5 mg PO qd (men and pre-menopausal women) or 10 mg PO qd (postmenopausal women not taking estrogen). Increase bone mass in men with osteoporosis: 10 mg PO qd. Paget's disease: 40 mg PO qd x 6 months.

PEDS - Not approved in children.

UNAPPROVED ADULT - Glucocorticoid-induced osteoporosis treatment: 35 mg PO weekly (men and pre-menopausal women) or 70 mg PO weekly (postmenopausal women not taking estrogen). Increase bone mass in men with osteoporosis: 70 mg PO weekly.

FORMS - Trade: Tabs 5, 10, 35, 40, 70 mg.

NOTES - May cause esophagitis; take 30 minutes before first food, beverage, or medication of the day with a full glass of plain water only. Remain in upright position for ≥30 minutes following dose. Avoid if CrCl < 35 ml/min.

etidronate (*Didronel*) ▶K ♀C ◗? $$$$

ADULT - Hypercalcemia: 7.5 mg/kg in 250 ml NS IV over ≥2h qd for 3 days. May start oral therapy the day following the last IV dose at 20 mg/kg/day x 30 days. Paget's disease: 5-10 mg/kg PO qd x 6 months or 11-20 mg/kg qd x 3 months. Heterotopic ossification with hip replacement: 20 mg/kg/day PO x 1 month before and 3 months after surgery. Heterotopic ossifi-

cation with spinal cord injury: 20 mg/kg/day PO x 2 weeks, then 10 mg/kg/day PO x 10 weeks.
PEDS - Not approved in children.
UNAPPROVED ADULT - Postmenopausal osteoporosis: 400 mg PO qd x 14 days every 3 months (intermittent cyclical therapy).
FORMS - Trade: Tabs 200, 400 mg.
NOTES - May divide oral dose if GI discomfort occurs. Avoid food, vitamins with minerals, or antacids within 2 h of dose.

pamidronate (*Aredia*) ▶K ♀C ▶? $$$$$
ADULT - Moderate hypercalcemia (corrected Ca =12-13.5 mg/dl): 60-90 mg IV single dose; infuse 60 mg dose over ≥4 h and 90 mg over 24 hours. Severe hypercalcemia (Ca >13.5 mg/dl): 90 mg IV single dose infused over 24 hours. Wait ≥7 days before considering retreatment. Paget's disease: 30 mg IV over ≥4 h qd x 3 days. Osteolytic bone lesions: 90 mg IV over ≥4 h once monthly. Osteolytic bone metastases: 90 mg IV over 2 h q3-4 weeks.
PEDS - Not approved in children.
UNAPPROVED ADULT - Mild hypercalcemia: 30 mg IV single dose over ≥4 hours. Osteoporosis treatment: 30-60 mg IV q month.
NOTES - Fever occurs in 20% of patients.

risedronate (*Actonel*) ▶K ♀C ▶? $$$
ADULT - Paget's disease: 30 mg PO qd x 2 months. Postmenopausal and glucocorticoid-induced osteoporosis prevention and treatment: 5 mg PO qd.
PEDS - Not approved in children.
FORMS - Trade: Tabs 5, 30 mg.
NOTES - May cause esophagitis; take 30 minutes before first food, beverage, or medication of the day with a full glass of plain water only. Remain in upright position for ≥30 minutes following dose.

tiludronate (*Skelid*) ▶K ♀C ▶? $$$$$
ADULT - Paget's disease: 400 mg PO qd x 3 months.
PEDS - Not approved in children.
FORMS - Trade: Tabs 200 mg.
NOTES - May cause esophagitis; take 30 minutes before first food, beverage, or medication of the day with a full glass of water only. Remain in upright position for ≥30 minutes following dose.

CORTICOSTEROIDS	*Approximate equivalent dose (mg)*	*Relative anti-inflammatory potency*	*Relative mineralocorticoid potency*	*Biologic Half-life (hours)*
betamethasone	0.6-0.75	20-30	0	36-54
cortisone	25	0.8	2	8-12
dexamethasone	0.75	20-30	0	36-54
hydrocortisone	20	1	2	8-12
methylprednisolone	4	5	0	18-36
prednisolone	5	4	1	18-36
prednisone	5	4	1	18-36
triamcinolone	4	5	0	18-36

ENDOCRINE & METABOLIC: Corticosteroids

NOTE: See also dermatology, ophthalmology.

betamethasone (*Celestone*, ✤*Beben*) ▶L ♀C ▶- $$$$$
ADULT - Anti-inflammatory/Immunosuppressive: 0.6- 7.2 mg/day PO divided bid- qid or up to 9 mg/day IM. 0.25-2.0 ml intraarticular depending on location and size of joint.
PEDS - Dosing guidelines not established.
UNAPPROVED PEDS - Anti-inflammatory/ Immunosuppressive: 0.0175-0.25 mg/kg/day PO divided tid-qid . Fetal lung maturation, maternal antepartum: 12 mg IM q24h x 2 doses.
FORMS - Trade: Tabs 0.6 mg. Syrup 0.6 mg/5 ml.
NOTES - Avoid prolonged use in children due to possible bone growth retardation. Monitor growth & development if prolonged therapy is necessary.

cortisone (*Cortone*) ▶L ♀C ▶- $
ADULT - Adrenocortical insufficiency: 25-300 mg PO qd or 10-150 mg IM q12h.
PEDS - Dosing guidelines not established.
UNAPPROVED PEDS - Adrenocortical insufficiency: 0.5-0.75 mg/kg/day PO divided q8h or 0.25-0.35 mg/ kg IM qd.
FORMS - Trade: Tabs 5, 10 mg. Generic/Trade:

Tabs 25 mg.

dexamethasone (*Decadron, Dexone, ♣Dexasone, Hexadrol*) ▸L ♀C ▸- $

ADULT - Anti-inflammatory/Immunosuppressive: 0.5-9 mg/day PO/IV/IM divided bid- qid. Cerebral edema: 10-20 mg IV load, then 4 mg IM q6h or 1-3 mg PO tid.

PEDS - Dosage in children < 12 yo of age has not been established.

UNAPPROVED PEDS - Anti-inflammatory/ immunosuppressive: 0.08-0.3 mg/kg/day PO/IV/IM divided q6-12h.

FORMS - Generic/Trade: Tabs 0.25, 0.5, 0.75, 1.0, 1.5, 2, 4, 6 mg. elixir/ solution 0.5 mg/5 ml. Trade only: oral solution 0.5 mg/ 0.5 ml. Decadron unipak (0.75 mg-12 tabs).

NOTES - Avoid prolonged use in children due to possible bone growth retardation. Monitor growth & development if prolonged therapy is necessary.

fludrocortisone (*Florinef*) ▸L ♀C ▸? $

ADULT - Adrenocortical insufficiency/ Addison's disease: 0.1 mg PO 3 times weekly to 0.2 mg PO qd. Salt-losing adrenogenital syndrome: 0.1-0.2 mg PO qd.

PEDS - Not approved in children.

UNAPPROVED ADULT - Postural hypotension: 0.05-0.4 mg PO qd.

UNAPPROVED PEDS - Adrenocortical insufficiency: 0.05-0.2 mg PO qd.

FORMS - Trade: Tabs 0.1 mg.

NOTES - Pure mineralocorticoid. Usually given in conjunction with cortisone or hydrocortisone for adrenocortical insufficiency.

hydrocortisone (*Cortef, Solu-Cortef*) ▸L ♀C ▸- $

ADULT - Adrenocortical insufficiency: 20-240 mg/day PO divided tid-qid or 100-500 mg IV/IM q2-10h prn (sodium succinate).

PEDS - Dosing guidelines have not been established.

UNAPPROVED PEDS - Adrenocortical insufficiency: 0.56-8 mg/kg/day PO divided tid-qid or 0.16-1 mg/kg IV/IM qd-bid.

FORMS - Trade: Tabs 5, 10 mg. suspension 10 mg/ 5 ml. Generic/Trade: Tabs 20 mg.

NOTES - Agent of choice for adrenocortical insufficiency because of mixed glucocorticoid and mineralocorticoid properties at doses >100 mg/day.

methylprednisolone (*Solu-Medrol, Medrol, Depo-Medrol*) ▸L ♀C ▸- $$$

ADULT - Anti-inflammatory/ Immunosuppressive: Parenteral (Solu-Medrol) 10- 250 mg IV/IM q4h prn. Oral (Medrol) 4- 48 mg PO qd. Medrol Dosepak tapers 24 to 0 mg PO over 7d. IM/ joints (Depo-Medrol) 4- 120 mg IM q1-2 weeks.

PEDS - Dosing guidelines not established.

UNAPPROVED PEDS - Anti-inflammatory/ Immunosuppressive: 0.5-2 mg/kg/day PO/IV/IM divided q6-12h.

FORMS - Trade only: Tabs 2, 8, 16, 24, 32 mg. Generic/Trade: Tabs 4 mg. Medrol Dosepak (4 mg-21 tabs).

prednisolone (*Prelone, Pediapred, Orapred*) ▸L ♀C ▸+ $$

ADULT - Anti-inflammatory/ Immunosuppressive: 5- 60 mg/day PO/IV/IM.

PEDS - Dosing guidelines have not been established.

UNAPPROVED PEDS - Anti-inflammatory/ Immunosuppressive: 0.14-2 mg/kg/day PO divided qid or 0.04-0.25 mg/kg/day IV/IM divided qd-bid.

FORMS - Generic/Trade: Tabs 5 mg. syrup 15 mg/ 5 ml (Prelone; wild cherry flavor). Trade only: solution 5 mg/5 ml (Pediapred; raspberry flavor); solution 15 mg/5 ml (Orapred; grape flavor).

prednisone (*Deltasone, Meticorten, Pred-Pak, Prednisone Intensol, Sterapred, ♣Winpred, Metreton*) ▸L ♀C ▸+ $

ADULT - Anti-inflammatory/ Immunosuppressive: 5-60 mg/day PO qd or divided bid-qid.

PEDS - Dosing guidelines have not been established.

UNAPPROVED PEDS - Anti-inflammatory/ Immunosuppressive: 0.05-2 mg/kg/day divided qd-qid.

FORMS - Generic/Trade: Tabs 1, 5, 10, 20, 50 mg. Trade only: Tabs 2.5 mg. Sterapred (5 mg-21& 48 tabs), Sterapred DS (10 mg-21,48, & 49 tabs) & Pred-Pak (5 mg- 45 & 79 tabs) taper packs. solution 5 mg/5 ml & 5 mg/ml (Intensol).

NOTES - Conversion to prednisolone may be impaired in liver disease.

triamcinolone (*Aristocort, Kenalog, ♣Aristospan*) ▸L ♀C ▸- $$$$

ADULT - Anti-inflammatory/ Immunosuppressive: 4-48 mg/day PO divided qd-qid. 2.5-60 mg IM qd (Kenalog). 40 mg IM q week (Aristocort)

PEDS - Dosing guidelines not established.

UNAPPROVED PEDS - Anti-inflammatory/ Immunosuppressive: 0.117-1.66 mg/kg/day PO divided qid.

FORMS - Generic/Trade: Tabs 4 mg. Trade only: injection 10 mg/ml, 25 mg/ml, 40 mg/ml.

NOTES - Parenteral form not for IV use.

ENDOCRINE & METABOLIC: Diabetes-Related - Sulfonylureas - 1st Generation

chlorpropamide (*Diabinese*) ▸LK ♀C ◗- $
ADULT - Initiate therapy with 100-250 mg PO qd. Titrate after 5-7 days by increments of 50-125 mg at intervals of 3-5 days to obtain optimal control. Max 750 mg/day.
PEDS - Not approved in children.
FORMS - Generic/Trade: Tabs 100, 250 mg.
NOTES - Long half-life can predispose to hypoglycemia. Accumulates in renal impairment. Avoid in elderly. May cause disulfiram reaction with alcohol.

tolazamide (*Tolinase*) ▸LK ♀C ◗? $
ADULT - Initiate therapy with 100 mg PO qd in patients with FBS < 200 mg/dl, and in patients who are malnourished, underweight, or elderly. Initiate therapy with 250 mg PO qd in patients with FBS > 200 mg/dl. Give with breakfast or the first main meal of the day. If daily doses exceed 500 mg, divide the dose bid. Max 1,000 mg/day.
PEDS - Not approved in children.
FORMS - Generic/Trade: Tabs 100,250,500 mg.

tolbutamide (*Orinase, Tol-Tab*) ▸LK ♀C ◗+ $
ADULT - Start 1g PO qd. Maintenance dose is usually 250 mg to 2 g PO qd. Total daily dose may be taken in the morning, divide doses if GI intolerance occurs. Max 3 g/day.
PEDS - Not approved in children.
FORMS - Generic/Trade: Tabs 500 mg.

DIABETES NUMBERS*		*Criteria for diagnosis of diabetes*		*Control*	*Hb A1c*
Self-monitoring glucose goals		*(repeat to confirm on subsequent day)*		Excellent	<7%
Preprandial	80-120 mg/dL	Fasting plasma glucose	≥126 mg/dL	Good	≤8%
Bedtime	100-140 mg/dL	Random plasma glucose	≥200 mg/dL	Take action	>8%

Management Schedule: *At every visit*: Measure weight and BP (goal <130/85 mmHg; <125/75 mmHg if proteinuria >1 g/day†); foot exam for high-risk feet; review self-monitoring blood glucose record; review/adjust meds; review self-management skills, dietary needs, and physical activity; counsel on smoking cessation. *Twice a year*: HbA1c in patients meeting treatment goals with stable glycemia (quarterly if not). *Annually*: Fasting lipid profile (goal LDL ≤100 mg/dL§), creatinine, UA for protein (check microalbumin if no overt proteinuria on UA); dilated eye exam; dental exam; flu vaccine; foot exam for low risk feet.

*http://ndep.nih.gov †JNC VI. *Arch Intern Med* 1997;157:2413-46. §*Diabetes Care* 2001;24(Suppl 1):S33-43 and *JAMA* 2001;285:2486-2497.

ENDOCRINE & METABOLIC: Diabetes-Related - Sulfonylureas - 2nd Generation

glimepiride (*Amaryl*) ▸LK ♀C ◗- $
ADULT - Diabetes: initiate therapy with 1-2 mg PO qd. Start with 1 mg PO qd in elderly, malnourished patients or those with renal or hepatic insufficiency. Give with breakfast or the first main meal of the day. Titrate in increments of 1-2 mg at 1-2 week intervals based on response. Usual maintenance dose is 1-4 mg PO qd, max 8 mg/day.
PEDS - Not approved in children.
FORMS - Trade: Tabs 1, 2, 4 mg.

glipizide (*Glucotrol, Glucotrol XL*) ▸LK ♀C ◗? $
ADULT - Diabetes: initiate therapy with 5 mg PO qd. Give 2.5 mg PO qd to geriatric patients or those with liver disease. Adjust dose in increments of 2.5-5 mg to a usual maintenance dose of 10-20 mg/day, max 40 mg/day. Doses >15 mg should be divided bid. Extended release (Glucotrol XL): initiate therapy with 5 mg PO qd. Usual dose is 5-10 mg PO qd, max 20 mg/day.
PEDS - Not approved in children.
FORMS - Generic/Trade: Tabs 5, 10 mg. Trade only: extended release Tabs (Glucotrol XL) 2.5, 5, 10 mg.

glyburide (*Micronase, DiaBeta, Glynase PresTab*, ✤*Euglucon*) ▸LK ♀B ◗? $
ADULT - Diabetes: initiate therapy with 2.5-5 mg PO qd. Start with 1.25 mg PO qd in elderly or malnourished patients or those with renal or hepatic insufficiency. Give with breakfast or the first main meal of the day. Titrate in increments of ≤2.5 mg at weekly intervals based on re-

sponse. Usual maintenance dose is 1.25-20 mg PO qd or divided bid, max 20 mg/day. Micronized tabs: initiate therapy with 1.5-3 mg PO qd. Start with 0.75 mg PO qd in elderly, malnourished patients or those with renal or hepatic insufficiency. Give with breakfast or the first main meal of the day. Titrate in increments of ≤1.5 mg at weekly intervals based on response. Usual maintenance dose is 0.75-12 mg PO qd, max 12 mg/day. May divide dose bid if > 6 mg/day.

PEDS - Not approved in children.

FORMS - Generic/Trade: Tabs 1.25, 2.5, 5 mg. micronized Tabs 1.5, 3, 6 mg.

ENDOCRINE & METABOLIC: Diabetes-Related Agents - Other

acarbose (*Precose*, ✤*Prandase*) ▶Gut/K ♀B ◗- $$

ADULT - Diabetes: initiate therapy with 25 mg PO tid with the first bite of each meal. Start with 25 mg PO qd to minimize GI adverse effects. May increase to 50 mg PO tid after 4-8 weeks. Usual range is 50-100 mg PO tid. Maximum dose for patients ≤60 kg is 50 mg tid, >60 kg is 100 mg tid.

PEDS - Not approved in children.

FORMS - Trade: Tabs 25, 50, 100 mg.

NOTES - Acarbose administered alone should not cause hypoglycemia. If hypoglycemia occurs, use oral glucose rather than sucrose (table sugar). Adverse GI effects (i.e. flatulence, diarrhea, abdominal pain) may occur with initial therapy.

dextrose (*Glutose, B-D Glucose, Insta-Glucose*) ▶L ♀C ◗? $

ADULT - Hypoglycemia: 0.5-1 g/kg (1-2 ml/kg) up to 25 g (50 ml) of 50% solution by slow IV injection. Hypoglycemia in conscious diabetics: 10-20 g PO q10-20 min prn.

PEDS - Hypoglycemia in neonates: 250-500 mg/kg/dose (5-10 ml of 25% dextrose in a 5 kg infant). Severe hypoglycemic cases or older infants may require larger doses up to 10-12 ml of 25% dextrose along with continuous IV infusion of 10% dextrose.

FORMS - OTC/Trade only: chew Tabs 5 g. gel 40%.

NOTES - Do not exceed an infusion rate of 0.5 g/kg/hr.

diazoxide (*Proglycem*) ▶L ♀C ◗- $$$$$

ADULT - Hypoglycemia: initially 3 mg/kg/day PO divided equally q8h, usual maintenance dose 3-8 mg/kg/day divided equally q8-12 hours, max 10-15 mg/kg/day.

PEDS - Hypoglycemia: neonates and infants, initially 10 mg/kg/day divided equally q8h, usual maintenance dose 8-15 mg/kg/day divided equally q8-12h; children, same as adult.

FORMS - Trade: susp 50 mg/ ml.

glucagon (*Glucagon, GlucaGen*) ▶LK ♀B ◗? $$$

ADULT - Hypoglycemia in adults: 1 mg IV/IM/SC. If no response in 5-20 minutes, may repeat dose 1-2 times.

PEDS - Hypoglycemia in children >20 kg: same as adults. Hypoglycemia in children <20 kg: 0.5 mg IV/IM/SC or 20-30 mcg/kg. If no response in 5-20 minutes, may repeat dose 1-2 times.

FORMS - Trade: injection 1 mg.

NOTES - Advise patients to educate family members and co-workers how to administer a dose. Give supplemental carbohydrates when patient responds.

glucose home testing (*Chemstrip bG, Dextrostix, Diascan, Glucometer, Glucostix, Clinistix, Clinitest, Diastix, Tes-Tape, GlucoWatch*) ▶None ♀+ ◗+ $$

ADULT - Use for home glucose monitoring

PEDS - Use for home glucose monitoring

FORMS - Blood: Chemstrip bG, Dextrostix, Diascan, Glucometer, Glucostix; Urine: Clinistix, Clinitest, Diastix, Tes-Tape, GlucoWatch

NOTES - GlucoWatch monitors glucose levels q20 min for 12 h by sending small electric currents through the skin (a thin plastic sensor is attached to the back of the watch each time it is strapped on to extract glucose from fluid in skin cells). GlucoWatch may cause skin irritation. Home HgbA1C monitors also available.

***Glucovance* (glyburide + metformin)** ▶KL ♀B ◗? $$

WARNING - Lactic acidosis can occur due to metformin accumulation and may be fatal.

ADULT - Diabetes, initial therapy: Start 1.25/250 mg PO qd or bid with meals; maximum 10/2000 mg daily. Diabetes, second-line therapy: Start 2.5/500 or 5/500 mg PO bid with meals; maximum 20/2000 mg daily.

PEDS - Not approved in children.

FORMS - Trade: Tabs 1.25/250, 2.5/500, 5/500 mg

NOTES - Hold at the time of or prior to IV contrast agents and for 48 h after. Avoid if ethanol abuse, CHF, renal or hepatic insufficiency.

INSULIN*	*Preparation*	*Onset (h)*	*Peak (h)*	*Duration (h)*
Rapid-acting:	Insulin aspart (*Novolog*)	¼	¾	3-5
	Insulin lispro (*Humalog*)	0-¼	½-1½	6-8
	Regular	½-1	2½-5	6-8
Intermediate-acting:	NPH	1-1½	4-12	24
	Lente	1-2½	7-15	24
Long-acting:	Ultralente	4-8	10-30	>36
	Insulin glargine (*Lantus*)	Slow, prolonged absorption†		

*These are general guidelines, as onset, peak, and duration of activity are affected by the site of injection, physical activity, body temperature, and blood supply.

†Relatively constant concentration/time profile over 24 h with no pronounced peak.

insulin (*Novolin, Novolog, Humulin, Humalog, Lantus*) ▶LK ♀B/C ▶+ $$

ADULT - Diabetes: Humalog/Novolog: maintenance dose 0.5-1 unit/kg/day SC in divided doses, but doses vary. Lantus: Start 10 units SC qhs in insulin naïve patients, adjust to usual dose of 2-100 units/day. When transferring from twice daily NPH human insulin, the initial Lantus dose should be reduced by ~20% from the previous total daily NPH dose, then adjust dose based on patient response. Other insulins are OTC products and have no FDA approved indications.

PEDS - Diabetes age > 3 yo (Humalog): maintenance dose 0.5-1 unit/kg/day SC in divided doses, but doses vary. Age 6-15 yo (Lantus): Start 10 units SC qhs in insulin naïve patients, adjust to usual dose of 2-100 units/day . When transferring from twice daily NPH human insulin, the initial Lantus dose should be reduced by ~20% from the previous total daily NPH dose, then adjust dose based on patient response. Other insulins are not approved in children.

UNAPPROVED ADULT - Diabetes: 0.3-0.5 unit/kg/day SC in divided doses (Type 1), and 1-1.5 unit/kg/day SC in divided doses (Type 2), but doses vary. Severe hyperkalemia: 5-10 units regular insulin plus concurrent dextrose IV. Profound hyperglycemia (eg, DKA): 0.1 unit/kg regular insulin IV bolus, then IV infusion 100 units in 100 ml NS (1 unit/ml) at 0.1 units/kg/hr. 70 kg: 7 units/h (7 ml/h). Titrate to clinical effect.

UNAPPROVED PEDS - Diabetes: maintenance: 0.5-1 unit/kg/day SC, but doses vary. Humalog may be given after meals. Profound hyperglycemia (eg, DKA): 0.1 unit/kg regular insulin IV bolus, then IV infusion 100 units in 100 ml NS (1 unit/ml) at 0.1 units/kg/hr. Titrate to clinical effect. Severe hyperkalemia: 0.1 units/kg regular insulin IV with glucose over 30 min. May repeat in 30-60 min or start 0.1 units/kg/hr.

FORMS - Trade: injection NPH, regular, lente, ultralente, insulin lispro (Humalog), Insulin lispro protamine suspension/ insulin lispro (Humalog Mix 75/25), insulin glargine (Lantus), insulin aspart (Novolog), NPH and regular mixtures (70/30 or 50/50).

NOTES - Do not mix Lantus with other insulins in a syringe.

metformin (*Glucophage, Glucophage XR*, ✤*Glycon*) ▶K ♀B ▶? $$$

WARNING - Lactic acidosis can occur due to metformin accumulation and may be fatal.

ADULT - Diabetes: Glucophage: Start 500 mg PO qd-bid or 850 mg PO qd with meals. Increase by 500 mg q week or 850 mg q other week to a maximum of 2550 mg/day. Higher doses may be divided tid with meals. Glucophage XR: 500 mg PO qd with evening meal; increase by 500 mg q week to max 2000 mg/day (may divide 1000 mg PO bid).

PEDS - Diabetes 10-16 yo: Start 500 mg PO qd-bid (Glucophage) with meals, increase by 500 mg q week to max 2000 mg/day in divided doses. Glucophage XR is not approved in children.

UNAPPROVED ADULT - Polycystic ovary syndrome: 500 mg PO tid.

FORMS - Trade: Tabs 500, 850, 1000 mg; extended release 500 mg.

NOTES - Hold metformin at the time of or prior to IV contrast agents and for 48 h after. Avoid if ethanol abuse, CHF, renal or hepatic insufficiency. May be given concomitantly with sulfonylureas or insulin.

miglitol (*Glyset*) ▶K ♀B ▶- $$$

ADULT - Diabetes: Initiate therapy with 25 mg PO tid with the first bite of each meal. Use 25 mg PO qd to start if GI adverse effects. May increase dose to 50 mg PO tid after 4-8 weeks, max 300 mg/day.

PEDS - Not approved in children.

FORMS - Trade: Tabs 25, 50, 100 mg.
NOTES - Miglitol administered alone should not cause hypoglycemia. If hypoglycemia occurs, use oral glucose rather than sucrose (table sugar). Adverse GI effects (i.e. flatulence, diarrhea, abdominal pain) may occur with initial therapy.

nateglinide (*Starlix*) ▶L ♀C ▶? $$$
ADULT - Diabetes, monotherapy or in combination with metformin: 120 mg PO tid 1-30 min before meals; use 60 mg PO tid in patients who are near goal HbA1c.
PEDS - Not approved in children.
FORMS - Trade: Tabs 60, 120 mg.
NOTES - Not to be used as monotherapy in patients inadequately controlled with glyburide or other anti-diabetic agents previously.

pioglitazone (*Actos*) ▶L ♀C ▶- $$$
ADULT - Diabetes monotherapy or in combination with a sulfonylurea, metformin, or insulin: Start 15-30 mg PO qd, may adjust dose after 3 months to max 45 mg/day.
PEDS - Not approved in children.
FORMS - Trade: Tabs 15, 30, 45 mg.
NOTES - Use with caution in patients with edema or heart failure. May cause resumption of ovulation in premenopausal anovulatory patients with insulin resistance; recommend contraception use. Avoid if liver disease or ALT >2.5 x normal. Monitor LFTs before therapy & periodically thereafter. Discontinue if ALT >3 x normal.

repaglinide (*Prandin*, ✤*Gluconorm*) ▶L ♀C ▶? $$$
ADULT - Diabetes: 0.5- 2 mg PO tid within 30 minutes before a meal. Allow 1 week between dosage adjustments. Usual range is 0.5-4 mg PO tid-qid, max 16 mg/day.
PEDS - Not approved in children.
FORMS - Trade: Tabs 0.5, 1, 2 mg.
NOTES - May take dose immediately preceding meal to as long as 30 minutes before the meal.

rosiglitazone (*Avandia*) ▶L ♀C ▶- $$$
ADULT - Diabetes monotherapy or in combination with metformin or sulfonylurea: Start 4 mg PO qd or divided bid, may increase after 12 weeks to max 8 mg/day as monotherapy or in combination with metformin. There is no experience with doses greater than 4 mg/day in combination with sulfonylureas.
PEDS - Not approved in children < 18 yo.
FORMS - Trade: Tabs 2, 4, 8 mg.
NOTES - Use with caution in patients with edema or heart failure. May cause resumption of ovulation in premenopausal anovulatory patients with insulin resistance; recommend contraception use. Avoid if liver disease or ALT > 2.5 x normal. Monitor LFTs before therapy, q2 months for the first year, and periodically thereafter. Discontinue if ALT >3x normal.

ENDOCRINE & METABOLIC: Gout-Related

allopurinol (*Zyloprim*) ▶K ♀C ▶? $
ADULT - Mild gout or recurrent calcium oxalate stones: 200-300 mg PO qd. Moderately severe gout: 400-600 mg PO qd. Secondary hyperuricemia: 600-800 mg PO qd. Doses in excess of 300 mg should be divided. Max 800 mg/day. Reduce dose in renal insufficiency (CrCl 10-20 ml/ min= 200 mg/day, CrCl < 10 ml/min = 100 mg/day).
PEDS - Secondary hyperuricemia: age <6 yo = 150 mg PO qd; age 6-10 yo = 300 mg PO qd or 1 mg/kg/day divided q6h to a maximum of 600 mg/day.
FORMS - Generic/Trade: Tabs 100, 300 mg.
NOTES - May precipitate an acute gout flare; use NSAIDs or colchicine to prevent. Incidence of rash is increased in renal impairment. Discontinue if rash or allergic symptoms. Drug interaction with warfarin and azathioprine. Normal serum uric acid levels are usually achieved after 1-3 weeks of therapy.

colchicine ▶L ♀C(oral), D(IV) ▶+ $
ADULT - Acute gouty arthritis: start 1-1.2 mg PO, then 0.5-1.2 mg PO q1-2h until pain relief or unacceptable side effects (eg, diarrhea, GI upset); or 2 mg IV over 2-5 minutes, followed by 0.5 mg IV q6h. Max 8 mg/day PO or 4 mg IV per treatment course. Gout prophylaxis: 0.5-1 mg PO qd-bid.
PEDS - Not approved in children.
FORMS - Generic/Trade: Tabs 0.5, 0.6 mg.
NOTES - Reserve IV form when GI side effects are intolerable or a rapid response is needed. May cause severe infiltration/ extravasation injuries. Accumulation of the drug and toxicity may occur; wait 3-7 days before giving a second course.

probenecid, ✤***Benemid, Benuryl*** ▶KL ♀B ▶? $
ADULT - Gout: 250 mg PO bid x 7 days, then 500 mg PO bid. May increase by 500 mg/day q4 weeks not to exceed 2 g/day. Adjunct to

penicillin: 2 g/day PO in divided doses. Reduce dose to 1 g/day in renal impairment.
PEDS - Adjunct to penicillin in children 2-14 yo: 25 mg/kg PO initially, then 40 mg/kg/day divided qid. For children > 50 kg, use adult dose. Contraindicated in children < 2 yo.
FORMS - Generic: Tabs 500 mg.
NOTES - Decrease dose if GI intolerance occurs. Maintain alkaline urine. Begin therapy 2-3 weeks after acute gouty attack subsides.

INTRAVENOUS SOLUTIONS (ions in mEq/l)

Solution	*Dextrose*	*Cal/l*	*Na*	*K*	*Ca*	*Cl*	*Lactate*	*Osm*
0.9 NS	0 g/l	0	154	0	0	154	0	310
LR	0 g/l	9	130	4	3	109	28	273
D5 W	50 g/l	170	0	0	0	0	0	253
D5 0.2 NS	50 g/l	170	34	0	0	34	0	320
D5 0.45 NS	50 g/l	170	77	0	0	77	0	405
D5 0.9 NS	50 g/l	170	154	0	0	154	0	560
D5 LR	50 g/l	179	130	4	2.7	109	28	527

ENDOCRINE & METABOLIC: Minerals

calcium acetate (*PhosLo*) ▸K ♀+ ◗? $
ADULT - Hyperphosphatemia in end-stage renal failure: initially 2 tabs/caps PO tid with each meal. Titrate dose based on serum phosphorus.
PEDS - Not approved in children.
UNAPPROVED PEDS - Titrate to response.
FORMS - Trade only: tab/cap 667 mg (169 mg elem Ca).
NOTES - Higher doses more effective, but beware of hypercalcemia, especially if given with vitamin D. Most patients require 3-4 tabs/meal.

calcium carbonate (*Tums, Os-Cal, Os-Cal+D, Caltrate*) ▸K ♀+ ◗? $
ADULT - 1-2 g elem Ca/day or more PO with meals divided bid-qid. Prevention of osteoporosis: 1000-1500 mg elem Ca/day PO divided bid-tid with meals. Hypocalcemia: 1-2 g elem Ca/day or more PO in 3-4 divided doses. The adequate intake in most adults is 1000-1200 mg elem Ca/day.
PEDS - Hypocalcemia: Neonates: 50-150 mg elem Ca/kg/day PO in 4-6 divided doses; Children: 45-65 mg elem Ca/kg/day PO divided qid. Adequate intake for children (in elem calcium): <6 mo: 210 mg/day when consuming human milk and 315 mg/day when consuming cow's milk; 6-12 mo: 270 mg/day when consuming human milk+solid food and 335 mg/day when consuming cow's milk+solid food; 1-3 yo: 500 mg/day; 4-8 yo: 800 mg/day; 9-18 yo 1300 mg/day.
UNAPPROVED ADULT - May lower BP with HTN. May reduce PMS symptoms such as fluid retention, pain, and negative affect.
FORMS - OTC Generic/Trade: tab 650,667, 1250,1500 mg, chew tab 750,1250 mg, cap 1250 mg, susp 1250 mg/5 ml.
NOTES - Calcium carbonate is 40% elem calcium and contains 20 mEq of elem calcium/g calcium carbonate. Not more than 500-600 mg elem Ca/dose. Drug interaction with levothyroxine, tetracycline, and fluroquinolones. Os-Cal 250 + D contains 125 units vitamin D/tab, Os-Cal 500 + D contains 200 units vitamin D/tab.

calcium chloride ▸K ♀+ ◗? $
ADULT - Hypocalcemia: 500-1000 mg IV q1-3 days. Magnesium intoxication: 500 mg IV. Hyperkalemic ECG changes: dose based on ECG.
PEDS - Hypocalcemia: 0.2 ml/kg IV up to 10 ml/day. Cardiac resuscitation: 0.2 ml/kg IV.
UNAPPROVED ADULT - Has been used in calcium channel blocker toxicity and to treat or prevent calcium channel blocker-induced hypotension.
UNAPPROVED PEDS - Has been used in calcium channel blocker toxicity.
FORMS - Generic: injectable 10% (1000 mg/10 ml) 10 ml ampules, vials, syringes.
NOTES - Calcium chloride contains 14.4 mEq Ca++/g versus calcium gluconate 4.7 mEq Ca++/g. For IV use only; do not administer IM or SC. Avoid extravasation. Administer no faster than 0.5-1 ml/min. Use cautiously in patients receiving digoxin; inotropic and toxic effects are synergistic and may cause arrhyth-

mias. Usually not recommended for hypocalcemia associated with renal insufficiency because calcium chloride is an acidifying salt.

calcium citrate (*Citracal*) ▶K ♀+ ▶? $

ADULT - 1-2 g elem Ca/day or more PO with meals divided bid-qid. Prevention of osteoporosis: 1000-1500 mg elem Ca/day PO divided bid-tid with meals. Hypocalcemia: 1-2 g elem Ca/day or more PO in 3-4 divided doses. The adequate intake in most adults is 1000-1200 mg elem Ca/day.

FORMS - OTC: Trade: tab 200 mg elem Ca, 250 mg elem Ca with 125 units vitamin D, 315 mg elem Ca with 200 units vitamin D, 250 mg elem Ca with 62.5 units magnesium stearate vitamin D, effervescent tab 500 mg elem Ca.

NOTES - Calcium citrate is 21% elem Ca. Not more than 500-600 mg elem Ca/dose. Drug interaction with levothyroxine, tetracycline and fluroquinolones.

calcium gluconate ▶K ♀+ ▶? $

ADULT - Emergency correction of hypocalcemia: 7-14 mEq IV prn. Hypocalcemic tetany: 4.5-16 mEq IM prn. Hyperkalemia with cardiac toxicity: 2.25-14 mEq IV while monitoring ECG. May repeat after 1-2 minutes. Magnesium intoxication: 4.5-9 mEq IV, adjust dose based on patient response. If IV administration not possible, give 2-5 mEq IM. Exchange transfusions: 1.35 mEq calcium gluconate IV concurrent with each 100 ml of citrated blood. Oral calcium gluconate: 1-2 g elem Ca/day or more PO with meals divided bid-qid. Prevention of osteoporosis: 1000-1500 mg elem Ca/day PO with meals in divided doses. Hypocalcemia: 1-2 g elem Ca/day or more PO in 3-4 divided doses.

PEDS - Emergency correction of hypocalcemia: Children: 1-7 mEq IV prn. Infants: 1 mEq IV prn. Hypocalcemic tetany: Children: 0.5-0.7 mEq/kg IV tid-qid. Neonates: 2.4 mEq/kg/day IV in divided doses. Exchange transfusions: Neonates: 0.45 mEq IV/100 ml of exchange transfusions. Oral calcium gluconate: Hypocalcemia: Neonates: 50-150 mg elem Ca/kg/day PO in 4-6 divided doses; children: 45-65 mg elem Ca/kg/day PO divided qid.

UNAPPROVED ADULT - Has been used in calcium channel blocker toxicity and to treat or prevent calcium channel blocker-induced hypotension.

UNAPPROVED PEDS - Has been used in calcium channel blocker toxicity.

FORMS - Generic: injectable 10% (1000 mg/10 ml, 4.65mEq/10 ml) 10,50,100,200 ml. OTC generic: tab 500,650,975,1000 mg.

NOTES - Calcium gluconate is 9.3% elem calcium and contains 4.6 mEq elem calcium/g calcium gluconate. Administer IV calcium gluconate not faster than 0.5-2 ml/min. Use cautiously in patients receiving digoxin; inotropic and toxic effects are synergistic and may cause arrhythmias.

ferrous gluconate (*Fergon*) ▶K ♀+ ▶+ $

ADULT - Iron deficiency: 800-1600 mg ferrous gluconate (100-200 mg elem iron) PO divided tid. Iron supplementation: RDA (elem iron) is: adult males (≥19 yo): 8 mg; adult premenopausal females (11-50 yo) 18 mg; adult females (≥51yo): 8 mg; pregnancy: 27 mg; lactation: 14-18 yo: 10 mg; 19-50 yo: 9 mg. Upper limit: 45 mg/day.

PEDS - Mild-moderate iron deficiency: 3 mg/kg/day of elem iron PO in 1-2 divided doses; severe iron deficiency: 4-6 mg/kg/day PO in 3 divided doses. Iron supplementation: RDA (elem iron) is: < 6 mo: 6 mg; 7-12 mo: 6.9 mg; 1-3 yo: 7 mg; 4-8 yo: 10 mg; 9-13 yo: 8 mg; males 14-18 yo: 11 mg; females 14-18 yo: 15 mg.

UNAPPROVED ADULT - Adjunct to epoetin to maximize hematologic response: 200 mg elem iron/day PO.

UNAPPROVED PEDS - Adjunct to epoetin to maximize hematologic response: 2-3 mg/kg elem iron/day PO.

FORMS - OTC Generic/Trade: tab 240,300,324, 325 mg.

NOTES - Ferrous gluconate is 12% elem iron. For iron deficiency, 4-6 months of therapy generally necessary to replete stores even after hemoglobin has returned to normal. Do not take within 2 h of antacids, tetracyclines, levothyroxine or fluoroquinolones. May cause black stools, constipation or diarrhea.

ferrous polysaccharide (*Niferex*) ▶K ♀+ ▶+ $

ADULT - Iron deficiency: 50-200 mg PO divided qd-tid. Iron supplementation: RDA (elem iron) is: adult males (≥19yo): 10 mg; adult females (11-50yo) 15 mg; adult females (≥51yo): 10 mg; pregnancy: 30 mg; lactation: 15 mg.

PEDS - Mild-moderate iron deficiency: 3 mg/kg/day of elem iron PO in 1-2 divided doses. Severe iron deficiency: 4-6 mg/kg/day PO in 3 divided doses. Iron supplementation: RDA (elem iron) is: < 6 mo: 6 mg; 7-12 mo: 6.9 mg; 1-3 yo: 7 mg; 4-8 yo: 10 mg; 9-13 yo: 8 mg; males 14-18 yo: 11 mg; females 14-18 yo: 15 mg.

UNAPPROVED ADULT - Adjunct to epoetin to maximize hematologic response: 200 mg elem iron/day PO.

UNAPPROVED PEDS - Adjunct to epoetin to maximize hematologic response: 2-3 mg/kg elem iron/day PO.

FORMS - OTC Generic/Trade: (strength in terms of elem mg iron): tab 50 mg, cap 150 mg, liquid 100 mg/5 ml.

NOTES - For iron deficiency, 4-6 months of therapy generally necessary. Do not take within 2 h of antacids, tetracyclines, levothyroxine, or fluoroquinolones. May cause black stools, constipation or diarrhea.

ferrous sulfate (*Fer-in-Sol, FeoSol Tabs*) ▶K ♀+ ▶+ $

ADULT - Iron deficiency: 500-1000 mg iron sulfate (100-200 mg elem iron) PO divided tid. Liquid: 5-10 ml tid. Iron supplementation: RDA (elem iron) is: adult males (≥19 yo): 8 mg; adult premenopausal females (11-50 yo): 18 mg; adult females (≥51 yo): 8 mg; pregnancy: 27 mg; lactation: 14-18 yo: 10 mg; 19-50 yo: 9 mg. Upper limit: 45 mg/day.

PEDS - Mild-moderate iron deficiency: 3 mg/kg/day of elem iron PO in 1-2 divided doses; severe iron deficiency: 4-6 mg/kg/day PO in 3 divided doses. Iron supplementation: RDA (elem iron) is: < 6 mo: 6 mg; 7-12 mo: 6.9 mg; 1-3 yo: 7 mg; 4-8 yo: 10 mg; 9-13 yo: 8 mg; males 14-18 yo: 11 mg; females 14-18 yo: 15 mg.

UNAPPROVED ADULT - Adjunct to epoetin to maximize hematologic response: 200 mg elem iron/day PO.

UNAPPROVED PEDS - Adjunct to epoetin to maximize hematologic response: 2-3 mg/kg elem iron/day PO.

FORMS - OTC Generic/Trade: tab 324,325 mg, liquid 220 mg/5 ml, drops 75 mg/0.6 ml.

NOTES - Iron sulfate is 20% elem iron. For iron deficiency, 4-6 months of therapy generally necessary. Do not take within 2 h of antacids, tetracyclines, levothyroxine, fluoroquinolones. May cause black stools, constipation, diarrhea.

fluoride (*Luride*, ✤*Flur-A-Day*) ▶K ♀? ▶? $

ADULT - Prevention of dental cavities: 10 ml of topical rinse swish and spit qd.

PEDS - Prevention of dental caries: Dose based on age and fluoride concentrations in water. See chart.

FORMS - Generic: chew tab 0.5,1 mg, tab 1 mg, drops 0.125 mg/dropperful, 0.25 mg/dropperful, 0.5 mg/dropperful, lozenges 1 mg, solution 0.2 mg/ml, gel 0.1%,0.5%,1.23%, rinse (sodium fluoride) 0.05,0.1,0.2%).

NOTES - In communities without fluoridated water, fluoride supplementation should be used until 13-16 years of age. Chronic overdosage of fluorides may result in dental fluorosis (mottling of tooth enamel) and osseous changes. Use rinses and gels after brushing and flossing and before bedtime.

FLUORIDE: Pediatric qd dose is based on drinking water fluoride (shown in ppm)

Age (*years*)	*<0.3* *ppm*	*0.3-0.6* *ppm*	*>0.6* *ppm*
0-0.5	none	none	none
0.5-3	0.25mg	none	none
3-6	0.5mg	0.25mg	none
6-16	1 mg	0.5 mg	none

iron dextran (*InFed, DexFerrum*, ✤*Dexiron*) ▶KL ♀- ▶? $$$$

WARNING - Parenteral iron therapy has resulted in anaphylactic reactions. Potentially fatal hypersensitivity reactions have been reported with iron dextran injection. Facilities for CPR must be available during dosing. Use only when clearly warranted.

ADULT - Iron deficiency: Dose based on patient weight and hemoglobin. Total dose (ml) = 0.0442 x (desired hgb - observed hgb) x weight (kg) + [0.26 x weight (kg)]. For weight, use lesser of lean body weight or actual body weight. Iron replacement for blood loss: replacement iron (mg) = blood loss (ml) x hematocrit. Maximum daily IM dose 100 mg.

PEDS - Not recommended for infants <4 months of age. Iron deficiency in children > 5 kg: Dose based on patient weight and hemoglobin. Dose (ml) = 0.0442 x (desired hgb - observed hgb) x weight (kg) + [0.26 x weight (kg)]. For weight, use lesser of lean body weight or actual body weight. Iron replacement for blood loss: replacement iron (mg) = blood loss (ml) x hematocrit. Maximum daily IM dose: infants < 5 kg: 25 mg; children 5-10 kg: 50 mg; children > 10 kg 100 mg.

UNAPPROVED ADULT - Adjunct to epoetin to maximize hematologic response. Has been given by slow IV infusion. Total dose iron infusion (325-1500 mg) as a single, slow (6 mg/min) IV infusion has been used.

UNAPPROVED PEDS - Adjunct to epoetin to maximize hematologic response.

NOTES - A 0.5 ml IV test dose (0.25 ml dose in infants) over at least 30 seconds should be given at least 1 h before therapy. Infuse IV iron no faster than 50 mg/min. For IM iron administration, use Z-track technique.

iron sucrose (*Venofer*) ▶KL ♀B ▶? $$$$$

WARNING - Potentially fatal hypersensitivity reactions have been rarely reported with iron sucrose injection. Facilities for CPR must be available during dosing.
ADULT - Iron deficiency in chronic hemodialysis patients: 5 ml (100 mg elem iron) IV over 5 min or diluted in 100 ml NS IV over ≥15 minutes.
PEDS - Not approved in children.
UNAPPROVED ADULT - Iron deficiency: 5 ml (100 mg elem iron) IV over 5 min or diluted in 100 ml NS IV over ≥15 min.
NOTES - Most hemodialysis patients require 1 g of elem iron over 10 consecutive hemodialysis session.

magnesium gluconate (*Almore, Magtrate, Maganate*) ▸K ♀A ▸+ $
ADULT - Dietary supplement: 500-1000 mg/day PO divided tid. RDA (elem Mg): Adult males: 19-30 yo: 400 mg;>30 yo: 420 mg. Adult females: 19-30 yo: 310 mg; >30 yo: 320 mg.
PEDS - Not approved in children.
UNAPPROVED ADULT - Hypomagnesemia: 300 mg elem magnesium PO divided qid. Has also been used as oral tocolysis following IV magnesium sulfate.
UNAPPROVED PEDS - Hypomagnesemia: 10-20 mg elem magnesium/kg/dose PO qid. RDA (elem Mg): 1-3 yo: 80 mg; 4-8 yo: 130 mg; 9-13 yo: 240 mg; 14-18 yo (males): 410 mg; 14-18 yo (females): 360 mg.
FORMS - OTC Generic: tab 500 mg, liquid 54 mg elem Mg/5 ml.
NOTES - 500 mg tabs of magnesium gluconate contain 27-29 mg elem magnesium. May cause diarrhea. Use caution in renal failure; may accumulate.

magnesium oxide (*Mag-200, Mag-Ox 400*) ▸K ♀A ▸+ $
ADULT - Dietary supplement: 400-800 mg PO qd. RDA (elem Mg): Adult males: 19-30 yo: 400 mg;>30 yo 420 mg. Adult females: 19-30 yo: 310 mg; >30yo: 320 mg.
PEDS - Not approved in children.
UNAPPROVED ADULT - Hypomagnesemia: 300 mg elem magnesium PO qid. Has also been used as oral tocolysis following IV magnesium sulfate and in the prevention of calcium-oxalate kidney stones.
UNAPPROVED PEDS - Hypomagnesemia: 10-20 mg elem magnesium/kg/dose PO qid. RDA (elem Mg): 1-3 yo: 80 mg; 4-8 yo: 130 mg; 9-13 yo: 240 mg; 14-18 yo (males): 410 mg; 14-18 yo (females): 360 mg.
FORMS - OTC Generic/Trade: cap 140,250, 400,420,500 mg.
NOTES - Magnesium oxide is approximately 60% elem magnesium. May accumulate in renal insufficiency.

magnesium sulfate ▸K ♀A ▸+ $
ADULT - Hypomagnesemia: mild deficiency: 1g IM q6h x 4 doses; severe deficiency: 2 g IV over 1 h (monitor for hypotension). Hyperalimentation: maintenance requirements not precisely known; adults generally require 8-24 mEq/day.
PEDS - Not approved in children.
UNAPPROVED ADULT - Has been used for inhibition of premature labor (tocolysis), as an adjunct in the treatment of acute asthma as a bronchodilator (1-2 g IV), to reduce early mortality when given ASAP after acute MI (controversial), and in chronic fatigue syndrome.
UNAPPROVED PEDS - Hypomagnesemia: 25-50 mg/kg IV/IM q6-8h for 3-4 doses, maximum single dose 2 g. Hyperalimentation: maintenance requirements not precisely known; infants require 2-10 mEq/day. Acute nephritis: 20-40 mg/kg (in 20% solution) IM prn. Has been used as an adjunct in the treatment of acute asthma as a bronchodilator.
NOTES - 1000 mg magnesium sulfate contains 8 mEq elem magnesium. Do not give faster than 1.5 ml/min (of 10% solution) except in eclampsia or seizures. Use caution in renal failure; may accumulate. Monitor urine output, patellar reflex, respiratory rate and serum magnesium level.

phosphorous (*Neutra-Phos, K-Phos*) ▸K ♀C ▸? $
ADULT - Dietary supplement: 1 cap/packet (Neutra-Phos) or 1-2 tab (K-Phos) dissolved in 75 ml water PO qid after meals and at bedtime. Severe hypophosphatemia (<1 mg/dl): 0.08-0.16 mmol/kg IV over 6 h. In TPN, 310-465 mg/day (10-15 mM) IV usually adequate, although higher amounts may be necessary in hypermetabolic states. RDA for adults is 700 mg.
PEDS - Normal daily requirements for elem phosphorous are: 0-6 mo: 300 mg; 6-12 mo: 500 mg; 1-10 yo: 800 mg; 15-18 yo: 1200 mg. Severe hypophosphatemia (< 1 mg/dl): 0.25-0.5 mmol/kg IV over 4-6 h. Infant TPN: 1.5-2 mmol/kg/day in TPN. RDA for children 1-3 yo: 460 mg; 4-8 yo: 500 mg; 9-18 yo: 1250 mg.
FORMS - OTC: Trade: (Neutra-Phos, Neutra-Phos K) tab/cap/packet 250 mg (8 mmol) phosphorous. Rx: Trade: (K-Phos) tab 250 mg (8 mmol) phosphorous.
NOTES - Dissolve caps/tabs/powder in water prior to ingestion.

POTASSIUM, oral forms

Liquids
20 mEq/15 ml: *Cena-K, Kaochlor 10%, Kay Ciel, Kaon*
40 mEq/15 ml: *Cena-K, Kaon-Cl 20%*
Powders
20 mEq/pack: *Kay Ciel, K-Lor, Klor-Con EF, Klorvess*
25 mEq/pack: *Klor-Con 25*
Effervescent Tablets
25 mEq: *K-Lyte Cl, Klor-Con, K-Vescent*
50 mEq: *K-Lyte DS, K-Lyte Cl 50*
Tablets/Capsules
8 mEq: *Klor-Con 8, Slow-K, Micro-K*
10 mEq: *Kaon-Cl 10, Klor-Con 10, Klotrix, K-Tab, K-Dur 10, Micro-K 10*
20 mEq: *K-Dur 20*

potassium ▶K ♀C ▶? $

ADULT - Treatment of hypokalemia: 20-40 mEq/day or more PO/IV. Intermittent infusion dose: 10-20 mEq/dose infused over 1-2 h prn. Hypokalemia prevention: 20-40 mEq/day PO qd-bid.

PEDS - Not approved in children.

UNAPPROVED ADULT - Diuretic-induced hypokalemia: 20-60 mEq/day PO.

UNAPPROVED PEDS - Treatment of hypokalemia: 2.5 mEq/kg/day given IV/PO qd-bid. Intermittent infusion dose: 0.5-1 mEq/kg/dose IV at 0.3-0.5 mEq/kg/h prn.

FORMS - Injectable, many different products in a variety of salt forms (i.e. chloride, bicarbonate, citrate, acetate, gluconate), available in Tabs, Caps, liquids, effervescent Tabs, and packets. Potassium gluconate available OTC.

NOTES - When hypokalemia is associated with alkalosis, use potassium chloride; when associated with acidosis, use potassium bicarbonate, citrate, acetate, or gluconate.

sodium ferric gluconate complex (*Ferrlecit*) ▶KL ♀B ▶? $$$$$

WARNING - Potentially fatal hypersensitivity reactions have been rarely reported with sodium ferric gluconate complex. Facilities for CPR must be available during dosing.

ADULT - Iron deficiency in chronic hemodialysis patients: 125 mg elem iron IV over 10 min or diluted in 100 ml NS IV over 1 h. Most hemodilaysis patients require 1 g of elem iron over 8 consecutive hemodialysis session.

PEDS - Not approved in children.

UNAPPROVED ADULT - Iron deficiency: 125 mg elem iron IV over 10 min or diluted in 100 ml NS IV over 1 hr.

NOTES - Serious hypotensive events in 1.3%.

PEDIATRIC REHYDRATION SOLUTIONS (ions in mEq/l)

Brand	*Glucose*	*Cal/l*	*Na*	*K*	*Cl*	*Citrate*	*Phos*	*Ca*	*Mg*
Lytren	20 g/l	80	50	25	45	30	0	0	0
Pedialyte	25 g/l	100	45	20	35	30	0	0	0
Rehydrate	25 g/l	100	75	20	65	30	0	0	0
Resol	20 g/l	80	50	20	50	34	5	4	4

ENDOCRINE & METABOLIC: Nutritionals

banana bag ▶KL ♀+ ▶+ $

UNAPPROVED ADULT - Alcoholic malnutrition (one formula): Add thiamine 100 mg + magnesium sulfate 2g + IV multivitamins to 1 liter NS and infuse over 4h. "Banana bag" is jargon and not a valid drug order; specify individual components.

fat emulsion (*Intralipid, Liposyn*) ▶L ♀C ▶? $$$$$

WARNING - Deaths have occurred in preterm infants after infusion of IV fat emulsions. Autopsy results showed intravascular fat accumulation in the lungs. Strict adherence to total daily dose and administration rate is mandatory. Premature and small for gestational age infants have poor clearance of IV fat emulsion. Monitor infant's ability to eliminate fat (i.e. triglycerides or plasma free fatty acid levels).

ADULT - Calorie and essential fatty acids source: As part of TPN, fat emulsion should comprise no more than 60% of total calories. Initial infusion rate 1 ml/min IV (10% fat emulsion) or 0.5 ml/min (20% fat emulsion) IV for first 15-30 min. If tolerated increase rate. If using 10% fat emulsioninfuse 500 ml first day and increase the following day. Maximum daily dose 2.5 g/kg. If using 20% fat emulsion, infuse 250 ml (Liposyn II) or 500 ml (Intralipid) first day and increase the following day. Maximum daily dose 3 g/day.

PEDS - Calorie and essential fatty acids source: As part of TPN, fat emulsion should comprise no more than 60% of total calories. Initial infusion rate 0.1 ml/min IV (10% fat emulsion) or 0.05 ml/min (20% fat emulsion) for first 10-15 min. If tolerated increase rate to 1 g/kg in 4 h. Max daily dose 3g/kg. For premature infants, start at 0.5 g/kg/day and increase based on infant's ability to eliminate fat.

NOTES - Do not use in patients with severe egg allergy; contains egg yolk phospholipids. Use caution in patients with severe liver disease, pulmonary disease, anemia, blood coagulation disorders, when there is the danger of fat embolism or in jaundiced or premature infants. Monitor CBC, blood coagulation, LFTs, plasma lipid profile and platelet count.

formulas - infant (*Enfamil, Similac, Isomil, Nursoy, Prosobee, Soyalac, Alsoy*) ▶L ♀+ ◗+ $

ADULT - Not used in adults.

PEDS - Infant meals.

FORMS - OTC: Milk-based (Enfamil, Silmilac, SMA) or soy-based (Isomil, Nursoy, Prosobee, Soyalac, Alsoy).

levocarnitine (*Carnitor*) ▶KL ♀B ◗? $$$$$

ADULT - Prevention of levocarnitine deficiency in dialysis patients: 10-20 mg/kg IV at each dialysis session. Titrate dose based on serum concentration.

PEDS - Prevention of deficiency in dialysis patients: 10-20 mg/kg IV at each dialysis session. Titrate dose based on serum concentration.

NOTES - Adverse neurophysiologic effects may occur with long term, high doses of oral levocarnitine in patients with renal dysfunction. Only the IV formulation is indicated in patients receiving hemodialysis.

omega-3-fatty acids (*Promega, Max EPA*) ▶L ♀- ◗? $

ADULT - Dietary supplement in patients at risk for early coronary artery disease: 1-2 cap PO tid with meals.

PEDS - Not approved in children.

UNAPPROVED ADULT - Adjunctive treatment in rheumatoid arthritis: 20 g/day PO. Psoriasis: 10-15 g/day PO. Prevention of early restenosis after coronary angioplasty in combination with dipyridamole and aspirin: 18 g/day PO.

FORMS - OTC Generic/Trade: cap 600,1000,1200 mg (with varying ratios of EPA:DHA).

NOTES - May increase bleeding time and inhibit platelet aggregation; use caution in patients receiving anticoagulants or aspirin. Monitor blood sugar in NIDDM patients.

rally pack ▶KL ♀C ◗- ?

UNAPPROVED ADULT - Alcoholic malnutrition: Add thiamine 100 mg + magnesium sulfate 2g + IV multivitamins to 1 liter NS and infuse over 4h. "Rally pack" is jargon and not a valid drug order; specify individual components.

ENDOCRINE & METABOLIC: Thyroid Agents

iodine (*Thyro-Block, Lugol's Solution*) ▶L ♀D ◗- $

WARNING - Do not use for obesity.

ADULT - Thyroidectomy preparation: 2-6 gtts (Lugol's) PO tid x 10 days prior to surgery. Thyroid storm: 1 ml (Lugol's) PO tid at least 1h after initial propylthiouracil or methimazole dose. Thyroid blocking in radiation emergency: 130 mg PO qd x 10 days or as directed by state health officials.

PEDS - Thyroid blocking in radiation emergency >1 yo: 130 mg PO qd x 10 days. <1 year of age: 65 mg PO qd x 10 days

FORMS - Trade: Tabs 130 mg. Soln (Lugol's).

NOTES - Tabs available to state and federal authorities only.

levothyroxine (*T4, Synthroid, Levoxyl, Levothroid, L-thyroxine*, ✤*Levotec, Eltroxin, Levo-T*) ▶L ♀A ◗? $

WARNING - Do not use for obesity.

ADULT - Hypothyroidism : Start 100-200 mcg PO qd (healthy adults) or 12.5-50 mcg PO qd (elderly or CV disease), increase by 12.5-25 mcg/day at 3-8 week intervals. Usual maintenance dose 100-200 mcg PO qd, max 300 mcg/day.

PEDS - Hypothyroidism 0-6 months: 8-10 mcg/kg/day PO; 6- 12 months: 6-8 mcg/kg/day PO; 1-5 yo: 5-6 mcg/kg/day PO; 6- 12 yo: 4-5 mcg/kg/day PO; > 12 yo: 2-3 mcg/kg/day PO, max 300 mcg/day.

UNAPPROVED ADULT - Hypothyroidism: 1.6 mcg/kg/day PO; start with lower doses (25 mcg PO qd) in elderly & those with cardiac disease.

FORMS - Generic/Trade: Tabs 25, 50, 75, 100, 125, 150, 200, 300 mcg. Trade only: Tabs 88, 112, 137, 175 mcg.

NOTES - May crush tabs for infants and ch

dren. May give IV or IM at ½ oral dose in adults and ½ - ¾ oral dose in children; then adjust based on tolerance and therapeutic response.

liothyronine (*T3, Cytomel*) ▸L ♀A ◗? $

WARNING - Do not use for obesity.

ADULT - Mild hypothyroidism: 25 mcg PO qd, increase by 12.5-25 mcg/day at 1-2 week intervals to desired response. Usual maintenance dose 25-75 mcg PO qd. Goiter: 5 mcg PO qd, increase by 5-10 mcg/day at 1-2 week intervals. Usual maintenance dose 75 mcg PO qd. Myxedema: 5 mcg PO qd, increase by 5-10 mcg/day at 1-2 week intervals. Usual maintenance dose 50-100 mcg/day.

PEDS - Congenital hypothyroidism: 5 mcg PO qd, increase by 5 mcg/day at 3-4 day intervals to desired response.

FORMS - Trade only: Tabs 5 mcg. Generic/Trade: Tabs 25, 50 mcg.

NOTES - Start therapy at 5 mcg/d in children & elderly and increase by 5 mcg increments only. Rapidly absorbed from the GI tract. Monitor T3 and TSH.

methimazole (*Tapazole*) ▸L ♀D ◗+ $$$

ADULT - Mild hyperthyroidism: 5 mg PO tid. Moderate hyperthyroidism: 10 mg PO tid. Severe hyperthyroidism: 20 mg PO tid (q8h intervals). Maintenance dose = 5- 30 mg/day.

PEDS - Hyperthyroidism: 0.4 mg/kg/day PO divided q8h. Maintenance dose = ½ initial dose, max 30 mg/day.

UNAPPROVED ADULT - Start 10-30 mg PO qd, then adjust.

FORMS - Generic/Trade: Tabs 5, 10 mg.

NOTES - Monitor CBC for evidence of marrow suppression if fever, sore throat, or other signs of infection. Propylthiouracil preferred over methimazole in pregnancy.

propylthiouracil (*PTU*) ▸L ♀D (but preferred over methimazole) ◗+ $

ADULT - Hyperthyroidism: 100-150 mg PO tid. Severe hyperthyroidism and/or large goiters: 200-400 mg PO tid. Continue initial dose for approximately 2 months. Adjust dose to desired response. Usual maintenance dose 100-150 mg/day. Thyroid storm: 200 mg PO q4-6h x 1 day, decrease dose gradually to usual maintenance dose.

PEDS - Hyperthyroidism in children age 6-10 yo: 50 mg PO qd-tid. Children ≥10 yo: 50-100 mg PO tid. Continue initial dose for 2 months, then maintenance dose is 1/3 to 2/3 intial dose.

UNAPPROVED PEDS - Hyperthyroidism in neonates: 5-10 mg/kg/day PO divided q8h. Children: 5-7 mg/kg/day PO divided q8h.

FORMS - Generic: Tabs 50 mg.

NOTES - Monitor CBC for evidence of marrow suppression if fever, sore throat, or other signs of infection. Propylthiouracil preferred over methimazole in pregnancy.

thyroid - dessicated (*Thyroid USP, Armour Thyroid*) ▸L ♀A ◗? $

WARNING - Do not use for obesity.

ADULT - Obsolete; use thyroxine instead. Hypothyroidism: Start 30 mg PO qd, increase by 15 mg/day at 2-3 week intervals to a maximum dose of 180 mg/day.

PEDS - Congenital hypothyroidism: 15 mg PO qd. Increase at 2 week intervals.

FORMS - Generic/Trade: Tabs 15,30,60,65,90, 120,180,300 mg. Trade only: Tabs 240 mg.

NOTES - 60 mg thyroid dessicated is roughly equivalent to 50-60 mcg thyroxine. Combination of levothyroxine (T4) and liothyronine (T3); content varies.

***Thyrolar* (liotrix, levothyroxine + liothyronine)** ▸L ♀A ◗? $

WARNING - Do not use for obesity.

ADULT - Hypothyroidism: 1 PO qd, starting with small doses initially (¼ - ½ strength), then increase at 2 week intervals.

PEDS - Not approved in children.

FORMS - Trade: Tabs T4/T3 12.5/3.1 (¼ strength), 25/6.25 (½ strength), 50/12.5 (#1), 100/25 (#2), 150/37.5 (#3) mcg.

NOTES - Combination of levothyroxine (T4) and liothyronine (T3).

ENDOCRINE & METABOLIC: Vitamins

ascorbic acid (*vitamin C*) ▸K ♀C ◗? $

ADULT - Prevention of scurvy: 70-150 mg/day PO. Treatment of scurvy: 300-1000 mg/day PO. RDA females: 75 mg/day; males: 90 mg/day. Smokers: add 35 mg/day more than nonsmokers.

PEDS - Prevention of scurvy: Infants: 30 mg/day PO. Treatment of scurvy: Infants: 100-300 mg/day PO. Adequate daily intake for infants 0-6 mo: 40 mg; 7-12 mo: 50 mg. RDA for children: 1-3 yo: 15 mg; 4-8 yo: 25 mg; 9-13 yo: 45 mg; 14-18 yo: 75 mg (males), 65 mg (females).

UNAPPROVED ADULT - Urinary acidification with methenamine: > 2 g/day PO. Idiopathic methemoglobinemia: 150 mg/day or more PO. Wound healing: 300-500 mg/day or more PO for 7-10 days. Severe burns: 1-2 g/day PO. High doses of vitamin C have been tried for the prevention of the common cold, treatment of asthma, atherosclerosis, schizophrenia, and cancer.

FORMS - OTC: Generic: tab 25,50,100,250, 500,1000 mg, chew tab 100,250,500 mg, time released tab 500 mg, 1000,1500 mg, time released cap 500 mg, lozenge 60 mg, liquid 35 mg/0.6 ml, oral solution 100 mg/ml, syrup 500 mg/5 ml.

NOTES - Use IV/IM/SC ascorbic acid for acute deficiency or when oral absorption is uncertain. Avoid excessive doses in diabetics, patients prone to renal calculi, those undergoing stool occult blood tests (may cause false-negative), those on sodium restricted diets and those taking anticoagulants (may decrease INR). Doses in adults >2 g/day may cause osmotic diarrhea.

calcitriol (*Rocaltrol, Calcijex*) ▸L ♀C ◗? $$

ADULT - Hypocalcemia in chronic renal dialysis: 0.25 mcg PO qd, increase by 0.25 mcg every 4-8 weeks until normocalcemia achieved, or 1-2 mcg, 3 times a week IV, increase dose by 0.5-1 mcg every 2-4 weeks until normocalcemia achieved. Most hemodialysis patients require 0.5-1 mcg/day PO. Hyperparathyroidism: 0.25 mcg PO qd; increase dose in 2-4 weeks if inadequate response. Secondary hyperparathyroidism in predialysis patients: 0.25 mcg/day PO.

PEDS - Hyperparathyroidism 1-5 yo: 0.25-0.75 mcg PO qd; >6 yo: 0.5-2 mcg PO qd. Secondary hyperparathyroidism in predialysis patients > 3 yo: 10-15 ng/kg/day PO.

UNAPPROVED ADULT - Psoriatic vulgaris: 0.5 mcg/day PO or 0.5 mcg/g petrolatum topically qd.

FORMS - Trade only: cap 0.25,0.5 mcg, oral soln 1mcg/ml.

NOTES - Calcitriol is the activated form of vitamin D. During titration period, monitor serum calcium at least twice weekly.

cyanocobalamin (*vitamin B12, Nascobal*) ▸K ♀C ◗+ $

ADULT - Nutritional deficiency: 25-250 mcg/day PO or 500 mcg intranasal weekly. Nutritional deficiency due to malabsorption (i.e. pernicious anemia): 100 mcg IM/SC qd, for 6-7 days, then qod for 7 doses, then q 3-4 days for 2-3 weeks, then q month. Others with B12 deficiency: 30 mcg IM qd for 5-10 days, then 100-200 mcg IM q month. RDA for adults is 2.4 mcg.

PEDS - Nutritional deficiency: Hematologic signs: 10-50 mcg/day IM/SC for 5-10 days, then 100-250 mcg/dose every 2-4 weeks; Neurologic signs: 100 mcg/day IM/SC for 10-15 days, then 1-2 times/week for several months, then tapering to 250-1000 mcg monthly. Adequate daily intake for infants: 0-5 mo: 0.4 mcg; 6-11 mo: 0.5 mcg. RDA for children: 1-3 yo: 0.9 mcg; 4-8 yo: 1.2 mcg; 9-13 yo: 1.8 mcg; 14-18 yo: 2.4 mcg.

UNAPPROVED ADULT - Prevention and treatment of cyanide toxicity associated with nitroprusside.

UNAPPROVED PEDS - Prevention and treatment of cyanide toxicity associated with nitroprusside.

FORMS - OTC Generic: tab 25,50,100,250 mcg. RX Trade only: nasal gel 500 mcg/0.1 ml.

NOTES - Pricing for nasal form (Nascobal) is $$$. Although official dose for deficiency states is 100-200 mcg IM q month, some give 1000 mcg IM periodically. Oral therapy is usually not recommended for pernicious anemia. The maximum amount that can be absorbed from a single oral dose is 1-5 mcg. The percent absorbed decreases with increasing doses.

dihydrotachysterol (*vitamin D, DHT*) ▸L ♀C ◗? $$

ADULT - Treatment of acute, chronic, and latent forms of postoperative tetany, idiopathic tetany and hypoparathyoidism: Initial dose 0.75-2.5 mg PO qd for several days, then maintenance dose of 0.2-1.75 mg PO qd to maintain normocalcemia.

PEDS - Safe dosing exceeding the RDA and in children undergoing dialysis has not been established.

UNAPPROVED PEDS - Hypoparathyoidism: Neonates: 0.05-0.1 mg PO qd. Infants and young children: 0.1-0.5 mg PO qd. Older children: 0.5-1 mg PO qd. Nutritional rickets: 0.5 mg PO for 1 dose or 13-50 mcg/day PO until healing occurs. Renal osteodystrophy: 0.125-0.5 mg PO qd.

FORMS - Generic: tab 0.125,0.2, 0.4 mg, cap 0.125 mg, oral solution 0.2 mg/ml.

NOTES - Monitor serum calcium. Dose may be supplemented with calcium therapy.

doxercalciferol (*Hectorol*) ▸L ♀C ◗? $$$$

ADULT - Secondary hyperparathyroidism in dialysis patients: Initial dose 10 mcg PO or 4 mcg IV three times a week.

PEDS - Not approved in children.

FORMS - Trade only: cap 2.5 mcg.

NOTES - Monitor PTH, serum calcium and

phosphorus weekly during dose titration.

folic acid (*folate, Folvite*) ▶K ♀A ◗+ $

ADULT - Megaloblastic anemia: 1 mg PO/IM/IV/SC qd. When symptoms subside and CBC normalizes, give maintenance dose of 0.4 mg/day and 0.8 mg/day in pregnant and lactating females. RDA for adults 0.4 mg, 0.6 mg for pregnant females, and 0.5 mg for lactating women. Max recommended daily dose 1 mg.

PEDS - Megaloblastic anemia: 0.5-1 mg PO qd. Maintenance dose for infants is 0.1 mg/day, and up to 0.3 mg/day for children < 4 yo. Adequate daily intake for infants: 0-5 mo: 65 mcg; 6-11 mo: 80 mcg. RDA for children: 1-3 yo: 150 mcg; 4-8 yo: 200 mcg; 9-13 yo: 300 mcg, 14-18 yo: 400 mcg.

FORMS - OTC Generic: tab 0.4,0.8 mg. Rx generic 1 mg.

NOTES - Folic acid doses > 0.1 mg may obscure pernicious anemia. Prior to conception all women should receive 0.4 mg/day to reduce the risk of neural tube defects in infants. Consider high dose (up to 4 mg) in women with prior history of infant with neural tube defect. Use oral route except in cases of severe intestinal absorption.

multivitamins (*MVI*) ▶LK ♀+ ◗+ $

ADULT - Dietary supplement: Dose varies by product.

PEDS - Dietary supplement: Dose varies by product.

FORMS - OTC & Rx: Many different brands and forms available with and without iron (tab, cap, chew tab, drops, liquid).

NOTES - Do not take within 2 h of antacids, tetracyclines, levothyroxine or fluoroquinolones.

niacin (*vitamin B3, Niacor, Slo-Niacin, Niaspan*) ▶K ♀C ◗? $

ADULT - Niacin deficiency: 100 mg PO qd. Pellegra: up to 500 mg PO qd. RDA is 16 mg for males and 14 mg for females. See cardiovascular section for lipid-lowering dose.

PEDS - Safety and efficacy in children have not been established in doses which exceed nutritional requirements. Adequate daily intake for infants: 0-5 mo: 2 mg; 6-11mo: 3 mg. RDA for children: 1-3 yo: 6 mg; 48 yo: 8 mg; 9-13 yo: 12 mg; 14-18 yo: 16 mg (males) and 14 mg (females).

FORMS - OTC: Generic: tab 50,100,250,500 mg, timed release cap 125,250, 400 mg, timed release tab 250, 500 mg, liquid 50 mg/5 ml. Trade: 250,500,750 mg (Slo-Niacin). Rx: Trade only: tab 500 mg (Niacor), timed release cap 500 mg, timed release tab 500,750,1000 mg (Niaspan, $$).

NOTES - Begin with small doses and increase gradually to minimize adverse effects. May cause flushing, usually within 2 h of ingestion; pretreat with 325 mg aspirin 30-60 min prior to niacin ingestion. Use caution in diabetics, patients with gout, peptic ulcer, liver, gallbladder or coronary disease.

paricalcitol (*Zemplar*) ▶L ♀C ◗? $$$$$

ADULT - Prevention/treatment of secondary hyperparathyroidism with CRF: Initially 0.04-0.1 mcg/kg (2.8-7.0 mcg) IV 3 times/week during dialysis. Can increase dose based on PTH at 2-4 week intervals. Max dose 16.8 mcg (0.24 mcg/kg).

PEDS - Not approved in children.

NOTES - Monitor serum PTH, calcium and phosphorous.

phytonadione (*vitamin K, Mephyton, AquaMephyton*) ▶L ♀C ◗+ $

WARNING - Severe reactions, including fatalities, have occurred during and immediately after IV injection, even with diluted injection and slow administration. Restrict IV use to situations where other routes of administration are not feasible.

ADULT - Anticoagulant-induced prothrombin deficiency: Dose varies based on INR. INR 5-9: 1-2.5 mg PO (2-4 mg PO may be given if rapid reversal necessary); INR > 9 with no bleeding: 3-5 mg PO; INR> 20: 10 mg slow IV. Hypoprothrombinemia due to other causes: 2.5-25 mg PO/IM/SC. Adequate daily intake 120 mcg (males) and 90 mcg (females).

PEDS - Hemorhagic disease of the newborn: Prophylaxis: 0.5-1 mg IM 1 hr after birth; Treatment: 1 mg SC/IM.

FORMS - Trade only: tab 5 mg.

NOTES - Excessive doses of vitamin K in a patient receiving warfarin may cause warfarin resistance for up to a week. Avoid IM administration in patients with a high INR.

pyridoxine (*vitamin B6*) ▶K ♀A ◗? $

ADULT - Dietary deficiency: 10-20 mg PO qd for 3 weeks. Prevention of deficiency due to isoniazid in high-risk patients: 10-25 mg PO qd. Treatment of neuropathies due to INH: 50-200 mg PO qd. INH overdose (>10 g): Give an equal amount of pyridoxine: 4 g IV followed by 1 g IM q 30 min. RDA for adults: 19-50 yo: 1.3 mg; > 50 yo: 1.7 mg (males), 1.5 mg (females). Max recommended: 100 mg/day.

PEDS - Not approved in children. Adequate daily intake for infants: 0-5 mo: 0.1 mg; 5-11 mo: 0.3 mg. RDA for children: 1-3 yo: 0.5 mg;

4-8 yo: 0.6 mg; 9-13 yo: 1 mg; 14-18 yo: 1.3 (boys) and 1.2 mg (girls).

UNAPPROVED ADULT - PMS: 50-500 mg/day PO. Hyperoxaluria type I and oxalate kidney stones: 25-300 mg/day PO. Prevention of oral contraceptive-induced deficiency; 25-40 mg PO qd. Pregnancy hyperemesis: 10-50 mg PO q8h. Has been used in hydrazine poisoning.

UNAPPROVED PEDS - Dietary deficiency: 5-10 mg PO qd for 3 weeks. Prevention of deficiency due to isoniazid: 1-2 mg/kg/day PO qd. Treatment of neuropathies due to INH: 10-50 mg PO qd. Pryridoxine-dependent epilepsy: neonatal: 25-50 mg/dose IV; older infants and children: 100 mg/dose IV for 1 dose then 100 mg PO qd.

FORMS - OTC Generic: tab 25,50,100 mg, timed release tab 100 mg.

riboflavin (*vitamin B2*) ▶K ♀A ▶+ $

ADULT - Deficiency: 5-25 mg/day PO. RDA for adults is 1.3 mg (males) and 1.1 mg (females), 1.4 mg for pregnant women and 1.6 mg for lactating women.

PEDS - Deficiency: 5-10 mg/day PO. Adequate daily intake for infants: 0-5 mo: 0.3 mg; 5-11 mo: 0.4 mg. RDA for children: 1-3 yo: 0.5 mg; 4-8 yo: 0.6 mg; 9-13 yo: 0.9 mg; 14-18 yo: 1.3 mg (males) and 1.0 mg (females).

UNAPPROVED ADULT - Prevention of migraine headaches: 400 mg PO qd.

FORMS - OTC Generic: tab 25,50,100 mg.

NOTES - May cause yellow/orange discoloration of urine.

thiamine (*vitamin B1*) ▶K ♀A ▶? $

ADULT - Beriberi: 10-20 mg IM 3 times/week for 2 weeks. Wet beriberi with myocardial infarction: 10-30 mg IV tid. Wernicke encephalopathy: 50-100 mg IV and 50-100 mg IM for 1 dose then 50-100 mg IM qd until patient resumes normal diet. Give before starting glucose. RDA for adults is 1.2 mg (males) and 1.1 mg (females).

PEDS - Beriberi: 10-25 mg IM qd or 10-50 mg PO qd for 2 weeks then 5-10 mg PO qd for 1 month. Adequate daily intake infants: 0-5 mo: 0.2 mg; 5-11 mo: 0.3 mg. RDA for children: 1-3 yo: 0.5 mg; 4-8 yo: 0.6 mg; 9-13 yo: 0.9 mg; 14-18 yo: 1.2 mg (males), 1.0 mg (females).

UNAPPROVED ADULT - Oral thiamine has been studied as a mosquito repellant.

FORMS - OTC Generic: tab 50,100,250,500 mg, enteric coated tab 20 mg.

tocopherol (*vitamin E*) ▶L ♀A ▶? $

ADULT - RDA is 22 units (natural, d-alpha-tochopherol) or 33 units (synthetic, d,l-alpha-tochopherol) or 15 mg (alpha-tocopherol). Max receommended 1000 mg (alpha-tocopherol).

PEDS - Adequate daily intake (alpha-tocopherol): infants 0-5 mo: 4 mg; 6-12 mo: 6 mg. RDA for children (alpha-tocopherol): 1-3 yo: 6 mg; 4-8 yo: 7 mg; 9-13 yo: 11 mg; 14-18 yo: 15 mg.

UNAPPROVED ADULT - Antioxidant: 400-800 units PO qd. Alzheimer's disease: 1000 units PO bid. Has been used in cancer, skin conditions, Parkinson's disease, tardive dyskinesia, nocturnal leg cramps, sexual dysfunction, heart disease, aging, PMS, and to increase athletic performance.

UNAPPROVED PEDS - Has been used to reduce the toxic effects of oxygen on the lung parenchyma and retina in premature babies and to prevent hemolytic anemia and prevent periventricular hemorrhage.

FORMS - OTC Generic: tab 200,400 units, cap 73.5, 100, 147, 165, 200, 330, 400, 500, 600, 1000 units, drops 50 mg/ml.

NOTES - Natural vitamin E (d-alpha-tochopherol) recommended over synthetic (d,l-alpha-tocopherol). Large randomized trials have failed to confirm convincing cardioprotective effect. Do not exceed 1500 units natural vit E/day. Higher doses may increase bleeding risk.

vitamin A ▶L ♀A (C if exceed RDA, X in high doses) ▶+ $

ADULT – Deficiency treatment: 100,000 units IM qd x 3 days, then 50,000 units IM qd x 2 weeks. RDA: 1000 mcg RE (males), 800 mcg RE (females). Max recommended daily dose in non-deficiency 3000 mcg.

PEDS - Treatment of deficiency states: Infants: 7,500 - 15,000 units IM qd x 10 days; children 1-8 yo: 17,500 - 35,000 units IM qd x 10 days. Kwashiorkor: 30 mg IM of water miscible palmitate followed by 5,000-10,000 units PO qd x 2 months. Xerophthalmia: > 1 yo: 110 mg retinyl palmitate PO or 55 mg IM plus 110 mg PO the following day. Administer another 110 mg PO prior to discharge. Vitamin E (40 IU) should be co-administered to increase efficacy of retinol.

UNAPPROVED ADULT - Acne: 100,000 - 300,000 units PO qd (efficacy not established). Test for fat absorption: 7000 IU/kg (2100 RE/kg) PO x 1. Measure serum vitamin A concentrations at baseline and 4 hr after ingestion. Dermatologic disorders such as follicularis keratosis: 50,000 - 500,000 units PO qd x several weeks. Has been tried in promyelocytic leukemia, diminishing malignant cell growth, enhancing immune system, and prevention of lung cancer and cardiovascular disease.

UNAPPROVED PEDS - Has been tried in reduction of malaria episodes in children > 12 mo and to reduce the mortality in HIV-infected children.
FORMS - OTC: Generic: cap 10,000, 15,000 units. Trade: tab 5,000 units. Rx: Generic: 25,000 units. Trade: soln 50,000 IU/ml.
NOTES - 1 RE (retinol equivalent) = 1 mcg retinol or 6 mcg beta-carotene.

vitamin D (*vitamin D2, ergocalciferol*) ▶L ♀A (C if exceed RDA) ◗+ $
ADULT - Osteomalacia: 25-125 mcg PO qd. Familial hypophosphatemia: 250-1500 mcg PO qd. Hypoparathyroidism: 0.625-5 mg PO qd. Anticonvulsant-induced osteomalacia: 50-1250 mcg PO qd. Adequate daily intake adults: 19-50 yo: 5 mcg (200 units); 51-70 yo: 10 mcg (400 units; > 70 yo: 15 mcg (600 units). Max recommended daily dose in non-deficiency 50 mcg (2000 units).
PEDS - Adequate daily intake infants and children: 5 mcg (200 units) . Hypoparathyroidism: 1.25-5 mg PO qd.
UNAPPROVED ADULT - Osteoporosis prevention: 10-20 mcg (400-800 units) PO qd with calcium supplements. Fanconi syndrome: 1.25-5 mg PO qd.
UNAPPROVED PEDS - Fanconi syndrome: 6.25-1250 mcg PO qd.
FORMS - OTC: Generic: 400 units. Rx: Trade: cap 50,000 units,soln 8000 units/ml.
NOTES - 1 mcg ergocalciferol = 40 units vitamin D. IM therapy may be necessary if malabsorption exists.

ENDOCRINE & METABOLIC: Other

bromocriptine (*Parlodel*) ▶L ♀B ◗- $$$$
ADULT - Start 1.25-2.5 mg PO qhs with food, increase q3-7 days, usual effective dose 2.5-15 mg/day, max 40 mg/day (hyperprolactinemia) or 20-30 mg/day, max 100 mg/day (acromegaly). Doses >20 mg/day have been divided bid. Take with food to minimize dizzines and nausea.
PEDS - Not approved in children.
UNAPPROVED ADULT - Hyperprolactinemia: 2.5-7.5 mg vaginally qd if GI intolerance to PO dose.
FORMS - Generic/Trade: Tabs 2.5 mg. Caps 5 mg.
NOTES - Seizures, stroke, HTN, and MI have been reported. Should not be used for postpartum lactation suppression. Monitor serum prolactin levels.

cabergoline (*Dostinex*) ▶L ♀B ◗- $$$$$
ADULT - Hyperprolactinemia: initiate therapy with 0.25 mg PO twice weekly. Increase by 0.25 mg twice weekly at 4 week intervals up to a maximum of 1 mg twice weekly.
PEDS - Not approved in children.
FORMS - Trade: Tabs 0.5 mg.
NOTES - Monitor serum prolactin levels. Use caution in hepatic insufficiency.

calcitonin-salmon (*Calcimar, Miacalcin, ✤Caltine*) ▶Plasma ♀C ◗? $$$
ADULT - Osteoporosis: 100 units SC/IM qd or 200 units intranasal qd (alternate nostrils). Paget's disease: 50-100 units SC/IM qd or 3 times weekly. Hypercalcemia: 4 units/kg SC/IM q12h. May increase after 2 days to maximum of 8 units/kg q6h.
PEDS - Not approved in children.
UNAPPROVED PEDS - Osteogenesis imperfecta age 6 mos-15 yo: 2 units/kg SC/IM three times weekly with oral calcium supplements.
FORMS - Trade: nasal spray 200 units/activation in 2 ml bottle (minimum of 14 doses/bottle).
NOTES - Skin test before using injectable product: 1 unit intradermally and observe for local reaction.

cosyntropin (*Cortrosyn*, *✤Synacthen*) ▶L ♀C ◗? $
ADULT - Rapid screen for adrenocortical insufficiency: 0.25 mg IM/ IV over 2 min; measure serum cortisol before & 30-60 min after.
PEDS - Rapid screen for adrenocortical insufficiency: 0.25 mg (0.125 mg if <2 yo) IM/IV over 2 min; measure serum cortisol before & 30-60 min after.

desmopressin (*DDAVP, Stimate*, *✤Octostim*) ▶LK ♀B ◗? $$$$
ADULT - Diabetes insipidus: 10-40 mcg (0.1-0.4 ml) intransally qd -tid. or 0.05-1.2 mg PO daily or divided bid-tid. or 0.5-1 ml (2-4 mcg) SC/IV daily in 2 divided doses.
PEDS - Diabetes insipidus 3 mo-12 yo: 5-30 mcg (0.05-0.3 ml) intranasally qd-bid or 0.05 mg PO qd.
FORMS - Trade only: Tabs 0.1, 0.2 mg. nasal solution 1.5 mg/ml (150 mcg/ spray). Generic/Trade: nasal solution 0.1 mg/ml (10 mcg/ spray). Note difference in concentration of nasal solutions.

NOTES - Monitor serum sodium. Prime the nasal spray pump. IV/SC doses are approximately 1/10th the intranasal dose.

growth hormone human (*Protropin, Genotropin, Norditropin, Nutropin, Humatrope, Serostim, Saizen*) ▶K ♀B/C ▶? $$$$$

ADULT - Somatotropin deficiency syndrome (Humatrope): 0.006 mg/kg/day SC. Maximum dose = 0.0125 mg/kg/day. AIDS wasting or cachexia (Serostim): > 55 kg = 6 mg SC qhs, 45-55 kg = 5 mg SC qhs, 35-45 kg = 4 mg SC qhs, < 35 kg = 0.1 mg/kg SC qhs.

PEDS - Growth failure: doses vary according to product used. Turner syndrome (Nutropin, Humatrope): 0.375 mg/kg/week SC divided into 3-7 equal doses.

FORMS - Single dose vials (powder for injection with diluent).

raloxifene (*Evista*) ▶L ♀X ▶- $$$

ADULT - Postmenopausal osteoporosis prevention and treatment: 60 mg PO qd.

PEDS - Not approved in children.

FORMS - Trade: Tabs 60 mg.

NOTES - Hot flashes and leg cramps may occur. Contraindicated if history of DVT. Discontinue use 72 h prior to and during prolonged immobilization because of increased DVT risk. Interactions with warfarin and cholestyramine.

sevelamer (*Renagel*) ▶Not absorbed ♀C ▶? $$$$

ADULT - Hyperphosphatemia: 800-1600 mg PO tid with meals, adjust according to serum phosphorus concentration.

PEDS - Not approved in children.

FORMS - Trade: Caps 403 mg. Tabs 400, 800 mg.

NOTES - Titrate by one tab/cap per meal at 2 week intervals to keep phosphorus ≤6 mg/dl.

sodium polystyrene sulfonate (*Kayexalate*) ▶Fecal excretion ♀C ▶? $$$$

ADULT - Hyperkalemia: 15 g PO qd- qid or 30-50 g retention enema (in sorbitol) q6h prn. Retain for 30 minutes to several h. Irrigate with tap water after enema to prevent necrosis.

PEDS - Hyperkalemia: 1 g/kg PO q6h.

UNAPPROVED PEDS - Hyperkalemia: 1 g/kg PR q2-6h.

FORMS - Generic: suspension 15 g/ 60 ml. Powdered resin.

NOTES - 1 g binds approximately 1 mEq of potassium. Give powdered resin with a suitable laxative (e.g. sorbitol).

spironolactone (*Aldactone*) ▶LK ♀D ▶? $

ADULT - Primary hyperaldosteronism, maintenance therapy: 100-400 mg/day PO until surgery or indefinitely if surgery not an option.

UNAPPROVED ADULT - Hirsutism: 50-200 mg PO daily, maximal regression of hirsutism in 6 months.

FORMS - Generic/Trade: Tabs 25,50,100 mg.

NOTES - May cause menstrual irregularities.

tamoxifen (*Nolvadex*, ✤*Tamofen, Tamone*) ▶L ♀D ▶- $$$$

ADULT - Breast cancer: 10-20 mg PO bid x 5 years. Breast cancer prevention: 20 mg PO qd x 5 years.

PEDS - Not approved in children.

UNAPPROVED ADULT - Mastalgia: 10 mg PO qd x 4 months. Anovulation: 5-40 mg PO bid x 4 days.

FORMS - Generic/Trade: Tabs 10,20 mg.

NOTES - Use with caution in women with history of DVT. Safe for use in male breast cancer. Interacts with warfarin. May cause hot flashes. Increased risk of endometrial cancer.

vasopressin (*Pitressin*, ✤*Pressyn*) ▶LK ♀C ▶? $$$$$

ADULT - Diabetes insipidus: 5-10 units IM/SC bid-qid prn

PEDS - Diabetes insipidus: 2.5-10 units IM/SC bid-qid prn.

UNAPPROVED PEDS - Growth hormone and corticotropin provocative test: 0.3 units/kg IM, max 10 units. GI hemorrhage: start 0.002-0.005 units/kg/min IV, increase prn to 0.01 units/kg/min.

NOTES - Monitor serum sodium. Injectable form may be given intranasally.

ENT: Antihistamines - Nonsedating

NOTE: Antihistamines ineffective when treating the common cold.

fexofenadine (*Allegra*) ▶LK ♀C ▶? $$$

ADULT - Allergic rhinitis: 60 mg PO bid or 180 mg PO qd. Urticaria: 60 mg PO bid; 60 mg PO qd if decreased renal function.

PEDS - Allergic rhinitis, urticaria: 6-12 yo: 30 mg PO bid; 30 mg PO qd if decreased renal function.

FORMS - Trade: Tabs 30, 60, & 180 mg. Caps 60 mg.

NOTES - Avoid taking with fruit juice due to a large decrease in bioavailability.

loratadine (*Claritin*) ▶LK ♀B ▶+ $$$

ADULT - Allergic rhinitis/urticaria: 10 mg PO qd.
PEDS - Allergic rhinitis/urticaria ≥6 yo: use adult dose. 2-5 yo: 5 mg PO qd (syrup).
FORMS - Trade: Tabs 10 mg, fast-dissolve Reditabs 10 mg. Syrup 1 mg/ml.
NOTES - Decrease dose in liver failure or renal insufficiency. Reditabs dissolve on tongue without water.

ENT: Antihistamines - Sedating

NOTES: Antihistamines ineffective when treating the common cold. Contraindicated in narrow angle glaucoma, BPH, stenosing peptic ulcer disease, & bladder obstruction. Use half the normal dose in the elderly. May cause drowsiness and/or sedation, which may be enhanced with alcohol, sedatives, tranquilizers, etc.

azatadine (*Optimine*) ▶LK ♀B ▶- $$$
ADULT - Allergic rhinitis/urticaria: 1-2 mg PO bid.
PEDS - Allergic rhinitis/urticaria age ≥12 yo: 1-2 mg PO bid.
FORMS - Trade: Tabs 1 mg, scored.

cetirizine (*Zyrtec*, *✱Reactine*) ▶LK ♀B ▶- $$$
ADULT - Allergic rhinitis/urticaria: 5-10 mg PO qd.
PEDS - Allergic rhinitis/urticaria: 6-11 yo: use adult dose. 2-5 yo: 2.5 mg PO qd-bid.
FORMS - Trade: Tabs 5, 10 mg. Syrup 5 mg/5 ml.
NOTES - Decrease dose in renal or hepatic impairment.

chlorpheniramine (*Chlor-Trimeton, Chlo-Amine, Aller-Chlor*) ▶LK ♀B ▶- $
ADULT - Allergic rhinitis: 4 mg PO q4-6h. 8 mg PO q8-12h (timed release) or 12 mg PO q12h (timed release), max 24 mg/day.
PEDS - Allergic rhinitis ≥12 yo: use adult dose. 6-11 yo: 2 mg PO q4-6h, max 12 mg/day.
UNAPPROVED PEDS - Allergic rhinitis 2-5yo: 1 mg PO q4-6h, max 6 mg/day. Timed release 6-11 yo: 8 mg PO q12h prn.
FORMS - OTC: Trade: Tabs chew 2 mg. Generic/Trade: Tabs 4 mg. Syrup 2 mg/5 ml. Generic/Trade: Tabs, Timed-release 8 mg. Trade only: Tabs, Timed-release 12 mg.

clemastine (*Tavist*) ▶LK ♀B ▶- $
ADULT - Allergic rhinitis: 1.34 mg PO bid, max 8.04 mg/day. Urticaria/angioedema: 2.68 mg PO qd-tid, max 8.04 mg/day.
PEDS - Allergic rhinitis ≥12 yo: use adult dose. 6-12 yo: 0.67 mg PO bid, max 4.02 mg/day. Urticaria/angioedema ≥12 yo: use adult dose. 6-12 yo: 1.34 mg PO bid, max 4.02 mg/day.
UNAPPROVED PEDS - Allergic rhinitis < 6yo: 0.05 mg/kg/day (as clemastine base) PO divided bid-tid; max dose: 1 mg/day.
FORMS - OTC: Generic/Trade: Tabs 1.34 mg. Rx; Generic/Trade: Tabs 2.68 mg. Trade only: Syrup 0.67 mg/5 ml.
NOTES - 1.34 mg = 1 mg clemastine base

cyproheptadine (*Periactin*) ▶LK ♀B ▶- $
ADULT - Allergic rhinitis/urticaria: Start 4 mg PO tid, usual effective dose is 12-16 mg/day, max 32 mg/day.
PEDS - Allergic rhinitis/urticaria: 2-6 yo: Start 2 mg PO bid-tid, max 12 mg/day; 7-14 yo: Start 4 mg PO bid-tid, max 16 mg/day.
UNAPPROVED ADULT - Appetite stimulant: 2-4 mg PO tid 1h ac. Prevention of cluster headache 4 mg PO qid.
FORMS - Generic/Trade: Tabs 4 mg (trade scored). Syrup 2 mg/5 ml.

dexchlorpheniramine maleate (*Polaramine*) ▶LK ♀? ▶- $$
ADULT - Allergic rhinitis/urticaria: 2 mg PO q4-6h. Timed release tabs: 4 or 6 mg PO at qhs or q8-10h.
PEDS - Immediate Release tabs & syrup: ≥ 12 years: use adult dose. 6-11 yo: 1 mg PO q4-6h. 2-5 yo: 0.5 mg PO q4-6h. Timed Release Tabs: 6-12 yo: 4 mg PO qd, preferably at qhs.
FORMS - Trade: Tabs, Immediate Release 2 mg. Syrup 2 mg/5 ml. Generic/Trade: Tabs, Timed Release: 4, 6 mg.

diphenhydramine (*Benadryl*, *✱Allerdryl, Allernix*) ▶LK ♀B(- in 1st trimester) ▶- $
ADULT - Allergic rhinitis, urticaria, hypersensitivity reactions: 25-50 mg PO/IM/IV q4-6h, max 300-400 mg/day. Motion sickness: 25-50 mg PO pre-exposure & q4-6h prn. Drug-induced Parkinsonism: 10-50 mg IV/IM. Antitussive: 25 mg PO q4h, max 100 mg/day.
PEDS - Hypersensitivity reactions: ≥12 yo: use adult dose. 6-11 yo: 12.5-25 mg PO q4-6h or 5 mg/kg/day PO/IV/IM divided qid, max 150 mg/day. Antitussive (syrup): 6-12 yo 12.5 mg PO q4h, max 50 mg/day. 2-5 yo 6.25 mg PO q4h, max 25 mg/day.
FORMS - OTC: Trade: Tabs 25, 50 mg, chew tabs 12.5 mg. OTC & Rx: Generic/Trade: Caps 25, 50 mg, softgel cap 25 mg. OTC: Generic/Trade: Liquid 6.25 mg/5 ml & 12.5 mg/5 ml.

hydroxyzine (*Atarax, Vistaril*) ▶L ♀C ▶- $
ADULT - Pruritus: 25-100 mg IM/PO qd-qid or prn.
PEDS - Pruritus: < 6 yo: 50 mg/day PO divided qid; ≥ 6 yo: 50-100 mg/day PO divided qid.
FORMS - Generic/Trade: Tabs 10, 25, 50. Trade only: 100 mg. Generic/Trade: Caps 25, 50, 100 mg. Syrup 10 mg/5 ml (Atarax). Trade: Suspension 25 mg/5 ml (Vistaril).
NOTES - Atarax (hydrochloride salt), Vistaril (pamoate salt).

promethazine (*Phenergan*) ▶LK ♀C ▶- $
ADULT - Hypersensitivity reactions: 25 mg IM/IV, may repeat in 2 hours. Allergic conditions: 12.5 mg PO/PR/IM/IV qid or 25 mg PO/PR qhs.
PEDS - Hypersensitivity reactions: > 2 yo: 6.25-12.5 mg PO/PR/IM/IV q6h prn.
FORMS - Trade: Tabs 12.5 mg, scored. Generic/Trade: Tabs 25, 50 mg. Syrup 6.25 mg/5 ml. Trade only: Phenergan Fortis Syrup 25 mg/5 ml. Trade: Suppositories 12.5 & 25 mg. Generic/Trade: Suppositories 50 mg.
NOTES - Inject IV at ≤25 mg/min.

ENT: Antitussives / Expectorants

benzonatate (*Tessalon, Tessalon Perles*) ▶L ♀C ▶? $
ADULT - Cough: 100-200 mg PO tid, max 600 mg/day.
PEDS - >10 yo: use adult dose.
FORMS - Generic: Caps, softgel 100,200 mg. Trade: Perles 100 mg. Caps 200 mg.
NOTES - Swallow whole. Do not chew. Numbs mouth, possible choking hazard.

dextromethorphan (*Benylin, Delsym, Vick's*) ▶L ♀+ ▶+ $
ADULT - Cough: 10- 20 mg PO q4h or 30 mg PO q6-8h; 60 mg PO q12h (Delsym).
PEDS - Cough >12 yo: use adult dose; 6-12 yo: 5-10 mg PO q4h or 15 mg PO q6-8h; 30 mg PO q12h (sustained action liquid). 2-5 yo: 2.5-5 mg PO q4h or 7.5 mg PO q6-8h; 15 mg PO q12h (sustained action liquid).
FORMS - OTC: Trade: Caps 30 mg. Lozenges 2.5, 5, 7.5, 15 mg. Liquid 3.5, 5, 7.5, 10, 12.5, 15 mg/5 ml; 10 & 15 mg/15 ml (Generic/Trade). Trade (Delsym): Sustained action liquid 30 mg/5 ml.

guaifenesin (*Robitussin, Humibid LA, Hytuss, Guiatuss, Fenesin, Guaifenex LA*) ▶L ♀C ▶+ $
ADULT - Expectorant: 100-400 mg PO q4h or 600-1200 mg PO q12h (extended release), max 2.4g/day.
PEDS - Expectorant >12 yo: use adult dose. 6-11 yo: 100-200 mg PO q4h or 600 mg PO q12h (extended release), max 1.2g/day. 2-5 yo: 50-100 mg PO q4h or 300 mg PO q12h (extended release), max 600 mg/day.
FORMS - OTC: Trade: Tabs 100 & 200 mg.Trade: Caps 200 mg. Trade: Syrup 100 & 200 mg/5 ml. Rx:Trade: Tabs 200 & 1200mg. Generic/Trade: Tabs, extended release 600 & 1200 mg.Trade: Caps, sustained release 300 mg. Trade: Syrup 100/5 ml.
NOTES - Lack of convincing studies to document efficacy.

ENT: Decongestants

NOTES: See ENT - Nasal Preparations for topical nasal spray decongestants (oxymetazoline, phenylephrine). Systemic decongestants are sympathomimetic, and accordingly may aggravate hypertension. Use in such patients should be undertaken with caution.

pseudoephedrine (*Sudafed, Sudafed 12 Hour, Efidac/24, PediaCare Infants' Decongestant Drops, Triaminic Oral Infant Drops*) ▶L ♀C ▶+ $
ADULT - Nasal Congestion: 60 mg PO q4-6h. 120 mg PO q12h (extended release). 240 mg PO qd (extended release), max 240 mg/day.
PEDS - Nasal Congestion >12 yo: use adult dose. 6-11 yo: 30 mg PO q4-6h, max 120 mg/day. 2-5 yo: 15 mg PO q4-6h, max 60 mg/day. Pediacare Infant Drops & Triaminic Infant Drops: Give PO q4-6h prn; max of 4 doses/day. 2-3 yo: 1.6 ml. 12-23 mo: 1.2 ml. 4-11 mo: 0.8 ml. ≤ 3 mo: 0.4 ml.
FORMS - OTC: Generic/Trade: Tabs 30, 60 mg. Chewable tabs 15 mg. Trade only: Tabs, extended release 120, 240 mg. Trade only: Liquid 15 mg/5 ml. Generic/Trade: Liquid 30 mg/5 ml. Infant drops 7.5 mg/0.8 ml.
NOTES - 12 to 24-hour extended release dosage forms may cause insomnia; use a shorter-acting form if this occurs.

ENT: Ear Preparations

Auralgan **(benzocaine + antipyrine)** ▶Not absorbed ♀C ▶? $

ADULT - Otitis media, adjunct: Instill 2-4 drops (or enough to fill the ear canal) tid-qid or q1-2h prn. Cerumen removal: Instill 2-4 drops (or enough to fill the ear canal) tid x 2-3 days to detach cerumen, then prn for discomfort. Insert cotton plug moistened with soln after instillation.

PEDS - Otitis media, adjunct: use adult dose. Cerumen removal: use adult dose.

FORMS - Generic/Trade: Otic soln 10 & 15 ml.

carbamide peroxide (*Debrox, Murine Ear*) ▶Not absorbed ♀? ▶? $

ADULT - Cerumen removal: Instill 5-10 drops into ear bid x 4 days.

PEDS - Not approved in children.

FORMS - OTC: Trade: Otic soln 6.5% ,15 or 30 ml bottle.

NOTES - Drops should remain in ear > 15 minutes. Do not use for > 4 days. Remove excess wax by flushing with warm water using a rubber bulb ear syringe.

Cipro HC Otic **(ciprofloxacin + hydrocortisone)** ▶Not absorbed ♀C ▶- $$$

ADULT - Otitis externa: Instill 3 drops into affected ear(s) bid x 7 days.

PEDS - Otitis externa ≥1 yo: use adult dose.

FORMS - Trade: Otic suspension 10 ml bottle.

NOTES - Shake well; contains benzyl alcohol.

Cortisporin Otic **(hydrocortisone + polymyxin + neomycin)** ▶Not absorbed ♀? ▶? $$

ADULT - Otitis externa: Instill 4 drops in affected ear(s) tid-qid up to 10 days.

PEDS - Otitis externa: Instill 3 drops in affected ear(s) tid-qid up to 10 days.

FORMS - Generic/Trade: Otic soln or suspension 7.5 & 10 ml.

NOTES - Use suspension and cotton plug if TM perforation.

Cortisporin TC Otic **(hydrocortisone + neomycin + thonzonium + colistin)** ▶Not absorbed ♀? ▶? $$

ADULT - Otitis externa: Instill 5 drops in affected ear(s) tid-qid up to 10 days.

PEDS - Otitis externa: Instill 4 drops in affected ear(s) tid-qid up to 10 days.

FORMS - Trade: Otic suspension, 10 ml.

docusate sodium (*Colace*) ▶Not absorbed ♀+ ▶+ $

UNAPPROVED ADULT - Cerumen removal: Instill 1 ml in affected ear.

UNAPPROVED PEDS - Cerumen removal: Instill 1 ml in affected ear.

FORMS - Generic/Trade: Liquid 150 mg/15 ml.

NOTES - Allow to remain in ear(s) for 10-15 min. Irrigate with 50 ml lukewarm NS if necessary. Use liquid, not syrup.

Domeboro Otic **(acetic acid + aluminum acetate)** ▶Not absorbed ♀? ▶? $

ADULT - Otitis externa: Instill 4-6 drops in affected ear(s) q2-3h.

PEDS - Otitis externa: Instill 2-3 drops in affected ear(s) q3-4h.

FORMS - Generic/Trade: Otic soln 60 ml bottle.

NOTES - Insert a saturated wick. Keep moist x 24 hours.

ofloxacin (*Floxin Otic*) ▶Not absorbed ♀C ▶- $$

ADULT - Otitis externa: Instill 10 drops in affected ear(s) bid x 10 days. Chronic suppurative otitis media: Instill 10 drops in affected ear(s) bid x 14 days.

PEDS - Otitis externa >12 yo: use adult dose. 1-12 yo: Instill 5 drops in affected ear(s) bid x 10 days. Chronic suppurative otitis media >12 yo: use adult dose. Acute otitis media with tympanostomy tubes 1-12 yo: Instill 5 drops in affected ear(s) bid x 10 days.

FORMS - Trade: Otic soln 0.3% 5 ml bottle.

Otobiotic **(hydrocortisone + polymyxin B)** ▶Not absorbed ♀? ▶? $

ADULT - Otitis externa: Instill 4 drops in affected ear(s) tid-qid up to 10 days.

PEDS - Otitis externa: Instill 3 drops in affected ear(s) tid-qid up to 10 days.

FORMS - Trade: Otic soln 0.5%, 15 ml.

NOTES - Good choice if neomycin allergy.

Pediotic **(hydrocortisone + polymyxin + neomycin)** ▶Not absorbed ♀? ▶? $$

ADULT - Otitis externa: Instill 4 drops in affected ear(s) tid-qid up to 10 days.

PEDS - Otitis externa: Instill 3 drops in affected ear(s) tid-qid up to 10 days.

FORMS - Trade: Otic suspension 7.5 ml.

NOTES - Insert cotton plug prior to medication if TM perforation.

Swim-Ear **(isopropyl alcohol + anhydrous glycerins)** ▶Not absorbed ♀? ▶? $

ADULT - Otitis externa, prophylaxis: Instill 4-5 drops in ears after swimming, showering, or bathing.

PEDS - Otitis externa, prophylaxis: use adult dose.

FORMS - OTC: Trade: Otic soln 30 ml bottle.

triethanolamine (*Cerumenex*) ▶Not absor-

bed ♀C ▶- $$
ADULT - Cerumen removal: Fill ear canal with soln, insert cotton plug for 15-30 minutes, then flush with warm water.
PEDS - Not approved in children.
UNAPPROVED PEDS - Cerumen removal: use adult dose.
FORMS - Trade: Otic soln 6 & 12 ml bottle with dropper.
NOTES - Do not use for > 4 days. Remove excess wax by flushing with warm water using a rubber bulb ear syringe.

VoSol otic **(acetic acid + propylene glycol)** ▶Not absorbed ♀? ▶? $
ADULT - Otitis externa: Instill 5 drops in affected ear(s) tid-qid. Insert cotton plug moistened with 3-5 drops q4-6h for the first 24 hrs.
PEDS - Otitis externa >3 yo: Instill 3-4 drops in affected ear(s) tid-qid. Insert cotton plug moistened with 3-4 drops q4-6h for the first 24 hours.
FORMS - Generic/Trade: Otic soln 2% 15 & 30 ml bottle.
NOTES - VoSol HC adds hydrocortisone 1%.

ENT: ENT Combination Products - OTC

NOTES: Some ENT combination products contain decongestants which may aggravate HTN. Use cautiously in such patients. Certain products may contain sedating antihistamines. May cause drowsiness and/or sedation, which may be enhanced by alcohol, sedatives, tranquilizers, etc.

Actifed Cold & Allergy **(pseudoephedrine + triprolidine)** ▶L ♀C ▶+ $
ADULT - Allergic rhinitis/nasal congestion: 1 tab PO q4-6h, max 4 tabs/day.
PEDS - Allergic rhinitis/nasal congestion: >12 yo: use adult dose. 6-12 yo: 1/2 tab q4-6h, max 2 tabs/day.
FORMS - OTC: Trade: Tabs 60 mg pseudoephedrine/2.5 mg triprolidine
NOTES - Cold & Sinus: 30 mg pseudoephedrine /1.25 mg triprolidine/500 mg acetaminophen.

Allerfrim **(pseudoephedrine + triprolidine)** ▶L ♀C ▶+ $
ADULT - Allergic rhinitis/nasal congestion: 1 tab or 10 ml PO q4-6h, max 4 tabs/day or 40 ml/d.
PEDS - Allergic rhinitis/nasal congestion: >12 yo: use adult dose. 6-12 yo: 1/2 tab or 5 ml PO q4-6h, max 2 tabs/day or 20 ml/day.
FORMS - OTC: Trade: Tabs 60 mg pseudoephedrine/2.5 mg triprolidine. Syrup 30 mg pseudoephedrine/1.25 mg triprolidine/5 ml.

Aprodine **(pseudoephedrine + triprolidine)** ▶L ♀C ▶+ $
ADULT - Allergic rhinitis/nasal congestion: 1 tab or 10 ml PO q4-6h, max 4 tabs/day or 40 ml/day.
PEDS - Allergic rhinitis/nasal congestion: >12 yo: use adult dose; 6-12 yo: 1/2 tab or 5 ml PO q4-6h, max 2 tabs/day or 20 ml/day.
FORMS - OTC: Trade: Tabs 60 mg pseudoephedrine/2.5 mg triprolidine. Syrup 30 mg pseudoephedrine/1.25 mg triprolidine/5 ml.

Cheracol D Cough **(guaifenesin + dextromethorphan,** ***✤BenylinDME*****)** ▶L ♀C ▶? $
ADULT - Cough: 10 ml PO q4h
PEDS - Cough ≥12 yo: use adult dose; 6-11 yo: 5 ml PO q4h, max 30 ml/day; 2- 5 yo: 2.5 ml PO q4h, max 15 ml/day.
FORMS - OTC: Generic/Trade: Syrup 100 mg guaifenesin/10 mg dextromethorphan/5 ml.

Dimetapp Cold & Allergy **(pseudoephedrine + brompheniramine)** ▶LK ♀C ▶- $
ADULT - Allergic rhinitis/nasal congestion: 20 ml PO q4h; max 4 doses/24h.
PEDS - Allergic rhinitis/nasal congestion: ≥12 yo: use adult dose. 6-11 yo: 10ml PO q4h. 2-5 yo: 5 ml PO q4h. Max: 4 doses/24h.
UNAPPROVED PEDS - Allergic rhinitis/nasal congestion: 12-23 mo: ¾ tsp PO q6-8h. 6-11mo: ½ tsp PO q6-8h. Max: 4 doses/24h.
FORMS - OTC: Trade: Elixir 15 mg pseudoephedrine/ 1 mg brompheniramine/5 ml.
NOTES - Grape flavor, alcohol-free.

Dimetapp Cold & Fever **(pseudoephedrine + brompheniramine + acetaminophen)** ▶LK ♀C ▶- $
ADULT - Nasal congestion/fever/sore throat: 20 ml PO q4h; max 4 doses/24h.
PEDS - Nasal congestion/fever/sore throat: ≥12 yo: use adult dose. 6-11 yo: 10 ml PO q4h. 2-5 yo: 5 ml PO q4h. Max: 4 doses/24h.
UNAPPROVED PEDS - Nasal congestion/fever/sore throat: 12-23 mo: ¾ tsp PO q6-8h. 6-11mo: ½ tsp PO q6-8h. Max: 4 doses/24h.
FORMS - OTC: Trade: Suspension 15 mg pseudoephedrine/1 mg brompheniramine/160 mg acetaminophen/5 ml.
NOTES - Grape flavor, alcohol-free.

Dimetapp Decongestant Plus Cough Infant Drops **(pseudoephedrine + dextromethorphan)** ▶LK ♀C ▶- $

ADULT - Not recommended.
PEDS - Nasal congestion/cough: 2-3 yo: 1.6 ml PO q4-6h. Max: 4 doses/24h.
UNAPPROVED PEDS - Nasal congestion/cough: 12-23 mo: 1.2 ml PO q6h. 6-11mo: 0.8 ml PO q6h. Max: 4 doses/24h.
FORMS - OTC: Trade: Infant drops 7.5 mg pseudoephedrine/2.5 mg dextromethorphan/0.8 ml.
NOTES - Alcohol-free.

Dimetapp DM Cold & Cough **(pseudoephedrine + brompheniramine + dextromethorphan)** ▶LK ♀C ▶- $
ADULT - Nasal congestion/cough: 20 ml PO q4h; max 4 doses/24h.
PEDS - Nasal congestion/cough: ≥12 yo: use adult dose. 6-11 yo: 10 ml PO q4h. 2-5 yo: 5 ml PO q4h. Max: 4 doses/24h.
UNAPPROVED PEDS - Nasal congestion/cough: 12-23 mo: ¾ tsp PO q6-8h. 6-11mo: ½ tsp PO q6-8h. Max: 4 doses/24h.
FORMS - OTC: Trade: Elixir 15 mg pseudoephedrine/1 mg brompheniramine/5 mg dextromethorphan/5 ml.
NOTES - Red grape flavor, alcohol-free.

Dimetapp Nighttime Flu **(pseudoephedrine + dextromethorphan + acetaminophen + brompheniramine)** ▶LK ♀C ▶- $
ADULT - Nasal congestion/runny nose/fever/cough/sore throat: 20 ml PO q4h; max 4 doses/24h.
PEDS - Nasal congestion/runny nose/fever/cough/sore throat ≥12 yo: use adult dose. 6-11 yo: 10 ml PO q4h. 2-5 yo: 5 ml PO q4h. Max: 4 doses/24h.
UNAPPROVED PEDS - Nasal congestion/runny nose/fever/cough/sore throat: 12-23 mo: ¾ tsp PO q6-8h. 6-11mo: ½ tsp PO q6-8h. Max: 4 doses/24h.
FORMS - OTC: Trade: Syrup 15 mg pseudoephedrine/5 mg dextromethorphan/160 mg acetaminophen/1 mg brompheniramine/5 ml.
NOTES - Bubble gum flavor, alcohol-free.

Dimetapp Non-Drowsy Flu **(pseudoephedrine + dextromethorphan + acetaminophen)** ▶LK ♀C ▶- $
ADULT - Nasal congestion/fever/cough/sore throat: 20 ml PO q4h; max 4 doses/24h.
PEDS - Nasal congestion/fever/cough/sore throat ≥12 yo: use adult dose. 6-11 yo: 10 ml PO q4h. 2-5 yo: 5 ml PO q4h. Max: 4 doses/24h.
UNAPPROVED PEDS - Nasal congestion/fever/cough/sore throat: 12-23 mo: ¾ tsp PO q6-8h. 6-11mo: ½ tsp PO q6-8h. Max: 4 doses/24h.
FORMS - OTC: Trade: Syrup 15 mg pseudoephedrine/5 mg dextromethorphan/160 mg acetaminophen/5 ml.
NOTES - Fruit flavor, alcohol-free.

Drixoral Cold & Allergy **(pseudoephedrine + dexbrompheniramine)** ▶LK ♀C ▶- $
ADULT - Allergic rhinitis/nasal congestion: 1 tab PO q12h.
PEDS - Allergic rhinitis/nasal congestion ≥12 yo: use adult dose.
FORMS - OTC: Trade: Tabs, sustained-action 120 mg pseudoephedrine/6 mg dexbrompheniramine.

Guiatuss PE **(pseudoephedrine + guaifenesin)** ▶L ♀C ▶- $
ADULT - Nasal congestion/cough: 10 ml PO q4h, max 40 ml/day.
PEDS - Nasal congestion/cough: ≥12 yo: use adult dose; 6-11 yo: 5 ml PO q4h, max 20 ml/day; 2-5 yo: 2.5 ml PO q4h, max 10 ml/day.
FORMS - OTC: Trade: Syrup 30 mg pseudoephedrine/100 mg guaifenesin/5 ml.
NOTES - PE = pseudoephedrine

Mytussin DM **(guaifenesin + dextromethorphan)** ▶L ♀C ▶? $
ADULT - Cough: 10 ml PO q4h, max 60 ml/day.
PEDS - Cough: ≥12 yo: use adult dose; 6-11 yo: 5 ml PO q4h, max 30 ml/day; 2- 5 yo: 2.5 ml PO q4h, max 15 ml/day.
FORMS - OTC: Generic/Trade: Syrup 100 mg guaifenesin/10 mg dextromethorphan/5 ml.
NOTES - DM = dextromethorphan.

Robitussin CF **(pseudoephedrine + guaifenesin + dextromethorphan)** ▶L ♀C ▶- $
ADULT - Nasal congestion/cough: 10 ml PO q4h.
PEDS - Nasal congestion/cough: ≥12 yo: use adult dose. 6-11 yo: 5 ml PO q4h. 2-5 yo: 2.5 ml PO q4h.
FORMS - OTC: Trade: Syrup 30 mg pseudoephedrine + 100 mg guaifenesin + 10 mg dextromethorphan/5 ml.
NOTES - CF= cough formula.

Robitussin DM **(guaifenesin + dextromethorphan)** ▶L ♀C ▶+ $
ADULT - Cough: 10 ml PO q4h, max 60 ml/day.
PEDS - Cough: ≥12 yo: use adult dose. 6-11 yo: 5 ml PO q4h, max 30 ml/day. 2- 5 yo: 2.5 ml PO q4h, max 15 ml/day.
FORMS - OTC: Generic/Trade: Syrup 100 mg guaifenesin/10 mg dextromethorphan/5 ml.
NOTES - Alcohol-free. DM = dextromethorphan.

Robitussin PE **(pseudoephedrine + guaifenesin)** ▶L ♀C ▶- $
ADULT - Nasal congestion/cough: 10 ml PO

q4h, max 40 ml/day.
PEDS - Nasal congestion/cough: ≥12 yo: use adult dose. 6-11 yo: 5 ml PO q4h, max 20 ml/day. 2-5 yo: 2.5 ml PO q4h, max 10 ml/day.
FORMS - OTC: Trade: Syrup 30 mg pseudoephedrine/100 mg guaifenesin/5 ml.
NOTES - PE = pseudoephedrine.

Triaminic Chest Congestion **(pseudoephedrine + guaifenesin)** ▶LK ♀C ▶- $
ADULT - Chest/nasal congestion: 20 ml PO q4-6h.
PEDS - Chest/nasal congestion ≥12 yo: use adult dose. 6-11 yo: 10 ml PO q4-6h. 2-5 yo: 5 ml PO q4-6h.
UNAPPROVED PEDS - 13-23 mo: 2.5 ml PO q4-6h. 4-12 mo: 1.25 ml PO q4-6h.
FORMS - OTC: Trade: Syrup, 15 mg pseudoephedrine/50 mg guaifenesin/5 ml, citrus flavor.

Triaminic Cold & Allergy **(pseudoephedrine + chlorpheniramine)** ▶LK ♀C ▶- $
ADULT - Allergic rhinitis/nasal congestion: 20 ml PO q4-6h.
PEDS - Allergic rhinitis/nasal congestion ≥12 yo: use adult dose. 6-11 yo: 10 ml PO q4-6h. Softchew tab: 6-11 yo: 2 tabs q4-6h.
UNAPPROVED PEDS - Allergic rhinitis/nasal congestion: Give PO q4-6h: 2-5 yo: 5 ml. 13-23 mo: 2.5 ml. 4-12 mo: 1.25 ml.
FORMS - OTC: Trade: Syrup, softchew tabs 15 mg pseudoephedrine/1 mg chlorpheniramine/5 ml, orange flavor.

Triaminic Cold & Cough **(pseudoephedrine + chlorpheniramine + dextromethorphan)** ▶LK ♀C ▶- $
ADULT - Nasal congestion/ runny nose/cough: 20 ml PO q4h or 4 tabs q4-6h.
PEDS - Nasal congestion/runny nose/cough ≥12 yo: use adult dose. 6-11 yo: 10 ml PO q4h.Softchew tab: 6-11 yo: 2 tabs q4-6h.
UNAPPROVED PEDS - 13-23 mo: 2.5 ml PO q4h. 4-12 mo: 1.25 ml PO q4h.
FORMS - OTC: Trade: Syrup, softchew tabs 15 mg pseudoephedrine/1 mg chlorpheniramine/5 mg dextromethorphan/5 ml, cherry flavor.

Triaminic Cough **(pseudoephedrine + dextromethorphan)** ▶LK ♀C ▶- $
ADULT - Nasal congestion/cough: 20 ml PO q4h.
PEDS - Nasal congestion/cough ≥12 yo: use adult dose. 6-11 yo: 10 ml PO q4h. 2-5 yo: 5 ml PO q4h. Softchew tab: 6-11 yo: 2 tabs q4-6h.
UNAPPROVED PEDS - 13-23 mo: 2.5 ml PO q4h. 4-12 mo: 1.25 ml PO q4h.
FORMS - OTC: Trade: Syrup, softchew tabs 15 mg pseudoephedrine/ 5 mg dextromethorphan/5 ml, berry flavor

Triaminic Cough & Sore Throat **(pseudoephedrine + dextromethorphan + acetaminophen)** ▶LK ♀C ▶- $
ADULT - Nasal congestion/cough/sore throat: 20 ml PO q4h.
PEDS - Nasal congestion/cough/sore throat ≥12 yo: use adult dose. 6-11 yo: 10 ml PO q4h. 2-5 yo: 5 ml PO q4h. Softchew tab: 6-11 yo: 2 tabs q4-6h.
UNAPPROVED PEDS - 13-23 mo: 2.5 ml PO q4h. 4-12 mo: 1.25 ml PO q4h.
FORMS - OTC: Trade: Syrup, 15 mg pseudoephedrine/ 5 mg dextromethorphan / 160 mg acetaminophen /5 ml, berry flavor. Softchew tab, 15 mg pseudoephedrine/ 7.5 mg dextromethorphan / 160 mg acetaminophen.

ENT: ENT Combination Products - Rx Only

NOTES: Some ENT combination products contain decongestants which may aggravate HTN. Use cautiously in such patients. Certain products may contain sedating antihistamines. May cause drowsiness and/or sedation, which may be enhanced by alcohol, sedatives, tranquilizers, etc.

Allegra-D **(pseudoephedrine + fexofenadine)** ▶LK ♀C ▶- $$$
ADULT - Allergic rhinitis/nasal congestion: 1 tab PO q12h.
PEDS - Not approved in children.
FORMS - Trade: Tabs, extended release 120 mg pseudoephedrine/60 mg fexofenadine.
NOTES - Decrease dose to 1 tablet PO qd with decreased renal function. Take on an empty stomach. Avoid taking with fruit juice due to a large decrease in bioavailability.

Bromfenex **(pseudoephedrine + brompheniramine)** ▶LK ♀C ▶- $
ADULT - Allergic rhinitis/nasal congestion: 1 cap PO q12h, max 2 caps/day.
PEDS - Allergic rhinitis/nasal congestion: >12 yo: use adult dose. 6-11 yo: 1 cap PO qd.
FORMS - Generic/Trade: Caps, sustained release 120 mg pseudoephedrine/12 mg brompheniramine.

Bromfenex PD **(pseudoephedrine + brompheniramine)** ▶LK ♀C ▶- $
ADULT - Allergic rhinitis/nasal congestion: 1-2 caps PO q12h, max 4 caps/day.

PEDS - Allergic rhinitis/nasal congestion: >12 yo: 1 cap PO q12h, max 2 caps/day.
FORMS - Generic/Trade: Caps, sustained release 60 mg pseudoephedrine + 6 mg brompheniramine.
NOTES - PD = pediatric.

Carbodec DM **(pseudoephedrine + carbinoxamine + dextromethorphan) ▶L♀C▶- $**
ADULT - Allergic rhinitis/nasal congestion/cough: 5 ml PO qid.
PEDS - Allergic rhinitis/nasal congestion/cough > 6 yo: 5 ml PO qid. 18 mo-5 yo: 2.5 ml PO q6h. Infant Drops: Give PO qid: 1-3 mo: 0.25 ml. 4-6 mo: 0.5 ml. 7-9 mo: 0.75 ml. 10 mo-17 mo: 1 ml.
FORMS - Generic/Trade: Syrup 60 mg pseudoephedrine/4 mg carbinoxamine/15 mg dextromethorphan/5 ml (Carbodec DM Syrup). Generic/Trade: Drops 25 mg pseudoephedrine/2 mg carbinoxamine/4 mg dextromethorphan/ ml, grape flavor 30 ml w/dropper (Carbodec DM Oral Infant Drops).
NOTES - Carbinoxamine has potential for sedation similar to diphenhydramine. DM = dextromethorphan.

Chlordrine SR **(pseudoephedrine + chlorpheniramine) ▶LK ♀C ▶- $**
ADULT - Allergic rhinitis/nasal congestion: 1 cap PO q12h, max 2 caps/day.
PEDS - Allergic rhinitis/nasal congestion >12 yo: use adult dose. 6-11 yo: 1 cap PO qd.
FORMS - Generic/Trade: Caps, sustained release 120 mg pseudoephedrine/8 mg chlorpheniramine.

Claritin-D 12 hour **(pseudoephedrine + loratadine) ▶LK ♀B ▶- $$$**
ADULT - Allergic rhinitis/nasal congestion: 1 tab PO q12h.
PEDS - Not approved in children.
FORMS - Trade: Tabs, 12-hour extended release: 120 mg pseudoephedrine/5 mg loratadine.
NOTES - Decrease dose to 1 tab PO qd with CrCl < 30 ml/min. Avoid in patients with hepatic insufficiency.

Claritin-D 24 hr **(pseudoephedrine + loratadine) ▶LK ♀B ▶- $$$**
ADULT - Allergic rhinitis/nasal congestion: 1 tab PO qd.
PEDS - Not approved in children.
FORMS - Trade: Tabs, 24-hour extended release tabs: 240 mg pseudoephedrine/10 mg loratadine.
NOTES - Decrease dose to 1 tab PO qod with CrCl < 30 ml/min. Avoid in patients with hepatic insufficiency.

Cydec Drops **(pseudoephedrine + carbinoxamine) ▶L ♀C ▶- $**
PEDS - Allergic rhinitis/nasal congestion: Give PO qid: 1-3 mo: 0.25 ml. 3-6 mo: 0.5 ml.6-9 mo: 0.75 ml. 9 mo-5 yo: 1.0 ml.
FORMS - Generic/Trade: Drops 25 mg pseudoephedrine/2 mg carbinoxamine/ml, raspberry flavor, 30 ml.
NOTES - Carbinoxamine has potential for sedation similar to diphenhydramine.

Deconamine **(pseudoephedrine + chlorpheniramine) ▶LK ♀C ▶- $**
WARNING - Multiple strengths; see FORMS & write specific product on Rx.
ADULT - Allergic rhinitis/nasal congestion: 1 tab or 10 ml PO tid-qid, max 6 tabs or 60 ml/day. Sustained release: 1 cap PO q12h, max 2 caps/day.
PEDS - Allergic rhinitis/nasal congestion: >12 yo: use adult dose. 6-11 yo: ½ tab or 5 ml PO tid-qid, max 3 tabs or 30 ml/day.
FORMS - Trade: Tabs 60 mg pseudoephedrine/4 mg chlorpheniramine, scored (Deconamine). Syrup 30 mg pseudoephedrine/2 mg chlorpheniramine/5 ml (Deconamine). Generic/Trade: Caps, sustained release 120 mg pseudoephedrine/8 mg chlorpheniramine (Deconamine SR).

Deconsal II **(pseudoephedrine + guaifenesin) ▶L ♀C ▶- $**
ADULT - Nasal congestion/cough: 1-2 tabs PO q12h, max 4 tabs/day.
PEDS - Nasal congestion/cough: >12 yo: use adult dose. 6-12 yo: 1 tab PO q12h, max 2 tabs/day. 2-5 yo: ½ tab PO q12h, max 1 tab/day.
FORMS - Generic/Trade: Tabs, sustained release 60 mg pseudoephedrine/600 mg guaifenesin, scored.

Defen-LA **(pseudoephedrine + guaifenesin) ▶L ♀C ▶- $**
ADULT - Nasal congestion/cough: 1-2 tabs PO q12h.
PEDS - Nasal congestion/cough: >12 yo: use adult dose.
FORMS - Trade: Tabs, long-acting 60 mg pseudoephedrine/600 mg guaifenesin, scored.

Detussin **(pseudoephedrine + hydrocodone, ✤*Novahistex*) ▶L ♀C ▶- ©III $**
ADULT - Nasal congestion/cough: 5 ml PO qid prn.
PEDS - Nasal congestion/cough 22-40 kg: 2.5 ml PO qid prn. 12-22 kg: 1.25 ml PO qid prn.
FORMS - Generic/Trade: Liquid 60 mg pseu-

doephedrine/5 mg hydrocodone/5 ml.

Dimetane-DX Cough Syrup **(pseudoephedrine + brompheniramine + dextromethorphan)** ▶L ♀C ▶- $$

ADULT - Nasal congestion/rhinitis/cough: 10 ml PO q4h prn.

PEDS - Nasal congestion/rhinitis/cough: >12 yo: use adult dose. 6-11 yo: 5 ml PO q4h. 2-5 yo: ½ tsp PO q4h. 22-40 kg: 2.5 ml PO qid prn. 12-22 kg: 1.25 ml PO qid prn.

FORMS - Trade: Liquid 30 mg pseudoephedrine/2 mg brompheniramine/10 mg dextromethorphan/5 ml, butterscotch flavor.

Duratuss **(pseudoephedrine + guaifenesin)** ▶L ♀C ▶- $

ADULT - Nasal congestion/cough: 1 tab PO q12h.

PEDS - Nasal congestion/cough: >12 yo: use adult dose. 6-12 yo: ½ tab PO q12h.

FORMS - Trade: Tabs, long-acting 120 mg pseudoephedrine/600 mg guaifenesin, scored.

Duratuss GP **(pseudoephedrine + guaifenesin)** ▶L ♀C ▶- $

ADULT - Nasal congestion/cough: 1 tab PO q12h.

FORMS - Trade: Tabs, long-acting 120 mg pseudoephedrine/1200 mg guaifenesin.

Duratuss HD **(hydrocodone + pseudoephedrine + guaifenesin)** ▶L ♀C ▶- ©III $$$

ADULT - Cough/nasal congestion: 10 ml PO q4-6h.

PEDS - Cough/nasal congestion: > 12 yo: use adult dose; 6-12yo: 5 ml PO q4-6h.

FORMS - Trade: Elixir 2.5 mg hydrocodone/30 mg pseudoephedrine/ 100 mg guaifenensin/5 ml; 5% alcohol, fruit punch flavored.

Entex PSE **(pseudoephedrine + guaifenesin)** ▶L ♀C ▶- $

ADULT - Nasal congestion/cough: 1 tab PO q12h.

PEDS - Nasal congestion/cough: >12 yo: use adult dose. 6-12 yo: ½ tab PO q12h.

FORMS - Trade: Tabs, long-acting 120 mg pseudoephedrine/600 mg guaifenesin, scored.

NOTES - PSE = pseudoephedrine.

Fenesin DM **(guaifenesin + dextromethorphan)** ▶L ♀C ▶? $

ADULT - Cough: 1-2 tabs PO q12h, max 4 tabs/day.

PEDS - Cough ≥12 yo: use adult dose. 6-12 yo: 1 tab PO q12h, max 2 tabs/day. 2-5 yo: ½ tab PO q12h, max 1 tab/day.

FORMS - Trade: Tabs, sustained release 600 mg guaifenesin/30 mg dextromethorphan.

NOTES - DM = dextromethorphan.

Gani-Tuss NR **(guaifenesin + codeine)** ▶L ♀C ▶? ©V $

ADULT - Cough: 10 ml PO q4h, max 60 ml/day.

PEDS - Cough ≥12 yo: use adult dose. 6-11 yo: 5 ml PO q4h, max 30 ml/day. 2-5 yo: 2.5-5 ml PO q4h, max 30 ml/day. 6-23 mo: 1.25-2.5 ml PO q4h, max 15 ml/day.

FORMS - Trade: Syrup 100 mg guaifenesin/10 mg codeine/5 ml, raspberry flavor.

Guaifenex DM **(guaifenesin + dextromethorphan)** ▶L ♀C ▶? $

ADULT - Cough: 1-2 tabs PO q12h, max 4 tabs/day.

PEDS - Cough ≥12 yo: use adult dose. 6-12 yo: 1 tab PO q12h, max 2 tabs/day. 2-6 yo: ½ tab PO q12h, max 1 tab/day.

FORMS - Trade: Tabs, sust'd release 600 mg guaifenesin/30 mg dextromethorphan, scored.

NOTES - DM = dextromethorphan.

Guaifenex PSE **(pseudoephedrine + guaifenesin)** ▶L ♀C ▶- $

WARNING - Multiple strengths; see FORMS & write specific product on Rx.

ADULT - Nasal congestion/cough: PSE 60: 1-2 tabs PO q12h, max 4 tabs/day. PSE 120: 1 tab PO q12h.

PEDS - Nasal congestion/cough: PSE 60: >12 yo: use adult dose. 6-12 yo: 1 tab PO q12h, max 2 tabs/day. 2-6 yo: ½ tab PO q12h, max 1 tab/day. PSE 120: >12 yo: use adult dose. 6-12 yo: ½ tab PO q12h.

FORMS - Generic/Trade: Tabs, extended release 60 mg pseudoephedrine/600 mg guaifenesin, scored (Guaifenex PSE 60). Trade: Tabs, extended release 120 mg pseudoephedrine/600 mg guaifenesin (Guaifenex PSE 120).

NOTES - PSE = pseudoephedrine.

Guaitex II SR/PSE **(pseudoephedrine + guaifenesin)** ▶L ♀C ▶- $

WARNING - Multiple strengths; see FORMS & write specific product on Rx.

ADULT - Nasal congestion/cough: 1-2 tabs PO q12h, max 4 tabs/day (Guaitex II SR). 1 tab PO q12h, max 2 tabs/day (Guaitex PSE).

PEDS - Nasal congestion/cough: >12 yo: use adult dose. 6-12 yo: 1 tab PO q12h, max 2 tabs/day. 2-5 yo: ½ tab PO q12h, max 1 tab/day (Guaitex II SR). >12 yo: use adult dose. 6-12 yo: ½ tab PO q12h (Guaitex PSE).

FORMS - Generic/Trade: Tabs, sustained release 60 mg pseudoephedrine/600 mg guaifenesin (Guaitex II SR). Trade: Tabs, long-acting 120 mg pseudoephedrine/600 mg guaifenesin (Guaitex PSE).

NOTES - PSE=pseudoephedrine.

Guiatuss AC **(guaifenesin + codeine)** ▶L ♀C ◗? ©V $

ADULT - Cough: 10 ml PO q4h, max 60 ml/day.

PEDS - Cough ≥12 yo: use adult dose. 6-11 yo: 5 ml PO q4h, max 30 ml/day.

FORMS - Generic/Trade: Syrup 100 mg guaifenesin/10 mg codeine/5 ml.

NOTES - AC = and codeine

Guiatussin DAC **(pseudoephedrine + guaifenesin + codeine)** ▶L ♀C ◗- ©V $

ADULT - Nasal congestion/cough: 10 ml PO q4h, max 40 ml/day.

PEDS - Nasal congestion/cough ≥12 yo: use adult dose. 6-11 yo: 5 ml PO q4h, max 20 ml/day.

FORMS - Trade: Syrup 30 mg pseudoephedrine/100 mg guaifenesin/10 mg codeine/5 ml.

NOTES - DAC = decongestant and codeine.

Halotussin AC **(guaifenesin + codeine)** ▶L ♀C ◗? ©V $

ADULT - Cough: 10 ml PO q4h, max 60 ml/day.

PEDS - Cough ≥12 yo: use adult dose. 6-11 yo: 5 ml PO q4h, max 30 ml/day.

FORMS - Trade: Syrup 100 mg guaifenesin/10 mg codeine/5 ml.

NOTES - AC = and codeine

Halotussin DAC **(pseudoephedrine + guaifenesin + codeine)** ▶L ♀C ◗- ©V $

ADULT - Nasal congestion/cough: 10 ml PO q4h, max 40 ml/day.

PEDS - Nasal congestion/cough: ≥12 yo: use adult dose. 6-11 yo: 5 ml PO q4h, max 20 ml/d.

FORMS - Trade: Syrup 30 mg pseudoephedrine/100 mg guaifenesin/10 mg codeine/5 ml, cherry-raspberry flavor.

NOTES - DAC = decongestant and codeine.

Histinex HC **(phenylephrine + chlorpheniramine + hydrocodone)** ▶L ♀C ◗- ©III $

ADULT - Allergic rhinitis/congestion/cough: 10 ml PO q4h, max 40 ml/day.

PEDS - Allergic rhinitis/congestion/cough: >12 yo: use adult dose. 6-12 yo: 5 ml PO q4h, max 20 ml/day.

FORMS - Trade: Syrup 5 mg phenylephrine/2 mg chlorphenir/2.5 mg hydrocodone/5 ml.

Histussin D **(pseudoephedrine + hydrocodone)** ▶L ♀C ◗- ©III $

ADULT - Nasal congestion/cough: 5 ml PO qid prn.

PEDS - Nasal congestion/cough: 22-40kg: 2.5 ml PO qid prn. 12-22kg: 1.25 ml PO qid prn.

FORMS - Generic/Trade: Liquid 60 mg pseudoephedrine/5 mg hydrocodone/5 ml, cherry/black raspberry flavor.

Histussin HC **(phenylephrine + chlorpheniramine + hydrocodone)** ▶L ♀C ◗- ©III $$

ADULT - Allergic rhinitis/congestion/cough: 10 ml PO q4h, max 40 ml/day.

PEDS - Allergic rhinitis/congestion/cough: >12 yo: use adult dose. 6-12 yo: 5 ml PO q4h, max 20 ml/day.

FORMS - Trade: Syrup 5 mg phenylephrine/2 mg chlorphenir/2.5 mg hydrocodone/5 ml.

Humibid DM **(guaifenesin + dextromethorphan)** ▶L ♀C ◗? $

ADULT - Cough: 1-2 tabs PO q12h, max 4 tabs/day.

PEDS - Cough: ≥12 yo: use adult dose. 6-12 yo: 1 tab PO q12h, max 2 tabs/day. 2-5 yo: ½ tab PO q12h, max 1 tab/day.

FORMS - Trade: Tabs, sust'd release 600 mg guaifenesin/30 mg dextromethorphan, scored.

NOTES - DM = dextromethorphan.

Hycodan **(hydrocodone + homatropine)** ▶L ♀C ◗- ©III $

ADULT - Antitussive: 1 tab or 5 mL PO q4-6h, max 6 doses/day.

PEDS - Antitussive >12 yo: use adult dose. 6-12 yo: 2.5 mg (based on hydrocodone) PO q4-6h prn, max 15 mg/day.

FORMS - Trade: Tabs 5 mg hydrocodone/1.5 mg homatropine methylbromide. Generic/Trade; Syrup 5 mg hydrocodone/1.5 mg homatropine methylbromide/5ml.

NOTES - May cause drowsiness/sedation. Dosing based on hydrocodone content.

Hycotuss **(hydrocodone + guaifenesin)** ▶L ♀C ◗- ©III $$

ADULT - Cough: 5 ml PO pc & qhs, max 6 doses/day.

PEDS - Cough: > 12 yo: use adult dose. 6-12 yo: 2.5 ml PO pc & qhs, max 6 doses/day.

FORMS - Trade: Syrup 5 mg hydrocodone/100 mg guaifenesin/5 ml; butterscotch flavor.

Novafed A **(pseudoephedrine + chlorpheniramine)** ▶LK ♀C ◗- $

ADULT - Allergic rhinitis/nasal congestion: 1 cap PO q12h, max 2 caps/day.

PEDS - Allergic rhinitis/nasal congestion: >12 yo: use adult dose. 6-12 yo: 1 cap PO qd.

FORMS - Generic/Trade: Caps, sustained release 120 mg pseudoephedrine/8 mg chlorpheniramine.

Phenergan VC **(phenylephrine + promethazine)** ▶LK ♀C ◗? $

ADULT - Allergic rhinitis/congestion: 5 ml PO q4-6h, max 30 ml/day.

PEDS - Allergic rhinitis/congestion: ≥12 yo: use adult dose. 6-11 yo: 2.5-5 ml PO q4-6h, max 20 ml/day. 2-5 yo: 1.25-2.5 ml PO q4-6h, max

15 ml/day.
FORMS - Generic/Trade: Syrup 6.25 mg promethazine/5 mg phenylephrine/5 ml.
NOTES - VC = vasoconstrictor

Phenergan VC w/codeine **(phenylephrine + promethazine + codeine)** ▶LK♀C▶? ©V $
ADULT - Allergic rhinitis/congestion/cough: 5 ml PO q4-6h, max 30 ml/day.
PEDS - Allergic rhinitis/congestion/cough: ≥12 yo: use adult dose. 6-11 yo: 2.5-5 ml PO q4-6h, max 20 ml/day. 2-5 yo: 1.25-2.5 ml PO q4-6h, max 10 ml/day.
FORMS - Generic/Trade: Syrup 5 mg phenylephrine/6.25 mg promethazine/10 mg codeine/5 ml.

Phenergan/Dextromethorphan **(promethazine + dextromethorphan)** ▶LK ♀C ▶? $
ADULT - Allergic rhinitis/cough: 5 ml PO q4-6h, max 30 ml/day.
PEDS - Allergic rhinitis/cough: ≥12 yo: use adult dose. 6-11 yo: 2.5-5 ml PO q4-6h, max 20 ml/day. 2-5 yo: 1.25-2.5 ml PO q4-6h, max 10 ml/day.
FORMS - Generic/Trade: Syrup 6.25 mg promethazine/15 mg dextromethorphan/5 ml.

Polyhistine **(phenyltoloxamine + pyrilamine + pheniramine)** ▶L ♀? ▶? $
ADULT - Allergic/vasomotor rhinitis, allergic conjunctivitis, urticaria: 10 ml PO q4h.
PEDS - Allergic/vasomotor rhinitis, allergic conjunctivitis, urticaria: 6-12 yo: 5 ml PO q4h. 2-5 yo: 2.5 ml PO q4h.
FORMS - Trade: Elixir phenyltoloxamine 4 mg/pyrilamine 4 mg/pheniramine 4 mg/5 ml.

Pseudo-Chlor **(pseudoephedrine + chlorpheniramine)** ▶LK ♀C ▶- $
ADULT - Allergic rhinitis/nasal congestion: 1 cap PO q12h, max 2 caps/day.
PEDS - Allergic rhinitis/nasal congestion: >12 yo: use adult dose.
FORMS - Trade: Generic/Trade: Caps, sustained release 120 mg pseudoephedrine/8 mg chlorpheniramine.

Robitussin AC **(guaifenesin + codeine)** ▶L ♀C ▶? ©V $
ADULT - Cough: 10 ml PO q4h, max 60 ml/day.
UNAPPROVED PEDS - Cough: ≥ 12 yo, use adult dose. 6 -11 yo 5-10 ml PO q4h. 2-5 yo 2.5-5 ml PO q4h. 6 -23 mo 1.25-2.5 ml PO q4h.
FORMS - Generic/Trade: Syrup 100 mg guaifenesin/10 mg codeine/5 ml.
NOTES - AC = and codeine

Robitussin DAC **(pseudoephedrine + guaifenesin + codeine)** ▶L ♀C ▶- ©V $
ADULT - Nasal congestion/cough: 10 ml PO q4h, max 40 ml/day.
PEDS - Nasal congestion/cough: ≥12 yo: use adult dose. 6-11 yo: 5 ml PO q4h, max 20 ml/day.
FORMS - Trade: Syrup 30 mg pseudoephedrine/100 mg guaifenesin/10 mg codeine/5 ml.
NOTES - DAC = decongestant and codeine.

Rondec **(pseudoephedrine + brompheniramine)** ▶L ♀C ▶- $$
ADULT - Allergic rhinitis/nasal congestion: 5 ml syrup PO qid.
PEDS - Allergic rhinitis/nasal congestion > 6 yo: 5 ml syrup PO qid. 18 mo-5 yo: 2.5 ml PO qid.
FORMS - Generic/Trade: Syrup 60 mg pseudoephedrine/4 mg brompheniramine/5 ml, berry flavor.

Rondec DM **(pseudoephedrine + carbinoxamine + dextromethorphan)** ▶L ♀C ▶- $$
WARNING - Multiple strengths; see FORMS & write specific product on Rx.
ADULT - Allergic rhinitis/nasal congestion/cough: 5 ml syrup PO qid.
PEDS - Allergic rhinitis/nasal congestion/cough >6 yo: 5 ml syrup PO qid. 18 mo-5 yo: 2.5 ml syrup PO qid. Infant Drops: Give PO qid: 1-3 mo: 0.25 ml. 4-6 mo: 0.5 ml. 7-9 mo: 0.75 ml.10 mo-17 mo: 1 ml.
FORMS - Generic/Trade: Syrup 60 mg pseudoephedrine/4 mg carbinoxamine/15 mg dextromethorphan/5 ml (Rondec DM Syrup). Generic/Trade: Drops 25 mg pseudoephedrine/2 mg carbinoxamine/4 mg dextromethorphan/ml, grape flavor 30 ml w/dropper (Rondec DM Infant Drops).
NOTES - Carbinoxamine is a sedating antihistamine similar to diphenhydramine. DM = dextromethorphan.

Rondec Infant Drops **(pseudoephedrine + carbinoxamine)** ▶L ♀C ▶- $$
PEDS - Allergic rhinitis/nasal congestion: Give PO qid: 1-3 mo: 0.25 ml. 4-6 mo: 0.5 ml. 7-9 mo: 0.75 ml. 10 mo-17 mo: 1 ml.
FORMS - Trade: Drops 15 mg pseudoephedrine/2 mg carbinoxamine/ml, berry flavor 30 ml.
NOTES - Carbinoxamine is a sedating antihistamine similar to diphenhydramine.

Ryna-12 S **(phenylephrine + pyrilamine)** ▶L ♀C ▶- $$
PEDS - Nasal congestion, allergic rhinitis, sinusitis: > 6 yo: 5-10 ml PO q12h. 2-6 yo 2.5-5 ml PO q12h. < 2 yo titrate dose individually.
FORMS - Trade: Suspension 5 mg phenylephrine/30 mg pyrilamine/5 ml strawberry-currant flavor w/graduated oral syringe.

Rynatan **(azatadine + pseudoephedrine)** ▶LK ♀C ▶- $$
ADULT - Allergic rhinitis/nasal congestion: 1 tab PO q12h.
PEDS - Allergic rhinitis/nasal congestion: ≥12 yo: 1 tab PO q12h.
FORMS - Trade: Tabs, extended release: 1 mg azatadine/120 mg pseudoephedrine.

Rynatan Pediatric Suspension **(phenylephrine + chlorpheniramine)** ▶L ♀C ▶- $$
PEDS - Nasal congestion, allergic rhinitis, sinusitis >6 yo: 5-10 ml PO q12h. 2-6 yo 2.5-5 ml PO q12h. <2 yo titrate dose individually.
FORMS - Trade: Suspension 5 mg phenylephrine/4.5 mg chlorpheniramine//5 ml strawberry-currant flavor.

Semprex-D **(pseudoephedrine + acrivastine)** ▶LK ♀C ▶- $$$
ADULT - Allergic rhinitis/nasal congestion: 1 cap PO q4-6h up to 4 caps/day.
FORMS - Trade: Caps 60 mg pseudoephedrine/8 mg acrivastine.

Tanafed **(pseudoephedrine + chlorpheniramine)** ▶L ♀C ▶- $$
ADULT - Allergic rhinitis/nasal congestion: 10-20 ml PO q12h, max 40 ml/day.
PEDS - Allergic rhinitis/nasal congestion: ≥12 yo: use adult dose. 6-11 yo: 5-10 ml PO q12h, max 20 ml/day. 2-5 yo: 2.5-5 ml PO q12h, max 10 ml/day.
FORMS - Trade: Suspension 75 mg pseudoephedrine/4.5 mg chlorpheniramine/5 ml, strawberry-banana flavor.

Triacin-C **(pseudoephedrine + triprolidine + codeine)** ▶L ♀C ▶+ ©V $
ADULT - Allergic rhinitis/nasal congestion/cough: 10 ml PO q4-6h, max 40 ml/day.
PEDS - Allergic rhinitis/nasal congestion/cough: ≥12 yo: use adult dose. 6-11 yo: 2.5-5 ml PO q4-6h, max 20 ml/day.
FORMS - Trade: Syrup 30 mg pseudoephedrine /1.25 mg triprolidine/10 mg codeine /5 ml.

Tuss-HC **(phenylephrine + chlorpheniramine + hydrocodone)** ▶L ♀C ▶- ©III $
ADULT - Allergic rhinitis/congestion/cough: 10 ml PO q4h, max 40 ml/day.
PEDS - Allergic rhinitis/congestion/cough: >12 yo: use adult dose. 6-12 yo: 5 ml PO q4h, max 20 ml/day.
FORMS - Trade: Syrup 5 mg phenylephrine/2 mg chlorpheniramine/2.5 mg hydrocodone/5 ml.

Zephrex-LA **(pseudoephedrine + guaifenesin)** ▶L ♀C ▶- $
ADULT - Nasal congestion/cough: 1 tab PO q12h.
PEDS - Nasal congestion/cough: >12 yo: use adult dose. 6-12 yo: ½ tab PO q12h.
FORMS - Trade: Tabs, extended release 120 mg pseudoephedrine/600 mg guaifenesin.

ENT: Mouth & Lip Preparations

amlexanox (*Aphthasol*) ▶LK ♀B ▶? $
ADULT - Aphthous ulcers: Apply ¼ inch paste to ulcer in mouth qid after oral hygiene.
PEDS - Not approved in children.
FORMS - Trade: Oral paste 5%, 5g tube.

chlorhexidine gluconate (*Peridex, Periogard*) ▶Fecal excretion ♀B ▶? $
ADULT - Gingivitis: For gingivitis with redness and swelling, including bleeding upon probing. Use bid as an oral rinse, morning & evening after brushing teeth. Rinse with 15 ml of undiluted soln for 30 seconds. Do not swallow. Spit after rinsing.
FORMS - Trade: Oral rinse 0.12% 473-480 ml bottles.
NOTES - May also be part of a periodontal maintenance program, which includes good oral hygiene and scaling and root planing.

clotrimazole (*Mycelex*) ▶L ♀C ▶? $$$
ADULT - Oral candidiasis: 1 troche dissolved slowly in mouth 5x/day x 14 days. Prevention of oropharyngeal candidiasis in immunocompromised patients: 1 troche dissolved slowly in mouth tid until end of chemotherapy/high-dose corticosteroids.
PEDS - Treatment of oropharyngeal candidiasis: ≥3 yo: use adult dose.
FORMS - Trade: Oral troches 10 mg.
NOTES - Monitor LFTs.

docosanol (*Abreva*) ▶? ♀B ▶? $
ADULT - Herpes labialis (cold sores): At 1st sign of infection apply 5x/day until healed.
PEDS - ≥ 12 yo: use adult dose.
FORMS - OTC: Trade: 10% cream in 2g tube.
NOTES - Dries clear. Cosmetics may be applied over docosanol using a separate applicator to avoid spreading the infection. Contains benzyl alcohol.

doxycycline (*Periostat*) ▶L ♀D ▶- $$$
ADULT - Adjunct to scaling & root planing in periodontitis: 20 mg PO bid.
PEDS - Not approved in children.

FORMS - Trade: Caps 20 mg.
NOTES - Used in studies for up to 9 months.

lidocaine viscous (*Xylocaine*) ▶LK ♀B ◗+ $
WARNING - Instruct patients not to swallow if intended for oral or labial use. It may cause lidocaine toxicity from GI absorption.Tell patients to measure the dose exactly. Patients may apply to small areas in the mouth with a cotton-tipped applicator.
ADULT - Mouth or lip pain: 15-20 ml topically or swish & spit q3h, max 8 doses/day.
PEDS - Use with extreme caution, as therapeutic doses approach potentially toxic levels. Use the lowest effective dose. Mouth or lip pain >3 yo: 3.75-5 ml topically or swish and spit up to q3h.
FORMS - Generic/Trade: soln 2%, 20 ml unit dose, 50, 100, 450 ml bottles.
NOTES - Be aware of adverse effects and the high risk for overdose in children. Consider benzocaine as a safer alternative. Clearly communicate the amount, frequency, max daily dose, & mode of administration (eg, cotton pledget to individual lesions, 1/2 dropper to each cheek q4h, or 20 minutes before meals). Do not prescribe on a "PRN" basis without specified dosing intervals.

***magic mouthwash* (Benadryl + Mylanta (Maalox) + Carafate)** ▶LK ♀B(- in 1st trimester) ◗- $$$
UNAPPROVED ADULT - Stomatitis: 5 ml PO swish & spit or swish & swallow tid before meals and prn.
UNAPPROVED PEDS - Stomatitis: Apply small amounts to lesions prn.
FORMS - Compounded suspension. A standard mixture is 30 ml diphenhydramine liquid (12.5 mg/5 ml) + 60 ml Mylanta or Maalox + 4g Carafate.
NOTES - Variations of this formulation are available. The dose and decision to swish and spit or swallow may vary with the indication and/or ingredient. Some preparations may contain: Kaopectate, nystatin, tetracycline, hydrocortisone, 2% lidodcaine, cherry syrup (for children). Check local pharmacies for customized formulations. Avoid Benadryl formulations with alcohol - may cause stinging of mouth sores.

nystatin (*Mycostatin*) ▶Not absorbed ♀C ◗? $$
ADULT - Thrush: 5 ml PO swish & swallow qid with ½ of dose in each cheek or 1-2 oral lozenges 4- 5 times/day for up to 14 days.
PEDS - Thrush in infants: 1 ml PO in each cheek qid. Premature and low birth weight infants: 0.5 ml PO in each cheek qid.
FORMS - Generic/Trade: Suspension 100,000 units/ml 60 & 480 ml bottle. Trade: Oral lozenges (Pastilles) 200,000 units.
NOTES - Allow oral lozenge to dissolve on tongue. May apply oral suspension in infants using a cotton swab.

penciclovir (*Denavir*) ▶Not absorbed ♀B ◗- $
ADULT - Herpes labialis (cold sores): apply cream q2h while awake x 4 days. Start at first sign of symptoms.
PEDS - Not approved in children.
FORMS - Trade: Cream 1%, 1.5g tube.
NOTES - For moderate to severe cases of herpes labialis, systemic treatment with acyclovir, famciclovir, or valacyclovir may be preferred.

triamcinolone acetonide (*Kenalog in Orabase*) ▶L ♀C ◗? $
ADULT - Apply with finger about 1/2 cm of paste to oral lesion and a thin film will develop. Apply paste bid-tid, ideally pc & qhs.
FORMS - Generic/Trade: 0.1% oral paste 5g tubes
NOTES - Re-evaluate cause if lesion has not healed in 7 days.

ENT: Nasal Preparations

NOTES: For ALL nasal sprays except saline, oxymetazoline, & phenylephrine, tell patients to prime pump before 1st use and shake well before each subsequent use. For nasal steroids, decrease to the lowest effective dose for maintenance therapy.

azelastine (*Astelin*) ▶L ♀C ◗? $$
ADULT - Allergic/vasomotor rhinitis: 2 sprays in each nostril bid.
PEDS - Allergic rhinitis: ≥12 yo: use adult dose. ≥5 yo: 1 spray in each nostril bid. Vasomotor rhinitis ≥12 yo: use adult dose.
FORMS - Trade: Nasal spray, 100 sprays/bottle (17 ml).

beclomethasone (*Vancenase, Vancenase AQ Double Strength, Beconase, Beconase AQ*) ▶L ♀C ◗? $$
ADULT - Allergic rhinitis/nasal polyp prophylaxis: Vancenase, Beconase: 1 spray in each nostril bid-qid. Beconase AQ: 1-2 spray(s) in each nostril bid. Vancenase AQ Double Strength: 1-2 spray(s) in each nostril qd.

PEDS - Allergic rhinitis/nasal polyp prophylaxis: Vancenase/Beconase: >12 yo: adult dose; 6-12 yo: 1 spray in each nostril tid. Beconase AQ: > 6 yo 1-2 spray(s) in each nostril bid. Vancenase AQ Double Strength: > 6 yo: 1-2 spray(s) in each nostril qd.

FORMS - Trade: Nasal inhalation aerosol (Beconase, Vancenase) 42 mcg/spray, 80 & 200 sprays/bottle. Nasal aqueous suspension (Beconase AQ) 42 mcg/spray, 200 sprays/bottle. Nasal aqueous suspension double strength (Vancenase AQ Double Strength) 84 mcg/spray, 120 sprays/bottle.

NOTES - AQ (aqueous) formulation may cause less stinging.

budesonide (*Rhinocort, Rhinocort Aqua*) ▶L ♀C ▶? $$

ADULT - Allergic rhinitis: 2 sprays/nostril bid or 4 sprays/nostril/day (Rhinocort). 1-4 sprays/ nostril/day (Rhinocort Aqua).

PEDS - Allergic rhinitis ≥6 yo: 2 sprays per nostril bid or 4 sprays qd (Rhinocort). 1-2 sprays/ nostril/day (Rhinocort Aqua).

FORMS - Trade: (Rhinocort): Nasal inhaler 200 sprays/bottle. (Rhinocort Aqua): Nasal inhaler 60 sprays/bottle.

cromolyn (*NasalCrom, Children's NasalCrom*) ▶LK ♀B ▶+ $

ADULT - Allergic rhinitis: 1 spray per nostril tid-qid up to 6 times/day.

PEDS - Allergic rhinitis ≥2 yo: use adult dose.

FORMS - OTC: Generic/Trade: Nasal inhaler 200 sprays/bottle. Trade: 100 sprays/bottle. Children's NasalCrom w/special “child-friendly” applicator.

NOTES - Therapeutic effects may not be seen for 1-2 weeks.

flunisolide (*Nasalide, Nasarel*, ✱*Rhinalar*) ▶L ♀C ▶? $$

ADULT - Allergic rhinitis: 2 sprays per nostril bid, may increase to tid, max 8 sprays/nostril/day.

PEDS - Allergic rhinitis 6-14 yo: 1 spray per nostril tid or 2 sprays per nostril bid, max 4 sprays/nostril/day.

FORMS - Trade: Nasal soln 0.025%, 200 sprays/bottle (25 ml). Nasalide with pump unit. Nasarel with meter pump & nasal adapter.

fluticasone (*Flonase*) ▶L ♀C ▶? $$$

ADULT - Allergic rhinitis: 2 sprays per nostril qd or 1 spray per nostril bid, decrease to 1 spray per nostril qd when appropriate.

PEDS - Allergic rhinitis: > 4 yo: 1-2 sprays per nostril qd, max 2 sprays/nostril/day.

FORMS - Trade: Nasal spray 0.05%, 120 sprays/bottle (16 ml).

ipratropium (*Atrovent Nasal Spray*) ▶L ♀B ▶? $$

ADULT - Rhinorrhea due to allergic rhinitis: 2 sprays (0.03%) per nostril bid-tid Rhinorrhea due to common cold: 2 sprays (0.06%) per nostril tid-qid.

PEDS - Rhinorrhea due to allergic rhinitis ≥5 yo: 2 sprays (0.03%) per nostril tid. Rhinorrhea due to common cold ≥12 yo: use adult dose.

UNAPPROVED ADULT - Vasomotor rhinitis: 2 sprays (0.06%) in each nostril tid-qid.

FORMS - Trade: Nasal spray 0.03%, 345 sprays/bottle (30 ml) & 0.06%, 165 sprays/bottle (15 ml).

mometasone (*Nasonex*) ▶L ♀C ▶? $$$

ADULT - Allergic rhinitis: 2 sprays per nostril qd.

PEDS - Allergic rhinitis ≥12 yo: use adult dose. 3-11 yo: 1 spray per nostril qd.

FORMS - Trade: Nasal spray, 120 sprays/bottle (17 ml).

oxymetazoline (*Afrin, Dristan 12 Hr Nasal, Nostrilla*) ▶L ♀C ▶? $

ADULT - Nasal congestion: 2-3 sprays or drops (0.05%) per nostril bid x 3 days.

PEDS - Nasal congestion ≥6 yo: 2-3 sprays or drops (0.05%) per nostril bid x 3 days. 2-5 yo: 2-3 drops (0.025%) per nostril bid x 3 days.

FORMS - OTC: Generic/Trade: Nasal spray 0.05%, 15 & 30 ml bottles. Nose drops 0.025% & 0.05%, 20 ml w/dropper.

NOTES - Overuse (>3-5 days) may lead to rebound congestion. If this occurs, taper to use in one nostril only, alternating sides, then discontinue. Substituting an oral decongestant or nasal steroid may also be useful.

phenylephrine (*Neo-Synephrine, Sinex, Nostril*) ▶L ♀C ▶? $

ADULT - Nasal congestion: 2-3 sprays or drops (0.25 or 0.5%) per nostril q4h prn x 3 days. Use 1% soln for severe congestion.

PEDS - Nasal congestion: >12 yo: use adult dose. 6-12 yo: 2-3 drops or sprays (0.25%) per nostril q4h prn x 3 days. 1-5 yo: 2-3 drops (0.125% or 0.16%) per nostril q4h prn x 3 days. 6-11 mo: 1-2 drops (0.125% or 0.16%) per nostril q4h prn x 3 days.

FORMS - OTC: Trade: Nasal drops 0.125, 0.16%. Generic/Trade: Nasal spray/drops 0.25, 0.5, 1%.

NOTES - Overuse (>3-5 days) may lead to rebound congestion. If this occurs, taper to use in one nostril only, alternating sides, then discontinue. Substituting an oral decongestant or nasal steroid may also be useful.

saline nasal spray (*SeaMist, Pretz, NaSal, Ocean*, ✱*HydraSense*) ▶Not metabolized ♀A ▶+ $

ADULT - Nasal dryness: 1-3 sprays/nostril prn.

PEDS - Nasal dryness: 1-3 drops prn.

FORMS - Generic/Trade: Nasal spray 0.4,0.5, 0.6,0.65,0.75%. Nasal drops 0.4,0.65, 0.75%.

NOTES - May be prepared at home by combining: 1/4 teaspoon salt with 8 ounces warm water. Add 1/4 teaspoon baking soda (optional) and put in spray bottle, ear syringe, or any container with a small spout. Discard after one week.

triamcinolone (*Nasacort, Nasacort AQ*) ▶L ♀C ▶- $$

ADULT - Allergic rhinitis: Nasacort: Start 2 sprays per nostril qd, may increase to 2 sprays/nostril bid or 1 spray/nostril qid, max 4 sprays/nostril/day. Nasacort AQ: 2 sprays/nostril qd.

PEDS - Allergic rhinitis: ≥12 yo: use adult doses. 6-12 yo: 1-2 sprays per nostril qd (Nasacort & Nasacort AQ).

FORMS - Trade: Nasal inhaler 100 sprays/bottle, 10g (Nasacort). Nasal pump 120 sprays/bottle, 16.5g (Nasacort AQ).

NOTES - AQ (aqueous) formulation may cause less stinging. Decrease to lowest effective dose after allergy symptom improvement.

triamcinolone acetonide (*Tri-Nasal*) ▶L ♀C ▶? $$

ADULT - Allergic rhinitis: 2 sprays per nostril qd. Max of 4 sprays per nostril qd.

PEDS - Allergic rhinitis: =>12yo: use adult dosing.

FORMS - Trade: 50 mcg/spray, 120 sprays/bottle (15 ml).

GASTROENTEROLOGY: Antidiarrheals

attapulgite (*Kaopectate, Diasorb, Donnagel*) ▶Not absorbed ♀+ ▶+ $

ADULT - Symptomatic diarrhea: 1200-1500 mg PO after each loose BM; max 9000 mg/24hrs.

PEDS - Symptomatic diarrhea: Age < 3 yo: not recommended. 3-6 yo: 300-750 mg/dose PO up to 2250 mg/24hrs. 6-12 yo: 600-1500 mg/dose PO up to 4500 mg/24hrs.

FORMS - Generic/Trade: liquid 600 mg&750 mg/15 ml (Donnagel, Kaopectate), 750 mg/5 ml (Diasorb), tab 750, chew tab 300,600,750.

NOTES - Decreased absorption of orally administered clindamycin, tetracycline, penicillamine, digoxin. Do not use for pseudomembranous colitis or diarrhea due to toxogenic bacteria.

bismuth subsalicylate (*Pepto-Bismol*) ▶K ♀D ▶? $

WARNING - Avoid in children and teenagers with chickenpox or flu due to association with Reye's syndrome.

ADULT - Diarrhea: 2 tabs or 30 ml (262 mg/15 ml) PO q 30 min-60 min up to 8 doses/24h.

PEDS - Diarrhea: 100 mg/kg/day divided into 5 doses. Age 3-6 yo: 1/3 tab or 5 ml (262 mg/15 ml) every 30 min-60 min prn up to 8 doses/24h. 6-9 yo: 2/3 tab or 10 ml (262 mg/15 ml) every 30 min-1 hr prn up to 8 doses/24h. 9-12 yo: 1 tab or 15 ml (262 mg/15 ml) every 30 min-1 hr prn up to 8 doses/24h.

UNAPPROVED ADULT - Prevention of traveler's diarrhea: 2.1g/24h or 2 tab qid before meals and qhs. Has been used as part of a multi-drug regimen to eradicate H pylori.

UNAPPROVED PEDS - Chronic infantile diarrhea: Age 2-24 mo: 2.5 ml (262 mg/15 ml) PO q4h. 24-48 mo: 5 ml (262 mg/15 ml) q4h. 48-70 mo: 10 ml (262 mg/15 ml) q4h.

FORMS - OTC Generic/Trade: chew tab 262 mg, susp 262 & 524 mg/15 ml. Generic only: susp 130 mg/15 ml. Trade only: caplets 262 mg.

NOTES - Use with caution in patients already taking salicylates. Decreases absorption of tetracycline. May darken stools, tongue.

***Lomotil* (diphenoxylate + atropine)** ▶L ♀C ▶- ©V $

ADULT - Diarrhea: 2 tabs or 10 ml PO qid.

PEDS - Diarrhea: 0.3-0.4 mg diphenoxylate/kg/24h in 4 divided dose. Age <2 yo: not recommended. 2 yo: 1.5-3 ml PO qid; 3 yo: 2-3 ml PO qid; 4 yo: 2-4 ml PO qid; 5 yo: 2.5-4.5 ml PO qid; 6-8 yo: 2.5-5 ml PO qid; 9-12 yo: 3.5-5 ml PO qid.

FORMS - Generic/Trade: solution 2.5 mg diphenoxylate + 0.025 mg atropine per 5 ml, tab 2.5 mg diphenoxylate + 0.025 mg atropine per tab.

NOTES - Give with food to decrease GI upset. May cause atropinism in children, esp with Down's syndrome, even at recommended doses. Can cause delayed toxicity. Has been reported to cause severe respiratory depression, coma, brain damage, death after overdose in children. Naltrexone reverses toxicity. Do not use for pseudomembranous colitis or diarrhea due to toxogenic bacteria.

loperamide (*Imodium, Imodium AD*, ♣*Loperacap*) ▶L ♀B ▶+ $

ADULT - Diarrhea: 4 mg PO initially, then 2 mg after each unformed stool to max 16 mg/day.

PEDS - Diarrhea (first day): Age 2-5 yo (13-20 kg): 1 mg PO tid. 6-8 yo (20-30 kg): 2 mg po bid. 9-12 yo (>30 kg): 2 mg PO tid. After first day, give 1 mg/10 kg PO after each loose stool; daily dose not to exceed daily dose of first day.

UNAPPROVED ADULT - Chronic diarrhea or ileostomy drainage : 4 mg initially then 2 mg after each stool until symptoms are controlled, then reduce dose for maintenance treatment, average adult maintenance dose 4-8 mg daily as a single dose or in divided doses.

UNAPPROVED PEDS - Chronic diarrhea: limited information. Average doses of 0.08-0.24 mg/kg/day PO in 2-3 divided doses.

FORMS - Generic/Trade: cap 2 mg, tab 2 mg. OTC generic/trade: liquid 1 mg/5 ml.

NOTES - Do not use for pseudomembranous colitis or diarrhea due to toxogenic bacteria.

***Motofen* (difenoxin + atropine)** ▶L ♀C ▶- ©IV $

ADULT - Diarrhea: 2 tabs PO initially, then 1 after each loose stool q3-4 h prn. Maximum of 8 tabs in a 24h period.

PEDS - Not approved in children. Contraindicated in children < 2 yo.

FORMS - Trade only: tab difenoxin 1 mg + atropine 0.025 mg.

NOTES - Do not use for pseudomembranous colitis or diarrhea due to toxogenic bacteria. May cause atropinism in children, esp with Down's syndrome, even at recommended doses. Can cause delayed toxicity. Has been reported to cause severe respiratory depression, coma, brain damage, death after overdose in children.

opium (*opium tincture, paregoric*) ▶L ♀B (D with long-term use) ▶? ©II (opium tincture), III (paregoric) $

ADULT - Diarrhea: 5-10 ml paregoric PO qd-qid or 0.3-0.6 ml PO opium tincture qid.

PEDS - Diarrhea: 0.25-0.5 ml/kg paregoric PO qd-qid or 0.005-0.01 ml/kg PO opium tincture q3-4h, max 6 doses/day.

FORMS - Trade: opium tincture 10% (deodorized opium tincture). Generic: paregoric (camphorated opium tincture, 2 mg morphine equiv./5 ml).

NOTES - Opium tincture contains 25 times more morphine than paregoric.

GASTROENTEROLOGY: Antiemetics - 5-HT3 Receptor Antagonists

dolasetron (*Anzemet*) ▶LK ♀B ▶? $$$

ADULT - Prevention of nausea/vomiting with chemo: 1.8 mg/kg up to 100 mg IV/PO single dose 30 min (IV) or 60 min (PO) before chemo. Prevention/treatment of post-op N/V: 12.5 mg IV as a single dose 15 min before end of anesthesia or as soon as N/V starts. Alternative for prevention 100 mg PO 2 h before surgery.

PEDS - Prevention of nausea/vomiting with chemo in children 2-16 yo: 1.8 mg/kg up to 100 mg IV/PO single dose 30 min (IV) or 60 min (PO) before chemo. Prevention/treatment of post-op N/V in children 2-16 yo: 0.35 mg/kg IV as single dose 15 minutes before end of anesthesia or as soon as N/V starts. Max 12.5 mg. Prevention alternative 1.2 mg/kg PO to max of 100 mg 2 h before surgery.

UNAPPROVED ADULT - N/V due to radiotherapy: 40 mg IV as a single dose. Alternatively, 0.3 mg/kg IV as a single dose.

FORMS - Trade only: tab 50,100 mg.

NOTES - Use caution in patients who have or may develop prolongation of QT interval (i.e. hypokalemia, hypomagnesemia, concomitant antiarrhythmic therapy, cumulative high-dose anthracycline therapy).

granisetron (*Kytril*) ▶L ♀B ▶? $$$

ADULT - Prevention of nausea/vomiting with chemo: 10 mcg/kg over 5 min IV 30 mins prior to chemo. Oral: 1 mg PO bid x 1 day only. Radiation induced nausea and vomiting: 2 mg PO 1 hr before first irradiation fraction of each day.

PEDS - Children 2-16 yo: Prevention of nausea/vomiting with chemo: 10 mcg/kg IV 30 minutes prior to chemo. Oral form not approved in children.

UNAPPROVED ADULT - N/V after surgery: 1-3 mg IV.

FORMS - Trade only: tab 1 mg.

ondansetron (*Zofran*) ▶L ♀B ▶? $$$

ADULT - Prevention of nausea/vomiting with chemo: 32 mg IV as a single dose over 15 min, or 0.15 mg/kg IV 30 minutes prior to chemo and repeated at 4 and 8 hrs after first dose. Alternatively, 8 mg PO 30 min before chemo and 8 h later. Post-op nausea: 4 mg IV/IM over 2-5 min or 16 mg PO 1 hr before anesthesia. Prevention of post-op N/V associated with radiotherapy: 8 mg PO tid.

PEDS - Prevention of nausea/vomiting with chemo: IV: Age > 3 yo: 0.15 mg/kg 30 minutes prior to chemo and repeated at 4 and 8 hrs after first dose. PO: Children 4-11 yo: 4 mg 30 minutes prior to chemo and repeated at 4 and 8 hrs after first dose. Children ≥12 yo:8 mg PO 30 min before chemo and 8 h later.

UNAPPROVED ADULT - Has been used in hyperemesis associated with pregnancy.

FORMS - Trade only: tab 4,8,24 mg,orally disintegrating tab 4, 8 mg, solution 4 mg/5 ml.

NOTES - Most common adverse effects - headache, fever, constipation, diarrhea. No experience using ondansetron in post-op nausea in children. Maximum oral dose in patients with severe liver disease is 8 mg/day.

GASTROENTEROLOGY: Antiemetics - Other

dimenhydrinate (*Dramamine*, ✤*Gravol*) ▸LK ♀B ▸- $

ADULT - Nausea: 50-100 mg/dose PO/IM/IV q4-6h prn. Maximum PO dose 400 mg/24h, maximum IM dose 300 mg/24h.

PEDS - Nausea: Age < 2 yo: not recommended. 2-6 yo: 12.5-25 mg PO q6-8h or 5 mg/kg/24h divided q6h. Children 6-12 yo: 25-50 mg PO q6-8h. Maximum daily PO doses: 2-6 yo: 75 mg/24h, 6-12 yo: 150 mg/24h.

FORMS - OTC: Generic/Trade: tab/cap 50 mg, liquid 12.5 mg/4 ml. Trade only: chew tab 50 mg, liquid 12.5 mg/ 4 ml (Children's Dramamine), 12 mg/5 ml. Rx: Generic/Trade: liquid 15.62 mg/5 ml.

NOTES - May cause drowsiness. Use with caution in conditions which may be aggravated by anticholinergic effects (i.e. prostatic hypertrophy, asthma, narrow-angle glaucoma).

doxylamine (*Unisom Nighttime Sleep Aid, others*) ▸L ♀A ▸? $

UNAPPROVED ADULT - Nausea and vomiting associated with pregnancy: 12.5 mg PO bid; often used in combination with pyridoxine.

FORMS - OTC Trade/Generic: tab 25 mg.

dronabinol (*Marinol*) ▸L ♀C ▸- ©III $$$$$

ADULT - Nausea with chemo: 5 mg/m2 1-3 h before chemo then 5 mg/m2/dose q2-4h after chemo for 4-6 doses/day. Dose can be increased to max 15 mg/m2. Anorexia associated with AIDS: Initially 2.5 mg PO bid before lunch and dinner. Maximum 20 mg/day.

PEDS - Not approved in children.

UNAPPROVED PEDS - Nausea with chemo: 5 mg/m2 1-3 h before chemo then 5 mg/m2/dose q2-4h after chemo for 4-6 doses/day. Dose can be increased to max 15 mg/m2.

FORMS - Trade only: cap 2.5,5,10 mg.

NOTES - Additive CNS effects with alcohol, sedatives, hypnotics, psychomimetics. Additive cardiac effects with amphetamines, antihistamines, anticholinergic medications, tricyclic antidepressants.

droperidol (*Inapsine*) ▸L ♀C ▸? $

ADULT - Antiemetic premedication : 0.625-2.5 mg IV or 2.5-10 mg IM.

PEDS - Preop: Age 2-12 yo: 0.088-0.165 mg/kg IV. Post-op antiemetic: 0.01-0.03 mg/kg/dose IV q 6-8h prn.

UNAPPROVED ADULT - Chemo-induced nausea: 2.5-5 mg IV/IM q 3-4h prn.

UNAPPROVED PEDS - Chemo-induced nausea: 0.05-0.06 mg/kg/dose IV/IM q 4-6h prn.

NOTES - Has no analgesic or amnestic effects. Consider lower doses in geriatric, debilitated, or high-risk patients such as those receiving other CNS depressants. May cause hypotension or tachycardia, extrapyramidal reactions, drowsiness.

meclizine (*Antivert, Bonine, Medivert, Meclicot, Meni-D*) ▸L ♀B ▸? $

ADULT - Motion sickness: 25-50 mg PO 1 hr before travel. May repeat q24h prn.

PEDS - Not approved in children.

FORMS - Rx/OTC/Generic/Trade: Tabs 12.5, 25 mg. chew Tabs 25 mg. Rx/Trade only: Tabs 30, 50 mg. Caps 25 mg.

NOTES - May cause dizziness and drowsiness.

metoclopramide (*Reglan*, ✤*Maxeran*) ▸K ♀B ▸+ $$

ADULT - Gastroesophageal reflux: 10-15 mg PO qid 30 min before meals and qhs. Diabetic gastric stasis: 10 mg PO/IV/IM 30 min before meals and bedtime. Prevention of chemo-induced emesis: 1-2 mg/kg 30 min before chemo and then q2h for 2 doses then q3h for 3 doses prn. Prevention of post-op nausea: 10-20 mg IM/IV near end of surgical procedure, may repeat q3-4 h prn. Intubation of small intestine: 10 mg IV. Radiographic exam of upper GI tract: 10 mg IV.

PEDS - Intubation of small intestine: Age < 6 yo: 0.1 mg/kg IV. 6-14 yo: 2.5-5 mg IV. Radiographic exam of upper GI tract: Age < 6 yo: 0.1

mg/kg IV; 6-14 yo: 2.5-5 mg IV.

UNAPPROVED ADULT - Prevention/treatment of chemo-induced emesis: 3 mg/kg over 1h followed by continuous IV infusion of 0.5 mg/kg/h for 12h. To improve patient response to ergotamine, analgesics and sedatives in migraines: 10 mg PO 5-10 min before ergotamine/analgesic/sedative.

UNAPPROVED PEDS - Gastroesophageal reflux: 0.4-0.8 mg/kg/day in 4 divided doses. Prevention of chemo-induced emesis: 1-2 mg/kg 30 min before chemo and then q3h prn.

FORMS - Generic/Trade: tabs 5,10 mg, liquid 5 mg/5 ml.

NOTES - If extrapyramidal reactions occur (especially with high IV doses) give diphenhydramine IM/IV. Adjust dose in renal dysfunction. May cause drowsiness, agitation, seizures, hallucinations, galactorrhea, constipation, diarrhea. Increases aspirin, diazepam, ethanol, lithium absorption. Do not use if bowel perforation or mechanical obstruction present. Levodopa decreases metoclopramide effects. Tardive dyskinesia in <1% with long-term use.

phosphorated carbohydrates (*Emetrol*) ▶L ♀A ▶+ $

ADULT - Nausea: 15-30 ml PO q15min until nausea subsides or up to 5 doses.

PEDS - Nausea: 2-12 yo: 5-10 ml q15min until nausea subsides or up to 5 doses.

UNAPPROVED ADULT - Morning sickness: 15-30 ml PO upon rising, repeat q3h prn. Motion sickness or nausea due to drug therapy or anesthesia: 15 ml/dose.

UNAPPROVED PEDS - Regurgitation in infants: 5-10 ml PO 10-15 min prior to each feeding. Motion sickness or nausea due to drug therapy or anesthesia: 5 ml/dose.

FORMS - OTC Generic/Trade: Solution containing dextrose and fructose.

NOTES - Do not dilute. Do not ingest fluids before or for 15 min after dose. Monitor blood glucose in diabetic patients.

prochlorperazine (*Compazine*, ♣*Stemetil*) ▶LK ♀C ▶? $

ADULT - Nausea and vomiting: 5-10 mg PO/IM tid-qid max 40 mg/day; 15-30 mg PO qd or 10 mg PO q12h of sustained release or 15 mg PO qam of sustained release; 25 mg PR q12h; 5-10 mg IV over at least 2 min q3-4h prn max 40 mg/day; 5-10 mg IM q3-4h prn max 40 mg/day.

PEDS - Nausea and vomiting: Age <2 yo or <10 kg: not recommended. >2 yo: 0.4 mg/kg/day PO/PR in 3-4 divided doses; 0.1-0.15 mg/kg/dose IM; IV not recommended.

UNAPPROVED PEDS - N/V during surgery: 5-10 mg IM 1-2 hr before anesthesia induction, may repeat in 30 min; 5-10 mg IV 15-30 min before anesthesia induction, may repeat once.

FORMS - Generic/Trade: tabs 5,10,25 mg, supp 25 mg. Trade only: extended release (Compazine Spansules) 10,15,30 mg, supp 2.5,5 mg, liquid 5 mg/5 ml.

NOTES - May cause extrapyramidal reactions, hypotension (with IV), arrhythmias, sedation, seizures, gynecomastia, dry mouth, constipation, urinary retention, leukopenia, thrombocytopenia.

promethazine (*Phenergan*) ▶LK ♀C ▶- $

ADULT - Nausea and vomiting: 12.5-25 mg q4-6h PO/IM/PR prn. Motion sickness: 25 mg PO 30-60 min prior to departure and q12h prn.

PEDS - Nausea and vomiting: 0.25-0.5 mg/kg/dose PO/IM/PR q4-6h prn. Motion sickness: 0.5 mg/kg PO 30-60 min prior to departure and q12h prn.

UNAPPROVED ADULT - Nausea and vomiting: 12.5-25 mg IV q4h prn.

UNAPPROVED PEDS - Nausea and vomiting: 0.25-0.5 mg/kg/dose IV q4h prn.

FORMS - Generic/Trade: tab 25,50 mg, syrup 6.25 mg/5 ml, supp 50 mg. Trade only: tab 12.5 mg, syrup 25 mg/5 ml, supp 12.5,25 mg.

NOTES - May cause sedation, extrapyramidal reactions (esp. with high IV doses), hypotension with rapid IV administration, anticholinergic side effects, eg, dry mouth, blurred vision.

scopolamine (*Transderm Scop*, ♣*Transderm-V*) ▶L ♀C ▶+ $

ADULT - Motion sickness: 1 disc behind ear at least 4h before travel and q3 days prn. Prevention of post-op nausea/vomiting: Apply patch behind ear 4 h before surgery, remove 24 h after surgery.

PEDS - Not approved in children < 12 yo.

FORMS - Trade only: topical disc 1.5 mg/72h, box of 4.

NOTES - Dry mouth common. Also causes drowsiness, blurred vision.

thiethylperazine (*Torecan*) ▶L ♀? ▶? $

ADULT - Nausea/vomiting:10 mg PO/IM 1-3 times/day.

PEDS - Not approved in children.

FORMS - Trade only: tab 10 mg.

trimethobenzamide (*Tigan*) ▶LK ♀C but + ▶? $

ADULT - Nausea and vomiting: 250 mg PO q6-8h, 200 mg PR/IM q6-8h.

PEDS - N/V: Children < 13.6kg (except neonates): 100 mg PR q6-8h. Children 13.6-40.9

kg: 100-200 mg PO/PR q6-8h.
FORMS - Trade only: cap 100 mg. Generic/ Trade: cap 250 mg, supp 100,200 mg.
NOTES - Not for IV use. May cause sedation.

GASTROENTEROLOGY: Antiulcer - Antacids

aluminum hydroxide (*Alternagel, Amphojel, Alu-tab*) ▶K ♀+ (? 1st trimester) ◗? $
ADULT - Hyperphosphatemia in chronic renal failure (short term treatment only to avoid aluminum accumulation): 30-60 ml PO with meals. Upset stomach, indigestion: 5-10 ml or 1-2 tabs PO 6 times/day, between meals & qhs & prn.
PEDS - Not approved in children.
UNAPPROVED ADULT - Hyperphosphatemia in chronic renal failure (short term treatment only to avoid aluminum accumulation): 30-60 ml PO with meals. Symptomatic reflux: 15-30 ml PO q30-60 min. For long-term management of reflux disease: 15-30 ml PO 1 and 3 h after meals and qhs prn. Peptic ulcer disease: 15-45 ml or 1-3 tab PO 1 and 3h after meals and qhs. Prophylaxis against GI bleeding (titrate dose to maintain gastric pH > 3.5): 30-60 ml or 2-4 tab PO q1-2h.
UNAPPROVED PEDS - Peptic ulcer disease: 5-15 ml PO 1 and 3h after meals and qhs. Prophylaxis against GI bleeding (titrate dose to maintain gastric pH > 3.5): Neonates 0.5-1 ml/kg/dose PO q4h. Infants 2-5 ml PO q1-2h. Child: 5-15 ml PO q1-2h.
FORMS - OTC Generic/Trade: tabs 300,475, 500,600 mg, susp 320,450,600,675 mg/5 ml.
NOTES - For concentrated suspensions, use ½ the recommended dose. May cause constipation. Avoid administration with tetracyclines, digoxin, iron, isoniazid, buffered/enteric aspirin, diazepam.

calcium carbonate (*Tums, Mylanta Children's, Titralac, Rolaids Calcium Rich, Surpass*) ▶K ♀+ (? 1st trimester) ◗? $
ADULT - Antacid: 1000-3000 mg (2-4 tab) PO q2h prn or 1-2 pieces gum chewed prn, max 8000 mg/day.
PEDS - Safe dosing above the RDA has not been established.
UNAPPROVED PEDS - Hypocalcemia: 20-65 mg/kg/day elem Ca PO in 4 divided doses.
FORMS - OTC Generic/Trade: tabs 350,400, 420,500,550,650,750, 850,1000 mg, susp 400, 1250 mg/5 ml, gum (Surpass) 300, 450 mg.
NOTES - May cause constipation. Avoid concomitant administration with tetracyclines.

***Maalox* (aluminum & magnesium hydroxide)** ▶K ♀+ (? 1st trimester) ◗? $
ADULT - Heartburn/indigestion: 10-20 ml or 1-4 tab PO qid, after meals and qhs and prn.
PEDS - Not approved in children.
UNAPPROVED ADULT - Peptic ulcer disease: 15-45 ml PO 1 & 3h after meals & qhs. Symptomatic reflux: 15-30 ml PO q30-60 min prn. For long-term management of reflux disease: 15-30 ml PO 1 and 3 h after meals & qhs prn. Prophylaxis against GI bleeding (titrate dose to maintain gastric pH > 3.5): 30-60 ml PO q1-2h.
UNAPPROVED PEDS - Peptic ulcer disease: 5-15 ml PO 1 and 3h after meals and qhs. Prophylaxis against GI bleeding (titrate dose to maintain gastric pH > 3.5): Neonates 1 ml/kg/dose PO q4h. Infants 2-5 ml PO q1-2h. Child: 5-15 ml PO q1-2h.
FORMS - OTC Generic/Trade: chew tabs, susp.
NOTES - Maalox Extra Strength and Maalox TC are more concentrated than Maalox. Maalox Plus has added simethicone. May cause constipation or diarrhea. Avoid concomitant administration with tetracyclines, digoxin, iron, isoniazid, buffered/enteric aspirin, diazepam. Avoid chronic use in patients with renal dysfunction due to potential for magnesium accumulation.

magaldrate (*Riopan*) ▶K ♀+ (? 1st trimester) ◗? $
ADULT - Relief of upset stomach: 5-10 ml between meals and qhs and prn.
PEDS - Not approved in children.
UNAPPROVED PEDS - Peptic ulcer disease: 5-10 ml PO 1 and 3h after meals and qhs.
FORMS - OTC Generic/Trade: susp 540 mg/5 ml. (Riopan Plus available as susp 540, 1080 mg/5 ml, chew tab 480, 1080).
NOTES - Riopan Plus has added simethicone. Avoid concomitant administration with tetracyclines, digoxin, iron, isoniazid, buffered/enteric aspirin, diazepam Avoid chronic use in patients with renal failure.

***Mylanta suspension* (aluminum & magnesium hydroxide + simethicone)** ▶K ♀+ (? 1st trimester) ◗? $
ADULT - Heartburn/indigestion: 10-45 ml or 2-4 tab PO qid, after meals and qhs and prn.
PEDS - Safe dosing has not been established.
UNAPPROVED ADULT - Peptic ulcer disease: 15-45 ml PO 1 and 3h after meals and qhs.

Symptomatic reflux: 15-30 ml PO q30-60 min. For long-term management of reflux: 15-30 ml PO 1 and 3 h postprandially and qhs prn.
UNAPPROVED PEDS - Peptic ulcer disease: 5-15 ml PO 1 and 3h after meals and qhs.
FORMS - OTC Generic/Trade: Liquid, double strength liquid, tab, double strength tab.
NOTES - Mylanta Gelcaps contain calcium carbonate and magnesium hydroxide. May cause constipation or diarrhea. Avoid concomitant administration with tetracyclines, digoxin, iron, isoniazid, buffered/enteric aspirin, diazepam. Avoid in renal dysfunction.

GASTROENTEROLOGY: Antiulcer - H2 Antagonists

cimetidine (*Tagamet, Tagamet HB*) ▶LK ♀B ◗+ $$$
ADULT - Treatment of duodenal or gastric ulcer: 800 mg PO qhs or 300 mg PO qid with meals and qhs or 400 mg PO bid. Prevention of duodenal ulcer: 400 mg PO qhs. Erosive esophagitis: 800 mg PO bid or 400 mg PO qid. Heartburn: (otc product only approved for this indication) 200 mg PO prn max 400 mg/day. Hypersecretory conditions: 300 mg PO qid with meals and qhs. Patients unable to take oral medications: 300 mg IV/IM q6-8h or 37.5 mg/h continuous IV infusion. Prevention of upper GI bleeding in critically ill patients: 50 mg/h continuous infusion.
PEDS - Not approved in children.
UNAPPROVED ADULT - Prevention of aspiration pneumonitis during surgery: 400-600 mg PO or 300 mg IV 60-90 min prior to anesthesia.
UNAPPROVED PEDS - Treatment of duodenal or gastric ulcers, erosive esophagitis, hypersecretory conditions: Neonates and infants: 10-20 mg/kg/day PO/IV/IM divided q6h. Children: 20-40 mg/kg/day PO/IV/IM divided q6h. Chronic viral warts in children: 25-40 mg/kg/day PO in divided doses.
FORMS - Generic/Trade: tab 200,300,400,800 mg, liquid 300 mg/5 ml. OTC, trade only: tab 100 mg, susp 200 mg/20 ml.
NOTES - May cause dizziness, drowsiness, headache, diarrhea, nausea. Decreased absorption of ketoconazole, itraconazole. Increased levels of carbamazepine, cyclosporine, diazepam, labetolol, lidocaine, theophylline, phenytoin, procainamide, quinidine, propranolol, tricyclic antidepressants, valproic acid, warfarin. Stagger doses of cimetidine and antacids. Decrease dose with Clcr < 40 ml/min.

famotidine (*Pepcid, Pepcid RPD, Pepcid AC*) ▶LK ♀B ◗? $$$$
ADULT - Treatment of duodenal ulcer: 40 mg PO qhs or 20 mg PO bid. Maintenance of duodenal ulcer: 20 mg PO qhs. Treatment of gastric ulcer: 40 mg PO qhs. GERD: 20 mg PO bid. Treatment or prevention of heartburn: (otc product only approved for this indication) 10 mg PO prn max 20 mg/day. Hypersecretory conditions: 20 mg PO q6h. Patients unable to take oral medications: 20 mg IV q12h.
PEDS - Not approved in children.
UNAPPROVED ADULT - Prevention of aspiration pneumonitis during surgery: 40 mg PO/IM prior to anesthesia. Upper GI bleeding: 20 mg IV q12h.
UNAPPROVED PEDS - Treatment of duodenal or gastric ulcers, GERD, hypersecretory conditions: 0.6-0.8 mg/kg/day IV in 2-3 divided doses or 1-1.2 mg/kg/day PO in 2-3 divided doses, maximum 40 mg/day.
FORMS - Generic/Trade: tab 10 mg (OTC, Pepcid AC Acid Controller), 20, 30 mg. Trade only: orally disintegrating tab (Pepcid RPD) 20, 40 mg, suspension 40 mg/5 ml.
NOTES - May cause dizziness, headache, constipation, diarrhea. Decreased absorption of ketoconazole, itraconazole. Adjust dose in patients with Clcr < 60 ml/min.

nizatadine (*Axid, Axid AR*) ▶K ♀C ◗? $$$$
ADULT - Treatment of duodenal or gastric ulcer: 300 mg PO qhs or 150 mg PO bid. Maintenance of duodenal ulcer: 150 mg PO qhs. GERD: 150 mg PO bid. Treatment or prevention of heartburn: (otc product only approved for this indication) 75 mg PO prn, max 150 mg/day.
PEDS - Not approved in children.
UNAPPROVED PEDS - 6 mos-11 yo (limited data): 6-10 mg/kg/day PO in 2 divided doses.
FORMS - Trade only: tabs 75 mg (OTC, Axid AR), cap 150,300 mg.
NOTES - May cause dizziness, headache, constipation, diarrhea. Decreased absorption of ketoconazole, itraconazole. Adjust dose in patients with Clcr < 80 ml/min.

***Pepcid Complete* (famotidine + calcium carbonate + magnesium hydroxide)** ▶LK ♀B ◗? $
ADULT - Treatment of heartburn: 1 tab PO prn.

Max 2 tabs/day.

PEDS - Not approved in children.

FORMS - OTC: Trade only: chew tab famotidine 10 mg with calcium carbonate 800 mg & magnesium hydroxide 165 mg.

ranitidine (*Zantac, Zantac 75, Peptic Relief*) ▶K ♀B ▶? $$$

ADULT - Treatment of duodenal ulcer: 150 mg PO bid or 300 mg qhs. Treatment of gastric ulcer or GERD: 150 mg PO bid. Maintenance of duodenal or gastric ulcer: 150 mg PO qhs. Treatment of erosive esophagitis: 150 mg PO qid. Maintenance of erosive esophagitis: 150 mg PO bid. Treatment of heartburn: (otc product only approved for this indication) 75 mg PO prn, max 150 mg/day. Hypersecretory conditions: 150 mg PO bid. Patients unable to take oral meds: 50 mg IV/IM q6-8h or 6.25 mg/h continuous IV infusion.

PEDS - Not approved in children.

UNAPPROVED ADULT - Prevention of upper GI bleeding in critically ill patients: 6.25 mg/h continuous IV infusion (150 mg/d).

UNAPPROVED PEDS - Treatment of duodenal or gastric ulcers, GERD, hypersecretory conditions: Neonates: 2-4 mg/kg/24h PO divided q8-12h or 2 mg/kg/24h IV divided q6-8h. Infants and children: 4-5 mg/kg/24h PO divided q8-12h or 2-4 mg/kg/24h IV/IM divided q6-8h.

FORMS - Generic/Trade: tabs 75 mg (OTC, Zantac 75), 150,300 mg, syrup 75 mg/5 ml. Trade only: effervescent tab 150 mg, caps 150,300 mg, granules 150 mg.

NOTES - May cause dizziness, sedation, headache, drowsiness, rash, nausea, constipation, diarrhea. Variable effects on warfarin, decreased absorption of ketoconazole, itraconazole. Dissolve granules & effervescent tablet in water. Stagger doses of ranitidine & antacids. Adjust dose in patients with Clcr < 50 ml/min.

GASTROENTEROLOGY: Antiulcer - Helicobacter pylori Treatment

*Regimen**	*Dosing*	*Eradication*
lansoprazole, and clarithromycin, and amoxicillin *(PrevPac)*	30 mg PO bid x 14 days 500 mg PO bid x 14 days 1g PO bid x 14 days EQUALS 1 *Prevpac* dose PO bid x 2 wks	86%
omeprazole, and clarithromycin, and amoxicillin	20 mg PO bid x 14 days 500 mg PO bid x 14 days 1 g PO bid x 14 days	80-86%
lansoprazole, <u>or</u> omeprazole, and clarithromycin, and metronidazole	30 mg PO bid x 14 days <u>or</u> 20 mg PO bid x 14 days 500 mg PO bid x 14 days 500 mg PO bid x 14 days	≥ 80%
lansoprazole, <u>or</u> omeprazole, and BSS, and metronidazole and tetracycline	30 mg PO qd x 14 days <u>or</u> 20 mg PO qd x 14 days 525mg PO qid x 14 days 500 mg PO tid x 14 days 500 mg PO qid x 14 days	83-95%
famotidine, <u>or</u> ranitidine, <u>or</u> nizatidine, and BSS, and metronidazole, and tetracycline**	40 mg/d PO qd/bid x 28 days <u>or</u> 300 mg/day PO qd/bid x 28 days <u>or</u> 300 mg/day PO qd/bid x 28 days 525 mg PO qid x initial14 days 250 mg PO qid x initial14 days 500 mg PO qid x initial14 days	≥ 80%

**American College of Gastroenterology Guidelines (Am J Gastroenterol 1998; 93:2330). BSS = bismuth subsalicylate (Pepto-Bismol) **BSS,metronidazole, tetracycline available as Helidac.*

***Helidac* (bismuth subsalicylate + metronidazole + tetracycline)** ▶LK ♀D ▶- $$

ADULT - Active duodenal ulcer associated with Helicobacter pylori: 1 dose (2 bismuth subsalicylate Tabs, 1 metronidazole tab and 1 tetracycline cap) PO qid, at meals and qhs for 2 weeks with an H2 antagonist.

PEDS - Not approved in children.

UNAPPROVED ADULT - Active duodenal ulcer associated with Helicobacter pylori: Same dose

as in "adult", but substitute proton pump inhibitor for H2 antagonist.
FORMS - Trade only: Each dose: bismuth subsalicylate 524 (2x262 mg) + metronidazole 250 mg + tetracycline 500 mg.
NOTES - Tetracycline decreases effectiveness of oral contraceptives; use another form of contraception during therapy. Avoid alcohol. May cause photosensitivity, darkening of tongue and stools, nausea.

PrevPac **(lansoprazole + amoxicillin + clarithromycin, ✱*Hp-Pac*)** ▶LK ♀C ▶? $$$$$
ADULT - Active duodenal ulcer associated with Helicobacter pylori: 1 dose PO bid x 14 days.
PEDS - Not approved in children.
FORMS - Trade only: lansoprazole 30 mg + amoxicillin 1 g (2x500 mg), clarithromycin 500 mg.
NOTES - See components.

Tritec **(ranitidine bismuth citrate)** ▶K ♀C ▶? $$$
ADULT - Product discontinued by Glaxo. Active duodenal ulcers associated with H pylori: 400 mg PO bid x 4 weeks in conjunction with clarithromycin 500 mg PO tid for the first 2 weeks.
PEDS - Not approved in children.
FORMS - Trade only: tab 400 mg.
NOTES - May cause darkening of stools and tongue. Variable effects on warfarin, decreased absorption of ketoconazole, itraconazole. Use caution in patients with renal dysfunction. Do not use if Clcr < 25 ml/min.

GASTROENTEROLOGY: Antiulcer - Other

Bellergal-S **(phenobarbital + belladonna + ergotamine)** ▶LK ♀X ▶- $$
ADULT - Hypermotility/hypersecretion: 1 tab PO bid.
PEDS - Not approved in children.
FORMS - Generic/Trade: tab phenobarbital 40 mg, ergotamine 0.6 mg, belladonna 0.2 mg.
NOTES - May decrease INR in patients receiving warfarin. Variable effect on phenytoin levels. May cause sedation especially with alcohol, phenothiazines, narcotics, or tricyclic antidepressants. Additive anticholinergic effects with tricyclic antidepressants.

dicyclomine (*Bentyl, Bentylol*) ▶LK♀B ▶- $$
ADULT - Treatment of functional bowel/irritable bowel syndrome (irritable colon, spastic colon, mucous colon): Initiate with 20 mg PO qid and increase to 40 mg PO qid, if tolerated. Patients who are unable to take oral medications: 20 mg IM q6h.
PEDS - Not approved in children.
UNAPPROVED PEDS - Treatment of functional / irritable bowel syndrome: Infants > 6 months: 5 mg PO tid-qid. Children: 10 mg PO tid-qid.
FORMS - Generic/Trade: tab 20 mg, cap 10 mg, syrup 10 mg/5 ml. Generic only: cap 20 mg.
NOTES - Although some use lower doses (i.e., 10-20 mg PO qid), the only adult oral dose proven to be effective is 160 mg/day.

Donnatal **(phenobarbital + atropine + hyoscyamine + scopolamine)** ▶LK ♀C ▶- $
ADULT - Adjunctive therapy of irritable bowel syndrome or adjunctive treatment of duodenal ulcers: 1-2 tabs/caps or 5-10 ml PO tid-qid or 1 extended release tab PO q8-12h.
PEDS - Adjunctive therapy of irritable bowel syndrome: 0.1 ml/kg/dose PO q4h, maximum dose 5 ml. Adjunctive treatment of duodenal ulcers: 0.1 ml/kg/dose q4h. Alternative dosing regimen: Weight 4.5kg: 0.5 ml PO q4h or 0.75 ml PO q6h; 9.1kg: 1 ml PO q4h or 1.5 ml PO q6h; 13.6kg: 1.5 ml PO q4h or 2 ml PO q6h; 22.7kg: 2.5 ml PO q4h or 3.75 ml PO q6h; 34kg: 3.75 ml PO q4h or 5 ml PO q6h; 45.5kg: 5 ml PO q4h or 7.5 ml PO q6h.
FORMS - Generic/Trade: Phenobarbital 16.2 mg + hyoscyamine 0.1 mg + atropine 0.02 mg + scopolamine 6.5 mcg in each tab, cap or 5 ml. Each extended release tab has phenobarbital 48.6 mg + hyoscyamine 0.3111 mg + atropine 0.0582 mg + scopolamine 0.0195 mg.
NOTES - The FDA has classified Donnatal as "possibly effective" for treatment of irritable bowel syndrome and duodenal ulcer. Heat stroke may occur in hot weather. Can cause anticholinergic side effects; use caution in narrow-angle glaucoma, BPH, etc.

GI cocktail (*green goddess*) ▶LK ♀See individual ▶See individual $
UNAPPROVED ADULT - Acute GI upset: mixture of Maalox/Mylanta 30 ml + viscous lidocaine (2%) 10 ml + Donnatal 10 ml administered PO in a single dose.
NOTES - Avoid repeat dosing due to risk of lidocaine toxicity.

hyoscyamine (*Levsin, NuLev*) ▶LK ♀C ▶- $
ADULT - Control gastric secretion, GI hypermotility, irritable bowel syndrome, and others: 0.125-0.25 mg PO/SL q4h prn; 0.375-0.75 mg PO q12h of sustained release preparations.

PEDS - Control gastric secretion, GI hypermotility, irritable bowel syndrome, and others: Initial oral dose by weight for children < 2 yo: 12.5 mcg (2.3 kg), 16.7 mcg (3.4 kg), 20.8 mcg (5 kg), 25 mcg (7 kg), 31.3-33.3 mcg (10 kg), and 45.8 mcg (15 kg). Doses can be repeated q4h prn, but maximum daily dose is six times initial dose. Initial oral dose by weight for children 2-12 yo: 31.3-33.3 mcg (10kg), 62.5 mcg (20kg), 93.8 mcg (40kg), and 125 mcg (50kg). Doses may be repeated q4h, but maximum daily dose should not exceed 750 mcg.

FORMS - Generic/Trade: tab 0.125,0.15 mg, SL tab 0.125 mg, solution 0.125 mg/ml. Trade only: extended release tab/cap 0.375 mg, orally disintegrating tab 0.125 mg (NuLev), elixir 0.125 mg/5 ml.

NOTES - May cause drowsiness, dizziness, blurred vision. Can cause anticholinergic side effects so use caution in narrow-angle glaucoma, BPH, etc.

misoprostol (*Cytotec*) ▶LK ♀X ◗- $$$$

WARNING - Contraindicated in pregnant women because of its abortificant properties. Do not use in women of child-bearing potential unless patient requires NSAID and is at high risk of complications from gastric ulcer. If misoprostol is used in such patients, they must receive oral and written warnings, have a negative serum pregnancy test within 2 weeks before starting therapy, begin therapy on 2nd or 3rd day of next normal menstrual period and use effective contraceptive measures.

ADULT - Prevention of NSAID-induced gastric ulcers: 200 mcg PO qid. If not tolerated, use 100 mcg PO qid.

PEDS - Not approved in children.

UNAPPROVED ADULT - Treatment of duodenal ulcers: 100 mcg PO qid. Prevention of NSAID-induced gastric ulcers: 200 mcg PO bid-tid.

UNAPPROVED PEDS - Improvement in fat absorption in cystic fibrosis in children 8 - 16 yo: 100 mcg PO qid.

FORMS - Trade only: tab 100,200 mcg.

NOTES - Many practitioners start at 100 mcg PO qid and increase to 200 mcg PO qid, if tolerated. Does not prevent duodenal ulcers in patients on NSAIDs. Take with food. May cause diarrhea (13-40%) and abdominal pain (7-20%).

propantheline (*Pro-Banthine*) ▶LK ♀C ◗- $$$

ADULT - Adjunctive therapy in peptic ulcer disease: 7.5-15 mg PO 30 min before meals and qhs.

PEDS - Not approved in children.

UNAPPROVED ADULT - Irritable bowel, pancreatitis, urinary bladder spasms: 7.5-15 mg PO qid.

UNAPPROVED PEDS - Antisecretory effects: 1.5 mg/kg/day PO in 3-4 divided doses. Antispasmodic effects: 2-3 mg/kg/day PO divided q4-6h and qhs.

FORMS - Generic/Trade: tab 15 mg. Trade only: tab 7.5 mg.

NOTES - For elderly adults and those with small stature use 7.5 mg dose. May cause constipation, dry mucous membranes.

simethicone (*Mylicon, Gas-X, Phazyme*) ▶Not absorbed ♀C but + ◗? $

ADULT - Excessive gas in GI tract: 40-160 mg PO after meals and qhs prn, max 500 mg/day.

PEDS - Excessive gas in GI tract: < 2 yo: 20 mg PO qid prn, maximum of 240 mg/d. Children 2-12 yo: 40 mg PO qid prn.

UNAPPROVED PEDS - Has been used to treat infant colic in dose above for gas.

FORMS - OTC: Generic/Trade: tab 60,95 mg, chew tab 40,80,125 mg, cap 125 mg, drops 40 mg/0.6 ml.

NOTES - For administration to infants, may mix dose in 30 ml of liquid. chew Tabs should be chewed thoroughly.

sucralfate (*Carafate*, ✤*Sulcrate*) ▶Not absorbed ♀B ◗? $$$

ADULT - Duodenal ulcer: 1g PO qid, 1h before meals and qhs. Maintenance therapy of duodenal ulcer: 1g PO bid.

PEDS - Not approved in children.

UNAPPROVED ADULT - Gastric ulcer, reflux esophagitis, NSAID-induced GI symptoms, stress ulcer prophylaxis: 1g PO qid 1h before meals & qhs. Oral and esophageal ulcers due to radiation/chemo/sclerotherapy: (suspension only) 5-10 ml swish and spit /swallow qid.

UNAPPROVED PEDS - Reflux esophagitis, gastric or duodenal ulcer, stress ulcer prophylaxis: 40-80 mg/kg/day PO divided q6h. Alternative dosing: children < 6 yo: 500 mg PO qid, children > 6 yo: 1g PO qid.

FORMS - Generic/Trade: tab 1 g. Trade only: susp 1 g/10 ml.

NOTES - May cause constipation. May reduce the absorption of cimetidine, ciprofloxacin, digoxin, ketoconazole, itraconazole, norfloxacin, phenytoin, ranitidine, tetracycline, theophylline and warfarin; separate doses by at least 2 hours. Antacids should be separated by at least 30 minutes.

GASTROENTEROLOGY: Antiulcer - Proton Pump Inhibitors

esomeprazole (*Nexium*) ▶L ♀B ▶? $$$$

ADULT - Erosive esophagitis: 20-40 mg PO qd x 4-8 weeks. Maintenance of erosive esophagitis: 20 mg PO qd. GERD: 20 mg PO qd x 4 weeks. H pylori eradication: 40 mg PO qd x 10 days with amoxicillin & clarithromycin.

PEDS - Not approved in children.

FORMS - Trade only: delayed release cap 20, 40 mg.

NOTES - May decrease absoption of ketoconazole, itraconazole, digoxin, iron, and ampicillin.

lansoprazole (*Prevacid*) ▶L ♀B ▶? $$$$

ADULT - Erosive esophagitis: 30 mg PO qd. Maintenance therapy following healing of erosive esophagitis: 15 mg PO qd. NSAID-induced gastric ulcer 30 mg PO qd x 8 weeks (treatment), 15 mg PO qd for up to 12 weeks (prevention). GERD: 15 mg PO qd. Duodenal ulcer treatment and maintenance: 15 mg PO qd. Gastric ulcer: 30 mg PO qd. Part of a multidrug regimen for Helicobacter pylori eradiaction: 30 mg PO qd-bid depending on regimen (see table). Hypersecretory conditions: 60 mg PO qd.

PEDS - Not approved in children.

FORMS - Trade only: cap 15,30 mg. Susp 15,30 mg packets.

NOTES - Take before meals. Avoid concomitant administration with sucralfate. May decrease absorption of ketoconazole, itraconazole, ampicillin, digoxin and iron.

omeprazole (*Prilosec, Losec*) ▶L♀C▶? $$$$

ADULT - GERD: 20 mg PO qd. Maintenance therapy following healing of erosive esophagitis: 20 mg PO qd. Duodenal ulcer: 20 mg PO qd. Gastric ulcer: 40 mg PO qd. Hypersecretory conditions: 60 mg PO qd.

PEDS - Not approved in children.

UNAPPROVED PEDS - GERD, gastric or duodenal ulcers, hypersecretory states: 0.7-3.3 mg/kg/dose PO qd.

FORMS - Trade only: cap 10,20,40 mg.

NOTES - Take before meals. Caps contain enteric-coated granules; do not chew. Caps may be opened and administered in acidic liquid (i.e. apple juice). May increase levels of diazepam, warfarin, and phenytoin. May decrease absorption of ketoconazole, itraconazole, iron, ampicillin, and digoxin. Avoid administration with sucralfate.

pantoprazole (*Protonix, Pantoloc*) ▶L ♀B ▶? $$$

ADULT - GERD: 40 mg PO qd for 8-16 weeks, or 40 mg IV qd x 7-10 days until taking PO. Maintenance therapy following healing of erosive esophagitis: 40 mg PO qd.

PEDS - Not approved in children.

FORMS - Trade only: tab 40 mg.

NOTES - May decrease absoption of ketoconazole, itraconazole, digoxin, iron, and ampicillin.

rabeprazole (*Aciphex*) ▶L ♀B ▶? $$$$

ADULT - GERD: 20 mg PO qd x8-16 weeks. Duodenal ulcers: 20 mg PO qd x 4 weeks. Zollinger-Ellison syndrome: 60 mg PO qd, may increase up to 100 mg qd or 60 mg bid.

PEDS - Not approved in children.

FORMS - Trade only: tab 20 mg.

NOTES - May decrease absorption of ketoconazole, itraconazole, digoxin, iron, and ampicillin.

GASTROENTEROLOGY: Laxatives

bisacodyl (*Correctol, Dulcolax, Feen-a-Mint*) ▶L ♀+ ▶? $

ADULT - Constipation/colonic evacuation prior to a procedure: 10-15 mg PO qd prn, 10 mg PR qd prn.

PEDS - Constipation/colonic evacuation prior to a procedure: 0.3 mg/kg/d PO qd prn. Children < 2 yo: 5 mg PR prn. 2-11 yo: 5-10 mg PR prn. >11 yo: 10 mg PR prn.

FORMS - OTC Generic/Trade: tab 5 mg, supp 10 mg.

NOTES - Oral tablet has onset of 6-10 h. Onset of action of suppository is approximately 15-60 min. Do not chew Tabs, swallow whole. Do not give within 1h of antacids or dairy products. Chronic use of stimulant laxatives may lead to a poorly functioning colon.

cascara ▶L ♀C ▶+ $

ADULT - Constipation: 325 mg PO qhs prn or 5 ml/day of aromatic fluid extract PO qhs prn.

PEDS - Constipation: Infants: 1.25 ml/day of aromatic fluid extract PO qd prn. Children 2-11 yo: 2.5 ml/day of extract PO qd prn.

FORMS - OTC Generic: tab 325 mg, liquid aromatic fluid extract.

NOTES - Cascara sagrada fluid extract is 5 times more potent than cascara sagrada aromatic fluid extract.

castor oil (*Purge, Fleet Flavored Castor Oil*) ▶Not absorbed ♀- ▶? $

ADULT - Constipation: 15 ml PO qd prn. Colonic evacuation prior to procedure: 15-30 ml of castor oil or 30-60 ml emulsified castor oil PO as a single dose 16h prior to procedure.

PEDS - Colonic evacuation prior to procedure: Children < 2 yo: 1-5 ml of castor oil or 5-15 ml emulsified castor oil PO as a single dose 16h prior to procedure. 2-11 yo: 5-15 ml of castor oil or 7.5-30 ml of emulsified castor oil PO as a single dose 16h prior to procedure.

FORMS - OTC Generic/Trade: liquid 30,60,120, 480 ml, emulsified susp 45,60,90,120 ml.

NOTES - Emulsions somewhat mask the bad taste. Onset of action approximately 2-6h. Do not give at bedtime. Chill or administer with juice to improve taste.

docusate calcium (*Surfak*) ▶L ♀+ ▶? $

ADULT - Constipation: 240 mg PO qd.

PEDS - Safe dosing has not been established.

UNAPPROVED PEDS - Constipation: 50-150 mg PO qd.

FORMS - OTC Generic/Trade: cap 240 mg. Trade only: cap 50 mg.

NOTES - Takes 1-3 days to notably soften stools.

docusate sodium (*Colace*) ▶L ♀+ ▶? $

ADULT - Constipation: 50-400 mg/day PO in 1-4 divided doses.

PEDS - Constipation: Children < 3 yo: 10-40 mg/day PO in 1-4 divided doses. 3-6 yo: 20-60 mg/day PO in 1-4 divided doses. 6-12 yo: 40-150 mg/day PO in 1-4 divided doses.

UNAPPROVED ADULT - Constipation: Can be given as a retention enema: Mix 50-100 mg docusate liquid with saline or oil retention enema for rectal use.

FORMS - OTC Generic/Trade: cap 50,100,240, 250 mg, tab 50,100 mg, liquid 10 & 50 mg/5 ml, syrup 16.75 & 20 mg/5 ml.

NOTES - Takes 1-3 days to notably soften stools. Use higher doses initially. Liquids (not syrups) should be mixed with juice, milk or formula to mask bitter taste.

glycerin ▶Not absorbed ♀C ▶? $

ADULT - Constipation: 1 adult supp PR prn.

PEDS - Constipation: Neonates: 0.5 ml/kg/dose PR prn. Children <6 yo: 1 infant supp or 2-5 ml rectal solution as an enema PR prn. Children ≥6 yo: 1 adult supp or 5-15 ml of rectal solution as enema PR prn.

FORMS - OTC Generic/Trade: supp infant & adult, solution (Fleet Babylax) 4 ml/applicator.

lactulose (*Chronulac, Cephulac, Kristalose, ✤Acilac*) ▶Not absorbed ♀B ▶? $$

ADULT - Constipation: 15-30 ml (syrup) or 10-20 g (powder for oral solution) PO qd. Evacuation of barium following barium procedures: 5-10 ml (syrup) PO bid. Acute hepatic encephalopathy: 30-45 ml syrup/dose PO q1h until laxative effect observed. Prevention of encephalopathy: 30-45 ml syrup PO tid-qid or 300 ml in 700 ml water or saline PR as a retention enema q4-6h.

PEDS - Prevention or treatment of encephalopathy: Infants: 2.5-10 ml/day (syrup) PO in 3-4 divided doses. Children/adolescents: 40-90 ml/day (syrup) PO in 3-4 divided doses.

UNAPPROVED ADULT - Restoration of bowel movements in hemorrhoidectomy patients: 15 ml syrup PO bid on day before surgery and for 5 days following surgery.

UNAPPROVED PEDS - Constipation: 7.5 ml syrup PO qd, after breakfast.

FORMS - Generic/Trade: syrup 10 g/15 ml. Trade only (Kristalose): 10, 20 g packets for oral solution.

NOTES - May be mixed in water, juice or milk to improve palatability. Packets for oral solution should be mixed in 4 oz of water. Titrate dose to produce 2-3 soft stools/day.

magnesium citrate ▶K ♀+ ▶? $

ADULT - Evacuate bowel prior to procedure: 150-300 ml PO divided qd-bid.

PEDS - Evacuate bowel prior to procedure: Children < 6 yo: 2-4 ml/kg/24h PO divided qd-bid. Children 6-12 yo: 100-150 ml/24h PO divided qd-bid.

FORMS - OTC Generic: solution 300 ml/bottle.

NOTES - Use caution with impaired renal function. May decrease absorption of phenytoin, ciprofloxacin, benzodiazepines, and glyburide. May cause additive CNS depression with CNS depressants. Chill to improve palatability.

magnesium hydroxide (*Milk of Magnesia*) ▶K ♀+ ▶? $

ADULT - Laxative: 30-60 ml PO as a single dose or divided doses. Antacid: 5-15 ml/dose PO qid prn or 622-1244 mg PO qid prn.

PEDS - Laxative: Age < 2 yo: 0.5 ml/kg PO as a single dose. 2-5 yo: 5-15 ml/day PO as a single dose or in divided doses. 6-11 yo: 15-30 ml PO in a single dose or in divided doses. Antacid (children > 12yo): 2.5-5 ml/dose PO qid prn.

FORMS - OTC Generic/Trade: liquid 400 & 800 (concentrated) mg/5 ml, chew tab 311 mg.

NOTES - Milk of magnesia concentrated liquid contains 800 mg/5 ml, so use half of the dose. Use caution with impaired renal function.

methylcellulose (*Citrucel*) ▶Not absorbed ♀+ ▶? $

ADULT - Laxative: 1 heaping tablespoon in 8 ounces cold water PO qd-tid.

PEDS - Laxative: Age 6-12 yo: 1½ heaping teaspoons in 4 ounces cold water qd-tid PO prn.

FORMS - OTC Trade only: Packets, multiple use canisters.

NOTES - Must be taken with water to avoid esophageal obstruction or choking.

mineral oil (*Agoral, Kondremul, Fleet Mineral Oil Enema*) ▶Not absorbed ♀C ▶? $

ADULT - Laxative: 15-45 ml PO in a single dose or in divided doses, 120 ml PR.

PEDS - Laxative: Children 6-11 yo: 5-20 ml PO in a single dose or in divided doses. Children 2-11 yo: 30-60 ml PR.

FORMS - OTC Generic/Trade: plain mineral oil, mineral oil emulsion (Agoral, Kondremul).

NOTES - Although usual directions for plain mineral oil are to administer at bedtime, this increases risk of lipid pneumonitis. Mineral oil emulsions may be administered with meals.

***Peri-Colace* (docusate + casanthranol)** ▶L ♀C ▶? $

ADULT - Constipation: 1-2 cap or 15-30 ml PO qhs prn.

PEDS - Constipation: 5-15 ml PO qhs prn.

FORMS - OTC Generic/Trade: cap 100 mg docusate + 30 mg casanthranolol/cap, syrup 60 mg docusate + 30 mg casanthranolol/15 ml.

NOTES - Dilute syrup in 6-8 oz. of juice, milk or infant formula to prevent throat irritation.

polycarbophil (*FiberCon, Fiberall, Konsyl Fiber, Equalactin*) ▶Not absorbed ♀+ ▶? $

ADULT - Laxative: 1 g PO qid prn.

PEDS - Laxative: Children 3-5 yo: 500 mg PO qd-bid prn. ≥6 yo: 500 mg PO qd-tid prn.

UNAPPROVED ADULT - Diarrhea: 1 g PO q30min prn. Max daily dose 6 g.

UNAPPROVED PEDS - Diarrhea: Children 3-5 yo: 500 mg PO q30min prn. Max daily dose 1.5 g. >6 yo: 500 mg PO qd-tid or prn. Max daily dose 3 g.

FORMS - OTC Generic/Trade: tab 500,625 mg, chew tab 500,1000 mg.

NOTES - When used as a laxative, take dose with at least 8 ounces of fluid. Do not administer concomitantly with tetracycline; separate by at least 2 hours.

polyethylene glycol (*Miralax*) ▶Not absorbed ♀C ▶? $

ADULT - Constipation: 1 heaping tablespoon in 8 oz. water PO qd.

PEDS - Not approved in children.

FORMS - Trade only: powder for oral solution.

NOTES - Takes 2-4 days to produce bowel movement. Indicated for up to 14 days.

polyethylene glycol with electrolytes (*GoLytely, CoLyte*, ✤*Klean-Prep, Lyte-prep*) ▶Not absorbed ♀C ▶? $

ADULT - Bowel cleansing prior to GI examination: 240 ml PO every 10 min or 20-30 ml/min NG until 4L are consumed or rectal effluent is clear.

PEDS - Not approved in children.

UNAPPROVED ADULT - Chronic constipation: 125-500 ml/day PO qd-bid.

UNAPPROVED PEDS - Bowel cleansing prior to GI examination: 25-40 ml/kg/h PO for 4-10 h or until rectal effluent is clear or 20-30 ml/min NG until 4L are consumed or rectal effluent is clear. Acute iron OD: children <3 yo: 0.5 L/h.

FORMS - Generic/Trade: powder for oral soln.

NOTES - Solid food should not be given within 2 h of solution. Effects should occur within 1-2 hours. Chilling improves palatability.

psyllium (*Metamucil, Fiberall, Konsyl, Hydrocil*) ▶Not absorbed ♀+ ▶? $

ADULT - Laxative: 1 rounded tsp in liquid, 1 packet in liquid or 1 wafer with liquid PO qd-tid.

PEDS - Laxative (children 6-11yo): ½-1 rounded tsp in liquid, ½-1 packet in liquid or 1 wafer with liquid PO qd-tid.

UNAPPROVED ADULT - Reduction in cholesterol: 1 rounded tsp in liquid, 1 packet in liquid or 1-2 waferswith liquid PO tid.

FORMS - OTC: Generic/Trade: powder, granules, wafers, including various flavors and various amounts of psyllium.

NOTES - Powders and granules must be mixed with liquid prior to ingestion. Start with 1 dose/day and gradually increase to minimize gas and bloating. Can bind with warfarin, digoxin, potassium-sparing diuretics, salicylates, tetracycline and nitrofurantoin; space at least 3 h apart.

senna (*Senokot, SenokotXTRA, Ex-Lax, Fletcher's Castoria*) ▶L ♀C ▶+ $

ADULT - Laxative or evacuation of the colon for bowel or rectal examinations: 1 tsp granules in water or 10-15 ml or 2 tabs PO or 1 supp PR qhs. Max daily dose 4 tsp of granules, 30 ml of syrup, 8 tabs or 2 supp.

PEDS - Laxative: 10-20 mg/kg/dose PO qhs. Alternative regimen: 1 mo-1 yo: 55-109 mg PO qhs, max 218 mg/day; 1-5yo: 109-218 mg PO qhs, max 436 mg/day; 5-15 yo: 218-436 mg PO qhs, max 872 mg/day. Children >27kg: ½ supp PR qhs.

FORMS - OTC Generic/Trade: granules 15mg/tsp, syrup 8.8 mg/5 ml, liquid 33.3 mg/ml senna concentrate, 25 mg/15 ml, tab 6, 8.6, 15, 17, 25 mg.
NOTES - Effects occur 6-24 h after oral administration. Use caution in renal dysfunction.

***Senokot-S* (senna + docusate)** ▶L ♀C ▶+ $
ADULT - 2 tabs PO qd, maximum 4 tabs/day.
PEDS - 6-12 yo: 1 tab PO qd, max 2 tabs/day. 2-6 yo: ½ tab PO qd, max 1 tab/day.
FORMS - OTC Trade: tab 8.6 mg senna concentrate/50 mg docusate.
NOTES - Effects occur 6-24 h after oral administration. Use caution in renal dysfunction.

sodium phosphate (*Fleet enema, Fleet Phospho-Soda, Visicol*) ▶Not absorbed ♀C ▶? $
ADULT - 1 adult or pediatric enema PR or 20-30 ml of oral soln PO prn. Visicol: Evening before colonoscopy: 3 tabs with 8 oz clear liquid q15 min until 20 tabs are consumed. Day of colonoscopy: starting 3-5 h before procedure, 3 tabs with 8 oz clear liquid q15 min until 20 tabs are consumed.
PEDS - Laxative: 1 pediatric enema (67.5 ml) PR prn or 5-9 yo: 5 ml of oral solution PO prn. 10-12 yo: 10 ml of oral solution PO prn.
FORMS - OTC Trade only: pediatric & adult enema, oral solution. Visicol tab (trade $$): 1.5 g.

sorbitol ▶Not absorbed ♀+ ▶? $
ADULT - Laxative: 30-150 ml (of 70% solution) PO or 120 ml (of 25-30% solution) PR.
PEDS - Laxative: Children 2-11 yo: 2 ml/kg (of 70% solution) PO or 30-60 ml (of 25-30% solution) PR.
FORMS - Generic: solution 70%.

GASTROENTEROLOGY: Other GI Agents

balsalazide (*Colazal*) ▶Minimal absorption ♀B ▶? $$$
ADULT - Ulcerative colitis: 2.25 g PO tid x 8-12 weeks.
PEDS - Not approved in children.
FORMS - Trade: cap 750 mg.
NOTES - Contraindicated in salicylate allergy.

cisapride (*Propulsid*, *✤Prepulsid*) ▶LK ♀C ▶? $
WARNING - Available only through limited-access protocol through manufacturer. Can cause potentially fatal cardiac arrhythmias. Many drug and disease interactions.
ADULT - 10 mg PO qid, at least 15 min before meals and qhs. Some patients may require 20 mg PO qid. Max 80 mg/day.
PEDS - Not approved in children.
UNAPPROVED PEDS - Gastroesophageal refulux disease: 0.2-0.3 mg/kg/dose PO tid-qid.
FORMS - Trade: Tab 10,20 mg, susp 1 mg/1 ml.

glycopyrrolate (*Robinul, Robinul Forte*) ▶K ♀B ▶? $$$
ADULT - Drooling: 0.1 mg/kg PO bid-tid, max 8 mg/day.
PEDS - Not approved in children.
UNAPPROVED PEDS - Drooling: 0.1 mg/kg PO bid-tid, max 8 mg/day.
FORMS - Trade: tab 1, 2 mg.

infliximab (*Remicade*) ▶Serum ♀C ▶? $$$$$
WARNING - Serious, life-threatening infections, including sepsis & disseminated TB have been reported. Evaluate patients for latent TB, and treat if necessary, prior to initiation of infliximab. Hypersensitivity reactions may occur.
ADULT - Crohn's disease: 5 mg/kg IV infusion. Fistualizing Crohn's disease: 5 mg/kg IV infusion at 0, 2, and 6 weeks.
PEDS - Not approved in children.
NOTES - Up to 16% patients experience adverse effects, eg, headache, nausea, infections, abdominal pain, fever.

lactase (*Lactaid*) ▶Not absorbed ♀+ ▶+ $
ADULT - Swallow or chew 3 caplets (Original strength), 2 caplets (Extra strength), 1 caplet (Ultra) with first bite of dairy foods. Adjust dose based on response.
PEDS - Titrate dose bsaed on response.
FORMS - OTC trade/generic: caplets, chew tab.

***Librax* (clidinium + chlordiazepoxide)** ▶K ♀D ▶- $
ADULT - Irritable bowel syndrome: 1 cap PO tid-qid.
PEDS - Not approved in children.
FORMS - Generic/Trade: cap clidinium 2.5 mg + chlordiazepoxide 5 mg.
NOTES - May cause drowsiness. After prolonged use, gradually taper to avoid withdrawal symptoms.

mercaptopurine (*Purinethol*) ▶L ♀D ▶? $$$
UNAPPROVED ADULT - Inflammatory bowel dz: Start at 50 mg PO qd, titrate to response. Typical dose range 0.5-1.5 mg/kg PO qd.
UNAPPROVED PEDS - 1.5 mg/kg PO qd.
FORMS - Trade: tab 50 mg.
NOTES - May cause severe toxicity including hepatitis in up to 10% of patients.

mesalamine (*Asacol, Pentasa, Rowasa, Canasa*, ✱*Mesasal*) ▶Gut ♀B ▶? $$$$

ADULT - Ulcerative colitis: Tab: 800 mg PO tid. Cap: 1 g PO qid. Rowasa supp: 500 mg PR retained for 1-3h or longer bid. Canasa supp: 500 mg PR bid-tid. Susp: 4 g (60 ml) PR retained for 8h qhs. Maintenance of ulcerative colitis: 1600 mg/day PO in divided doses.

PEDS - Not approved in children.

UNAPPROVED PEDS - Tab: 50 mg/kg/day PO divided q6-12h. Cap: 50 mg/kg/day PO divided q8-12h.

FORMS - Trade only: delayed release tab 400 mg (Asacol), controlled release cap 250 mg (Pentasa), supp 500 mg (Rowasa), rectal susp 4 g/60 ml (Rowasa).

NOTES - Avoid in salicylate sensitivity. May decrease digoxin levels. May discolor urine yellow-brown. Most common adverse effects include headache, abdominal pain, fever, rash.

neomycin (*Mycifradin*) ▶Minimally absorbed ♀D ▶? $$$

ADULT - Suppression of intestinal bacteria (given with erythromycin): 1 g PO at 19h, 18h and 9h prior to procedure (i.e. 1 pm, 2 pm, 11 pm on prior day). Alternative regimen 1 g PO q1h for 4 doses then 1 g PO q4h for 5 doses. Hepatic encephalopathy: 4-12 g/day PO divided q6h. Diarrhea caused by enteropathogenic E. coli: 3 g/day PO divided q6h.

PEDS - Suppression of intestinal bacteria (given with erythromycin): 25 mg/kg PO at 19h, 18h and 9h prior to procedure (i.e. 1 pm, 2 pm, 11 pm on prior day). Alternative regimen 90 mg/kg/day PO divided q4h for 2-3 days. Hepatic encephalopathy: 50-100 mg/kg/day PO divided q6-8h. Diarrhea caused by enteropathogenic E. coli: 50 mg/kg/day PO divided q6h.

FORMS - Generic/Trade: tab 500 mg, solution 125 mg/5 ml.

NOTES - Increased INR with warfarin, decreased levels of digoxin, methotrexate.

octreotide (*Sandostatin*) ▶LK ♀B ▶? $$$$$

ADULT - Diarrhea associated with carcinoid tumors: 100-600 mcg/day SC/IV in 2-4 divided doses. Diarrhea associated with vasoactive intestinal peptide-secreting tumors: 200-300 mcg/day SC/IV in 2-4 divided doses.

PEDS - Not approved in children.

UNAPPROVED ADULT - Variceal bleeding: Bolus 25-50 mcg IV followed by 25-50 mcg/h continuous IV infusion. AIDS diarrhea: 100-500 mcg SC tid. Irritable bowel syndrome: 100 mcg as a single dose to 125 mcg SC bid. GI fistulas: 50-200 mcg SC/IV q8h. Other uses.

UNAPPROVED PEDS - Diarrhea: initially 1-10 mcg/kg SC/IV q12h.

FORMS - Trade only: vials for injection 0.05,0.1,0.2,0.5,1 mg.

NOTES - For the treatment of variceal bleeding, most studies treat for 5 days. Individualize dose based on response. Dosage reduction often necessary in elderly. May cause hypoglycemia, hyperglycemia, hypothyroidism, cardiac arrhythmias.

olsalazine (*Dipentum*) ▶L ♀C ▶- $$$$

ADULT - Maintenance of remission of ulcerative colitis in patients intolerant to sulfasalazine: 500 mg PO bid.

PEDS - Not approved in children.

FORMS - Trade only: cap 250 mg.

NOTES - Diarrhea in up to 17%. Avoid in salicylate sensitivity.

orlistat (*Xenical*) ▶Gut ♀B ▶? $$$$

ADULT - Weight loss and weight management: 120 mg PO tid with meals or up to 1 h after meals.

PEDS - Not approved in children.

FORMS - Trade only: cap 120 mg.

NOTES - May cause fatty stools, fecal urgency, flatus with discharge and oily spotting in > 20% of patients. GI adverse effects greater when taken with high fat diet.

pancreatin (*Creon, Donnazyme, Ku-Zyme*, ✱*Entozyme*) ▶Gut ♀C ▶? $$$

ADULT - Enzyme replacement (initial dose): 8,000-24,000 units lipase (1-2 cap/tab) PO with meals and snacks.

PEDS - Enzyme replacement (initial dose): < 1 yo: 2,000 units lipase PO with meals. 1-6 yo: 4,000-8,000 units lipase PO with meals, 4,000 units lipase with snacks. 7-12 yo: 4,000-12,000 units lipase PO with meals and snacks.

FORMS - Tab, cap with varying amounts of pancreatin, lipase, amylase and protease.

NOTES - Titrate dose to stool fat content. Products are not interchangeable. Avoid concomitant calcium carbonate and magnesium hydroxide since these may affect the enteric coating. Do not crush/chew microspheres or Tabs. Possible association of colonic strictures and high doses of lipase (>16,000 units/kg/meal) in pediatric patients.

pancrelipase (*Viokase, Pancrease, Cotazym, Ku-Zyme HP*) ▶Gut ♀C ▶? $$$

ADULT - Enzyme replacement (initial dose): 4,000-33,000 units lipase (1-3 cap/tab) PO with meals and snacks.

PEDS - Enzyme replacement (initial dose): 6 mo -1 yo: 2,000 units lipase or 1/8 tsp PO with

feedings. 1-6 yo: 4,000-8,000 units lipase PO with meals, 4,000 units lipase with snacks. 7-12 yo: 4,000-12,000 units lipase PO w/ meals/snacks.
FORMS - Tab, cap, powder with varying amounts of lipase, amylase and protease.
NOTES - Titrate dose to stool fat content. Products are not interchangeable. Avoid concomitant calcium carbonate and magnesium hydroxide since these may affect the enteric coating. Do not crush/chew microspheres or Tabs. Possible association of colonic strictures and high doses of lipase (>16,000 units/kg/ meal) in pediatric patients.

sibutramine (*Meridia*) ▶L ♀C ◗- $$$
ADULT - Weight loss:10 mg PO qd; can increase to 15 mg qd after 4 weeks.
PEDS - Not approved in children.
FORMS - Trade only: cap 5,10,15 mg.
NOTES - Monitor BP and heart rate. Use for up to 1 year. Avoid concurrrent use of SSRIs, MAO inhibitors, sumatriptam, ergotamine and other serotonin agents to avoid development of serotonin syndrome.

sulfasalazine (*Azulfidine, Azulfidine EN-tabs*, *✤Salazopyrin, Salazopyrin EN*) ▶K ♀- ◗? $$
ADULT - Ulcerative colitis: Initially, 500-1000 mg PO qid. Maintenance: 500 mg PO qid.
PEDS - Ulcerative colitis, > 2yo: Initially 30-60 mg/kg/day PO divided into 3-6 doses. Maintenance: 30 mg/kg/day PO divided qid.
FORMS - Generic/Trade: tab 500 mg.
NOTES - Contraindicated in children < 2yo. Avoid in sulfonamide or salicylate sensitivity. Monitor CBC, LFTs. May decrease folic acid, digoxin, and iron levels. May discolor contact lenses skin, urine. May cause photosensitivity. Enteric coated (Azulfidine EN, Salazopyrin EN) Tabs may cause fewer GI adverse effects.

ursodiol (*Actigall, Ursofalk, Urso*) ▶Bile ♀B ◗? $$$$
ADULT - Radiolucent gallstone dissolution (Actigall): 8-10 mg/kg/day PO divided in 2-3 doses. Prevention of gallstones associated with rapid weight loss (Actigall): 300 mg PO bid. Primary biliary cirrhosis (Urso): 13-15 mg/kg/day PO divided in 4 doses.
PEDS - Not approved in children.
UNAPPROVED PEDS - Biliary atresia, cystic fibrosis with liver disease: 10-15 mg/kg/day PO divided tid.
FORMS - Trade/generic: cap 300 mg. Trade only: Tab 250 mg (Urso).
NOTES - Gallstone dissolution requires months of therapy. Complete dissolution does not occur in all patients and 5-year recurrence up to 50%. Does not dissolve calcified cholesterol stones, radiopaque stones or radiolucent bile pigment stones. Avoid concomitant antacids, cholestyramine, colestipol, estrogen, oral contraceptives.

vasopressin (*Pitressin, ADH*, *✤Pressyn*) ▶LK ♀C ◗? $$$$$
UNAPPROVED ADULT - Bleeding esophageal varices: 0.2-0.4 units/min initially (max 0.9 units /min).
UNAPPROVED PEDS - Bleeding esophageal varices: 0.002-0.005 units/kg/min initially (max 0.01 units/kg/min).
NOTES - Carbamazepine and chlorpropamide potentiate vasopressin. Use with caution in coronary artery disease. May cause tissue necrosis with extravasation.

HEMATOLOGY: Anticoagulants - Low-Molecular-Weight Heparins & Heparinoids

NOTES: See cardiology section for antiplatelet drugs and thrombolytics. LMWHs & heparinoids contraindicated in active major bleeding or pork allergy. Avoid spinal punctures before/during treatment with LMWHs & heparinoids due to risk of spinal/epidural hematomas. Monitor platelets, hemoglobin, stool for occult blood.

dalteparin (*Fragmin*) ▶KL ♀B ◗+ $$$$$
ADULT - DVT prophylaxis, abdominal surgery: 2,500 units SC 1-2 h preop and qd postop x 5-10 days. DVT prophylaxis, abdominal surgery in patients with malignancy: 5,000 units SC evening before surgery and qd postop x 5-10 days. Alternatively, 2,500 units SC 1-2 h preop and 12 h later, then 5,000 units SC qd x 5-10 days. DVT prophylaxis, hip replacement: Give SC for up to 14 days. Preop start regimens: 2,500 units 2 h preop and 4-8h postop, then 5,000 units qd starting ≥6h after second dose. Alternatively, 5,000 units q evening starting the evening before surgery. Postop start regimen: 2,500 units 4-8h postop, then 5,000 units qd starting ≥6h after first dose. Unstable angina or non-Q-wave MI: 120 units/kg up to 10,000 units SC q12h with aspirin (75-165 mg/day PO) until clinically stable.
PEDS - Not approved in children.
UNAPPROVED ADULT - Therapeutic antico-

agulation: 200 units/kg SC qd or 100-120 units/kg SC bid. DVT prophylaxis, orthopedic surgery: 5,000 units SC 8-12 h preop and qd starting 12 h postop. DVT prophylaxis, medical conditions: 2,500 units SC qd. Venous thromboembolism in pregnancy. Prevention: 5000 units SC qd. Treatment: 200 units/kg SC qd. To avoid unwanted anticoagulation during delivery, stop LMWH 24 h before elective induction of labor.

FORMS - Trade: Single-dose syringes 2,500 & 5,000 anti-Xa units/0.2 ml; multi-dose vial 10,000 units/ml, 10 ml.

NOTES - Contraindicated in heparin allergy, history of heparin-induced thrombocytopenia. Not for treatment of unstable angina/non-Q-wave MI in patients receiving regional anesthesia. Use cautiously in renal/liver failure. In obesity or renal failure, adjust dose based on anti-Xa level taken 4h after second SC dose. With q12h SC dosing, therapeutic range is 0.6 to 1.0 anti-Xa units/mL. In obesity, additional testing not required after correct dose is established.

danaparoid (*Orgaran*) ▶K ♀B ▶? $$$$$

ADULT - DVT prophylaxis, hip replacement: 750 anti-Xa units SC q12h starting 1-4 h preop x 7-10 days. Second dose not <2 h postop.

PEDS - Not approved in children.

UNAPPROVED ADULT - DVT prophylaxis, high-risk general surgery: 750 anti-Xa units 1-4 h preop & bid postop. DVT prophylaxis, medical conditions: 750 anti-Xa units SC bid. Heparin-induced thrombocytopenia. IV infusion for therapeutic anticoagulation: 2,250 unit bolus (1,500 units if < 50 kg; 3,000 units if 75-90 kg; 3,750 units if > 90 kg), then 400 units/h for 4 h, then 300 units/h for 4 h. Maintenance infusion of 150-200 units/h to maintain anti-Xa levels at 0.5-0.8 units/ml. Can also give 1,500 units SC q8-12h after initial bolus. Prophylactic anticoagulation: 750 units SC q12h (750 units q8h if 75-90 kg; 1,500 units q12h if > 90 kg). Anti-Xa level is usually 0.1 units/ml on day 1 and increases to 0.15-0.35 units/ml by day 5 (measured mid-interval, 6 h after morning dose).

UNAPPROVED PEDS - Therapeutic anticoagulation: 30 units/kg load, then 1.2-2.0 units/kg/h with anti-factor Xa goal of 0.4-0.8 units/ml.

NOTES - Careful monitoring if serum creatinine >2 mg/dl. PT unreliable within 5 h of dose.

enoxaparin (*Lovenox*) ▶KL ♀B ▶+ $$$$$

ADULT - DVT prophylaxis, hip/knee replacement: 30 mg SC q12h starting 12-24 h postop for ≤14 days. Alternative for hip replacement: 40 mg SC qd starting 12 h preop. After hip replacement may continue 40 mg SC qd x 3 wks. DVT prophylaxis, abdominal surgery: 40 mg SC qd starting 2 h preop for ≤12 days. DVT prophylaxis, acute medical illness with restricted mobility: 40 mg SC qd for ≤14 days. Outpatient treatment of DVT without pulmonary embolus: 1 mg/kg SC q12h. Inpatient treatment of DVT with/without pulmonary embolus: 1 mg/kg SC q12h or 1.5 mg/kg SC q24h. Give at the same time each day. Continue enoxaparin for ≥ 5 days after warfarin is started and until INR is therapeutic. Unstable angina or non-Q-wave MI: 1 mg/kg SC q12h with aspirin (100-325 mg PO qd) for ≥2 days and until clinically stable.

PEDS - Not approved in children.

UNAPPROVED ADULT - Prevention of venous thromboembolism. After major trauma: 30 mg SC q12h starting 12-36 h postinjury if hemostatically stable. Acute spinal cord injury: 30 mg SC q12h. Recurrent thromboembolism: 40 mg SC qd. Venous thromboembolism in pregnancy. Prevention: 40 mg SC qd. Treatment: 1 mg/kg SC q12h. To avoid unwanted anticoagulation during delivery, stop LMWH 24 h before elective induction of labor.

UNAPPROVED PEDS - Therapeutic anticoagulation: Age <2 mo: 1.5 mg/kg/dose SC q12h. Age >2 mo: 1 mg/kg/dose SC q12h with anti-factor Xa goal of 0.5-1.0 units/ml. DVT prophylaxis: Age <2 mo: 0.75 mg/kg/dose q12h. Age >2 mo: 0.5 mg/kg/dose q12h.

FORMS - Trade: Syringes 30,40 mg; graduated syringes 60, 80, 100 mg; ampules 30 mg.

NOTES - Contraindicated in patients with heparin allergy, history of heparin-induced thrombocytopenia. Consider reduced dose if weight <45 kg and/or CrCl <30 ml/min. In obesity or renal failure, adjust dose based on anti-Xa level taken 4h after 2nd SC dose. With q12h SC dosing, therapeutic range is 0.6 to 1.0 anti-Xa units/mL. In obesity, additional testing not required after correct dose is established. Monitor anti-Xa levels in abnormal coagulation/bleeding.

tinzaparin (*Innohep*) ▶K ♀B ▶+ $$$$$

ADULT - DVT with/without pulmonary embolus: 175 anti-Xa units/kg SC qd for ≥6 days and until adequate anticoagulation with warfarin.

PEDS - Not approved in children.

UNAPPROVED ADULT - DVT prophylaxis. Moderate-risk general surgery: 3,500 units SC given 2 h preop and qd postop. Orthopedic surgery: 75 units/kg SC qd starting 12-24h postop or 4,500 units SC given 12h preop and qd postop.

FORMS - Trade: 20,000 anti-Xa units/ml, 2 ml multi-dose vial.
NOTES - Contraindicated if history of heparin-induced thrombocytopenia, or allergy to heparin, sulfites, or benzyl alcohol. Can cause thrombocytopenia, priapism (rare), increased AST/ALT. Tinzaparin may slightly prolong PT; draw blood for INR just before giving tinzaparin. In obesity or renal failure, adjust dose based on anti-Xa level taken 4h after second SC dose. With q12h SC dosing, therapeutic range is 0.6 to 1.0 anti-Xa units/mL. In obesity, additional testing not required after correct dose is established.

HEMATOLOGY: Anticoagulants - Other

aprotinin (*Trasylol*) ▶lysosomal enzymes & K ♀B ◗? $$$$$
WARNING - Anaphylaxis can occur even with test dose. Risk low in previously unexposed patients. Risk high with reexposure ≤6 months after first dose; use special precautions.
ADULT - Reduction of blood loss during cardiopulmonary bypass in coronary artery bypass graft surgery: 1 ml IV test dose ≥10 min before loading dose. Give IV loading dose over 20-30 min to supine patient, after anesthesia induction, but before sternotomy. Choice of two regimens based upon perceived bleeding risk. Regimen A: 200 ml (280 mg) loading dose, then 200 ml (280 mg) pump prime dose, then 50 ml/h (70 mg/h). Regimen B: 100 ml (140 mg) loading dose, then 100 ml (140 mg) pump prime dose, then 25 ml/h (35 mg/h). Give through central line with no other meds.
PEDS - Safety and efficacy not established in children.
FORMS - For hospital/clinic use; not intended for outpatient prescribing. Trasylol contains 10,000 Kallikrein inhibitor units (KIUs)/ml. 10,000 KIUs=1.4 mg.
NOTES - Rapid administration can cause hypotension. Prolongation of activated clotting time (ACT) by aprotinin may overestimate heparin anticoagulation. Effect of aprotinin on ACT may vary by ACT formulation. Determine the dose of protamine to reverse heparin based on the heparin dose rather than ACT value.

argatroban ▶L ♀B ◗- $$$$$
ADULT - Prevention/treatment of thrombosis in heparin-induced thrombocytopenia: Start 2 mcg/kg/min IV infusion. Get APTT at baseline and 2 h after starting infusion. Adjust dose (not >10 mcg/kg/min) until APTT is 1.5-3 times baseline (not >100 seconds).
PEDS - Not approved in children.
NOTES - Argatroban prolongs INR with warfarin. Check INR daily after warfarin is started. For argatroban doses ≤2 mcg/kg/min, INR >4 on combo therapy corresponds to INR of 2-3 with warfarin alone. When INR>4 on combo therapy, stop argatroban and re-measure INR 4-6 h later. If INR is too low, restart argatroban until warfarin dose is therapeutic. INR cannot be predicted if argatroban dose >2 mcg/kg/min. Reduce argatroban to 2 mcg/kg/min and measure INR 4-6 h later. Can return to higher dose of argatroban while awaiting INR result. Dosage adjustment in adults with liver dysfunction: 0.5 mcg/kg/min initially.

bivalirudin (*Angiomax*) ▶proteolysis/K ♀B ◗? $$$$$
ADULT - Anticoagulation in patients with unstable angina undergoing PTCA: 1 mg/kg IV bolus just prior to PTCA, then infuse 2.5 mg/kg/h for 4 h. Can infuse 0.2 mg/kg/h for up to 20 h more. Intended for use with aspirin 300-325 mg PO qd.
PEDS - Not approved in children.
NOTES - Former trade name Hirulog. Contraindicated in active major bleeding. Monitor activated clotting time and consider reduced dose if CrCl <60 ml/min.

heparin, ✷***Hepalean*** ▶Reticuloendothelial system ♀C but + ◗+ $
ADULT - Venous thrombosis/pulmonary embolus treatment: Load 80 units/kg IV, then mix 25,000 units in 250 ml D5W (100 units/ml) and infuse at 18 units/kg/h. 63 kg adult: Load 5,000 units, then infuse at 11 ml/h. Adjust based on coagulation testing (APTT). DVT prophylaxis: 5000 units SC q8-12h. Adjusted-dose for prevention of venous thromboembolism: 3,500 units SC q8h initially. Adjust up/down by 500 units/dose to maintin mid-interval APTT at high normal value. Low-dose for prevention of thromboembolism in pregnancy: 5,000-10,000 units SC q12h. Treatment of thromboembolism in pregnancy: 80 units/kg IV load, then infuse ≥ 30,000 units/24h with dose titrated to achieve full anticoagulation for ≥ 5 days. Then adjusted-dose prophylaxis with ≥ 10,000 units SC q8-12h to achive APTT of 1.5-

2.5 x control. To avoid unwanted anticoagulation during delivery, stop adjusted-dose heparin 24 h before elective induction of labor.

PEDS - Venous thrombosis/pulmonary embolus treatment: Load 50 units/kg IV, then 25 units/kg/h infusion.

UNAPPROVED ADULT - Adjunct to thrombolytics for acute MI. For use with alteplase, reteplase, or tenecteplase: 5,000 unit IV load, then infuse 1,000 units/h. Or 60 units/kg IV load (max 4,000 units), then infuse 12 units/kg/h (max 1,000 units/h). Duration of therapy is usually 48 h. For use with streptokinase: 12,500 units SC q12h x 48 h. IV heparin only for patients receiving streptokinase/ anistreplase who are at high risk for systemic/ venous thromboemolism. Do not start heparin until ≥ 4 h after start of streptokinase/ anistreplase and APTT <70 s. Anticoagulation for acute MI not treated with thrombolytics: 75 units/kg IV load, then infuse 1,000-1,200 units/h. Unstable angina: 75 units/kg IV load, then infuse 1,250 units/h. Goal APTT for all regimens is 1.5-2 x control (50-70 seconds).

UNAPPROVED PEDS - Venous thrombosis/pulmonary embolus treatment: Load 75 units/kg IV over 10 minutes, then 28 units/kg/h if age <1 yo, 20 units/kg/h if age >1 yo.

FORMS - Generic: 2500,5000,7500,10,000, 20,000 units/ml in various vial & syringe sizes.

NOTES - Beware of heparin-induced thrombocytopenia (heparin antibodies with unexplained decrease in platelet count of >50% or skin lesions at injection site), elevated LFTs, hyperkalemia/ hypoaldosteronism. Osteoporosis with long-term use. Bleeding risk increased by high dose; concomitant thrombolytic or platelet GPIIb/IIIa receptor inhibitor; recent surgery, trauma, or invasive procedure; concomitant hemostatic defect.

WEIGHT-BASED HEPARIN DOSING*

Initial dose: 80 units/kg IV bolus, then 18 units/kg/h. Check APTT in 6 h.
APTT <35 seconds (<1.2 x control): 80 units/kg IV bolus, then ↑ infusion rate by 4 units/kg/h.
APTT 35-45 seconds (1.2-1.5 x control): 40 units/kg IV bolus, then ↑ infusion by 2 units/kg/h.
APTT 46-70 seconds (1.5-2.3 x control): No change.
APTT 71-90 seconds (2.3-3 x control): ↓ infusion rate by 2 units/kg/h.
APTT >90 seconds (>3 x control): Hold infusion for 1 h, then ↓ infusion rate by 3 units/kg/h.

*APTT = Activated partial thromboplastin time. Monitor APTT q6h during first 24h of therapy and 6h after each heparin dosage adjustment. The frequency of APTT monitoring can be reduced to q morning when APTT is stable within therapeutic range. Check platelet count between days 3 to 5. Can begin warfarin on first day of heparin; continue heparin for at least ≥4 to 5 days of combined therapy. Adapted from *Ann Intern Med* 1993;119:874; *Chest* 2001:119:69S, and *Circulation* 2001; 103:2994.

lepirudin (*Refludan*) ▶K ♀B ▶? $$$$$

ADULT - Thromboembolism in heparin-induced thrombocytopenia: Bolus 0.4 mg/kg up to 44 mg IV over 15-20 seconds, then infuse 0.15 mg/kg/h up to 16.5 mg/h x 2-10 days. Adjust dose to maintain APTT ratio of 1.5-2.5.

PEDS - Not approved in children.

UNAPPROVED ADULT - Adjunct to thrombolytics for acute MI in patients with known/suspected heparin-induced thrombocytopenia: 0.1 mg/kg IV bolus, then infuse 0.15 mg/h.

NOTES - Renal impairment: Bolus 0.2 mg/kg IV followed by 0.075 mg/kg/h for CrCl 45-60 ml/min, 0.045 mg/kg/h for CrCl 30-44 ml/min, 0.0225 mg/kg/h for CrCl 15-29 ml/min. Hemodialysis/CrCl <15 ml/min: Bolus 0.1 mg/kg IV qod if APTT ratio <1.5.

warfarin (*Coumadin*) ▶L ♀X ▶+ $

WARNING - Many important drug interactions that increase/decrease INR, see table.

ADULT - Oral anticoagulation: Start 5 mg PO qd x 2-4 days, then adjust dose to PT/INR. Higher loading doses no longer recommended. Consider initial dose <5 mg/day if elderly, malnourished, liver disease, or high bleeding risk. Target INR of 2-3 for most indications except mechanical heart valves (usual target INR of 2.5 to 3.5). See table for target INRs and duration of anticoagulation for specific indications.

PEDS - Not approved in children.

FORMS - Generic/Trade: Tabs 1, 2, 2.5, 3, 4, 5, 6, 7.5, 10 mg.

NOTES - Tissue necrosis in protein C or S deficiency. Many important drug interactions that increase/decrease INR, see table. Warfarin onset of action is 4-5 days. Most patients can begin warfarin at the same time as heparin/LMWH. Continue heparin/LMWH treatment for thrombosis until the INR has been in the therapeutic range for ≥4 days.

WARFARIN – SELECTED DRUG INTERACTIONS

Assume possible interactions with any new medication. When starting/stopping a medication, the INR should be checked weekly for ≥2-3 weeks and dose adjusted accordingly, especially in patients with intensive anticoagulation (INR 2.5-3.5). Similarly monitor if significant change in diet (including supplements) or illness resulting in decreased oral intake.

Increased anticoagulant effect of warfarin and increased risk of bleeding

• *Monitor INR when agents below started, stopped, or dosage changed.*

acetaminophen ≥2	**corticosteroids¶**	fluvoxamine	miconazole, in-	propoxyphene
g/d for ≥3-4 d	cyclophosphamide	gemcitabine	travaginal	quinidine
allopurinol	delavirdine	glucagon	modafinil	quinine
amiodarone*	efavirenz	glyburide	neomycin (PO for	rofecoxib
amprenavir	fenofibrate	ifosfamide	>1-2 days)	sertraline
cefazolin	fluconazole	isoniazid	olsalazine	tamoxifen
cefoxitin	**fluoroquinolones**	itraconazole ke-	omeprazole	**tetracyclines**
ceftriaxone	fluorouracil	toconazole le-	penicillin, high-	tramadol
celecoxib	fluoxetine	vamisole	dose IV	valproate
cisapride	flutamide	levothyroxine#	pentoxifylline	vitamin E
			propafenone	zileuton

• *Consider alternative to agents below, or monitor INR when started, stopped, or dosage changed.*

cimetidine†	**macrolides‡**	nalidixic acid	paroxetine	**statins§**	**sulfonamides**	zafirlukast

• *Avoid unless benefit justifies risk; monitor INR when started, stopped, or dosage changed.*

anabolic steroids	aspirin¶	danazol	gemfibrozil	**NSAIDs¶**
androgens	clofibrate	disulfiram	metronidazole	sulfinpyrazone

• *Avoid agents below; benefits do not justify risks*

cefoperazone	danshen (Chinese herb)	fish oil	ginkgo
cefotetan	dong quai (Chinese herb)	garlic supplements	

Decreased anticoagulant effect of warfarin and increased risk of thrombosis

• *Monitor INR when agents below started, stopped, or dosage changed.*

aminoglutethimide	dicloxacillin	methimazole#	phenytoin (consi-	rifapentine
azathioprine	efavirenz	mitotane	der alternative)	rifampin (avoid unless
barbiturates	griseofulvin	nafcillin	primidone	benefit justifies risk)
carbamazepine	mercaptopurine	panax ginseng	propylthiouracil#	St John's wort
coenzyme Q-10	mesalamine		raloxifene	*Trazodone*
			rifabutin	Vitamin C, high-dose

• *Use alternative to agents below. Or give at different times of day and monitor INR when agent started, stopped, dose/dosing schedule changed.*

cholestyramine	colestipol (likely lower risk than cholestyramine)	sucralfate

• *Avoid unless benefit justifies risk. If used, monitor INR when started, stopped, or form changed.*

Oral contraceptives (Does not necessarily decrease INR, but may induce hypercoagulability)

*Interaction may be delayed; monitor INR for several weeks after starting & several months after stopping amiodarone. May need to decrease warfarin dose by 33% to 50%.

† Ranitidine, famotidine, nizatidine are alternatives.

‡ Azithromycin appears to have lower risk of interaction than clarithromycin or erythromycin.

§ Pravastatin appears to have lower risk of interaction.

Hyperthyroidism increases and hypothyroidism decreases response to warfarin.

¶ Does not necessarily increase INR , but increases bleeding risk. Check INR frequently and monitor for GI bleeding. COX-2 inhibitors (celecoxib, rofecoxib) may be preferred (less GI toxicity, no effect on platelet aggregation), but INR monitoring still recommended.

Table adapted from: www.coumadin.com, *Am Fam Phys* 1999;59:635, *Chest* 2001; 114: 11S; *Hansten and Horn's Drug Interactions Analysis and Management*.

THERAPEUTIC GOALS FOR ORAL ANTICOAGULATION

Indication	*INR**	*Duration of Therapy*
Prophylaxis of venous thromboembolism after high-risk surgery†	2-3	≥7-10 days for total hip/knee replacement; clinical judgment otherwise
Treatment of venous thromboembolism/pulm embolus		
First episode, reversible/time-limited risk factor ‡	2-3	3-6 months
First episode, continuing risk factor §	2-3	12 months to indefinite
First episode, idiopathic	2-3	At least 6 months
Recurrent, idiopathic or with clotting predisposition	2-3	12 months to indefinite
Isolated symptomatic calf vein thrombosis	2-3	At least 6-12 weeks
Coronary heart disease		
Acute MI with increased embolic risk ‖	2-3	1-3 months
Acute MI with atrial fibrillation	2-3	Indefinite
Recurrent ischemic episodes following acute MI ¶	1.5	Clinical judgment
Unstable angina with contraindication to aspirin	2.5	Several months
Primary prevention in men at high risk of cardiovascular events #	1.5	Indefinite
Valvular heart disease		
After thrombotic event or if left atrial diameter >5.5 cm	2-3	Indefinite
Atrial fibrillation		
Chronic/intermittent in patient with ≥1 high-risk or ≥2 moderate-risk factors **	2-3	Indefinite
Elective cardioversion for atrial fibrillation >48h Duration	2-3	From 3 weeks before cardioversion until NSR maintained for 4 weeks
Prosthetic heart valves, mechanical		
Bileaflet aortic valve	2-3	Indefinite
Tilting disc aortic valve ††	2-3	Indefinite
Bileaflet aortic valve plus atrial fibrillation ††	2.5-3.5	Indefinite
Bileaflet mitral valve ††	2.5-3.5	Indefinite
Tilting disc mitral valve ††	2.5-3.5	Indefinite
Caged ball/caged disc valve ‡‡	2.5-3.5	Indefinite
Mechanical valve plus additional risk factors ‡‡	2.5-3.5	Indefinite
Systemic embolism despite adequate anticoagulation in patient with mechanical valve ‡‡	2.5-3.5	Indefinite
Bioprosthetic heart valves		
Mitral/aortic	2-3	3 months
History of systemic embolism	2.5-3	3-12 months
Acute spinal cord injury, rehab phase	2-3	Not defined
Postpartum anticoagulation for venous thromboembolism during pregnancy	2-3	At least 6 weeks

Adapted from: *Chest* suppl *2001;119:129S,187S,203S,215S, 247S; Am Fam Physician 1999;59:635*

*Aim for an INR in the middle of the INR range (e.g. 2.5 for a range of 2.0-3.0 and 3.0 for a range of 2.5-3.5).

†General surgery in very high risk patient, total hip/knee replacement, hip fracture surgery

‡Transient immobilization, trauma, surgery, or estrogen use.

§Cancer (until resolved), anticardiolipin antibody, antithrombin III deficiency. Therapy duration unclear for 1st event associated with homozygous factor V Leiden (activated protein C resistance), homocystinemia, protein C or S deficiency, prothrombin gene mutation 20210, or multiple thrombophilias.

‖ Anterior AMI or AMI complicated by severe LV dysfunction, CHF, previous emboli, or echocardiographic evidence of mural thrombosis. Warfarin (target INR 2.5) is also an alternative when aspirin is contraindicated in patients with acute MI or unstable angina.

¶Plus aspirin 75-81 mg/day.
#Consider the addition of aspirin 75-81 mg/day in men at very high risk of cardiovascular events
**High-risk factors: Prior TIA, stroke, or systemic embolus; history of HTN; poor left ventricular systolic function; rheumatic mitral valve disease; prosthetic heart valve; age >75 years. Moderate-risk factors: age 65-75 years; diabetes mellitus; CAD with preserved left ventricular systolic function. Patients with one moderate risk factor can receive warfarin (INR target 2.5, range 2-3) or aspirin 325 mg/day. Patients <65 years without clinical or echocardiographic evidence of cardiovascular disease and patients with no moderate- or high-risk factors should receive aspirin.
††A target INR of 2.5 (range 2-3) plus aspirin 81-100 mg/day is an option for patients with aortic bileaflet mechanical valves and atrial fibrillation, mitral bileaflet mechanical valves, or tilting disc valves.
‡‡Plus aspirin 81-100 mg/day.

HEMATOLOGY: Other Hematological Agents

See endocrine section for vitamins and minerals.

aminocaproic acid (*Amicar*) ▶K ♀D ▶? $$

ADULT - To improve hemostasis when fibrinolysis contributes to bleeding: 4-5 g IV/PO over 1h, then 1 g/h for 8 h or until bleeding controlled.

PEDS - Not approved in children.

UNAPPROVED ADULT - Prevention of recurrent subarachnoid hemorrhage: 6 g IV/PO q4h (6 doses/day). Reduction of postop bleeding after cardiopulmonary bypass: 5 g IV, then 1 g/h x 6-8 h.

UNAPPROVED PEDS - To improve hemostasis when fibrinolysis contributes to bleeding: 100 mg/kg or 3 g/m2 IV infusion during first h, then continuous infusion of 33.3 mg/kg/h or 1 g/m2/h. Max dose of 18 g/m2/day. IV prep contains benzyl alcohol - do not use in newborns.

FORMS - Generic/Trade: Syrup 250 mg/ml. Trade: Tabs 500.

NOTES - Contraindicated in active intravascular clotting. Do not use in DIC without heparin. Can cause intrarenal thrombosis, hyperkalemia. Skeletal muscle weakness, necrosis with prolonged use - monitor CPK. Use with estrogen/oral contraceptives can cause hypercoagulability. Rapid IV administration can cause hypotension, bradycardia, arrhythmia.

anagrelide (*Agrylin*) ▶LK ♀C ▶? $$$$$

ADULT - Essential thrombocythemia: Start 0.5 mg PO qid or 1 mg PO bid, then after 1 week adjust to lowest effective dose that maintains platelet count < 600,000 mcL. Max 10 mg/day or 2.5 mg as a single dose.

PEDS - Not approved in children.

FORMS - Trade: Caps, 0.5,1 mg.

NOTES - Use with caution in patients with heart disease. May cause vasodilation, tachycardia, palpitations, CHF. Ensure women maintain effective contraception while on this drug.

desmopressin (*DDAVP, Stimate*) ▶LK ♀B ▶? $$$$$

ADULT - Hemophilia A, von Willebrand's disease: 0.3 mcg/kg IV over 15-30 min; 300 mcg intranasally if ≥50 kg (1 spray in each nostril), 150 mcg intranasally if <50 kg (single spray in 1 nostril).

PEDS - Hemophilia A, von Willebrand's disease (age ≥3 mo for IV, age ≥11 mo - 12 yo for nasal spray): 0.3 mcg/kg IV over 15-30 min; 300 mcg intranasally if ≥50 kg (1 spray in each nostril), 150 mcg intranasally if <50 kg (single spray in 1 nostril).

UNAPPROVED ADULT - Uremic bleeding: 0.3 mcg/kg IV single dose or q12h (onset 1-2h; duration 6-8h after single dose). Intranasal is 20 mcg/day (onset 24-72 h; duration 14 days during 14-day course).

FORMS - Trade: Stimate nasal spray 150 mcg/0.1 ml (1 spray), 2.5 ml bottle (25 sprays). DDAVP nasal spray: 10 mcg/0.1 ml (1 spray), 5 ml bottle (50 sprays). Note difference in concentration of nasal solutions.

NOTES - Avoid excessive fluid intake to prevent water intoxication/hyponatremia. Do not give if type IIB von Willebrand's disease. Changes in nasal mucosa may impair absorption of nasal spray. Refrigerate nasal spray - stable for 3 weeks at room temperature. 10 mcg = 40 units desmopressin.

erythropoietin (*Epogen, Procrit, epoetin alfa,* ♣*Eprex*) ▶L ♀C ▶? $$$$$

ADULT - Anemia of chronic renal failure: Initial dose 50-100 units/kg IV/SC 3 times/week. Target hematocrit: 30-36%. Zidovudine-induced anemia in HIV-infected patients: 100-300 units/kg IV/SC 3 times/week. Hold and reduce dose if hematocrit of ≥40%. Anemia in cancer chemo patients with erythropoietin levels ≤200 mU/ml: 150-300 units/kg SC 3 times/week.

Hold and reduce dose if hematocrit of ≥40%. Reduction of allogeneic blood transfusion in surgical patients: 300 units/kg/day SC x 10 days preop, on the day of surgery, and 4 days postop. Or 600 units/kg SC once weekly starting 21 days preop and ending on day of surgery (4 doses).

PEDS - Not approved in children.

UNAPPROVED PEDS - Anemia of chronic renal failure: Initial dose 50-100 units/kg IV/SC 3 times/week. Zidovudine-induced anemia in HIV-infected patients: 100 units/kg SC 3 times/week; max of 300 units/kg/dose.

FORMS - Trade: Single-dose 1 ml vials 2,000, 3,000, 4,000, 10,000, 20,000 40,000 units/ml. Multi-dose vials 10,000 units/ml 2 ml & 20,000 units/ml 1 ml.

NOTES - Contraindicated in uncontrolled HTN. Not for immediate correction of anemia. Monitor, control BP in chronic renal failure. Monitor hematocrit twice weekly in chronic renal failure, once weekly in HIV-infected and cancer patients until stable. Consider iron deficiency if no response. Single-dose vials contain no preservatives. Use one dose per vial; do not reenter vial. Discard unused portion. Multi-dose vials contain benzoyl alcohol; do not use in newborns.

factor IX ▶L ♀C ▶? $$$$$

ADULT - Hemophilia B: individualize factor IX dose.

PEDS - Hemophilia B: individualize factor IX dose.

NOTES - Risk of HIV/hepatitis transmission varies by product. Products that contain factors II, VII, & X may cause thrombosis in at-risk patients. Stop infusion if signs of DIC.

factor VIII ▶L ♀C ▶? $$$$$

ADULT - Hemophilia A: individualize factor VIII dose.

PEDS - Hemophilia A: individualize factor VIII dose.

NOTES - Risk of HIV/hepatitis transmission varies by product. Reduced response with development of factor VIII inhibitors. Hemolysis with large/repeated doses in patients with A, B, AB blood type.

filgrastim (*G-CSF, Neupogen*) ▶L ♀C ▶? $$$$$

ADULT - Reduction of febrile neutropenia after chemo for non-myeloid malignancies: 5 mcg/kg/day SC/IV for ≤2 weeks until post-nadir ANC is ≥10,000/mm3. Can increase by 5 mcg/kg/day with each cycle prn.

PEDS - Reduction of febrile neutropenia after chemo for non-myeloid malignancies: 5 mcg/kg/day SC/IV.

UNAPPROVED ADULT - AIDS: 0.3-3.6 mcg/kg/day.

FORMS - Trade: Single-dose vials 300 mcg/1 ml, 480 mcg/1.6 ml.

NOTES - Allergic-type reactions, bone pain, cutaneous vasculitis. Do not give within 24 h before/after cytotoxic chemotherapy.

oprelvekin (*Neumega*) ▶K ♀C ▶? $$$$$

ADULT - Prevention of severe thrombocytopenia in high-risk patients after chemo for nonmyeloid malignancies: 50 mcg/kg SC qd starting 6-24 h after chemo and continuing until post-nadir platelet count is ≥50,000 cells/mcL.

PEDS - Not approved in children.

UNAPPROVED PEDS - Prevention of severe thrombocytopenia in high-risk patients after chemo for nonmyeloid malignancies: 75-100 mcg/kg SC qd starting 6-24 h after chemo and continuing until post-nadir platelet count is ≥50,000 cells/mcL.

FORMS - Trade: 5 mg single-dose vials with diluent.

NOTES - Fluid retention - monitor fluid and electrolyte balance. Transient atrial arrhythmias, visual blurring, papilledema.

protamine ▶Plasma ♀C ▶? $

ADULT - Heparin overdose: 1 mg antagonizes ~100 units heparin. Give IV over 10 minutes in doses of not >50 mg.

PEDS - Not approved in children.

UNAPPROVED ADULT - Low molecular weight heparin overdose: 1 mg protamine per 100 anti-Xa units of ardeparin, dalteparin, or tinzaparin. Give additional 0.5 mg protamine per 100 anti-Xa units of tinzaparin if PTT remains prolonged 2-4 h after first infusion of protamine. 1 mg protamine per 1 mg enoxaparin.

UNAPPROVED PEDS - Heparin overdose: <30 min since last heparin dose, give 1 mg protamine per 100 units of heparin received; 30-60 min since last heparin dose, give 0.5-0.75 mg protamine per 100 units of heparin received; 60-120 min since last heparin dose, give 0.375-0.5 mg protamine per 100 units of heparin; >120 min since last heparin dose, give 0.25-0.375 mg protamine per 100u of heparin.

NOTES - Severe hypotension/anaphylactoid reaction with too rapid administration. Allergic reactions in patients with fish allergy, previous exposure to protamine (including insulin). Risk of allergy unclear in infertile/vasectomized men with anti-protamine antibodies. Additional doses of protamine may be required in some situations (neutralization of SC heparin, heparin rebound after cardiac surgery). Monitor APTT to confirm heparin neutralization.

sargramostim (*GM-CSF, Leukine*) ▶L ♀C ▶? $$$$$

ADULT - Specialized dosing for leukemia, bone marrow transplantation.

PEDS - Not approved in children.

CHILDHOOD IMMUNIZATION SCHEDULE*						*Months*				*Years*		
Age	*Birth*	*1*	*2*	*4*	*6*	*12*	*15*	*18*	*24*	*4-6*	*11-12*	*14-16*
Hepatitis B	HB-1											
		HB-2			HB-3							
DPT†			DTP	DTP	DTP		DTP			DTP	Td	
H influenza b			Hib	Hib	Hib	Hib						
Pneumococci			PCV	PCV	PCV	PCV						
Polio§			IPV	IPV	IPV					IPV		
MMR						MMR				MMR		
Varicella						Varicella						
Hepatitis A¶									HA (some areas)			

*2001 schedule from the CDC, ACIP, AAP, & AAFP, see www.aap.org/family/parents/immunize.htm for updates & expanded discussion, including catch-up doses. †Acellular form preferred for all DTP doses. § Inactivated form (IPV) preferred for all doses. ¶Recommended for selected high-risk areas, consult local public health authorities.

IMMUNOLOGY: Immunizations

BCG vaccine (*Tice BCG*) ▶? ♀C ▶? $$$$

ADULT - 0.2-0.3 ml multidose puncture disc (using 1 ml sterile water for reconstitution).

PEDS - Age > 1 month: use adult dose. Age < 1 month: 0.2-0.3 ml multidose puncture disc (decrease dose by 50% using 2 ml sterile water for reconstitution). May revaccinate with full dose (adult dose) after 1 yo if necessary.

cholera vaccine (*Cholera vaccine*) ▶? ♀C ▶? $

ADULT - 0.2 ml ID x 2 doses, separated by 1 week to 1 month or more.

PEDS - Age 6 months- 4 yo: 0.2 ml SC or IM x 2 doses; age 5-10 yo: 0.3 ml SC or IM x 2 doses; age > 10 yo: 0.5 ml SC or IM x 2 doses. Age ≥ 5 yo: 0.2 ml ID x 2 doses. Doses should be separated by 1 week to 1 month or more.

NOTES - Higher antibody levels may be achieved in children < 5 yo using the SC or IM route. May consider booster dose q6 months in endemic areas.

***Comvax* (haemophilus b + hepatitis B vaccine)** ▶L ♀C ▶? $$$

ADULT - Do not use in adults.

PEDS - Infants born of HbsAg (-) mothers: 0.5 ml IM x 3 doses at 2, 4, & 12-15 months old.

NOTES - Combination is made of PedvaxHIB (haemophilus b vaccine) + Recombivax HB (hepatitis B vaccine).

diphtheria tetanus & acellular pertussis vaccine (*DTaP, Tripedia, Infanrix*) ▶L ♀C ▶- $

ADULT - Do not use in adults.

PEDS - Check immunization history: DTaP is preferred for all DTP doses. Give first dose of 0.5 ml IM at approximately 2 mos, second dose at 4 mos, third dose at 6 mos, fourth dose at 15-18 mos, and fifth dose (booster) at 4-6 yo.

NOTES - Do not immunize persons ≥7 yo with pertussis vaccine. When feasible, use same brand for first 3 doses. Do not give if prior DTP vaccination caused anaphylaxis or encephalopathy within 7 days.

diphtheria-tetanus toxoid (*Td, DT*) ▶L ♀C ▶? $

ADULT - Age ≥7 yo: 0.5 ml IM, second dose 4-8 weeks later, and third dose 6-12 months later. Give 0.5 ml booster dose at 10 year intervals. Use adult formulation (Td) for adults and children ≥7 years of age.

PEDS - Age 6 weeks- 6 yo: 0.5 ml IM , second dose 4-8 weeks later, and third dose 6-12 months later using DT for pediatric use. If immunization of infants begins in the first year of life using DT rather than DTP (i.e. pertussis is contraindicated), give three 0.5 ml doses 4- 8 weeks apart, followed by a fourth dose 6- 12 months later.

FORMS - Injection DT (pediatric: 6 weeks- 6 yo). Td (adult and children: ≥7 years).

NOTES - Current shortage of Td is expected to last until 2002. Health care providers can order directly from Aventis Pasteur (1-800-822-2463) for priority indications. DTaP is preferred for most children <7 years of age. Td is preferred for adults and children ≥7 yo.

haemophilus b vaccine (*ActHIB, HibTITER, OmniHIB, PedvaxHIB*) ▶L ♀C ◗? $

PEDS - Doses vary depending on formulation used and age at first dose. ActHIB/ OmniHIB/ HibTITER: 2- 6 months- 0.5 ml IM x 3 doses at two month intervals. 7- 11 months- 0.5 ml IM x 2 doses at two month intervals. 12- 14 months- 0.5 ml IM x 1 dose. A single 0.5 ml IM (booster) dose is given to children ≥ 15 months old, and at least 2 months after the previous injection. 15- 60 months: 0.5 ml IM x 1 dose (no booster). PedvaxHIB: 2- 14 months- 0.5 ml IM x 2 doses at two month intervals. If the 2 doses are given before 12 months of age, a third 0.5 ml IM (booster) dose is given at least 2 months after the second dose. 15- 60 months- 0.5 ml IM x 1 dose (no booster).

UNAPPROVED ADULT - Asplenia, prior to elective splenectomy, or immunodeficiency: 0.5 ml IM x 1 dose of any Hib conjugate vaccine.

UNAPPROVED PEDS - Asplenia, prior to elective splenectomy, or immunodeficiency age ≥ 5 yo: 0.5 ml IM x 1 dose of any Hib vaccine.

NOTES - Not for IV use. No data on interchangeability between brands; AAP & ACIP recommend use of any product in children > 12- 15 months of age.

hepatitis A vaccine (*Havrix, Vaqta*) ▶L ♀C ◗+ $$$

ADULT - Havrix ≥18 yo: 1 ml (1440 ELU) IM, then 1 ml (1440 ELU) IM booster dose 6- 12 months later. Vaqta ≥18 yo: 1 ml (50 U) IM, then 1 ml (50 U) IM booster 6 months later.

PEDS - Havrix 2-18 yo: 0.5 ml (720 ELU) IM x 1 dose, then 0.5 ml (720 ELU) IM booster 6-12 months after first dose. Vaqta 2-18 yo: 0.5 ml (25 U) IM x 1 dose, then 0.5 ml (25 U) IM booster 6- 18 months later.

FORMS - Single dose vial (specify pediatric or adult)

NOTES - Do not inject IV, SC, or ID. Brands may be used interchangeably. Post-exposure prophylaxis with hepatitis A vaccine alone is not recommended. Should be given 4 weeks prior to travel to endemic area. May be given at the same time as immune globulin, but preferably at different site.

hepatitis B vaccine (*Engerix-B, Recombivax HB*) ▶L ♀C ◗+ $$$

ADULT - Engerix-B ≥20 yo: 1 ml (20 mcg) IM, repeat in 1 and 6 months. Hemodialysis: Give 2.0 ml (40 mcg) IM, repeat in 1, 2, & 6 months. Give 2.0 ml (40 mcg) IM booster when antibody levels <10 mIU/ml. Recombivax HB: 1 ml (10 mcg) IM, repeat in 1 and 6 months. Hemodialysis: 1 ml (40 mcg) IM, repeat in 1 & 6 months. Give 1 ml (40 mcg) IM booster when antibody levels <10 mIU/ml.

PEDS - Specialized dosing based on age and maternal HbsAg status. Infants of hepatitis B negative and positive mothers, children, adolescents < 20 years: Engerix-B 10 mcg (0.5 ml) IM 0,1,6 months. Recombivax 5 mcg (0.5 ml) IM 0,1,6 months. In adolescents 11-15 year, a 2-dose schedule can be used (Recombivax HB 10 mcg (1.0 ml) IM 0, 4-6 months).

NOTES - Infants born to hepatitis B positive mothers should also receive hepatitis B immune globulin and hepatitis B vaccine within 12 hours of birth. Not for IV or ID use. May interchange products. Recombivax HB Dialysis Formulation is intended for adults only. Avoid if yeast allergy.

influenza vaccine (*Fluzone, Fluvirin, FluShield*, *♣Fluviral*) ▶L ♀C ◗+ $

ADULT - 0.5 ml IM (any formulation) single dose once yearly.

PEDS - Age 6- 35 months: 0.25 ml IM, repeat dose ≥4 weeks. Age 3- 8 yo: 0.5 ml IM, repeat dose ≥4 weeks. Age 9- 12 yo: same as adult. Use only the split virus vaccine (i.e. subvirion or purified surface antigen) in children 6 months- 8 yo. Give repeat dose only in previously unvaccinated children.

NOTES - Avoid in allergy to chicken eggs or thimerosal. Optimal administration October to November.

Japanese encephalitis vaccine (*JE-Vax*) ▶? ♀C ◗? $$$$$

ADULT - 1 ml SC x 3 doses on days 0, 7, & 30.

PEDS - Age ≥ 3 yo: 1.0 ml SC x 3 doses on days 0, 7, and 30. Age 1-3 yo: 0.5 ml SC x 3 doses on days 0, 7, and 30.

NOTES - Give at least 10 days before travel to endemic areas. An abbreviated schedule on days 0, 7, & 14 can be given if time constraints. A booster dose may be given after 2 years.

lyme disease vaccine (*LYMErix*) ▶L ♀C ◗? $$$

ADULT - ≥15 yo: 30 mcg IM, repeat in 1 and 12

months.
PEDS - Not approved in children.
UNAPPROVED ADULT - ≥15 yo: 30 mcg IM, repeat in 1 and 2 months or 1 and 6 months.
NOTES - Need for boosters is unclear. Avoid in patients with rheumatoid arthritis, chronic Lyme disease, or allergy to yeast or kanamycin. Do not inject IV, ID, or SC.

measles mumps & rubella vaccine (*M-M-R II*) ▶L ♀C ▶+ $$
ADULT - 0.5 ml (1 vial) SC.
PEDS - 12-15 months of age: 0.5 ml (1 vial) SC. Revaccinate prior to elementary and/or middle school according to local health guidelines. If measles outbreak, may immunize infants 6-12 months old with 0.5 ml SC; then start 2 dose regimen between 12-15 months of age.
NOTES - Do not inject IV. Contraindicated in pregnancy. Advise women to avoid pregnancy for 3 months following vaccination. Live virus, contraindicated in immunocompromised patients. Avoid if allergic to neomycin; caution in patients with egg allergies.

meningococcal polysaccharide vaccine (*Menomune-A/C/Y/W-135*) ▶? ♀C ▶? $$$
ADULT - 0.5 ml SC
PEDS - age ≥ 2 yo: 0.5 ml SC
UNAPPROVED PEDS - age 3-18 months: 0.5 ml SC x 2 doses separated by 3 months
NOTES - Give 2 weeks before elective splenectomy or travel to endemic areas. May consider revaccination q3-5 yrs in high risk patients. Do not inject IV. Contraindicated in pregnancy. Consider vaccinating college students living in dormitories.

plague vaccine (*Plague vaccine*) ▶? ♀C ▶+ $
ADULT - Age 18-61 yo: 1 ml IM x 1 dose, then 0.2 ml IM 1-3 months after the 1st injection, then 0.2 ml IM 5-6 months after 2nd injection.
PEDS - Not approved in children.
NOTES - Up to 3 booster doses (0.2 ml) may be administered at 6 month intervals in high risk patients. Jet injector gun may be used for IM administration.

pneumococcal 7-valent conjugate vaccine (*Prevnar*) ▶L ♀C ▶? $$$
ADULT - Not approved in adults
PEDS - 0.5 ml IM x 3 doses 6-8 weeks apart starting at 2-6 months of age, followed by a 4th dose of 0.5 ml IM at 12-15 months. For previously unvaccinated older infants and children age 7-11 months: 0.5 ml x 2 doses 6-8 weeks apart, followed by a 3rd dose of 0.5 ml at 12-15 months. Age 12-23 months: 0.5 ml x 2 doses 6-8 weeks apart. Age 2-9 yo: 0.5 ml x 1 dose; give 2nd dose 4 weeks later in immunocompromised or chronically ill children. .
NOTES - For IM use only; do not inject IV. Shake susp vigorously prior to administration.

pneumococcal vaccine (*Pneumovax, Pnu-Imune, ✤Pneumo 23*) ▶L ♀C ▶+ $
ADULT - 0.5 ml IM/SC. Routine revaccination in immunocompetent patients is not recommended. Consider revaccination once in patients ≥65 yo or patients at high risk of developing serious pneumococcal infection if > 5 years from initial vaccine.
PEDS - ≥2 yo: 0.5 ml IM/SC. Consider revaccination once in patients at high risk of developing serious pneumococcal infection after 3-5 yo from initial vaccine in patients that would be ≤10 yo at revaccination.
NOTES - Do not give IV or ID. May be given in conjunction with influenza virus vaccine at different site.

poliovirus vaccine (*Orimune (Sabin), IPOL (inactivated)*) ▶L ♀C ▶? $$
ADULT - Not generally recommended. Previously unvaccinated adults at increased risk of exposure should receive a complete primary immunization series of 3 doses of IPV (two doses at intervals of 4-8 weeks; a third dose at 6-12 months after the second dose). Accelerated schedules are available. Travelers to endemic areas who have received primary immunization should receive a single booster (IPV) in adulthood.
PEDS - An all-IPV schedule is now recommended: 0.5 ml IM or SC (IPV, IPOL) at 2 months of age. Second dose at 4 months, third dose at 6- 18 months, and fourth dose at 4- 6 yo. OPV (Orimune) may be used in special circumstances.

rabies vaccine (*RabAvert, Imovax Rabies, Imovax Rabies ID, Biorab, Rabies Vaccine Adsorbed*) ▶L ♀C ▶? $$$$$
ADULT - Post-exposure prophylaxis: Give rabies immune globulin (20 IU/ kg) immediately after exposure, then give rabies vaccine 1 ml IM in deltoid region on days 0, 3, 7, 14, and 28. If patients have received pre-exposure immunization, give 1 ml IM rabies vaccine on days 0 & 3 only without rabies immune globulin. Pre-exposure immunization: 1 ml IM rabies vaccine on days 0, 7, and between days 21-28. Or 0.1 ml ID on days 0, 7, and between days 21-28. (Imovax Rabies I.D. vaccine formula only). Repeat q2-5 years based on antibody titer.
PEDS - Same as adults.

NOTES - Do not use ID preparation for post-exposure prophylaxis.

tetanus toxoid ▶L ♀C ◗+ $

WARNING - Td is preferred in adults and children ≥7 yo. DTP is preferred in children <7 yo. Use fluid tetanus toxoid in assessing cell-mediated immunity only.

ADULT - 0.5 ml IM (adsorbed) x 2 doses 4-8 wks apart. Give third dose 6-12 months after 2nd injection. Give booster q10 yrs. Assess cell-mediated immunity: 0.1 ml of 1:100 diluted skin-test reagent or 0.02 ml of 1: 10 diluted skin-test reagent injected intradermally.

PEDS - 0.5 ml IM (adsorbed) x 2 doses 4-8 wks apart. Give third dose 6-12 months after 2nd injection. Give booster q10 years.

NOTES - May use tetanus toxoid fluid for active immunization in patients hypersensitive to the aluminum adjuvant of the adsorbed formulation: 0.5 ml IM or SC x 3 doses at 4- 8 week intervals. Give fourth dose 6- 12 months after third injection. Give booster dose q10 years.

***TriHibit* (haemophilus b+DTaP)** ▶L ♀C ◗- $$

PEDS - For 4th dose only, 15-18 mos: 0.5 ml IM.

NOTES - Tripedia (DtaP) is used to reconstitute ActHIB (Haemophilus b) to make TriHibit and will appear whitish in color. Use within 30 min.

***Twinrix* (hepatitis A inactivated + hepatitis B recombinant vaccines)** ▶L ♀C ◗? $$$

ADULT - ≥18 yo: 1 ml IM, repeat in 1 & 6 months.

PEDS - Not approved in children.

NOTES - Not for IV or ID use. 1 ml = 720 ELU inactivated hepatitis A + 20 mcg hepatitis B surface antigen.

typhoid vaccine (*Vivotif Berna, Typhim Vi, Typhoid Vaccine*) ▶? ♀C ◗? $$

ADULT - Typhim Vi: 0.5 ml IM x 1 dose given at least 2 weeks prior to potential exposure. May consider revaccination q2 yrs in high risk patients. Typhoid Vaccine, USP: 0.5 ml SC x 2 doses separated by 4 weeks. May consider revaccination q3 yrs in high risk patients. Vivotif Berna: One cap 1 hr before a meal with cold or luke warm drink qod x 4 doses to be completed ≥1 week prior to potential exposure. May consider revaccination q5 yrs in high risk patients.

PEDS - age ≥ 6 yo: Typhim Vi- same as adult dose. Age ≥ 10 yo: Typhoid Vaccine, USP-same as adult dose; age < 10 yo: 0.25 ml SC x 2 doses separated by 4 weeks. Age ≥ 2 yo: Vivotif Berna- same as adult dose.

FORMS - Trade only: Caps

NOTES - Recommended for travel to endemic areas. Typhoid vaccine, USP has more adverse reactions, but is no more effective than Typhim Vi or Vivotif Berna.

varicella vaccine (*Varivax*) ▶L ♀C ◗+ $$$

ADULT - 0.5 ml SC. Repeat 4- 8 weeks later.

PEDS - age 1- 12 yo: 0.5 ml SC x 1 dose. Age ≥13 yo: same as adult dose. Not recommended for infants < 1 yo.

UNAPPROVED PEDS - Postexposure prophylaxis: 0.5 ml SC within 3-5 days of exposure.

NOTES - Do not inject IV. Avoid pregnancy for 3 months following vaccination. The need for booster doses is not defined. Varicella vaccine is a live vaccine and is contraindicated in immunocompromised patients.

yellow fever vaccine (*YF-Vax*) ▶? ♀C ◗+ $$$

ADULT - 0.5 ml SC

PEDS - age 6 months-3 yo: 0.5 ml SC into the thigh; Age ≥ 3 yo: 0.5 ml SC into the deltoid region.

NOTES - Approval by state and/or federal authorities required to obtain vaccine. A booster dose (0.5 ml) may be administered q10 years.

TETANUS WOUND MANAGEMENT www.cdc.gov/nip/publications/pink/tetanus.pdf

Prior tetanus immunizations	*Non tetanus prone wound**	*Tetanus prone wound**
Uncertain or less than 3	Td§	Td§, TIG†
3 or more	Td if >10y since last dose	Td if >5y since last dose

* Non-tetanus prone are clean & minor. Tetanus prone include those with dirt or other contamination, punctures, or crush components. † Tetanus immune glob 250 units IM at site other than dT. § DT if <7 yo.

IMMUNOLOGY: Immunoglobulins

NOTE: Adult IM injections should be given in the deltoid region; injection in the gluteal region may result in suboptimal response.

antivenin - crotalidae immune Fab ovine polyvalent (*CroFab*) ▶? ♀C ◗? $$$$$

ADULT - Rattlesnake envenomation: Give 4-6

vials IV infusion over 60 minutes, <6 h of bite if possible. Administer 4-6 additional vials if no initial control of envenomation syndrome, then 2 vials q6h for up to 18 h (3 doses) after initial control has been established.

PEDS - Same as adults, although specific studies in children have not been conducted.

NOTES - Contraindicated in allergy to papaya or papain. Start IV infusion slowly over the first 10 minutes at 25-50 ml/hr and observe for allergic reaction, then increase to full rate of 250 ml/hr.

antivenin - crotalidae polyvalent ▶L ♀C ▶? $$$$$

ADULT - Pit viper envenomation: minimal envenomation: 20- 40 ml (2- 4 vials) IV infusion; moderate envenomation: 50- 90 ml (5- 9 vials) IV infusion; severe envenomation: ≥100- 150 ml (10- 15 vials) IV infusion. Administer within 4 h of bite, less effective after 8 hours, and of questionable value after 12 hours. May give additional 10- 50 ml (1- 5 vials) IV infusion based on clinical assessment and response to initial dose.

PEDS - Larger relative doses of antivenin are needed in children and small adults because of small volume of body fluid to dilute the venom. The dose is not based on weight.

NOTES - Test first for sensitivity to horse serum. Serum sickness may occur 5-24 days after dose. IV route is preferred. May give IM.

antivenin - latrodectus mactans ▶L♀C▶? $$

ADULT - Specialized dosing for black widow spider toxicity; consult poison center.

PEDS - Specialized dosing for black widow spider toxicity; consult poison center.

NOTES - Test first for horse serum sensitivity. Serum sickness may occur after 5-24 days.

hepatitis B immune globulin (*H-BIG, BayHep B, NABI-HB*) ▶L ♀C ▶? $$$

ADULT - Post-exposure prophylaxis (i.e. needlestick, ocular, mucosal exposure): 0.06 ml/kg IM (usual dose 3- 5 ml) within 24 h of exposure. Initiate hepatitis B vaccine series within 7 days. Consider a second dose of hepatitis B immune globulin (HBIG) one month later if patient refuses hepatitis B vaccine series. Post-exposure prophylaxis (i.e. sexual exposure): 0.06 ml/kg IM within 14d of sexual contact. Initiate hepatitis B vaccine series.

PEDS - Prophylaxis of infants born to HBsAG (+) mothers: 0.5 ml IM within 12 h of birth. Initiate hepatitis B vaccine series within 7 days. If hepatitis B vaccine series is refused, repeat HBIG dose at 3 and 6 months. Household exposure < 12 months of age: 0.5 ml IM within 14d of exposure. Initiate hep B vaccine series.

NOTES - HBIG may be administered at the same time or up to 1 month prior to hepatitis B vaccine without impairing the active immune response from hepatitis B vaccine.

immune globulin (*Gamimune, Polygam, Sandoglobulin, Gammagard, Gammar, Venoglobulin, Baygam*) ▶L ♀C ▶? $$$$$

ADULT - IV dosage varies by indication and formulation used. Hepatitis A post-exposure prophylaxis (i.e. household or institutional contacts): 0.02 ml/kg IM within 2 weeks of exposure. Hepatitis A pre-exposure prophylaxis (i.e. travel to endemic area): < 3 months length of stay = 0.02 ml/kg IM. > 3 months length of stay = 0.06 ml/kg IM and repeat q4- 6 months. Measles: 0.2-0.25 ml/ kg IM within 6 days of exposure, max 15 ml.

PEDS - Pediatric HIV: 400 mg/kg IV infusion q28 days. Measles: 0.2-0.25 ml/ kg IM within 6 days of exposure. In susceptible immunocompromised children use 0.5 ml/ kg IM (max 15 ml) immediately after exposure. Acute idiopathic thrombocytic purpura (ITP): 0.8-1 g/kg IV in 1 or 2 doses. Kawasaki's Disease: 2 g/kg IV x 1.

NOTES - Infusion-rate related adverse events occur; monitor vital signs continuously throughout infusion. Human derived product, increased infection risk.

rabies immune globulin human (*Imogam, BayRab*) ▶L ♀C ▶? $$$$$

ADULT - Post-exposure prophylaxis: 20 units/ kg (0.133 ml/kg), with as much as possible infiltrated around the bite and the rest given IM. Give as soon as possible after exposure. Administer with the first dose of vaccine, but in a different extremity.

PEDS - Not approved in children.

UNAPPROVED PEDS - Use adult dosing.

NOTES - Do not repeat dose once rabies vaccine series begins. Do not give to patients who have been completely immunized with rabies vaccine. Do not administer IV.

RHO immune globulin (*RhoGAM, MICRhoGAM, BayRho-D, WinRho SDF*) ▶L ♀C ▶? $$$$

ADULT - Post-partum prophylaxis: 1 vial (300 mcg) IM within 72 hours of Rh-incompatible delivery. Doses >1 vial may be needed if large fetal-maternal hemorrhage occurs during delivery (see complete prescribing information to determine dose). Antepartum prophylaxis: 1 vial (300 mcg) IM at 26- 28 weeks gestation and 1 vial 72 hours after an Rh-incompatible delivery.

Following amniocentesis, miscarriage, abortion, or ectopic pregnancy ≥13 weeks gestation: 1 vial (300 mcg) IM. <12 weeks gestation: 1 vial (50 mcg) microdose IM. Rh-incompatible transfusion: specialized dosing. Immune thrombocytopenic purpura (ITP), nonsplenectomized (WinRho): 250 units/kg/dose (50 mcg/kg/dose) IV x 1 if hemoglobin > 10 g/dL or 125-200 units/kg/dose (25-40 mcg/kg/dose) IV x 1 if hemoglobin < 10 g/dL. Additional doses of 125-300 units/kg/dose (25-60 mcg/kg/dose) IV may be given as determined by patient's response.

PEDS - Immune thrombocytopenic purpura (ITP), nonsplenectomized (WinRho): 250 units/kg/dose (50 mcg/kg/dose) IV x 1 if hemoglobin > 10g/dL or 125-200 units/kg/dose (25-40 mcg/kg/dose) IV x 1 if hemoglobin < 10 g/dL. Additional doses of 125-300 units/kg/dose (25-60 mcg/kg/dose) IV may be given as determined by patient's response.

NOTES - Do not give IV. If the dose required is ≥2 vials, may inject as divided doses at different injection sites or divide the total dose and inject at intervals within 72 hours.

RSV immune globulin (*RespiGam*) ▶Plasma ♀C ◗? $$$$$

PEDS - RSV prophylaxis in children <24 months: 1.5 ml/kg/hr x 15 minutes. Increase rate as clinical condition permits to 3 ml/kg/hr x 15 minutes, then to a maximum rate of 6 ml/kg/hr. Max total dose/ month is 750 mg/kg.

NOTES - May cause fluid overload; monitor vital signs frequently during IV infusion. RSV season is typically November-April.

tetanus immune globulin (*BayTet*) ▶L ♀C ◗? $$$$

ADULT - See tetanus wound management table. Post-exposure prophylaxis in tetanus prone wounds in patients ≥7 years of age: if <3 doses of tetanus vaccine have been administered or if history is uncertain, give 250 units IM x 1 dose along with dT. If ≥3 doses of tetanus vaccine have been administered in the past, do not give tetanus immune globulin. Tetanus treatment: 3000-6000 units IM in combination with other therapies.

PEDS - <7 yo: 4 units/ kg IM or 250 units IM. Initiate tetanus toxoid vaccine (DTP or DT).

NOTES - Do not give tetanus immune globulin for clean, minor wounds. May be given at the same time as tetanus toxoid active immunization. Do not inject IV.

varicella-zoster immune globulin (*VZIG*) ▶L ♀C ◗? $$$$$

ADULT - Specialized dosing for post-exposure prophylaxis.

PEDS - Specialized dosing for post-exposure prophylaxis.

IMMUNOLOGY: Immunosuppression

basiliximab (*Simulect*) ▶Plasma ♀B ◗? $$$$$

ADULT - Specialized dosing for organ transplantation.

PEDS - Specialized dosing for organ transplantation.

cyclosporine (*Sandimmune, Neoral, Gengraf*) ▶L ♀C ◗- $$$$$

ADULT - Specialized dosing for organ transplantation and rheumatoid arthritis.

PEDS - Not approved in children.

FORMS - Generic/Trade: microemulsion Caps 25, 100 mg. Trade only: Caps (Sandimmune) 25, 100 mg. Solution (Sandimmune) 100 mg/ml. Microemulsion solution (Neoral, Gengraf) 100 mg/ml.

NOTES - Monitor cyclosporine blood concentrations closely. Many drug interactions. Monitor patients closely when switching from Sandimmune to microemulsion formulations.

daclizumab (*Zenapax*) ▶L ♀C ◗? $$$$$

ADULT - Specialized dosing for organ transplantation.

PEDS - Not approved in children.

mycophenolate mofetil (*Cellcept*) ▶? ♀C ◗? $$$$$

ADULT - Specialized dosing for organ transplantation.

PEDS - Not approved in children.

FORMS - Trade only: Caps 250 mg. Tabs 500 mg. Oral suspension 200 mg/ml.

sirolimus (*Rapamune*) ▶L ♀C ◗- $$$$$

ADULT - Specialized dosing for organ transplantation.

PEDS - Not approved in children.

FORMS - Trade: oral solution 1 mg/ml.

tacrolimus (*Prograf, FK 506*) ▶L ♀C ◗- $$$$$

ADULT - Specialized dosing for organ transplantation.

PEDS - Specialized dosing for organ transplantation.

FORMS - Trade only: Caps 1,5 mg.

IMMUNOLOGY: Other

tuberculin PPD (*Aplisol, Tubersol, Mantoux, PPD*) ▶L ♀C ◗+ $

ADULT - 5 TU (0.1 ml) intradermally.

PEDS - Same as adult dose. AAP recommends screening at 12 months, 4- 6 yo, and 14- 16 yo.

NOTES - Avoid SC injection. Read 48- 72 h after intradermal injection. Repeat testing in patients with known prior positive PPD may cause scarring at injection site.

NEUROLOGY: Alzheimer's Dementia

NOTE: Used for mild to moderate (Folstein MMSE 10-26) Alzheimer's dementia.

donepezil (*Aricept*) ▶LK ♀C ◗? $$$$

ADULT - Alzheimer's dementia: Start 5 mg PO qhs. May increase to 10 mg PO qhs in 4-6 weeks.

PEDS - Not approved in children.

FORMS - Trade: Tabs 5, 10 mg.

NOTES - Some clinicians start 5 mg PO qod to minimize GI side effects.

galantamine (*Reminyl*) ▶K ♀B ◗? $$$$

ADULT - Alzheimer's dementia: Start 4 mg PO bid, increase to 8 mg bid after 4 weeks. May increase to 12 mg PO bid after 4 weeks at previous dose. Usual dose 16-24 mg/day.

PEDS - Not approved in children.

FORMS - Trade: tabs 4,8,12 mg.

NOTES - Administer with am & pm meals. Do not exceed 16 mg/day with renal or hepatic impairment. Avoid use with anticholinergics; use caution with CYP3A4 and CYP2D6 inhibitors (e.g. cimetidine, ranitidine, ketoconazole, erythromycin, paroxetine).

rivastigmine (*Exelon*) ▶L ♀B ◗? $$$$

ADULT - Alzheimer's dementia: Start 1.5 mg PO bid, increase to 3 mg bid after 2 weeks. Usual effective dose is 6-12 mg/day, maximum 12 mg/day.

PEDS - Not approved in children.

FORMS - Trade: Caps 1.5, 3, 4.5, 6 mg. Oral solution 2 mg/ml.

NOTES - To reduce severe vomiting, reinitiate treatment with the lowest daily dose (i.e. 1.5 mg PO bid) if patients have interrupted therapy for several days. Take with food. GI adverse effects include nausea, vomiting, anorexia, and weight loss. Avoid with anticholinergic drugs.

tacrine (*Cognex*) ▶L ♀C ◗? $$$$

ADULT - Alzheimer's dementia: Start 10 mg PO qid for 4 weeks, then increase to 20 mg qid. Titrate to higher doses q4 weeks based on tolerability, max 160 mg/day.

PEDS - Not approved in children.

FORMS - Trade: Caps 10, 20, 30, 40 mg.

NOTES - Hepatotoxicity may occur. Monitor LFTs q2 weeks x 16 weeks, then q3 months.

NEUROLOGY: Anticonvulsants

carbamazepine (*Tegretol, Tegretol XR, Carbatrol, Epitol*) ▶LK ♀D ◗+ $

WARNING - Aplastic anemia and agranulocytosis. Monitor CBC and platelets at baseline and periodically.

ADULT - Epilepsy: Start 200 mg PO bid, increase by 200 mg/day at weekly intervals divided tid- qid (regular release) or bid (extended release) up to a maximum dose of 1,600 mg/day. Trigeminal neuralgia: Start 100 mg PO bid or 50 mg PO qid (suspension), increase by 200 mg/day until pain relief, not to exceed 1,200 mg/day.

PEDS - Epilepsy age > 12 yo: Start 200 mg PO bid, or 100 mg PO qid (suspension), increase by 200 mg/day at weekly intervals divided tid-qid (regular release) or bid (extended release) up to maximum dose of 1,000 mg/day (age 12-15 yo) or 1,200 mg/day (age > 15 yo). Epilepsy age 6-12 yo: 100 mg PO bid or 50 mg PO qid (suspension), increase by 100 mg/day at weekly intervals divided tid-qid (regular release) or bid (extended release) up to maximum of 1,000 mg/day. Epilepsy age < 6 yo: 10-20 mg/kg/day PO bid- qid. Maximum dose = 35 mg/kg/day.

UNAPPROVED ADULT - Migraine prophylaxis: 600 mg/day.

FORMS - Generic/Trade: Tabs 200 mg. chew tabs 100 mg. Suspension 100 mg/5 ml. Trade only: ext'd release tabs 100, 200, 300, 400 mg.

NOTES - Therapeutic range = 4- 12 mcg/ml. Stevens-Johnson Syndrome and hepatitis may occur. Monitor LFTs. Many drug interactions.

clonazepam (***Klonopin***, ***✦Clonapam, Rivotril***) ▶LK ♀D ▶? ©IV $$$

ADULT - Epilepsy: Start 0.5 mg PO tid, increase by 0.5- 1 mg q3 days, max 20 mg/day.

PEDS - Epilepsy ≤10 yo or ≤30 kg: 0.01- 0.03 mg/kg/day PO divided bid- tid, increase by 0.25- 0.5 mg q3 days up to 0.1- 0.2 mg/kg/day divided tid.

UNAPPROVED ADULT - Neuralgias: 2- 4 mg/day PO. Restless legs syndrome: 0.5-4 mg PO qhs.

FORMS - Generic/Trade: Tabs 0.5, 1, 2 mg.

NOTES - Therapeutic range = 20- 80 ng/ml.

diazepam (***Valium, Diastat***, ***✦Vivol, E Pam***) ▶LK ♀D ▶- ©IV $

ADULT - Status epilepticus: 5- 10 mg IV, repeat in 10- 15 minutes to maximum dose of 30 mg. Epilepsy, adjunctive therapy: 2- 10 mg PO bid-qid. Increased seizure activity: 0.2- 0.5 mg/kg PR (rectal gel) up to max dose of 20 mg/day.

PEDS - Status epilepticus: age 1 month- 5 yo: 0.2- 0.5 mg/kg IV slowly q2-5 minutes to maximum of 5 mg. Age > 5 yo: 1 mg IV slowly q2-5 minutes to maximum of 10 mg. Repeat q2-4h prn. Epilepsy, adjunctive therapy age > 1 month: 1- 2.5 mg PO tid- qid, gradually increase to maximum of 30 mg/day. Increased seizure activity: 0.5 mg/kg PR for 2-5 yo, 0.3 mg/kg PR for 6-11 yo, 0.2 mg/kg PR for > 12 yo up to max 20 mg.

UNAPPROVED ADULT - Restless legs syndrome: 0.5-4.0 mg PO qhs.

FORMS - Generic/Trade: Tabs 2, 5, 10 mg. solution 5 mg/ 5 ml. Trade only: concentrated solution (Intensol) 5 mg/ml. rectal gel (Diastat) 2.5, 5, 10, 15, 20 mg.

NOTES - Respiratory depression may occur.

ethosuximide (***Zarontin***) ▶LK ♀C ▶+ $$$$

ADULT - Epilepsy: 500 mg PO qd or divided bid, increase by 250 mg/day q4-7 days to maximum dose of 1.5 g/day.

PEDS - Epilepsy age 3-6 yo: 250 mg PO qd or divided bid. Age > 6 yo: 500 mg PO qd or divided bid. Optimal peds dose 20 mg/kg/day. Age <3 yo: Not approved.

UNAPPROVED PEDS - Epilepsy age 3-6 yo: 15 mg/kg/day divided bid, increase prn q4-7d. Usual maintenance 15-40 mg/kg/day divided bid, max 500 mg/d.

FORMS - Trade only: Caps 250 mg. Generic/ Trade: syrup 250 mg/ 5 ml.

NOTES - Therapeutic range = 40- 100 mcg/ml. Monitor CBC for blood dyscrasias.

felbamate (***Felbatol***) ▶KL ♀C ▶- $$$$

WARNING - Aplastic anemia and fatal hepatic failure have occurred.

ADULT - Epilepsy: Start 400 mg PO tid, increase by 600 mg/day q2 weeks to max 3,600 mg/day.

PEDS - Lennox- Gastaut syndrome, adjunctive therapy age 2- 14 yo: Start 15 mg/kg/day PO in 3-4 divided doses, increase by 15 mg/kg/day at weekly intervals to max 45 mg/kg/day.

FORMS - Trade: Tabs 400, 600 mg. suspension 600 mg/ 5 ml.

NOTES - Do not use without discussing the risks and obtaining written informed consent. Many drug interactions.

fosphenytoin (***Cerebyx***) ▶L ♀D ▶+ $$$$$

ADULT - Status epilepticus: 15- 20 mg PE/kg IV no faster than 100- 150 mg PE/minute. Non-emergent loading dose: 10- 20 mg PE/kg IM/IV at rate ≤150 mg/min. Maintenance dose: 4- 6 mg PE/kg/day for up to 5 days.

PEDS - Not approved in children.

UNAPPROVED PEDS - Status epilepticus: 15-20 mg PE/kg IV at a rate < 2 mg PE/kg/min.

NOTES - Therapeutic range = 10- 20 mcg/ml. Fosphenytoin is prescribed in phenytoin equivalents (PE). Monitor ECG & vital signs continuously during and after infusion. Many drug interactions.

gabapentin (***Neurontin***) ▶K ♀C ▶? $$$$

ADULT - Epilepsy, adjunctive therapy: Start 300 mg PO qhs, increase by 300 mg/day over a few days to usual dose of 300- 600 mg PO tid. Maximum dose is 3,600 mg/day.

PEDS - Epilepsy, adjunctive therapy ≥12 yo: Use adult dose. 3-12 yo: Start 10-15 mg/kg/day PO divided tid. Titrate over 3 days to usual dose of 25-40 mg/kg/day, max 50 mg/kg/day.

UNAPPROVED ADULT - Neuropathic pain: 300 mg PO tid, max 3,600 mg/day. Restless leg syndrome: 300- 2,700 mg/day PO. Mania: Start 300 mg PO qhs, titrate to 900- 2,400 mg/day in divided doses. Migraine prevention: Start 300 mg/day PO, titrate to 400-900 mg/day, then increase to 1200-2400 mg/day in divided doses.

FORMS - Trade: Caps 100, 300, 400 mg. Tabs 600, 800 mg. soln 50 mg/ml.

NOTES - Decrease dose in renal impairment. Discontinue gabapentin and/or add other anticonvulsants gradually over ≥1 week.

lamotrigine (***Lamictal, Lamictal CD***) ▶LK ♀C ▶- $$$$

WARNING - Severe, potentially life-threatening rashes (e.g. Stevens-Johnson Syndrome, toxic epidermal necrolysis) have been reported in 1:1000 adults and 1:50 children, usually within 2-8 weeks of initiation.

ADULT - Epilepsy, adjunctive therapy with valproic acid: Start 25 mg PO qod x 2 weeks, then 25 mg PO qd x 2 weeks. Increase by 25-50 mg/day q1-2 weeks to usual maintenance dose of 100-400 mg/day given qd or bid. Epilepsy, adjunctive therapy with enzyme-inducing antiepileptic drugs: Start 50 mg PO qd x 2 weeks, then 50 mg PO bid x 2 weeks. Increase by 100 mg/day q1-2 wks to usual maintenance dose of 150-250 mg PO bid.

PEDS - Lennox-Gastaut, adjunctive therapy with valproic acid age 2-12 yo: Start 0.15 mg/kg/day PO given qd or bid x 2 weeks, then 0.3 mg/kg/day PO given qd or bid x 2 weeks. Increase q1-2 weeks to usual maintenance dose of 1-5 mg/kg/day, maximum 200 mg/day. Adjunctive therapy with enzyme-inducing antiepileptic drugs age 2-12 yo: Start 0.6 mg/kg/day PO divided bid x 2 weeks, then 1.2 mg/kg/day PO divided bid x 2 weeks. Increase q1-2 weeks to usual maintenance dose of 5-15 mg/kg/day, maximum 400 mg/day.

UNAPPROVED ADULT - Bipolar depression: Start 25-50 mg PO qd, titrate to 100- 500 mg/day divided bid.

FORMS - Trade: Tabs 25, 100, 150, 200 mg. chew tabs 5, 25 mg.

NOTES - Drug interactions with enzyme-inducing antiepileptic drugs (eg, carbamazepine, phenobarbital, phenytoin, primidone) and valproic acid; may need to adjust dose.

levetiracetam (*Keppra*) ▶LK ♀C ▶? $$$$$

ADULT - Epilepsy, adjunctive therapy: Start 500 mg PO BID, increase by 1000 mg/day q2 weeks to maximum dose of 3000 mg/day.

PEDS - Not approved in children.

FORMS - Trade: Tabs 250, 500, 750 mg.

NOTES - Drug interactions are unlikely. Decrease dose in renal dysfunction. Taper off slowly when discontinuing therapy.

lorazepam (*Ativan*) ▶LK ♀D ▶- ©IV $$$

PEDS - Not approved in children.

UNAPPROVED ADULT - Status epilepticus: 0.05-0.1 mg/kg IV over 2-5 min or 4 mg IV. May repeat in 5-15 min. Max dose in 12 hour period is 8 mg.

UNAPPROVED PEDS - Status epilepticus: 0.05-0.1 mg/kg IV over 2-5 min. May repeat 0.05 mg/kg x 1 in 10-15 min. Do not exceed 4 mg/kg as single dose.

oxcarbazepine (*Trileptal*) ▶L ♀C ▶- $$$$

ADULT - Epilepsy, monotherapy: Start 300 mg PO bid, increase by 300 mg/day q3 days to usual dose of 1200 mg/day. May increase dose to 2400 mg/day in patients converted from other antiepileptic drugs. Epilepsy, adjunctive: Start 300 mg PO bid, increase by 600 mg/day at weekly intervals to usual dose of 1200 mg/day. Maximum dose 2400 mg/day.

PEDS - Epilepsy, adjunctive age 4- 16 yo: start 8- 10 mg/kg/day divided bid (maximum starting dose 600 mg/day), titrate to usual dose of 900 mg/day (20-29 kg children), 1200 mg/day (29.1- 39 kg children), and 1800 mg/day (> 39 kg children).

FORMS - Trade: Tabs 150, 300, 600 mg. Oral suspension 300 mg/5 ml.

NOTES - Decrease dose by one-half in patients with renal dysfunction (CrCl < 30 mL/min). Oxcarbazepine inhibits CYP 2C19 and induces CYP 3A4/5. Drug interactions with other antiepileptic drugs, oral contraceptives, and dihydropyridine calcium antagonists. Monitor sodium levels for possible hyponatremia.

phenobarbital (*Luminal*) ▶L ♀D ▶- ©IV $

ADULT - Epilepsy: 100-300 mg/day PO divided bid-tid. Status epilepticus: 200- 600 mg IV at rate ≤60 mg/ min up to total dose of 20 mg/ kg.

PEDS - Epilepsy: 3-5 mg/kg/day PO divided bid-tid. Status epilepticus: 100- 400 mg IV at rate ≤60 mg/ min up to 20 mg/ kg.

UNAPPROVED ADULT - Status epilepticus: may give up to total dose of 30 mg/kg IV.

UNAPPROVED PEDS - Status epilepticus: 15-20 mg/kg/dose IV load, may give an additional 5 mg/kg doses q15-30 minutes to total dose of 30 mg/kg. Epilepsy, maintenance dose: 3-5 mg/kg/day divided qd-bid (neonates), 5-6 mg/kg/day divided qd-bid (infants), 6-8 mg/kg/day divided qd-bid (age 1-5 yo), 4-6 mg/kg/day divided qd-bid (age 6-12 yo), and 1-3 mg/kg/day divided qd-bid (age >12 yo).

FORMS - Generic/Trade: Tabs 15, 16, 30, 32, 60, 65, 100 mg. elixir 20 mg/5 ml.

NOTES - Therapeutic range = 15- 40 mcg/ml. Decrease dose in renal or hepatic dysfunction. Many drug interactions.

phenytoin (*Dilantin, Diphen*) ▶L ♀D ▶+ $

ADULT - Epilepsy: oral loading dose: 400 mg PO initially, then 300 mg in 2h and 4h. Maintenance dose: 300 mg PO qd or divided tid. Status epilepticus: 10- 20 mg/kg IV at rate ≤50 mg/ min, then 100 mg IV/PO q6-8h.

PEDS - Epilepsy age > 6 yo: 5 mg/kg/day PO divided bid- tid, to max 300 mg/day. Status epilepticus: 10-20 mg/kg IV at ≤1-3 mg/kg/min (but most clinicians prefer 0.5 mg/kg/min).

FORMS - Generic/Trade: Caps 100 mg. Suspension 125 mg/5 ml. Extended release Caps 100 mg. Trade only: Extended release Caps 30 mg. chew Tabs 50 mg.

NOTES - Therapeutic range = 10- 20 mcg/ml. Monitor ECG and vital signs when administering IV. Many drug interactions. Monitor serum levels closely when switching between forms (some are free acid and some sodium salt). QD dosing only recommended with extended release caps.

primidone (*Mysoline*) ▶LK ♀D ▶- $

ADULT - Epilepsy: 100- 125 mg PO qhs, increase over 10 days to usual maintenance dose of 250 mg PO tid- qid. Maximum dose is 2 g/day.

PEDS - Epilepsy <8 yo: 50 mg PO qhs, increase over 10 days to usual maintenance dose of 125- 250 mg PO tid or 10- 25 mg/kg/day.

UNAPPROVED ADULT - Essential tremor: 250 mg PO tid.

FORMS - Trade only: Tabs 50 mg. suspension 250 mg/ 5 ml. Generic/Trade: Tabs 250 mg.

NOTES - Therapeutic range = 5- 12 mcg/ ml. Metabolized to phenobarbital.

tiagabine (*Gabitril*) ▶LK ♀C ▶- $$$$

ADULT - Epilepsy, adjunctive therapy: 4 mg PO qd, increase by 4-8 mg q1 week up to maximum dose of 56 mg/day divided bid- qid.

PEDS - Epilepsy, adjunctive therapy 12- 18 yo: 4 mg PO qd, increase by 4 mg q1-2 weeks up to maximum dose of 32 mg/day divided bid-qid. Age <12 yo: Not approved.

FORMS - Trade: Tabs 2, 4, 12, 16, 20 mg.

NOTES - Take with food.

topiramate (*Topamax*) ▶K ♀C ▶? $$$$$

ADULT - Epilepsy, adjunctive therapy: Start 25-50 mg PO qhs, increase by 25-50 mg/day q week to usual dose of 200 mg PO bid. Maximum dose is 1,600 mg/day.

PEDS - Epilepsy, adjunctive therapy 2-16 yo: Start 1-3 mg/kg/day (or 25 mg/day, whichever less) PO qhs, increase by 1-3 mg/kg/day q 1-2 wks up to 5-9 mg/kg/day in two divided doses .

UNAPPROVED ADULT - Bipolar disorder: Start 25-50 mg/day PO, titrate prn to max 400 mg/day.

FORMS - Trade only: Tabs 25, 100, 200 mg. Sprinkle Caps 15, 25 mg.

NOTES - Give ½ usual adult dose to those with renal impairment (CrCl < 70 ml/min). Confusion, renal stones, and weight loss may occur.

valproic acid (*Depakene, Depakote, Depakote ER, Depacon*, ✤*Epiject, Epival, Deproic*) ▶L ♀D ▶+ $$$$

WARNING - Fatal hepatic failure has occurred; monitor LFTs during first 6 months. Life-threatening cases of pancreatitis have been reported after initial or prolonged use. Evaluate for abdominal pain, nausea, vomiting, and/or anorexia and discontinue valproate if pancreatitis is diagnosed.

ADULT - Seizures: 10- 15 mg/kg/day PO or IV infusion over 60 mins (≤20 mg/min). Increase dose by 5- 10 mg/kg/day at weekly intervals to a max dose of 60 mg/kg/day. Doses >250 mg/day should be divided bid-qid (Depakote). Migraine prophylaxis: 250 mg PO bid (Depakote), or start 500 mg PO qd x 1 week, then 1000 mg PO qd (Depakote ER), max 1,000 mg/day.

PEDS - Seizures >2 yo: 10- 15 mg/kg/day PO or IV infusion over 60 minutes (≤20 mg/min). Increase dose by 5-10 mg/kg/day at weekly intervals to a maximum dose of 60 mg/kg/day. Divide doses >250 mg/day into bid- qid.

FORMS - Trade only: Tabs, delayed release (Depakote) 125, 250, 500 mg. Tabs, extended release (Depakote ER) 500 mg. Caps, sprinkle (Depakote) 125 mg. Generic/Trade: syrup (Depakene) 250 mg/5 ml. Caps (Depakene) 250 mg.

NOTES - Therapeutic range = 50- 150 mcg/ml. Depakote and Depakote ER are not interchangeable. Depakote releases divalproex sodium over 8-12h (qd-qid dosing) and Depakote ER releases divalproex sodium over 18-24h (qd dosing). Contraindicated in hepatic dysfunction. Many drug interactions. Reduce dose in elderly. GI irritation, thrombocytopenia may occur. Children receiving other anticonvulsants may require higher doses of valproic acid. Depakene (valproic acid), Depakote (divalproex sodium).

zonisamide (*Zonegran*) ▶LK ♀C ▶- $$$$

ADULT - Epilepsy, adjunctive: Start 100 mg PO qd, increase to 200 mg PO qd after two weeks. May increase to 300-400 mg/day divided qd or bid with at least two weeks between dose titrations to achieve steady state. Maximum dose 600 mg/day.

PEDS - Not approved in children.

FORMS - Trade: Caps 100 mg.

NOTES – Contraindicated in sulfonamide allergy. Fatalities and severe reactions including Stevens-Johnson syndrome, toxic epidermal necrolysis, fulminant hepatic necrosis, agranulocytosis, aplastic anemia, and other blood dyscrasias have occurred. Discontinue drug if signs of hypersensitivity or other reactions occur. Drug interactions with enzyme-inducers (e.g. phenytoin, carbamazepine, phenobarbital). Renal stones may occur.

NEUROLOGY: Migraine Therapy - 5-HT1 Receptor Agonists

NOTE: Avoid with coronary artery disease, uncontrolled HTN, & ergot drugs.

almotriptan (*Axert*) ▶LK ♀C ▶? ?
ADULT - Migraine treatment: 6.25-12.5 mg PO, may repeat in 2h. Max dose 25 mg/day.
PEDS - Not approved in children.
FORMS - Trade: tabs 6.25, 12.5 mg.
NOTES - Contraindicated in coronary artery disease, uncontrolled HTN, and concurrent MAO inhibitor or ergot drug use. Use lower doses (6.25 mg) in renal/hepatic dysfunction.

naratriptan (*Amerge*) ▶KL ♀C ▶? $$
ADULT - Migraine treatment: 1- 2.5 mg PO, may repeat in 4h for max dose of 5 mg/ 24h.
PEDS - Not approved in children.
FORMS - Trade: Tabs 1, 2.5 mg.
NOTES - Contraindicated in severe renal or hepatic impairment, coronary artery disease, uncontrolled HTN and ergot drug use.

rizatriptan (*Maxalt, Maxalt MLT*) ▶LK ♀C ▶? $$
ADULT - Migraine treatment: 5- 10 mg PO, may repeat in 2h to maximum dose of 30 mg/ 24h.
PEDS - Not approved in children.
FORMS - Trade: Tabs 5, 10 mg. orally disintegrating Tabs (MLT) 5, 10 mg.
NOTES - Contraindicated in coronary artery disease, uncontrolled HTN, and concurrent MAO inhibitor or ergot drug use. MLT form dissolves on tongue without liquids.

sumatriptan (*Imitrex*) ▶K ♀C ▶? $$
ADULT - Migraine treatment: 6 mg SC, may repeat after 1h to maximum dose of 12 mg/day or 25 mg PO, may repeat q2h with 25- 100 mg doses to maximum of 200- 300 mg/day. Alternative 5- 20 mg intranasally, may repeat q2h to maximum of 40 mg/day. Cluster headache treatment: 6 mg SC, may repeat after 1h to maximum dose of 12 mg/day.
PEDS - Not approved in children.
FORMS - Trade: Tabs 25, 50 mg. nasal spray 5, 20 mg/ spray. injection 6 mg/0.5 ml.
NOTES - Contraindicated in coronary artery disease, uncontrolled HTN, and with MAO inhibitors or ergot drugs. Avoid IM/IV route.

zolmitriptan (*Zomig*) ▶L ♀C ▶? $$
ADULT - Migraine treatment: 1- 2.5 mg PO q2h to maximum dose of 10 mg/ 24 hours.
PEDS - Not approved in children.
FORMS - Trade: Tabs 2.5, 5 mg.
NOTES - Contraindicated in coronary artery disease, uncontrolled HTN, and concurrent MAO inhibitor or ergot drug use. Use lower doses (< 2.5 mg) in hepatic dysfunction. May break 2.5 mg Tabs in half.

GLASGOW COMA SCALE

Eye Opening	*Verbal Activity*	*Motor Activity*
		6. Obeys commands
	5. Oriented	5. Localizes pain
4. Spontaneous	4. Confused	4. Withdraws to pain
3. To command	3. Inappropriate	3. Flexion to pain
2. To pain	2. Incomprehensible	2. Extension to pain
1. None	1. None	1. None

NEUROLOGY: Migraine Therapy - Other

***Cafergot* (ergotamine + caffeine)** ▶L♀X ▶- $
ADULT - Migraine and cluster headache treatment: 2 Tabs PO at onset, then 1 tab q30 minutes prn up to 6 Tabs/ attack, max 10 tabs/ week. May give suppositories up to 2/ attack, max 5 supp/ week.
PEDS - Not approved in children.
UNAPPROVED PEDS - Migraine treatment: 1 tab PO at onset, then 1 tab q 30 min prn up to max 3 Tabs/attack.
FORMS - Trade: Tabs 1 mg ergotamine/100 mg caffeine. suppositories 2 mg ergotamine/100 mg caffeine.
NOTES - Contraindicated in sepsis, peripheral vascular or coronary artery disease, impaired hepatic or renal function, malnutrition, severe pruritus, or HTN.

dihydroergotamine (*DHE 45, Migranal*) ▶L ♀X ▶- $$
ADULT - Migraine treatment: 1 mg IV/IM/SC, may repeat q1h prn up to maximum dose of 2 mg (IV) or 3 mg (IM/SC) per 24 hours. Or 1

spray (0.5 mg) in each nostril, may repeat in 15 minutes up to maximum dose of 6 sprays (3 mg)/ 24 h or 8 sprays (4 mg)/ week.

PEDS - Not approved in children.

FORMS - Trade: nasal spray 0.5 mg/ spray.

NOTES - Contraindicated in sepsis, peripheral vascular or coronary artery disease, vascular surgery, impaired hepatic or renal function, uncontrolled HTN, and with concurrent ergotamine, methysergide, or 5-HT1 agonist use.

Duradrin **(isometheptene + dichloralphenazone + acetaminophen)** ▶L ♀? ▶? ©IV $

ADULT - Tension and vascular headache treatment: 1- 2 Caps PO q4h, up to maximum of 8 caps/day. Migraine treatment: 2 caps PO, then 1 cap q1h up to maximum of 5 caps/ 12 hours.

PEDS - Not approved in children.

FORMS - Trade: Caps 65 mg isometheptene/ 100 mg dichloralphenazone/325 mg acetaminophen

NOTES - FDA has classified Duradrin as "possibly" effective for migraine treatment. Contraindicated in glaucoma, severe renal disease, HTN, heart disease, hepatic disease, and concurrent MAO inhibitor use.

Excedrin Migraine **(acetaminophen + aspirin + caffeine)** ▶LK ♀D ▶? $

ADULT - Migraine: 2 Tabs PO q6h, maximum 8 Tabs/day.

FORMS - OTC/Generic/Trade: Tabs acetaminophen 250 mg/ aspirin 250 mg/ caffeine 65 mg.

methysergide (*Sansert*) ▶L ♀D ▶- $$$$

WARNING - May cause fibrosis of retroperitoneum, pleura, and cardiac valves with long-term use.

ADULT - Migraine and cluster headache prophylaxis: Start with 2 mg PO qd and titrate to 4-8 mg/day PO in divided doses with meals. Include a drug-free interval of 3-4 weeks after each 6-month course of therapy. Gradually wean over 2-3 weeks prior to discontinuation to avoid rebound headache.

PEDS - Not approved in children.

FORMS - Trade: Tabs 2 mg.

NOTES - Contraindicated in patients with peripheral vascular or coronary artery disease, severe HTN, phlebitis or cellulitis of lower limbs, pulmonary disease, collagen diseases, fibrotic processes, impaired hepatic or renal function, valvular heart disease, debilitated states, and serious infections.

Midrin **(isometheptene + dichloralphenazone + acetaminophen)** ▶L ♀? ▶? ©IV $

ADULT - Tension and vascular headache treatment: 1- 2 Caps PO q4h, up to maximum of 8 Caps/day. Migraine treatment: 2 Caps PO, then 1 cap q1h up to maximum of 5 Caps/ 12 hours.

PEDS - Not approved in children.

FORMS - Trade: Caps 65 mg isometheptene/ 100 mg dichloralphenazone/325 mg acetaminophen.

NOTES - FDA has classified Midrin as "possibly" effective for migraine treatment. Contraindicated in glaucoma, severe renal disease, HTN, heart disease, hepatic disease, and concurrent MAO inhibitor use.

valproic acid (*Depakene, Depakote, Depakote ER*, ✦*Epiject, Epival, Deproic*) ▶L ♀D ▶+ $$

WARNING - Fatal hepatic failure has occurred; monitor LFTs during first 6 months. Life-threatening cases of pancreatitis have been reported after initial or prolonged use. Evaluate for abdominal pain, nausea, vomiting, and/or anorexia and discontinue valproate if pancreatitis is diagnosed.

ADULT - Migraine prophylaxis: 250 mg PO bid (Depakote) or start 500 mg PO qd x 1 week, then 1000 mg PO qd (Depakote ER), max 1,000 mg/day.

PEDS - Not approved for migraine prophylaxis in children.

FORMS - Trade only: Tabs, delayed release (Depakote) 125, 250, 500 mg. Tabs, extended release (Depakote ER) 500 mg. Caps, sprinkle (Depakote) 125 mg. Generic/Trade: syrup (Depakene) 250 mg/ 5 ml. Caps (Depakene) 250 mg.

NOTES - Contraindicated in hepatic dysfunction. Many drug interactions. Reduce dose in elderly. GI irritation, thrombocytopenia. Depakene (valproic acid), Depakote (divalproex sodium).

LUMBOSACRAL NERVE ROOT COMPRESSION	Root	Motor	Sensory	Reflex
	L4	quadriceps	medial foot	knee-jerk
	L5	dorsiflexors	dorsum of foot	medial hamstring
	S1	plantarflexors	lateral foot	ankle-jerk

DERMATOMES

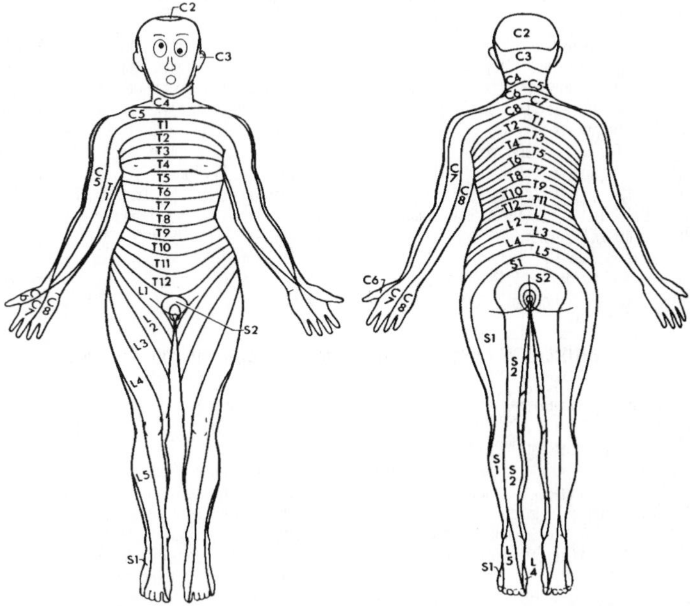

NEUROLOGY: Parkinsonian Agents - Anticholinergics

benztropine mesylate (*Cogentin*, ✤*Bensylate*) ▶LK ♀C ◗? $
ADULT - Parkinsonism: 0.5- 2 mg/day PO/IM/IV, increase by 0.5 mg increments at weekly intervals to a max 6 mg/day. May divide doses qd-qid. Drug-induced extrapyramidal disorders: 1-4 mg PO/IM/IV qd-bid.
PEDS - Not approved in children.
UNAPPROVED PEDS - Parkinsonism: >3 yo: 0.02- 0.05 mg/kg/dose qd- bid. Use with caution due to anticholinergic side effects. Contraindicated in children < 3 yo.
FORMS - Generic/Trade: Tabs 0.5, 1, 2 mg.

biperiden (*Akineton*) ▶LK ♀C ◗? $$
ADULT - Parkinsonism: 2 mg PO tid-qid, titrate to max dose of 16 mg/day. Drug-induced extrapyramidal disorders: 2 mg PO qd-tid or 2 mg IM/IV q30 minutes prn up to max of 8 mg/24h.
PEDS - Not approved in children.
FORMS - Trade: Tabs 2 mg
NOTES - Contraindicated in glaucoma, bowel obstruction, and megacolon.

trihexyphenidyl (*Artane*) ▶LK ♀C ◗? $
ADULT - Parkinsonism: 1 mg PO qd, increase by 2 mg/day at 3-5 day intervals to 6-10 mg/day. Divide doses tid w/ meals max 15 mg/day.
PEDS - Not approved in children.
FORMS - Generic/Trade: Tabs 2, 5 mg. elixir 2 mg/ 5 ml.
NOTES - Adjust dose of levodopa and trihexyphenidyl when used concurrently.

MOTOR FUNCTION BY NERVE ROOTS

Level	*Motor function*
C3/C4/C5	Diaphragm
C5/C6	Deltoid / biceps
C7/C8	Triceps
C8/T1	Finger flexion / intrinsics
T1-T12	Intercostal / abd muscles
L2/L3	Hip flexion
L2/L3/L4	Hip adduction / quads
L4/L5	Ankle dorsiflexion
S1/S2	Ankle plantarflexion
S2/S3/S4	rectal tone

NEUROLOGY: Parkinsonian Agents - COMT Inhibitors

entacapone (*Comtan*) ▶L ♀C ▶? $$$$

ADULT - Parkinsonism, adjunctive: Start 200 mg PO with each dose of levodopa/carbidopa up to a maximum of 8 times/day (1600 mg).

PEDS - Not approved in children.

FORMS - Trade: Tabs 200 mg.

NOTES - Adjunct to levodopa/carbidopa in patients who have end-of-dose "wearing off" effect. Entacapone has no antiparkinsonian effect on its own. Avoid with non-selective MAO inhibitors, possible interaction.

tolcapone (*Tasmar*) ▶LK ♀C ▶? $$$$

WARNING - Fatal hepatic failure has occurred. Use only in patients on carbidopa/levodopa who are unresponsive or cannot take alternative therapies. Discontinue if no clinical benefit after 3 weeks of therapy or if LFT elevation. Monitor LFTs at baseline and q2 weeks.

ADULT - Parkinsonism, adjunctive: Start 100 mg PO tid, increase to 200 mg PO tid only if expected benefit is justified. Max 600 mg/day.

PEDS - Not approved in children.

FORMS - Trade: Tabs 100, 200 mg.

NOTES - Adjunct to carbidopa/ levodopa only. Monitor LFTs. Avoid use with non-selective MAOIs.

NEUROLOGY: Parkinsonian Agents - Dopaminergic Agents

amantadine (*Symmetrel*, *✤Endantadine*) ▶K ♀C ▶- $

ADULT - Parkinsonism: 100 mg PO bid, max 400 mg/day. Drug- incuded extrapyramidal disorders: 100 mg PO bid, max 300 mg/day.

PEDS - Not approved in children <1 yo.

FORMS - Trade only: Tabs 100 mg. Generic: caps 100 mg. Generic/Trade: syrup 50 mg/5 ml.

NOTES - Decrease dose in CHF, peripheral edema, orthostatic hypotension, impaired renal function, seizure disorders, or age >65 years. Side effects are nausea, dizziness, insomnia, and livedo reticularis.

***Atamet* (carbidopa + levodopa)** ▶L♀C▶- $$$

ADULT - Parkinsonism: Start 1 tab (25/100) PO tid, increase by 1 tab/day q1-2 days prn up to maximum of 8 Tabs/day (200 mg carbidopa/ 800 mg levodopa). Use 1 tab (25/250) PO tid-qid when higher levodopa doses are needed. Increase by ½- 1 tab q1-2 days to maximum of 8 Tabs/day (200 mg carbidopa/ 2 g levodopa). Maximum 200 mg/day carbidopa.

PEDS - Not approved in children.

UNAPPROVED ADULT - Restless legs syndrome: start 1/2 -1 tab (25/100) PO qhs, increase q3-4d to max 50/200 qhs.

FORMS - Generic/Trade: Tabs 25/100, 25/250.

NOTES - Provide at least 70- 100 mg/day carbidopa to reduce N/V.

bromocriptine (*Parlodel*) ▶L ♀B ▶- $$$$

ADULT - Parkinson's disease: 1.25 mg PO bid, increase by 2.5 mg/day q14-28 days to 10- 40 mg/day. Max 100 mg/day.

PEDS - Not approved in children.

UNAPPROVED ADULT - Neuroleptic malignant syndrome: 2.5- 5 mg PO 2-6 times/day.

FORMS - Generic/Trade: Tabs 2.5 mg. Caps 5 mg.

NOTES - Adverse effects are nausea, vomiting, dizziness, hypotension, and erythromelalgia. Take with food to minimize dizzines & nausea.

levodopa (*Laradopa*) ▶L ♀- ▶- $$

ADULT - Parkinsonism: 250- 500 mg PO bid, increase by 100- 750 mg/day q3-7 days to max 8 g/day.

PEDS - Not approved in children.

FORMS - Trade: Tabs 100, 250, 500 mg.

NOTES - Therapeutic response seen in 3-6 months. Rarely used alone, usually in combination with carbidopa.

pergolide (*Permax*) ▶K ♀B ▶? $$$$$

ADULT - Parkinsonism: 0.05 mg PO qd x2 days, increase by 0.1-0.15 mg/day q3 days x12 days, then increase by 0.25 mg/day q3 days to response. Usual dose is 1 mg tid, max 5 mg/day.

PEDS - Not approved in children.

UNAPPROVED ADULT - Restless legs syndrome: 0.05 mg PO taken 2h before bedtime, increase to max 0.5 mg.

FORMS - Trade: Tabs 0.05, 0.25, 1 mg.

NOTES - Adjunct to carbidopa/ levodopa. Titrate dose slowly to avoid hypotension.

pramipexole (*Mirapex*) ▶K ♀C ▶? $$$$

ADULT - Parkinsonism: Start 0.125 mg PO tid, increase by 0.125 mg/dose at weekly intervals to 0.5- 1.5 mg PO tid.

PEDS - Not approved in children.

UNAPPROVED ADULT - Restless legs syndrome: start 0.125 mg PO qhs, increase q7d to max 0.75 mg qhs.

FORMS - Trade: Tabs 0.125,0.25,0.5,1,1.5 mg.

NOTES - Decrease dose in renal impairment. Titrate slowly to avoid orthostatic hypotension.

ropinirole (*Requip*) ▶L ♀C ▶? $$$

ADULT - Parkinsonism: 0.25 mg PO tid, increase by 0.25 mg/dose at weekly intervals up to 1 mg PO tid. Max 24 mg/day.

PEDS - Not approved in children.

UNAPPROVED ADULT - Restless legs syndrome: start 0.25 mg PO qhs or bid, increase to max 12 mg/day.

FORMS - Trade: Tabs 0.25, 0.5, 1, 2, 4, 5 mg.

NOTES - Syncope and/or hypotension may occur. Titrate slowly.

selegiline (*Eldepryl, Atapryl, Carbex, Selpak*) ▶LK ♀C ▶? $$$

ADULT - Parkinsonism: 5 mg PO q am and q noon. Max 10 mg/day.

PEDS - Not approved in children.

FORMS - Generic/Trade: Caps 5 mg. Tabs 5 mg.

NOTES - Adjunct to carbidopa/ levodopa. Contraindicated with meperidine and other opioids. Risk of non-selective MAO inhibition at higher than recommended doses. Do not exceed maximum recommended dose.

***Sinemet* (carbidopa + levodopa)** ▶L ♀C ▶- $$$

ADULT - Parkinsonism: Start 1 tab (25/100) PO tid, increase by 1 tab/day q1-2 days prn up to maximum of 8 Tabs/day (200 mg carbidopa/ 800 mg levodopa). May start 1 tab (10/100) PO tid-qid, increase by 1 tab q1-2 days prn to maximum of 8 Tabs/day (80 mg carbidopa/ 800 mg levodopa). Use 1 tab (25/250) PO tid-qid when higher levodopa doses are needed. Increase by ½- 1 tab q1-2 days to maximum of 8 Tabs/day (200 mg carbidopa/ 2 g levodopa). Maximum 200 mg/day carbidopa. Sinemet CR: Start 1 tab (50/200) PO bid, separate doses by at least 6 hrs. Increase as needed at intervals ≥3 days.

PEDS - Not approved in children.

UNAPPROVED ADULT - Restless legs syndrome: start 1/2 -1 tab (25/100) PO qhs, increase q3-4d to max 1 tab (50/200) qhs.

FORMS - Generic/Trade: Tabs 10/100, 25/100, 25/250. Tabs, sust'd release 25/100, 50/200.

NOTES - Motor fluctuations & dyskinesias may occur. Provide at least 70- 100 mg/day carbidopa to reduce N/V. Extended release formulations are less bioavailable than conventional preps and may require increased dosage.

NEUROLOGY: Other Agents

***Aggrenox* (aspirin + dipyridamole)** ▶LK ♀D ▶? $$$

ADULT - Stroke risk reduction: one cap PO bid.

PEDS - Not approved in children.

FORMS - Trade: Caps 25 mg aspirin/ 200 mg extended-release dipyridamole.

alteplase (*t-PA, Activase*) ▶L ♀C ▶? $$$$$

ADULT - Acute ischemic stroke within 3 h of symptom onset: 0.9 mg/kg (maximum 90 mg). Give 10% of total dose as IV bolus over 1 min and remainder as IV infusion over 60 min.

PEDS - Not approved in children.

NOTES - Multiple exclusion criteria.

dexamethasone (*Decadron*, ✤*Dexasone, Hexadrol*) ▶L ♀C ▶- $$$

ADULT - Cerebral edema: 10- 20 mg IV/IM load, then 4 mg IV/IM q6h or 1-3 mg PO tid.

PEDS - Not approved in children.

UNAPPROVED ADULT - Cerebral edema: 1-2 mg/kg PO/IV/IM x 1 load, then 1-1.5 mg/kg/day divided q4-6h; max 16 mg/day. Bacterial meningitis (controversial): 0.15 mg/kg IV q6h x 2-4 days; start before the first dose of antibiotic.

UNAPPROVED PEDS - Bacterial meningitis (controversial): 0.15 mg/kg IV q6h x 2-4 days; start dexamethasone before the first dose of antibiotic.

FORMS - Generic/Trade: Tabs 0.25, 0.5, 0.75, 1.0, 1.5, 2, 4, 6 mg. elixir/ solution 0.5 mg/5 ml. Trade only: solution concentrate 0.5 mg/ 0.5 ml (Intensol)

NOTES - Avoid prolonged use of corticosteroids in children due to possible bone growth retardation. Monitor growth and development if chronic therapy is necessary.

edrophonium (*Tensilon, Enlon, Reversol*) ▶Plasma ♀C ▶? $

ADULT - Evaluation for myasthenia gravis: 2 mg IV over 15-30 seconds (test dose), then 8 mg IV after 45 seconds.

PEDS - Evaluation for myasthenia gravis, weight ≤34 kg: 1 mg IV (test dose), then 1 mg IV q30-45 seconds. If >34 kg: 2 mg IV (test dose) , then 2 mg IV q30- 45 seconds. Max 5 mg in children ≤34 kg and 10 mg in children >34 kg.

NOTES - Not for maintenance therapy of myasthenia gravis because of short duration of action (5- 10 minutes). May give IM. Monitor cardiac function. Atropine should be readily available in case of cholinergic reaction.

glatiramer (*Copaxone*) ▶Serum ♀B ◗? $$$$$

ADULT - Multiple sclerosis: 20 mg SC qd.

PEDS - Not approved in children.

FORMS - Trade: injection 20 mg single dose vial.

NOTES - Do not inject IV.

interferon beta-1A (*Avonex*, ✱*Rebif*) ▶L ♀C ◗? $$$$$

ADULT - Multiple sclerosis: 30 mcg (6 million units) IM q week.

PEDS - Not approved in children.

FORMS - Trade: injection 33 mcg (6.6 million units) single dose vial.

NOTES - Use interferons with caution in patients with depression.

interferon beta-1B (*Betaseron*) ▶L ♀C ◗? $$$$$

ADULT - Multiple sclerosis: 0.25 mg (8 million units) SC qod.

PEDS - Not approved in children.

FORMS - Trade: injection 0.3 mg (9.6 million units) single dose vial.

NOTES - Use interferons with caution in patients with depression.

mannitol (*Osmitrol, Resectisol*) ▶K ♀C ◗? $$$

ADULT - Intracranial HTN: 0.25- 2 g/kg IV over 30-60 minutes as a 15, 20, or 25% solution.

PEDS - Not approved in children.

UNAPPROVED ADULT - Increased ICP/ Head trauma: 0.25-1 g/kg IV push over 20 minutes, repeat q4-6h prn.

UNAPPROVED PEDS - Increased ICP/ Cerebral edema: 0.25-1 g/kg/dose IV push over 20-30 min, then 0.25-0.5 g/kg/dose IV q4-6h prn.

NOTES - Monitor fluid and electrolyte balance. Filter IV solutions ≥ 20%; crystals may be present.

meclizine (*Antivert, Bonine, Medivert, Meclicot, Meni-D*, ✱*Bonamine*) ▶L ♀B ◗? $

ADULT - Motion sickness: 25- 50 mg PO 1 hour prior to travel, then 25- 50 mg PO qd.

PEDS - Not approved in children.

UNAPPROVED ADULT - Vertigo: 25 mg PO qd-qid prn.

FORMS - Rx/OTC/Generic/Trade: Tabs 12.5, 25 mg. chew Tabs 25 mg. Rx/Trade only: Tabs 30, 50 mg. Caps 25 mg.

NOTES - FDA classifies meclizine as "possibly effective" for vertigo. May cause dizziness and drowsiness.

methylprednisolone (*Solu-Medrol, Medrol, Depo-Medrol*) ▶L ♀C ◗- $$$$$

ADULT - See endocrine section.

PEDS - Not approved in children.

UNAPPROVED ADULT - Spinal cord injury: 30 mg/kg IV over 15 min, followed in 45 min by 5.4 mg/kg/h IV infusion x 23h if initiated within 3h of injury or x 47h if initiated within 3-8h of injury.

UNAPPROVED PEDS - Spinal cord injury: 30 mg/kg IV over 15 min, followed in 45 min by 5.4 mg/kg/h IV infusion x 23h.

neostigmine (*Prostigmin*) ▶L ♀C ◗? $$$

ADULT - Myasthenia gravis: 15- 375 mg/day PO in divided doses or 0.5 mg IM/SC when oral therapy is not possible.

PEDS - Not approved in children.

UNAPPROVED PEDS - Myasthenia gravis: 7.5-15 mg PO tid-qid; or 0.03 mg/kg IM q2-4h.

FORMS - Trade: Tabs 15 mg.

NOTES - Oral route preferred when possible.

nimodipine (*Nimotop*) ▶L ♀C ◗- $$$$$

ADULT - Subarachnoid hemorrhage: 60 mg PO q4h x 21 days.

PEDS - Not approved in children.

UNAPPROVED PEDS - Subarachnoid hemorrhage: 0.35 mg/kg PO q4h x 21 days. May titrate to 0.7-1 mg/kg (not to exceed adult dose).

FORMS - Trade: Caps 30 mg.

NOTES - Give 1 hour before or 2 h after meals. Begin therapy within 96 h of subarachnoid hemorrhage. May give cap contents via NG tube or SL. Decrease dose in hepatic failure.

pyridostigmine (*Mestinon, Regonal*) ▶L ♀C ◗+ $$$

ADULT - Myasthenia gravis: Start 60 mg PO tid, increase gradually to usual dose of 200 mg PO tid. Or give 180 mg PO qd-bid (extended release). Max 1,500 mg/day. May give 2 mg IM or slow IV injection q2-3h.

PEDS - Not approved in children.

UNAPPROVED PEDS - Myasthenia gravis, neonates: 5 mg PO q4-6h or 0.05- 0.15 mg/kg IM/IV q4-6h. Myasthenia gravis, children: 7 mg/kg/day PO in 5-6 divided doses or 0.05-0.15 mg/kg/dose IM/IV q4-6h. Max 10 mg IM/IV single dose.

FORMS - Trade: Tabs 60 mg. extended release Tabs 180 mg. syrup 60 mg/ 5 ml.

NOTES - Give injection at 1/30th of oral dose when oral therapy is not possible.

riluzole (*Rilutek*) ▶LK ♀C ◗- $$$$$

ADULT - Amyotrophic lateral sclerosis: 50 mg PO q12h.

PEDS - Not approved in children.

FORMS - Trade: Tabs 50 mg.

NOTES - Take 1 hour before or 2 h after meals. Monitor LFTs.

OB/GYN: Estrogens

NOTE: See also Vaginal Preps, Hormone Replacement Combinations. Unopposed estrogens increase the risk of endometrial cancer in postmenopausal women. When uterus intact a progestin may be administered daily throughout the month or for the last 10-12 days of the month. Do not use during pregnancy. May increase the risk of DVT/PE, gallbladder disease. Interactions with warfarin, certain anticonvulsants, barbiturates, rifampin, corticosteroids, St. John's wort.

esterified estrogens (*Menest, Estratab*) ▶L ♀X ▶- $

ADULT - Menopausal vasomotor symptoms: 1.25 mg PO qd. Atrophic vaginitis: 0.3 to 1.25 mg PO qd. Female hypogonadism: 2.5 - 7.5 mg PO qd in divided doses for 20 days followed by a 10-day rest period. Repeat until bleeding occurs. Female castration & primary ovarian failure: 1.25 mg PO qd. Breast cancer palliation in certain patients: 10 mg PO tid ≥ 3 months. Prevention of postmenopausal osteoporosis: 0.3 - 1.25 mg PO qd.

PEDS - Not approved in children.

FORMS - Trade: Tabs 0.3, 0.625, 1.25, 2.5 mg.

NOTES - Typical regimen consists of a daily estrogen dose with a progestin added either daily or for the last 10-12 days of the cycle.

estradiol (*Estrace, Estradiol*) ▶L ♀X ▶- $

ADULT - Menopausal vasomotor symptoms & atrophic vaginitis, female hypogonadism, female castration & primary ovarian failure: 1-2 mg PO qd. Breast cancer palliation in certain patients: 10 mg PO tid ≥3 months. Postmenopausal osteoporosis prevention: 0.5 mg PO qd.

PEDS - Not approved in children.

FORMS - Generic/Trade: Tabs, micronized 0.5, 1, 2 mg, scored.

NOTES - Typical regimen consists of a daily estrogen dose with a progestin added either daily or for the last 10-12 days of the cycle.

estradiol cypionate (*depGynogen, Depo-Estradiol Cypionate, DepoGen*) ▶L ♀X ▶- $

ADULT - Menopausal vasomotor symptoms: 1-5 mg IM q3-4 weeks. Female hypogonadism: 1.5-2 mg IM q month.

PEDS - Not approved in children.

estradiol transdermal system (*Alora, Climara, Esclim, Estraderm, FemPatch, Vivelle, Vivelle Dot*) ▶L ♀X ▶- $$

ADULT - Menopausal vasomotor symptoms & atrophic vaginitis, female hypogonadism, female castration & primary ovarian failure: initiate with 0.025 - 0.05 mg/day patch once or twice weekly, depending on the product (see FORMS). Prevention of postmenopausal osteoporosis: 0.025-0.1 mg/day patch.

PEDS - Not approved in children.

FORMS - Trade: Transdermal patches doses in mg/day: Climara (q week) 0.025,0.05, 0.075, 0.1. FemPatch (q week) 0.025. Esclim (twice/week) 0.025, 0.0375, 0.05, 0.075, 0.1. Vivelle, Vivelle Dot (twice/week) 0.025 (not Dot), 0.0375, 0.05, 0.075, 0.1. Estraderm (twice/week) 0.05, & 0.1. Alora (twice/week) 0.05, 0.075, 0.1. Generic: Estradiol transdermal patches: (q week) 0.05 & 0.1.

NOTES - Rotate application sites; avoid waistline. Transdermal may be preferable when high triglycerides or chronic liver disease.

estradiol valerate (*Delestrogen, Gynogen L.A. 20, Valergen 20, Estra-L 40, Valergen 40*) ▶L ♀X ▶- $

ADULT - Menopausal vasomotor symptoms & atrophic vaginitis: 10-20 mg IM q4 weeks. Female hypogonadism, female castration & primary ovarian failure: 10-20 mg IM q4 weeks.

PEDS - Not approved in children.

estrogens conjugated (*Premarin, C.E.S., Congest*) ▶L ♀X ▶- $

ADULT - Menopausal vasomotor symptoms, atrophic vaginitis, & urethritis: 0.3-1.25 mg PO qd. Female hypogonadism: 2.5-7.5 mg PO qd in divided doses x 20 days, followed by a 10-day rest period. Female castration & premature ovarian failure: 1.25 mg PO qd. Prevention of postmenopausal osteoporosis: 0.625 mg PO qd. Breast cancer palliation in certain patients: 10 mg PO tid ≥ 3 months. Abnormal uterine bleeding: 25 mg IV/IM q6-12 hours until bleeding stops.

PEDS - Not approved in children.

UNAPPROVED ADULT - Normalizing bleeding time in patients with AV malformations or underlying renal impairment: 30-70 mg IV/PO qd until bleeding time normalized.

FORMS - Trade: Tabs 0.3, 0.625, 0.9, 1.25, 2.5 mg.

NOTES - Typical regimen consists of a daily estrogen dose with a progestin either daily or for the last 10-12 days of the cycle.

estrogens synthetic conjugated (*Cenestin*) ▶L ♀X ▶- $

ADULT - Menopausal vasomotor symptoms: 0.625-1.25 mg PO qd.

PEDS - Not approved in children.

FORMS - Trade: Tabs 0.625, 0.9, 1.25 mg.

ORAL CONTRACEPTIVES* ▸L ♀X **Monophasic**	*Estrogen* (mcg)	*Progestin* (mg)
Nelova 1/50M, Norinyl 1+50, Ortho-Novum 1/50, Necon 1/50	50 mestranol	1 norethindrone
Ovcon-50	50 ethinyl estradiol	
Demulen 1/50, Zovia 1/50E		1 ethynodiol
Ovral, Ogestrel		0.5 norgestrel
Nelova 1/35E, Norinyl 1+35, Ortho-Novum 1/35, Necon 1/35, Nortrel 1/35	35 ethinyl estradiol	1 norethindrone
Brevicon, Modicon, Nelova 0.5/35E, Necon 0.5/35, Nortrel 0.5/35		0.5 norethindrone
Ovcon-35		0.4 norethindrone
Ortho-Cyclen		0.25 norgestimate
Demulen 1/35, Zovia 1/35E		1 ethynodiol
Loestrin 21 1.5/30, Loestrin Fe 1.5/30	30 ethinyl estradiol	1.5 norethindrone
Lo/Ovral, Low-Ogestrel		0.3 norgestrel
Apri, Desogen, Ortho-Cept		0.15 desogestrel
Levlen, Levora, Nordette		0.15 levonorgestrel
Yasmin		3 drospirenone
Loestrin 21 1/20, Loestrin Fe 1/20	20 ethinyl estradiol	1 norethindrone
Alesse, Aviane, Levlite		0.1 levonorgestrel
Progestin-only		
Micronor, Nor-Q.D.	none	0.35 norethindrone
Ovrette		0.075 norgestrel
Biphasic *(estrogen & progestin contents vary)*		
Mircette	20/10 eth estradiol	0.15/0 desogestrel
Jenest 28 (7/14)	35 ethinyl estradiol	0.5/1 norethindrone
Ortho Novum 10/11, Necon 10/11, Nelova 10/11		0.5/1 norethindrone
Triphasic *(estrogen & progestin contents vary)*		
Cyclessa	25 ethinyl estradiol	0.100/0.125/0.150 desogestrel
Ortho-Novum 7/7/7	35 ethinyl estradiol	0.5/0.75/1 norethindrone
Tri-Norinyl		0.5/1/0.5 norethindrone
Tri-Levlen, Triphasil, Trivora-28	30/40/30 ethinyl estradiol	0.5/0.75/0.125 levonorgestrel
Ortho Tri-Cyclen	35 ethinyl estradiol	0.18/0.215/0.25 norgestimate
Estrostep Fe	20/30/35 ethinyl estradiol	1 norethindrone

*__All__: Not recommended in smokers. Increase risk of thromboembolism, stroke, MI, hepatic neoplasia & gallbladder disease. Nausea, breast tenderness, & breakthrough bleeding are common transient side effects. Effectiveness reduced by hepatic enzyme-inducing drugs such as certain anticonvulsants and barbiturates,rifampin, rifabutin, griseofulvin, & protease inhibitors. Coadministration with antibiotics or St. John's wort may decrease efficacy. Consider an additional form of birth control in above circumstances. See product insert for instructions on missing doses. Most available in 21 and 28 day packs. **Progestin only**: Because much of the literature regarding adverse effects associated with oral contraceptives pertains mainly to combination products containing estrogen and progestins, the extent to which progestin-only contraceptives cause these effects is unclear. No significant interaction has been found with broad-spectrum antibiotics. The effect of St. Johns wort is unclear. Available in 28 day packs. Readers may find the following website useful: www.managingcontraception.com.

NOTES - Typical regimen consists of a daily estrogen dose with a progestin either daily or for the last 10-12 days of the cycle.

estrone (*Kestrone 5, Primestrin, EstraGyn 5*) ▶L ♀X ▶- $

ADULT - Menopausal vasomotor symptoms, female hypogonadism, female castration, primary ovarian failure: 0.1-1 mg IM weekly in single or divided doses. Senile vaginitis & vulvitis: 0.1-0.5 mg IM 2-3x/week. Abnormal uterine bleeding: 2-5 mg IM qd for several days. Breast cancer palliation in certain patients: 5 mg IM ≥ 3 times a week.

PEDS - Not approved in children.

NOTES - Administer IM only. Shake vial and syringe well. Use a 21- to 23-gauge needle.

estropipate (*Ogen, Ortho-Est*) ▶L ♀X ▶- $

ADULT - Menopausal vasomotor symptoms, vulvar & vaginal atrophy: 0.625-5 mg PO qd. Female hypogonadism, female castration, or primary ovarian failure: 1.25-7.5 mg PO qd. Prevention of osteoporosis: 0.625 mg PO qd.

PEDS - Not approved in children.

FORMS - Generic/Trade: Tabs 0.625, 1.25, 2.5, 5 mg.

NOTES - Typical regimen consists of a daily estrogen dose with a progestin either daily or for the last 10-12 days of the cycle.

ethinyl estradiol (*Estinyl*) ▶L ♀X ▶- $

ADULT - Menopausal vasomotor symptoms: 0.02-0.05 mg PO qd. Female hypogonadism: 0.05 mg PO qd-tid x 2 weeks, followed by progesterone x 2 weeks. Breast cancer palliation in certain patients: 1 mg PO tid.

PEDS - Not approved in children.

FORMS - Trade: Tabs 0.02, 0.05, 0.5 mg.

NOTES - Typical regimen consists of a daily estrogen dose with a progestin either daily or for the last 10-12 days of the cycle.

EMERGENCY CONTRACEPTION within 72 hours of unprotected sex: Take first dose ASAP, then identical dose 12h later. Each dose is either 2 pills of *Ovral or Ogestrel,* 4 pills of *Levlen, Levora, Lo/Ovral, Nordette, Tri-Levlen, Triphasil, Trivora, or Low Ogestrel,* or 5 pills of *Alesse, Aviane,* or *Levlite* If vomiting occurs within 1 hour of taking either dose of medication, consider whether or not to repeat that dose and give an antiemetic 1h prior. *Preven* kit includes patient info booklet, urine pregnancy test, & blister pack of 4 tablets containing levonorgestrel 0.25mg & ethinyl estradiol 0.05mg. Each dose is 2 pills. *Plan B* kit contains two levonorgestrel 0.75mg tablets. Each dose is 1 pill. The progestin-only method causes less nausea & may be more effective.

Readers may find the following website useful: www.not-2-late.com.

OB/GYN: GnRH Agents

cetrorelix acetate (*Cetrotide*) ▶Plasma ♀X ▶- $$$$$

ADULT - Infertility: Multiple dose regimen: 0.25mg SC qd during the early to mid follicular phase. Continue treatment qd until the day of hCG administration. Single dose regimen: 3mg SC x 1 usually on stimulation day 7.

PEDS - Not approved in children.

FORMS - Trade: Injection 0.25 mg in 1 & 7-dose kits. 3 mg in 1 dose kit.

NOTES - Best sites for SC self-injection are on the abdomen around the navel. Storage in original carton: 0.25 mg refrigerated (36-46F); 3 mg room temperature (77F).

ganirelix acetate (*Antagon Kit*) ▶Plasma ♀X ▶? $$$$$

ADULT - Infertility: 250 mcg SC qd during the early to mid follicular phase. Continue treatment qd until the day of hCG administration.

PEDS - Not approved in children.

FORMS - Trade: Injection 250 mcg/0.5 ml in pre-filled, disposable syringes with 3 vials follitropin beta.

NOTES - Best sites for SC self-injection are on the abdomen around the navel or upper thigh. Store at room temperature (77F). Protect from light. Packaging contains natural rubber latex which may cause allergic reactions.

goserelin (*Zoladex*) ▶LK ♀X ▶- $$$$$

ADULT - Endometriosis: 3.6 mg implant SC q 28 days or 10.8 mg implant q12 weeks x 6 months. Palliative treatment of breast cancer: 3.6 mg implant SC q28 days indefinitely. Endometrial thinning prior to ablation for dysfunctional uterine bleeding: 3.6 mg SC 4 weeks prior to surgery or 3.6 mg SC q4 weeks x 2 with surgery 2-4 weeks after last dose.

PEDS - Not approved in children.

NOTES - Transient increases in symptoms may occur with initiation of therapy in patients with breast cancer. Hypercalcemia may occur in patients with bone metastases. Vaginal bleeding may occur during the first 2 months of treatment & should stop spontaneously.

leuprolide (*Lupron*) ▶L ♀X ▶- $$$$$

ADULT - Endometriosis or uterine leiomyomata (fibroids): 3.75 mg IM q month or 11.25 mg IM q3 months for total therapy of 6 months (endometriosis) or 3 months (fibroids). Administer concurrent iron for fibroid-associated anemia.

PEDS - Central precocious puberty: Injection: 50 mcg/kg/day SC. Increase by 10 mcg/kg/day until total down regulation. Depot: 0.3 mg/kg/4 weeks IM (minimum dose 7.5 mg). Increase by 3.75 mg q4 weeks until adequate down regulation.

NOTES - A fractional dose of the 3-month depot preparation is not equivalent to the same dose of the monthly formulation. Rotate the injection site periodically. Anaphylaxis has occurred with synthetic GnRH.

nafarelin (*Synarel*) ▶L ♀X ▶- $$$$$

ADULT - Endometriosis: 200 mcg spray into one nostril q am & the other nostril q pm. May be increased to one 200 mcg spray into each nostril bid. Duration of treatment: 6 months.

PEDS - Central precocious puberty: two sprays into each nostril q am & q pm for a total of 1600 mcg/day. May increase to 1800 mcg/day. Allow 30 seconds to elapse between sprays.

FORMS - Trade: Nasal soln 2 mg/ml in 8 ml bottle (200 mcg per spray) about 80 sprays/bottle.

NOTES - Ovarian cysts have occurred in the first 2 months of therapy. Symptoms of hypoestrogenism may occur. Elevations of phosphorus & eosinophil counts, and decreases in serum calcium & WBC counts have been documented.

DRUGS GENERALLY ACCEPTED AS SAFE IN PREGNANCY (selected)

Analgesics: acetaminophen, hydrocodone/acetaminophen, codeine*, meperidine*, methadone*. Antimicrobials: penicillins, cephalosporins, erythromycins (not estolate), azithromycin, nystatin, clotrimazole, metronidazole**, nitrofurantoin***, *Nix*. Antivirals:acyclovir, valacyclovir, famciclovir. CV: labetalol, methyldopa, hydralazine. Derm: erythromycin, clindamycin, benzoyl peroxide. Endo: insulin, liothyronine, levothyroxine. ENT: chlorpheniramine, diphenhydramine**, dimenhydrinate, dextromethorphan, guaifenesin, nasal steroids, nasal cromolyn. GI: trimethobenzamide, antacids*, simethicone, cimetidine, famotidine, ranitidine, psyllium, metoclopramide, bisacodyl, docusate, doxylamine, meclizine. Psych: fluoxetine, desipramine, doxepin. Pulmonary: short-acting inhaled beta-2 agonists, cromolyn, nedocromil, beclomethasone, budesonide, theophylline, prednisone**. Other - heparin. **Except if used long-term or in high does at term* ***Except 1st trimester.* ****Contraindicated at term and during labor and delivery.*

OB/GYN: Hormone Replacement

NOTE: See also vaginal preparations and estrogens. Unopposed estrogens increase the risk of endometrial cancer in postmenopausal women.In women with an intact uterus, a progestin may be administered daily throughout the month or for the last 10-12 days of the month. Do not use during pregnancy. May increase the risk of DVT/PE, gallbladder disease. Interactions with oral anticoagulants, phenytoin, rifampin, barbiturates, corticosteroids and St. John's wort. For preparations containing testosterone derivatives, observe women for signs of virilization.

***Activella* (estradiol + norethindrone)** ▶L ♀X ▶- $$

ADULT - Menopausal vasomotor symptoms, vulvar & vaginal atrophy, prevention of postmenopausal osteoporosis: 1 tab PO qd.

PEDS - Not approved in children.

FORMS - Trade: Tab 1 mg estradiol/0.5 mg norethindrone acetate in calendar dial pack dispenser.

***CombiPatch* (estradiol + norethindrone)** ▶L ♀X ▶- $$

ADULT - Menopausal vasomotor symptoms, vulvar & vaginal atrophy, female hypogonadism, castration, & primary ovarian failure, prevention of postmenopausal osteoporosis: 1 patch twice weekly.

PEDS - Not approved in children.

FORMS - Trade: Transdermal patch 0.05 estradiol/ 0.14 norethindrone & 0.05 estradiol/0.25 norethindrone in mg/day, 8 patches/box.

NOTES - Rotate application sites; avoid waistline.

***Estratest* (esterified estrogens + methyltestosterone)** ▶L ♀X ▶- $$

ADULT - Menopausal vasomotor symptoms: 1 tab PO qd.

PEDS - Not approved in children.
UNAPPROVED ADULT - Menopause-associated decrease in libido: 1 tab PO qd.
FORMS - Trade: Tabs 1.25 mg esterified estrogens/2.5 mg methyltestosterone.

Estratest H.S. **(esterified estrogens + methyltestosterone)** ▶L ♀X ▶- $$
ADULT - Menopausal vasomotor symptoms: 1 tab PO qd.
PEDS - Not approved in children.
UNAPPROVED ADULT - Menopause-associated decrease in libido: 1 tab PO qd.
FORMS - Trade: Tabs 0.625 mg esterified estrogens/1.25 mg methyltestosterone.
NOTES - HS = half-strength.

FemHRT 1/5 **(ethinyl estradiol + norethindrone)** ▶L ♀X ▶- $
ADULT - Menopausal vasomotor symptoms, prevention of postmenopausal osteoporosis: 1 tab PO qd.
PEDS - Not approved in children.
FORMS - Trade: Tabs 5 mcg ethinyl estradiol/1 mg norethindrone, 28/blister card.

Ortho-Prefest **(estradiol + norgestimate)** ▶L ♀X ▶- $$
ADULT - Menopausal vasomotor symptoms, vulvar atrophy, atrophic vaginitis, prevention of postmenopausal osteoporosis: 1 pink tab PO qd x 3 days followed by 1 white tab PO qd x 3 days, sequentially throughout the month.
FORMS - Trade: Tabs in 30-day blister packs 1 mg estradiol (15 pink) & 1 mg estadiol/0.09 mg norgestimate (15 white).

Premphase **(conjugated estrogens + medroxyprogesterone)** ▶L ♀X ▶- $$
ADULT - Menopausal vasomotor symptoms, vulvar/vaginal atrophy, & prevention of postmenopausal osteoporosis: 0.625 mg conjugated estrogens PO qd days 1-14 & 0.625 mg conjugated estrogens/5 mg medroxyprogesterone PO qd days 15-28.
PEDS - Not approved in children.
FORMS - Trade: Tabs in 28-day EZ-Dial dispensers: 0.625 mg conjugated estrogens (14) & 0.625 mg/5 mg conjugated estrogens/medroxyprogesterone (14).

Prempro **(conjugated estrogens + medroxyprogesterone)** ▶L ♀X ▶- $$
ADULT - Menopausal vasomotor symptoms, vulvar/vaginal atrophy, & prevention of postmenopausal osteoporosis: 1 PO qd.
PEDS - Not approved in children.
FORMS - Trade: Tabs in 28-day EZ-Dial dispensers: 0.625 mg/5 mg or 0.625 mg/2.5 mg conjugated estrogens/medroxyprogesterone.
NOTES - Two strengths available, specify dose on Rx.

OB/GYN: Labor Induction / Cervical Ripening

dinoprostone (*PGE2, Prepidil, Cervidil*) ▶Lung ♀C ▶? $$$$
ADULT - Cervical ripening: Gel - one syringe via catheter placed into cervical canal below the internal os. May be repeated q6h to a max of 3 doses. Insert - one insert in the posterior fornix of the vagina.
PEDS - Not approved in children.
FORMS - Trade: Gel (Prepidil) 0.5 mg/3 g syringe. Vaginal insert (Cervidil) 10 mg.
NOTES - Patient should remain supine for 15 - 30 minutes after gel and 2 h after vaginal insert. For hospital use only. Caution with asthma or glaucoma.

misoprostol (*PGE1, Cytotec*) ▶LK ♀X ▶- $
WARNING - Contraindicated in desired early or preterm pregnancy due to its abortifacient property. Pregnant women should avoid contact/exposure to the tabs.
ADULT - Prevention of NSAID- (including aspirin) induced gastric ulcers.
PEDS - Not approved in children.
UNAPPROVED ADULT - Cervical ripening and labor induction: 25-100 mcg intravaginally q3-4h up to 500 mcg in 24 hours; 50 mcg PO q4h up to 6 doses or 200 mcg PO q6-8h up to 2 doses. Medical abortion ≤56 days gestation: w/mifepristone, see mifepristone; w/methotrexate: 800 mcg intravaginally 5-7 days after 50 mg/m2 PO or IM methotrexate. Preop cervical ripening in 1st trimester: 400 mcg intravaginally 3-4h before suction curettage. Missed abortion: 200 mcg q4h or 800 mcg x 1 intravaginally.
FORMS - Trade: Oral tabs 100 & 200 mcg.
NOTES - Contraindicated with prior C-section. Oral tabs can be inserted into the vagina for labor induction/cervical ripening. Monitor for uterine hyperstimulation & abnormal fetal heart rate.

oxytocin (*Pitocin*) ▶LK ♀ ▶- $
WARNING - Not approved for elective labor induction, although widely used.
ADULT - Induction/stimulation of labor: 10 units

in 1000 ml NS, 1-2 milliunits/min IV as a continuous infusion (6-12 ml/hr). Increase in increments of 1-2 milliunits/min q30 minutes until a contraction pattern is established, up to a max of 20 milliunits/min.
PEDS - Not approved in children.
NOTES - Use a pump to accurately control the infusion while patient is under continuous observation. Continuous fetal monitoring is required. Concurrent sympathomimetics may result in postpartum hypertension. Anaphylaxis and severe water intoxication have occurred.

APGAR SCORE	*Heart rate*	0. Absent	1. <100	2. >100
	Respirations	0. Absent	1. Slow/irreg	2. Good/crying
	Muscle tone	0. Limp	1. Some flexion	2. Active motion
	Reflex irritability	0. No response	1. Grimace	2. Cough/sneeze
	Color	0. Blue	1. Blue extremities	2. Pink

OB/GYN: Progestins

NOTE: Do not use in pregnancy. DVT, PE, cerebrovascular disorders, & retinal thrombosis occasionally occur. Effectiveness may be reduced by hepatic enzyme-inducing drugs such as certain anticonvulsants and barbiturates, rifampin, rifabutin, griseofulvin & protease inhibitors. The effects of St. Johns wort-containing products on progestin only pills is currently unknown.

hydroxyprogesterone caproate (*Hylutin*) ▶L ♀X ◗? $
ADULT - Amenorrhea, dysfunctional uterine bleeding, metorrhagia: 375 mg IM. Production of secretory endometrium and desquamation: 125-250 mg IM on 10th day of the cycle, repeat q7days until suppression no longer desired.
PEDS - Not approved in children.
UNAPPROVED ADULT - Endometrial hyperplasia: 500 mg IM weekly.

levonorgestrel (*Norplant*) ▶L ♀X ◗+ $$$$$
WARNING - Bleeding irregularities, delayed follicular atresia, ocular lesions, foreign body carcinogenesis, & thromboembolic events are possible.
ADULT - Contraception: Implant all 6 caps within 7 days after the onset of menses. Insertion is subdermal in the mid-portion of the upper arm about 8-10cm above the elbow crease. Distribute caps in a fan-like pattern, about 15 degrees apart, for a total of 75 degrees. Effective contraception for up to 5 years. Remove the caps at the end of the 5th year.
PEDS - Not approved in children.
FORMS - Trade: Kit: set of 6 caps each containing 36 mg levonorgestrel & instruments needed for insertion.
NOTES - Menstrual bleeding irregularities & thrombophlebitis occasionally occur. Cost over 5 years approximates $9.00/month.

medroxyprogesterone acetate (*Provera, Cycrin, Amen, Curretab*) ▶L ♀X ◗+ $
ADULT - Secondary amenorrhea: 5-10 mg PO qd x 5-10 days. Abnormal uterine bleeding: 5-10 mg PO qd x 5-10 days beginning on the 16th or 21st day of the cycle (after estrogen priming). Withdrawal bleeding usually occurs 3-7 days after therapy ends.
PEDS - Not approved in children.
UNAPPROVED ADULT - Add to estrogen replacement therapy to prevent endometrial hyperplasia: 10 mg PO qd for last 10-12 days of month, or 2.5-5 mg PO qd daily. Endometrial hyperplasia: 10-30 mg PO qd (long-term); 40-100 mg PO qd (short-term) or 500 mg IM twice/week.
FORMS - Generic/Trade: Tabs 2.5, 5, & 10 mg, scored.
NOTES - Breakthrough bleeding/spotting may occur. Amenorrhea usually after 6 months of continuous dosing.

medroxyprogesterone acetate (injectable contraceptive) (*Depo-Provera*) ▶L ♀X ◗+ $
ADULT - Contraception: 150 mg IM q13 weeks.
PEDS - Not approved in children.
NOTES - Breakthrough bleeding/spotting may occur. Amenorrhea usually after 6 months. Weight gain is common. To ensure absence of pregnancy give only during the first 5 days after the onset of a normal menstrual period. May be given immediately postpartum, including breastfeeding women. May be given as often as 11 weeks apart. If the period between injections is >14 weeks, exclude pregnancy before administering.

megestrol (*Megace*) ▶L ♀D ◗? $$$$$
ADULT - AIDS anorexia: 800 mg (20 ml) suspension PO qd. Palliative treatment of advan-

ced carcinoma of the breast: 40 mg (tabs) PO qid. Endometrial carcinoma: 40-320 mg/day (tabs) in divided doses.
PEDS - Not approved in children.
UNAPPROVED ADULT - Endometrial hyperplasia: 40-160 mg PO qd x 3-4 months. Cancer-associated anorexia/cachexia: 80-160 mg PO qid.
FORMS - Generic/Trade: Tabs 20 & 40 mg. Trade: Suspension 40 mg/ml in 237 ml (pint).
NOTES - In HIV-infected women, breakthrough bleeding/spotting may occur.

norethindrone (*Aygestin, Norlutate*) ▶L ♀D ◗? $
ADULT - Amenorrhea, abnormal uterine bleeding: 2.5-10 mg PO qd x 5-10 days during the second half of the menstrual cycle. Endometriosis: 5 mg PO qd x 2 weeks. Increase by 2.5 mg q 2 weeks to 15 mg/day.
PEDS - Not approved in children.
FORMS - Trade: Tabs 5 mg, scored.

progesterone micronized (*Prometrium*) ▶L ♀B ◗+ $
WARNING - Contraindicated in patients allergic to peanuts since caps contain peanut oil.
ADULT - Hormone replacement therapy to prevent endometrial hyperplasia: 200 mg PO qhs 10-12 days per month. Secondary amenorrhea: 400 mg PO qhs x 10 days.
PEDS - Not approved in children.
UNAPPROVED ADULT - Hormone replacement therapy to prevent endometrial hyperplasia: 100 mg qhs daily.
FORMS - Caps 100 & 200 mg.
NOTES - Breast tenderness, dizziness, headache & abdominal cramping may occur.

OB/GYN: Selective Estrogen Receptor Modulators

raloxifene (*Evista*) ▶L ♀X ◗- $$$
WARNING - Do not use during pregnancy.
ADULT - Osteoporosis prevention/treatment: 60 mg PO qd.
PEDS - Not approved in children.
UNAPPROVED ADULT - Breast cancer prevention: 60-120 mg PO qd.
FORMS - Trade: Tabs 60 mg.
NOTES - Interactions with oral anticoagulants & cholestyramine. May increase risk of DVT/PE. Does not decrease (and may increase) hot flushes. Leg cramps.

tamoxifen (*Nolvadex, Tamone*) ▶L ♀D ◗- $$$
WARNING - Do not use during pregnancy.
ADULT - Breast cancer prevention in high-risk women: 20 mg PO qd x 5 years.
PEDS - Not approved in children.
FORMS - Generic/Trade: Tabs 10 & 20 mg.
NOTES - May increase the risk of DVT/PE & uterine cancer. Interacts with oral anticoagulants. Does not decrease hot flushes.

OB/GYN: Tocolytics

NOTE: Although tocolytics prolong pregnancy, they have not been shown to improve perinatal or neonatal outcomes & have adverse effects on women in preterm labor.

indomethacin (*Indocin, Indocid*) ▶L ♀? ◗- $
WARNING - Premature closure of the ductus arteriosus & fetal pulmonary hypertension have been reported. Oligohydramnios has been observed. There tends to be a higher rate of postpartum hemorrhage in women treated with indomethacin for tocolysis.
UNAPPROVED ADULT - Preterm labor: initial 50-100 mg PO/PR followed by 25 mg PO/PR q6-12h up to 48 hrs.
FORMS - Generic/Trade: Immediate release caps 25 & 50 mg. Sustained release caps 75 mg. Trade: Oral suspension 25 mg/5 ml. Suppositories 50 mg.
NOTES - 2nd or 3rd line agent for tocolysis. Effective for stopping premature labor and delaying delivery for several hours, but some consider the potential for complications in the mother and fetus to be too risky.

magnesium sulfate ▶K ♀A ◗+ $$
ADULT - Seizure prevention in pre-eclampsia or eclampsia: 1-4 g IV over 2-4 min. 5 g in 250 ml D5W IV infusion not exceeding 3 ml/min. 4-5 g of a 50% soln IM q4h prn.
PEDS - Not approved in children.
UNAPPROVED ADULT - Premature labor: 6 g IV over 20 minutes, then 2-3 g/h titrated to decrease contractions.
NOTES - Concomitant use with terbutaline may lead to fatal pulmonary edema. Caution in renal insufficiency. Hypermagnesemia may occur in the newborn if administered >24h. Watch for

signs of magnesium intoxication including decreased respirations & reflexes. Symptomatic hypocalcemia has occurred. If needed, may reverse effects with calcium gluconate 1 g IV.

nifedipine (*Procardia, Adalat, Procardia XL, Adalat CC*) ▸L ♀C ◗- $

WARNING - Excessive hypotension is possible.

UNAPPROVED ADULT - Preterm labor: loading dose 10 mg PO q20-30 min if contractions persist up to 40 mg within the first hour. (SL or bite & swallow regimens result in SLIGHTLY earlier plasma concentrations but may cause more side effects). After contractions are controlled, maintenance dose: 10-20 mg PO q4-6h or 60-160 mg extended release PO qd. Duration of treatment has not been established.

FORMS - Generic/Trade: immediate release caps 10 & 20 mg. Extended release tabs 30, 60, 90 mg.

NOTES - Vasodilation & flushing may occur frequently. Headache & nausea are possible, but usually transient. Hepatotoxicity has been reported and concomitant treatment with magnesium may result in neuromuscular blockade.

ritodrine ▸K ♀B ◗- $$$$

WARNING - Maternal pulmonary edema & death have occurred, sometimes after delivery. Avoid fluid overload, which may be aggravated by beta agonists & corticosteroids.

ADULT - Preterm labor: 0.05 mg/min IV infusion; increase by 0.05 mg/min q10min until desired result. Usual range 0.15-0.35 mg/min for at least 12h until contractions cease. Use a controlled infusion device.

PEDS - Not approved in children.

NOTES - 150 mg in 500 ml D5W = 0.3 mg/ml. Monitor maternal pulse & BP, fetal heart rate. Contraindicated before the 20th week of pregnancy. Magnesium sulfate may increase hypotension. Palpitations occur in 1/3 of patients.

terbutaline (*Brethine, Bricanyl*) ▸L ♀B ◗+ $

UNAPPROVED ADULT - Preterm labor: 0.25 mg SC q30 min up to 1 mg in four hours. Infusion: 2.5-10 mcg/min IV, gradually increased to effective max doses of 17.5-30 mcg/min. Maintenance: 2.5-5 mg PO q4-6h until term.

FORMS - Tabs 2.5, 5 mg.

NOTES - Concomitant use with magnesium sulfate may lead to fatal pulmonary edema. Tachycardia, transient hyperglycemia, hypokalemia, arrhythmias, pulmonary edema, cerebral & cardiac ischemia & increased fetal heart rate may occur.

OB/GYN: Uterotonics

carboprost (*Hemabate, 15-methyl-prostaglandin F2 alpha*) ▸LK ♀C ◗? $$

ADULT - Refractory postpartum uterine bleeding: 250 mcg deep IM. If necessary, may repeat at 15-90 minute intervals up to a total dose of 2 mg (8 doses).

PEDS - Not approved in children.

NOTES - Transient fever, HTN, nausea & flushing. May augment oxytocics.

methylergonovine (*Methergine*) ▸LK ♀C ◗? $

ADULT - To increase uterine contractions & decrease postpartum bleeding: 0.2 mg IM after delivery of the placenta, delivery of the anterior shoulder, or during the puerperium. Repeat q2-4h prn. 0.2 mg PO tid-qid in the puerperium for a max of 1 wk.

PEDS - Not approved in children.

FORMS - Trade: Tabs 0.2 mg.

NOTES - Contraindicated in pregnancy-induced hypertension/pre-eclampsia. Avoid IV route due to risk of sudden HTN and stroke. If IV absolutely necessary, give slowly over no less than 1 min, monitor BP.

oxytocin (*Pitocin*) ▸LK ♀? ◗? $

WARNING - Not approved for elective labor induction, although widely used.

ADULT - Uterine contractions/postpartum bleeding: 10 units IM after delivery of the placenta. 10-40 units in 1000 ml NS IV infusion.

PEDS - Not approved in children.

NOTES - Concurrent sympathomimetics may result in postpartum HTN. Anaphylaxis & severe water intoxication have occurred.

OB/GYN: Vaginal Preparations

NOTE: See STD/vaginitis table in antimicrobial section. Many experts recommend 7 day antifungal therapy for candida during pregnancy. Many creams & suppositories are oil-based and may weaken latex condoms & diaphragms. Do not use latex products for 72 hrs after last dose.

butoconazole (*Femstat 3, Gynazole-1*) ▶LK ♀C ▶? $(OTC)

ADULT - Local treatment of vulvovaginal candidiasis, nonpregnant patients: Femstat 3: 1 applicatorful (~5g) intravaginally qhs x 3 days, up to 6 days, if necessary. Pregnant patients: (2nd & 3rd trimesters only) 1 applicatorful (~5g) intravaginally qhs x 6 days. Gynazole-1: 1 applicatorful (~5g) intravaginally qhs x 1.

PEDS - Not approved in children.

FORMS - OTC: Trade (Femstat 3): 2% vaginal cream in 5 g pre-filled applicators (3s) & 20 g tube with applicators. Rx: Trade (Gynazole-1): 2% vaginal cream in 5 g pre-filled applicator.

NOTES - Do not use if abdominal pain, fever or foul-smelling vaginal discharge is present. Since small amount may be absorbed from the vagina, use during the 1st trimester only when essential. During pregnancy, use of a vaginal applicator may be contraindicated & manual insertion may be preferred. Vulvar/vaginal burning may occur. Avoid vaginal intercourse during treatment.

clindamycin phosphate (*Cleocin*, ♣*Dalacin*) ▶L ♀B ▶+ $$

ADULT - Bacterial vaginosis: 1 applicatorful (~ 100 mg clindamycin phosphate in 5g cream) intravaginally qhs x 7 days, or one supp qhs x 3 days.

PEDS - Not approved in children.

FORMS - Trade: 2% vaginal cream in 40 g tube with 7 disposable applicators. Vag supp (Ovules) 100 mg (3) w/applicator.

NOTES - Cervicitis, vaginitis, & vulvar irritation may occur. Avoid vaginal intercourse during treatment.

clotrimazole (*Mycelex, Gyne-Lotrimin, Femcare, Sweet'n fresh, Trivagizole 3*, ♣*Canestin*) ▶LK ♀B ▶? $

ADULT - Local treatment of vulvovaginal candidiasis: 1 applicatorful 1% cream qhs x 7 days. 1 applicatorful 2% cream qhs x 3 days. 100 mg tablet intravaginally qhs x 7 days. 200 mg tablet qhs x 3 days. 500 mg tablet intravaginally x 1. Topical cream for external symptoms bid x 7 days.

PEDS - Not approved in children.

FORMS - OTC: Generic/Trade: 1% vaginal cream with applicator (some pre-filled). Trade (Gyne-Lotrimin-3, Trivagizole 3): 2% vaginal cream with applicator. Generic/Trade: vaginal tablets 100 mg (7). Trade: vaginal tablets 200 mg (3) & 500 mg (1) with applicators. 1% topical cream in some combination packs.

NOTES - Do not use if abdominal pain, fever or foul-smelling vaginal discharge is present. Since small amounts of these drugs may be absorbed from the vagina, use during the 1st trimester only when essential. During pregnancy, use of a vaginal applicator may be contraindicated; manual insertion of tabs may be preferred. Skin rash, lower abdominal cramps, bloating, vulvar irritation may occur. Avoid vaginal intercourse during treatment.

estradiol vaginal ring (*Estring*) ▶L ♀X ▶- $$

WARNING - Do not use during pregnancy.

ADULT - Menopausal atrophic vaginitis: insert ring into upper 1/3 of the vaginal vault and replace after 90 days.

PEDS - Not approved in children.

FORMS - Trade: 2 mg ring single pack.

NOTES - Should the ring fall out or be removed during the 90 day period, rinse in lukewarm water and re-insert. Minimal systemic absorption, probable lower risk of adverse effects than systemic estrogens.

estradiol vaginal tab (*Vagifem*) ▶L ♀X ▶- $$

WARNING - Do not use during pregnancy.

ADULT - Menopausal atrophic vaginitis, initial: insert one tab vaginally qd x 2 weeks. Maintenance: one tab vaginally 2x/week.

PEDS - Not approved in children.

FORMS - Trade: Vaginal tab: 25 mcg in disposable single-use applicators, 15/pack.

estrogen cream (*Premarin, Estrace, Ogen, Ortho Dienestrol*) ▶L ♀X ▶? $$

WARNING - Unopposed estrogens increase the risk of endometrial cancer in postmenopausal women. In women with an intact uterus, a progestin may be administered daily throughout the month or for the last 10-12 days of the month.

ADULT - Atrophic vaginitis: Premarin: 0.5-2 g intravaginally qd. Estrace: 2-4 g intravaginally qd for 1-2 weeks. Gradually reduce to a maintenance dose of 1 g 1-3 x/week. Ogen: 2-4 g intravaginally qd. Ortho Dienestrol: 1-2 applicatorsful intravaginally qd for 1-2 weeks. Gradually reduce to a maintenance dose of 1 applicatorful 1-3 x/week.

PEDS - Not approved in children.

FORMS - Trade: Vaginal cream. Premarin: 0.625 mg conjugated estrogens/g in 42.5 g with or w/o calibrated applicator. Estrace: 0.1 mg estradiol/g in 42.5 g w/calibrated applicator. Ogen: 1.5 mg estropipate/g in 42.5 g with calibrated applicator. Ortho Dienestrol: 0.01% dienestrol in 78 g with or w/o applicator.

NOTES - Possibility of absorption through the vaginal mucosa. Uterine bleeding might be pro-

provoked by excessive use in menopausal women. Breast tenderness & vaginal discharge due to mucus hypersecretion may result from excessive estrogenic stimulation. Endometrial withdrawal bleeding may occur if use is discontinued.

metronidazole (*MetroGel-Vaginal*) ▶LK ♀B ◗? $$

ADULT - Bacterial vaginosis: 1 applicatorful (~ 5 g containing ~ 37.5 mg metronidazole) intravaginally qhs or bid x 5 days.

PEDS - Not approved in children.

FORMS - Trade: 0.75% gel in 70 g tube with applicator.

NOTES - Cure rate same with qhs and bid dosing. Vaginally applied metronidazole could be absorbed in sufficient amounts to produce systemic effects. Caution in patients with CNS diseases due to rare reports of seizures, neuropathy & numbness. Do not administer to patients who have taken disulfiram within the last 2 weeks. Interaction with ethanol. Caution with warfarin. Candida cervicitis & vaginitis, & vaginal, perineal or vulvar itching may occur. Avoid vaginal intercourse during treatment.

miconazole (*Monistat-3, Monistat-7, Monistat Dual Pak, Femizol, M-Zole, Micozole, Monazole*) ▶LK ♀+ ◗? $

ADULT - Local treatment of vulvovaginal candidiasis: 1 applicatorful 2% cream intravaginally qhs x 3 or 7 days. 100 mg supp intravaginally qhs x 7 days or 200 mg qhs x 3 days. 1200 mg vaginal insert qhs x 1. Topical cream for external symptoms bid x 7 days.

PEDS - Not approved in children.

FORMS - OTC: Generic/Trade: 2% vaginal cream in 45 g with 1 applicator or 7 disposable applicators. OTC: Trade: Vaginal suppositories 100 mg (7) & 200 mg (3) with applicator. OTC: Trade: 2% vaginal cream in 3 prefilled applicators. Combination pack: 200 mg (3) vaginal suppositories w/2% miconazole cream for external use. Rx: Trade: Monistat Dual Pak ($$): 1200 mg single dose soft gel vaginal insert plus 2% miconazole cream for external use.

NOTES - Do not use if abdominal pain, fever or foul-smelling vaginal discharge is present. Since small amounts of these drugs may be absorbed from the vagina, use during the 1st trimester only when essential. During pregnancy, use of a vaginal applicator may be contraindicated; manual insertion of suppositories may be preferred. Vulvovaginal burning, itching, irritation & pelvic cramps may occur. Avoid vaginal intercourse during treatment. May increase warfarin effect.

nystatin (*Mycostatin*, ✱*Candistatin*) ▶Not metabolized ♀A ◗? $$

ADULT - Local treatment of vulvovaginal candidiasis: 100,000 units tab intravaginally qhs x 2 weeks.

PEDS - Not approved in children.

FORMS - Generic/Trade: Vaginal Tabs 100,000 units in 15s & 30s with or without applicator(s).

NOTES - Topical azole products more effective. Do not use if abdominal pain, fever or foul-smelling vaginal discharge is present. During pregnancy use of a vaginal applicator may be contraindicated, manual insertion of tabs may be preferred. Avoid vaginal intercourse during treatment.

terconazole (*Terazol*) ▶LK ♀C ◗- $$

ADULT - Local treatment of vulvovaginal candidiasis: 1 applicatorful 0.4% cream intravaginally qhs x 7 days. 1 applicatorful 0.8% cream intravaginally qhs x 3 days. 80 mg supp intravaginally qhs x 3 days.

PEDS - Not approved in children.

FORMS - Trade: Vaginal cream 0.4% in 45 g tube with applicator. Vaginal cream 0.8% in 20 g tube with applicator. Vaginal suppositories 80 mg (3) with applicator.

NOTES - Do not use if abdominal pain, fever or foul-smelling vaginal discharge is present. Since small amounts of these drugs may be absorbed from the vagina, use during the 1st trimester only when essential. During pregnancy, use of a vaginal applicator may be contraindicated; manual insertion of suppositories may be preferred. Avoid vaginal intercourse during treatment. Vulvovaginal itching, burning, & pruritus may occur.

tioconazole (*Monistat-1, Vagistat-1*, ✱*Gynecure*) ▶Not absorbed ♀C ◗- $

ADULT - Local treatment of vulvovaginal candidiasis: 1 applicatorful (~ 4.6 g) intravaginally qhs x 1.

PEDS - Not approved in children.

FORMS - OTC: Trade: Vaginal ointment: 6.5% (300 mg) in 4.6 g prefilled single-dose applicator.

NOTES - Do not use if abdominal pain, fever or foul-smelling vaginal discharge is present. Since small amounts of these drugs may be absorbed from the vagina, use during the 1st trimester only when essential. During pregnancy, use of a vaginal applicator may be contraindicated. Avoid vaginal intercourse during treatment. Vulvovaginal burning & itching may occur.

OB/GYN: Other OB/GYN Agents

betamethasone sodium phosphate (*Celestone*) ▸L ♀C ◗- $
PEDS - Not approved in children.
UNAPPROVED ADULT - Fetal lung maturation, maternal antepartum: 12 mg IM q24h x 2 doses.

choriogonadotropin alfa (*Ovidrel*) ▸L ♀X ◗? $$$
ADULT - Specialized dosing for ovulation induction.
PEDS - Not approved in children.
FORMS - Trade: Injection 250 mcg w/sterile water.
NOTES - Best site for self-injection is on the abdomen below the navel. Beware of multiple pregnancy & multiple adverse effects. Store in original package & protect from light.

clomiphene (*Clomid, Serophene*) ▸L ♀D ◗? $$
ADULT - Specialized dosing for ovulation induction.
PEDS - Not approved in children.
FORMS - Generic/Trade: Tabs 50 mg, scored.
NOTES - Beware of multiple pregnancy & multiple adverse effects.

clonidine (*Catapres, Catapres-TTS*) ▸KL ♀C ◗? $
UNAPPROVED ADULT - Menopausal flushing: 0.1-0.4 mg/day PO divided bid-tid. Transdermal system applied weekly 0.1 mg/day.
FORMS - Generic/Trade: Tabs 0.1, 0.2, & 0.3 mg. Trade: Transdermal weekly patch: 0.1, 0.2, & 0.3 mg/day.
NOTES - Hypotension and sedation may occur.

danazol (*Danocrine*, ✤*Cyclomen*) ▸L ♀X ◗- $$$$$
ADULT - Endometriosis: Start 400 mg PO bid, then titrate downward to a dose sufficient to maintain amenorrhea x 3-6 months, up to 9 months. Fibrocystic breast disease: 100-200 mg PO bid x 4-6 months.
PEDS - Not approved in children.
UNAPPROVED ADULT - Menorrhagia: 100-400 mg PO qd x 3 months.
FORMS - Generic/Trade: Caps 50, 100, 200 mg.
NOTES - Contraindications: impaired hepatic, renal or cardiac function. Androgenic effects may not be reversible even after the drug is discontinued. Hepatic dysfunction has occurred. Insulin requirements may increase in diabetics. Prolongation of PT/INR has been reported with concomitant warfarin.

dexamethasone (*Decadron*) ▸L ♀C ◗- $
ADULT - Fetal lung maturation, maternal antepartum: 6 mg IM q12h x 4 doses.

fluconazole (*Diflucan*) ▸K ♀C ◗- $
ADULT - Vaginal candidiasis: 150 mg PO x 1.
PEDS - Approved in children for oral, esophageal & systemic but not vaginal candidiasis.
FORMS - Trade: Tabs 50, 100, 150, & 200 mg; Suspension 10 mg/ml & 40 mg/ml.
NOTES - Headache, nausea, abdominal pain & diarrhea may occur. Single dose fluconazole exposure in the 1st trimester of pregnancy does not appear to increase the risk of congenital disorders.

gonadotropins (*menotropins, FSH/LH, Pergonal, Humegon, Repronex*, ✤*Propasi HP*) ▸L ♀X ◗? $$$$$
ADULT - Specialized dosing for ovulation induction.
PEDS - Not approved in children.
NOTES - Beware of multiple pregnancy & numerous adverse effects.

levonorgestrel (*Plan B*) ▸L ♀X ◗- $
ADULT - Emergency contraception: 1 tab PO ASAP but within 72h of intercourse. 2nd tab 12h later.
PEDS - Not approved in children.
FORMS - Trade: Kit contains two 0.75 mg tabs.
NOTES - If vomiting occurs within 1h, initial dose must be given again. Patients should be instructed to then contact their healthcare providers. Can be used at any time during the menstrual cycle.

***Lunelle* (medroxyprogesterone + estradiol)** ▸L ♀X ◗- $$
WARNING - Not recommended in women who smoke. Increase risk of thromboembolism, stroke, MI, hepatic neoplasia & gallbladder disease. Nausea, breast tenderness, & breakthrough bleeding are common transient side effects. Coadministration with antibiotics, anticonvulsants or products that contain St. John's wort may lead to a decrease in efficacy. An additional form of birth control may be advisable.
ADULT - Contraception: 0.5 ml IM q 28-30 days into deltoid, gluteus maximus or anterior thigh.
PEDS - Not approved in children.
NOTES - Initial injection during 1st 5 days of menstrual cycle. Do not exceed 33 days between injections. Do not use earlier than 4 weeks postpartum if not breastfeeding or 6 weeks if breastfeeding.

mifepristone (*Mifeprex, RU-486*) ▶L ♀X ◗? $$$$$

WARNING - Surgical intervention may be necessary with incomplete abortions. Provide info on where such services are available & what do in case of an emergency.

ADULT - Termination of pregnancy, up to 49 days: Day 1: 600 mg PO. Day 3: 400 mcg misoprostol (unless abortion confirmed). Day 14: confirmation of pregnancy termination.

PEDS - Not approved in children.

FORMS - Trade: Tabs 200 mg.

NOTES - Bleeding/spotting & cramping most common side effects. Contraindications: ectopic pregnancy, IUD use, adrenal insufficiency & long-term steroid use, use of anticoagulants, hemorrhagic disorders & porphyrias. CYP3A4 inducers may increase metabolism & lower levels. Available through physician offices only.

***Premesis-Rx* (B6 + folic acid + B12 + calcium carbonate)** ▶L ♀A ◗+ $

ADULT - Treatment of pregnancy-induced nausea: 1 tab PO qd.

PEDS - Unapproved in children.

FORMS - Trade: Tabs 75 mg vitamin B6 (pyridoxine), sustained-release, 12 mcg vitamin B12 (cyanocobalamin), 1 mg folic acid, and 200 mg calcium carbonate.

NOTES - May be taken in conjunction with prenatal vitamins.

***Preven* (levonorgestrel + ethinyl estradiol)** ▶L ♀X ◗- $

ADULT - Emergency contraception: 2 tabs PO ASAP but within 72h of intercourse. 2 tabs 12h later.

PEDS - Not approved in children.

FORMS - Trade: Kit contains patient info booklet, pregnancy test, & 4 tabs 0.25mg levonorgestrel/5 mcg ethinyl estradiol.

NOTES - Consider adding antiemetic regimen. If vomiting occurs within 1h, initial dose must be given again. Patients should be instructed to then contact their healthcare providers. Can be used at any time during the menstrual cycle.

RHO immune globulin (*RhoGAM, Gamulin Rh, HypRho-D, MICRhoGAM, Mini-Gamulin Rh, HypRho-D Mini-Dose*) ▶L ♀C ◗? $$$$

ADULT - 300 mcg vial IM. Prevention of isoimmunization in Rh-negative women following spontaneous or induced abortion or termination of ectopic pregnancy up to and including 12 weeks gestation: 50 mcg (Microdose) IM.

PEDS - Not approved in children.

NOTES - Do not give IV. One 300 mcg vial prevents maternal sensitization to the Rh factor if the fetal packed RBC volume that entered the mother's blood due to fetomaternal hemorrhage is less than 15 ml (30 ml of whole blood). When the fetomaternal hemorrhage exceeds this, administer more than one 300 mcg vial.

***Women's Tylenol Menstrual Relief* (acetaminophen + pamabrom)** ▶LK ♀B ◗+ $

ADULT - Menstrual cramps: 2 caplets PO q4-6h.

PEDS - >12 yo: use adult dose.

FORMS - OTC: Caplets 500 mg acetaminophen/25 mg pamabrom (diuretic).

NOTES - Hepatotoxicity with chronic use, especially in alcoholics.

ONCOLOGY

Variable dosages. **Alkylating agents:** busulfan (*Myleran, Busulfex*), carboplatin (*Paraplatin*), carmustine (*BCNU, BiCNU, Gliadel*), chlorambucil (*Leukeran*), cisplatin (*Platinol-AQ*), cyclophosphamide (*Cytoxan, Neosar,* ♣*Procytox*), dacarbazine (*DTIC-Dome*), ifosfamide (*Ifex*), lomustine (CCNU, *CeeNu*), mechlorethamine (*Mustargen*), melphalan (*Alkeran*), procarbazine (*Matulane*), streptozocin (*Zanosar*), temozolomide (*Temodar*), thiotepa (*Thioplex*). **Antibiotics:** bleomycin (*Blenoxane*), dactinomycin (*Cosmegen*), daunorubicin (*DaunoXome, Cerubidine*), doxorubicin (*Adriamycin, Rubex, Doxil*), epirubicin (*Ellence,* ♣*Pharmorubicin*), idarubicin (*Idamycin*), mitomycin (*Mutamycin*), mitoxantrone (*Novantrone*), plicamycin (mithramycin, *Mithracin*), valrubicin (*Valstar*). **Antimetabolites:** capecitabine (*Xeloda*), cladribine (*Leustatin*), cytarabine (*Cytosar-U, Tarabine, Depo-Cyt*), floxuridine (*FUDR*), fludarabine (*Fludara*), fluorouracil (*Adrucil, 5-FU*), gemcitabine (*Gemzar*), hydroxyurea (*Hydrea*), mercaptopurine (6-MP, *Purinethol*), methotrexate (*Rheumatrex*), pentostatin (*Nipent*), thioguanine (♣*Lanvis*). **Hormones**: anastrozole (*Arimidex*), bicalutamide (*Casodex*), estramustine (*Emcyt*), exemestane (*Aromasin*), flutamide (*Eulexin,* ♣*Euflex*), goserelin (*Zoladex*), irinotecan (*Camptosar*), letrozole (*Femara*), leuprolide (*Leupron*), nilutamide (*Nilandron,* ♣*Anandron*), tamoxifen (*Nolvadex, Tamone*), topotecan (*Hycamtin*), toremifene (*Fareston*), triptorelin (*Trelstar Depot*). **Immunomodulators**: aldesleukin (Interleukin-2)

(*Proleukin*), BCG (Bacillus of Calmette & Guerin, *TheraCys, TICE BCG*), denileukin diftitox (*Ontak*), interferon alfa-2a (*Roferon-A*), interferon alfa-2b (*Intron A*), interferon alfa-n3 (*Alferon N*), rituximab (*Rituxan*), trastuzumab (*Herceptin*). **Mitotic Inhibitors**: docetaxel (*Taxotere*), etoposide (*VP-16, Etopophos, Toposar, VePesid*), paclitaxel (*Taxol*), teniposide (VM-26, *Vumon*), vinblastine (VLB, *Velban*, ♣*Velbe*), vincristine (VCR) (*Oncovin, Vincasar*), vinorelbine (*Navelbine*). **Radiopharmaceuticals**: samarium 153 (*Quadramet*), strontium-89 (*Metastron*). **Miscellaneous**: altretamine (*Hexalen*), arsenic trioxide (*Trisenox*), asparaginase (*Elspar*, ♣*Kidrolase*), bexarotene (*Targretin*), levamisole (*Ergamisol*), mitotane (*Lysodren*), pegaspargase (*Oncaspar*), porfimer (*Photofrin*), tretinoin (*Vesanoid*).

OPHTHALMOLOGY: Antibacterials - Aminoglycosides

gentamicin (*Garamycin*, ♣*Alcomicin*) ▶K ♀C ◗? $

ADULT - Ocular infections: 1-2 gtts q4h or ½ inch ribbon of ointment bid- tid.

PEDS - Not approved in children.

UNAPPROVED PEDS - Ocular infections: 1-2 gtts q4h or ½ inch ribbon of ointment bid-tid.

FORMS - Generic/Trade: solution 0.3%, ointment 0.3%.

NOTES - For severe infections, use up to 2 gtts every hour.

tobramycin (*Tobrex*) ▶K ♀B ◗- $

ADULT - Ocular infections, mild to moderate: 1-2 gtts q4h or ½ inch ribbon of ointment bid-tid. Ocular infections, severe: 2 gtts q1h, then taper to q4h or ½ inch ribbon of ointment q3-4h, then taper to bid-tid.

PEDS - Not approved in children.

UNAPPROVED PEDS - Ocular infections: 1-2 gtts q4h or ½ inch ribbon of ointment bid-tid.

FORMS - Generic/Trade: solution 0.3%. Trade only: ointment 0.3%.

OPHTHALMOLOGY: Antibacterials - Fluoroquinolones

ciprofloxacin (*Ciloxan*) ▶LK ♀C ◗? $$

ADULT - Corneal ulcers/ keratitis: 2 gtts q15 minutes x 6 hours, then 2 gtts q30 minutes x 1 day; then, 2 gtts q1h x 1 day, and 2 gtts q4h x 3-14 days. Conjunctivitis: 1-2 gtts q2h while awake x 2 days, then 1-2 gtts q4h while awake x 5 days; or ½ inch ribbon ointment tid x 2 days, then ½ inch ribbon bid x 5 days.

PEDS - Use adult dose for age ≥1 yo (solution) and ≥2 yo (ointment). Not approved below these ages.

FORMS - Trade only: solution 0.3%, ointment 0.3%.

NOTES - Avoid the overuse of fluoroquinolones for conjunctivitis. May cause white precipitate of active drug at site of epithelial defect that may be confused with a worsening infection. Resolves within 2 weeks and does not necessitate discontinuation. Ocular administration has not been shown to cause arthropathy.

levofloxacin (*Quixin*) ▶KL ♀C ◗? $$

ADULT - Ocular infections: 1-2 gtts q2h while awake up to 8 times/day on days 1&2, then 1-2 gtts q4h up to 4 times/day on days 3-7.

PEDS - <1 yo: Not approved. >1yo: Ocular infections: 1-2 gtts q2h while awake up to 8 times/day on days 1&2, then 1-2 gtts q4h up to 4 times/day on days 3-7.

FORMS - Trade only: solution 0.5%.

NOTES - Avoid the overuse of fluoroquinolones for conjunctivitis. Ocular administration has not been shown to cause arthropathy.

norfloxacin (*Chibroxin, Noroxin*) ▶LK ♀C ◗? $

ADULT - Ocular infections: 1-2 gtts qid x 7 days. Severe infections may require 1-2 gtts q2h x 1-2 days, then qid.

PEDS - Ocular infections >1 year of age: 1-2 gtts qid x 7 days.

FORMS - Trade only: solution 0.3%.

NOTES - Avoid the overuse of fluoroquinolones for conjunctivitis. Ocular administration has not been shown to cause arthropathy.

ofloxacin (*Ocuflox*) ▶LK ♀C ◗? $$

ADULT - Corneal ulcers/keratitis: 1-2 gtts q30 minutes while awake and 1-2 gtts 4-6 h after retiring x 2 days, then 1-2 gtts q1h while awake x 5 days, then 1-2 gtts qid x 3 days. Conjunctivitis: 1-2 gtts q2-4 h x 2 days, then 1-2 gtts qid x 5 days.

PEDS - Age ≥1 yo: Use adult dose. <1 yo: Not approved.

FORMS - Trade only: solution 0.3%.

NOTES - Avoid the overuse of fluoroquinolones

for conjunctivitis. Ocular administration has not been shown to cause arthropathy.

OPHTHALMOLOGY: Antibacterials - Other

bacitracin (*AK Tracin*) ▶Minimal absorption ♀C ▶? $
ADULT - Ocular infections: apply ½ inch ribbon of ointment q3-4h or bid-qid.
PEDS - Not approved in children.
UNAPPROVED PEDS - Ocular infections: apply ½ inch ribbon of ointment q3-4h or bid-qid.
FORMS - Generic/Trade: ointment 500 units/g.

erythromycin (*Ilotycin, AK-Mycin*) ▶L ♀B ▶+ $
ADULT - Ocular infections: ½ inch ribbon of ointment to affected eye(s) q3-4h. For chlamydial infections: bid x 2 months or bid x 5 days/month for 6 months .
PEDS - Ophthalmia neonatorum prophylaxis: ½ inch ribbon to both eyes within 1 hour of birth.
FORMS - Generic/Trade: ointment 0.5%.

***Neosporin Ointment* (neomycin + bacitracin + polymyxin B)** ▶K ♀C ▶? $
ADULT - Ocular infections: ½ inch ribbon of ointment q3-4 h x 7-10 days.
PEDS - Not approved in children.
UNAPPROVED PEDS - ½ inch ribbon of ointment q3-4h x 7-10 days.
FORMS - Generic/Trade: ointment.
NOTES - Contact dermatitis can occur after prolonged use.

***Neosporin solution* (neomycin + polymyxin + gramicidin)** ▶K ♀C ▶? $$
ADULT - Ocular infections:1-2 gtts q1-6h x 7-10 days.
PEDS - Not approved in children.
UNAPPROVED PEDS - 1-2 gtts q1-6h x 7-10 days.
FORMS - Trade/generic: solution
NOTES - Contact dermatitis can occur after prolonged use.

***Polysporin* (polymyxin B + bacitracin)** ▶K ♀C ▶? $
ADULT - Ocular infections: ½ inch ribbon of ointment q3-4h x 7-10 days.
PEDS - Not approved in children.
UNAPPROVED PEDS - Ocular infections: ½ inch ribbon of ointment q3-4h x 7-10 days.
FORMS - Generic/Trade: ointment.

***Polytrim* (polymyxin B + trimethoprim)** ▶K ♀C ▶? $
ADULT - Ocular infections: 1 gtt q3-6h x 7-10 days. Maximum dose = 6 gtts/day.
PEDS - Age ≥2 mo: Use adult dose. < 2 mo: Not approved.
FORMS - Trade only: solution.

sulfacetamide (*Sulamyd, Bleph-10, Sulf-10, Isopto Cetamide*) ▶K ♀C ▶- $
ADULT - Ocular infections: 1-2 gtts q2-3h initially, then taper by decreasing frequency as condition allows x 7- 10 days or ½ inch ribbon of ointment q3-4h initially, then taper x 7-10 days. Trachoma: 2 gtts q2h with systemic antibiotic such as doxycycline or azithromycin.
PEDS - Age ≥2 mo: Use adult dose. < 2 mo: Not approved.
FORMS - Generic/Trade: solution 1%, 10%, 15%, 30%. ointment 10%.
NOTES - Ointment may be used as an adjunct to solution.

OPHTHALMOLOGY: Antiviral Agents

fomivirsen (*Vitravene*) ▶Exonuclease ♀C ▶- $$$$$
ADULT - CMV retinitis in AIDS patients with failure/intolerance to other treatments: 330 mcg by intravitreal injection q2 weeks x 2 doses, then q 4 weeks.
PEDS - Not approved in children.
NOTES - Corticosteroid-responsive ocular inflammation, transient increase in intraocular pressure. Not for patients who have received cidofovir in past 2-4 weeks.

trifluridine (*Viroptic*) ▶Minimal absorption ♀C ▶- $$$
ADULT - HSV keratitis/keratoconjunctivitis: 1 gtt q2h to maximum 9 gtts/day. After re-epithelialization, decrease dose to 1 gtt q4h (minimum 5 gtts/day) while awake x 7-14 days.
PEDS - Age ≥6 yo: Use adult dose. < 6 yo: Not approved.
FORMS - Trade only: solution 1%.
NOTES - Avoid continuous use >21 days; may cause keratitis and conjunctival scarring. Urge frequent use of topical lubricants (ie, tear substitutes) to minimize surface damage.

vidarabine (*Vira-A*) ▶Cornea ♀C ▶? $$$
ADULT - HSV keratitis/keratoconjunctivitis: ½

inch ribbon of ointment 5 times daily divided q3h while awake. After re-epithelialization, decrease dose to ½ inch ribbon bid x 5-7 days.

PEDS - Age ≥2 yo: Use adult dose. < 2 yo: Not approved.

FORMS - Trade only: ointment 3%.

OPHTHALMOLOGY: Corticosteroid & Antibacterial Combinations

NOTE: Recommend that only ophthalmologists or optometrists prescribe due to infection and glaucoma risk.

Blephamide **(prednisolone + sodium sulfacetamide; *Vasocidin, FML-S*)** ▶KL♀C◗?$

ADULT - Start 1-2 gtts q1h during the day and q2h during the night, then 1 gtt q4-8h; or ½ inch ribbon (ointment) tid-qid initially, then qd-bid thereafter.

PEDS - Not approved in children.

FORMS - Generic/Trade: suspension, ointment.

NOTES - Shake well before using suspension. Gradually taper when discontinuing.

Cortisporin **(neomycin + polymyxin + hydrocortisone)** ▶LK ♀C ◗? $

ADULT - 1-2 gtts or ½ inch ribbon of ointment q3-4h or more frequently prn.

PEDS - Not approved in children.

UNAPPROVED PEDS - 1-2 gtts or ½ inch ribbon of ointment q3-4h.

FORMS - Generic/Trade: suspension, ointment.

NOTES - Shake well before using suspension. Gradually taper when discontinuing.

Maxitrol **(dexamethasone + neomycin + polymyxin; Dexacidin)** ▶KL ♀C ◗? $

ADULT - Start 1-2 gtts q1h during the day and q2h during the night, then 1 gtt q4-8h; or ½ -1 inch ribbon (ointment) tid-qid initially, then qd-bid thereafter.

PEDS - Not approved in children.

FORMS - Generic/Trade: suspension, ointment.

NOTES - Shake well before using suspension. Gradually taper when discontinuing.

Pred G **(prednisolone acetate + gentamicin)** ▶KL ♀C ◗? $$

ADULT - Start 1-2 gtts q1h during the day and q2h during the night, then 1 gtt q4-8h or ½ inch ribbon of ointment bid-qid.

PEDS - Not approved in children.

FORMS - Trade: suspension, ointment.

NOTES - Shake well before using suspension. Gradually taper when discontinuing.

TobraDex **(tobramycin + dexamethasone)** ▶L ♀C ◗? $$

ADULT - 1-2 gtts q2h x 1-2 days, then 1-2 gtts q4-6h; or ½ inch ribbon of ointment bid-qid.

PEDS - Not approved in children.

FORMS - Trade only: ointment. Trade/generic: suspension.

NOTES - Shake well before using suspension. Gradually taper when discontinuing.

OPHTHALMOLOGY: Corticosteroids

NOTE: Recommend that only ophthalmologists or optometrists prescribe due to infection and glaucoma risk.

fluorometholone (*FML, FML Forte, Flarex*) ▶L ♀C ◗? $$

ADULT - 1-2 gtts q1-2h or ½ inch ribbon of ointment q4h x 1-2 days, then 1-2 gtts bid-qid or ½ inch of ointment qd-tid.

PEDS - Age ≥2 yo: Use adult dose. < 2 yo: Not approved.

FORMS - Generic/Trade: suspension 0.1%. Trade only: suspension 0.25%. solution 0.1%, ointment 0.1%.

NOTES - Shake well before using suspension. Gradually taper when discontinuing.

loteprednol (*Alrex, Lotemax*) ▶L ♀C ◗? $$

ADULT - 1-2 gtts qid, may increase to 1 gtt q1h during first week of therapy prn.

PEDS - Not approved in children.

FORMS - Trade only: suspension 0.2% (Alrex), 0.5% (Lotemax).

NOTES - Shake well before using suspension. Gradually taper when discontinuing.

prednisolone (*AK-Pred, Pred Forte, Pred Mild, Inflamase Forte*) ▶L ♀C ◗? $$

ADULT - Start 1-2 gtts q1h during the day and q2h during the night, then 1-2 gtts q3-12h.

PEDS - Not approved in children.

FORMS - Generic/Trade: suspension 0.12, 0.125, 1%, solution 0.125,1%.

NOTES - Shake well before using suspension. Gradually taper when discontinuing.

rimexolone (*Vexol*) ▶L ♀C ◗? $$

ADULT - Post-operative inflammation: 1-2 gtts qid x 2 weeks. Uveitis: 1-2 gtts q1h while awake x 1 week, then 1 gtt q2h while awake x

1 week, then taper.
PEDS - Not approved in children.
FORMS - Trade only: suspension 1%.
NOTES - Shake well before using suspension. Gradually taper when discontinuing.

OPHTHALMOLOGY: Glaucoma Agents - Beta Blockers

NOTE: May be absorbed and cause effects, side effects and drug interactions associated with systemic beta-blocker therapy. Use caution in cardiac conditions and asthma.

betaxolol (*Betoptic, Betoptic S*) ▸LK ♀C ◗? $$
ADULT - Glaucoma: 1-2 gtts bid.
PEDS - Not approved in children.
FORMS - Trade only: suspension 0.25%. Generic/Trade: solution 0.5%.
NOTES - More selective beta1-blocking agent.

carteolol (*Ocupress*) ▸KL ♀C ◗? $
ADULT - Glaucoma: 1 gtt bid.
PEDS - Not approved in children.
FORMS - Generic/Trade: solution 1%.

levobetaxolol (*Betaxon*) ▸KL ♀C ◗? ?
ADULT - Glaucoma: 1 gtt bid.
PEDS - Not approved in children.
FORMS - Trade only: solution 0.5%.

levobunolol (*Betagan*) ▸? ♀C ◗- $
ADULT - Glaucoma: 1-2 gtts (0.5%) qd-bid or 1-2 gtts (0.25%) bid.
PEDS - Not approved in children.
FORMS - Generic/Trade: solution 0.25, 0.5%.

timolol (*Timoptic, Timoptic XE*) ▸LK♀C◗+ $
ADULT - Glaucoma: 1 gtt (0.25 or 0.5%) bid or 1 gtt of gel (0.25 or 0.5% Timoptic XE) qd.
PEDS - Not approved in children.
FORMS - Generic/Trade: solution 0.25%, 0.5%, gel forming solution 0.25, 0.5% (Timoptic XE).

OPHTHALMOLOGY: Glaucoma Agents - Carbonic Anhydrase Inhibitors

NOTE: Sulfonamide derivatives; verify absence of sulfa allergy before prescribing.

acetazolamide (*Diamox*) ▸LK ♀C ◗+ $$
ADULT - Glaucoma: immediate-release, 250 mg PO qd-qid, extended-release, 500 mg PO qd-bid. Acute glaucoma: 500 mg IV, followed by oral therapy .
PEDS - Not approved in children.
UNAPPROVED PEDS - Glaucoma: 8-30 mg/kg/day PO, divided tid. Acute glaucoma: 5-10 mg/kg IV every 6h .
FORMS - Generic/Trade: Tabs 125, 250 mg. Trade only: extended release Caps 500 mg.
NOTES - May cause metallic taste, anorexia, or diarrhea in >10 % of patients.

brinzolamide (*Azopt*) ▸LK ♀C ◗? $
ADULT - Glaucoma: 1 gtt tid.
PEDS - Not approved in children.
FORMS - Trade only: suspension 1%.
NOTES - Do not administer while wearing soft contact lenses. Wait ≥15 minutes after administration before inserting lenses.

dorzolamide (*Trusopt*) ▸KL ♀C ◗- $$
ADULT - Glaucoma: 1 gtt tid.
PEDS - Not approved in children.
FORMS - Trade only: solution 2%.
NOTES - Do not administer while wearing soft contact lenses. Wait ≥15 minutes after administration before inserting lenses.

methazolamide (*Neptazane*) ▸LK ♀C ◗? $
ADULT - Glaucoma: 100-200 mg PO initially, then 100 mg PO q 12h until desired response. Maintenance dose: 25-50 mg PO qd-tid.
PEDS - Not approved in children.
FORMS - Generic/Trade: Tabs 25, 50 mg.

OPHTHALMOLOGY: Glaucoma Agents - Prostaglandin Analogs

bimatoprost (*Lumigan*) ▸LK ♀C ◗? $$
ADULT - Glaucoma: 1 gtt qhs.
PEDS - Not approved in children.
FORMS - Trade only: solution 0.03%.
NOTES - May gradually change hazel eye color to brown & darken eyelids/lashes. Do not administer while wearing soft contacts. Wait ≥15 min after administration before inserting lenses. May aggravate intraocular inflammation.

latanoprost (*Xalatan*) ▸LK ♀C ◗? $$
ADULT - Glaucoma: 1 gtt qhs.
PEDS - Not approved in children.
FORMS - Trade only: solution 0.005%.
NOTES - May gradually change hazel eye color to brown. Do not administer while wearing soft contact lenses. Wait ≥15 minutes after admini-

stration before inserting lenses. May aggravate intraocular inflammation.

travoprost (*Travatan*) ▶L ♀C ◗? $$

ADULT - Glaucoma: 1 gtt qhs.

PEDS - Not approved in children.

FORMS - Trade only: solution 0.004%.

NOTES - May gradually change hazel eye color to brown and darken eyelids and lashes. Do not administer while wearing soft contact lenses. Wait ≥15 minutes after administration before inserting lenses. May aggravate intraocular inflammation.

unoprostone (*Rescula*) ▶Plasma, K ♀C ◗? $$

ADULT - Glaucoma: 1 gtt bid.

PEDS - Not approved in children.

FORMS - Trade only: solution 0.15%.

NOTES - Indicated for patients intolerant to or who have failed other glaucoma medications. May gradually change hazel eye color to brown and darken eyelids and lashes. Do not administer while wearing soft contact lenses. Wait ≥15 minutes after administration before inserting lenses. May aggravate intraocular inflammation.

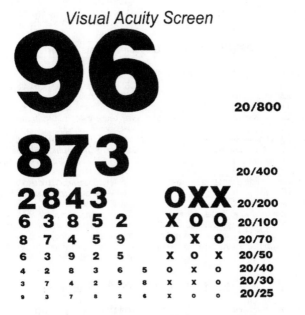

Visual Acuity Screen

9	6								20/800
8	7	3							20/400
2	8	4	3			O	X	X	20/200
6	3	8	5	2		X	O	O	20/100
8	7	4	5	9		O	X	O	20/70
6	3	9	2	5		X	O	X	20/50
4	2	8	3	6	5	O	X	O	20/40
3	7	4	2	5	8	X	X	O	20/30
9	3	7	8	2	6	X	O	O	20/25

Hold card in good light 14 inches from eye. Record vision for each eye separately with and without glasses. Presbyopic patients should read through bifocal glasses. Myopic patients should wear glasses only.

Pupil Diameter (mm)

JG Rosenbaum, MD. Pocket Vision Screen. Beachwood, Ohio

OPHTHALMOLOGY: Glaucoma Agents - Sympathomimetics

apraclonidine (*Iopidine*) ▸KL ♀C ▸? $$$
ADULT - Glaucoma: 1-2 gtts (0.5%) tid. Perioperative IOP elevations: 1 gtt (1%) 1h prior to surgery, then 1 gtt immediately after surgery.
PEDS - Not approved in children.
FORMS - Trade only: solution 0.5,1%.
NOTES - Rapid tachyphylaxis may occur. Do not administer while wearing soft contact lenses. Wait ≥15 minutes after administration before inserting lenses.

brimonidine (*Alphagan, Alphagan P*) ▸L ♀B ▸? $$
ADULT - Glaucoma: 1 gtt tid.
PEDS - Not approved in children.
FORMS - Trade only: solution 0.15% (Alphagan P) 0.2% (Alphagan).
NOTES - Contraindicated in patients receiving MAO inhibitors. Do not administer while wearing soft contact lenses. Wait ≥15 minutes after administration before inserting lenses. Local allergic reactions may occur in 10-30%. Alphagan P may be associated with fewer side effects.

dipivefrin (*Propine*) ▸Eye, plasma ♀B ▸? $
ADULT - Glaucoma: 1 gtt q12h.
PEDS - Not approved in children.
FORMS - Generic/Trade: solution 0.1%.
NOTES - Do not administer while wearing soft contact lenses. Wait ≥15 minutes after administration before inserting lenses.

OPHTHALMOLOGY: Glaucoma Agents - Other

***Cosopt* (dorzolamide + timolol)** ▸LK ♀C ▸- $$
ADULT - Glaucoma: 1 gtt bid.
PEDS - Not approved in children.
FORMS - Trade only: solution (dorzolamide 2% + timolol 0.5%).
NOTES - Do not administer while wearing soft contact lenses. Wait ≥15 minutes after administration before inserting lenses. See beta-blocker warnings.

echothiophate iodide (*Phospholine Iodide*) ▸? ♀C ▸- $$
ADULT - Glaucoma: 1 gtt qd-bid.
PEDS - Accommodative esotropia, diagnosis: 1 gtt (0.125%) in both eyes qhs x 2-3 weeks. Treatment: 1 gtt (0.125%) in both eyes qod or 1 gtt (0.06%) qd. Gradually taper to lowest possible concentration. Maximum dose = 1 gtt (0.125%) qd.
FORMS - Trade only: solution 0.03, 0.06, 0.125, 0.25%.
NOTES - Extreme caution with succinylcholine. May cause ciliary spasm, blurred vision and poor vision in dim light.

pilocarpine (*Pilocar, Pilopine qhs, Isopto Carpine*, ✤*Diocarpine*) ▸Plasma ♀C ▸? $
ADULT - Glaucoma: 1-2 gtts up to tid-qid or ½ inch ribbon (4% gel) qhs.
PEDS - Not approved in children.
FORMS - Generic/Trade: solution 0.5, 1, 2, 3, 4, 6, 8%. Trade only: 0.25,5,10%, gel 4%.
NOTES - Do not administer while wearing soft contact lenses. Wait ≥15 minutes after administration before inserting lenses. Causes miosis. May cause blurred vision and difficulty with adaptation in dark.

OPHTHALMOLOGY: Mydriatics & Cycloplegics

NOTE: Use caution in infants.

atropine (*Isopto Atropine*) ▸K ♀C ▸+ $
ADULT - Uveitis: 1-2 gtts (0.5 or 1% solution) up to qid or ¼ inch ribbon (1% ointment) up to tid. Refraction: 1-2 gtts (1% solution) 1 h before procedure or 1/8-1/4 inch ribbon qd-tid.
PEDS - Uveitis: 1-2 gtts (0.5%) up to tid or 1/8-1/4 inch ribbon up to tid. Refraction: 1-2 gtts (0.5%) bid x 1-3 days before procedure or 1/8 inch ribbon (1% ointment) x 1-3 days before procedure.
FORMS - Generic/Trade: solution 1, 2%, ointment 1%. Trade only: solution 0.5%.
NOTES - Cycloplegia lasts 5-10 days, mydriasis lasts 7-14 days. Each drop of a 1% solution contains 0.5 mg atropine.

cyclopentolate (*AK-Pentolate, Cyclogyl, Pentolair*) ▸? ♀C ▸? $
ADULT - Refraction: 1-2 gtts (1-2%), repeat in 5-10 min prn. Give 45 min before procedure.
PEDS - May cause CNS disturbances in children. Refraction: 1-2 gtts (0.5,1, or 2%), repeat in 5-10 min prn. Give 45 min before procedure.
FORMS - Generic/Trade: solution 1%. Trade

only: 0.5,2%.

NOTES - Cycloplegia lasts 6-24 hours, mydriasis lasts 1 day.

homatropine (*Isopto Homatropine*) ▶? ♀C ▶? $

ADULT - Refraction: 1-2 gtts (2%) or 1 gtt (5%) in eye(s) immediately before procedure, repeat q5-10 minutes prn. Uveitis: 1-2 gtts (2-5%) bid-tid or as often as q3-4h.

PEDS - Refraction: 1 gtt (2%) in eye(s) immediately before procedure, repeat q10 minutes prn. Uveitis: 1 gtt (2%) bid-tid.

FORMS - Trade only: solution 2%. Generic/ Trade: solution 5%.

NOTES - Cycloplegia & mydriasis last 1-3 days.

phenylephrine (*Neo-Synephrine, Mydfrin, Relief*) ▶Plasma ♀C ▶? $

ADULT - Ophthalmologic exams: 1-2 gtts (2.5, 10%) before procedure. Ocular surgery: 1-2 gtts (2.5, 10%) before surgery. Uveitis: 1-2 gtts (2.5, 10%) tid with atropine.

PEDS - Not routinely used in children.

FORMS - OTC Generic/Trade: solution 0.12, 2.5, 10%.

NOTES - Overuse can cause rebound dilation of blood vessels. No cycloplegia; mydriasis lasts 5hours. Systemic absorption may be associated with sympathetic stimulation (eg, tachycardia).

tropicamide (*Mydriacyl*) ▶? ♀? ▶? $

ADULT - Fundus exam: 1-2 gtts (0.5%) in eye(s) 15- 20 minutes before exam, repeat q30 minutes prn.

PEDS - Not approved in children.

FORMS - Generic/Trade: solution 0.5, 1%.

NOTES - Mydriasis last 6 hours.

OPHTHALMOLOGY: Nonsteroidal Anti-Inflammatories

diclofenac (*Voltaren*, *✤Vofenal*) ▶L♀B ▶? $$

ADULT - Post-op inflammation following cataract removal: 1 gtt qid x 2 weeks. Ocular irritation and pain associated with ocular surgery: 1 gtt to operative eye(s) 1 h prior to surgery and 1 gtt within 15 minutes after surgery, then 1 gtt qid prn for ≤ 3 days.

PEDS - Not approved in children.

FORMS - Generic/Trade: solution 0.1%.

NOTES - Contraindicated for use with soft contact lenses.

ketorolac (*Acular*) ▶L ♀C ▶? $$$

ADULT - Allergic conjunctivitis: 1 gtt (0.25 mg) qid. Post-op inflammation following cataract removal: 1 gtt (0.25 mg) to affected eye(s) qid beginning 24 h after surgery x 2 weeks.

PEDS - Age ≥12 yo: Use adult dose. < 12 yo: Not approved.

FORMS - Trade only: solution 0.5%.

NOTES - Do not administer while wearing soft contact lenses. Wait ≥15 minutes after administration before inserting lenses.

OPHTHALMOLOGY: Ocular Antihistamines

azelastine (*Optivar*) ▶L ♀C ▶? $$

ADULT - Allergic conjunctivitis: 1 gtt in each eye bid.

PEDS - Age ≥3 yo: Use adult dose. <3yo: Not approved.

FORMS - Trade only: solution 0.05%.

NOTES - Wait 10 minutes after use before inserting contact lenses. Do not use contacts if red eyes.

levocabastine (*Livostin*) ▶? ♀C ▶? $$$

ADULT - Seasonal allergic conjunctivitis: 1 gtt in each eye qid for up to 2 weeks.

PEDS - Age ≥12 yo: Use adult dose. < 12 yo: Not approved.

FORMS - Trade only: suspension 0.05%.

NOTES - Do not administer while wearing soft contact lenses. Wait ≥15 minutes after administration before inserting lenses.

OPHTHALMOLOGY: Ocular Decongestants

naphazoline (*Albalon, AK-Con, Vasocon, Naphcon, Allerest, Clear Eyes*) ▶?♀C ▶? $

ADULT - Ocular vasoconstrictor/decongestant: 1 gtt q3-4h prn up to qid.

PEDS - Not approved in children.

FORMS - OTC Generic/Trade: solution 0.012, 0.02, 0.03. Rx generic/trade: 0.1%.

NOTES - Overuse can cause rebound dilation of blood vessels. Do not administer while wearing soft contact lenses. Wait ≥15 minutes after administration before inserting lenses.

***Naphcon-A* (naphazoline + pheniramine)**

▶L ♀C ▶? $

ADULT - Eye decongestant: 1-2 gtts bid-qid prn.

PEDS - Age ≥6 yo: Use adult dose. < 6 yo: Not approved.

FORMS - OTC Generic/Trade: solution (0.025% naphazoline + 0.3% pheniramine).

NOTES - Overuse can cause rebound dilation of blood vessels. Do not administer while wearing soft contact lenses. Wait ≥15 minutes after administration before inserting lenses.

OPHTHALMOLOGY: Ocular MAST Cell Stabilizers

cromolyn sodium (*Crolom, Opticrom*) ▶LK ♀B ▶? $$$

ADULT - Allergic ocular disorders: 1-2 gtts in each eye 4-6 times/day at regular intervals.

PEDS - Age ≥4 yo: Use adult dose. < 4 yo: Not approved.

FORMS - Generic/Trade: solution 4%.

NOTES - Works best as preventative agent; use continually during at risk season. Do not administer while wearing soft contact lenses. Wait ≥15 minutes after administration before inserting lenses. Response may take several days to weeks.

ketotifen (*Zaditor*) ▶Minimal absorption ♀C ▶? $$

ADULT - Allergic conjunctivitis: 1 gtt in each eye q8-12h.

PEDS - Allergic conjunctivitis children > 3yo: 1 gtt in each eye q8-12h.

FORMS - Trade only: soln 0.025%.

lodoxamide tromethamine (*Alomide*) ▶K ♀B ▶? $$$

ADULT - Allergic ocular disorders: 1-2 gtts in each eye qid for up to 3 months.

PEDS - Age ≥2 yo: Use adult dose. < 2 yo: Not approved.

FORMS - Trade only: solution 0.1%.

NOTES - Works best as preventative agent; use continually during at risk season. Do not administer while wearing soft contact lenses. Wait ≥15 minutes after administration before inserting lenses.

nedocromil (*Alocril*, ✤*Mireze*) ▶L ♀B ▶? $$

ADULT - Allergic conjunctivitis: 1-2 gtts in each eye bid.

PEDS - Children > 3 yo: Allergic conjunctivitis: 1-2 gtts bid. Not approved in children < 3yo.

FORMS - Trade only: solution 2%.

NOTES - Solution normally appears slightly yellow. Works best as preventative agent; use continually during at risk season.

olopatadine (*Patanol*) ▶K ♀C ▶? $$$

ADULT - Allergic conjunctivitis: 1-2 gtts in each eye bid at an interval of 6-8h.

PEDS - Age ≥3 yo: Use adult dose. < 3 yo: Not approved.

FORMS - Trade only: solution 0.1%.

NOTES - Do not administer while wearing soft contact lenses. Wait ≥15 minutes after administration before inserting lenses.

pemirolast (*Alamast*) ▶? ♀C ▶? $$

ADULT - Allergic conjunctivitis: 1-2 gtts in each eye qid.

PEDS - Not approved in children < 3 yo. Children > 3 yo: 1-2 gtts qid.

FORMS - Trade only: solution 0.1%.

NOTES - Works best as preventative agent; use continually during at risk season. Decreased itching may be seen within a few days, but full effect may require up to four weeks.

OPHTHALMOLOGY: Other Ophthalmologic Agents

artificial tears (*Tears Naturale, Hypotears, Refresh Tears, Lacrilube*) ▶Minimal absorption ♀A ▶+ $

ADULT - Eye lubricant: 1-2 gtts tid-qid prn.

PEDS - Eye lubricant: 1-2 gtts tid-qid prn.

FORMS - OTC solution.

dapiprazole (*Rev-Eyes*) ▶Minimal absorption ♀B ▶? $

ADULT - Reversal of diagnostic mydriasis: 2 gtts in each eye, repeat in 5 minutes.

PEDS - Age ≥4 yo: Use adult dose. <4 yo: Not approved.

FORMS - Trade only: solution 0.5%.

NOTES - Wait 10 min after use before inserting contact lenses. Do not use contacts if red eyes.

petrolatum (*Lacrilube, Dry Eyes, Refresh PM*) ▶Minimal absorption ♀A ▶+ $

ADULT - Ophthalmic lubricant: Apply ¼ inch ointment to inside of lower lid prn.

PEDS - Ophthalmic lubricant: Apply ¼ inch ointment to inside of lower lid prn.

FORMS - OTC ointment.

proparacaine (*Ophthaine, Ophthetic*, ✤*Alcaine*) ▶L ♀C ▶? $

ADULT - Do not prescribe for unsupervised use. Corneal toxicity may occur with repeated use. Local anesthetic: 1-2 gtts before procedure. Repeat q5-10 minutes x 1-3 doses (suture or foreign body removal) or x 5-7 doses (cataract or glaucoma surgery).
PEDS - Not approved in children.
FORMS - Generic/Trade: solution 0.5%.

tetracaine (*Pontocaine*) ▶Plasma ♀C ▶? $
ADULT - Do not prescribe for unsupervised use. Corneal toxicity may occur with repeated use. Local anesthetic: 1-2 gtts or ½-1 inch ribbon of ointment before procedure.
PEDS - Not approved in children.
FORMS - Generic/Trade: solution 0.5%.

verteporfin (*Visudyne*) ▶L/plasma ♀C ▶? $$$$$
ADULT - Treatment of age-related macular degeneration: 6 mg/m2 IV over 10 minutes; laser light therapy 15 minutes after start of infusion.
PEDS - Not approved in children.
NOTES - Risk of photosensitivity x 5 days.

PSYCHIATRY: Antidepressants - Monoamine Oxidase Inhibitors (MAOIs)
serotonin, norepinephrine, and dopamine

NOTE: Must be on tyramine-free diet, stay on diet for 2 weeks after stopping. Risk of hypertensive crisis and serotonin syndrome with many medications, including OTC. Evaluate thoroughly for drug interactions. Allow ≥2 weeks wash-out between MAOIs and SSRIs (up to 6 weeks with fluoxetine), TCAs, and other antidepressants.

isocarboxazid (*Marplan*) ▶L ♀C ▶? $$$
ADULT - Depression: Start 10 mg PO bid, increase by 10 mg q2-4 days. Usual effective dose is 20- 40 mg/day. Maximum dose is 60 mg/day divided bid-qid.
PEDS - Not approved in children < 16 yo.
FORMS - Trade: Tabs 10 mg.
NOTES - May interfere with sleep; avoid qhs dosing.

phenelzine (*Nardil*) ▶L ♀C ▶? $$
ADULT - Depression: Start 15 mg PO tid. Usual effective dose is 60-90 mg/day divided doses.
PEDS - Not approved in children <16 yo.
FORMS - Trade: Tabs 15 mg.
NOTES - May interfere with sleep; avoid qhs dosing.

tranylcypromine (*Parnate*) ▶L ♀C ▶- $$$
ADULT - Depression: Start 10 mg PO qam, increase by 10 mg/day at 1-3 week intervals to usual effective dose of 10-40 mg/day divided bid. Maximum dose is 60 mg/day.
PEDS - Not approved in children <16 yo.
FORMS - Trade: Tabs 10 mg.
NOTES - May interfere with sleep; avoid qhs dosing.

PSYCHIATRY: Antidepressants - Selective Serotonin Reuptake Inhibitors
SSRIs – serotonin

NOTE: Avoid sibutramine and cisapride with the SSRIs. Gradually taper when discontinuing SSRIs (except fluoxetine) to avoid withdrawal symptoms after prolonged use.

citalopram (*Celexa*) ▶LK ♀C ▶- $$$
ADULT - Depression: Start 20 mg PO qd, increase by 20 mg at > 1 week intervals. Maximum dose is 60 mg/day.
PEDS - Not approved in children.
FORMS - Trade: Tabs 10, 20, 40 mg. oral solution 10 mg/5 ml.
NOTES - Don't use with MAOIs or tryptophan.

fluoxetine (*Prozac, Prozac Weekly*) ▶L ♀C ▶- $$$
ADULT - Depression & OCD: Start 20 mg PO qam, increase after several weeks to usual effective dose of 20-40 mg/day. Max dose 80 mg /day. Depression, maintenance therapy: 90 mg PO once weekly; start 7 days after last dose of 20 mg/day. Bulimia: 60 mg PO qam; may need to titrate up to 60 mg/day over several days.
PEDS - Not approved in children.
UNAPPROVED PEDS - Depression > 5 yo: 5-10 mg PO qd .
FORMS - Trade: tablets 10, 20 mg. Capsules 10, 40 mg.Capsules, delayed release (Prozac Weekly) 90 mg, Oral solution 20 mg/5 ml. Generic/Trade: capsules 20 mg.
NOTES - Half life is 7- 9 days. Contraindicated with thioridazine. Don't use with cisapride, thioridazine, tryptophan, or MAOIs; caution with lithium, phenytoin, TCAs, and warfarin.

fluvoxamine (*Luvox*) ▶L ♀C ▶- $$$$
ADULT - OCD: 50 mg PO qhs, increase by 50 mg/day q4-7 days to usual effective dose of 100-300 mg/day divided bid. Maximum dose is

300 mg/day.
PEDS - OCD and ≥8 yo: 25 mg PO qhs, increase by 25 mg/day q4-7 days to usual effective dose of 50- 200 mg/day divided bid. Maximum dose is 200 mg/day if age 8-11 yo; max 300 mg/day if >11 yo. Therapeutic effect may be seen with lower doses in girls.
FORMS - Generic/Trade: Tabs 25, 50, 100 mg.
NOTES - Contraindicated with thioridazine. Don't use with cisapride, diazepam, tryptophan, pimozide, or MAOIs; caution with benzodiazepines, theophylline, TCAs, and warfarin.

paroxetine (*Paxil*) ▸LK ♀C ▸? $$$
ADULT - Depression: Start 20 mg PO qam, increase by 10 mg/day at intervals ≥ 1 week to usual effective dose of 20-50 mg/day. Max 50 mg/day. OCD: Start 20 mg PO qam, increase by 10 mg/day at intervals ≥ 1 week to usual effective dose of 20-60 mg/day. Max 60 mg/day. Panic disorder: Start 10 mg PO qam, increase by 10 mg/day at intervals ≥ 1 week to usual effective dose of 10-60 mg/day. Max 60 mg/day. Social phobia: Start 20 mg PO qam, max 60 mg/day. Generalized anxiety disorder: Start 20 mg PO qam, max 50 mg/day.
PEDS - Not approved in children.
UNAPPROVED PEDS - Depression <14 yo: Start 10 mg PO qd.
FORMS - Trade: Tabs 10, 20, 30, 40 mg. oral suspension 10 mg/ 5 ml.
NOTES - Do not exceed 40 mg/day in elderly or debilitated patients or those with renal or hepatic impairment. Contraindicated with thioridazine. Don't use with MAOIs or tryptophan; caution with barbiturates, cimetidine, phenytoin, theophylline, TCAs, and warfarin.

sertraline (*Zoloft*) ▸LK ♀C ▸+ $$$
ADULT - Depression/ OCD: 50 mg PO qd, may increase after 1 week. Usual effective dose is 50-200 mg/day. Maximum dose is 200 mg/day. Panic disorder/Posttraumatic stress disorder: 25 mg PO qd, may increase after 1 week to 50 mg PO qd. Usual effective dose is 50-200 mg/day. Maximum dose is 200 mg/day.
PEDS - OCD and 6-12 yo: 25 mg PO qd, max 200 mg/day. OCD and ≥ 13yo: Adult dosing.
FORMS - Trade: Tabs 25, 50, 100 mg. oral concentrate 20 mg/ml.
NOTES - Don't use with cisapride, tryptophan, or MAOIs; caution with cimetidine, warfarin, or TCAs. Must dilute oral concentrate before administration.

PSYCHIATRY: Antidepressants - Heterocyclic Compounds

NOTE: Gradually taper dose when discontinuing cyclic antidepressants to avoid withdrawal symptoms after prolonged use.

amitriptyline (*Elavil, Vanatrip*) ▸L ♀D ▸- $
ADULT - Depression: Start 25-100 mg PO qhs, gradually increase to usual effective dose of 50-300 mg/day.
PEDS - Depression, adolescents: Use adult dosing. Not approved in children <12 yo.
UNAPPROVED ADULT - Chronic pain/migraine 10-100 mg/day.
UNAPPROVED PEDS - Depression, children: Start 1 mg/kg/day PO divided tid x 3 days, then increase to 1.5 mg/kg/day to max 5 mg/kg/day.
FORMS - Generic/Trade: Tabs 10, 25, 50, 75, 100, 150 mg.
NOTES - Tricyclic, tertiary amine - primarily serotonin. Demethylated to nortriptyline. Therapeutic range is 150-300 ng/ml (amitriptyline + nortriptyline). Orthostatic hypotension, arrhythmias, and anticholinergic side effects. Don't use with MAOIs.

amoxapine (*Asendin*) ▸L ♀C ▸- $$$
ADULT - Rarely used; other drugs preferred. Depression: Start 25-50 mg PO bid-tid, increase by 50- 100 mg bid- tid after 1 week. Usual effective dose is 150- 400 mg/day. Maximum dose is 600 mg/day.
PEDS - Not approved in children <16 yo.
FORMS - Generic/Trade: Tabs 25, 50, 100, 150 mg.
NOTES - Tetracyclic - primarily norepinephrine. Dose ≤300 mg/day may be given as a single bedtime dose. Don't use with MAO inhibitors.

clomipramine (*Anafranil*) ▸L ♀C ▸+ $$$
ADULT - OCD: Start 25 mg PO qhs, gradually increase over 2 weeks to usual effective dose of 150-250 mg/day, max 250 mg/day.
PEDS - OCD and ≥10 yo: Start 25 mg PO qhs, gradually increase over 2 weeks to 3 mg/kg/day or 100 mg/day, max 200 mg/day. <10 yo: Not approved.
UNAPPROVED ADULT - Depression: 100- 250 mg/day. Panic disorder: 12.5- 150 mg/day. Chronic pain: 100- 250 mg/day.
FORMS - Generic/Trade: Caps 25, 50, 75 mg.
NOTES - Tricyclic, tertiary amine- primarily serotonin. May cause seizures, orthostatic hypotension, arrhythmias, and anticholinergic side effects. Don't use with MAOIs.

desipramine (*Norpramin*) ▶L ♀C ▶+ $

ADULT - Depression: Start 25 mg PO qd or in divided doses. Gradually increase to usual effective dose of 100-300 mg/day.

PEDS - Not approved in children.

FORMS - Generic/Trade: Tabs 10, 25, 50, 75, 100, 150 mg.

NOTES - Tricyclic, secondary amine- primarily norepinephrine. Therapeutic range is 125-300 ng/ml. May cause less anticholinergic side effects than tertiary amines. Orthostatic hypotension, arrhythmias. Don't use with MAOIs.

doxepin (*Sinequan, Zonalon*) ▶L ♀C ▶- $

ADULT - Depression and/or anxiety: Start 25 mg PO qhs, gradually increase to usual effective dose of 75- 300 mg/day.

PEDS - Adolescents : Use adult dose. Not approved in children < 12 yo.

UNAPPROVED ADULT - Chronic pain: 50- 300 mg/day.

FORMS - Generic/Trade: Caps 10, 25, 50, 75, 100, 150 mg. oral concentrate 10 mg/ml.

NOTES - Tricyclic, tertiary amine - primarily norepinephrine. Do not mix oral concentrate with carbonated beverages. Orthostatic hypotension, arrhythmias, and anticholinergic side effects. Don't use with MAOIs.

imipramine (*Tofranil*) ▶L ♀D ▶- $

ADULT - Depression: Start 25 mg PO qhs, gradually increase to usual effective dose of 50-300 mg/day. May give IM up to 100 mg/day.

PEDS - Not approved in children < 12 yo.

UNAPPROVED ADULT - Panic disorder: Start 10 mg PO qhs, titrate to usual effective dose of 50-300 mg/day.

UNAPPROVED PEDS - Depression, children: Start 1.5 mg/kg/day PO divided tid, increase by 1-1.5 mg/kg/day q3-4 days to max 5 mg/kg/d.

FORMS - Generic/Trade: Tabs 10, 25, 50 mg. Trade only: Caps 75, 100, 125, 150 mg.

NOTES - Tricyclic, tertiary amine - mixed serotonin and norepinephrine. Demethylated to desipramine. Orthostatic hypotension, arrhythmias, and anticholinergic side effects. Don't use with MAOIs.

maprotiline (*Ludiomil*) ▶KL ♀B ▶? $$

ADULT - Rarely used; other drugs preferred. Depression: Start 25 mg PO qd, gradually increase by 25 mg q2 weeks to a maximum dose of 225 mg/day. Usual effective dose is 150-225 mg/day. Chronic use maximum dose is 200 mg/day.

PEDS - Not approved in children.

FORMS - Generic/Trade: Tabs 25, 50, 75 mg.

NOTES - Tetracyclic- primarily norepinephrine. May cause seizures. Don't use with MAOIs.

nortriptyline (*Aventyl, Pamelor*) ▶L ♀D ▶+ $

ADULT - Depression: Start 25 mg PO qd-qid . Gradually increase to usual effective dose of 50-150 mg/day.

PEDS - Not approved in children.

UNAPPROVED ADULT - Panic disorder: Start 25 mg PO qhs, titrate to usual effective dose of 50-150 mg/day.

UNAPPROVED PEDS - Depression 6-12 yo: 1-3 mg/kg/day PO divided tid-qid or 10-20 mg/day PO.

FORMS - Generic/Trade: Caps 10, 25, 50, 75 mg. Trade only: oral solution 10 mg/ 5 ml.

NOTES - Tricyclic, secondary amine- primarily norepinephrine. Therapeutic range is 50-150 ng/ml. May cause less anticholinergic side effects than tertiary amines. Orthostatic hypotension, arrhythmias. Don't use with MAOIs.

protriptyline (*Vivactil*, ✤*Triptil*) ▶L ♀C ▶+ $$

ADULT - Depression: 15-40 mg/day PO divided tid-qid. Maximum dose is 60 mg/day.

PEDS - Not approved in children.

FORMS - Generic/Trade: Tabs 5, 10 mg.

NOTES - Tricyclic, secondary amine - primarily norepinephrine. May cause less anticholinergic side effects than tertiary amines. Orthostatic hypotension, arrhythmias. Don't use with MAOIs. Increases in dose should be made in the morning.

trimipramine (*Surmontil*) ▶L ♀C ▶? $$$

ADULT - Depression: Start 25 mg PO qhs, increase gradually to 75-150 mg/day. Max 300 mg/day.

PEDS - Not approved in children.

FORMS - Trade: Caps 25, 50, 100 mg.

NOTES - Tricyclic, tertiary amine- primarily norepinephrine. Orthostatic hypotension, arrhythmias, and anticholinergic side effects. Don't use with MAOIs.

PSYCHIATRY: Antidepressants - Other

bupropion (*Wellbutrin, Wellbutrin SR*) ▶LK ♀B ▶- $$$

ADULT - Depression: Start 100 mg PO bid (immediate release) or 100-150 mg PO qam (sustained release), after 4-7 days may increase to 100 mg tid (immediate release) or 150 mg bid

(sustained release). Usual effective dose is 300-450 mg/day. Maximum dose is 150 mg/ dose and 450 mg/day (immediate release) or 400 mg/day (sustained release). Allow 6-8h between doses with last dose no later than 5 pm.
PEDS - Not approved in children.
UNAPPROVED ADULT - ADHD: 150-450 mg/ day PO. Increase sexual drive in women: 150 mg PO qd-bid.
UNAPPROVED PEDS - ADHD: 1.4-5.7 mg/kg/ day PO.
FORMS - Generic/Trade: Tabs 75,100 mg. Trade only: sustained release Tabs 100, 150 mg (Wellbutrin SR).
NOTES - Weak inhibitor of dopamine reuptake. Contraindicated in seizure disorders, bulimia, anorexia, or with MAO inhibitors. Seizures in 0.4% of patients taking 300- 450 mg/ day. Wellbutrin SR is same drug as Zyban for smoking cessation.

mirtazapine (*Remeron, Remeron SolTab*) ▶LK ♀C ◗? $$$
ADULT - Depression: Start 15 mg PO qhs, increase after 1-2 weeks to usual effective dose of 15-45 mg/day.
PEDS - Not approved in children.
FORMS - Trade: Tabs 15, 30, 45 mg. Tabs, orally disintegrating (SolTab) 15, 30, 45 mg.
NOTES - Enhances norepinephrine and serotonin release, inhibits 5-HT2 and 5-HT3 receptors. 0.1% risk of agranulocytosis. May cause drowsiness and increased appetite/weight gain. Don't use with MAOIs.

nefazodone (*Serzone*) ▶L ♀C ◗? $$$
ADULT - Depression: Start 100 mg PO bid, increase by 100-200 mg/day at ≥ 1 week intervals to usual effective dose of 150-300 mg PO bid. Maximum dose is 600 mg/day. Start 50 mg PO bid in elderly or debilitated patients.
PEDS - Not approved in children.
FORMS - Trade: Tabs 50,100,150,200,250 mg.
NOTES - Inhibits 5-HT2 receptors, inhibits serotonin reuptake. Don't use with cisapride, MAOIs, pimozide, or triazolam; caution with alprazolam. Many other drug interactions.

trazodone (*Desyrel*) ▶L ♀C ◗- $$
ADULT - Depression: Start 50-150 mg/day PO in divided doses, increase by 50 mg/day q3-4 days. Usual effective dose is 400-600 mg/day in divided doses.
PEDS - Not approved in children.
UNAPPROVED ADULT - Insomnia: 25-75 mg qhs PO.
UNAPPROVED PEDS - Depression 6-18 yo: Start 1.5-2 mg/kg/day PO divided bid-tid, may increase q3-4 days to max 6 mg/kg/day.
FORMS - Generic/Trade: Tabs 50, 100, 150. Trade only: Tabs 300 mg.
NOTES - Inhibits 5-HT2 receptors, inhibits serotonin reuptake. May cause priapism. Rarely used as monotherapy for depression; most often used as a sleep aid and adjunct to another antidepressant.

venlafaxine (*Effexor, Effexor XR*) ▶LK ♀C ◗? $$$$
ADULT - Depression: Start 37.5-75 mg PO qd (Effexor XR) or 75 mg/day PO divided bid-tid (Effexor). Increase in 75 mg increments q4 days to usual effective dose of 150-225 mg/day, max 225 mg/day (Effexor XR) or 375 mg/day (Effexor). Generalized anxiety disorder: Start 37.5-75 mg PO qd (Effexor XR), increase in 75 mg increments q4 days to max 225 mg/day.
PEDS - Not approved in children.
FORMS - Trade: Caps, extended release 37.5, 75, 150 mg. Tabs 25, 37.5, 50, 75, 100 mg.
NOTES - Non-cyclic, serotonin-norepinephrine reuptake inhibitor (SNRI). Decrease dose in renal or hepatic impairment. Monitor for increases in BP. Don't give with MAOIs; caution with cimetidine and haloperidol. Gradually taper dose when discontinuing therapy to avoid withdrawal symptoms after prolonged use.

PSYCHIATRY: Antimanic (Bipolar) Agents

carbamazepine (*Tegretol, Tegretol XR, Carbatrol, Epitol, Mazepine*) ▶LK ♀D ◗+ $
WARNING - Aplastic anemia and agranulocytosis have been reported. Monitor CBC and platelets at baseline and periodically.
ADULT - See neurology section.
PEDS - See neurology section.
UNAPPROVED ADULT - Mania: 200 mg PO qd-bid, increase by 200 mg/day q2-4 days. Mean effective dose = 1,000 mg/day.
FORMS - Generic/Trade: Tabs 200 mg, chew Tabs 100 mg, susp 100 mg/ 5 ml. Trade only: extended release tabs 100, 200, 300, 400 mg.
NOTES - Therapeutic range = 4-12 mcg/ml. Stevens-Johnson Syndrome and hepatitis. Monitor LFTs. Many drug interactions.

gabapentin (*Neurontin*) ▶K ♀C ◗? $$$$
UNAPPROVED ADULT - Bipolar disorder: Start

300 mg PO qhs, titrate over a few days to 300-600 mg PO tid, max 3600 mg/day. Frequently used as adjunctive therapy with valproate, lithium, or carbamazepine.

FORMS - Trade: Caps 100, 300, 400 mg. Tabs 600, 800 mg. solution 50 mg/ml.

NOTES - Decrease dose in renal impairment. Discontinue gabapentin gradually over ≥1 week.

lamotrigine (*Lamictal, Lamictal CD*) ▸LK ♀C ▸- $$$$

WARNING - Severe, potentially life-threatening rashes (e.g. Stevens-Johnson Syndrome, toxic epidermal necrolysis) have been reported in 1:1000 adults and 1:50 children.

UNAPPROVED ADULT - Bipolar disorder: Start 25-50 mg PO qd, titrate to 100-500 mg/day divided bid. Frequently used as adjunctive therapy with valproate, lithium, or carbamazepine.

FORMS - Trade: Tabs 25, 100, 150, 200 mg. chew Tabs 5, 25 mg.

NOTES - Drug interactions with enzyme-inducing antiepileptic drugs (i.e. carbamazepine, phenobarbital, phenytoin, primidone) and valproic acid; may need to adjust dose.

lithium (*Eskalith, Eskalith CR, Lithobid, Lithonate*, ✤*Lithane, Carbolith, Duralith*) ▸K ♀D ▸- $

WARNING - Lithium toxicity can occur at therapeutic levels.

ADULT - Acute mania: Start 300-600 mg PO bid -tid, usual effective dose is 900-1,800 mg/day.

PEDS - Adolescents: Adult dosing. Not approved in children <12 yo.

UNAPPROVED PEDS - Mania: Start 15-60 mg/kg/day PO divided tid-qid, adjust weekly based on therapeutic levels.

FORMS - Generic/Trade: caps 150, 300, 600 mg. tabs 300 mg. Trade only: extended release tabs 300 (Lithobid), 450 mg (Eskalith CR). syrup 300 mg/5 ml.

NOTES - 300 mg = 8 mEq or mmol. Steady state in 5 days (longer in elderly or renally impaired patients). Trough levels for acute mania 1.0-1.5 mEq/L, maintenance 0.6-1.2 mEq/L. Dose increase of 300 mg/day raises level by approx 0.2 mEq/L. Monitor renal, thyroid function. Diuretics and ACE inhibitors increase levels. NSAIDs may increase lithium levels (ASA & sulindac OK). Avoid dehydration, salt restriction. Monitor for thirst, fluid intake, and urine output; polyuria and polydipsia can occur. Concentration-related side effects (e.g. tremors, GI upset) may be decreased by extending the dosing interval to tid- qid or using the extended release product.

topiramate (*Topamax*) ▸K ♀C ▸? $$$$$

UNAPPROVED ADULT - Bipolar disorder: Start 25-50 mg/day PO, titrate prn to max 400 mg/day.

FORMS - Trade only: tabs 25, 100, 200 mg. sprinkle caps 15, 25 mg.

NOTES - Give ½ usual adult dose to patients with renal impairment (CrCl < 70 ml/ min). Confusion, renal stones, and weight loss may occur.

valproic acid (*Depakene, Depakote, Depakote ER, Depacon*, ✤*Epiject, Epival, Deproic*) ▸L ♀D ▸+ $

WARNING - Fatal hepatic failure has occurred especially in children < 2 yo with multiple anticonvulsants and co-morbities. Monitor LFTs during first 6 months. Life-threatening cases of pancreatitis have been reported after initial or prolonged use. Evaluate for abdominal pain, nausea, vomiting, and/or anorexia and discontinue valproate if pancreatitis is diagnosed.

ADULT - Mania: 250 mg PO tid (Depakote), titrate to therapeutic trough level of 50-100 mcg/ml or to a maximum dose of 60 mg/kg/day.

PEDS - Not approved for mania in children.

FORMS - Generic/Trade: Caps (Depakene) 250 mg. syrup (Depakene) 250 mg/ 5 ml. Trade only: sprinkle Caps (Depakote) 125 mg. Tabs, delayed release (Depakote) 125, 250, 500 mg. Tabs, ext'd release (Depakote ER) 500 mg.

NOTES - Therapeutic range = 50-100 mcg/ml. Contraindicated in hepatic dysfunction. Many drug interactions. Reduce dose in elderly. GI irritation, thrombocytopenia may occur. Depakene (valproic acid); Depakote (divalproex sodium).

PSYCHIATRY: Antipsychotics - Atypical

Serotonin Dopamine Receptor Antagonists (SDAs)

clozapine (*Clozaril*) ▸L ♀B ▸- $$$$$

WARNING - Risk of agranulocytosis is 1-2%, monitor WBC counts q week x 6 months, then q2 weeks. Contraindicated if WBC < 3,500 cells/ mm3. Discontinue if WBC < 3,000 cells/ mm3. Risk of seizures, orthostatic hypotension, respiratory/ cardiac arrest.

ADULT - Treatment refractory schizophrenia:

Start 12.5 mg PO qd- bid, increase by 25- 50 mg/day to usual effective dose of 300- 450 mg/day. Maximum dose is 900 mg/day.

PEDS - Not approved in children.

FORMS - Generic/Trade: Tabs 25, 100 mg.

NOTES - Low EPS and tardive dyskinesia risk. May be effective for treatment resistant patients who have not responded to conventional agents. Associated with significant weight gain and increased risk of developing new onset diabetes - monitor weight, fasting blood glucose, and triglycerides before initiation and at regular intervals during treatment.

olanzapine (*Zyprexa, Zyprexa Zydis*) ▶L ♀C ◗- $$$$$

ADULT - Psychotic disorders: Start 5-10 mg PO qd, increase weekly to usual effective dose of 10-15 mg/day. Max 20 mg/day. Bipolar mania: Start 10-15 mg PO qd, adjust dose at intervals ≥ 24 h in 5 mg/day increments to usual effective dose of 5-20 mg/day. Max 20 mg/day.

PEDS - Not approved in children.

FORMS - Trade: Tabs 2.5, 5, 7.5, 10, 15 mg. Tabs, orally disintegrating 5,10 mg (Zydis)

NOTES - Low EPS and tardive dyskinesia risk. Use for short-term (3-4 weeks) acute manic episodes associated with bipolar disorder. Associated with significant weight gain and increased risk of developing new onset diabetes - monitor weight, fasting blood glucose, and triglycerides before initiation and at regular intervals during treatment.

quetiapine (*Seroquel*) ▶LK ♀C ◗- $$$$$

ADULT - Psychotic disorders: Start 25 mg PO bid, increase by 25- 50 mg bid-tid on day 2-3, to a target dose of 300-400 mg/day divided bid-tid. Usual effective dose is150-750 mg/day. Maximum dose is 800 mg/day.

PEDS - Not approved in children.

FORMS - Trade: Tabs 25, 100, 200 mg.

NOTES - Eye exam for cataracts recommended q 6 months. Low EPS, tardive dyskinesia risk.

risperidone (*Risperdal*) ▶LK ♀C ◗- $$$$$

ADULT - Psychotic disorders: Start 1 mg PO bid, increase by 1 mg bid on the 2nd & 3rd day, then at intervals ≥ 1 week (some patients may require slower titration). Start 0.5 mg/dose in the elderly, debilitated, renally or hepatically impaired, or hypotensive patients. Titrate by ≤ 0.5 mg BID. Usual effective dose is 4-8 mg/day divided qd-bid; max dose is 16 mg/day.

PEDS - Not approved in children.

UNAPPROVED PEDS - Psychotic disorders, mania: 0.5-1.5 mg/day PO.

FORMS - Trade: Tabs 0.25, 0.5, 1, 2, 3, 4 mg. oral solution 1 mg/ml.

NOTES - Low EPS and tardive dyskinesia risk. Solution is compatible with water, coffee, orange juice, and low-fat milk; is NOT compatible with cola or tea.

ziprasidone (*Geodon*) ▶L ♀C ◗- $$$$$

ADULT - Schizophrenia: Start 20 mg PO bid with food, adjust at >2 day intervals to max 80 mg PO bid.

PEDS - Not approved in children.

FORMS - Trade: Caps 20,40,60,80 mg.

NOTES - May prolong QT interval. Drug interactions with carbamazepine and ketoconazole.

Psychiatry: Antipsychotics - D2 Antagonists - High Potency
1-5 mg = 100 mg CPZ

NOTE: Extrapyramidal side effects may occur with this class of typical antipsychotics. Can be given in qhs doses, but may be divided initially to decrease side effects and increase daytime sedation.

fluphenazine (*Prolixin, Permitil*, ✤*Modecate, Moditen*) ▶LK ♀C ◗? $$

ADULT - Psychotic disorders: Start 0.5- 10 mg/day PO divided q6-8h. Usual effective dose 1-20 mg/day. Maximum dose is 40 mg/day PO or 1.25- 10 mg/day IM divided q6-8h. Maximum dose is 10 mg/day IM. May use long-acting formulations (enanthate/ decanoate) when patients are stabilized on a fixed daily dose. Approximate conversion ratio: 12.5- 25 mg IM/ SC (depot) q3 weeks = 10- 20 mg/day PO.

PEDS - Not approved in children.

FORMS - Generic/Trade: Tabs 1, 2.5, 5, 10 mg. elixir 2.5 mg/5 ml. oral concentrate 5 mg/ml.

NOTES - Do not mix oral concentrate with coffee, tea, cola, or apple juice. 2 mg = 100 CPZ.

haloperidol (*Haldol*) ▶LK ♀C ◗- $

ADULT - Psychotic disorders/Tourette's: 0.5-5 mg PO bid-tid. Usual effective dose is 6-20 mg/day, max dose 100 mg/day or 2-5 mg IM q1-8h prn. May use long-acting (depot) form when patients are stabilized on a fixed daily dose. Approximate conversion ratio: 100- 200 mg IM (depot) q4 weeks = 10 mg/day PO haloperidol.

PEDS - Psychotic disorders age 3- 12 yo: 0.05-0.15 mg/kg/day PO divided bid-tid. Tourette's or non-psychotic behavior disorders age 3- 12 yo: 0.05- 0.075 mg/kg/day PO divided bid-tid. Increase dose by 0.5 mg q week to maximum dose of 6 mg/day. Not approved for IM administration in children.

UNAPPROVED ADULT - Acute psychoses and combative behavior: 5-10 mg IV/IM, repeat in 10-30 min.

UNAPPROVED PEDS - Psychosis 6-12 yo: 1-3 mg/dose IM (as lactate) q4-8h, max 0.15 mg/kg/day.

FORMS - Generic/ Trade: Tabs 0.5, 1, 2, 5, 10, 20 mg. oral concentrate 2 mg/ml.

NOTES - Therapeutic range is 2- 15 ng/ml. 2 mg = 100 mg CPZ.

perphenazine (*Trilafon*) ▶LK ♀C ▶? $$

ADULT - Psychotic disorders: Start 4-8 mg PO tid or 8-16 mg PO bid-qid (hospitalized patients), max PO dose is 64 mg/day. Can give 5-10 mg IM q6h, max IM dose is 30 mg/day.

PEDS - Not approved for children < 12 yo.

FORMS - Generic/Trade: Tabs 2, 4, 8, 16 mg. Trade only: oral concentrate 16 mg/5 ml.

NOTES - Do not mix oral concentrate with coffee, tea, cola, apple juice. 10 mg=100 mg CPZ.

pimozide (*Orap*) ▶L ♀C ▶- $$$

ADULT - Tourette's: Start 1-2 mg/day PO in divided doses, increase q2 days to usual effective dose of 1-10 mg/day. Maximum dose is 0.2 mg/kg/day up to 10 mg/day.

PEDS - Tourette's age > 12 yo: 0.05 mg/kg PO qhs, increase q3 days to maximum of 0.2 mg/kg/day up to 10 mg/day.

FORMS - Trade only: Tabs 1, 2 mg.

NOTES - QT prolongation may occur. Monitor ECG at baseline and periodically throughout therapy. Contraindicated with macrolide antibiotics. 0.3-0.5 mg = 100 mg CPZ.

thiothixene (*Navane*) ▶LK ♀C ▶? $$

ADULT - Psychotic disorders: Start 2 mg PO tid. Usual effective dose is 20-30 mg/day, maximum dose is 60 mg/day PO. Can give 4 mg IM bid-qid. Usual effective dose is 16-20 mg/day IM, maximum dose is 30 mg/day IM.

PEDS - Adolescents: Adult dosing. Not approved in children < 12 yo.

FORMS - Generic/Trade: Caps 1, 2, 5, 10. oral concentrate 5 mg/ml. Trade only: Caps 20 mg.

NOTES - 4 mg = 100 mg CPZ.

trifluoperazine (*Stelazine*) ▶LK ♀C ▶- $$

ADULT - Psychotic disorders: Start 2-5 mg PO bid. Usual effective dose is 15- 20 mg/day, some patients may require ≥ 40 mg/day. Can give 1-2 mg IM q4-6h prn, maximum IM dose is 10 mg/day. Anxiety: 1-2 mg PO bid for up to 12 weeks. Maximum dose is 6 mg/day.

PEDS - Psychotic disorders 6-12 yo: 1 mg PO qd-bid, gradually increase to maximum dose of 15 mg/day. Can give 1 mg IM qd-bid.

FORMS - Generic/Trade: Tabs 1, 2, 5, 10 mg. Trade only: oral concentrate 10 mg/ml.

NOTES - 5 mg = 100 mg CPZ. Dilute oral concentrate just before giving.

PSYCHIATRY: Antipsychotics - D2 Antagonists - Mid Potency (10 mg = 100 mg CPZ)

NOTE: Extrapyramidal side effects may occur with this class of typical antipsychotics.

loxapine (*Loxitane*, 🍁*Loxapac*) ▶LK ♀C ▶- $$$

ADULT - Psychotic disorders: Start 10 mg PO bid, usual effective dose is 60-100 mg/day divided bid- qid. Maximum dose is 250 mg/day. Can give 12.5- 50 mg IM q4-12h.

PEDS - Not approved in children.

FORMS - Generic/Trade: Caps 5, 10, 25, 50 mg. Trade only: oral concentrate 25 mg/ml.

NOTES - 15 mg = 100 mg CPZ.

molindone (*Moban*) ▶LK ♀C ▶? $$$$$

ADULT - Psychotic disorders: Start 50- 75 mg/day PO divided tid- qid, usual effective dose is 50- 100 mg/day. Maximum dose is 225 mg/day.

PEDS - Adolescents: Adult dosing. Not approved in children <12 yo.

FORMS - Trade: Tabs 5, 10, 25, 50, 100 mg. oral concentrate 20 mg/ml.

NOTES - 10 mg = 100 mg CPZ.

PSYCHIATRY: Antipsychotics - D2 Antagonists - Low Potency (50-100 mg = 100 mg CPZ)

NOTE: Extrapyramidal side effects may occur with this class of typical antipsychotics.

chlorpromazine (*Thorazine*, 🍁*Largactil*) ▶LK ♀C ▶- $

ADULT - Psychotic disorders: 10- 50 mg PO bid-qid or 25-50 mg IM, can repeat in 1 hour.

Severe cases may require 400 mg IM q4-6h up to max of 2,000 mg/day IM. Hiccups: 25-50 mg PO/IM tid-qid. Persistent hiccups may require 25-50 mg in 0.5-1 L NS by slow IV infusion.
PEDS - Severe behavioral problems/ psychotic disorders age 6 months-12 yo: 0.5 mg/kg PO q4-6h prn or 1 mg/kg PR q6-8h prn or 0.5 mg/kg IM q6-8h prn.
FORMS - Generic/Trade: Tabs 10, 25, 50, 100, 200 mg. oral concentrate 30 mg/ml, 100 mg/ml. Trade only: sustained release Caps 30, 75, 150 mg. syrup 10 mg/5 ml. suppositories 25, 100 mg.
NOTES - Monitor for hypotension with IM or IV use.

mesoridazine (*Serentil*) ▶LK ♀C ▶- $$$$
WARNING - Can cause prolongation of the QT interval; reserve for patients inadequately controlled or unable to tolerate other antipsychotics.
ADULT - Schizophrenia: 50 mg PO tid, usual effective dose is 100-400 mg/day. Behavior problems: 25 mg PO tid, usual effective dose is 75-300 mg/day.
PEDS - Not approved in children.
FORMS - Trade: Tabs 10, 25, 50, 100 mg. oral concentrate 25 mg/ml.
NOTES - 50 mg = 100 mg CPZ.

thioridazine (*Mellaril*) ▶LK ♀C ▶? $
WARNING - Can cause QTc prolongation, torsade de pointes-type arrhythmias, and sudden death.
ADULT - Psychotic disorders: Start 50-100 mg PO tid, usual effective dose is 200-800 mg/day divided bid-qid. Maximum dose is 800 mg/day.
PEDS - Behavioral disorders 2- 12 yo: 10- 25 mg PO bid-tid, maximum dose is 3 mg/kg/day.
FORMS - Generic/Trade: Tabs 10, 15, 25, 50, 100, 150, 200 mg. oral concentrate 30, 100 mg/ml. Trade only: oral suspension 25, 100 mg/5 ml.
NOTES - Not recommended as first-line therapy. Contraindicated in patients with a history of cardiac arrhythmias, congenital long QT syndrome, or those taking fluvoxamine, propranolol, pindolol, drugs that inhibit CYP 2D6 (e.g. fluoxetine, paroxetine), and other drugs that prolong the QTc interval. Only use for patients with schizophrenia who do not respond to other antipsychotics. Monitor baseline ECG and potassium. Pigmentary retinopathy with doses > 800 mg/day. 100 mg = 100 mg CPZ.

Psychiatry: Anxiolytics / Hypnotics - Benzodiazepines - Long Half-Life (25-100 hours)

NOTE: To avoid withdrawal, gradually taper when discontinuing after prolonged use. Use cautiously in the elderly; may accumulate and lead to side effects, psychomotor impairment.

chlordiazepoxide (*Librium*) ▶LK ♀D ▶- ©IV $
ADULT - Anxiety: 5-25 mg PO tid- qid or 25-50 mg IM/IV tid-qid (acute/severe anxiety). Acute alcohol withdrawal: 50-100 mg PO/IM/IV, repeat q3-4h prn up to 300 mg/day.
PEDS - Anxiety and >6 yo: 5-10 mg PO bid-qid.
FORMS - Generic/Trade: Caps 5, 10, 25 mg.
NOTES - Half-life 5-30 h.

clonazepam (*Klonopin*, ✤*Clonapam, Rivotril*) ▶LK ♀D ▶? ©IV $$
ADULT - Panic disorder: 0.25 mg PO bid, increase by 0.125- 0.25 mg q3 days to maximum dose of 4 mg/day.
PEDS - Not approved for panic disorder in children.
UNAPPROVED ADULT - Restless legs syndrome: 0.5-4 mg PO qhs.
FORMS - Generic/Trade: Tabs 0.5, 1, 2 mg.
NOTES - Half-life 18- 50 h.

clorazepate (*Tranxene*) ▶LK ♀D ▶- ©IV $$
ADULT - Anxiety: Start 7.5-15 mg PO qhs or bid -tid, usual effective dose is 15-60 mg/day. Acute alcohol withdrawal: 60-90 mg/day on first day divided bid-tid, gradually reduce dose to 7.5-15 mg/day over 5 days. Max dose is 90 mg/day. May transfer patients to single-dose tabs (Tranxene-SD) when dose stabilized.
PEDS - Not approved in children <9 yo.
FORMS - Generic/Trade: Tabs 3.75, 7.5, 15 mg. Trade only: sust'd release tabs 11.25, 22.5 mg.
NOTES - Half-life 40-50 h.

diazepam (*Valium*, ✤*Vivol, E Pam*) ▶LK ♀D ▶- ©IV $
ADULT - Anxiety: 2-10 mg PO bid-qid or 2-20 mg IM/ IV, repeat dose in 3-4h prn.
PEDS - Not approved for anxiety in children.
UNAPPROVED ADULT - Restless legs syndrome: 5 mg PO bid.
FORMS - Generic/Trade: Tabs 2, 5, 10 mg. oral solution 5 mg/ 5 ml. Trade only: oral concentrate (Intensol) 5 mg/ml.
NOTES - Half-life 20-80h. Respiratory depression may occur.

flurazepam (*Dalmane*, ✤*Somnol, Som*

***Pam*)** ▸LK ♀X ◗- ©IV $
ADULT - Insomnia: 15-30 mg PO qhs.
PEDS - Not approved in children <15 yo.
FORMS - Generic/Trade: Caps 15, 30 mg.
NOTES - Half-life 70-90h. For short term treatment of insomnia.

PSYCHIATRY: Anxiolytics / Hypnotics - Benzodiazepines - Medium Half-Life (10-15 hours)

NOTE: To avoid withdrawal, gradually taper when discontinuing after prolonged use.

estazolam (*ProSom*) ▸LK ♀X ◗- ©IV $$
ADULT - Insomnia: 1-2 mg PO qhs for up to 12 weeks. Reduce dose to 0.5 mg in elderly, small, or debilitated patients.
PEDS - Not approved in children.
FORMS - Generic/Trade: Tabs 1, 2 mg.
NOTES - For short term treatment of insomnia.

lorazepam (*Ativan*) ▸LK ♀D ◗- ©IV $$$
ADULT - Anxiety: Start 0.5-1 mg PO bid-tid, usual effective dose is 2-6 mg/day. Maximum dose is 10 mg/day PO. Anxiolytic/sedation: 0.04-0.05 mg/kg IV/IM; usual dose 2 mg, max 4 mg. Insomnia: 2-4 mg PO qhs.
PEDS - Not approved in children.
UNAPPROVED PEDS - Anxiolytic/Sedation: 0.05 mg/kg/dose q4-8h PO/IV, max 2 mg/dose.
FORMS - Generic/Trade: Tabs 0.5, 1, 2 mg. Trade only: oral concentrate 2 mg/ml.
NOTES - Half-life 10-20h. No active metabolites. For short term treatment of insomnia.

temazepam (*Restoril*) ▸LK ♀X ◗- ©IV $
ADULT - Insomnia: 7.5- 30 mg PO qhs x 7-10 d.
PEDS - Not approved in children.
UNAPPROVED ADULT - Restless legs syndrome: 15-30 mg PO qhs.
FORMS - Generic/Trade: Caps 7.5, 15, 30 mg.
NOTES - Half-life 8-25h. For short term treatment of insomnia.

PSYCHIATRY: Anxiolytics / Hypnotics - Benzodiazepines - Short Half-Life (<12 hours)

NOTE: To avoid withdrawal, gradually taper when discontinuing after prolonged use.

alprazolam (*Xanax*) ▸LK ♀D ◗- ©IV $
ADULT - Anxiety: Start 0.25- 0.5 mg PO tid, may increase q3-4 days to a maximum dose of 4 mg/day. Use 0.25 mg PO bid in elderly or debilitated patients. Panic disorder: Start 0.5 mg PO tid, may increase by 1 mg/day q3-4 days to usual effective dose of 5-6 mg/day, maximum dose is 10 mg/day.
PEDS - Not approved in children.
FORMS - Generic/Trade: Tabs 0.25, 0.5, 1, 2 mg. Trade only: oral concentrate 1 mg/ml.
NOTES - Half-life 12h, but need to give tid. Divide administration time evenly during waking h to avoid interdose symptoms. Don't give with antifungals (i.e. ketoconazole, itraconazole); use caution with macrolides, propoxyphene, oral contraceptives, TCAs, cimetidine, antidepressants, anticonvulsants, and others that inhibit CYP 3A4.

oxazepam (*Serax*) ▸LK ♀D ◗- ©IV $$
ADULT - Anxiety: 10-30 mg PO tid-qid. Acute alcohol withdrawal: 15-30 mg PO tid-qid.
PEDS - Not approved in children <6 yo.
FORMS - Generic/Trade: Caps 10, 15, 30 mg.
NOTES - Half-life 8 hours.

triazolam (*Halcion*) ▸LK ♀X ◗- ©IV $
ADULT - Hypnotic: 0.125- 0.25 mg PO qhs x 7-10 days, maximum dose is 0.5 mg/day. Start 0.125 mg/day in elderly or debilitated patients.
PEDS - Not approved in children.
UNAPPROVED ADULT - Restless legs syndrome: 0.125-0.5 mg PO qhs.
FORMS - Generic/Trade: Tabs 0.125, 0.25 mg.
NOTES - Half-life 2-3 hours. Anterograde amnesia may occur. Don't use with protease inhibitors, ketoconazole, itraconazole, or nefazodone; use caution with macrolides, cimetidine, and other CYP 3A4 inhibitors.

PSYCHIATRY: Anxiolytics / Hypnotics - Other

buspirone (*BuSpar*, *🍁Bustab, Buspirex*) ▸K ♀B ◗- $$$
ADULT - Anxiety: Start 15 mg "dividose" daily (7.5 mg PO bid), increase by 5 mg/day q2-3 days to usual effective dose of 30 mg/day, maximum dose is 60 mg/day.

PEDS - Not approved in children.
FORMS - Generic/Trade: tabs 5, 7.5,10, 15 mg. Trade only: dividose tab 15,30 mg (scored to be easily bisected or trisected).
NOTES - Slower onset of action as compared to other anxiolytics; optimum effect requires 3-4 wks of therapy. Don't use with MAOIs; caution with itraconazole, cimetidine, nefazodone, erythromycin, and other CYP 3A4 inhibitors.

butabarbital (*Butisol*) ▶LK ♀D ▶? ©III $$
ADULT - Rarely used; other drugs preferred. Sedative: 15-30 mg PO tid-qid. Hypnotic: 50-100 mg PO qhs for up to 2 weeks.
PEDS - Pre-op sedation: 2-6 mg/kg PO before procedure, maximum 100 mg.
FORMS - Trade: Tabs 30, 50 mg. elixir 30 mg/5 ml.

chloral hydrate (*Somnote, Aquachloral Supprettes*, ✤*Noctec*) ▶LK ♀C ▶+ ©IV $
ADULT - Sedative: 250 mg PO/PR tid after meals. Hypnotic: 500- 1,000 mg PO/PR qhs. Acute alcohol withdrawal: 500- 1,000 mg PO/PR q6h prn.
PEDS - Sedative: 25 mg/kg/day PO/PR divided tid-qid, up to 500 mg tid. Hypnotic: 50 mg/kg PO/PR qhs, up to maximum of 1 g. Pre-anesthetic: 25- 50 mg/kg PO/PR before procedure.
UNAPPROVED PEDS - Sedative: higher than approved doses 75-100 mg/kg PO/PR.
FORMS - Generic/Trade: Caps 500 mg. syrup 500 mg/ 5 ml. suppositories 500 mg. Trade only: suppositories: 324, 648 mg.
NOTES - Give syrup in ½ glass of fruit juice or water.

diphenhydramine (*Benadryl, Banaril, Allermax, Diphen, Dytuss, Sominex, Tusstat, Truxadryl*, ✤*Allerdryl, Allernix*) ▶LK ♀B(- in 1st trimester) ▶- $
ADULT - Insomnia: 25-50 mg PO qhs.
PEDS - Insomnia age ≥12 yo: 25-50 mg PO qhs.
FORMS - OTC/Generic/Trade: Tabs 25, 50 mg. OTC/Trade only: chew Tabs 12.5 mg. OTC/Rx/Generic/Trade: Caps 25, 50 mg. oral solution 12.5 mg/5 ml.

mephobarbital (*Mebaral*) ▶LK ♀D ▶? ©IV $
ADULT - Rarely used; other drugs preferred. Sedative: 32-100 mg PO tid-qid, usual dose is 50 mg PO tid-qid.
PEDS - Sedative: 16- 32 mg PO tid-qid.
FORMS - Generic/Trade: Tabs 32, 50, 100 mg.

pentobarbital (*Nembutal*) ▶LK ♀D ▶? ©II $
ADULT - Rarely used; other drugs preferred. Sedative: 20 mg PO tid-qid. Hypnotic: 100 mg PO qhs or 120-200 mg PR or 150-200 mg IM or 100 mg IV at a rate of 50 mg/min, maximum dose is 500 mg.
PEDS - Sedative: 2-6 mg/kg/day PO/PR. Hypnotic age 2 months-1 yo: 30 mg PR, age 1-4 yo: 30-60 mg PR, age 5-12 yo: 60 mg PR, age 12-14 yo: 60-120 mg PR. Can give 2-6 mg/kg IM.
UNAPPROVED PEDS - Hypnotic <4 yo: 3-6 mg/kg PO/PR qhs. Age ≥ 4 yo: 1.5-3 mg/kg PO/PR qhs.
FORMS - Trade: Caps 50, 100 mg. suppositories 60, 200 mg.

secobarbital (*Seconal*) ▶LK ♀D ▶+ ©II $
ADULT - Rarely used; other drugs preferred. Hypnotic: 100 mg PO or 100- 200 mg IM qhs for up to 2 weeks.
PEDS - Pre-anesthetic: 2-6 mg/kg PO up to 100 mg.
FORMS - Trade: Caps 100 mg.

***Tuinal* (amobarbital + secobarbital)** ▶LK ♀D ▶? ©II $
ADULT - Rarely used; other drugs preferred. Hypnotic: 1 cap PO qhs.
PEDS - Not approved in children.
FORMS - Trade: Caps 100 (50 mg amobarbital + 50 mg secobarbital).

zaleplon (*Sonata*, ✤*Starnoc*) ▶L ♀C ▶- ©IV $$$
ADULT - Insomnia: 5-10 mg PO qhs prn, maximum 20 mg.
PEDS - Not approved in children.
FORMS - Trade: Caps 5, 10 mg.
NOTES - Half-life = 1 hour. Useful if problems with sleep initiation or morning grogginess. For short term treatment of insomnia. Take immediately before bedtime or after going to bed and experiencing difficulty falling asleep. Use 5 mg dose in patients with mild to moderate hepatic impairment, elderly patients, and in patients taking cimetidine. Possible drug interactions with rifampin, phenytoin, carbamazepine, and phenobarbital. Do not use for benzodiazepine or alcohol withdrawal.

zolpidem (*Ambien*) ▶L ♀B ▶+ ©IV $$$
ADULT - Hypnotic: 5- 10 mg PO qhs. Maximum dose is 10 mg.
PEDS - Not approved in children.
FORMS - Trade: Tabs 5, 10 mg.
NOTES - Half-life = 2.5 hours. Useful if problems with early morning awakening. For short term treatment of insomnia. Do not use for benzodiazepine or alcohol withdrawal.

PSYCHIATRY: Combination Drugs

Etrafon **(perphenazine + amitriptyline)** ▶LK ♀D ▶? $

ADULT - Rarely used; other drugs preferred. Depression/ Anxiety: 1 tab (2-25 or 4-25) PO tid-qid or 1 tab (4-50) PO bid. max 8 Tabs/day (2-25 or 4-25) or 4 Tabs/day (4-50).

PEDS - Not approved in children.

FORMS - Generic/Trade: Tabs, perphenazine/ amitriptyline: 2/10, 2/25, 4/10, 4/25, 4/50.

Limbitrol **(chlordiazepoxide + amitriptyline)** ▶LK ♀D ▶- ©IV $$

ADULT - Rarely used; other drugs preferred. Depression/ Anxiety: 1 tab PO tid-qid, may increase up to 6 Tabs/day.

PEDS - Not approved in children <12 yo.

FORMS - Generic/Trade: Tabs, chlordiazepoxide/ amitriptyline: 5/12.5, 10/25.

Triavil **(perphenazine + amitriptyline)** ▶LK ♀D ▶? $

ADULT - Rarely used; other drugs preferred. Depression/ Anxiety: 1 tab (2-25 or 4-25) PO tid-qid or 1 tab (4-50) PO bid. max 8 Tabs/day (2-25 or 4-25) or 4 Tabs/day (4-50).

PEDS - Not approved in children.

FORMS - Generic/Trade: Tabs, perphenazine/ amitriptyline: 2/10, 2/25, 4/10, 4/25, 4/50.

PSYCHIATRY: Drug Dependence Therapy

bupropion (*Zyban*) ▶LK ♀B ▶- $$$

ADULT - Smoking cessation: Start 150 mg PO qam x 3 days, then increase to 150 mg PO bid x 7-12 wks. Allow 8h between doses with last dose no later than 5 pm. Maximum dose is 150 mg PO bid. Target quit date should be after at least 1 wk of therapy to achieve steady state. Stop if no progress towards abstinence by 7th wk. Write "dispense behavioral modification kit" on first script.

PEDS - Not approved in children.

FORMS - Trade: sust'd release tabs 150 mg.

NOTES - Zyban is same drug as antidepressant Wellbutrin SR. Contraindicated in seizure disorders, bulimia, anorexia, or those taking MAO inhibitors. Seizures occur in 0.4% of patients taking 300- 450 mg/day.

clonidine (*Catapres, Catapres TTS*) ▶LK ♀C ▶? $

PEDS - Not approved in children <12 yo.

UNAPPROVED ADULT - Opioid withdrawal: 0.1 mg PO tid-qid or 0.015-0.017 mg/kg/day divided tid-qid. Alcohol withdrawal, adjunct: 0.3-0.6 mg PO q6h. Smoking cessation: 0.15-0.4 mg/day PO divided tid-qid or 0.2 mg patch (TTS-2) q week. ADHD: 5 mcg/kg/day PO x 8 weeks.

FORMS - Generic/Trade: Tabs 0.1, 0.2, 0.3 mg. Trade only: patch TTS-1, TTS- 2, TTS- 3.

NOTES - Rebound HTN with abrupt discontinuation. Transdermal Therapeutic System (TTS) is designed for seven day use so that a TTS-1 delivers 0.1 mg/day x 7 days. May supplement first dose of TTS with oral x 2-3 days until therapeutic level is achieved.

disulfiram (*Antabuse*) ▶L ♀C ▶? $

WARNING - Never give to an intoxicated pt.

ADULT - Sobriety: 125-500 mg PO qd.

PEDS - Not approved in children.

FORMS - Generic/Trade: Tabs 250, 500 mg.

NOTES - Patient must abstain from any alcohol for ≥12 h before using. Disulfiram-alcohol reaction may occur for up to 2 weeks after discontinuing disulfiram. Metronidazole and alcohol in any form (eg, cough syrups, tonics) contraindicated. Hepatotoxicity.

methadone (*Dolophine, Methadose*) ▶L ♀B ▶? ©II $$

ADULT - Narcotic dependence: 15-60 mg PO q6-8h.

PEDS - Not approved in children.

FORMS - Generic/Trade: Tabs 5, 10, 40 mg. oral solution 5 & 10 mg/5 ml. oral concentrate 10 mg/ml.

NOTES - Treatment >3 wks is maintenance and only permitted in approved treatment programs. Drug interactions leading to decreased methadone levels with enzyme-inducing HIV drugs (I.e. efavirenz, nevirapine); monitor for opiate withdrawal symptoms and increase methadone if necessary.

naltrexone (*ReVia, Depade*) ▶LK ♀C ▶? $$$$

WARNING - Hepatotoxicity with higher than approved doses.

ADULT - Alcohol dependence: 50 mg PO qd. Narcotic dependence: Start 25 mg PO qd, increase to 50 mg PO qd if no signs of withdrawal.

PEDS - Not approved in children.

FORMS - Generic/Trade: Tabs 50 mg.

NOTES - Avoid if recent (past 7-10 days) ingestion of opioids.

nicotine gum (*Nicorette, Nicorette DS*) ▶LK ♀X ▶- $$$$$

ADULT - Smoking cessation: Gradually taper 1 piece (2 mg) q1-2h x 6 weeks, 1 piece (2 mg) q2-4h x 3 weeks, then 1 piece (2 mg) q4-8h x 3 weeks. Max 30 pieces/day of 2 mg gum or 24 pieces/day of 4 mg gum. Use 4 mg pieces (Nicorette DS) for high cigarette use (> 24 cigarettes/day).

PEDS - Not approved in children.

FORMS - OTC/Generic/Trade: gum 2, 4 mg.

NOTES - Chew slowly and park between cheek and gum periodically. May cause N/V, hiccups. Coffee, juices, wine, and soft drinks may reduce absorption. Avoid eating/ drinking x 15 minutes before/during gum use. Available in original, orange, or mint flavor. Do not use beyond 6 months.

nicotine inhalation system (*Nicotrol Inhaler*) ▶LK ♀D ▶- $$$$$

ADULT - Smoking cessation: 6-16 cartridges/ day x 12 weeks.

PEDS - Not approved in children.

FORMS - Trade: Oral inhaler 10 mg/cartridge (4 mg nicotine delivered), 42 cartridges/box.

nicotine nasal spray (*Nicotrol NS*) ▶LK ♀D ▶- $$$$$

ADULT - Smoking cessation: 1-2 doses each hour, with each dose = 2 sprays, one in each nostril (1 spray = 0.5 mg nicotine). Minimum recommended: 8 doses/day, max 40 doses/day.

PEDS - Not approved in children.

FORMS - Trade: nasal solution 10 mg/ml (0.5 mg/inhalation); 10 ml bottles.

nicotine patches (*Habitrol, Nicoderm, Nicotrol*) ▶LK ♀D ▶- $$$

ADULT - Smoking cessation: Start one patch (14- 22 mg) qd and taper after 6 weeks. Total duration of therapy is 12 weeks.

PEDS - Not approved in children.

FORMS - OTC/Rx/Generic/Trade: patches 11, 22 mg/ 24 hours. 7, 14, 21 mg/ 24 h (Habitrol & Nicoderm). OTC/Trade: 15 mg/ 16 h (Nicotrol).

NOTES - Ensure patient has stopped smoking. Dispose of patches safely; can be toxic to kids, pets.

BODY MASS INDEX* Heights are in feet and inches; weights are in pounds

BMI	Classification	4'10"	5'0"	5'4"	5'8"	6'0"	6'4"
<19	Underweight	<91	<97	<110	<125	<140	<156
19-24	Healthy Weight	91-119	97-127	110-144	125-163	140-183	156-204
25-29	Overweight	120-143	128-152	145-173	164-196	184-220	205-245
30-40	Obese	144-191	153-204	174-233	197-262	221-293	246-328
>40	Very Obese	>191	>204	>233	>262	>293	>328

*BMI = kg/m^2 = (weight in pounds)(703)/(height in inches)^2. Anorectants appropriate if BMI ≥30 (with comoribidities ≥27); surgery an option if BMI >40 (with comorbidities 35-40). www.nhlbi.nih.gov

PSYCHIATRY: Sympathomimetics / Stimulants / Anorexiants

***Adderall* (dextroamphetamine + racemic amphetamine)** ▶L ♀C ▶- ©II $$

WARNING - Chronic overuse/abuse can lead to marked tolerance and psychic dependence; caution with prolonged use.

ADULT - Narcolepsy: Start 10 mg PO qam, increase by 10 mg q week, maximum dose is 60 mg/day divided bid-tid at 4-6h intervals.

PEDS - Narcolepsy: 6-12 yo: Start 5 mg PO qd, increase by 5 mg q week. Age > 12 yo: Start 10 mg PO qam, increase by 10 mg q week, maximum dose is 60 mg/day divided bid-tid at 4-6h intervals. ADHD: 3-5 yo: Start 2.5 mg PO qd, increase by 2.5 mg q week. Age ≥ 6 yo: Start 5 mg PO qd-bid, increase by 5 mg q week, maximum dose is 40 mg/day divided bid-tid at 4-6h intervals. Not recommended for children < 3 yo.

FORMS - Trade: Tabs 5, 10, 20, 30 mg.

NOTES - Avoid evening doses. Monitor growth and use drug holidays when appropriate. May increase pulse and BP.

caffeine (*NoDoz, Vivarin, Caffedrine, Stay Awake, Quick-Pep*) ▶L ♀B ▶? $

ADULT - Fatigue: 100- 200 mg PO q3-4h prn.

PEDS - Not approved in children <12 yo.

FORMS - OTC/Generic/Trade: Tabs 200 mg. OTC/Trade: extended release Tabs 200 mg.

dextroamphetamine (*Dexedrine, Dextrostat*) ▶L ♀C ▶- ©II $$

WARNING - Chronic overuse/abuse can lead to marked tolerance and psychic dependence;

caution with prolonged use.

ADULT - Narcolepsy: Start 10 mg PO qam, increase by 10 mg q wk, max 60 mg/day divided qd (sust'd release) or bid-tid at 4-6h intervals.

PEDS - Narcolepsy: 6-12 yo: Start 5 mg PO qam, increase by 5 mg q week. Age > 12 yo: Start 10 mg PO qam, increase by 10 mg q week, max 60 mg/day divided qd (sustained release) or bid-tid at 4-6h intervals. ADHD: age 3-5 yo: Start 2.5 mg PO qd, increase by 2.5 mg q week. Age ≥ 6 yo: Start 5 mg PO qd-bid, increase by 5 mg q week, max 40 mg/day divided qd-tid at 4-6h intervals. Not recommended for patients < 3 yo.

FORMS - Trade: Tabs 5, 10 mg. Caps, sustained release 5, 10, 15 mg.

NOTES - Avoid evening doses. Monitor growth and use drug holidays when appropriate. May increase pulse and BP.

methylphenidate (*Ritalin, Ritalin-SR, Methylin, Methylin ER, Metadate ER, Metadate CD, Concerta*) ▶LK ♀C ▶? ©II $

WARNING - Chronic overuse/abuse can lead to marked tolerance and psychic dependence; caution with prolonged use.

ADULT - Narcolepsy: 10 mg PO bid-tid before meals. Usual effective dose is 20-30 mg/day, max 60 mg/day. Use sustained release Tabs when the 8-hour dosage corresponds to the titrated 8-hour dosage of the conventional Tabs.

PEDS - ADHD age ≥ 6 yo: Start 5 mg PO bid before breakfast and lunch, increase gradually by 5-10 mg/day at weekly interval to max 60 mg/day. Start 18 mg PO qam (extended release); titrate in 18 mg increments at weekly intervals to max 54 mg/day. Consult product labeling for dose conversion from other methylphenidate regimens. Discontinue after 1 month if no improvement observed.

FORMS - Generic/Trade: tabs 5,10,20 mg. Sustained release tabs 10,20 mg. Trade only: extended release caps 20 mg (Metadate CD), extended release tabs 18,36,54 mg (Concerta).

NOTES - Avoid evening doses. Monitor growth and use drug holidays when appropriate. May increase pulse and BP.

modafinil (*Provigil, Alertec*) ▶L ♀C ▶? ©IV $$$$

ADULT - Narcolepsy: 200 mg PO qam.

PEDS - Not approved in children < 16 yo.

FORMS - Trade: Tabs 100, 200 mg.

NOTES - May increase levels of diazepam, phenytoin, TCAs, warfarin, or propranolol; may decrease levels of cyclosporine, oral contraceptives, or theophylline.

pemoline (*Cylert*) ▶LK ♀B ▶? ©IV $$$

WARNING – Not 1st line therapy for ADHD due to life-threatening hepatic failure.

PEDS - ADHD age > 6 yo: Start 37.5 mg PO q am, increase by 18.75 mg at 1 week intervals to usual effective dose of 56.25- 75 mg/day. Maximum dose is 112.5 mg/day.

UNAPPROVED ADULT - Narcolepsy: 50- 200 mg/day PO divided bid.

FORMS - Generic/Trade: tabs 18.75, 37.5, 75 mg. chew tabs 37.5 mg.

NOTES - Monitor ALT at baseline and q2 weeks thereafter; discontinue if > 2 x ULN. Avoid evening doses. Monitor growth and use drug holidays when appropriate.

phentermine (*Adipex-P, Ionamin, Phentride, Phentercot, Teramine, Pro-Fast, OBY-Trim*) ▶KL ♀C ▶- ©IV $

ADULT - Obesity: 8 mg PO tid before meals or 1-2 h after meals. May give 15-37.5 mg PO q am or 10-14 h before bedtime.

PEDS - Not approved in children <16 yo.

FORMS - Generic/Trade: Caps 15, 18.75, 30, 37.5 mg. Tabs 8, 37.5 mg. Trade only: extended release Caps 15, 30 mg (Ionamin).

NOTES - Indicated for short term (8-12 weeks) use only. Contraindicated for use during or within 14 days of MAOIs (hypertensive crisis).

sibutramine (*Meridia*) ▶KL ♀C ▶- ©IV $$$

ADULT - Obesity: Start 10 mg PO q am, may titrate to 15 mg/day after one month. Maximum dose is 15 mg/day.

PEDS - Not approved in children <16 yo.

FORMS - Trade: Caps 5, 10, 15 mg.

NOTES - May increase pulse and BP. Don't use in patients with uncontrolled HTN or heart disease. Caution using with SSRIs or other antidepressants. Contraindicated for use during or within 14 days of MAOIs (hypertensive crisis).

PSYCHIATRY: Other Agents

benztropine (*Cogentin, Bensylate*) ▶LK ♀C ▶? $

ADULT - Drug-induced extrapyramidal disorders: 1-4 mg PO/IM/IV qd-bid.

PEDS - Not approved in children

FORMS - Generic/Trade: Tabs 0.5, 1, 2 mg.

clonidine (*Catapres*) ▶LK ♀C ▶? $

PEDS - Not approved in children < 12 yo.

UNAPPROVED PEDS - ADHD: 5 mcg/kg/day PO x 8 weeks.
FORMS - Generic/Trade: Tabs 0.1, 0.2, 0.3 mg. Trade only: patch TTS-1, TTS-2, TTS-3.
NOTES - Rebound HTN with abrupt withdrawal.

diphenhydramine (*Benadryl, Banaril, Allermax Diphen, Dytuss, Sominex, Tusstat, Truxadryl, ✤Allerdryl, Allernix*) ▶LK ♀B(- in 1st trimester) ▶- $
ADULT - Drug-induced extrapyramidal disorders: 25-50 mg PO tid-qid or 10-50 mg IV/IM tid-qid.
PEDS - Drug-induced extrapyramidal disorders: 12.5-25 mg PO tid-qid or 5 mg/kg/day IV/IM divided qid, max 300 mg/day.
FORMS - OTC/Generic/Trade: Tabs 25, 50 mg. OTC/Trade only: chew Tabs 12.5 mg. OTC/Rx/Generic/Trade: Caps 25, 50 mg. oral solution 12.5 mg/5 ml.

fluoxetine (*Sarafem*) ▶L ♀C ▶- $$$
ADULT - Premenstrual Dysphoric Disorder (PMDD): 20 mg PO qd.
PEDS - Not approved in children.
FORMS - Trade: Caps 10, 20 mg.
NOTES - Sarafem is same drug as antidepressant Prozac. Half life is 7- 9 days. Contraindicated with thioridazine. Don't use with cisapride, thioridazine, tryptophan, or MAOIs; caution with lithium, phenytoin, TCAs, warfarin.

guanfacine (*Tenex*) ▶K ♀B ▶? $$
UNAPPROVED PEDS - ADHD: Start 0.5 mg PO qd, titrate by 0.5 mg q3-4 days as tolerated to 0.5 mg PO tid.
FORMS - Generic/Trade: Tabs 1, 2 mg.
NOTES - Less sedation and hypotension compared to clonidine.

PULMONARY: Beta Agonists

NOTE: Palpitations, tachycardia, tremor, lightheadedness, nervousness, headache, & nausea may occur; these effects may be more pronounced with systemic administration.

albuterol (*Ventolin, Ventolin HFA, Proventil, Proventil HFA, Volmax, Ventodisk, ✤Alromir, Asmavent, Salbutamol*) ▶L ♀C ▶? $
ADULT - Asthma: MDI: 2 puffs q4-6h prn; soln for inhalation: 2.5 mg inh tid-qid. Dilute 0.5 ml 0.5% soln with 2.5 ml NS. Deliver over ~ 5-15 min. One 3 ml unit dose (0.083%) nebulized tid-qid. Caps for inhalation: 200-400 mcg inh q4-6h via a Rotahaler device. 2-4 mg PO tid-qid or extended release 4-8 mg PO q12h up to 16 mg PO q12h.
PEDS - Asthma: MDI: ≥ 4 yo: 1-2 puffs q4-6 h prn. Soln for inhalation (0.5%): 2-12 yo: 0.1-0.15 mg/kg/dose not to exceed 2.5 mg tid-qid, diluted with NS to 3 ml. Caps for inhalation: ≥ 4 yo 200-400 mcg inhaled q4-6h via a Rotahaler device. Tabs, syrup 6-12 yo: 2-4 mg PO tid-qid, max dose 24 mg/d in divided doses. Syrup 2-5 yo: 0.1-0.2 mg/kg/dose PO tid up to 4 mg tid. Prevention of exercise-induced bronchospasm ≥ 4 yo (Proventil HFA, Ventolin HFA): 2 puffs 15 minutes before exercise.
UNAPPROVED ADULT - COPD: MDI, soln for inhalation: use asthma dose. Acute asthma: MDI, solnsoln for inhalation: dose as above q20min X 3 or until improvement.
UNAPPROVED PEDS - Prevention of exercise-induced bronchospasm: MDI: ≥ 4 yo 2 puffs 15 minutes before exercise. Acute asthma: Continuous nebulization: 0.3 mg/kg/h until improvement. MDI, soln for inhalation: dose as above q20min X 3 or until improvement.
FORMS - Generic/Trade: MDI 90 mcg/actuation, 200/canister. "HFA" inhalers use hydrofluoroalkane propellant instead of CFCs but are otherwise equivalent. Soln for inhalation 0.5% (5 mg/ml) in 20 ml with dropper. Nebules for inhalation 3 ml unit dose 0.083%. Trade only:1.25 mg & 0.63 mg/3 ml unit dose.Tabs 2 & 4 mg. Syrup 2 mg/5 ml. Trade: extended release tabs 4 & 8 mg. Caps for inhalation 200 mcg microfine in 24s & 96s w/ Rotahaler.

bitolterol (*Tornalate*) ▶L ♀C ▶? $$
ADULT - Asthma, acute: MDI: 2 puffs at an interval of at least 1-3 minutes, followed by a third inhalation prn. Soln for inhalation: 0.5-1 ml tid-qid via intermittent flow or 1.25 ml tid-qid via continuous flow. Asthma maintenance: 2 puffs q8h. Max dose 12 puffs/day divided q8h.
PEDS - Not approved in children.
UNAPPROVED ADULT - COPD: MDI: 2 puffs q8h. Max dose 12 puffs/day divided q8h.
UNAPPROVED PEDS - Asthma >4 yo MDI: 2 puffs q8h; inhalation soln: 0.5-1 ml tid-qid via intermittent flow or 1.25 ml tid-qid via continuous flow; allow ≥4 h between treatments.
FORMS - Trade: MDI 0.37 mg/actuation, ~300/canister. Soln for inhalation 0.2% (2 mg/ml) with dropper.

formoterol (*Foradil Aerolizer*) ▶L ♀C ▶? $$$
ADULT - Asthma maintenance: 1 puff bid. Pre-

vention of exercise-induced bronchospasm: 1 puff 15 min prior to exercise.

PEDS - Asthma maintenance ≥5 yo: 1 puff bid. Prevention of exercise-induced bronchospasm ≥12 yo: Use adult dose.

FORMS - Trade: DPI 12 mcg, 60 blisters/pack.

NOTES - Not for use for the relief of acute bronchospasm.

isoetharine ▸L ♀C ◗? $$$

ADULT - Asthma & emphysema: Soln for inhalation via aerosol nebulizer w/ NS: 0.25-0.5 ml of 1% soln q4h prn; via hand nebulizer: 3-7 inhalations, undiluted q4h prn.

FORMS - Generic: Soln for inhalation: 1% 10 & 30 ml with dropper.

levalbuterol (*Xopenex*) ▸L ♀C ◗? $$$$

ADULT - Asthma: Soln for inhalation: 0.63-1.25 mg nebulized q6-8h.

PEDS - Asthma: Soln for inhalation ≥12 yo: Use adult dose.

UNAPPROVED PEDS - Asthma: Soln for inhalation: 0.16-1.25 mg nebulized q8h.

FORMS - Trade: soln for inhalation 0.63 & 1.25 mg in 3 ml unit-dose vials.

NOTES - R-isomer of albuterol. Dyspepsia may occur.

metaproterenol (*Alupent, Metaprel, Pro-Meta*) ▸L ♀C ◗? $$

ADULT - Asthma: MDI: 2-3 puffs q3-4h; max dose 12 puffs/day. Soln for inhalation: 0.2-0.3 ml of 5% soln in 2.5 ml NS. 20 mg PO tid-qid.

PEDS - Asthma: soln for inhalation: >6 yo 0.1-0.3 ml of the 5% soln in 2.5 ml NS. Tabs or syrup: >9yo or > 60lbs: 20 mg PO tid-qid. 6-9 yo or <60lbs: 10 mg PO tid-qid. 2-5 yo: 1.3-2.6 mg/kg/day PO in divided doses tid-qid.

UNAPPROVED PEDS - Asthma: MDI: > 6yo 2-3 puffs q3-4h; max dose 12 puffs/day. Soln for inhalation: 0.1-0.3 ml of the 5% soln in 2.5 ml NS q4-6h prn or q20min until improvement. Tabs/syrup: < 2yo: 0.4 mg/kg/dose PO tid-qid.

FORMS - Trade: MDI 0.65 mg/actuation in 100 & 200/canister. Trade/Generic: Soln for inhalation 0.4, 0.6% in unit-dose vials; 5% in 10 & 30 ml with dropper. Syrup 10 mg/5 ml. Generic: Tabs 10 & 20 mg.

pirbuterol (*Maxair, Maxair Autohaler*) ▸L ♀C ◗? $$

ADULT - Asthma: MDI: 1-2 puffs q4-6h. Max dose 12 puffs/day.

PEDS - Not approved in children.

UNAPPROVED PEDS - Asthma ≥12 yo: Use adult dose.

FORMS - Trade: MDI 0.2 mg/actuation, 300/canister, 400/canister (Autohaler).

NOTES - Available with breath actuated autohaler.

salmeterol (*Serevent, Serevent Diskus*) ▸L ♀C ◗? $$$

ADULT - Asthma/ COPD maintenance: MDI: 2 puffs bid, 12 h apart. Inhalation powder (Diskus): 1 puff bid. Prevention of exercise-induced bronchospasm: MDI: 2 puffs 30-60 minutes before exercise.

PEDS - Asthma maintenance ≥4 yo: Diskus: 1 puff bid.

UNAPPROVED PEDS - Asthma maintenance ≥4 yo: MDI: 2 puffs bid.

FORMS - Trade: MDI: 25 mcg/actuation, 60 & 120/canister. DPI (Diskus): 50 mcg, 60 blisters.

NOTES - Not for use for the relief of acute bronchospasm.

terbutaline (*Brethine, Bricanyl*) ▸L ♀B ◗- $$

ADULT - Asthma: 2.5-5 mg PO q6h while awake. Max dose 15 mg/24h. 0.25 mg SC into lateral deltoid area; may repeat x1. Max dose 0.5 mg/4h.

PEDS - Not approved in children.

UNAPPROVED PEDS - Asthma: > 12yo: use adult dose, max 7.5 mg/24h; =< 12yo: 0.05 mg/kg/dose tid, increase to max of 0.15 mg/kg/dose tid, max 5 mg/day.

FORMS - Trade: Tabs 2.5 & 5 mg (Brethine scored).

PULMONARY: Combinations

***Advair Diskus* (fluticasone + salmeterol)** ▸L ♀C ◗? ?

ADULT - Asthma maintenance: 1 puff bid.

PEDS - Asthma maintenance ≥12 yo: Use adult dose.

FORMS - Trade: DPI: 100/50, 250/50, 500/50 mcg fluticasone propionate/mcg salmeterol per actuation.

NOTES - See components for additional info.

***Combivent* (albuterol + ipratropium)** ▸L ♀C ◗? $$

ADULT - COPD: MDI: 2 puffs qid. Max dose 12 puffs/24 hours.

PEDS - Not approved in children.

FORMS - Trade: MDI: 90 mcg albuterol/18 mcg ipratropium per actuation, 200/canister.

NOTES - Contraindicated with soy & peanut allergy. Refer to components.

DuoNeb **(albuterol + ipratropium)** ▶L ♀C ◗? $$$$

ADULT - COPD: One unit dose nebulized qid; may add 2 doses/day prn to max of 6 doses/day.

PEDS - Not approved in children.

FORMS - Trade: Unit dose: 3 mg albuterol sulfate/0.5 mg ipratropium bromide per 3 ml vial, premixed. 30 & 60 vials/carton.

NOTES - Refer to components

WHAT COLOR IS WHAT INHALER? (Body then cap - Generics may differ)

Advair	purple	*Flovent*	orange/ peach	*QVAR* 40 mcg	beige/grey
Aerobid	grey/purple	*Foradil*	grey/beige	*QVAR* 80 mcg	mauve/grey
Aerobid-M	grey/green	*Intal*	white/blue	*Serevent*	teal/light teal
Alupent	clear/blue	*Maxair*	blue/white	*Tilade*	white/white
Atrovent	clear/green	*Maxair Autohaler*	white/white	*Tornalate*	blue/blue
Azmacort	white/white			*Vanceril*	pink/maroon
Beclovent	cream/brown	*Proventil*	yellow/ orange	*Ventolin*	light blue/navy
Combivent	clear/orange	*Pulmicort*	white/brown		

PULMONARY: Inhaled Steroids

NOTE: See Endocrine-Corticosteroids when oral steroids necessary. Beware of adrenal suppression when changing from systemic to inhaled steroids. Inhaled steroids are not for treatment of acute asthma; higher doses may be needed for severe asthma and exacerbations. Adjust to lowest effective dose for maintenance. Use of a DPI, a spacing device, & rinsing the mouth with water after each use may decrease the incidence of thrush & dysphonia. Pharyngitis & cough may occur with all products.

beclomethasone dipropionate (*Beclovent, Vanceril, QVAR*, *✤Beclodisk*) ▶L ♀C ◗? $$

ADULT - Asthma maintenance (Beclovent, Vanceril): 2 puffs tid-qid or 4 puffs bid. Severe asthma: start with 12-16 puffs per day & adjust downward. QVAR: 40 mcg 1-4 puffs bid; 80 mcg 1-2 puffs bid.

PEDS - Asthma maintenance in 6-12 yo (Beclovent, Vanceril): 1-2 puffs tid-qid or 2-4 puffs bid.

UNAPPROVED ADULT - High-dose: Regular strength >20 puffs/day.

FORMS - Trade: Beclovent, Vanceril MDI: 42 mcg/actuation, 80 & 200/canister. QVAR MDI (non-CFC): 40 mcg & 80 mcg/actuation, 100 actuations/canister.

budesonide (*Pulmicort Turbuhaler, Pulmicort Respules*) ▶L ♀C ◗? $$$$

ADULT - Asthma maintenance: DPI: 1-2 puffs qd-bid up to 4 puffs bid.

PEDS - Asthma maintenance 6-12 yo: DPI: 1-2 puffs qd-bid. 12 mo - 8 yo: Suspension for inhalation (Respules): 0.5 mg - 1 mg qd or divided bid.

FORMS - Trade: DPI: 200 mcg powder/actuation, 200/canister. Respules: 0.25 mg/2 ml & 0.5 mg/2 ml unit dose.

NOTES - Respules should be delivered via a jet nebulizer with a mouthpiece or face mask. One DPI ~1½ to 3 months treatment.

flunisolide (*AeroBid, AeroBid-M*, *✤Rhinalar*) ▶L ♀C ◗? $$$

ADULT - Asthma maintenance: MDI: 2 puffs bid up to 4 puffs bid.

PEDS - Asthma maintenance: 6-15 yo: MDI: 2 puffs bid.

UNAPPROVED ADULT - High-dose: > 8 puffs/day.

FORMS - Trade: MDI: 250 mcg/actuation, 100/canister. AeroBid-M: menthol flavor.

fluticasone (*Flovent, Flovent Rotadisk*) ▶L ♀C ◗? $$$

ADULT - Asthma maintenance: MDI: 2 puffs bid up to 4 puffs bid. Max dose 880 mcg bid. DPI (Rotadisk): 1 puff bid up to 2 puffs bid. Max dose 500 mcg bid.

PEDS - Asthma maintenance 4-11 yo: DPI (Rotadisk): 1 puff bid up to max dose 100 mcg bid.

UNAPPROVED PEDS - Asthma maintenance 4-11 yo: MDI: 1-2 puffs (44mcg/puff) bid.

FORMS - Trade: MDI: 44, 110, 220 mcg/actuation in 60 & 120/canister. DPI (Rotadisk): 50, 100, & 250 mcg/actuation, in 4 blisters containing 15 Rotadisks (total of 60 doses) with inhalation device.

triamcinolone acetonide (*Azmacort*) ▶L ♀D ◗? $$$

ADULT - Asthma maintenance: MDI: 2 puffs tid-qid or 4 puffs bid. Max dose 16 puffs/day. Se-

vere asthma: 12-16 puffs/day and adjust downward.
PEDS - Asthma maintenance >12 yo: Use adult dose. 6-12 yo: 1-2 puffs tid-qid or 2-4 puffs bid. Max dose 12 puffs/day.
UNAPPROVED ADULT - High-dose: >20 puffs/day.
FORMS - Trade: MDI: 100 mcg/actuation, 240/canister. Built-in spacer.

INHALED STEROIDS: ESTIMATED COMPARATIVE DAILY ADULT DOSES*

Drug	*Form*	*Low Dose*	*Medium Dose*	*High Dose*
beclomethasone MDI	42 mcg/puff	4-12 puffs	12-20 puffs	>20 puffs
	84 mcg/puff	2-6 puffs	6-10 puffs	>10 puffs
budesonide DPI	200 mcg/dose	1-2 inhalations	2-3 inhalations	>3 inhalations
flunisolide MDI	250 mcg/puff	2-4 puffs	4-8 puffs	>8 puffs
fluticasone MDI	44 mcg/puff	2-6 puffs	-	-
	110 mcg/puff	2 puffs	2-6 puffs	>6 puffs
	220 mcg/puff	-	-	>3 puffs
fluticasone DPI	50 mcg/dose	2-6 inhalations	-	-
	100 mcg/dose	-	3-6 inhalations	>6 inhalations
	250 mcg/dose	-	-	>2 inhalations
triamcinolone MDI	100 mcg/puff	4-10 puffs	10-20 puffs	>20 puffs

*MDI=metered dose inhaler. DPI=dry powder inhaler. Reference: www.nhlbi.nih.gov/guidelines/asthma/asthgdln.htm

PULMONARY: Leukotriene Inhibitors

NOTE: Not for treatment of acute asthma. Abrupt substitution for corticosteroids may precipitate Churg-Strauss syndrome.

montelukast (*Singulair*) ▶L ♀B ▶? $$$
ADULT - Asthma maintenance: 10 mg PO q pm.
PEDS - Asthma maintenance 2-5 yo: 4 mg PO q pm. 6-14 yo: 5 mg PO q pm.
UNAPPROVED ADULT - Allergic rhinitis: 10 mg PO qd.
FORMS - Trade: Tabs 4, 5 mg (chew cherry flavored) & 10 mg.
NOTES - chew tabs contain phenylalanine. Levels decreased by phenobarbital & rifampin. Dyspepsia may occur.

zafirlukast (*Accolate*) ▶L ♀B ▶- $$$
ADULT - Asthma maintenance: 20 mg PO bid, 1h ac or 2h pc.
PEDS - Asthma maintenance ≥12 yo: use adult dose. 5-11 yo: 10 mg PO bid, at least 1h ac or 2h pc.
UNAPPROVED ADULT - Allergic rhinitis: 20 mg PO bid, 1h ac or 2h pc.
FORMS - Trade: Tabs 10, 20 mg.
NOTES - Potentiates warfarin & theophylline. Levels increased by erythromycin. Nausea may occur. If liver dysfunction is suspected, discontinue drug & manage accordingly.

zileuton (*Zyflo*) ▶L ♀C ▶? $$$$
WARNING - Contraindicated in active liver dz.
ADULT - Asthma maintenance: 600 mg PO qid.
PEDS - Asthma maintenance ≥12 yo: use adult dose.
FORMS - Trade: Tabs 600 mg.
NOTES - Monitor LFTs for elevation. Potentiates warfarin, theophylline, & propranolol. Dyspepsia & nausea may occur.

PREDICTED PEAK EXPIRATORY FLOW (liters/min) *Am Rev Resp Dis* 1963; 88:644

Age	Women *(height in inches)*					Men *(height in inches)*					Child *(height in inches)*	
(yrs)	55"	60"	65"	70"	75"	60"	65"	70"	75"	80"		
20	390	423	460	496	529	554	602	649	693	740	44"	160
30	380	413	448	483	516	532	577	622	664	710	46"	187
40	370	402	436	470	502	509	552	596	636	680	48"	214
50	360	391	424	457	488	486	527	569	607	649	50"	240
60	350	380	412	445	475	463	502	542	578	618	52"	267
70	340	369	400	432	461	440	477	515	550	587	54"	293

ASTHMA ACTION PLAN

Download copy: www.nhlbi.nih.gov/health/public/lung/asthma/asth_fs.htm

ASTHMA ACTION PLAN FOR ____________ Doctor's Name ____________ Date ________

Doctor's Phone Number ____________ Hospital/Emergency Room Phone Number ____________

GREEN ZONE: Doing Well

- No cough, wheeze, chest tightness, or shortness of breath during the day or night
- Can do usual activities

And, if a peak flow meter is used,
Peak flow: more than ________
(80% or more of my best peak flow)

My best peak flow is: ________

Take These Long-Term-Control Medicines Each Day (include an anti-inflammatory)

Medicine	How much to take	When to take it

Before exercise ❑ ____________ ❑ 2 or ❑ 4 puffs 5 to 60 minutes before exercise

YELLOW ZONE: Asthma Is Getting Worse

- Cough, wheeze, chest tightness, or shortness of breath, or
- Waking at night due to asthma, or
- Can do some, but not all, usual activities

-Or-

Peak flow: ______ to ______
(50% - 80% of my best peak flow)

FIRST **Add: Quick-Relief Medicine – and keep taking your GREEN ZONE medicine**

____________ ❑ 2 or ❑ 4 puffs, every 20 minutes for up to 1 hour
(short-acting $beta_2$-agonist) ❑ Nebulizer, once

SECOND **If your symptoms (and peak flow, if used) *return to GREEN ZONE* after 1 hour of above treatment:**
❑ Take the quick-relief medicine every 4 hours for 1 to 2 days.
❑ Double the dose of your inhaled steroid for ________ (7-10) days.
-Or-
If your symptoms (and peak flow, if used) *do not return to GREEN ZONE* after 1 hour of above treatment:
❑ Take: ____________ ❑ 2 or ❑ 4 puffs or ❑ Nebulizer
(short-acting $beta_2$-agonist)
❑ Add: ____________ ________ mg. per day For ________ (3-10) days
(oral steroid)
❑ Call the doctor ❑ before/ ❑ within ________ hours after taking the oral steroid.

RED ZONE: Medical Alert!

- Very short of breath, or
- Quick-relief medicines have not helped, or
- Cannot do usual activities, or
- Symptoms are same or get worse after 24 hours in Yellow Zone

-Or-

Peak flow: less than ________
(50% of my best peak flow)

Take this medicine:
❑ ____________ ❑ 4 or ❑ 6 puffs or ❑ Nebulizer
(short-acting $beta_2$-agonist)
❑ ____________ ________ mg.
(oral steroid)

Then call your doctor *NOW*. Go to the hospital or call for an ambulance if:
- You are still in the red zone after 15 minutes AND
- You have not reached your doctor.

DANGER SIGNS
- **Trouble walking and talking due to shortness of breath**
- **Lips or fingernails are blue**

- **Take ❑ 4 or ❑ 6 puffs of your quick-relief medicine *AND***
- **Go to the hospital or call for an ambulance (____________) *NOW!***

PULMONARY: Other Pulmonary Medications

acetylcysteine (*Mucomyst, Mucosil-10, Mucosil-20, Parvolex*) ▶L ♀B ▶? $$

ADULT - Mucolytic nebulization: 3-5 ml of the 20% soln or 6-10 ml of the 10% soln tid-qid. Instillation, direct or via tracheostomy: 1-2 ml of a 10% to 20% soln q1-4h; via percutaneous intratracheal catheter: 1-2 ml of the 20% soln or 2-4 ml of the 10% soln q1-4h.

PEDS - Mucolytic nebulization: Use adult dose.

FORMS - Generic/Trade: soln 10 & 20% in 4,10, & 30 ml vials.

NOTES - Increased volume of liquefied bronchial secretions may occur; maintain an open airway. Watch for bronchospasm in asthmatics. Stomatitis, nausea, vomiting, fever, & rhinorrhea may occur. A slight disagreeable odor may occur & should soon disappear. A face mask may cause stickiness on the face after nebulization; wash with water.

aminophylline ▶L ♀C ▶? $

ADULT - Asthma: loading dose if currently not receiving theophylline: 6 mg/kg IV over 20-30 min. Maintenance IV infusion 1g in 250 ml D5W (4 mg/ml) at 0.5-0.7 mg/kg/h (70kg: 0.7 mg/kg/h =11 ml/h). If currently on theophylline, each 0.6 mg/kg aminophylline will increase the serum theoph concentration by approximately 1mcg/ml. Maintenance: 200 mg PO bid-qid.

PEDS - Asthma loading dose if currently not receiving theophylline: 6 mg/kg IV over 20-30 min. Maintenance >6 mo: 0.8-1 mg/kg/hr IV infusion. >1 yo: 3-4 mg/kg/dose PO q6h.

UNAPPROVED PEDS - Neonatal apnea of prematurity: loading dose 5-6 mg/kg IV/PO. Main-

Maintenance: 1-2 mg/kg/dose q6-8 h IV/PO.

FORMS - Generic: Tabs 100 & 200 mg. Oral liquid 105 mg/5 ml. Trade: Tabs controlled release (12hr) 225 mg, scored.

NOTES - Aminophylline is 79% theophylline. Administer IV infusion ≤ 25 mg/min. Multiple drug interactions (especially ketoconazole, rifampin, carbamazepine, isoniazid, phenytoin, macrolides, zafirlukast & cimetidine). Review meds before initiating treatment. Irritability, nausea, palpitations & tachycardia may occur. Overdose may be life-threatening.

beractant (*Survanta*) ▶Lung ♀? ◗? $$$$$

PEDS - RDS (hyaline membrane disease) in premature infants: Specialized dosing.

calfactant (*Infasurf*) ▶Lung ♀? ◗? $$$$$

PEDS - RDS (hyaline membrane disease) in premature infants: Specialized dosing.

colfosceril palmitate (*Exosurf Neonatal*) ▶Lung ♀? ◗? $$$$$

PEDS - RDS (hyaline membrane disease) in premature infants: Specialized dosing.

cromolyn sodium (*Intal, Gastrocrom, Nalcrom*) ▶LK ♀B ◗? $$$

ADULT - Asthma maintenance: MDI: 2-4 puffs qid. Soln for inhalation: 20 mg inh qid. Prevention of exercise-induced bronchospasm: MDI: 2 puffs 10-15 min prior to exercise. soln for nebulization: 20 mg 10-15 min prior. Mastocytosis: 200 mg PO qid, 30 min ac & qhs.

PEDS - Asthma maintenance >5 yo: MDI: 2 puffs qid. >2 yo: soln for nebulization: 20 mg inh qid. Prevention of exercise-induced bronchospasm >5 yo: MDI: 2 puffs 10-15 min prior to exercise. >2 yo soln for nebulization: 20 mg 10-15 min prior. Mastocytosis: 2-12 yo: 100 mg PO qid 30 min ac & qhs.

FORMS - Trade: MDI 800 mcg/actuation, 112 & 200/canister. Oral concentrate 5 ml/100 mg in 8 amps/foil pouch. Generic/Trade: Soln for nebs: 20 mg/2 ml.

NOTES - Not for treatment of acute asthma. Pharyngitis may occur. Directions for oral concentrate: 1) Break open and squeeze liquid contents of ampule(s) into a glass of water. 2) Stir soln. 3) Drink all of the liquid.

dexamethasone (*Decadron*) ▶L ♀C ◗- $

PEDS - Not approved in children.

UNAPPROVED PEDS - Bronchopulmonary dysplasia in preterm infants: 0.5 mg/kg PO/IV divided q12h x 3 days, then taper. Croup: 0.15-0.6 mg/kg PO or IM x 1. Acute asthma: > 2 yo: 0.6 mg/kg to max 16 mg PO qd x 2 days.

FORMS - Generic/Trade: Tabs 0.25,0.5,0.75,1, 1.5,2,4,,6 mg, various scored. Elixir: 0.5 mg/5 ml. Oral soln: 0.5 mg/5 ml & 0.5 mg/0.5 ml.

dornase alfa (*Pulmozyme*) ▶L ♀B ◗? $$$$$

ADULT - Cystic fibrosis: 2.5 mg nebulized qd-bid.

PEDS - Cystic fibrosis ≥6 yo: 2.5 mg nebulized qd-bid.

UNAPPROVED PEDS - Has been used in a small number of children as young a 3mo w/similar efficacy & side effects.

FORMS - Trade: soln for inhalation: 1 mg/ml in 2.5 ml vials.

NOTES - Voice alteration, pharyngitis, laryngitis, & rash may occur.

epinephrine (*EpiPen, EpiPen Jr.*) ▶Plasma ♀C ◗- $

ADULT - Acute asthma & hypersensitivity reactions: 0.1 to 0.3 mg of 1:1,000 soln SC.

PEDS - Acute asthma: 0.01 ml/kg (up to 0.5 ml) of 1:1,000 soln SC; repeat q15min x 3-4 doses prn. Sustained release: 0.005 ml/kg (up to 0.15 ml) of 1:200 soln SC; repeat q8-12h prn. Hypersensitivity reactions: 0.01 mg/kg SC autoinjector.

FORMS - Soln for inj: 1:1,000 (1 mg/ml in 1 ml amps). Sust'd formulation (Sus-Phrine): 1:200 (5 mg/ml) in 0.3 ml amps or 5 ml multi-dose vials. Injectable allergy kit in single-dose autoinjectors: Epipen 0.3 mg, Epipen Jr 0.15 mg.

NOTES - Directions for injectable kit use: Remove cap. Place black tip end on thigh & push down to inject. Hold in place for 10 seconds. May be injected directly through clothing. Cardiac arrhythmias & hypertension may occur. For emergencies only.

epinephrine racemic (*AsthmaNefrin, MicroNefrin, Nephron, S-2*) ▶Plasma ♀C ◗- $

PEDS - Severe croup: inhalation soln: 0.05 ml/kg/dose diluted to 3 ml w/NS over 15 min prn not to exceed q1-2h dosing. Max dose 0.5 ml.

FORMS - Trade: soln for inhalation: 2.25% racepinephrine in 15 & 30 ml.

NOTES - Cardiac arrhythmias and hypertension may occur.

ipratropium (*Atrovent*) ▶Lung ♀B ◗? $$

ADULT - COPD maintenance: MDI: 2-3 puffs qid; max dose 12 puffs/day. Soln for inhalation: 500 mcg nebulized tid-qid.

PEDS - Not approved in children <12 yo.

UNAPPROVED PEDS - Asthma: MDI: >12 yo: use adult dose. =<12 yo: 1-2 puffs tid-qid. Soln for inhalation: >12 yo: 250-500 mcg/dose tid-qid; =<12 yo: 250 mcg/dose tid-qid. Acute asthma: 2-18yo: 500 mcg nebulized with 2nd & 3rd doses of albuterol.

FORMS - Trade: MDI: 18mcg/actuation, 200/

canister. Generic/Trade: Soln for nebulization: 0.02% (500 mcg/vial) in unit dose vials.
NOTES - Contraindicated with soy & peanut allergy. Caution with glaucoma, BPH, or bladder neck obstruction. Cough, dry mouth & blurred vision may occur.

methacholine (*Provocholine*) ▶Plasma ♀C ▶? $$
WARNING - Life-threatening bronchoconstriction can result; have resuscitation capability available.
ADULT - Diagnosis of bronchial airway hyperreactivity in non-wheezing patients with suspected asthma: 5 breaths each of ascending serial concentrations, 0.025 mg/ml to 25 mg/ml, via nebulization. The procedure ends when there is a ≥ 20% reduction in the FEV1 compared with baseline.
PEDS - Diagnosis of bronchial airway hyperreactivity: use adult dose.
NOTES - Avoid with epilepsy, bradycardia, vagotonia, peptic ulcer disease, thyroid disease, urinary tract obstruction or other conditions that could be adversely affected by a cholinergic agent. Do not inhale powder.

nedocromil (*Tilade*) ▶L ♀B ▶? $$
ADULT - Asthma maintenance: MDI: 2 puffs qid. Reduce dose as tolerated.
PEDS - Asthma maintenance > 6 yo: MDI: 2 puffs qid.
FORMS - Trade: MDI: 1.75 mg/actuation, 112/ canister.
NOTES - Not for treatment of acute asthma. Unpleasant taste & dysphonia may occur.

nitric oxide (*INOmax*) ▶Lung, K ♀C ▶? $$$$$
PEDS - Respiratory failure with pulmonary hypertension in infants > 34 weeks old: Specialized dosing.

poractant (*Curosurf*) ▶Lung ♀? ▶? $$$$$
PEDS - RDS (hyaline membrane disease) in premature infants: Specialized dosing.

theophylline (*Slo-Phyllin, Elixophyllin, Uni-Dur, Uniphyl, Theo-24, Theo-Dur, Slo-bid*) ▶L ♀C ▶+ $
ADULT - Asthma: 5-13 mg/kg/day PO in divided doses. Max dose 900 mg/day.
PEDS - Asthma, initial: >1 yo & <45 kg: 12-14 mg/kg/day PO divided q4-6h to max of 300 mg/24h. Maintenance: 16-20 mg/kg/day PO divided q4-6h to max of 600 mg/24h. >1 yo & ≥45 kg: Initial: 300mg/24h PO divided q6-8h. Maintenance: 400-600 mg/24h PO divided q6-8h. Infants 6-52 weeks: [(0.2 x age in weeks) + 5] x kg = 24hr dose in mg PO divided q6-8h.
UNAPPROVED ADULT - COPD: 10 mg/kg/day PO in divided doses.
UNAPPROVED PEDS - Apnea & bradycardia of prematurity: 3-6 mg/kg/day PO divided q6-8h. Maintain serum concentrations 3-5 mcg/ml.
FORMS - Slo-Phyllin, Elixophyllin, various: Tabs 100, 125, 200, 250, & 300 mg. Liquid 80 mg/15 ml, 150 mg/15 ml. Qd sustained release Uni-Dur, Uniphyl, Theo-24: 100, 200, 300, 400 & 600 mg. Bid sustained release Theo-Dur, Slo-bid, various generics: 100, 200, 300 & 450 mg.
NOTES - Multiple drug interactions (especially ketoconazole, rifampin, carbamazepine, isoniazid, phenytoin, macrolides, zafirlukast & cimetidine). Review meds before initiating treatment. Irritability, nausea, palpitations & tachycardia may occur. Overdose may be life-threatening.

TOXICOLOGY

acetylcysteine (*Mucomyst*) ▶L ♀B ▶? $$$
ADULT - Acetaminophen toxicity: loading dose 140 mg/kg PO or NG as soon as possible, then 70 mg/kg q4h x 17 doses.
PEDS - Acetaminophen toxicity: same as adult dosing.
UNAPPROVED ADULT - Renal impairment prophylaxis prior to contrast agents: 600 mg PO bid on the day before and on the day of administration of contrast agents.
FORMS - Generic/Trade: solution 10%, 20%.
NOTES - May be mixed in water or soft drink. IV use possible; consult poison center.

charcoal (*activated charcoal, Actidose-Aqua, CharcoAid*, ♣*Charcodate*) ▶Not absorbed ♀+ ▶+ $
ADULT - Gut decontamination: 25- 100 g (0.5-1 g/kg or 10 times the amount of poison ingested) PO or NG ASAP. Repeat q4h prn.
PEDS - Gut decontamination: 0.5-1g/kg or 10 times the amount of poison ingested PO or NG as soon as possible. Repeat q4h prn. Not approved in children <1 yo.
FORMS - OTC/Generic/Trade: Tabs 250 mg, Caps 260 mg, solution 25 g/ 120 ml.
NOTES - Some products may contain sorbitol to improve taste and reduce GI transit time. Not usually effective for toxic alcohols (methanol, ethylene glycol, isopropanol), heavy metals (lead, iron, bromide), arsenic, lithium, potas-

sium, hydrocarbons, and caustic ingestions (acids, alkalis).

deferoxamine (*Desferal*) ▶K ♀C ▶? $$$$$

ADULT - Chronic iron overload: 500 mg- 1000 mg IM qd and 2 g IV infusion (≤15 mg/kg/hr) with each unit of blood or 1-2 g SC qd (20- 40 mg/kg/day) over 8-12 h via continuous infusion pump. Specialized dosing for acute iron toxicity; consult poison center: 1g IM initially, then 500 mg IM q4h x 2 doses, then 500 mg IM q4-12h based on response. Max 6 g/day. Give by IV infusion (<15 mg/kg/hr) in cardiovascular collapse.

PEDS - Specialized dosing for acute iron toxicity; consult poison center.

NOTES - Contraindicated in renal failure/ anuria unless undergoing dialysis.

dimercaprol (*BAL in oil*) ▶KL ♀C ▶? $$$$$

ADULT - Specialized dosing for arsenic, mercury, gold, lead toxicity. Consult poison center. Mild arsenic or gold toxicity: 2.5 mg/kg IM qid x 2 days, then bid x 1 day, then qd x 10 days. Severe arsenic or gold toxicity: 3 mg/kg IM q4h x 2 days, then qid x 1 day, then bid x 10 days. Mercury toxicity: 5 mg/kg IM initially, then 2.5 mg/kg qd-bid x 10 days. Begin therapy within 1-2 h of toxicity. Acute lead encephalopathy: 4 mg/kg IM initially, then q4h in combination with calcium edetate x 2-7 days. May reduce dose to 3 mg/kg IM for less severe toxicity.

PEDS - Not approved in children.

edetate disodium (*EDTA, Endrate, Meritate*) ▶K ♀C ▶- $$$

WARNING - Beware of elevated intracranial pressure in lead encephalopathy.

ADULT - Consult poison center. Lead toxicity: 1000 mg/m2/day IM (divided into equal doses q8-12h) or IV (infuse total dose over 8-12h) x 5 days. Interrupt therapy for 2-4 days, then repeat same regimen. Two courses of therapy are usually necessary. Acute lead encephalopathy: edetate disodium alone or in combination with dimercaprol. Lead nephropathy: 500 mg/m2 q24h x 5 doses (creat 2-3 mg/dl), q48h x 3 doses (creat 3-4 mg/dl), or once weekly (creat >4 mg/dl). May repeat at one month intervals.

PEDS - Specialized dosing for lead toxicity; same as adult dosing. Consult poison center.

ethanol ▶L ♀D ▶+ ?

UNAPPROVED ADULT - Consult poison center. Specialized dosing for methanol, ethylene glycol toxicity if fomepizole is unavailable or delayed: 1000 mg/kg (10 ml/kg) of 10% ethanol (100 mg/ml) IV over 1-2h then 100 mg/kg/h (1 ml/kg/h) to keep ethanol level approximately 100 mg/dl.

flumazenil (*Romazicon*, ✱*Anexate*) ▶LK ♀C ▶? $$$

WARNING - Do not use in chronic benzodiazepine use or acute overdose with tricyclic antidepressants due to seizure risk.

ADULT - Benzodiazepine sedation reversal: 0.2 mg IV over 15 sec, then 0.2 mg q1 min prn up to 1 mg total dose. Usual dose is 0.6- 1 mg. Benzodiazepine overdose reversal: 0.2 mg IV over 30 sec, then 0.3-0.5 mg q30 sec prn up to 3 mg total dose.

PEDS - Not approved in children.

UNAPPROVED PEDS - Benzodiazepine overdose reversal: 0.01 mg/kg IV. Benzodiazepine sedation reversal: 0.01 mg/kg IV initially (max 0.2 mg), then 0.005-0.01 mg/kg (max 0.2 mg) q1 min to max total dose 1 mg. May repeat doses in 20 min, max 3 mg in 1 hour.

NOTES - For IV use only, preferably through an IV infusion line into a large vein. Local irritation may occur following extravasation.

fomepizole (*Antizol*) ▶L ♀C ▶? $$$$$

ADULT - Consult poison center. Ethylene glycol or methanol toxicity: 15 mg/kg IV (load), then 10 mg/kg IV q12h x 4 doses, then 15 mg/kg IV q12h until ethylene glycol or methanol level < 20 mg/dl. Administer doses as slow IV infusions over 30 minutes.

PEDS - Not approved in children.

ipecac syrup ▶Gut ♀C ▶? $

ADULT - Emesis: 15- 30 ml, then 3- 4 glasses of water.

PEDS - Emesis, <1 yo: 5- 10 ml, then ½ - 1 glass of water (controversial in children < 1 year). Emesis, 1- 12 yo: 15 ml, then 1-2 glasses of water. May repeat dose (15 ml) if vomiting does not occur within 20- 30 minutes.

FORMS - Generic/OTC: syrup.

NOTES - Do not use if any potential for altered mental status (eg, seizure, neurotoxicity) strychnine, beta blocker, calcium channel blocker, corrosive, or petroleum distillate ingestions.

methylene blue (*Urolene blue*) ▶K ♀C ▶? $$

ADULT - Methemoglobinemia: 1- 2 mg/kg IV over 5 minutes.

PEDS - Not approved in children.

UNAPPROVED PEDS - Methemoglobinemia: 1-2 mg/kg/dose IV over 5 min; may repeat in 1h.

NOTES - May turn urine blue-green.

penicillamine (*Cuprimine, Depen*) ▶K ♀D ▶- $$$

WARNING - Fatal drug-related adverse events

have occurred.
ADULT - Consult poison center: Specialized dosing for copper toxicity: 750 mg- 1.5 g/day PO x 3 months based on 24-hour urinary copper excretion, max 2 g/day. May start 250 mg/day PO in patients unable to tolerate.
PEDS - Specialized dosing for copper toxicity. Consult poison center.
FORMS - Trade: Caps 125, 250 mg; Tabs 250 mg.
NOTES - Patients may require supplemental pyridoxine.

pralidoxime (*Protopam*) ▶K ♀C ◗? $$$
ADULT - Consult poison center: Specialized dosing for organophosphate toxicity: 1-2 g IV infusion over 15-30 min or slow IV injection ≥ 5 min (max rate 200 mg/min). May repeat dose after 1 h if muscle weakness persists.
PEDS - Not approved in children.
UNAPPROVED ADULT - Organophosphate toxicity; consult poison center: 20-40 mg/kg/dose IV infusion over 15-30 min.
UNAPPROVED PEDS - Specialized dosing for organophosphate toxicity. Consult poison center.
NOTES - Administer <36h of exposure when possible. Give in conjunction with atropine. IM or SC may be used if IV access unavailable.

sorbitol ▶Not absorbed ♀+ ◗+ $
ADULT - Cathartic: 30-50 ml of 70% solution PO.
FORMS - Generic: oral solution 70%.
NOTES - Acts as an osmotic cathartic. May precipitate electrolyte imbalance.

succimer (*Chemet*) ▶K ♀C ◗? $$$$$
PEDS - Lead toxicity ≥ 1 yo: Start 10 mg/kg PO or 350 mg/m2 q8h x 5 days, then reduce the frequency to q12h x 2 weeks. Not approved in children <12 mo.
FORMS - Trade: Caps 100 mg.
NOTES - Can open cap and sprinkle medicated beads over food, or give them in a spoon and follow with fruit drink. Indicated for blood lead levels > 45 mcg/dl. Allow at least 4 weeks between edetate disodium and succimer treatment.

ANTIDOTES

Toxin	*Antidote/Treatment*	*Toxin*	*Antidote/Treatment*
acetaminophen	N-acetylcysteine	ethylene glycol	fomepizole
antidepressants	bicarbonate	heparin	protamine
arsenic, mercury	dimercaprol (BAL)	iron	deferoxamine
benzodiazepine	flumazenil	lead	EDTA, succimer
beta blockers	glucagon	methanol	fomepizole
calcium channel blockers	calcium chloride, glucagon	methemoglobin	methylene blue
		narcotics	naloxone
cyanide	Lilly cyanide kit	organophosphates	atropine+pralidoxime
digoxin	dig immune Fab	warfarin	vitamin K, FFP

UROLOGY: Benign Prostatic Hyperplasia

doxazosin (*Cardura*) ▶L ♀C ◗? $$
ADULT - BPH: Start 1 mg PO qhs, titrate by doubling the dose over at least 1-2 week intervals up to a maximum of 8 mg PO qhs.
PEDS - Not approved in children.
FORMS - Generic/Trade: Tabs 1, 2, 4, 8 mg.
NOTES - Beware of dizziness, drowsiness, syncope, lightheadedness, postural hypotension; monitor BP closely. If therapy is interrupted for several days, restart at 1 mg dose. Alpha blockers are considered 1st line treatment in men with more than minimal symptoms.

finasteride (*Proscar*) ▶L ♀X ◗- $$$
ADULT - BPH: 5 mg PO qd.
PEDS - Not approved in children.
FORMS - Trade: Tabs 5 mg.
NOTES - Therapy for 6-12 months may be needed to assess effectiveness. Pregnant or potentially pregnant women should not handle crushed Tabs because of possible absorption and fetal risk. Use with caution in hepatic insufficiency. Monitor PSA before therapy; finasteride will decrease PSA by 50% in patients with BPH, even with prostate cancer. Finasteride is most effective in men with prostate volumes >40 ml.

tamsulosin (*Flomax*) ▶LK ♀B ◗- $$
ADULT - BPH: 0.4 mg PO qd 30 min after the

same meal each day. If an adequate response is not seen after 2-4 wks, may increase dose to 0.8 mg PO qd. If therapy is interrupted for several days, restart at the 0.4 mg dose.
PEDS - Not approved in children.
FORMS - Trade: Caps 0.4 mg.
NOTES - Dizziness, headache, abnormal ejaculation. Less risk for postural hypotension than with other alpha blockers. Alpha blockers are generally considered to be first line treatment in men with more than minimal symptoms.

terazosin (*Hytrin*) ▶LK ♀C ▶? $$
ADULT - BPH: Start 1 mg PO qhs, titrate dose in a stepwise fashion to 2, 5, or 10 mg PO qhs to desired effect. Treatment with 10 mg PO qhs for 4-6 weeks may be needed to assess benefit. Maximum 20 mg/day.
PEDS - Not approved in children.
FORMS - Generic/Trade: Caps 1, 2, 5, 10 mg.
NOTES - Beware of dizziness, drowsiness, lightheadedness, syncope, postural hypotension; monitor BP closely. If therapy is interrupted for several days, restart at 1 mg dose. Alpha blockers are generally considered to be first line treatment in men with more than minimal symptoms.

UROLOGY: Bladder Agents

***B&O Supprettes* (belladonna and opium)** ▶L ♀C ▶? ©II $$$
ADULT - Bladder spasm: 1 suppository PR qd-bid, max 4 doses/day .
PEDS - Not approved in children < 12 yo.
FORMS - Generic/Trade: suppositories 30 mg opium [15A], 60 mg opium [16A].
NOTES - Store at room temperature. May cause dizziness, drowsiness, blurred vision, dry mouth, N/V, urinary retention. Contraindicated in glaucoma, obstructive conditions (e.g. pyloric or duodenal obstruction, obstructive intestinal lesions or ileus, achalasia, GI hemorrhage, and obstructive uropathies).

bethanechol (*Urecholine*, ✤*Duvoid, Myotonachol*) ▶L ♀C ▶? $
ADULT - Urinary retention: 10-50 mg PO tid-qid or 2.5-5 mg SC tid-qid. Take 1 hour before or 2 h after meals to avoid N/V. Determine the minimum effective dose by giving 5-10 mg PO initially and repeat at hourly intervals until response or to a maximum of 50 mg.
PEDS - Not approved in children.
UNAPPROVED PEDS - Urinary retention/abdominal distention: 0.6 mg/kg/day PO divided q6-8h or 0.12-0.2 mg/kg/day SC divided q6-8h.
FORMS - Generic/Trade: Tabs 5, 10, 25, 50 mg.
NOTES - May cause drowsiness, lightheadedness, and fainting. Not for obstructive urinary retention. Avoid with cardiac disease, hyperthyroidism, parkinsonism, peptic ulcer disease, and epilepsy.

desmopressin (*DDAVP*, ✤*Octostim*) ▶LK ♀B ▶? $$$$
ADULT - Primary nocturnal enuresis: 10- 40 mcg (0.1- 0.4 ml) intranasally qhs, administer ½ of dose per nostril or 0.2- 0.6 mg PO qhs.
PEDS - Primary nocturnal enuresis >6 yo: 20 mcg (0.2 ml) intransally qhs or 0.2-0.6 mg PO qhs.
FORMS - Trade: Tabs 0.1, 0.2 mg; nasal solution 0.1 mg/ml (10 mcg/ spray).
NOTES - Prime the nasal spray pump.

flavoxate (*Urispas*) ▶K ♀B ▶? $$$$
ADULT - Bladder spasm: 100 or 200 mg PO tid-qid. Reduce dose when improved.
PEDS - Not approved in children < 12 yo.
FORMS - Trade: Tabs 100 mg.
NOTES - May cause dizziness, drowsiness, blurred vision, dry mouth, N/V, urinary retention. Contraindicated in glaucoma, obstructive conditions (e.g. pyloric or duodenal obstruction, obstructive intestinal lesions or ileus, achalasia, GI hemorrhage, obstructive uropathies).

hyoscyamine (*Anaspaz, A-spaz, Cystospaz, ED Spaz, Hyosol, Hyospaz, Levbid, Levsin, Levsinex, Medispaz, NuLev, Spacol, Spasdel, Symax*) ▶LK ♀C ▶- $
ADULT - Bladder spasm: 0.125-0.25 mg PO q4h or prn; or 0.375-0.75 mg PO q12h (extended release). Max 1.5 mg/day.
PEDS - Bladder spasm >12 yo: Adult dosing.
FORMS - Generic/Trade: Tabs 0.125; sublingual Tabs 0.125 mg; extended release Tabs 0.375 mg; extended release Caps 0.375 mg; elixir 0.125 mg/5 ml; drops 0.125 mg/1 ml; Trade only: Tabs 0.15 mg (Hyospaz, Cystospaz). Tabs, orally disintegrating 0.125 (NuLev).
NOTES - May cause dizziness, drowsiness, blurred vision, dry mouth, N/V, urinary retention. Contraindicated in glaucoma, obstructive conditions (e.g. pyloric or duodenal obstruction, obstructive intestinal lesions or ileus, achalasia, GI hemorrhage, and obstructive uropathies), unstable cardiovascular status, and

myasthenia gravis.

imipramine (*Tofranil, Tofranil-PM*) ▶L ♀B ▶? $

PEDS - Enuresis ≥6 yo: 10- 25 mg/day PO given one hour before bedtime, then increase in increments of 10-25 mg at 1-2 week intervals not to exceed 50 mg/day in 6-12 yo children or 75 mg/day in children >12 yo. Do not exceed 2.5 mg/kg/day.

UNAPPROVED ADULT - enuresis: 25-75 mg PO qhs.

FORMS - Generic/Trade: Tabs 10, 25, 50 mg. Trade only: Caps (Tofranil-PM) 75, 100, 125, 150 mg.

NOTES - Contraindicated with MAO inhibitors, recent MI.

methylene blue (*Urolene blue*) ▶Gut/K ♀C ▶? $

ADULT - Dysuria: 65-130 mg PO tid after meals with liberal water.

PEDS - Not approved in children.

FORMS - Trade only: Tabs 65 mg.

NOTES - May turn urine, stool, skin, contact lenses, and undergarments blue-green.

oxybutynin (*Ditropan, Ditropan XL*, ✤*Oxybutyn*) ▶LK ♀B ▶? $

ADULT - Bladder instability: 5 mg PO bid-tid, max 5 mg PO qid; or start 5 mg PO qd (Ditropan XL), increase by 5 mg/day q week to max 30 mg/day.

PEDS - Bladder instability >5 yo: 5 mg PO bid, max dose: 5 mg PO tid.

UNAPPROVED PEDS - Bladder instability ≤5 yo: 0.2 mg/kg/dose PO bid-qid.

FORMS - Generic/Trade: Tabs 5 mg; syrup 5 mg/5 ml. Trade only: extended release tabs (Ditropan XL) 5, 10, 15 mg.

NOTES - May cause dizziness, drowsiness, blurred vision, dry mouth, urinary retention. Contraindicated with glaucoma, obstructive uropathy or GI disease, unstable cardiovascular status, and myasthenia gravis.

pentosan polysulfate (*Elmiron*) ▶K ♀B ▶? $$$$

ADULT - Interstitial cystitis: 100 mg PO tid 1 hour before or 2 h after a meal.

PEDS - Not approved in children.

FORMS - Trade: Caps 100 mg.

NOTES - May increase risk of bleeding. Use with caution in hepatic or splenic dysfunction.

phenazopyridine (*Pyridium, Azo-Standard, Urogesic, Prodium, Pyridiate, Urodol, Baridium, UTI Relief*, ✤*Pyronium, Phenazo Tab*) ▶K ♀B ▶? $

ADULT - Dysuria: 200 mg PO tid after meals x 2 days.

PEDS - Dysuria in children 6-12 yo: 12 mg/kg/day PO divided tid x 2 days.

FORMS - OTC/Generic/Trade: Tabs 95, 97.2 mg. Generic/Trade: Tabs 100, 200 mg.

NOTES - Turns urine & contact lenses orange. Contraindicated with hepatitis or renal insufficiency.

***Prosed/ DS* (methenamine + phenyl salicylate + methylene blue + benzoic acid + atropine sulfate + hyoscyamine sulfate)** ▶KL ♀C ▶? $$$

ADULT - Bladder spasm: 1 tab qid with liberal fluids.

PEDS - Not approved in children

FORMS - Trade only: Tabs (methenamine 81.6 mg + phenyl salicylate 36.2 mg + methylene blue 10.8 mg + benzoic acid 9.0 mg + atropine sulfate 0.06 mg + hyoscyamine sulfate 0.06 mg).

NOTES - May cause dizziness, drowsiness, blurred vision, dry mouth, nausea/vomiting, urinary retention. May turn urine and contact lenses blue.

tolterodine (*Detrol, Detrol LA*) ▶L ♀C ▶- $$$

ADULT - Overactive bladder: 2 mg PO bid (Detrol) or 4 mg PO qd (Detrol LA). Decrease dose to 1 mg PO bid (Detrol) or 2 mg PO qd (Detrol LA) if adverse symptoms, hepatic insufficiency or specific coadministered drugs (see notes).

PEDS - Not approved in children.

FORMS - Trade: Tabs 1, 2 mg. Caps, extended release 2, 4 mg.

NOTES - Contraindicated with urinary or gastric retention, or uncontrolled glaucoma. Drug interactions with CYP3A4 inhibitors (e.g. erythromycin, ketoconazole, itraconazole); decrease dose to 1 mg PO bid or 2 mg PO qd (Detrol LA).

***Urised* (methenamine + phenyl salicylate + atropine + hyoscyamine + benzoic acid + methylene blue)** ▶K ♀C ▶? $$$$

ADULT - Dysuria: 2 Tabs PO qid.

PEDS - Dysuria > 6 yo: reduce dose based on age and weight. Not recommended for children < 6 yo.

FORMS - Trade: tab (methenamine 40.8 mg + phenyl salicylate 18.1 mg + atropine 0.03 mg + hyoscyamine 0.03 mg + 4.5 mg benzoic acid + 5.4 mg methylene blue).

NOTES - Take with food to minimize GI upset. May precipitate urate crystals in urine. Avoid use with sulfonamides. May turn urine and contact lenses blue.

UROLOGY: Erectile Dysfunction

alprostadil (*Muse, Caverject, Edex*) ▶L ♀- ▶- $$$$$

ADULT - Erectile dysfunction: 1.25-2.5 mcg intracavernosal injection over 5-10 seconds initially using a ½ inch, 27 or 30 gauge needle. If no response, may give next higher dose after 1 hour, max 2 doses/day. May increase by 2.5 mcg and then 5-10 mcg incrementally on separate occasions. Dose range= 1-40 mcg. Alternative: 125 - 250 mcg intraurethral pellet (Muse). Increase or decrease dose on separate occasions until erection achieved. Maximum intraurethral dose 2 pellets/24h. The lowest possible dose to produce an acceptable erection should be used.

PEDS - Not approved in children.

FORMS - Trade: injection (Edex) 10,20,40 mcg; (Caverject) 6.15,11.9,23.3 mcg. pellet (Muse) 125, 250, 500, 1000 mcg.

NOTES - Contraindicated in patients at risk for priapism, with anatomical penile deformity, with penile implants, in women or children, in men for whom sexual activity is inadvisable, and for intercourse with a pregnant woman. Onset of effect is 5-20 minutes.

sildenafil (*Viagra*) ▶LK ♀B ▶- $$$$

WARNING - Contraindicated in patients taking nitrates in prior/subsequent 24 hours; risk of profound hypotension & death.

ADULT - Erectile dysfunction: 50 mg PO approximately 1h (range 0.5-4h) before sexual activity. Usual effective dose range: 25- 100 mg. Maximum 1 dose/day. Use lower dose (25 mg) if >65 yo, hepatic/renal impairment, or certain coadministered drugs (see notes). Not FDA-approved in women.

PEDS - Not approved in children.

FORMS - Trade: Tabs 25, 50, 100 mg. Unscored tab but can be cut in half.

NOTES - Drug interactions with cimetidine, erythromycin, ketoconazole, itraconazole, saquinavir, ritonavir and other CYP3A4 inhibitors; use 25 mg dose. Do not exceed 25 mg/48 h with ritonavir.

UROLOGY: Nephrolithiasis

acetohydroxamic acid (*Lithostat*) ▶K ♀X ▶? $$$

ADULT - Chronic UTI, adjunctive therapy: 250 mg PO tid-qid for a total dose of 10-15 mg/kg/day. Maximum dose is 1.5 g/day. Decrease dose in patients with renal impairment to no more than 1 g/day.

PEDS - Adjunctive therapy in chronic urea-splitting UTI: 10 mg/kg/day PO divided bid-tid.

FORMS - Trade: Tabs 250 mg.

NOTES - Do not use if CrCl < 20 ml/min. Administer on an empty stomach.

allopurinol (*Zyloprim*) ▶K ♀C ▶+ $

ADULT - Recurrent calcium oxalate stones : 200-300 mg PO qd-bid. Reduce dose in renal insufficiency (CrCl 10-20 ml/ min= 200 mg/day, CrCl < 10 ml/min = 100 mg/day).

PEDS - Not approved for urolithiasis in children.

FORMS - Generic/Trade: Tabs 100, 300 mg.

NOTES - Incidence of rash is increased in renal impairment. Discontinue if rash or allergic symptoms. Drug interaction with warfarin & azathioprine.

hydrochlorothiazide (*HCTZ, Esidrix, HydroDIURIL, Oretic, Microzide, Ezide, Hydrocot, Aquazide H*) ▶L ♀D ▶+ $

UNAPPROVED ADULT - nephrolithiasis: 50-100 mg PO qd.

FORMS - Generic/Trade: Tabs 25, 50, 100 mg; solution 50 mg/ 5 ml. Trade only: Caps 12.5 mg.

NOTES - Beware of azotemia, hypokalemia.

potassium citrate (*Polycitra-K, Urocit-K*) ▶K ♀C ▶? $$$

ADULT - Urinary alkalinization: 1 packet in water/juice PO tid-qid with meals. 15-30 ml PO solution tid-qid with meals. 10-20 mEq PO Tabs tid-qid with meals. Max 100 mEq/day.

PEDS - Urinary alkalinization: 5-15 ml PO qid with meals.

FORMS - Trade: Polycitra-K packet (potassium 3300 mg + citric acid 1002 mg). Polycitra-K oral solution (5 ml = potassium 1100 mg + citric acid 334 mg). Urocit-K wax Tabs 5, 10 mEq.

NOTES - Contraindicated in renal insufficiency, PUD, UTI, and hyperkalemia.

UROLOGY: Prostate Cancer

bicalutamide (*Casodex*) ▶L ♀X ◗- $$$$$
ADULT - Prostate cancer: 50 mg PO qd in combination with a LHRH analog (e.g. goserelin or leuprolide). Not indicated in women.
PEDS - Not approved in children.
FORMS - Trade: Tabs 50 mg.
NOTES - Monitor LFTs and PSA. May cause increased INR with warfarin. Gynecomastia and breast pain occur.

flutamide (*Eulexin*, *✤Euflex*) ▶KL ♀D ◗- $$$$$
ADULT - Prostate cancer: 250 mg PO q8h in combination with a LHRH analog (e.g. goserelin or leuprolide). Not indicated in women.
PEDS - Not approved in children.
FORMS - Trade: Caps 125 mg.
NOTES - Monitor LFTs and PSA. May cause increased INR with warfarin. Gynecomastia and breast pain occur.

goserelin (*Zoladex*) ▶L ♀X ◗- $$$$$
ADULT - Prostate cancer: 3.6 mg implant SC into upper abdominal wall every 28 days, or 10.8 mg implant SC q12 weeks.
PEDS - Not approved in children.
FORMS - Trade: implants 3.6, 10.8 mg.
NOTES - Transient increases in testosterone and estrogen occur.

leuprolide (*Lupron, Lupron Depot, Oaklide, Viadur*) ▶L ♀X ◗- $$$$$
ADULT - Prostate cancer: 1 mg SC qd, 7.5 mg IM q month (Lupron Depot), 22.5 mg IM q3 months (Lupron Depot), or 30 mg IM q4 months (Lupron Depot), or 65 mg SC implant q12 months (Viadur).
PEDS - Not approved for this indication.
NOTES - Transient increases in testosterone and estrogen occur.

nilutamide (*Nilandron*, *✤Anandron*) ▶K ♀C ◗? $$$$$
ADULT - Prostate cancer: 300 mg PO qd for 30 days, then 150 mg PO qd. Begin therapy on same day as surgical castration.
PEDS - Not approved in children.
FORMS - Trade: Tabs 50 mg.
NOTES - Contraindicated in severe hepatic or respiratory insufficiency. Beware of delay in eyes adapting to dark, interstitial pneumonitis, hepatitis, and aplastic anemia.

Index

B

E

F

N

S

T

Page left blank for notes

Page left blank for notes

E

Page left blank for notes

SFeP

Hemochromatosis

- C282Y / H63D

CHF
DM

- iron overload
  - * heart, liver, pancreas, jt,

Bronze DM

- inflammation
- fasting x 6wks
  - ⊖ ETOH ↑

>1000 ⊕ LFT ≠

- Gold liver bx
  - √ Fe
  - hepatic Fe index

Page left blank for notes

ADULT EMERGENCY DRUGS (selected)

ALLERGY	cimetidine (*Tagamet*): 300 mg IV/IM. diphenhydramine (*Benadryl*): 50 mg IV/IM. epinephrine: 0.1-0.5 mg SC (1:1000 solution), may repeat after 20 minutes. methylprednisolone (*Solu-Medrol*): 125 mg IV/IM.
DYSRHYTHMIAS / CARDIAC ARREST	adenosine (*Adenocard*): SVT (not A-fib/flutter): 6 mg rapid IV & flush, preferably through a central line. If no response after 1-2 minutes then 12 mg. A third dose of 12-18 mg may be given prn. amiodarone (*Cordarone, Pacerone*): Life-threatening ventricular arrhythmia: Load 150 mg IV over 10 min, then 1 mg/min x 6h, then 0.5 mg/min x 18h. atropine: 0.5-1.0 mg IV/ET. diltiazem (*Cardizem*): Rapid atrial fibrillation: bolus 0.25 mg/kg or 20 mg IV over 2 min. Infusion 5-15 mg/h. epinephrine: 1 mg IV/ET for cardiac arrest. [1:10,000 solution] lidocaine (*Xylocaine*): Load 1 mg/kg IV, then 0.5 mg/kg q8-10min as needed to max 3 mg/kg. Maintenance 2g in 250ml D5W (8 mg/ml) at 1-4 mg/min drip (7-30 ml/h). procainamide (*Pronestyl*): 100 mg IV q10min or run infusion below at 20 mg/min (150 ml/h) until: 1) QRS or PR widens >50%, 2) Dysrhythmia suppressed, 3) Hypotension, or 4) Total of 17 mg/kg or 1000 mg. Infusion 2g in 250ml D5W (8 mg/ml) at 2-6 mg/min (15-45 ml/h). vasopressin (*Pitressin,* ADH): Ventricular fibrillation: 40 units IV once.
PRESSORS	dobutamine (*Dobutrex*). 250 mg in 250ml D5W (1 mg/ml) at 2.5-15 mcg/kg/min. 70 kg: 21 ml/h = 5 mcg/kg/min. dopamine (*Intropin*). 400 mg in 250ml D5W (1600 mcg/ml) at 2-20 mcg/kg/min. 70 kg: 13 ml/h = 5 mcg/kg/min. Doses in mcg/kg/min: 2-5 = dopaminergic, 5-10 = beta, >10 = alpha. norepinephrine (*Levophed*): 4 mg in 500 ml D5W (8 mcg/ml) at 2-4 mcg/min. 20 ml/h = 3 mcg/min. phenylephrine (*Neo-Synephrine*): 50 mcg boluses IV. Infusion for hypotension: 20 mg in 250ml D5W (80 mcg/ml) at 40-180 mcg/min (35-160ml/h).
INTUBATION	etomidate (*Amidate*): 0.3 mg/kg IV. methohexital (*Brevital*): 1-1.5 mg/kg IV. rocuronium (*Zemuron*): 0.6-1.2 mg/kg IV. succinylcholine (*Anectine*): 1 mg/kg IV. Peds (<5 yo): 2 mg/kg IV preceded by atropine 0.02 mg/kg. thiopental (*Pentothal*): 3-5 mg/kg IV.
SEIZURES	diazepam (*Valium*): 5-10 mg IV, or 0.2-0.5 mg/kg rectal gel up to 20 mg PR. fosphenytoin (*Cerebyx*): Load 15-20 "phenytoin equivalents" per kg either IM, or IV no faster than 100-150 mg/min. lorazepam (*Ativan*): 0.05-0.15 mg/kg up to 3-4 mg IV/IM. magnesium sulfate: Eclampsia: 1-4 g IV over 2-4 min. phenobarbital: 200- 600 mg IV at rate ≤60 mg/min up to 20 mg/kg. phenytoin (*Dilantin*): Load 15-20 mg/kg up to 1000 mg IV no faster than 50 mg/min.

CARDIAC DYSRHYTHMIA PROTOCOLS (*Circulation* 2000; 102, suppl I)

Basic Life Support

All cases: Two initial breaths, then compressions 100 per minute

One or two rescuer: 15:2 ratio of compressions to ventilations

V-Fib, Pulseless V-Tach

CPR until defibrillator ready
Defibrillate 200 J
Defibrillate 200-300 J
Defibrillate 360 J
Intubate, IV, then *options:*

- Epinephrine 1 mg IV q3-5 minutes
- Vasopressin 40 units IV once only; switch to epi if no response
- Defibrillate 360 J after each drug dose

Options:

- Amiodarone 300 mg IV; repeat doses 150 mg
- Lidocaine 1.0-1.5 mg/kg IV q3-5 minutes to max 3 mg/kg
- Magnesium 1-2 g IV
- Procainamide 30 mg/min IV to max 17 mg/kg
- Bicarbonate 1 mEq/kg IV

Defibrillate 360 J after each drug dose

Pulseless Electrical Activity (PEA)

CPR, intubate, IV.

- Consider 5 H's: hypovolemia, hypoxia, H^+ acidosis, hyper / hypokalemia, hypothermia
- Consider 5 T's: "tablets"-drug OD, tamponade-cardiac, tension pneumothorax, thrombosis-coronary, thrombosis-pulmonary embolism

Epinephrine 1 mg IV q3-5 minutes
If bradycardia, atropine 1 mg IV q3-5 min to max 0.04 mg/kg

Asystole

CPR, intubate, IV, assess code status
Confirm asystole in >1 lead
Search for and treat reversible causes
Consider early transcutaneous pacing
Epinephrine 1 mg IV q3-5 minutes
Atropine 1 mg IV q3-5 min to max 0.04 mg/kg

Bradycardia (<60 bpm), symptomatic

Airway, oxygen, IV
Atropine 0.5-1 mg IV q3-5 min to max 0.04 mg/kg
Transcutaneous pacemaker
Options:

- Dopamine 5-20 mcg/kg/min
- Epinephrine 2-10 mcg/min

Unstable Tachycardia (>150 bpm)

Airway, oxygen, IV
Consider brief trial of medications
Premedicate whenever possible
Synchronized cardioversion 100 J
Synchronized cardioversion 200 J
Synchronized cardioversion 300 J
Synchronized cardioversion 360 J

Stable Monomorphic V-Tach

Airway, oxygen, IV
If no CHF, then choose just one top agent (procainamide, sotalol) or other agent (amiodarone, lidocaine)
If CHF (EF<40%), then DC cardioversion after pretreatment with either:

- Amiodarone 150 mg IV over 10 min; repeat q10-15 min prn
- Lidocaine 0.5-0.75 mg/kg IV; repeat q5-10 min prn to max 3 mg/kg

Stable Wide-Complex Tachycardia

Airway, oxygen, IV
If no CHF, then *options*:

- DC cardioversion
- Procainamide 20-30 mg/min IV to max 17 mg/kg
- Amiodarone

If CHF (EF<40%), then *options*:

- DC cardioversion
- Amiodarone

Stable Narrow-Complex SVT

Airway, oxygen, IV
Vagal stimulation
Adenosine
Further treatment based on specific rhythm (junctional tachycardia, PSVT, multifocal atrial tachycardia) and presence or absence of CHF.

Ordering Books From Tarascon Publishing

FAX	PHONE	INTERNET	MAIL
Fax credit card orders 24 hrs/day toll free to **877.929.9926**	For phone orders or customer service, call **800.929.9926**	Order through our OnLine store with your credit card at **www.tarascon.com**	Mail order & check to: **Tarascon Publishing PO Box 1159 Loma Linda, CA 92354**

Name		
Address		
City	State	Zip

Please send me:	*Number*	*Price ‡*
Tarascon Pocket Pharmacopoeia, Classic Shirt-Pocket Edition		$
Tarascon Pocket Pharmacopoeia, Deluxe Labcoat Pocket Ed.		$
Tarascon Pocket Orthopaedica		$
Tarascon Internal Medicine & Critical Care Pocketbook		$
Tarascon Adult Emergency Pocketbook		$
Tarascon Pediatric Emergency Pocketbook		$
How to be a Truly Excellent Junior Medical Student		$

‡ Price per Copy by Number of Copies Ordered

Total # of each ordered	1–9	10–49	50-99	≥100
Pocket Pharmacop Classic	$8.95	$7.95	$6.95	$5.95
Pocket Pharmacop Deluxe	$17.95	$15.25	$13.45	$12.55
Pocket Orthopaedica	$11.95	$9.90	$8.95	$8.35
Internal Med Pocketbook	$11.95	$9.90	$8.95	$8.35
Adult Emerg Pocketbook	$11.95	$9.90	$8.95	$8.35
Peds Emerg Pocketbook	$9.95	$8.25	$7.45	$6.95
How…Truly Excellent JMS	$9.95	$8.25	$7.45	$6.95

Shipping & Handling

If subtotal is →	<$10	$10-24	$25-99	$100-300
Standard shipping	$1.00	$2.50	$5.00	$8.00
UPS 2-day air*	$12.00	$12.00	$14.00	$18.00

No post office boxes

Subtotal	$
California only add 7.5% sales tax	$
Shipping and handling (table)	$
TOTAL	$

❒ **Charge credit card**: ❒ VISA ❒ Mastercard ❒ American Express

Card number		Exp Date
Signature	E-mail	Phone